Human Neuropsychology

G. NEIL MARTIN

MIDDLESEX UNIVERSITY

PRENTICE HALL

LONDON ■ NEW YORK ■ TORONTO ■ SYDNEY ■ TOKYO ■ SINGAPORE

MADRID ■ MEXICO CITY ■ MUNICH ■ PARIS

First published 1998 by
Prentice Hall Europe
Campus 400, Maylands Avenue
Hemel Hempstead
Hertfordshire, HP2 7EZ

Reprinted 1999

Typeset in 9.5/12pt Melior
by Photoprint, Torquay, Devon

Printed and bound in Great Britain by
Biddles Ltd, Guildford and King's Lynn

Library of Congress Cataloging-in-Publication Data

Martin, G. Neil.
  Human neuropsychology/G. Neil Martin.
    p. cm.
  Includes bibliographical references and index.
  ISBN 0–13–802331–X (pbk.)
  1. Neuropsychology. I. Title.
  [DNLM: 1. Neuropsychology. WL 103.5 M38th
1997]
QP360.M3515 1997
612.8 – dc21
DNLM/DLC
for Library of Congress   97-111667
                                                      CIP

British Library Cataloguing in Publication Data

A catalogue record for this book is available from
the British Library

ISBN 0–13–802331–X

1 2 3 4 5   02 01 00 99 98

Contents

Figures

Tables

Acknowledgements

Grateful acknowledgement is made to the following sources for permission to reproduce material in this book previously published elsewhere. Every effort has been made to trace copyright holders, but if any have been inadvertently overlooked the publisher will be pleased to make the necessary arrangement at the first opportunity.

Chapter 1

Figure 1.3 by permission of Romy and George Dunbar.

Figure 1.4 by permission of Neuroscience, Inc.

Figures 1.6, 1.7 reproduced by kind permission of John Polich.

Figure 1.9 from Carlson, N.R., *Foundations of Physiological Psychology* (3rd edition). © 1995 Allyn and Bacon; reproduced by permission.

Chapter 2

Figures 2.1, 2.2, 2.3, 2.4, 2.5, 2.6, 2.7, 2.8, 2.9, 2.10 from Kandel, E.R., Schwartz, J.H. and Jessell, T.M., *Essentials of Neural Science and Behaviour*, International edition. © 1995 Appleton and Lange, and by kind permission of Eric Kandel and Appleton and Lange.

Chapter 3

Figures 3.1, 3.6, 3.13, 3.14, 3.19, 3.20, 3.21, 3.23, 3.28 from Kandel, E.R., Schwartz, J.H. and Jessell, T.M., *Essentials of Neural Science and Behaviour*, International edition. © 1995 Appleton and Lange, and by kind permission of Eric Kandel and Appleton and Lange.

Figures 3.2, 3.4, 3.8, 3.9, 3.10(a), 3.10(b), 3.11(a) and 3.11(b) from Dearmond, S.J., Fusco, M.M. and Dewey, M.M., *Structure of the Human Brain: A photographic atlas.* © 1989 S.J. Dearmond, M.M. Fusco and M.M. Dewey; used by permission of Oxford University Press, Inc.

Figures 3.7, 3.12, 3.15, 3.16, 3.22, 3.24, 3.25, 3.26, 3.27 from Carlson, N.R., *Foundations of Physiological Psychology* (3rd edition). © 1995 Allyn and Bacon; reproduced by permission.

Figure 3.17 from Brodal, P., *The Central Nervous System*. © 1991 Oxford University Press.

Figures 3.18(a) and (b) reprinted from Barr, M.L. and Kiernan, J.A., *The Human Nervous System* (5th edition). © 1988 J.B. Lippincott Company.

Chapter 4

Figure 4.1 reproduced by kind permission of Martin Skinner.

Figures 4.2 and 4.3 adapted from Shepard, R.N. and Metzler, D., Mental rotation of three-dimensional objects, *Science*, **171** (1971), 701–3.

Figures 4.5(a) and (b) reproduced by kind permission of Doreen Kimura.

Chapter 6

Figure 6.1 from Crawford, J.R., Parker, D.M. and McKinlay, W.W. (1992), *A Handbook of Neuropsychological Assessment*. © 1992 Lawrence Erlbaum Associates. Reproduced by kind permission of Denis Parker and John Crawford.

Figure 6.3 from Goldstein, L.H., Bernard, S., Fenwick, P.B.C., Burgess, P.W. and McNeil, J., Unilateral frontal lobectomy can produce strategy application disorder. *Journal of Neurology, Neurosurgery and Psychiatry*, **56** (1993), 274–6. Reprinted by kind permission of Laura Goldstein.

Figures 6.4 and 6.5 reprinted from Damasio, H., Grabowski, T., Frank, R., Galaburda, A.M. and Damasio, A.R., The return of Phineas Gage: clues about the brain from the skull of a famous patient, *Science*, **264** (1994), 1102–5. Reprinted by kind permission of Hanna and Antonio Damasio.

Chapter 7

Figure 7.1 from Bruce, V. and Young, A., Understanding face recognition, *British Journal of Psychology*, **77** (1986), 305–27. By kind permission of Vicki Bruce and the British Psychological Society.

Figures 7.2, 7.3, 7.4, 7.5 from Halligan, P. and Marshall, J., Current issues in spatial neglect: an editorial introduction, *Neuropsychological Rehabilitation*, **4** (1994), 103–10. By kind permission of Peter Halligan.

Figure 7.6 from Guariglia, C., Padovani, A., Pantano, P. and Pizzamiglio, L., Unilateral neglect restricted to visual imagery, *Nature*, **364** (1993), 235–7. © 1994 Macmillan Magazines Limited, and with the kind permission of Luigi Pizzamiglio.

Chapter 8

Figure 8.1 from Carlson, N.R., *Foundations of Physiological Psychology* (3rd edition). © 1995 Allyn and Bacon; reproduced by permission.

Chapter 10

Figure 10.1 from Kandel, E.R., Schwartz, J.H. and Jessell, T.M., *Essentials of Neural Science and Behaviour*, International edition. © 1995 Appleton and Lange, and by kind permission of Eric Kandel and Appleton and Lange.

Figure 10.2 from LeDoux, J., In search of an emotional system in the brain. In M. Gazzaniga (ed.), *The Cognitive Neurosciences*, MIT Press. By kind permission of Joseph LeDoux.

Figure 10.3 from Adolphs, R., Tranel, D., Damasio, H. and Damasio, A.R., Fear and the human amygdala, *Journal of Neuroscience*, **15** (1995), 5879–91. © 1995 Society for Neuroscience; reprinted by permission.

Figure 10.4 from Schiff, B.B. and Lamon, M., Inducing emotion by unilateral contraction of facial muscles: a new look at hemispheric specialization and the experience of emotion, *Neuropsychologia*, **27** (1989), 923–35. © 1989; by kind permission of Elsevier Science Ltd and Bernard Schiff.

Figures 10.6 and 10.7 by kind permission of Jeffrey A. Gray.

Chapter 11

Figures 11.2 and 11.3 from Rabbitt, P., Does it all go together when it goes? The nineteenth Bartlett memorial lecture, *Quarterly Journal of Experimental Psychology*, **46A** (1993), 385–434. By kind permission of Patrick Rabbitt.

Chapter 12

Figure 12.1 from Cowan, W.M., The development of the brain, *Scientific American*, **241** (1979), 106–17. Reprinted by kind permission of W.H. Freeman and Company.

Figures 12.2(a) and 12.3 from Conel, J.L., *The Postnatal Development of the Human Cerebral Cortex*, volumes 1–8 (1939–67), Cambridge, MA: Harvard University Press. Reprinted by kind permission of Harvard University Press.

Figure 12.2(b) from Dekaban, A.S. and Sadowsky, D., Changes in brain weights during the span of human life: relation of brain weight to body heights and body weights, *Annals of Neurology*, **4** (1978), 345–56.

Preface

The United States Congress has declared the 1990s to be the Decade of the Brain. New advances and theoretical perspectives in neuroscience research are making this field a popular one both with scientists and with the public imagination. No other machine is so precious and yet so poorly understood as the brain. Like most problems in science, the answers that studies of the human brain yield provoke only further, more interesting questions. A decade of attention will not be sufficient to understand even the simplest of the human brain's processes, but it is a beginning.

The study of human neuropsychology, part of the grand edifice that is modern neuroscience, has blossomed in the past two decades. Much of this expansion in research and interest has been driven by newer and better neuromedical techniques of investigation. Twenty years ago, for example, it would have been impossible to perform a brain scan such as that undertaken during PET imaging while a subject completed a psychological task. Such methods did not exist in workable form. In terms of human brain anatomy, our scientific predecessors relied on very crude post-mortem dissection and staining measures to determine changes in brain structure and their relation to function. Twenty-five years ago, computerized axial tomography (CT) scans – the brain's own x-ray images – afforded an improved method for observing the human brain's living structure. Today, we have a much superior method in magnetic resonance imaging (MRI) which does a similar job, only better. In future, we look forward to *functional* magnetic resonance imaging which can be used to investigate brain function and not merely structure. These brain imaging techniques, together with measures of the brain's electrical activity such as the electroencephalogram (EEG), arm the neuroscientist with a formidable battery of methods and techniques that can be used to study the neuropsychology of the living human brain.

The meat and drink of neuropsychology, however, have traditionally been the study of those individuals with brain injury. Famous case histories in neuropsychology are a colourful, fortuitous catalog of the woefully and astonishingly brain-damaged. Who would have imagined that a diseased brain or a brain that had been penetrated by a fencing foil or damaged because of surgery to alleviate epilepsy could have provided science with insights, if that is the correct word, into the relationship between the human brain and its function? Yet these case studies did, and in the following chapters you will learn more about these individuals and others like them. Of course, they are often unique. It is not every person who, like Phineas Gage, has most of his frontal lobes demolished by having an iron rod propelled through his head. But these case studies frequently provide the fillip for theory, further research and new conceptions in neuropsychological science. Such accidents, should they occur often enough, provide more than simply a terrible anecdote: they help shape the way in which we think that the human brain works.

Human Neuropsychology aims to provide an up-to-date introduction to the issues and problems arising in modern neuropsychology. Knowledge concerning the neuroanatomy and neurophysiology of the human brain, the neuropsychology of the senses, motor disorders, sensory disorders, functional asymmetry, social behaviour, cognition, normal and abnormal emotion, degenerative diseases, development and recovery of function and neuropsychological assessment is drawn from a vast pool of data, including studies of healthy and clinical samples. The thirteen chapters of this book could form the basis of a semesterized course. The first three chapters provide an introduction to the subject, reviewing the history of neuropsychology and its methods and providing a brief background to the neurophysiology and neuroanatomy of the brain. Readers unfamiliar with the brain, its structure and its workings should familiarize themselves with these chapters before reading the others, as the later chapters assume a rudimentary knowledge of these topics. Readers who are already familar with these topics might like either to forgo these chapters or read them for revision.

Most of the topics covered in the book will be included in any traditional neuropsychology course, and some other topics are included that often do not make it onto these courses but are meaningful in a neuropsychological context nonetheless. A resurgence of interest in cognitive neuropsychology has occurred in the past twenty years and this is reflected in the content of some of these chapters.

The appendix provides a list of resources which you will find useful in your search for further information about human neuropsychology. Important journals in the discipline which you should try to consult regularly are listed, as are software programs which teach you about the neurochemistry, neurophysiology or neuroanatomy of the brain and its functions. Perhaps the most explosive information resource in recent years has been the Internet, the global, electronic information network. The appendix lists the addresses and brief content summaries of the best of the Web sites which provide information about neuropsychology. Like many Internet innovations, there is no guarantee that when you read this book these sites will still be in operation, but those listed have been operating for some time and look as if they will be in the future.

All knowledge is informed by its past and shaped by its context, and this book is no exception. I am indebted to the following individuals who have either commented on draft chapters or have offered their assistance and expertise in many other welcome and charitable ways. In alphabetical order, they are: Alan A.

Beaton (University College of Swansea, UK), Vicki Bruce (University of Stirling, UK), Alan Glass (University of Birmingham, UK), Mark Coulson (Middlesex University, UK), Antonio Damasio (University of Iowa, USA), Hanna Damasio (University of Iowa, USA), Romy and George Dunbar (University of Warwick, UK), Uta Frith (MRC Cognitive Development Unit, UK), Laura A. Goldstein (Institute of Psychiatry, UK), Jeffrey A. Gray (Institute of Psychiatry, UK), Monika Harvey (University of Bristol, UK), Peter W. Halligan (University of Oxford, UK), Graham Hole (University of Sussex, UK), Doreen Kimura (University of Western Ontario, Canada), Joseph LeDoux (New York University, USA), Judy McSorley (Middlesex University, UK), Denis Parker (Glasgow Caledonian University, UK), Anne-Marie Parr (Institute of Psychiatry, UK), Luigi Pizzamiglio (University of Rome, Italy), John Polich (Scripps Research Institute, USA) and Bernard Schiff (University of Toronto, Canada).

An especial thank you is reserved for Nicky Brunswick (Wellcome Department of Cognitive Neurology, London) who not only wrote Chapter 9 on the neuro-psychology of language and language disorders but provided invaluable material assistance and immeasurable help during the book's gestation. It is in no small part that this book was made possible by her.

I would also like to acknowledge the influence of and to thank those teachers who, whether they knew it or not, encouraged the production and intellectual shape of this book: Colin D. Gray, Maureen Lewis and Denis Parker. Finally, I would like to thank both Rupert Knight and Christina Wipf Perry, my editors at Prentice Hall, for their help and encouragement.

It is customary to end a personal acknowledgement section with the admission that any errors and flaws left in the book are the author's own. This custom is honoured here. I hope, however, that the influence of the above individuals will have made the author's shortcomings less obvious.

G. NEIL MARTIN
LONDON 1997

Men ought to know that from the brain, and from the brain only, arise our pleasures, joy, laughter and jests, as well as our sorrows, pains, griefs and tears. Through it, in particular, we think, see and hear, and distinguish the ugly from the beautiful, the bad from the good, the pleasant from the unpleasant.

(Hippocrates, *The Sacred Disease*, XVII)

Chapter One

Neuropsychology: its history, aims and methods

■ Neuropsychology: some history and definitions

> The key philosophical theme of modern neural science is that all behaviour is a reflection of brain function.
>
> (Kandel, 1991)

It is often surprising to discover, in these sophisticated neuropsychological times when the brain's activity can be monitored and captured in coloured, three-dimensional splendour, that the brain was once considered less important than other organs for maintaining and initiating thought and behaviour. Some ancient philosophers and physicians had very different views of the role of the brain.

Early theories of 'localization of function' focused on the heart as the organ responsible for mediating behaviour. Aristotle (384–322 BC), for example, argued that those organs located near the brain were connected to the heart via 'vascular channels' and that the brain existed in order to balance the heart's function, specifically to 'make the heat and the boiling in the heart well blent and tempered'. This viewpoint is called the **cardiocentric view**: the position that the nerves originated in the heart and that thought and sensation both resided here. It was challenged by Hippocrates (*c.* 430–350 BC) who argued that the brain was responsible for the behaviours and functions ascribed to the heart. This **cephalocentric view** was espoused in many of his writings. 'I hold that the brain is the most powerful organ of the human body', he wrote in *The Sacred Disease*, 'eyes, ears, tongue, hands and feet act in accordance with the discernment of the brain.' Earlier observers such as Alcmaeon of Croton (*c.* 500 BC) had also ascribed functional and behavioural significance to the brain.

While this flash of astonishing and prescient insight might seem to us to be obvious, Hippocrates' and his supporters' beliefs, such as those of the influential Greek physician Galen (AD 130–200) were the minority position. Indeed, it was not until the nineteenth century that experimental localization studies confirmed the importance of the brain, and specifically the outer layers of the brain, the **neocortex**, to human behaviour. Even mediaeval studies had placed greater emphasis on the brain's ventricles, the cavities within the brain, and not its actual inner and outer structure. The once minority view, however, is the starting point for modern neuropsychology – the hypothesis that the brain is responsible for the execution and maintenance of function.

The aim of human neuropsychology is to establish relationships between function such as motor/sensory behaviour, cognition, perception, mood, emotion and so on, and brain activity and structure. This is sometimes referred to as **functional localization**. A similar term is **functional lateralization** which refers to the proposition that a function may reside in one or either side (or **hemisphere**) of the brain. **Functional asymmetry, laterality** and functional lateralization are virtually synonymous.

According to Beaumont (1996a), 'if psychology is the science of mental life, to use George Miller's ingenious description, then neuropsychology is the scientific study of the relationship between the brain and mental life.' Neuropsychology is often characterized as being the study of the relationship between the brain and behaviour or function and there are some distinct subareas within the discipline. One of the more prominent is cognitive neuropsychology which 'represents a convergence of cognitive psychology and neuropsychology' (Ellis and Young, 1996) and, according to McCarthy and Warrington (1990), is a 'hybrid term applied to the analysis of those handicaps in human cognitive function which result from brain injury. Cognitive neuropsychology draws both on neurology and cognitive psychology for insights into the cerebral organisation of cognitive skills and abilities.'

In fact, much of the knowledge relating the brain function and activity derives from clinical studies of patients with damage to the central nervous system – the brain and spinal cord. Usually single-case studies, these examples illustrate vividly the effects of brain damage on behaviour and function. When considering the neurophysiological basis of language, for example, this type of information is important because animal ablation studies would not be able to give us much information about the neuropsychology of human language.

Together with studies of healthy individuals assessed using modern localizing techniques such as brain imaging, clinical observations hold great potential in helping to piece together a coherent picture of brain function. Each type of investigation is potentially complementary. Later in this chapter, both of these approaches and the techniques employed are described and evaluated in detail.

Development of human neuropsychology

Any good science benefits from an understanding of its origins, and human neuropsychology is no exception. One of the earliest documents describing the effects of brain damage on function dates from the seventeenth century BC, although it is probably a copy of an ancient composite manuscript dating from around 3000–2500 BC, supplemented by commentaries (Breasted, 1930). This ancient manuscript, called the *Edwin Smith Surgical Papyrus* after the Egyptologist who discovered it in Luxor, Egypt, in 1862, describes 48 observations of brain and spinal injury and its treatment. It is an extraordinary document in that it contains the first description of various parts of the brain, including the cranial sutures, the meninges, the brain's external surface and cerebrospinal fluid (Wilkins, 1992) and is probably the first scientific document to use the word 'brain'. It also contains the first reported case of disorders such as quadriplegia, urinary incontinence, priaprism and seminal emission following vertebral dislocation. Most cases are presented in the same format with title, examination, diagnosis and treatment described. For example, the description below is case two of the papyrus and describes a wound to the head.

Case two of the Edwin Smith Surgical Papyrus

Title: Instructions concerning a [gaping] wound [in his head], penetrating to the bone.

Examination: If thou examinest a man having a [gaping] wound [in] his [head], penetrating to the bone, thou shouldst lay thy hand upon it (and) [thou shouldst] pal[pate hi]s [wound]. If thou findest his skull [uninjured, not hav]ing a perforation in it . . .

Diagnosis: Thou shouldst say regarding [him]: 'One hav[ing a gaping wou]nd in his head. An ailment which I will treat.'

Treatment: [Thou] shouldst bind [fresh meat upon it the first day; thou shouldst apply for him two strips of linen, and treat afterward with grease, honey (and) lin]t every day until he recovers.

Gloss: As for "two strips of linen," [it means] two bands [of linen which one applies upon the two lips of the gaping wound in order to cause that one join] to the other.

(From Breasted, 1930)

Early cephalocentric theories of function, dating back to at least AD 4, had argued that the types of behaviour mediated by the brain were based on activity of the ventricles and the fluid in them. Much later on, Andreas Vesalius (1514–1564) described the principal method of brain dissection which involved (primarily) exposing the ventricles for observation. He noted, however, no difference between the ventricular volume of humans and that of animals, suggesting that the site responsible for function might be more 'cerebral' in nature. It was thought, for example, that sensory function was localized at the front of the brain, cognition, emotion and imagination were localized centrally and that memory was localized towards the brain's rear end. The ventricles appear to have a unique history in that they are thought to be the only cerebral structures mentioned in the physiology of antiquity (Wilkins, 1992). Remarkably, it has been noted that most of the accounts of cerebral localization before the seventeenth century appeared to be attempts at ventricular localization (Macmillan, 1995).

The quest for the localization of function continued in many guises during the seventeenth and eighteenth centuries. A large part of seventeenth century endeavours revolved around the localization of the seat of the soul or 'the mind'. René Descartes (1596–1650), for example, suggested that the pineal gland, a small brainstem structure, was the 'seat' of the soul. Or rather, it was seen as the place where sensory information would converge and go on to the soul. Separate sense impressions came together here, argued Descartes, 'before they reach the soul'. Descartes' localization of the mind/soul, if the most widely known, was not the only attempt at ascribing the localization of mental properties to brain structures. Other candidates for the source of the mind/soul included the corpus striatum, the white matter and the corpus callosum, structures that we shall discuss in Chapter 3.

However, the eighteenth and nineteenth centuries saw separate anatomical and neurophysiological discoveries which emphasized the way in which the brain functioned. One discovery was that the brain was composed of cells (neurons) that had various functional parts called the cell body, dendrites and axon. Camillo Golgi had discovered a means of tracing the structure of these cells by a form of 'staining' involving silver impregnation. These types of stain are called **Golgi stains**. Under a microscope, such staining showed clearly the structure of the tissues of the brain. This staining technique was used by another brain pioneer, Santiago Ramon y Cajal, who discovered that the brain comprised a network of communicating neurons. Cajal's enormously influential work led to the formulation of the **neuron doctrine** – the belief that the nervous system is made up of communicating cells or neurons. In recognition of this work, Golgi and Ramon y Cajal jointly won the Nobel prize in medicine and physiology in 1906.

Another important event, Luigi Galvani's discovery that nerve cells produced electricity, led to Emil DuBois-Reymond and Hermann von Helmholtz's discovery that nerve cells communicated with each other using electrical signals. This finding paved the way for discoveries in psychopharmacology and, specifically, the discovery that the surface of neurons – their receptor sites – was responsive to various chemicals called neurotransmitters. The most important of these are described in Chapter 2.

As these important discoveries in neuroanatomy and neurophysiology were becoming known, attempts at localization of human function continued. The most seriously proposed, although ultimately ridiculed and disregarded, theory of localization in the nineteenth century was that the brain comprised a number of separate organs each of which controlled a separate innate faculty. There were said to be twenty-seven of these faculties. Development of these organs led to prominences or 'bumps' in the individual's skull. A bump on the skull indicated a well developed underlying cortical gyrus and therefore a greater faculty for a particular behaviour. A skull depression, conversely, was a sign of an undeveloped gyrus and, therefore, a lack of function.

This notion was know as **phrenology** or **anatomical personology**, devised by the Viennese physician and anatomist Franz Joseph Gall and his co-worker, Johann Caspar Spurzheim (it was Spurzheim who actually coined the term). This pseudo-scientific theory of localization was easily challenged. It was, however, important in that it clearly localized function in the neocortex. Furthermore, Gall did make other, important contributions to neuropsychology. He suggested, for example, a relationship between damage to the front part of the brain on the left side and aphasia, the inability to produce or comprehend speech. In fact, Hippocrates had associated brain damage with aphasia and noted that damage to one side of the brain (unilateral damage) resulted in paralysis of the opposite side of the body. It is for the ill-fated phrenology, however, that Gall will probably be best remembered.

One of phrenology's fiercest critics was Pierre Flourens, a French neurologist who argued that no functional localization occurred in the cerebrum. In a series of experiments to determine the effects of removal of certain parts of the brain on function, he found that it was not the site of the removal which was important but the quantity of tissue removed. In other words, he argued that cerebral matter was **equipotential**: any part of the brain could perform another's function. This was also known as the **aggregate field** view of the brain. He noted this especially in birds and animals where recovery was possible following **ablation** (removal of parts of the brain). The notion of equipotentiality was a strong and popular one at the time. It was not long, however, before findings from clinical neurology cast some doubt on the theory's validity.

In 1861, a French surgeon, Pierre Paul Broca, published a report in which he described a form of production aphasia (the inability to produce speech) in one of his patients. This patient, Tan, was found to have injuries to the third left frontal convolution at post-mortem. During his lifetime, Tan could barely produce more than a few words, mainly uttering the word 'tan', hence his name. This form of **motor aphasia**, now called **Broca's aphasia**, and its localization in one hemisphere of the brain indicated that the brain did not behave as equipotentially as was thought. The region damaged is now known as Broca's area. This discovery was subsequently bolstered by the findings from other clinical studies. Jean Baptiste Brouillard, for example, highlighted the importance of the frontal lobes to speech and argued that since writing, drawing and painting are performed by the right hand, then the left hemisphere controls these functions (a precursor to cerebral dominance). Carl Wernicke had also reported an aphasic deficit, this time in patients who were unable to comprehend speech (**Wernicke's aphasia**). This type of aphasia was associated with left-hemisphere damage in a location below that of Broca's area. Importantly, Wernicke argued that not only were specific regions responsible for specific functions but that connections between regions were also responsible for function.

Much of the clinical evidence strongly suggested that localization of some functions, especially language-related functions, was probable. The year 1870 saw perhaps the clearest evidence at that time of cerebral localization of function and presaged the dawning of the modern science of cerebral localization and neuropsychology. Gustav Theodore Fritsch and Eduard Hitzig, two young German physicians, discovered that the neocortex was not only excitable by electrical stimulation but also selectively excitable (Fritsch and Hitzig, 1870). Using Frau Hitzig's dressing-table on which to operate (there was no suitable laboratory available), they found that selective stimulation of restricted portions of the anterior part of the brain in dogs elicited movement of particular body parts. It was another four years before a living human's brain was electrically stimulated.

Friedrich Goltz, however, argued that if these areas were important, then their removal would abolish the behaviour that they mediate. In fact, when Fritsch and Hitzig decorticated their dogs, i.e. removed the outer part of the brian, the cortex, functions were not abolished but reduced. This suggested to John Hughlings-Jackson, a British neurologist, that the nervous system consisted of a series of layers organized in a functional hierarchy with higher-level layers (the cerebral cortex) controlling more complex aspects of behaviour, and lower structures (spinal cord, medulla and pons) allowing lower-level function. Hughlings-Jackson's work in the field of focal epilepsy (seizures occurring in one part of the body) also localized sensory and motor functions to particular brain regions.

With this accumulating evidence, moves to map functions of the brain became widespread. A number of these maps seek to provide a taxonomy of the brain and include **projection maps** which trace sensory/motor axons to the brain from their respective systems and **functional maps** that are constructed from information provided from the observation of the effect of brain electrical stimulation on behaviour, recording the brain's electrical activity during some form of behaviour and associating damage to the brain with subsequent behavioural impairment. The most well known functional map is based on Wilder Penfield's studies of brain electrical stimulation during surgery (see below) and outlines the motor and somatosensory regions of the brain. One of the more widely used maps is Brodmann's **cytoarchitectonic map** (Brodmann, 1909), seen in Figure 1.1.

Cytoarchitectonic maps are complicated atlases constructed according to the type of cell that exists in specific regions of the brain. Brodmann's map assigns numbers to various areas of the brain that are distinguished by their cellular arrangement. There is a high correlation between Brodmann's areas and under-lying function. Area 44, for example, corresponds to Broca's area; the regions responsible for vision and motor function have specific cellular arrangements. Brodmann's map is widely used as a guide to the brain's regions and is referred to in this book.

Towards the tail-end of the nineteenth century, neuropsychology had found its modern beginning. The twentieth century, however, brought new discoveries and techniques which rapidly advanced the science of neuropsychology. These techniques included electroencephalogram (EEG) recording and brain imaging, both of which now contribute to the brain scientist's understanding of localization of function. Perhaps their greatest advantage is that these techniques can provide a picture of the human brain's function *in vivo*. Of course, with new developments, old generalizations are often disregarded and more specific observations replace them. Such is the case with neuropsychology. Some of the most commonly used techniques in human neuropsychological studies are described below. Each of these techniques has its advantages and disadvantages and it is likely that, towards the end of the twenty-first century, some of these techniques will have become obsolete and will have been replaced by more efficient technologies. Currently, however, they provide us with an expanding and informative range of technologies with which to examine brain function.

■ Techniques used in human neuropsychological studies

A large number of disciplines can and do contribute to the understanding of human brain function at many levels, from the molecular and biochemical level to

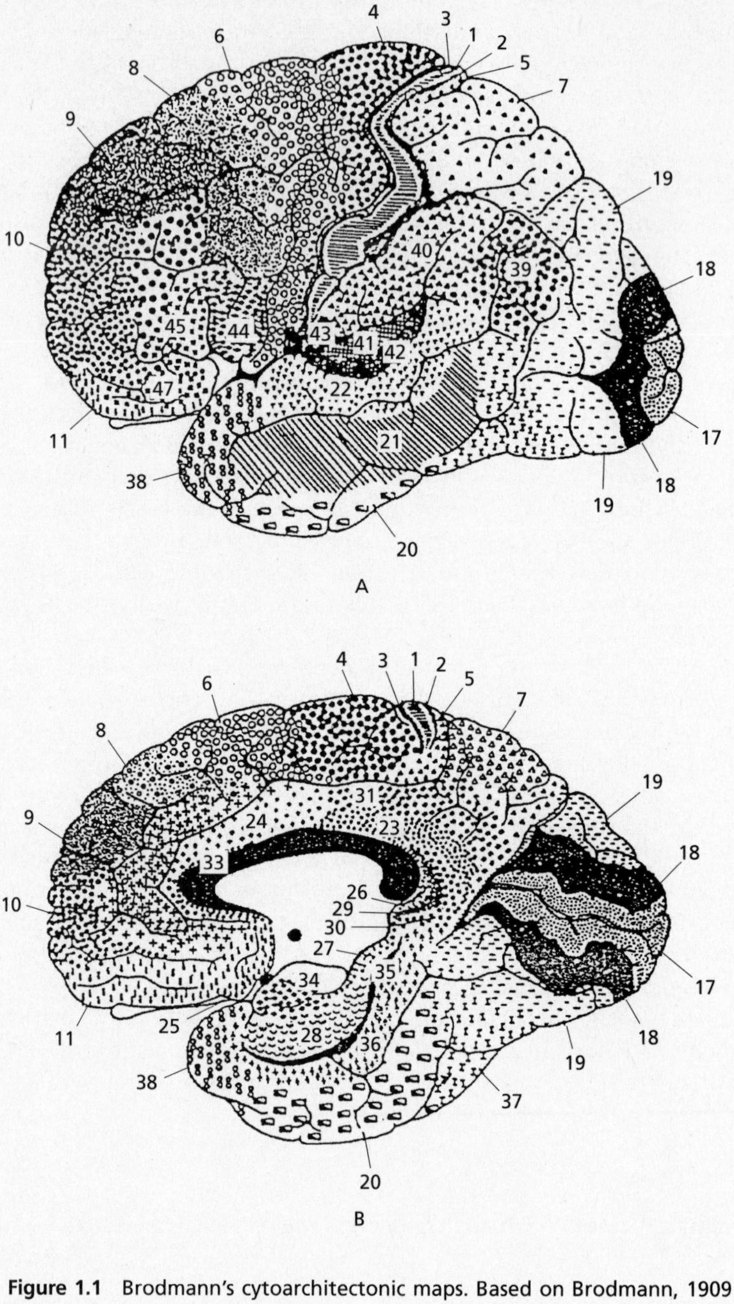

Figure 1.1   Brodmann's cytoarchitectonic maps. Based on Brodmann, 1909

the more gross neuronal level exemplified by the recording of the brain's electrical activity. The techniques used to examine brain/behaviour relationships reflect the multidisciplinary approach to brain function. Psychologists, psychiatrists, radiologists, pharmacologists, physiologists, biochemists and other scientists employ their own different but frequently overlapping techniques in the pursuit of this understanding. As a result, neuropsychologists have an enormously diverse armoury of methods and evidence to help them to establish brain and behaviour relationships.

Some of the commonest techniques used by neuropsychologists are tests of cognitive ability. These are tests which are thought to tap various cognitive functions such as verbal ability, visuospatial awareness, memory and so on and which might also be sensitive to brain injury. Thus, if an individual performs poorly on a test which is normally performed poorly by individuals with damage to a particular brain region and the subject performs within the same range as those with brain injury, then the neuropsychologist might recommend some form of neurological or radiological examination (such as CT/MRI scan – see the section below) to determine whether any trauma or lesion has occurred. Often, however, the procedure works the other way around. An individual may have sustained some form of brain injury via a trauma such as accident or disease, but the neuropsychologist wishes to know whether this injury has produced deficits in cognitive ability. This form of testing, called **neuropsychological testing**, is revisited in Chapter 13.

Techniques used in neuropsychological investigations are often employed on the basis of:

1. the type of subject examined;
2. the theoretical framework guiding the method; and
3. an expectation of what one wishes to find.

For example, there are techniques such as autoradiography, the Wada test or, more obviously, the split-brain operation which one would not use with normal, healthy controls for ethical, practical and theoretical reasons. Methods such as modern brain imaging or the measurement of brain electrical activity, however, can be used with both control and clinical groups. Each of these approaches has its advantages and disadvantages.

Brain damage/surgery

Brain lesions or brain damage provide an invaluable, if unfortunate, source of information regarding the relationship between brain and behaviour. Although strictly not a technique – neuroscientists do not deliberately go and damage their patients' brains for the purposes of research – lesioning or surgery does provide information concerning human brain function which is unique and which may complement non-invasive imaging techniques used with subjects who are free of brain damage. In fact, you will find as you read the many papers and books available on neuropsychology that much of the information about brain function is derived from studies of brain-damaged individuals, often in the form of case studies.

The forms of brain damage seen by clinicians can be caused by accidental head injury, disease, infection, virus or psychosurgery. Psychosurgery might involve the removal or lesioning of a particular part of the cortex to alleviate certain behavioural symptoms. To alleviate the symptoms of intractable epilepsy, for example, the structures connecting the two hemispheres of the brain may be severed almost completely, thus preventing the passage of the epileptic seizure from one hemisphere to another (this is called a commissurotomy). However, the severance of these connections appears to result in a lack of communication between the two hemispheres, giving rise to certain peculiarities and irregularities in the patients' behaviour after surgery (see Chapter 5). A common consequence of commissurotomy is that information processed by one hemisphere cannot be processed by the other. The surgical procedure is popularly known as 'split-brain' surgery and is described in Chapter 5.

Lesioning the human brain produces several functional consequences. It can produce a loss of function (normally, the larger the lesion, the greater the loss of function), a release of function (a new behaviour appears or an old behaviour increases) or functional disorganization (not being able to produce behaviour which requires sequential movement, for example). However, it is important when interpreting brain lesion studies to take into account three important points. First, it is advisable to have a description of the patient's behaviour before the trauma or to administer a test which can determine this. What is required here is a **pre-morbid** (meaning, before the damage) index of the patient's cognitive function behaviour. This is important because the test norms may not apply to the individual. For example, imagine a highly intelligent individual whose pre-morbid IQ was 150 but which decreases to 110 after head injury. Given that the population average is 100, this person is still performing effectively in comparison to the norm but his own function has markedly declined.

Secondly, meticulous identification and description of the locus of the damage is important. As human subjects' brain damage is often accidental or the result of factors beyond the experimenter's control, several brain areas may be damaged in unison. Localizing a behaviour to a given region or structure may, therefore, be difficult as other structures may be involved. Furthermore, the serendipitous nature of this research suggests that only a few individuals will present the form of brain damage studied. Many neuropsychological studies are based on single cases. This leads to the third important point.

Interpretation of the findings from studies involving single cases must be done circumspectly. Because findings are presented from a very small number of separate individuals, it is worth bearing in mind that the changes in behaviour observed may not be common to all individuals who present with the same form of brain damage. What may be needed is the assessment of several investigations involving single cases and the extraction of the common features that they share. An alternative consideration is to conduct a group study, where individuals with known damage to certain brain regions are tested as a homogeneous group. It is conceded, however, that this is difficult given the variation in the locus of damage. The pros and cons of single case studies have been a source of some controversy and debate in neuropsychology. Further discussion can be found in Shallice (1988), Sokol *et al.* (1991), Caramazza (1992), Kosslyn and Intriligator (1992), McCloskey (1993), Miller (1993) and Semenza (1996), all of which give the flavour of this particular debate.

Advantages	Disadvantages
▪ Valuable because human brain lesions cannot be performed experimentally ▪ Brain damage may highlight role of damaged region in function	▪ Invasive ▪ Subject to individual differences ▪ Locus of damage may not always be accurately described ▪ Previous level of functioning may be unknown ▪ Other damaged brain regions may be producing deficits ▪ There may be confounding factors such as medication use

Electroencephalography (EEG)

In 1875, Richard Caton, a British physiologist at the University of Liverpool, found that it was possible to record from the scalps of living monkeys, cats and rabbits, changes in electrical potentials arising from the brain's 'feeble currents'. Over fifty years later, Hans Berger, a German psychiatrist, reported what is thought to be the first recording of brain electrical activity in humans (Berger, 1929). This brain potential became known as the Berger or alpha wave. Over ten years after this discovery, which was not entirely accepted by the scientific community, Adrian and Mathews (1934) reported a study in which they were able to record electrical activity from the olfactory bulbs of hedgehogs. The currents they were recording were **electroencephalograms** (EEGs), sometimes colloquially known as brain-waves. The EEG technique is now a part of the clinician's modern battery and, used selectively, can provide useful clinical information as well as information of use to research scientists. The technique is usually non-invasive to humans: the organism is not 'invaded' by any piece of mechanical equipment because electrical activity of the brain is recorded by electrodes placed on the scalp. Electrodes may be either placed on the scalp individually according to an agreed placement system called the International Electrode Placement System, or fitted to an electrode cap which the subject wears on the head like a swimming cap (see Figures 1.2 and 1.3).

In animals, it is possible to implant *micro*electrodes in specific neurons or around a neuron or groups of neurons and monitor the electrical activity from within (intracellular) or outside (extracellular) these neurons as the animal behaves. For ethical reasons, this procedure is not normally used in humans. Instead, *macro*electrodes placed on the scalp which measure activity from millions of neurons are used. The number of electrodes used is determined by the researcher's theoretical position and may range from 2 or 3 to over 130.

The EEG technique is widely used in healthy and clinical groups to indicate the brain's level of electrical activity while it is processing a particular task or responding to a particular stimulus. The EEG signal is generated by the post-synaptic dendrites of millions of brain cells called pyramidal cells. The signal itself is very small (not more than a 100 microvolts) and, therefore, must be amplified many times before it is fed through to a line polygraph (or monitor, if the

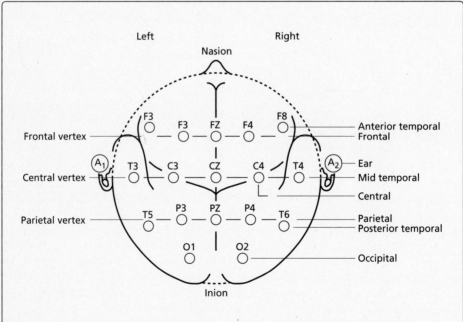

Figure 1.2 A selection of electrode sites from the 10–20 International Placement System

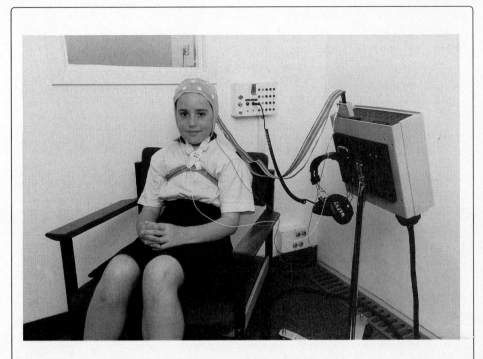

Figure 1.3   A typical experimental setting for recording of EEG

system is sophisticated enough) and seen as the EEG wave. The signal is the difference in potentials between two electrodes, where one electrode is a reference, i.e. it is placed at a site where little electrical activity is thought to occur (the earlobe, or an electrically inactive part of the body). There continues to be debate over which parts of the body are the best sites for non-active electrodes, however.

The EEG is divided into four classical wavebands. These wavebands describe how often a wave appears each second (its frequency, in hertz, Hz). From largest to smallest these are delta (1–4 Hz, i.e. the wave appears 1–4 times a second), theta (5–7 Hz), alpha (8–12 Hz) and beta (13–22 Hz), as seen in Figure 1.4.

Alpha is thought to be the human adult's resting EEG, normally seen under quiet, unstressful conditions (Niedermeyer, 1987). When there is a shift in frequency due to some cognitive activity or external stimulation, the neurons are thought to be desynchronized. This is sometimes called **alpha desynchronization** because alpha activity is replaced by the much faster beta activity.

The EEG is a measure of gross brain activity and function (activity from millions of cells is recorded by one electrode), although it does provide useful information

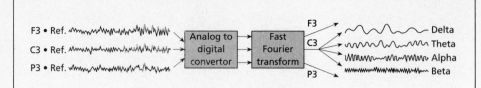

Figure 1.4   The conversion of the raw EEG from three electrode sites (F3, C3 and P3) into the four classical EEG frequencies: from slowest to fastest (delta, theta, alpha and beta)

about fluctuations in brain electrical activity and their relationship with function (Davidson, 1988). In an experimental setting, a 'baseline' EEG is recorded by having the subject sitting comfortably with eyes closed for two or more minutes or having them fixate on a spot ahead of them in the distance. This can then be used to compare with changes which might occur when the subject is performing a particular task, such as mental rotation or mental arithmetic. It is difficult to localize a function using this technique, however, since the generating source may be at some distance from the recording electrode. Often, there are other sources of evidence which guide the site of the electrodes chosen for recording. There is also the additional problem of 'smearing', i.e. the attenuation or impedance of the signal from the generating site to the recording site by the matter lying between these two areas.

A recent development in EEG has been brain electrical activity mapping (Duffy, 1986). This involves the conversion of recorded EEG, via a technique called fast-Fourier analysis, into coloured topographical maps. In this way, a section of the EEG record (called an epoch, lasting two and a half seconds, for example) is averaged and presented as a map indicating areas high or low in electrical activity. This technique makes EEG data look amazingly impressive and is an ornate method of presenting staid-looking data. The coloured representations, however, may be misleading in that areas of very low increases in activity show up as highly coloured. Different areas might look more or less activated depending on the epoch viewed. Researchers instead find it useful to analyze the numerical data provided by the technique (amplitude in microvolts, μV) and use the maps for illustration. The technique has been used, however, in areas as diverse as dyslexia (Duffy *et al.*, 1984; Duffy, 1986; Brunswick and Rippon, 1994) and human olfaction research (G.N. Martin, 1995a,b).

Advantages	Disadvantages
■ Non-invasive	■ Ability to localize function is weak
■ Has excellent temporal resolution	■ Activity is recorded from millions of groups of neurons
■ Relatively easy and cheap to operate	■ Signal may be attenuated and smeared
■ Can be used with healthy and clinical human subjects	■ Brain activity may fluctuate unpredictably and 'chaotically'
■ Can be used to record brain electrical activity in real time	■ Susceptible to movement artifact
■ Can be used to measure the brain's response to a number of psychological variables	

Event-related potentials (ERPs)

Event-related potentials (ERPs) are large, slow brainwaves which appear as a result of some sensory or cognitive stimulation. They are also called evoked potentials or averaged evoked potential waves. The ERP recording technique, like the EEG, is an electrophysiological one. That is, it is a measure of the brain's electrical activity. Under normal recording conditions, the EEG can be very 'messy' and 'busy': there is a lot of background noise. The ERP is useful in that it allows this background noise to be diminished through the repeated presentation of stimuli. This enhances what is called the **signal-to-noise ratio**.

For example, in a typical auditory evoked potential experiment, a series of stimuli (usually, a tone) is presented to the subject as EEG activity is being recorded from electrodes placed on the scalp. The brain's response to each stimulus is thus summed and averaged. Normally, a tone would not in itself have much effect in altering the EEG; repeated presentation of a stimulus, however, makes the effect on the EEG very clear. What appears above the noise is a large, clear, slow wave. These waves are given names such as N100, P200, N200 and P300, depending on **polarity** and **time of onset**, i.e. the direction of their peaks (N = a negative peak, usually meaning downward-pointing; P = positive peak, upward-pointing) and their time of appearance (in milliseconds, ms) following stimulus presentation. The polarity refers to the wave's **amplitude**; the time of onset refers to **latency**.

In addition to these 'standard' types of EP wave, there are others such as the N400. This is elicited when semantically inappropriate words end sentences presented to subjects word by word (Kutas and Hillyard, 1980). Even the P300 has been separated into two components, P3a and P3b. The early waves such as the N100 and P200 are thought to represent stimulus processing, the brain's initial response to sensory stimulation. These types of sensory stimulus are thought to elicit exogenous ERPs: evoked potentials that do not rely on 'cognitive' processing but which are the result of either the sensation or the perception of a sensory stimulus. An example of the types of change in electrical potentials is seen in Figure 1.5. The later waves, specifically the P300, are thought to reflect more endogenous components of processing such as decision-making, context-updating, cognitive processing or response to stimulus uncertainty. Because of this assumed function of the P300, researchers have paid considerable attention to it.

While many demand characteristics regulating the appearance of the P300 are known, the neural mechanisms underlying it are still something of a mystery.

The P300 was originally reported by Sam Sutton and his colleagues in 1965 (S. Sutton *et al.*, 1965). They found that if subjects were required to keep track of the number of stimuli in a series presented to them and the occasional stimulus did not appear, a late-going, positive wave (the P300) was elicited. In fact, the P300 is usually elicited when unusual, infrequent or unexpected stimuli appear in a series of frequent or expected stimuli (see Donchin and Coles (1988) and Polich and Kok (1995) for good reviews of the P300). One of the most common ERP tasks which

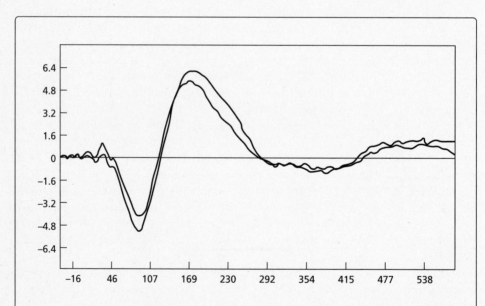

Figure 1.5 Example of the N100 (the negative peak) and P200 (the positive peak) elicited by an auditory stimulus. The two waves represent EPs recorded during exposure to two different odours

elicits the P300 is that called the 'auditory oddball'. Here, subjects count the number of low tones in a series of high and low tones where there are always fewer low tones (rare stimuli) than high (frequent stimuli). Presentation of the same type of tone does not produce the P300; the appearance of a different type of tone does. This can be seen in Figure 1.6.

Because of this change in brain activity to rare stimuli, it has been argued that the P300 reflects either the organism's decision-making process, i.e. deciding whether the tone is different, or context-updating, i.e. familiarization with new elements in the environment to accommodate the appearance of an unexpected stimulus in that environment.

The ERP technique has been used to study a number of cognitive processes including memory, language and attention. It has also been used to evaluate cognitive deterioration found in neuropsychiatric disorders (such as schizophrenia, anxiety, depression) and degenerative disorders (Alzheimer's disease, alcoholism, Korsakoff's disease, multi-infarct dementia, auto immune deficiency syndrome). If the P300 is a good index of successful processing, the argument goes, it may provide a useful indication of the onset of the types of cognitive deficit seen in these disorders (Polich and Kok, 1995). An example of the type of clinical evoked potential is seen in Figure 1.7.

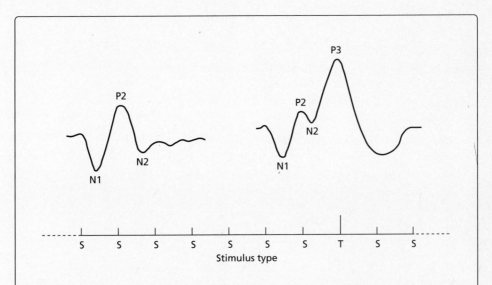

Figure 1.6 Two examples of EPs elicited by auditory stimuli. The waves on the left represent potentials evoked by a series of same-tone stimulus (e.g. a low tone); the waves on the right represent potentials elicited by a series of two different tones (e.g. a high and a low tone). In the latter condition, the P300 is evoked by the 'different-sounding' tone

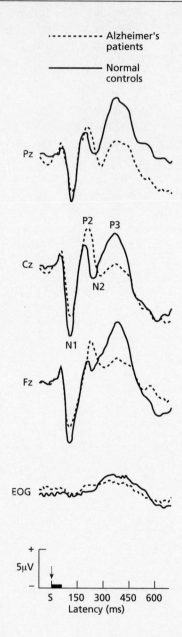

Figure 1.7   A comparison between the ERPs from patients with Alzheimer's disease and those from control subjects. A markedly reduced P300 is seen for the demented patients at each electrode site

Advantages	Disadvantages
▓ Can be used in healthy and clinical subjects	▓ Significance of some waves unknown
▓ Useful index of sensory function	▓ Mechanism underlying ERP poorly understood
▓ Possible measure of cognitive decline and normal cognitive function	
▓ Non-invasive	
▓ High temporal resolution (one millisecond)	
▓ Relatively easy to use and measure	

Magnetoencephalography (MEG)

A more recent electrophysiological technique is magnetoencephalography. Neurons, as well as generating electrical currents, also generate magnetic ones. These magnetic fields which accompany electrical activity can be measured via a machine called a superconducting quantum interference device (SQUID). The machine detects the activity of magnetic fields from a large number of neurons because the magnetic fields generated by single neurons are very weak. The subsequent recording is called the magnetoencephalograph or MEG. Unlike the EEG, MEG can be used to localize sources of activity fairly well and these sources can be plotted on a three-dimensional image of the subject's head. The significance of MEG to brain function is, as yet, unclear, however, and there continues to be controversy surrounding its use (see Ioannides (1991), Wikswo *et al.* (1993) and Hari and Salmelin (1997) for a complex discussion of these issues).

Advantages	Disadvantages
▓ Non-invasive.	▓ Subject cannot move during recording
▓ Superior to EEG in terms of localization	▓ Very expensive and requires magnetically-shielded room
▓ Signals not distorted by conduction between skull and sensor	

Computerized axial tomography (CT)

The first modern scientific method of imaging the brain was developed in the early 1960s and 1970s by Allan M. Cormack, a South African physicist, and Godfrey Hounsfield, a British engineer who worked independently on developing the technique (Cormack, 1963; Hounsfield, 1973). This technique, known as x-ray computerized tomography (x-ray CT), utilized the fact that different tissues absorb differing amounts of x-ray energy. If x-rays are passed through organs and tissues at various angles, the amount of radiation not absorbed by these tissues will allow the reconstruction of the structure of these organs and tissues. Computerized axial tomography (as it is now known) measures the amount of radiation not absorbed by the brain when x-rays are passed through the brain. A three-dimensional representation of the brain is produced as a result of the x-ray beam rotated through 180 degrees at 160 equally spaced positions. This became a useful technique to neurologists who could for the first time use such an image to detect structural anomalies in the living tissue of patients with brain trauma and lesions. Furthermore, an advantage was that the technique was relatively non-invasive and caused little discomfort to the patient.

A technique which owes much to the development of CT is **tissue radiography**. This method is used almost exclusively in animals and measures the distribution of radioactivity in a radioactively injected organ. After an injected animal is killed, post-mortem slices of the organ (e.g. the brain) are examined by placing them on film sensitive to radioactive materials. The developed film indicates the parts of the organ which were more or less radioactive. For example, a form of radio-actively labelled glucose will give information about brain metabolism because neurons derive energy from glucose (Sokoloff *et al.*, 1977). The principal problem with this technique for human subjects is the obvious need for *in vivo* measurement of function.

The basis for the development of human autoradiography was the idea that if the structure of an organ could be delineated by passing an x-ray through it, then it may be possible to trace the appearance of a radioactively labelled material, called a **radioisotope**, by measuring the degree of radioactivity emitted by particular living tissue. The radioisotopes that became used were those emitting positrons. The combination of a positron and electron would result in the annihilation of both, producing the emission of two gamma rays which travel in different directions. It was thought possible to detect these rays and locate their origin. This gave rise to positron emission tomography (PET).

Advantages	Disadvantages
▉ Provides structural image of the brain *in vivo*	▉ Poor spatial resolution
▉ Can be used in healthy and clinical subjects	▉ Provides measure of structure, not ongoing activity
▉ Indicates areas of brain abnormality	▉ Expensive and requires highly trained specialist staff
▉ Relatively non-invasive	

Positron emission tomography (PET)

Posner and Raichle (1994) observed that: 'A remarkable thing happened in the mid-1980s. For the first time we could actually look at pictures of the human brain while people thought. The pictures were of areas of increased blood flow caused by enhanced neural activity during mental effort'. The first reported study of increased regional cerebral blood flow during cognition was made in 1928 (Fulton, 1928). This noted increased blood flow over an arteriovenous malformation in the occipital lobe during reading. Positron emission tomography (PET), one of the newer brain imaging techniques, can provide a measure of brain function via the measurement of brain oxygen consumption, blood flow and glucose metabolism. Of these three measures, blood flow appears to be the most reliable (Raichle, 1994). Blood flow measures are described below but a brief description of the process of glucose metabolism gives the idea behind the workings of positron emission.

To measure glucose metabolism, radioactive glucose (usually 2-deoxyglucose, or 2DG) is injected into the subject and is taken up by metabolically active cells. The radioactive particles of the 2DG emit positrons which are detected by a scanner designed to detect the emission of these positrons. When positrons are emitted and collide with electrons, they form gamma rays which exit the head and are detected. Those areas high in metabolic activity will produce more gamma rays because they take up more glucose. The degree of gamma radiation is transformed into a three-dimensional colour-coded representation which indicates to the observer those regions that are high or low in metabolic activity or where there is increased blood flow.

Blood flow can also be measured by injecting radioactively labelled water (hydrogen and oxygen 15). When this water decays, positrons are emitted. It takes about a minute for the water to reach the brain; once there it can provide an image of blood flow, based on the principle that when neurons become active, blood flow to them increases. It is a relatively safe method, with oxygen 15 having a half-life of two minutes; it takes about ten minutes for the entire substance to decay and become non-radioactive (Raichle, 1994), thus reducing the chances of increased exposure to radiation.

To obtain a final image, PET investigations average responses across many subjects or conditions. The rationale is similar to that for ERP recording: averaging reduces background noise and highlights areas of genuine activity. PET also uses a method of subtraction to highlight those areas especially active during the performance of a particular task. Blood flow or radioactive counts obtained during the resting stage are subtracted from counts obtained during functional activation, i.e. when the subject is performing the task. The resulting image should then give an accurate representation of the specific regions activated by the task.

In a language task, for example, the control or resting state is subtracted from a condition in which the subject reads or listens to nouns (Petersen *et al.*, 1988). The reading/listening condition is then subtracted from a condition in which subjects may recite nouns. This illustrates those regions responsible for speech production. Finally, the recitation condition may be subtracted from a condition in which the subject utters a verb associated with the noun. This highlights those regions responsible for processing the semantic associations between words. This technique has been used to investigate a number of language tasks as well as memory, visual perception and recognition tasks.

PET provides quite a clear picture of areas of activity in living brains. It can highlight areas clearly to within three millimetres, providing good **spatial resolution**. However, what PET gains in spatial resolution it loses in temporal resolution (one minute) and in multiple averaging of subjects. This last limitation is important given the inter-individual variability in cortical anatomy and the claimed ability of PET to be able to focus on activity in small areas of the cortex.

Advantages	Disadvantages
▪ Can be used in clinical and healthy subjects	▪ Invasive
▪ High spatial resolution	▪ Poor temporal resolution (blood flow is slower than neural transmission)
▪ Measure of neuronal activity (indexed by blood flow/metabolism) *in vivo*	▪ Tasks must take longer than a minute
▪ Gives three-dimensional representation of regional activity	▪ Averaging does not take into account cortico-anatomical variation
▪ Can be used to measure brain activity during task performance	▪ Requires expensive technology (scanner, cyclotron and radiography department)
	▪ Often uses a small number of subjects

Functional magnetic resonance imaging (fMRI)

Functional magnetic resonance imaging (fMRI) is another brain imaging technique, developed during the 1980s. The technique is based on changes in the magnetic properties of atoms and was developed to observe the activity of atomic nuclei. It is an example of another technique developed independently by two people, Felix Bloch and Edward M. Purcell. It won them the Nobel prize in 1952. Originally called nuclear magnetic resonance imaging (NMRI), the term 'nuclear', with its connotations of radiation, was later dropped in favour of the less emotive magnetic resonance imaging (Maier, 1995).

NMRI can detect protons (hydrogen nuclei) which respond like compass needles in the presence of a magnetic field. The technique allows a magnetic field to pass through the subject's head, while the subject is lying inside a scanner (a narrow tube in which the entire body must fit). This scanner has a large magnet which ensures that protons are in the upright position. When a radiowave is passed through the head, the reverberations, or **precesses**, produced by the resonance of hydrogen molecules are then detected by the scanner. The reverberation produces an energy signal which is measured by the scanner as the protons return to their original state (D. Cohen *et al.*, 1993). This produces excellent anatomical images, as seen in Figure 1.8.

Until a short time ago, only structural images were possible with MRI, limiting its usefulness as a method of observing ongoing cognitive processing. Recently, however, it is has become possible to use the technique to detect signals which PET cannot detect (Cohen and Bookheimer, 1994). When neurons are active, increased oxygen reaches those active neurons. Yet these neurons exhibit anaerobic metabolism in that although increased blood flow accompanies increased neuronal activity (as PET can measure), the cells do not consume more oxygen. In fact, they use no more than if they were at rest. Thus, when increased blood flow occurs in the absence of oxygen consumption, the oxygen concentration of nearby blood vessels increases. It is this increase in oxygen concentration in blood flow that fMRI can detect. The relationship between oxygen, blood flow and MRI lies in the fact that the concentration of oxygen in blood can affect the magnetic properties of haemoglobin (Pauling, 1935). MRI is able to detect these magnetic changes (Ogawa *et al.*, 1990) and functionally induced changes (hence *functional* MRI).

Functional MRI has been used to detect responses to sensory and motor activation (Kwong *et al.*, 1992; Bandettini *et al.*, 1992), language tasks (G. McCarthy *et al.*, 1993) and motor and visual imagery tasks (see Cohen and Bookheimer, 1994). Functional MRI has several advantages over other brain imaging techniques, although it does also have its limitations.

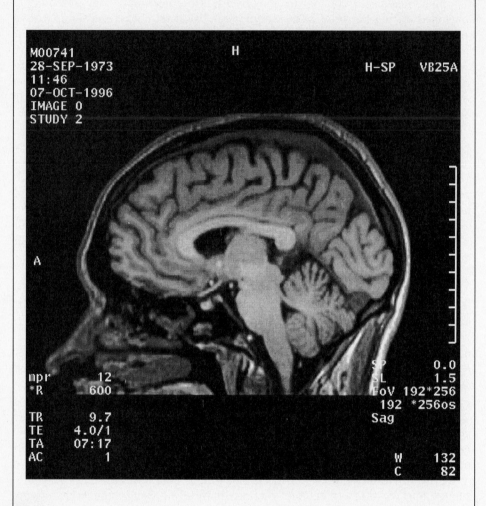

Figure 1.8 Sagittal view of an MRI scan of a living human brain

Advantages	Disadvantages
■ Measures direct changes in brain tissue from normal and clinical subjects	■ Decreases in venous oxygen content are not observed by MRI
■ Non-invasive and non-toxic	■ Procedure difficult if subject is claustrophobic
■ Allows structural and functional imaging	■ Poor temporal resolution (four images per second is current norm)
■ Provides the best spatial resolution of current imaging techniques (one to two millimetres)	■ Magnet precludes introduction of ferromagnetic materials
■ No known biological risk	■ Equipment producing radio frequencies must be shielded
■ More widely available and cheaper than PET	■ Some brain areas may be more efficient at regulating blood supply than others
	■ Obtaining good images from areas near to large cavities is difficult
	■ Is susceptible to movement artifact
	■ Transient scanner effects can produce one bad image out of ten or twenty
	■ Ensuring similar head placement for each subject is difficult
	■ Noisy procedure

Biochemical techniques

Sometimes a clearer picture of the neurophysiology of brain function can be provided by psychopharmacological techniques. Often these involve the administration of drugs to alleviate the symptoms of particular disorders. Therefore, alterations in symptoms brought about by the administration of the drug might allow scientists to examine the role of the drug and its induced neural changes in the appearance of a particular disorder. These disorders may be characterized by cognitive or behavioural irregularities or deficits such as chronic depression, mania, paranoia and thought disturbance (schizophrenia), motor disturbance (Parkinson's disease, Huntington's chorea), memory disturbances (Korsakoff's psychosis) and deteriorating intellectual performance (dementia). A number of the theories of localization of depressive illness, for example, have focused narrowly on a few neurotransmitters and their systems because these appear to be the ones primarily involved. These are discussed in Chapter 10.

Another biochemical technique used for quite different purposes is the Wada test, pioneered by Wada and Rasmussen in the 1950s and 1960s. This involves injecting sodium amytal into the carotid artery, briefly anaesthetizing the ipsilateral hemisphere, i.e. the one adjacent to the artery (Wada and Rasmussen, 1960). The technique utilizes the fact that humans have their language localized in one hemisphere. Its purpose is to localize the language areas of the patient's brain before he or she undergoes surgery. Localizing the function, therefore, will inform the surgeon of which areas to avoid during surgery.

At the beginning of the procedure, the patient begins counting from one to twenty with their arms raised, palms down and fingers spread. An injection of 100 g of amobarbitol sodium follows (this takes about four to five seconds). The patient is then requested to follow a command showing that they can identify their midline ('touch your nose'). Thirty to forty-five seconds after the injection, a memory test may also be administered. This takes the form of a series of eight objects presented to the patient and identified. The patients' recognition memory, i.e. the ability to recognize a series of target objects/names from a series of target and distractor objects/names, is tested after the language tasks.

During the anaesthesia, which lasts between four and ten minutes, the contralateral arm and leg become flaccid and there is little contralateral somatosensory response. Injection into the speech hemisphere results in an almost complete arrest of speech, lasting minutes; injection into the non-dominant hemisphere also produces speech impairments but these are brief. The language tasks used in this technique include expressive language and counting, e.g. the counting task described above; the recitation of the days of the week backwards and forwards, comprehension, e.g. the midline task above and other exercises such as following the command, 'stick out our tongue', naming, e.g. patients name drawings of a jacket or watch, or parts of them, and repetition and reading. Performance on all of these tests is rated according to severity of dysfunction. In surgical patients, this is the best technique for demonstrating localization of language function (Jones-Gotman et al., 1997).

Advantages	Disadvantages
▓ Provides best method of localizing language function	▓ Invasive
	▓ Cannot be used in healthy, non-clinical subjects
	▓ Cannot provide information at the molecular and regional level

Brain electrical stimulation

The technique of passing an electrical current across the brain using an electrode and observing its effects were most strikingly described by the American surgeon Wilder Penfield and his colleagues in the 1930s. Penfield found that stimulating certain parts of brains of patients undergoing surgery for epilepsy produced stereotypical behaviours such as reports of sensations (tingling or tickling) or uttering groans or cries (Penfield and Jasper, 1954). Penfield also reported that a patient whose brain was stimulated would recall a melody or a song from the distant past. However, the remarkable recall of memories and melodies only occurred in a small number of subjects (about 8 per cent).

The experiments usefully described the regions producing motor movements (Penfield and Rasmussen, 1950) and associated stimulation of the primary motor cortex (specifically a part called the precentral gyrus) with the movement of various parts of the body. When the results of stimulation are transposed onto a homunculus (a figure showing the parts of the body, with the size of the parts drawn in proportion to the number of receptors that each part has), the figure is characterized by large hands and a large face (see Figure 1.9. This is entirely due to that fact that these parts of the body perform the finest and most complex movements and, therefore, have the largest number of receptors.

Advantages	Disadvantages
▪ Good for localizing low-level behaviours such as sensation or motor movement	▪ Invasive
▪ Surgery provides an opportunity for brain stimulation not available in control subjects	▪ Cannot provide consistent information about higher function (e.g. memory)
	▪ Information is based on originally unhealthy subjects
	▪ Cannot be performed on healthy subjects

Lateralization techniques

Although fundamentally concerned with localization of function, neuropsychology is also interested in whether the different hemispheres perform different functions. The findings from studies of human brain lesions indicate that they do. Not surprisingly, there are various neuropsychological techniques for the measurement of laterality or asymmetry of function in normal, healthy individuals. EEG

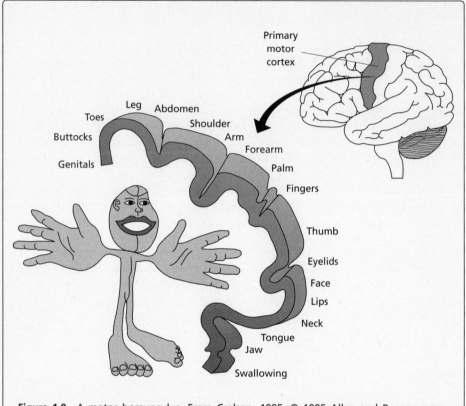

Figure 1.9 A motor homunculus. From Carlson, 1995. © 1995 Allyn and Bacon; reproduced by permission

and brain imaging techniques can provide such information, but other neuropsychological tests examine laterality more explicitly. The most commonly used techniques are dichotic listening, visual hemifield studies and lateral eye movement

Dichotic listening refers to the presentation of different auditory verbal stimuli (a word or an uttered digit or nonsense syllable) simultaneously to the two ears via headphones, as illustrated by Figure 1.10. When the subject has to say which word he or she heard, there is usually a **right ear advantage (REA)**, i.e. the subject identifies the word presented to the right ear. Doreen Kimura, in a well known study, presented her subjects with two different spoken digits in pairs to both ears. Patients with left temporal lobe damage performed more poorly than patients with right temporal lobe injury (Kimura, 1961). These lobes contain the sensory system responsible for hearing. The finding indicated that verbal auditory material could not be understood by the damaged left (language-based) hemisphere. However,

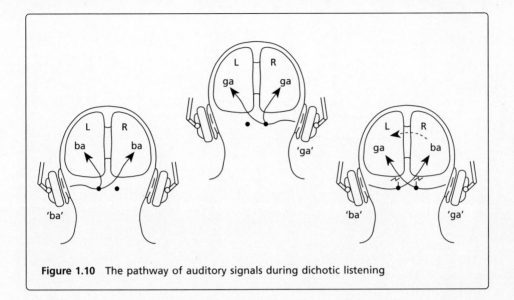

Figure 1.10   The pathway of auditory signals during dichotic listening

auditory information is received by both hemispheres. To account for this, Kimura argued that during dichotic listening, the ipsilateral auditory pathways (from the left ear to left hemisphere and right ear to right hemisphere) were suppressed by the contralateral pathway (the left ear to the right hemisphere and right ear to the left hemisphere). So, the superiority of the right ear could have been due to information not getting to the right hemisphere because the left hemisphere suppressed the signal or because the information that was transferred interhemispherically was lost on its way from the ipsilateral to contralateral hemisphere. Interestingly, although there appears to be a right ear advantage for verbal stimuli, there appears to be a left ear superiority for the processing of musical chords and melodies, at least in non-musicians (Gordon, 1980). Chapter 4 takes up these issues of localization and individual differences, and more information on the technique can be found in Hugdahl (1995).

Visual field studies, or visual hemifield studies, usually involve the projection of a visual stimulus to one half of the subject's visual field extremely quickly while the subject focuses on a central fixation spot (usually a cross on a white board). The machine presenting the stimulus, a tachistoscope, is capable of presenting images, words, shapes, objects etc. at millisecond speed. See Figure 1.11.

The technique is useful because the visual system is crossed: that is, at a point along its pathway, it transfers information to the side of the brain opposite that to which stimuli were presented. Figure 1.12 illustrates this system.

Using this technique, researchers have found that words flashed to the right visual field (RVF) and processed by the left hemisphere are better identified than words presented to the left visual field (LVF) and processed by the right hemisphere (Bryden, 1965). Right hemisphere (LVF) advantage has been found for

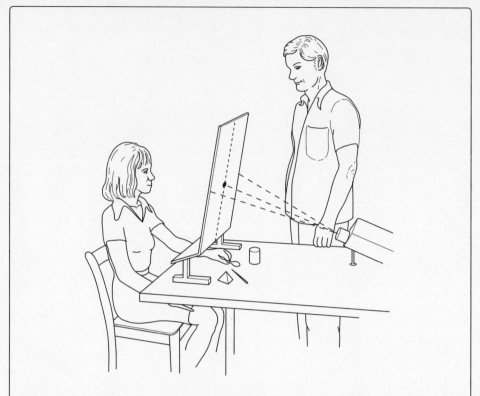

Figure 1.11   A typical testing session involving the tachistoscopic presentation of stimuli. As the subject fixates on a central spot, an image can be flashed to that spot or to its left or right

identification of pictorial stimuli and for identification requiring visuospatial skill (Kimura, 1969). This technique has been (and continues to be) widely used to examine the performance of split-brain patients and is used effectively with normal, healthy subjects (Resnick *et al.*, 1994), although a right visual field advantage at one testing session can evaporate at the next testing session.

Finally, **lateral eye movement (LEM,** also **conjugate lateral eye movement)** has been of interest to neuropsychologists because of its possible link with lateralization of function (Beaumont, 1996b). Early studies were encouraged by the finding that patients appeared to look either to the left or to the right when answering particular questions (Day, 1964). It was suggested that cognitive activity in one hemisphere produced movement in the contralateral (opposite) eye (Bakan, 1969). Questions with a verbal component, therefore, produced right lateral eye movements because verbal cognitive activity is undertaken in the left hemisphere,

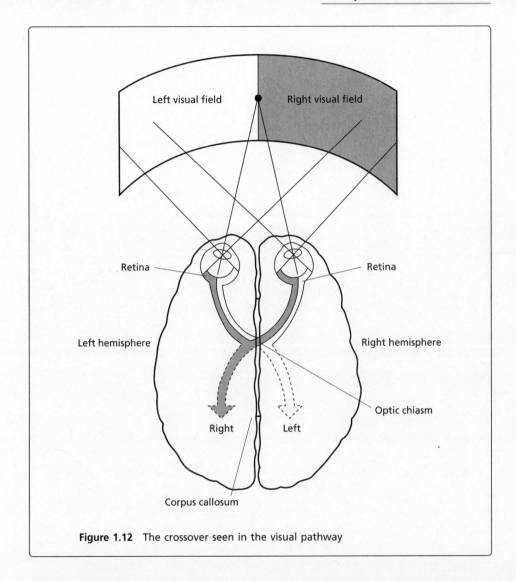

Figure 1.12 The crossover seen in the visual pathway

whereas questions requiring spatial analysis produced left lateral eye movement because activity is primarily being undertaken in the right hemisphere. There is no strong evidence that LEMs are a reliable indicator of hemispheric asymmetry, however, although there continues to be interest in the technique.

Advantages	Disadvantages
■ Non-invasive ■ Can be used in any subject with intact auditory and visual system ■ Inexpensive and easy to set up	■ Indirect measure of lateralization ■ Subjects' performance can be variable (ear and visual field advantage can change from one testing session to another)

DISCUSSION POINT

What is it like to undergo a brain scan?

The Wellcome Department of Cognitive Neurology in Queen Square, London, is part of the Institute of Neurology and houses one of the most active PET and MRI facilities in the world. It undertakes several projects involving cognition and emotion and how the brain behaves while it experiences these psychological phenomena. Among these projects are brain imaging studies of depression, memory, motor behaviour, dyslexia, and visual and spatial perception. One of its strongest research areas, however, is the study of the neuroanatomy of language: word recognition, reception, comprehension and production.

I had been asked by a colleague to participate in an experiment on word and symbol recognition. On arrival I was taken to the basement of the building which houses the PET and MRI scanners. I was struck by the spotlessness of the place: cleaners are constantly on duty.

A short length of bright white corridor brought us to the radiographers' room and, opposite that, the MRI and PET laboratories. I am told to remove all metal objects from my body (the MRI scanner *is* a magnet) and complete a form requesting information about my health. The radiographer leads me into a small, bare room with no defining features apart from an MRI scanner which has a narrow, bed-like structure emerging from a hole in the middle of the scanner. This is large enough to accommodate a prostrate human body. I am asked to lie on the bed and to wear a set of earplugs because the scanning is noisy, but not uncomfortably loud (it is about 9 decibels). I am given a panic button which I can press at any time when I am inside the scanner to attract attention. I am told to keep my head absolutely still (it is placed between two padded clamps) because any head movement can contaminate the spatial resolution of the image of my brain. The bed, remotely controlled by the radiographer, is moved inside the scanner.

My head gradually makes its way from the brightness of the room into the relative darkness of the cylindrical interior of the scanner. Even if I had wanted to move,

➠

there is not much room to do so. An intercom keeps me in contact with the radiologist at all times. Then, the scanning starts. Each scan sounds like an extremely loud but muffled buzz. The first stage of scanning ensures that my head is positioned at the right angle and that my image can be obtained clearly by the radiographer. Then, for what seems like twenty minutes but was actually about ten, the machine scans my brain. Although I have colleagues who found the procedure comfortable, the experience for me was claustrophobic. No true claustrophobe, I imagine, could sustain that length of time in a darkened cylinder.

The scanning over, the bed slides out of the scanner and I can move again. There is no disorientation but I feel a little woozy, not surprisingly given that I had been prostrate for ten minutes with plugs in my ears.

I am taken from the MRI room to the PET laboratory. Before participating, I am told to visit the lavatory because the experiment is about two hours long (twelve scans of six minutes each) and I will be lying still on my back for this time. There would be no opportunity for bladder-relief during the experiment.

The PET laboratory comprises two rooms: a small control room where the subject is monitored, stimuli are presented and images are collected, and another much larger room which houses the PET scanner. This scanner is a little like the MRI scanner in that it also has a cylindrical hole but is easier to walk around because it is not designed to accommodate the whole body. Before lying on the bed extending from the scanner, marks are placed on my face which act as the scanner's reference points. These are checked between scans. A plastic helmet with Velcro straps is placed on my head which helps to keep it in place while the imaging occurs. Lying down on the bed, my left arm is exposed and a canula is placed inside my vein by a clinician. It is a little like giving blood. The canula is then attached to a tube which automatically injects radioactive isotope into my bloodstream at prescribed intervals. Any kink in the tube results in the automatic ringing of an alarm, warning the experimenter that the flow has been obstructed. The level of radioactivity is low and harmless, the equivalent of taking a barium meal. Nonetheless, you are only allowed to be PET scanned once in twelve months for reasons of health and safety, and premenopausal women are never PET scanned because of possible complications with childbirth. It is also rare for children to be PET scanned in an experimental context.

Unlike the MRI procedure, the whole body does not enter the scanner during PET scanning. Instead, the top part of the head enters the hollow middle of the scanner. This allows the participant to observe any experimental stimuli presented. In this case, an overhead Macintosh computer monitor was placed in my line of vision in order to present stimuli to which I would respond using a keypad kept to my right. A blanket covered my body to prevent me getting cold (the cool environment is necessary for the computers to work efficiently). My task is to indicate whether real words, pseudowords (legally spelled but nonsense words), and false fonts (a type of print) contained letters that rose above the midline of the word (called ascenders). For example, no letter in the word 'car' rises above the midline, but the 't' in 'cat' does. The aim of the experiment is to discover whether normal and dyslexic readers use different parts of their cerebral machinery in making these decisions.

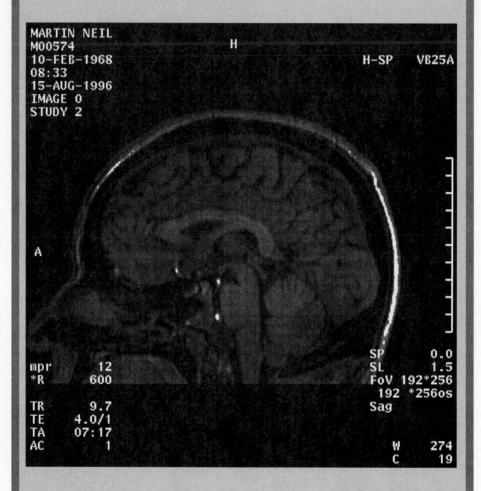

Figure 1.13 The author's MRI scan

The experimenter informs me that the experiment will begin in about two minutes, dims the lights and leaves the room. Two minutes later I have to indicate using one of two buttons next to my right hand whether a word has a letter above the midline in a series of about twelve presented words. Because PET relies on averaging activity across trials, there were a number of trials (hence the two hours lying still). After each trial, the experimenter checks that my head is in the correct position.

Lying in a supine position for two hours makes you relaxed (especially if you are tested at 8.30 in the morning) and after the experiment, I experienced no discomfort. I removed the helmet and was led out of the scanning room to observe my MRI scans which can be printed on a normal printer. An example of one of these appears in Figure 1.13. I am assured that this is normal.

Summary

☐ The aim of human neuropsychology is to understand the relationship between the brain's activity and structure and its function.

☐ Neuropsychology has a long history dating back to the ancient Greeks. Originally, it was the heart that was thought to be responsible for the functions we now ascribe to the brain.

☐ The first documented case of brain damage and behaviour is the *Edwin Smith Surgical Papyrus*, a document which dates back to the seventeenth century BC. This describes 48 cases of brain and skull injury, their consequences and their treatment.

☐ Modern landmarks in neuropsychology include Golgi's method of staining brain tissue which allows the observer to see the tissue's structure, Cajal's discovery that the nervous system was made up of neurons, Helmholtz's discovery that neurons communicate with each other via electrical signals, Gall's notion that skull protuberances resulted from underlying active cortical regions, Broca's post-mortem study of Leborgne ('Tan'), and Fritsch and Hitzig's studies of localization of motor function in dogs.

☐ Some of these techniques employed by neuropsychologists are relatively simple to use. These include dichotic listening and tachistoscopic presentations. Others, such as EEG, PET, CAT and fMRI, require considerable training and expertise.

☐ Measures of the brain's electrical activity include EEG (electroencephalography) and ERP (event-related potential) recording, and MEG (magneto-encephalography). Measures of regional cerebral blood flow include PET (positron emission tomography) and fMRI (functional magnetic resonance imaging). MRI and CT (computerized axial tomography) techniques are used to observe brain structure.

☐ Other localization techniques, e.g. dichotic listening, visual field procedures and lateral eye movement, are indirect measures of localization.

☐ Much of the information derived from brain function comes from the performance of brain-damaged individuals or individuals who have undergone brain surgery. This approach provides an excellent opportunity to see which behaviours are disrupted with brain damage but is restricted by limited samples, unclear description of damage and the variability of location of the damage.

☐ Each neuropsychological technique has its strengths and weaknesses. EEG and ERP recording, for example, have high temporal resolution but they are not particularly effective localizing tools. PET and fMRI, on the other hand, have excellent spatial resolution but are comparatively slow when compared with EEG and with the speed of the events in the brain that they measure.

☐ The future of the neuropsychology probably lies in the development of brain imaging techniques, perhaps in combination with other, electrophysiological techniques. Advances are currently being made towards implementing this sort of research strategy.

Recommended further general and specific reading

Key: (1) = introductory, (3) = intermediate, (5) = advanced

General

Andreassi, J.L. (1996) *Psychophysiology: Human behaviour and psychophysiological response* (3rd edition). Hillsdale, NJ: Lawrence Erlbaum Associates. *(3)*

Code, C., Wallesch, C-W., Joanette, Y. and Roch, A. (1996). *Classic Cases in Neuropsychology*. Hillsdale, NJ: Lawrence Erlbaum Associates. *(3)*

Feinberg, T.E. and Farah, M.J. (1997). *Behavioral Neurology and Neuropsychology*. New York: McGraw-Hill. *(2)*

Frakowiack, R.J.S., Friston, K.J., Frith, C.D., Dolan, R.J. and Mazziotta, J.C. (1997). *Human Brain Function*. Oxford: Academic Press. *(3)*

Hannay, H.J. (1986). *Experimental Techniques in Neuropsychology.* New York: Oxford University Press. *(3)*

Posner, M. and Raichle, M. (1994). *Images of Mind.* New York: Scientific American Library. *(2)*

Rugg, M.D. and Coles, M. (1995). *Electrophysiology of Mind.* New York: Oxford University Press. *(4)*

Shallice, T. (1988). *From Neuropsychology to Mental Structure.* Cambridge: Cambridge University Press. *(4)*

Specific

Beaumont, J.G. (1996) Lateral eye movement. In J.G. Beaumont, P.M. Keneally and M.J.C. Rogers (eds), *The Blackwell Dictionary of Neuropsychology.* Oxford: Blackwell. *(2)*

Cabeza, R. and Nyberg, L. (1997). Imaging cognition: an empirical review of PET studies with normal subjects. *Journal of Cognitive Neuroscience,* **9**(1), 1–26. *(2)*

Caramazza, A. (1986). On drawing inferences about the structure of normal cognitive systems from the analysis of patterns of impaired performance: the case for single-patient studies. *Brain and Cognition,* **5**, 41–66. *(3)*

Caramazza, A. (1992). Is cognitive neuropsychology possible? *Journal of Cognitive Neuroscience,* **4**(1), 80–95. *(3)*

Damasio, H. and Damasio, A.R. (1989). *Lesion Analysis in Neuropsychology.* Oxford: Oxford University Press. *(4)*

Davidson, R.J. (1988). EEG measures of cerebral asymmetry: conceptual and methodological issues. *International Journal of Neuroscience,* **39**, 71–89. *(3)*

Friston, K.J. (1997). Imaging cognitive anatomy. *Trends in Cognitive Sciences,* **1**(1), 21–7. *(2)*

Gold, S., Arndt, S., Johnson, D., O'Leary, D.S. and Andreasen, N.C. (1997). Factors that influence effect size in 15 O PET studies: a meta-analytic review. *Neuroimage,* **5**, 280–91. *(3)*

Hugdahl, K. (1995). Dichotic listening: probing temporal lobe functional integrity. In R.J. Davidson and K. Hugdahl (eds), *Brain Asymmetry.* Cambridge, MA: MIT Press. *(4)*

Jennings, J.M., McIntosh, A.R., Kapur, S., Tulving, E. and Houle, S. (1997). Cognitive subtractions may not add up: the interaction between semantic processing and response mode. *Neuroimage,* **5**, 229–39. *(3)*

Jones-Gotman, M., Rouleau, I. and Snyder, P.J. (1997). Clinical and research contributions to the intracarotid amobarbital procedure to neuropsychology. *Brain and Cognition,* **33**, 1–6. *(1)*

Kosslyn, S.M. and Intriligator, J.M. (1992). Is cognitive neuropsychology plausible? The perils of sitting on a one-legged stool. *Journal of Cognitive Neuroscience,* **4**(1), 96–106. *(3)*

Macmillan, M. (1995). Experimental and clinical studies of localisation before Flourens. *Journal of the History of Neuroscience,* **4**(3/4), 139–54. *(4)*

McCloskey, M. (1993). Theory and evidence in cognitive neuropsychology: a 'radical' response to Robertson, Knight, Rafal and Shimamura (1993). *Journal of Experimental Psychology: Learning, Memory and Attention,* **19**(3), 718–34. *(3)*

Polich, J. and Kok, A. (1995). Cognitive and biological determinants of P300: an integrative overview. *Biological Psychology,* **41**, 103–46. *(3)*

Raichle, M.E. (1994). Images of the mind: studies with modern imaging techniques. *Annual Review of Psychology,* **45**, 333–56. *(3)*

Raichle, M.E. (1994). Visualizing the mind. *Scientific American*, April, 36–42. *(2)*

Robertson, L.C., Knight, R.T., Rafal, R. and Shimamura, A.P. (1993). Cognitive neuropsychology is more than single-case studies. *Journal of Experimental Psychology: Learning, Memory and Attention*, **19**(3), 710–17. *(3)*

Snyder, P.J. and Harris, L.J. (1997). The intracarotid amobarbital procedure: an historical perspective. *Brain and Cognition*, **33**, 18–32. *(2)*

Sokol, S.M., McCloskey, M., Cohen, N.J. and Aliminosa, D. (1991). Cognitive representations and processes in arithmetic: inferences from the performance of brain-damaged subjects. *Journal of Experimental Psychology: Learning, Memory and Attention*, **17**(3), 355–76. *(4)*

Chapter Two

The brain I: basic neurophysiology

■ The nervous system and its two major divisions

The greyish, soft, 1400 gram jelly-like lump encased by the skull, together with the one-centimetre-thick cord extending from the back of it, provides the fundamental basis for adult human behaviour. The brain is part of the **nervous system (NS)**, the body's mass of interconnecting and interacting nervous tissue. The NS comprises two major parts: the **central nervous system (CNS)** and the **peripheral nervous system (PNS)**. The CNS consists of nervous tissue encased by the skull and the vertebral column, namely the brain and the spinal cord. The PNS consists of nervous tissue outside these bones: the cranial nerves, the spinal nerves and some sensory organ nerves. It contains two other distinct systems called the **somatic nervous system** (which receives sensory information from the muscles and skin and sends messages to skeletal muscles) and the **autonomic nervous system** (which innervates the body's glands and organs). The autonomic nervous system (ANS) has two branches: the sympathetic branch which is responsible for arousal of the body via increased heart rate, release of adrenaline and suppression of the digestive system, and the parasympathetic branch which has the opposite role of decreasing heart rate and facilitating the activity of the digestive system. Thus, one is energy-consuming, the other energy-conserving.

There is considerable interaction between the CNS and PNS. The PNS nerves can detect stimuli from outside the body and relay messages about these stimuli to the brain. Alternatively, the brain itself may send messages to the PNS. The cranial and spinal nerves of the PNS are considered in more detail in Chapter 3, as are the basic anatomy and structure of the brain. This chapter deals with the composition of the CNS and how the building blocks of the CNS behave and interact to allow behaviour to take place.

■ Cells in the nervous system

The CNS and PNS are made up of different types of cells. These cells are principally of two types: **nerve cells**, known as **neurons**, and **supporting cells**, known as **glial cells**. It has been estimated that between 100 billion and 1000 billion (1 000 000 000 000) neurons exist in the NS, although the exact number can never be known. Although this estimate is staggering enough, if you consider that neurons also communicate with other neurons which, in turn, communicate with other neurons, you can quickly see how challenging it is to understand and study the functions of the brain. It is estimated that neurons make 13 trillion (13 000 000 000 000) connections with each other. The complexity of communication is further compounded by the *ways* in which neurons communicate. This is returned to later in the chapter.

Glial cells are so called because, as their name suggests, they are thought to be the glue that keeps neurons together. Although this description is not strictly accurate (glial cells do not actually stick neurons together), they are closely attached to neurons and serve the purpose of attending to the needs of these neurons. Whereas neurons perform the functions of the CNS, glial cells give essential practical and physical support to those functioning neurons. They can repair neuronal damage, can shape the neuron and can control how the neuron develops. There are more glial cells than neurons in the CNS. If you imagine the neurons as the kings and queens of the NS, then glial cells are the valets and ladies-in-waiting.

Neurons communicate with each other via electrical signals. This electrical signal or discharge is called a **nerve impulse** and allows neurons to communicate with each other along great distances. The impulses are fast (in the order of milliseconds) and can be sent between neurons of the CNS and the PNS or from neurons in the CNS and PNS to other neurons in the NS.

■ The neuron

We are born with all the neurons that we will get in life – hundreds of billions. It has been estimated that we lose 100 000 of these a day from birth. Unlike other cells in the body, neurons cannot regenerate when they die (in fact, the quest to find a way of regenerating neurons has been described as the 'holy grail' of neurobiology). From birth onwards, therefore, we encounter a massive loss of neurons. Based on the above estimate, for example, we would lose about 36.5 million neurons in one year. This does not necessarily mean that we will be worse off, having to struggle with a few billion neurons. In fact, the neuronal loss is necessary because redundant neurons are shed and connections between the existing efficient neurons are increased (a topic returned to in Chapter 12).

The neuron has a number of identifiable characteristics and physical features which are made visible by staining techniques. These techniques involve special dyes that highlight specific parts of the neuron. Some techniques highlight some parts of the neuron, other techniques highlight other parts. The various parts sometimes appear as dark or coloured stains, contrasting with the light staining around them. The basic structure of the neuron can be seen in Figure 2.1.

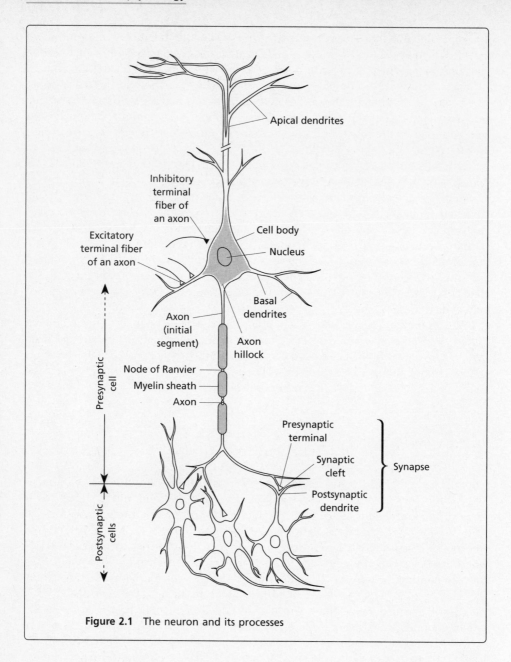

Figure 2.1   The neuron and its processes

A layer of lipids, called a **membrane**, covers the cell. This membrane exists to separate one neuron from another and contains substances which can (1) detect material outside the cell and (2) permit the exit of material from the cell. These substances actively transport material in and out of the cell. More importantly, the membrane has certain properties which enable it to carry nerve impulses, the electrical charge that enables neurons to communicate with each other.

The centre of the neuron is called the **cell body**. Other names for it include the **soma** and **perikaryon**. Inside the cell body is a nucleus and inside the nucleus, a **nucleolus**. The nucleus is large and makes the neuron clearly distinguishable from other NS cells. The neuron is surrounded by **extracellular fluid**, so called because it exists outside the cell (this is also known as interstitial fluid). Fluid inside the cell is called **intracellular fluid**. Several processes extend from the cell body which receive or send electrical signals. These are called **dendrites** and **axons**. There are usually several dendrites extending from the cell body but only one axon. The dendrites might branch out to form a mass of dendritic processes. This is advantageous because the role of the dendrites is to receive signals from other neurons. The dendrites might also have on them small spikes or **spines** which increase their surface area and therefore allow more information to be received. It is the axon which is responsible for carrying the nerve impulse to other neurons. Axons can be either short or very long (the longest is just over one metre). The advantage of having axons of differing lengths is that it permits them to communicate with neurons that are very far from or very near to the axon.

The axon leaves the cell body at a point called the **axon hillock** or **initial segment**. At the end of the axon there is a slight, knob-like enlargement called a **terminal**. This also has several other sobriquets including **bouton termineau**, **terminal button** and **synaptic knob**. The terminal is normally found close to the neuron receiving the axon's message. The point of contact between the terminal button and the other neuron is called the **synapse**. This is where information is sent from one neuron to another. In the PNS, terminal buttons may form synapses with muscle cells.

Communication at the synapse is made possible by the release of chemical substances known as a **neurotransmitters**. These are stored in the **synaptic vesicles** of the terminal button. Although there are many neurotransmitters, they are fairly hard to identify. They are released by the nerve impulse which prompts the neurotransmitter to leave the terminal button and enter the space between the button and the receiving neuron. This space is called the **synaptic cleft** and is approximately 20 nm wide (about 0.00002 mm). Because neurotransmitters are released by the terminal button and the proteins necessary for transmitting these chemicals are stored there, the membrane of the neuron facing the cleft (the terminal button) is thicker than that of the receiving neuron. This thicker membrane is called the **presynaptic membrane** because it is situated before the cleft (hence, *pre*synaptic). The surface of the cell contacted is called the **postsynaptic membrane**. Similarly, those neurons situated before the cleft are called **presynaptic neurons** whereas those receiving the neurotransmitter are called **postsynaptic neurons**. Synapses can occur almost anywhere on the neuron. For example, there can be synapses on the cell body (**axosomatic synapses**), the

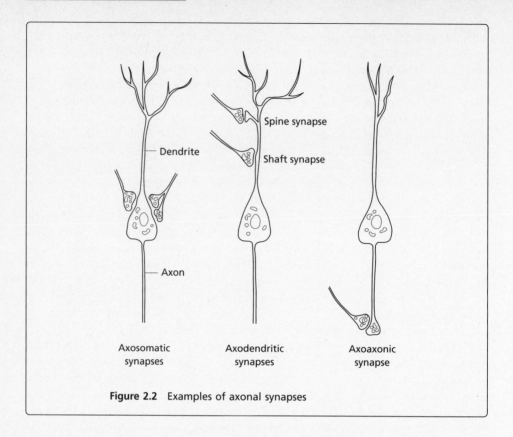

Spine synapse

Dendrite

Shaft synapse

Axon

Axosomatic
synapses

Axodendritic
synapses

Axoaxonic
synapse

Figure 2.2   Examples of axonal synapses

dendrites (**axodendritic synapses**) and on the axon itself (**axoaxonic synapses**), as seen in Figure 2.2.

There are hundreds, possibly thousands, of synapses made on each neuron. The number is so large that the Nobel prize-winning neurobiologist Gerald Edleman has estimated that it would take 32 million years to count the number of synapses in the CNS.

■ Inside the neuron

So far, we have considered the basic structure of the neuron and its processes. The internal parts of the neuron are what enable it to survive and function. The fluid inside the neuron is called **cytoplasm**. Various materials are present in cytoplasm which serve the neuron in various ways. For example, there are structures which utilize glucose and provide the neuron with the energy it requires. These are called **mitochondria**. There are materials which allow the synthesis of protein (these are called **free ribosomes**) and others which produce a substance that the neuron secretes (this is called **rough endoplasmic reticulum** or **rER**). The patches of rER are also called **Nissl bodies**. The substances produced by the rER are stored in the neuron's vesicles before they go on to be stored by the **Golgi apparatus**. From there the stored substances can be secreted by the neuron by a process called **exocytosis**. In exocytosis, the store of substances moves towards the membrane of the neuron and fuses with it, causing the store to burst and spill out its contents into the extracellular fluid. The substance (usually a neurotransmitter) can then be taken up by the receiving site.

Other materials inside the neuron include **chromosomes** (strands of **deoxyribonucleic acid** or **DNA**) which are found inside the nucleus. These are important for producing proteins (the individual blueprints for producing specific proteins are contained in the **genes**). Proteins are the essential builders of the cell, giving each neuron its structure. They also serve as enzymes, substances which work on molecules to alter their shape or function by bringing them together or splitting them.

The neuron also contains threads of protein called **neurofibrils**, which give the neuron its overall structure (**cytoskeleton**) and allow material to be transported by the neuron's processes. **Actin**, for example, consists of microfilaments found in axons and other processes. These actin filaments help to 'direct' the axon. At the end of an axon there is a **growth cone**, the part of the axon which, as its name suggests, grows. Actin helps to produce the movements of the cone as the axon develops and moves towards its final, target site.

Other threads are called **microtubules** (and **m-associated proteins** or **MAPs**). These define the shape of the processes in which they are found. The principal function of microtubules is to allow transport of materials within the neuron. In fact, a number of materials are transported in the axon from and to the cell body. **Anterograde axonal transport** describes the transport of material *from* the cell body to the axon's terminal; **retrograde axonal transport** describes the transport of materials *to* the cell body. The former is useful because it can transport materials that can only be synthesized in the cell body (e.g. mitochondria). The latter helps to bring substances to the cell body which could alter its function (such as changing the amount of neurotransmitter produced). It also brings back axonal debris which needs to be broken down by sacks of enzymes, called **lysosomes**, contained within the Golgi apparatus of the neuron. It is the function of lysosomes to break down materials and substances that the cell no longer requires and either reuse them or expel them from the cell. Of the two forms of transport, anterograde axonal transport is faster, moving material at about 5 mm per hour.

■ The axon and myelination

The axon is one of the most important processes extending from the cell body. It is covered in a membrane called the **axonal membrane** (or **axolemma**). Almost all axons in the CNS are surrounded by a **myelin sheath**. This sheath is made up of a number of layers (**lamellae**) of lipids (fats) and proteins called **myelin**, which insulates the axon from its surroundings and from other neurons. The sheath contains about 80 per cent lipid and 20 per cent protein. This insulation is advantageous because it helps the rapid conduction of nerve impulses. It does this by reducing the loss of the flow of current from the axon to the surrounding fluid. Axons covered in myelin are called **myelinated axons**; those not covered are called **unmyelinated axons**. The thicker the sheath the more rapid the speed of signal conduction. One way of estimating conduction velocity (the speed of the nerve impulse) is to multiply the diameter of the axon (in micrometres, μm) by six. Thus, an axon with a diameter of 20 μm (the maximum diameter) conducts at approximately 120 metres per second. A thinner axon with half that diameter would conduct at 60 metres per second. An unmyelinated axon with a diameter of 1 μm would conduct extremely slowly, at 1 metre or less per second. In some diseases, axons can become demyelinated (e.g. in multiple sclerosis). As a result, impulse conduction is either slowed down considerably or is stopped completely. If the disease progresses, the axon itself (as well as its myelin sheath) may degenerate.

The myelin sheath is cylindrical in shape, gives off a whitish appearance (because of the fat content) and is produced by a specific type of glial cell. The axon is not entirely covered in myelin, however. At intervals, the axonal membrane is unmyelinated, exposing it to the surrounding fluid. These unmyelinated points of the axon are called the **nodes of Ranvier** and separate the segments of myelinated axon (the nodes are about 1–2 μm in length; the myelinated segment is about 1 mm). These nodes assist in the speed of conduction by making the nerve impulse jump from one node to the next. This process is called **saltatory conduction** and is explained in more detail in the section, 'How neurons communicate II: neurotransmission' on page 56.

In the CNS, myelin is made from a type of glial cell called **oligodendrocytes** (or **oligodendroglia**). In the PNS, the myelin is produced by **Schwann cells**. Both of these cells are illustrated in Figure 2.3.

The structure of these sheaths in the two systems is virtually identical although the supporting cells themselves perform myelination differently. In the CNS, one oligodendrocyte sends out processes which produce myelin segments for several axons; in the PNS, one Schwann cell produces a myelin segment for one axon. Myelination is an important process in the NS since it is closely related to functional maturation. It begins before birth and continues until the age of two years, possibly ending during adolescence or young adulthood.

The insulation that glial cells provides is essential. All neurons are prone to the effects of mechanical stressors which might cause some damage or disruption to the structure of the NS. The insulation and protection that bone and glial cells provide to neurons in the CNS are much more secure than the protection afforded to neurons in the PNS. All neurons in the CNS are protected by bony casing externally and by supporting cells internally. Although PNS neurons do not receive the same degree of protection, they do receive some. For example, PNS nerves contain dense connective tissue called **collagen fibers** which prevent the

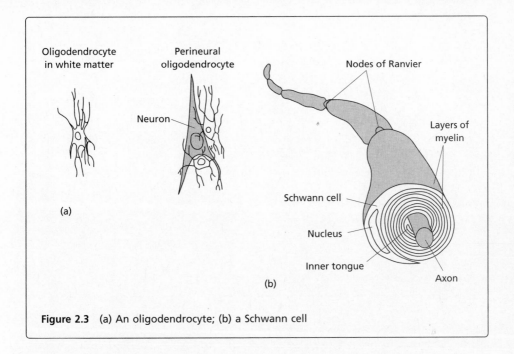

Figure 2.3   (a) An oligodendrocyte; (b) a Schwann cell

axons from stretching to the point of damage. Interestingly, those nerves that leave the skull and vertebrae are usually thicker than those remaining, presumably in order to give them the protection not given by bone.

Like the myelin sheath, protective connective tissue in the PNS is arranged in layers. The external layer is called the **epineurium**. The bundles of axons inside (called **fascicles**) are surrounded by another layer, the **perineurium**. This consists of several flattened cells which form a barrier to prevent substances from the outside entering the fascicles. There is another connective tissue, the **endoneurium**, which is found inside the fascicles but in very small quantities.

■ Different types of neuron

There are different types of neuron in the CNS which can be distinguished either by the length of their processes or by the number of processes extending from them. Some of these are illustrated in Figure 2.4.

For example, **projection neurons** send impulses via long axons to other neurons across long distances (these are also known as **Golgi type 1 cells**). There are examples of this type of neuron in the CNS and the PNS, e.g. the neurons projecting from the spinal cord to the muscles and the neurons projecting from the upper part of the brain (cerebral cortex) to the lower part (brain stem) and spinal

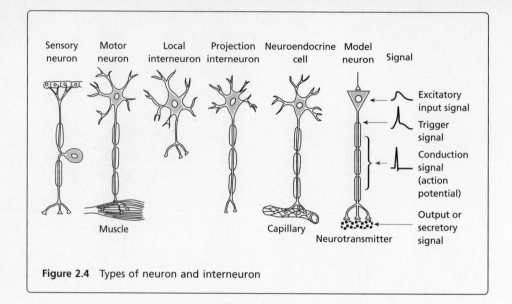

Figure 2.4　Types of neuron and interneuron

cord. The axons of projection neurons may also 'project' **axon collaterals** as they make their way to their target site. Collaterals – processes extending from the axon – might, therefore, terminate earlier and in different places from the parent axon.

A second type of neuron is called an **interneuron** (also called a **Golgi type 2 cell**). Interneurons have short processes that occur close to the cell body. One could argue that every neuron is an interneuron because every neuron sends signals to and receives signals from many other neurons and can therefore mediate the activity of other neurons. The term interneuron, however, is reserved for those neurons which communicate with only one group of neurons. Whereas these interneurons appear to be related to higher function (there are more of them in the CNS of humans than in the CNS of animals), the number of projection neurons depends on the organism's body size. Thus, the greater the body size, the larger the number of projection neurons. There are, however, instances where both types of cell appear to combine. Thus, a neuron could have short branches but a long axon.

Neurons are also described according to the number of axons and dendrites they send out, as seen in Figure 2.5.

Thus, **unipolar neurons** send one process which might bifurcate (divide into two) and are usually sensory in function (conveying information from the skin); **multipolar neurons** have several processes such as one axon and many dendrites and are the commonest type of neuron. **Bipolar neurons** have one axon and one dendrite which extend at opposite ends of the cell body. Certain sensory neurons are bipolar neurons, e.g. those found in the retina of the eye.

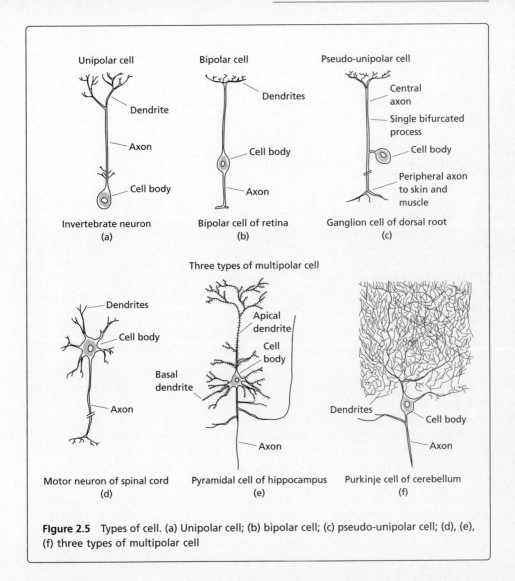

Figure 2.5 Types of cell. (a) Unipolar cell; (b) bipolar cell; (c) pseudo-unipolar cell; (d), (e), (f) three types of multipolar cell

The cell bodies of CNS neurons are often seen to congregate in groups. When this happens, the cell bodies form **nuclei** (or, when occurring in the PNS, **ganglia**). Groups of axons might leave these nuclei in close, near-parallel formation. When groups of axons extend from cell bodies in this fashion, they form a **tract** (in the PNS, they form a **nerve**). The axonal tracts are sometimes accompanied by smaller, parallel collections of axons which often branch off before the tracts terminate. These smaller bundles terminate on other neurons. It is the tract, however, which provides the greatest route for the nerve impulse. These tracts, because of their myelinated axons, give off a whitish colour. Tissue which contains large numbers of myelinated axons, therefore, is called **white matter**; tissue which contains primarily cell bodies and dendrites (as well as some axons) is called **grey matter** (because it looks grey). Despite the complexity of the system (consider again the number of connections and interconnections possible), there is organization in this complexity, as we see below.

■ Glial cells

Although they do not strictly glue parts of the nervous system together, glial or supporting cells do help bind neurons and their processes together. There are three main types of glial cell, all of which serve a distinct function and have a distinct structure. These three are not the only types of glial cell, however. There are other more specific ones found in various parts of the NS. For example, there are glial cells called **ependyma** which are found in the brain's cavities (ventricles). There are supporting **Muller cells** that are found in the retina and supporting **Bergman cells** that are found in the cerebellum.

Astrocytes (astroglia)

Astrocytes are the most common type of glial cell, and, in fact, of any type of brain cell. They are so called because of their star-shape and their function is to provide physical support for cells, as seen in Figure 2.6.

They are also responsible for **phagocytosis**, the process whereby dead cells are engulfed and digested. Because neurons die or are killed, it would be disadvantageous to have waste material and debris of this kind floating around the CNS. During phagocytosis, cells extend and retract their feet (called **pseudopodia**), reaching for these dead neurons. Once found, the astrocytes push against them, engulf them and finally digest them. What remains is a web of astrocytes, replacing the dead neurons. Astrocytes also produce scar tissue when the CNS is damaged or injured.

There are astrocytes with short processes (called **protoplasmic astrocytes**) and long processes (called **fibrillary astrocytes**). As well as contacting neurons and giving them support, astrocytes also contact blood capillaries. They perform all these support functions by wrapping the arms of their stars around the various processes.

Astrocytes are also useful in other ways. For example, they can exchange substances with neurons, they can remove or break down the neurotransmitters released into the synaptic gap thereby preventing too much neurotransmitter building up in the extracellular fluid, and they regulate the concentration of potassium ions in the extracellular fluid. As explained in the section on neurotransmission below, the excitability of neurons depends on the concentration of

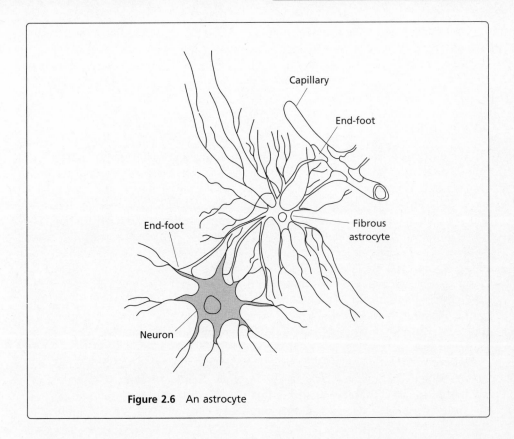

Figure 2.6   An astrocyte

potassium. If a neuron is 'overactivated', too much potassium can be left in the extracellular fluid. Astrocytes help in removing this excess substance.

Oligodendrocytes (oligodendroglia)

Oligodendroglia are another type of glial cell that supports the CNS. Their principal function is the production of myelin. Sometimes oligodendroglia are found very near the cell body. When this occurs, they are called **satellite cells**.

Microglial cells

Between 5 per cent and 20 per cent of glial cells are microglia, so called because they are small; they are evenly distributed throughout the CNS. Microglia have phagocytic properties and are thought to be activated in response to some insult to the brain such as inflammation, tumour or infection. They are sometimes called 'scavenger cells'. For example, they are thought to destroy invading organisms, remove dangerous material and promote tissue repair by secreting growth factor (Kreutzberg, 1996). Their small size makes them difficult to identify; they appear to have no clear-cut structural features. In fact, according to some authors, they may even be a variety of oligodendrocyte (Brodal, 1992).

Schwann cells

As we have seen from the section on myelination, the PNS has its own type of supporting cell, the Schwann cell, to help support and insulate that system's processes. Schwann cells also help give physical guidance to sprouting or damaged PNS axons. For example, when axons die, Schwann cells help in digesting the dead material and in arranging themselves cylindrically around the axon to guide its regrowth (unlike neurons, axons can regrow). The Schwann cell appears to develop only a certain distance ahead of its enveloped axon. If it developed way ahead of its axon it would probably die. This may serve a useful function of ensuring that excessive Schwann cell growth does not occur because excessive glial growth might result in pathology. Similar axonal resprouting can also be seen in the CNS but there is a slight problem in that scar tissue can often impede the pathway of any regrowing axon. To grow, therefore, a CNS axon has to penetrate this scar tissue.

There are Schwann cells that myelinate and others that do not. The non-myelinating Schwann cells are called **terminal Schwann cells**. There is some evidence to suggest that these cells maintain and repair neurons at neuromuscular synapses by sensing changes at the neuromuscular synapse and responding to them (Son *et al.*, 1996).

■ How neurons communicate I: the action potential

Neurons communicate with each other by sending electrical impulses called **action potentials**. Potential refers to source of electrical activity – the neuron's method of communication is thus electrical. This communication depends on the neuron's **excitability** – its capacity to react to a stimulus with an **electrical discharge** (or current or impulse – all of these words refer to the same thing).

The action potential is produced by charged particles called **ions** that pass through the cell membrane. The extracellular and intracellular fluid both contain ions. These ions are either positively charged (**cations**) or negatively charged (**anions**). The familiar phrase 'opposites attract' has its origin in electrolyte chemistry because while similarly charged ions repel, differently charged ions attract. The force produced by this repulsion and attraction is called **electrostatic pressure**. There are many different ions unevenly distributed inside and outside the cell membrane (intracellularly and extracellularly). It is this distribution which gives the membrane its electrical potential and is, therefore, called the **membrane**

potential. The membrane has an electrical charge because there are positive and negative ions both inside and outside the cell membrane.

The membrane is **selectively permeable** to ions. That is, it allows only certain ions in. Perhaps the most significant ions are **Na⁺ (sodium)**, **K⁺ (potassium)**, **Ca²⁺ (calcium)** and **Cl⁻ (chloride)**. Potassium, sodium and chloride ions are found in extracellular and intracellular fluid although there is more potassium in intracellular fluid and more sodium and chloride in extracellular fluid. Chloride is the more prominent extracellular anion. The type of channel-opening that is governed by neurotransmitters is called **transmitter-** or **ligand-gated**. Some channels are regulated by the magnitude of the membrane potential. These channels are called **voltage-gated** and it is these that are responsible for producing the action potential. The permeability of the membrane, i.e. its ability to allow potassium to enter or exit, is dependent not only on how many channels there are, how they are distributed and how much they open but also on the **concentration gradient** of the ion. The steeper this is, the greater the flow of ions.

The membrane potential

If the inside of the membrane is negative relative to the outside, positive ions will be attracted inside. As a result, positive ions will be forced out because, as you will recall, similarly charged ions repel. The degree of attraction or repulsion is determined by the membrane potential. For most neurons, the charge across this membrane is about 60–70 millivolts (mv) when it receives no stimulation. This charge is called the **resting potential**. Because there are more negative ions inside the cell, this resting potential has been arbitrarily defined as negative, i.e. as – 60/70 mv.

The potential is produced by the membrane's selective permeability to ions and the different concentrations of ions inside and outside the cell. The unequal distribution of ions is maintained by 'pumps' in the cell membrane. Potassium, for example, flows through the membrane quite easily when the cell is at rest, whereas sodium passes through with difficulty. Thus the expulsion of potassium results in the inside of the cell losing positive ions, producing a negative charge on the inside. Potassium does not leave the inside of the cell endlessly because at a certain point, the membrane will force potassium to flow *back into* the cell. At 70 mv, the strengths of the outward and inward flows of potassium are similar. This represents potassium's **equilibrium potential**. The resting potential is slightly lower than potassium's equilibrium potential because the membrane is also permeable (but only slightly) to positively charged sodium ions. Thus as potassium ions flow out, a small number of sodium ions enter the membrane, making the internal negative charge slightly less negative. The mechanism regulating the influx and efflux of sodium and potassium is the **sodium–potassium pump**. This forces out sodium ions in exchange for potassium ions, usually in the ratio of 3:2, that is for every three sodium ions expelled, two potassium ions are pushed in.

Depolarization and hyperpolarization

When sodium channels are opened, the cell becomes more permeable to sodium and the resting potential becomes more like the equilibrium potential for sodium (55 mv). The increased permeability and influx of sodium constitute what is called **depolarization**: the positive ions make the membrane potential less negative. If this continues and positive ions continue to flow into the cell, the intracellular charge reverses from negative to positive. Eventually, the resting potential is reached but is first overshot. When this happens the membrane is described as **hyperpolarized** and the process is called **hyperpolarization**. The time taken from depolarization to hyperpolarization is approximately 2–3 milliseconds (ms). This is the action potential: the depolarization and hyperpolarization of the cell membrane produced by an increase in the cell's permeability to sodium ions. To allow an action potential to occur, the membrane must reach the **threshold of excitation**. That is, it must be excited to a certain degree before an action potential is fired. The number of action potentials can reach 100 per second. Although this process might seem to require a large exchange of ions, the actual quantity of ions flowing in and out of the cell is small (1 for every 3000 ions in the case of potassium, for example). See Figure 2.7.

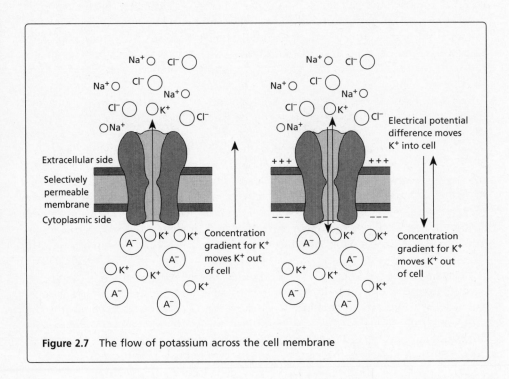

Figure 2.7   The flow of potassium across the cell membrane

The strength of an action potential is the same regardless of the strength of the stimulation. So, although a weak and a strong stimulus can both trigger an action potential, the strength of the action potential is the same. However, there are factors which influence the generation of the action potential. These are the *frequency* and the *pattern* of the stimulation. Sometimes one stimulus is not enough to precipitate an action potential: several bouts of stimulation are needed.

One ion so far unmentioned is **calcium**. Although this appears not to be as important as sodium and potassium in causing the action potential, calcium plays an important role in the extracellular regulation of the excitability of the cell membrane. The membrane does contain voltage-gated calcium channels. Calcium enters the cell during the action potential (actually, through sodium as well as calcium channels). Perhaps its most important role is intracellular. Its presence in the terminal buttons of axons is necessary for the release of neurotransmitters.

What happens after an action potential has occurred?

In the period following the action potential there is a period of relative calm before another action potential is fired. This resting state is called the cell's **refractory period**. This stage has been classed into two phases: the **absolute refractory period** where a cell is incapable of producing another action potential regardless of the strength or frequency of stimulation and the **relative refractory period** where stronger than normal depolarization is necessary.

How is the nerve impulse transmitted?

Although the axon can send an electrical current, it does so in a way quite unlike copper wire. It can lose particles and has high internal resistance: any normal electrical signal would soon fizzle out and die in such circumstances. The reason why the action potential does not die is that it is repropagated (or recharged) as it makes its way along the axon.

The course of the action potential is different depending on whether the axon is myelinated or unmyelinated. In unmyelinated axons, the impulse leaves the axon hillock, where depolarization occurs and where the action potential is triggered, and goes through repolarization. In myelinated axons, the impulse still continues for a short distance but is regenerated at the nodes of Ranvier, the unmyelinated parts of myelinated axons, which are directly exposed to the extracellular fluid. The passage of the impulse from the axon hillock to the first node is **electrotonic** (passive). This node becomes depolarized and another action potential occurs. The potential occurs because voltage-gated sodium channels are opened here. The electrical message is thus passed along the axon by being regenerated at each node. Whereas the passage of the action potential in unmyelinated axons is smooth, the course of the action potential in myelinated axons is slightly more jumpy because it is repropagated at each node. At each node, therefore, there is a slight delay before the impulse moves on because the membrane has to open channels and allow the flow of ions in and out.

How neurons communicate II: neurotransmission

The synapse

To recap: when an action potential is sent down the axon, depolarization occurs at the terminal button. This is not the end of the communication process. When depolarization occurs at the terminal button, calcium channels open, allowing this ion to enter the cell. The increased permeability to calcium and its presence in the cell is responsible for the secretion of a neurotransmitter from the vesicles. The neurotransmitter is released into the synaptic gap by a process called exocytosis. This means that the transmitter-containing vesicle moves up to the cell membrane of the presynaptic terminal button, pushes up against it and fuses with it. When this occurs, the vesicle releases the neurotransmitter which moves into the extracellular fluid of the synaptic gap where it binds to the postsynaptic, or receiving, terminal button of another neuron. A further stage of communication is then reached. Sometimes the neurotransmitter is released in small packets called **quanta**.

The neurotransmitter can alter the membrane potential and alter its permeability. Because of these effects, the neurotransmitter produces a **synaptic potential** which is slower than the action potential. If this potential is a depolarizing one, then the postsynaptic neuron may fire an action potential. When this happens, the effect of the neurotransmitter is **excitatory**: it excites a cell into producing an action potential and results from sodium and calcium ions going in and potassium ions being pushed out. This type of potential is called an **excitatory postsynaptic potential** (**EPSP**). See Figure 2.8.

The amount of transmitter released may be dependent on the amount of calcium entering the presynaptic neuron following depolarization. So, an increase in the amount of calcium entering the neuron becomes associated with larger amounts of neurotransmitter being released. Conversely, small amounts of calcium entering the neuron will be associated with little or perhaps no release of neurotransmitter. However, sometimes this relationship is not obvious: increased synaptic transmission may not follow increased inflow of calcium. What is more, decreased calcium is also found to accompany increases in neurotransmitter release. When this

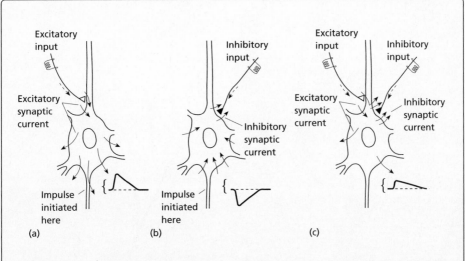

Figure 2.8 The effects of excitation and inhibition on the neuron. (a) Excitation; (b) inhibition; (c) excitation and inhibition

occurs, the release of neurotransmitter is said to be calcium-independent (Piccolino and Pignatelli, 1996). The mechanism for this is unknown.

It takes more than just one EPSP to produce an action potential in the receiving cell. Normally, repeated stimulation (many EPSPs) are needed before this can happen. There is a certain **threshold value** that these potentials must reach before the depolarization triggers an action potential. The process of repeated stimulation which produces an action potential is called **summation** because the effect of one EPSP is added to the next which is added to the next and so on until the threshold for depolarization is reached. This form of frequent repeated stimulation is called **temporal summation**.

Spatial summation also describes repeated stimulation but this time the stimulation does not come from one source repeatedly but from several other processes on the cell. When the postsynaptic membrane is stimulated and an EPSP is produced, the impulse is carried electrotonically from the postsynaptic process to the cell and the initial segment or axon hillock. This is the place where the possibility of producing an action potential is strongest. The closer the synapse is to this part, therefore, the greater the likelihood of an action potential occurring. Dendrites, being at some distance from the rest of the cell, transmit weaker signals because the impulse travels electrotonically. This means that the impulse has to reach the initial segment 'on its own' with no electrical assistance. An example of the course of the action potential is seen in Figure 2.9 which represents a reflex action. The apparatus employed for producing an action potential is illustrated by Figure 2.10.

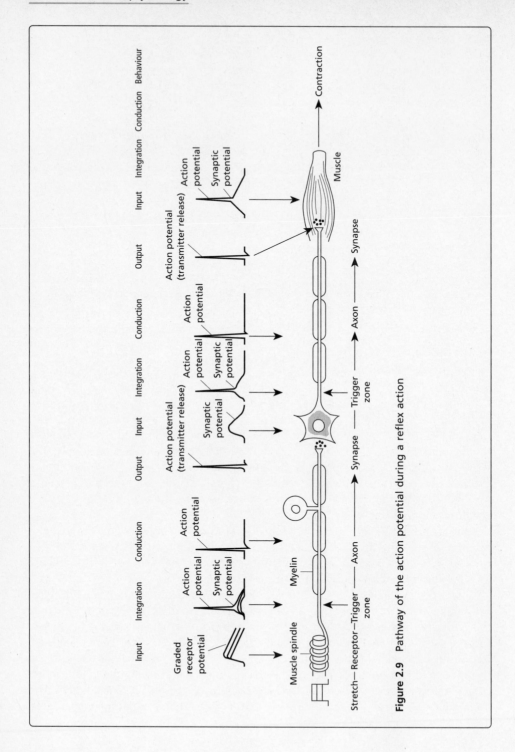

Figure 2.9 Pathway of the action potential during a reflex action

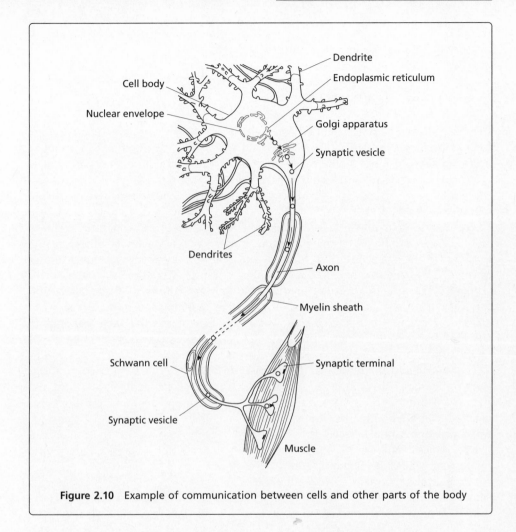

Dendrite
Cell body
Endoplasmic reticulum
Nuclear envelope
Golgi apparatus
Synaptic vesicle
Dendrites
Axon
Myelin sheath
Schwann cell
Synaptic terminal
Synaptic vesicle
Muscle

Figure 2.10 Example of communication between cells and other parts of the body

The opposite effect might happen at the postsynaptic button and the membrane could become hyperpolarized. This actually prevents the firing of an action potential by the postsynaptic button. When this occurs, the neurotransmitter's effect is called **inhibitory** and the potential produced by these transmitters is called the **inhibitory postsynaptic potential (IPSP)**. Here, potassium ions leave the membrane and negative chloride ions might be pumped in, making the inside of the cell negatively charged. The point of inhibition is that it prevents the neuron becoming overstimulated, as overstimulation could result in cell damage or death. Epileptic seizures result from an uncontrolled firing of impulses which is why many drugs to combat epilepsy help the inhibition of impulses. Because of the two different effects that neurotransmitters have, they are referred to as either **excitatory** or **inhibitory neurotransmitters**.

How long does a synaptic potential last?

The probability of a postsynaptic neuron firing an action potential depends on the total amount of stimulation it receives. The stimulation could be both inhibitory *and* excitatory. If stimulation is predominantly excitatory, an action potential is likely. If it is predominantly inhibitory, no action potential is likely. Furthermore, there may be neurons that excite strongly and others that excite weakly. If the stimulus is excited, depolarization lasts from a few seconds to a few minutes. There are slow synaptic potentials and there are fast ones. Slow potentials tend to result not from effects of the neurotransmitter on ion channels but from the binding of the transmitter to receptor sites which then triggers intracellular changes. These effects are called **modulatory synaptic effects** and the transmitters which produce them are called **modulatory neurotransmitters** (or **neuromodulators**) because they modulate the activity of the membrane that they come into contact with but do not change it directly. They make the membrane more susceptible to producing an action potential. At some synapses, transmitters will be modulatory; at others they will be excitatory.

The timecourse of neurotransmission and the efficacy of postsynaptic binding is thus dependent on a number of factors, including the concentration of the neurotransmitter and the desensitization of postsynaptic receptors after they have been activated. The number of postsynaptic receptors binding to a neurotransmitter is also important because this, together with desensitization, the number of quanta released and several other factors, influences the ability of the postsynaptic neuron to respond (Clements, 1996).

Interneurons can also be inhibitory. If one of these prevents a neuron from sending an impulse, then the phenomenon is called **recurrent inhibition**. However, this inhibitory interneuron may itself be excited or inhibited. Thus, the stimulation it receives determines the probability of recurrent inhibition increasing or decreasing. Perversely, the inhibitory interneuron may actually excite a neuron by inhibiting another inhibitory neuron. This prevention of a neuron inhibiting an action potential is called **disinhibition**.

■ What is a neurotransmitter?

So far we have described the effects of chemicals released by presynaptic buttons at the synapse on the activity of postsynaptic neurons. These chemicals send a signal to the postsynaptic button and can be inhibitory or excitatory. These are the properties of the neurotransmitter. The total number of possible neurotransmitters is unknown. With a system so complex and interacting, identifying one clear neurotransmitter (and modulator) is problematic. This said, techniques have identified a small number of certain neurotransmitters and neuromodulators. Those likely to be neurotransmitters are called **putative transmitters**.

Most of the more prominent neurotransmitters are protein-based. Neurotransmitters can be made up of **small** or **large protein molecules**. All small molecule neurotransmitters, except acetylcholine, are **amino acids** or a type of amino acid called **amines**. Larger molecules are made up of **peptides** (proteins that are made up of a small number of amino acids). Because of this they are called **neuropeptides**; their function is not as clear as that of the small-molecule transmitters. There are probably about 30–40 identifiable neuropeptides in the CNS.

The function of all neurotransmitters is not clear because the type of effect they produce depends on the type of receptor they bind to or communicate with. Neurotransmitters are made in the cell body and stored in the vesicles, as we saw in the section above. Usually, a terminal button contains one neurotransmitter and one or more neuropeptide. This complicates any understanding of the specific effects of each type of transmitter because the transmitters are released together.

Neurotransmitters are synthesized in the terminal button by enzymes travelling from the cell body. Neuropeptides, on the other hand, are synthesized in the cell body and travel down to the terminal button. The travelling nature of the peptides means that they are more prone than neurotransmitters to blockage. Blocked axons can prevent a neuropeptide from moving smoothly to the cell body; this problem does not arise for neurotransmitters.

Some of the known major neurotransmitters and the functions they appear to perform are described below.

Types of neurotransmitter

Acetylcholine

Acetylcholine is a small-molecule neurotransmitter which is synthesized by binding **choline** to **acetyl coenzyme A**. The binding is produced by the enzyme, **choline acetyltransferase (ChAT)**. Neurons which contain acetylcholine or ChAT are called **cholinergic neurons**. These are found mostly in the motor system, especially in brainstem and spinal cord motor neurons that innervate muscles of the skeleton. The chemical binds to **acetylcholine receptors**. This eventually produces an action potential which results in muscle contraction. Acetylcholine receptors are also known as **nicotinic receptors** because nicotine seems to produce the same effects on muscles as acetylcholine does. The receptors can be blocked, which sometimes results in motor impairments. **Curare** is one acetylcholine blocker; another is **atropine**. Atropine acts by blocking the stimulation of a particular acetylcholine receptor – called a **muscarinic receptor** – by **muscarine**. These types of receptor are usually only found in smooth muscles and are slower to respond than nicotinic receptors.

Monoamines (biogenic amines)

The monoamines are also small-molecule neurotransmitters and include **norepinephrine** (also known as **noradrenaline**), **epinephrine** (also known as **adrenaline**), **dopamine**, **serotonin** (also known as **5-HT** or **5-hydroxytryptamine**) and **histamine**. The first three are collectively known as the **catecholamines** and are synthesized from **tyrosine**, an amino acid. The last two are also synthesized from amino acids but these are **tryptophan** and **histidine**. The catecholamines appear to be involved in most of the important behaviours such as movement, mood and cognition.

The effects that these neurotransmitters have on postsynaptic neurons is complex. For example, each neurotransmitter has different types of receptor. For dopamine, there are so-called **D1** and **D2 receptors** which are different in function and distribution. Norepinephrine and epinephrine have **alpha** and **beta receptors** which sometimes produce completely different effects. Serotonin has several types of receptor. All of this receptor divergence means that a monoamine can both inhibit and excite depending on the type of receptor it contacts.

Glutamate

Glutamate is an excitatory amino acid and is served by three receptor types. The first two, known as **kainate** (K) and **quiscualate** (Q) **receptors**, are responsible for fast depolarization, the third is not. Glutamate-containing presynaptic neurons may control the release of the neurotransmitter from specific release sites (Sanchez-Prieto *et al.*, 1996). They may do this via presynaptic autoreceptors which give feedback about the action of previously released neurotransmitter.

Gamma-aminobutyric acid

Gamma-aminobutyric acid (or **GABA**) is the most common of the inhibitory amino acid CNS neurotransmitters. This transmitter produces hyperpolarization by opening either chloride channels or potassium channels. GABA has two types of receptor: **GABA** A and **GABA** B. The A receptor is responsible for inhibition presynaptically and mediates the membrane permeability of chloride; the B receptor mediates potassium permeability. Drugs such as benzodiazepines and barbiturates (so-called anti-anxiety drugs) bind to these receptor sites and enhance the effects of GABA either by increasing the frequency of opening of chloride channels or by prolonging this opening when it occurs. More information about the effects of these drugs can be found in Chapter 10.

Glycine

Glycine is another inhibiting neurotransmitter found in the brainstem and inter-neurons of the spinal cord. Its primary function appears to be the inhibition of motor neurons: for example, the glycine-receptor blocker, **strychnine**, causes muscle spasms.

How is neurotransmission stopped?

It is inadvisable for neurotransmission to continue ceaselessly for many of the reasons given for preventing perpetual excitatory or inhibitory stimulation. In fact, neurotransmission does have a set time and stops depending on the type of neurotransmitter and receptor it contacts. Furthermore, the surplus neurotransmit-ter in the extracellular fluid that does not bind to the postsynaptic membrane is cleaned away by reuptake mechanisms. That is, the neurotransmitter is taken back into the presynaptic button and either stored and reused or broken down. Some neurotransmitters, such as acetylcholine, also have enzymes in the synaptic gap that can break them down. Some chemicals, however, such as cocaine and amphetamine, prevent reuptake, thus potentiating the excitatory effect of the neurotransmitter.

Neurogeographical location of neurotransmitters

Certain neurotransmitters are found in groups of neurons (nuclei). These nuclei are distinct from each other in that some contain, for example, dopamine, while others contain epinephrine. Norepinephrine is most common in nuclei found in a part of the brainstem called the reticular formation (see Chapter 3). These nuclei form a distinct neuronal group called the nucleus locus coeruleus. Dopamine, however, is found mainly in large nuclei in the mesencephalon and substantia nigra (see Chapter 3). Serotonin is found predominantly in the raphe nuclei in the brainstem, whereas acetylcholine is found in the brainstem and parts of the forebrain, specifically in the nucleus basalis of Meynert.

In later chapters, especially those on emotion, dementia and motor system disorders and memory, we see how drugs act on the NS to produce changes in these 'neurotransmitter systems'.

■ The simplest of systems?

Up until now we have considered the neuron and its effects on other neurons as if one neuron communicates only with other single neurons. Of course, in the NS this never happens: *groups* of neurons exert effects on other groups of neurons. The simplest pathway – an axon from one neuron sending an action potential to only one other neuron – does not exist in the CNS. Usually, neurons contact many other neurons because their axons have collaterals which communicate with other neurons before the end of the axon reaches its destination. Thus, there is a divergence of neuronal connections. Conversely, there could be a convergence of connections with several neurons contacting one neuron. This neuron could be the end-target for the other neurons. There is also a strong presence of parallel pathways: two neurons send an action potential in parallel to another neuron. There are also intricate feedback loops. For example, a neuron could fire an action potential received by a neuron which, in turn, sends a message back to the sender. This return message can tell the neuron whether its effect was weak or strong. Sometimes a group of neurons do not send the same message. However, provided that enough do, the probability of having the desired effect on the postsynaptic neuron is increased. Because of these connections and interconnections, you will not be surprised to hear that the NS is never inactive in a living being with a nervous system.

Summary

☐ All behaviour depends on the normal, active functioning of the nervous system (NS). The NS comprises two major systems: the central nervous system (CNS) and the peripheral nervous system (PNS). The CNS represents the brain and the spinal cord; the PNS represents nervous tissue that lies outside the skull and vertebral column.

☐ Nervous tissue is made up of neurons (nerve cells) and supporting or glial cells (glia). There are slightly more glia than neurons.

☐ The neuron comprises a cell body (or perikaryon), an axon and dendrites. It contains and is surrounded by fluid (intracellular and extracellular fluid, respectively). The cell body contains materials essential for the neuron's survival. Mitochondria provide the cell with the energy it needs in order to function. Chromosomes produce essential protein. Neuro-fibrils allow materials to be transported in and out of the cell body. Microtubules define the shape of the neuron.

☐ Axons are the processes which send electrical messages to other neurons. Some of these are covered in insulating myelin (myelinated axons), others are not (unmyelinated axons). The myelin helps to protect the axon and assists the transport of the electrical impulse. A myelinated axon is covered by segments of myelin. There are small spaces or nodes of exposed axon between these segments, called the nodes of Ranvier.

☐ The two major types of neuron are the projection neuron (which sends axons across great distances) and interneurons. Axons often sprout axon collaterals which diverge and meet other neurons before the head of the axon contacts other neurons. Neurons are also described according to the number of processes they have extending from them. Unipolar neurons have one process, multipolar neurons have several (such as one axon and several dendrites). Bipolar neurons have an axon at one end and a dendrite at the other.

☐ Groups of cell bodies in the CNS are called nuclei; in the PNS they are called ganglia. Groups of axons which leave nuclei in parallel are called tracts. In the PNS, similar processes are called nerves. Tracts give off a whitish colour (largely owing to the colour of the myelin) and therefore comprise the CNS's white matter. Grey matter contains axons, cell bodies and dendrites.

☐ There are several types of glial cell. The main types are astrocytes, oligodendrocytes, microglia and Schwann cells. Astrocytes provide physical support to neurons and are responsible for phagocytosis, that is the digestion and elimination of detritus. They can also remove chemical substances from between neurons. Oligodendrocytes produce myelin for the insulation of axons. Microglia are also responsible for phagocytosis. Schwann cells are PNS cells that produce myelin (although some, called terminal Schwann cells, do not produce myelin). These cells also digest damaged axonal material and help to guide resprouting axons.

☐ Neurons communicate via electrical signals or impulses called action potentials. The potentials are produced by the activity of electrically charged particles called ions. The most important ions are sodium, potassium, calcium and chloride. These ions exist both inside and outside the cell. The inside of the membrane is negatively charged relative to the

➡

outside. When the neuron is not being stimulated, the resting potential is negative (between −60 and −70 millivolts).

☐ The cell membrane has channels through which it allows various ions in and out, i.e. it is selectively permeable. The maintenance of unequal distributions of ions inside and outside the membrane is provided by 'pumps'. For example, the mechanism responsible for the influx and efflux of sodium and potassium is called the sodium–potassium pump. The positive potassium ions exiting are replaced by positive sodium ions; the pump forces sodium ions out and replaces them with potassium ions.

☐ The increased permeability to sodium is called depolarization: the inside of the cell is made less negative relative to the outside. Eventually the charge on the inside of the cell will switch from negative to positive. The cell's charge does return to its normal resting state but is overshot. This is called hyperpolarization.

☐ Axon potentials are of the same strength regardless of the strength of the stimulus which activated them. Often, several stimuli are required for an action potential to be fired. In myelinated axons, the action potential jumps from myelinated segment to myelinated segment. This ensures that the impulse is regularly recharged and is called saltatory conduction. In unmyelinated axons, the impulse is sent electrotonically (passively; it is not regularly recharged).

☐ The action potential makes its way from the axon hillock, down the axon to the terminal button. This is where neurotransmitters, the chemicals which allow neurons to communicate with each other, are stored (in vesicles).

☐ Neurotransmitters are released from the terminal into the space between the sending (presynaptic) and receiving (postsynaptic) neurons. This space is called the synaptic gap. Transmitters are released by exocytosis: a process whereby vesicles make their way to the presynaptic membrane wall, fuse with it and expel the transmitter into the extracellular space.

☐ Neurotransmitters can excite or inhibit postsynaptic neurons, that is they can produce or prevent action potentials. The former are called excitatory neurotransmitters and produce excitatory postsynaptic potentials (EPSPs); the latter are called inhibitory neurotransmitters and elicit inhibitory postsynaptic potentials (IPSPs). It normally takes several EPSPs before an action potential is triggered – a threshold value must be reached. This is

⇒

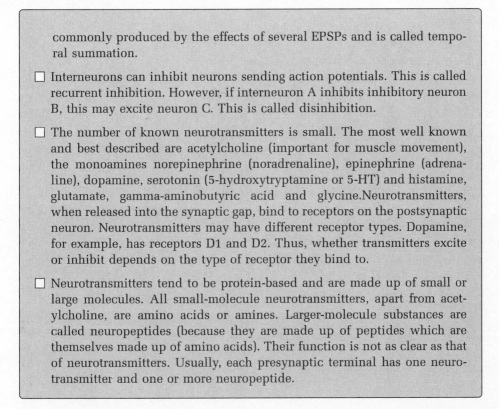

commonly produced by the effects of several EPSPs and is called temporal summation.

☐ Interneurons can inhibit neurons sending action potentials. This is called recurrent inhibition. However, if interneuron A inhibits inhibitory neuron B, this may excite neuron C. This is called disinhibition.

☐ The number of known neurotransmitters is small. The most well known and best described are acetylcholine (important for muscle movement), the monoamines norepinephrine (noradrenaline), epinephrine (adrenaline), dopamine, serotonin (5-hydroxytryptamine or 5-HT) and histamine, glutamate, gamma-aminobutyric acid and glycine.Neurotransmitters, when released into the synaptic gap, bind to receptors on the postsynaptic neuron. Neurotransmitters may have different receptor types. Dopamine, for example, has receptors D1 and D2. Thus, whether transmitters excite or inhibit depends on the type of receptor they bind to.

☐ Neurotransmitters tend to be protein-based and are made up of small or large molecules. All small-molecule neurotransmitters, apart from acetylcholine, are amino acids or amines. Larger-molecule substances are called neuropeptides (because they are made up of peptides which are themselves made up of amino acids). Their function is not as clear as that of neurotransmitters. Usually, each presynaptic terminal has one neurotransmitter and one or more neuropeptide.

Recommended further general and specific reading

Key: (1) = introductory, *(3)* = intermediate, *(5)* = advanced

General

Brodal, P. (1992). *The Central Nervous System: Structure and function.* Oxford: Oxford University Press. *(3)*

Carlson, N.R. (1995). *Foundations of Physiological Psychology.* New Jersey: Allyn and Bacon. *(2)*

Clarke, K.A. (1990). *Neurophysiology: Applications in the behavioural and medical sciences.* Chichester: Ellis Horwood. *(3)*

Kandel, E.R., Schwartz, J.H. and Jessell, T.M. (1995). *Essentials of Neural Science and Behaviour.* New Jersey: Prentice Hall International. *(2)*

Levitan, I.B. and Kaczmarek, L.K. (1991). *The Neuron.* Oxford: Oxford University Press. *(4)*

Peters, A., Palay, S.L. and Webster, H. de F. (1991). *The Fine Structure of the Nervous System: Neurons and their supporting cells* (3rd edition). New York: Oxford University Press. *(4)*

Shepard, G.M. (1988). *Neurobiology.* New York: Oxford University Press. *(4)*

Specific

Atwood, H.L. and Lnenicka, G.A. (1986). Structure and function in synapses: Emerging correlations. *Trends in Neurosciences*, **9**, 248–50. *(3)*

Kelly, R.B. (1993). Storage and release of neurotransmitters. *Cell* **72**/*Neuron* **10**, 43–53. *(3)*

Shepherd, G.M. (1990). *The Synaptic Organization of the Brain* (3rd edition). Oxford: Oxford University Press. *(4)*

Siegel, G.J., Agranoff, B.W., Albers, R.W. and Molinoff, P.B. (1994). *Basic Neurochemistry: Molecular, cellular and medical aspects* (5th edition). New York: Raven Press. *(4)*

Telgedy, G. (1987). *Neuropeptides and Brain Function*. Berlin: Karger. *(4)*

Unwin, N. (1993). Neurotransmitter action: opening of ligand-gated ion channels. *Cell* **72**/*Neuron* **10**, 31–41. *(4)*

Chapter Three

The brain II: basic neuroanatomy

▓ Introduction: coming to terms with terms

Opening any textbook on neuroanatomy can seem like encountering a new language. Strange, alien, polysyllabic terminology tends to mingle with convoluted and equally alien language. In fact, reading neuroanatomy is actually like reading many languages since many of the terms used to describe function or structure have Greek, French or Latin roots or may be a combination of these and other languages. Polyglotism is not essential for understanding neuroanatomy but it is an advantage. This is what appears most daunting to a student of neuropsychology: coming to terms with terms.

Aside from the terms in different languages, the student of neuropsychology will also encounter more than one term referring to the same function or structure. So, for example, Area 17, the striate cortex and the primary visual cortex all refer to the same area (the part at the back of the brain where visual information from the retina is processed). Area 44 is also known as Broca's area, the anterior language area or the frontal operculum. The effect of damage to this part of the brain is an inability to produce speech. This is known as Broca's aphasia. It is also known as motor aphasia, non-fluent aphasia, production aphasia or expressive aphasia. Damage to Wernicke's area (or the posterior language area) produces an inability to comprehend language. This is called Wernicke's aphasia, sensory aphasia or receptive aphasia. Throughout this book, alternative names are often given for structures when these structures are first encountered in the text but, for clarity's sake, only one term will be used thereafter.

▓ Positional terms

There are terms used in neuropsychology which describe the position of parts of the nervous system. A list of these appears in Table 3.1 and the most widely used are defined here.

The direction of structures is described according to a neuraxis, that is an imaginary line that can be drawn from the spinal cord to the brain, and parts are referred to as **rostral, caudal, dorsal** or **ventral**, as seen in Figure 3.1.

Rostral literally means towards the beak and normally refers to the anterior or front end of the region. Caudal (literally, towards the tail) refers to a region posterior to or towards the back end of other regions. The top of the head or back is referred to as the dorsal surface; the front end of the body (the part facing the ground) is referred to as the ventral surface. Two other descriptive terms, **lateral** and **medial**, are also used. Lateral means towards the side; medial means towards the midline. Frequently, these terms are joined together to form other terms. Thus, structures might be described as dorsomedial or ventrolateral.

Processes or structures may also be prefixed with **pre**, meaning before, and **post**, meaning after, as in presynaptic and postsynaptic neuron. Processes such as axons

Table 3.1 Some terms and prefixes frequently used to describe
neuroanatomical direction and position

Term	Definition
dys-	partial loss
a-	total loss
distal	far from
proximal	near to
afferent	moving towards
efferent	smoving away from
unilateral	on one side
bilateral	on both sides
coronal	vertical slice dividing into front and back halves
saggital	vertical slice dividing into left and right halves
transverse	horizontal section parallel to ground
medial	towards the midline
caudal	towards the tail-end
rostral	towards the front
anterior	towards the front
dorsal	top or back of
ventral	front end or ground-facing surface of
lateral	towards the side
ipsilateral	on the same side
contralateral	on the opposite side

may be **afferent**, meaning that they arrive at a particular region, or **efferent**, meaning that they are sent from a particular region. A useful mnemonic for learning the differences between these two is to think of afferents as arriving and efferent as exiting.

The prefix **inter** refers to a process that lies between two other processes; the prefix **intra** refers to a process than occurs within another process. Thus, inter-hemispheric refers to interactions between the two cerebral hemispheres whereas intrahemispheric refers to interactions within one cerebral hemisphere. A process may also be described as **ipsilateral**, meaning on the same side, or **contralateral**, meaning on the opposite side. Thus anaesthetizing the left hemisphere will produce paralysis of the contralateral limb (the right arm).

When sections or views of the brain or spinal cord are considered, there are special terms used to describe the ways in which the brain has been 'sliced'. This slicing is literal when the brain is studied post-mortem, metaphorical when the living brain is studied via imaging methods. A **coronal section** is made as if one is slicing salami from front to back end, as seen in Figures 3.2 and 3.3.

A **horizontal section** is one that is made parallel to the ground. Thus, if you imagine looking down onto the top of the brain, slices would be made as if taking off the top of an egg, as seen in Figures 3.4 and 3.5 on pages 76 and 77.

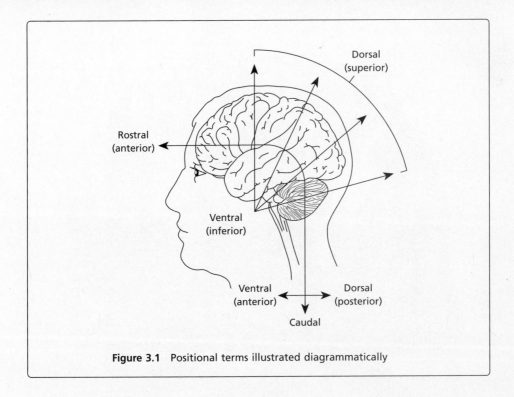

Figure 3.1 Positional terms illustrated diagrammatically

Finally, a **sagittal section** refers to slicing that is perpendicular to the ground. Again, imagine looking down onto the top of the brain but this time making slices from left to right.

Development of the central nervous system

A human embryo begins life as a hollow tube called a **neural tube**. As the embryo develops, the tube elongates and folds and its tissue thickens. The wall of the tube is made up of cells that will later become the glial cells and the neurons of the nervous system. At this stage, these cells are called **neuroepithelial cells**: the prospective glial cells are called **spongioblasts** and the prospective neurons are called **neuroblasts**. The inside of the tube is hollow, forming a canal which contains **cerebrospinal fluid (CSF)**, a clear, watery liquid which serves a number of functions in the CNS and is described more fully later on. The head of the embryo develops into the brain; the remainder straightens and becomes the spinal cord.

The canal develops four protuberances which later develop into the brain's four ventricles – chambers deep inside the brain – which contain CSF. The spinal cord end of the canal becomes one, long, fluid-filled canal which connects the four

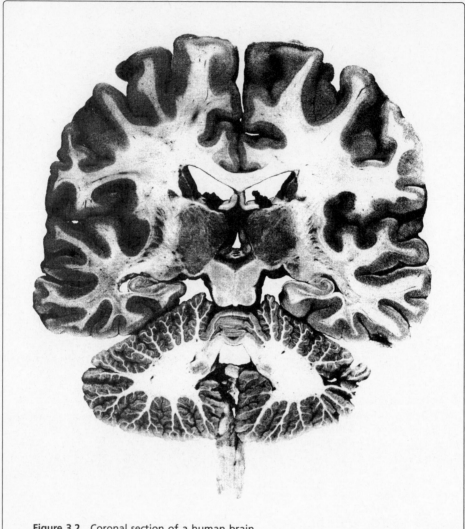

Figure 3.2 Coronal section of a human brain

ventricles of the brain. The ventricles help to divide the brain into various general regions called the forebrain, midbrain and hindbrain. The rostral ventricles are called the lateral and third ventricles. The region *surrounding* the lateral ventricles is called the endbrain or telencephalon and represents the most recently developed and most sophisticated part of the CNS, the cerebral cortex. The area surrounding the third ventricle becomes the diencephalon, or interbrain. These general, and further, subdivisions are seen in Figure 3.6 on page 78.

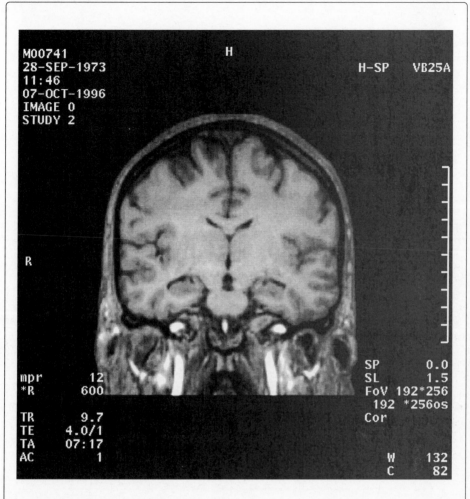

MO0741   H
28-SEP-1973   H-SP   VB25A
11:46
07-OCT-1996
IMAGE 0
STUDY 2

R

mpr   12
*R   600

TR   9.7
TE   4.0/1
TA   07:17
AC   1

SP   0.0
SL   1.5
FoV 192*256
     192 *256os
Cor

W   132
C   82

Figure 3.3   Coronal section seen via an MRI scan

■ Spinal cord

The spinal cord is about the size of your little finger in diameter, measures about 40–45 centimetres long and is cylindrical. It gives off a whitish colour because the outer part is made of axons. It is encased in a column of bone, called the **vertebral column**, a snake-like structure that covers more of spinal cord than there is and helps to protect the cord. The bone is made up of 24 vertebrae that are described according to the region that they protect. Thus, starting from the top of the cord,

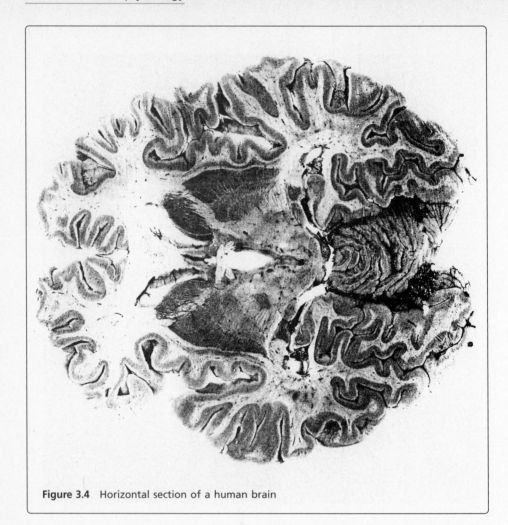

Figure 3.4   Horizontal section of a human brain

there are 7 **cervical** vertebrae, 12 **thoracic** and 5 **lumbar** vertebrae, as seen in Figure 3.7 on page 79.

The vertebrae protect the parts of the cord at the neck, chest and lower back areas, respectively. At certain points, the vertebrae are not separate but fused. These are the **saccral** and **coccygeal** vertebrae that are found towards the column's caudal part. The spinal cord runs along the inside of the column through a space called the **spinal foramen** (plural = foramina) which is found in each vertebra. As mentioned above, there is more column than there is cord. The reason for this is that the spinal cord ends in a collection of spinal roots called the **cauda equina** (literally, 'horse's tail' and so called because these roots look like a horse's tail).

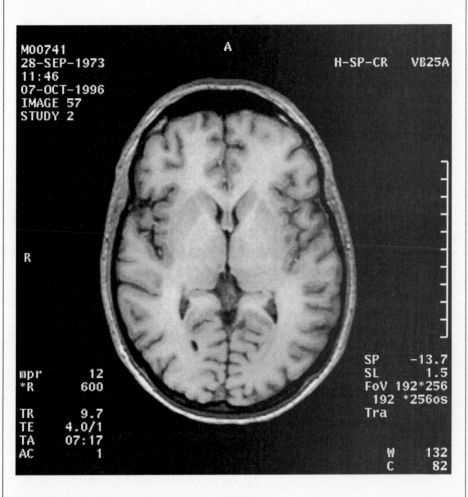

Figure 3.5 Horizontal section seen via an MRI scan

The cauda begins at the second lumbar vertebra and ends at the coccyx. Thus, vertebrae also extend to part of the cauda thereby protecting them too.

In relation to the body, the spinal column is found on the dorsal surface and at the midline of the back and extends to the second lumbar vertebra. The spinal cord extends to the bottom or inferior end of the brain, the brainstem, at a wedge-shaped structure area called the **medullary conus**. In fact, the cord is thicker at its brainstem or cervical end but is unequally thick along its course. Its other thicker aspect is in the lumbar region. The cord also exhibits narrow indentations, called **sulci**, where the **spinal nerves** reach the cord.

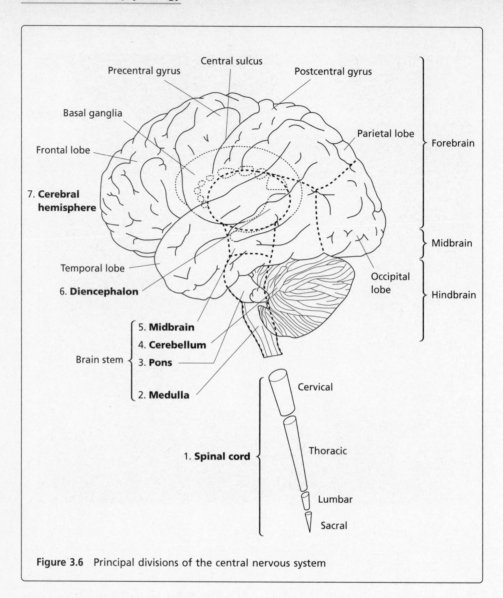

Precentral gyrus
Central sulcus
Postcentral gyrus
Basal ganglia
Parietal lobe
Forebrain
Frontal lobe
7. **Cerebral hemisphere**
Midbrain
Temporal lobe
Occipital lobe
6. **Diencephalon**
Hindbrain
5. **Midbrain**
4. **Cerebellum**
Brain stem
3. **Pons**
2. **Medulla**
Cervical
1. **Spinal cord**
Thoracic
Lumbar
Sacral

Figure 3.6 Principal divisions of the central nervous system

■ Spinal nerves

The spinal nerves make up part of the PNS, a system which helps to mediate communication between the CNS and other parts of the body. Given the importance of the spinal cord for motor and sensory behaviour, such connections are vital. Peripheral nerves enter and exit the spinal cord in small bundles of axons called **rootlets**. These eventually unite to form a thicker process called a **root**.

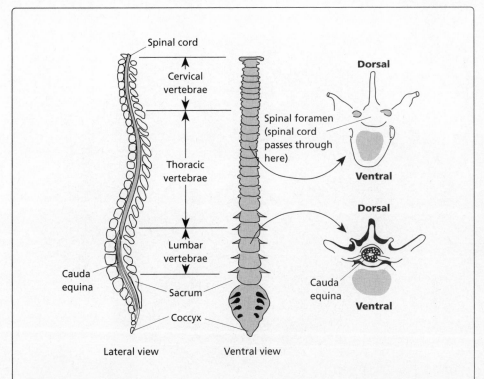

Figure 3.7 The spinal cord and vertebrae. From Carlson, 1995. © 1995 Allyn and Bacon; reproduced by permission

Thus, **dorsal** (posterior) and **ventral** (anterior) **roots** enter and exit the spinal cord. The dorsal root is special in that it has a swelling called a **spinal ganglion** which contains the cell bodies for sensory axons entering the cord. Together, the dorsal and ventral roots make up the **spinal nerve**. There are 31 pairs of spinal nerves, one on each side of the cord, and all but the first cervical pair leave the cord via spaces between vertebrae. There are 12 pairs of thoracic spinal nerves, 5 pairs of lumbar spinal nerves, 8 pairs of cervical spinal nerves, 5 pairs of saccral and 1 pair of coccygeal. The two types of root convey different types of information. The ventral root contains efferent motor fibers; the dorsal root contains afferent (sensory) fibers.

The symmetrical pairing of spinal nerves conveniently divides the spinal cord into **segments**. Each segment, when cut transversely, contains an outer covering of white matter and an inner, central area of grey matter arranged in an H-shape, as seen in Figures 3.8 and 3.9.

The white matter is divided into columns or **funiculi** which surrounds the H. The arms of the H are called **ventral** or **dorsal horns**, depending on the direction

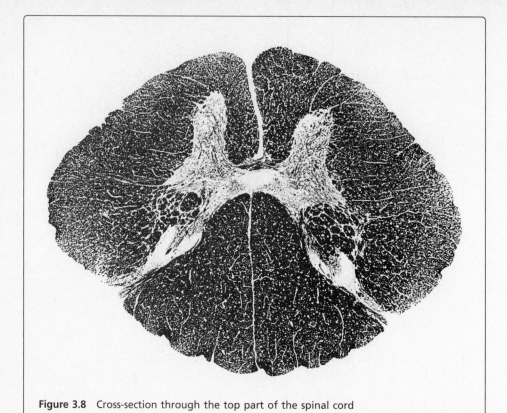

Figure 3.8   Cross-section through the top part of the spinal cord

of the arms. The extremities of the arms are called **zona terminalis**. If you imagine a transverse section of a spinal cord segment, then each half of the segment contains a **dorsal column** of white matter (from midline of cord to the dorsal horn), a **lateral column** (the matter between the dorsal and ventral horn) and a **ventral column** (between the ventral horn and the ventral median fissure, the groove which indents the cord along its length). The grey matter extends along the length of the cord and contains a very small and narrow central canal which ends before the cauda equina but extends upwards into the brain's ventricular system.

The ventral horn contains neurons which send axons from the CNS. Strictly, these neurons are found where the ventral and dorsal horns meet. The ventral horn itself contains motor neurons. The axons of these neurons leave the ventral root, exit through the spinal nerve and terminate in muscles of the skeleton (usually muscles that are under voluntary control). Another group of axons is sent to smooth muscles and glands.

The grey matter also contains neurons which send axons to the higher levels of the CNS. These are found in the dorsal horn side, or again, more strictly, in the area

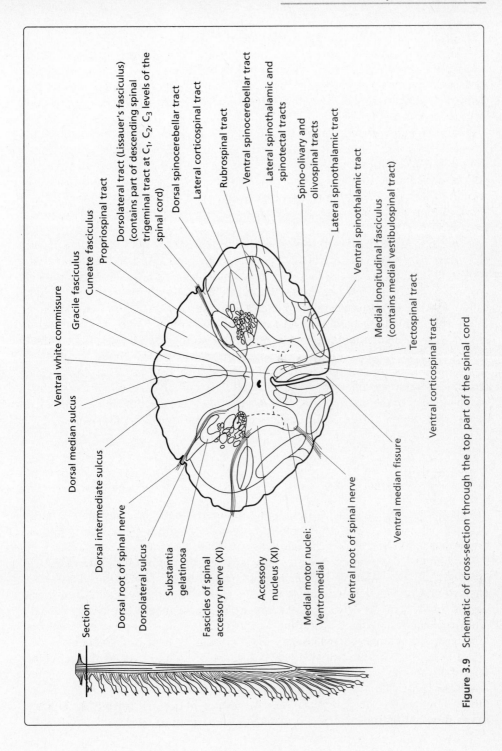

Section

Dorsal median sulcus

Ventral white commissure

Gracile fasciculus

Cuneate fasciculus

Propriospinal tract

Dorsolateral tract (Lissauer's fasciculus) (contains part of descending spinal trigeminal tract at C_1, C_2, C_3 levels of the spinal cord)

Dorsal spinocerebellar tract

Lateral corticospinal tract

Rubrospinal tract

Ventral spinocerebellar tract

Lateral spinothalamic and spinotectal tracts

Spino-olivary and olivospinal tracts

Lateral spinothalamic tract

Ventral spinothalamic tract

Medial longitudinal fasciculus (contains medial vestibulospinal tract)

Tectospinal tract

Ventral corticospinal tract

Ventral median fissure

Ventral root of spinal nerve

Medial motor nuclei: Ventromedial

Accessory nucleus (XI)

Fascicles of spinal accessory nerve (XI)

Substantia gelatinosa

Dorsolateral sulcus

Dorsal root of spinal nerve

Dorsal intermediate sulcus

Figure 3.9   Schematic of cross-section through the top part of the spinal cord

where dorsal and ventral horns meet, and inform the brain of the spinal cord's activities. For example, sensory receptors (from the skin, for instance) send information to the spinal cord via sensory afferent fibers. These enter the dorsal roots and branch out to form synapses with the grey matter's terminal buttons. Sensory neurons found in the spinal ganglion send dendrites to sense organs and an axon to the spinal cord.

Finally, the grey matter contains neurons which communicate with other neurons either within a segment or above and below a segment of the spinal cord. These are called **spinal interneurons** and are important because they form synapses with motor neurons which can mediate the motor response to sensory stimuli. There are also different types of spinal axon called **propriospinal fibers**. These belong to the axon of one neuron which sends collaterals to other spinal segments.

As we saw in Chapter 1, different parts of the CNS have neurons of a different shape and size, giving rise to what is known as cytoarchitecture. In the spinal cord, different types of neuron are found in bands or zones and different arrangements are found in the ventral and dorsal horns. Collectively, these arrangements are called laminae, or more accurately, **Rexed's laminae** after their discoverer. Outside the spinal foramen, the spinal nerves extend and form other branches. The thickest is called the **ventral ramus** (plural = rami); the thinner one is called the **dorsal ramus**. Each contains both spinal and motor neurons. The dorsal rami send processes to muscles and skin of the back; ventral rami send processes to the neck and the extremities amongst other regions. The spinal cord fibers do not act independently of the brain: the brain is responsible for controlling the action of the spinal cord. Much of this control occurs in the cortex and the brainstem.

▌ Brainstem

The brainstem is actually a continuation of the spinal cord. It is made up of fairly distinct regions including, from bottom to top, the **medulla oblongata**, the **pons**, the **mesencephalon** and **diencephalon**, as seen in Figure 3.6.

The brainstem is characterized by its ventricles, the fourth and third of which are found in the pons and diencephalon respectively. The brainstem is also characterized by nuclei which belong to 12 pairs of cranial nerves. All of these nerves apart from the first, the olfactory nerve, arise in the brainstem, and all twelve pairs are numbered according to where they emerge on the surface of the brainstem. The cranial nerves are described more fully later in the chapter.

In the core of the brainstem, there is a mass of neurons called the **reticular formation**, an interesting collection of fibers which is thought to be responsible for mediating quite different behaviours. Thus some parts of it are involved in sleep, others in respiration. Its activity has also been thought to provide a biological basis of the personality dimensions extroversion and neuroticism.

Medulla oblongata

The next major part of the brainstem is the medulla oblongata. The ventral median fissure, an indentation of the spinal cord, continues to the medulla oblongata, where it forms a longitudinal fissure. There are collections of processes called pyramids (because of their shape) on either side of the fissure. These are made up of axons belonging to the **pyramidal tract**, an important bundle of fibers (in fact, one million of them) which sends signals from the cortex to the spinal cord. At the bottom of the medulla, the axons cross over, forming a **pyramidal decussation**. The medulla also contains fibers from the dorsal column nuclei which form the **medial lemniscus**. This receives sensory information from the skin and muscle surrounding the joints.

Pons

The medulla oblongata extends into the pons (meaning bridge), a structure which contains a large-cell group called the **pontine nuclei**. These send projections to the **cerebellum**, connecting it to form the **middle cerebellar peduncle**. The pons is an important structure because several of the cranial nerves exit here.

Mesencephalon

The mesencephalon is the next clear region up from the pons and is quite short. On either side of the midline of the midbrain are the **cerebral peduncles** (crus cerebri). It contains four small, rounded bumps called **colliculi**. There are two pairs, **inferior colliculi** and **superior colliculi**, involved in the relay of auditory and visual information, respectively. As with other brainstem structures, the mesencephalon also contains cranial nerves. Near the colliculi is an aqueduct which joins the third and fourth cerebral ventricles. Surrounding this aqueduct is a region of grey matter called the **periaqueductal grey substance**, an important region for the sensation of pain. Finally, the mesencephalon contains the **substantia nigra** ('black substance'), an important area next to the crus cerebri which is involved the regulation of movement and is often referred to as part of the basal ganglia (see below).

Diencephalon

The next region up from the mesencephalon is the diencephalon which comprises two principal structures called the **thalamus** and **hypothalamus**. The thalamus is a structure which resides on either side of the third ventricle and has a flattened, egg-shaped appearance. It plays a vital role as a relay station for almost all information coming from the lower brainstem and CNS on its way to the cortex. To its side is a thick covering of white matter called the **internal capsule** which has fibers connecting the cerebral cortex with the rest of the CNS. This extends into another fiber structure, the **corpus callosum** which is a thick band of fibers that connects the two cerebral hemispheres.

A Y-shaped band of white matter, called the **internal medullary lamina**, divides the thalamus into different regions of nuclei. Among the thalamic nuclei that can be observed are the **medial thalamic nuclei**, the **lateral thalamic nucleus** and the **anterior thalamic nucleus**, all of which are described by their position. These nuclei can themselves be subdivided into smaller nuclei. One large set of nuclei in the posterior part, called the **pulvinar**, partly covers two other nuclei: the **lateral geniculate body** and the **medial geniculate body**. The first of these bodies acts as a relay station for visual information, the second as a relay station for auditory information. The importance of the diencephalon to vision does not end here. The optic nerves themselves, which deliver information from each retina, course under the diencephalon and meet, forming a chasm. Here, there is a partial crossing-over of fibers so that some axons cross to the contralateral hemisphere. Fibers leaving this chasm form an **optic tract**. The remainder of the visual pathway is described in the section on sensory and motor systems below.

Beneath and anterior to the thalamus lies the hypothalamus. This is another important structure and is responsible for mediating autonomic nervous system function and behaviours such as aggression, feeding and sexual activity. Protruding posteriorly from the hypothalamus are the **mammillary bodies**. The **fornix**, a thick arching collection of fibers, extends from the cerebral cortex and ends in the hypothalamus. Both the mammillary bodies and the fornix are thought to play a special role in memory and learning. The motor efferent fibers sent to the thalamus by the mammillary bodies form the **mammillothalamic tract**.

Finally, one other structure in the diencephalon is the **pituitary gland** which is important for the secretion of hormones.

▓ Cerebellum

The cerebellum (literally, little brain) extends from the pons and is responsible for the execution of movement and maintaining balance of posture. The cerebellum is located beneath the cortex and posterior to the brainstem. Its name, 'little brain', nicely describes the structure because it does look like a small brain attached to the back of the brainstem. It has its own covering or cortex of grey matter called the cerebellar cortex, beneath which lies white matter. The white matter itself contains the **cerebellar nuclei**; most of the cerebellum's efferent fibers originate here. The white matter has a distinctive appearance, like a mature, leafy tree. Because of this, it is called the **arbor vitae** (literally, tree of life).

Like the cerebral cortex, the surface of the cerebellum has a convoluted appearance, i.e. it has a number of folds called **folia** because they are like folded narrow sheets. It also displays various grooves on its surface which divide the structure into lobes. In the middle of the cerebellum is a narrow region called the **vermis**.

There are stalks connecting the brain stem to the cerebellum, called the **inferior**, **middle** and **superior peduncles**. Two of these bring information from various parts of the CNS and one sends fibers to the CNS. The two peduncles receiving afferents are the **inferior** (or **restiform body**) and **middle** (**brachium pontis**) peduncles. The former receives input from the spinal cord; the latter receives fibers from the cerebral cortex. The superior peduncle (or **brachium conjunctium**) sends efferents to the CNS. The fourth ventricle forms part of the cerebellum.

■ Cerebral cortex

The largest and outer part of the brain is called the cerebral cortex and fills most of the skull. A view of the brain from above shows that it has a curved and relatively smooth surface, in contrast to the underneath of the brain – the brainstem – which has an extremely uneven surface. The name cortex means bark, an appropriate name given the position of the tissue but one that does not describe its texture very well (this is soft and jelly-like).

The most obvious physical characteristic of the cortex (or **neocortex**) is its convoluted appearance. It looks wrinkly. The reason for this is that the cortex actually comprises several compressed sheets. Imagine trying to fit a sheet of A4 paper into a 4 × 4 inch wooden box without altering the shape of the paper. It would be impossible. If, however, you crumpled the paper, it would fit. The cortex has developed in similarly crumpled fashion in order to meet the constraints imposed by the skull. An advantage of this crumpling is that it increases the surface area of the brain that can be fitted inside the skull.

Fissures and sulci

The convolutions, or grooves, on the cortex are called **fissures** or **sulci** (singular = sulcus). They can be seen in Figures 3.10 and 3.11.

Fissures describe very deep grooves; sulci describe more superficial ones. The surfaces of the cortex lying between these grooves are called **gyri**. Each hemisphere contains one large fissure called the **lateral**, or **Sylvian**, fissure. This, as its name suggests, extends laterally and medially down each hemisphere. At the end of these fissures, there are gyri which form the region called the **insula**.

Although there is tremendous individual variation in the appearance and length of fissures and sulci, some are well described and are common. For example, one

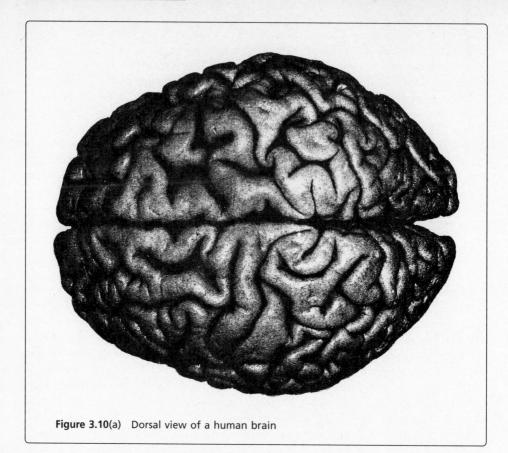

Figure 3.10(a)   Dorsal view of a human brain

groove in the middle of the brain extending inferiorly is called the **central sulcus** or **Rolandic fissure**. In front of this is the **precentral gyrus**. Together these two gyri form the cortical area responsible for motor movement. Damage to these gyri can result in paralysis in the contralateral side of the body. The gyrus appearing after the central sulcus is called the **postcentral gyrus** and is the region responsible for receiving sensory information from the skin and muscles. This is also called the **somatosensory cortex** or **SI**.

Lobes of the brain

The fissures and sulci appear to divide the brain into geographically distinct regions. These regions are called lobes and there are four of them: **frontal**, **temporal**, **parietal** and **occipital**, as seen in Figure 3.10(b).

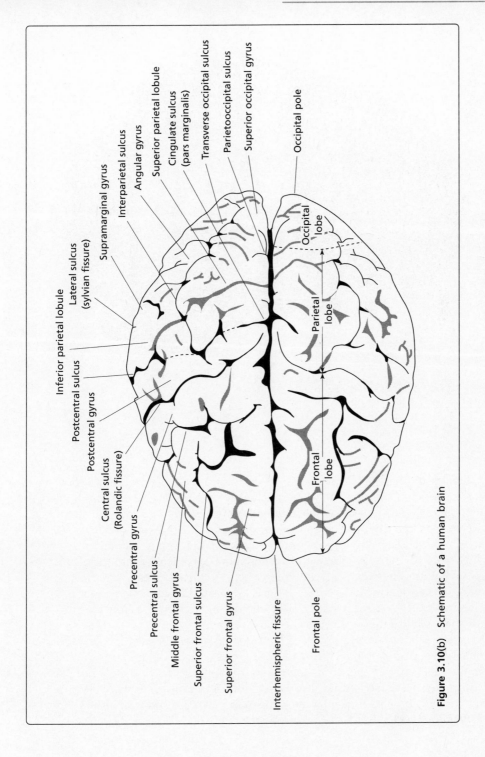

Figure 3.10(b)   Schematic of a human brain

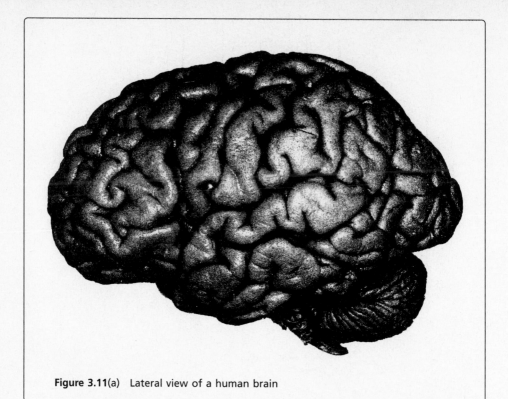

Figure 3.11(a) Lateral view of a human brain

There is no real underlying logic to the description of these lobes, however, because it is not based on the lobe's actual functional characteristics. It is true, however, that one lobe may be more responsible for a certain function than another. For example, the occipital lobes contain the primary visual cortex; the superior temporal gyrus of the temporal lobe contains the primary auditory cortex which receives impulses from the ear, or more specifically, the cochlea. These areas are thus described as the auditory cortex, the visual cortex, motor cortex and so on. In addition to these cortices, there are areas known as **association cortex areas** which lie outside the primary motor or sensory area but which have reciprocal connections with these regions.

The lobes of the cortex are, in fact, named after the skull bone that they underlie. Some lobes' names are very recent in origin. The part of the cortex called the occipital lobe also contains a white stripe running parallel to the cortex. Because of this, the occipital lobe is also called the **striate area/cortex**. The principal functions of the occipital lobe are considered later in this chapter. The frontal lobes occupy a chapter of their own (Chapter 6).

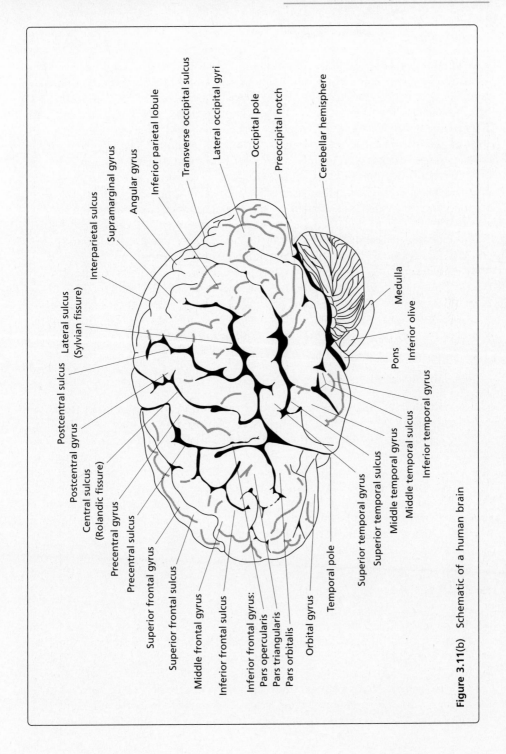

Figure 3.11(b)   Schematic of a human brain

Temporal lobe function

The temporal lobes are the brain regions primarily responsible for audition (hearing), language comprehension, memory and learning and, possibly, olfactory perception, detection and identification. These lobes are particularly important for hearing because they contain both the primary auditory cortex and the auditory association areas. Bilateral damage to Area 41 (Heschl's gyrus) might lead to cortical deafness. Unilateral lesions to this area result in less severe auditory consequences, such as a reduction in the threshold for auditory sensation. Damage to other regions of the auditory cortex can lead to musical deficits such as tone deafness or poor pitch/melody perception (musical agnosia) or an inability to comprehend non-verbal sounds (sound agnosia). Language comprehension is most affected by damage to unilateral lesions to Area 22 or Wernicke's area (see Chapter 9) and memory and learning deficits can also result from temporal lobe damage, as we see in Chapter 4. Inevitably, when memory and learning impairments arise from temporal damage, personality is changed as a result. Finally, damage to the right temporal (and orbitofrontal cortex) has been associated with deficits in odour recognition memory (Jones-Gotman and Zatorre, 1993). The cortical connections between the temporal cortex and the orbitofrontal region may also be important for olfactory perception and discrimination (Potter and Nauta, 1979).

Parietal lobe function

The parietal lobes contain the primary and association cortices for somatosensation. Damage to the parietal cortex, therefore, can produce deficits in behaviours such as tactile perception and touch discrimination. As the parietal lobe also contains the motor cortex, damage to the motor area can result in impairments in gross limb movement. Finally, parietal cortex damage is often associated with deficits in spatial representation such as spatial neglect, where the patient is unable to 'see' objects in one half of the visual field, a phenomenon discussed in Chapter 7, or constructional apraxia, the inability to copy a drawing in the absence of a neurological motor impairment, discussed in Chapter 8.

Basal ganglia

Inside the cortex there are a number of small structures which are integral to the functioning of the human brain and behaviour. One such collection is called the basal ganglia which is involved in certain aspects of movement, as illustrated by Figure 3.12.

The basal ganglia receive connections from parts of the cortex and send axons to the motor cortex. They have two main parts. The smallest is found anterior to the thalamus, has a long, curved tail and is called the **caudate nucleus**. The caudate

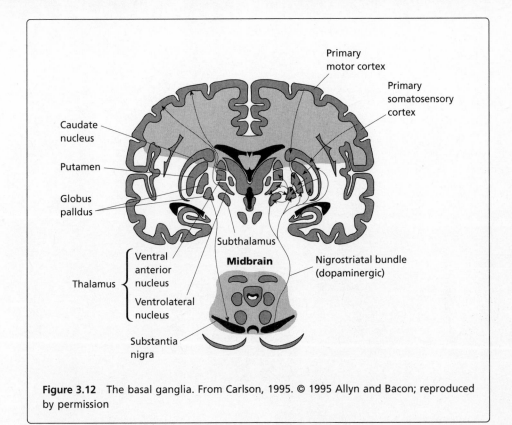

Figure 3.12   The basal ganglia. From Carlson, 1995. © 1995 Allyn and Bacon; reproduced by permission

has a large part (called the **caput**) and a tail-end (the **cauda**) which points upwards then backwards into the temporal lobe. The largest part of the basal ganglia, found laterally to the internal capsule, is called the **lentiform nucleus**. The lateral and external part of this is called the **putamen**. The medial and internal part is called the **globus pallidus**.

Limbic system

Another collection of structures important for behaviour represents part of the limbic system, a name given by the neuroanatomist Paul Maclean to a collection of subcortical structures which includes the **hippocampus**, the **septal nuclei**, the **amygdala**, the **cingulate gyrus**, the mammillary bodies and the hypothalamus (see Figure 3.13).

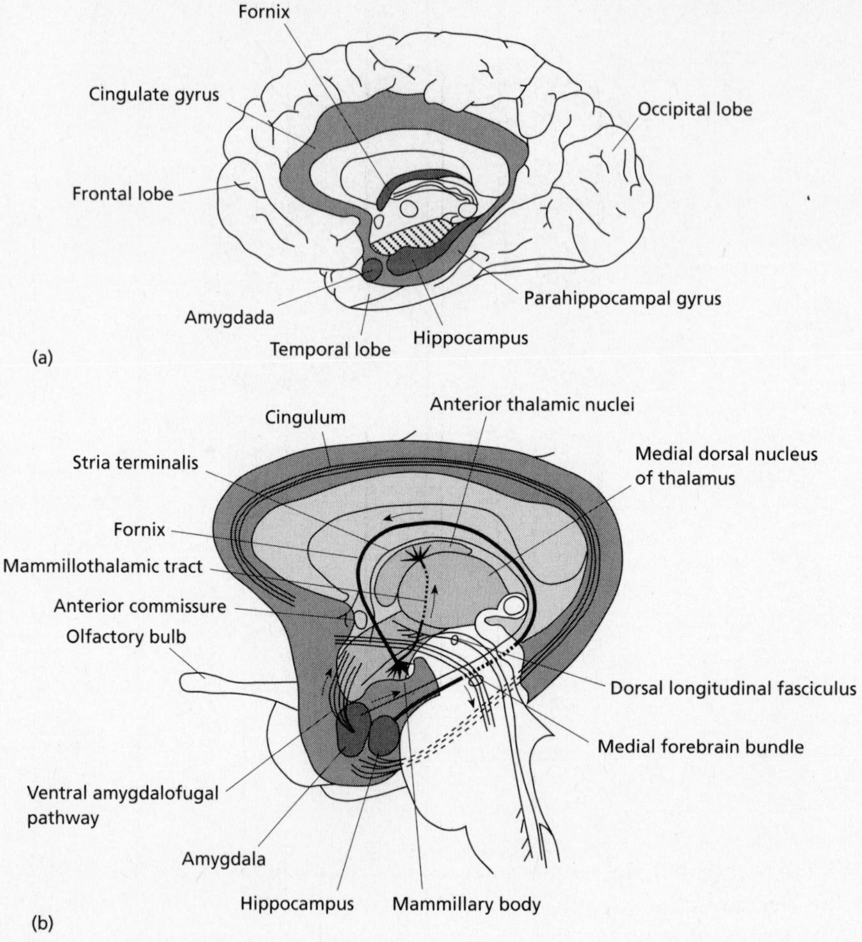

Figure 3.13 The limbic system. (a) General location of structures; (b) structures in detail

The limbic system is probably the oldest part of the brain and contains many of the structures involved in the most primitive behaviours such as feeding, copulating and aggressing. Originally, this part of the brain was called the rhinencephalon ('smell-brain') because it was thought to be heavily involved in the regulation of the olfactory system. Broca had earlier coined the term limbic lobe to describe these structures, before Maclean dignified them with the status of a system (there is still argument over whether these structures actually do constitute a system).

Whatever the merits and demerits of the description, the 'limbic system' is a useful shorthand description of connecting and interconnecting subcortical brain areas.

The hypothalamus, for example, has direct connections with most of the other parts of the limbic system. This structure in particular appears to be involved in the regulation of eating and drinking via connections with the amygdala. It also appears to be involved in regulating reproduction and body temperature. The amygdala, found in the temporal lobe anterior to the hippocampus and the horn of the third ventricle, has been thought to play a role in a number of behaviours including face recognition, emotion and aggression. In laboratory animals whose amygdala has been destroyed, normal aggressiveness is abolished. The limbic system's role in emotion is discussed more fully in Chapter 10. As we will see below, the limbic system receives connections from other parts of the brain and receives information from all the sensory systems via the **parahippocampal gyrus**.

Finally, there is an area between the globus pallidus and brain surface called the **substantia innominata**. This contains two important sets of nuclei: the **basal nucleus of Meynert (nucleus basalis of Meynert)** and the **nucleus of the diagonal band of Broca**. The former has cholinergic axons projecting to the amygdala and cortex, the latter to the hippocampus and septum. Lesions of the nucleus basalis result in a dramatic reduction in acetylcholine, and impairment of these nuclei has been associated with memory deficits.

■ Organization of the cerebral cortex

The six layers of the cortex

As well as being convoluted, the cortex is also made up of six parallel layers or laminae which are found perpendicular to the surface. The division of the cortex into six layers is made on the basis of cytoarchitecture: the number, size and density of cell bodies in the cortex. Neurons are not arranged randomly across the whole cortex.

About two-thirds of the neurons are **pyramidal cells**, so called because their cell bodies are shaped like pyramids. These tend to have a long axon and dendrite. The remainder of the neurons are non-pyramidal. In fact, there are other specific non-pyramidal cells which are given names which reflect their appearance. Thus, multipolar cells are called stellate cells. Chandelier and basket cells are named after their arrangement and appearance. The cortical layers contain neurons that either receive or send out axons; their main features are described in Table 3.2.

Table 3.2 The six layers of the cortex and the types of cell contained in them

Layer	Cell type
Layer 1: molecular layer	Contains few neurons and is made up primarily of axons and atypical dendrites from cell bodies in deeper layers
Layer 2: external granular layer	Contains a large number of small, rounded cell bodies, densely packed. It is called granular because these cell bodies are small and are like granules
Layer 3: external pyramidal layer	Contains pyramidal cells
Layer 4: internal granular layer	Like layer 2, contains small, densely packed cell bodies. It is well developed in sensory areas and is further laminated in the striate cortex where it is subdivided into layers 4a, 4b and 4c
Layer 5: internal pyramidal layer	Contains large pyramidal cells (larger than those in layer 3)
Layer 6: multiform layer	Contains a large number of spindle-shaped cells

Both layers 2 and 4 are *receiving* layers, receiving fibers mainly from sensory and association areas. Layers 3, 5 and 6 *send* fibers to the rest of the cortex. Layer 3 sends to association areas and the *commissures* (fibers which connect parts of the brain), whereas layer 6 sends axons to the thalamus. Layer 5 sends axons to the brainstem and spinal cord and is therefore much involved in regulating motor behaviour. Not surprisingly, this layer is well developed in the motor cortex and precentral gyrus. The laminar arrangement produces a complex network of receiving and sending axons.

Columns of the cortex

The cortex is also arranged in another way: it manifests distinct columns within these cortical layers. Each of these columns has a function that is not normally shared with immediately neighbouring columns. The existence of the columnar arrangement in the cortex was demonstrated by early electrophysiological studies in which electrodes were placed perpendicularly into the cortex. The neurons – regardless of the depth of the cortex reached – had the same receptive field. However, when the electrode was placed obliquely into the cortex, different receptive fields were recorded at each level. However, the columnar arrangement is not quite so simple. In a series of classic experiments, summarized by Hubel and

Wiesel (1979), it was found that the visual cortex is arranged in bands rather than columns. Thus, a column might reach a layer or two above or below but it would not reach all.

Connections between brain regions

There are quite specific connections made between certain brain regions. Perhaps the most important are connections between the thalamus and the cortex (**thalamocortical connections**), between region of the cortex and another (**corticocortical connections**) and between large areas of cortex and another (commissures). Corticocortical connections are usually reciprocal, i.e. the sending area receives fibers from the region that it sends to.

Thalamocortical connections

As we saw earlier, the thalamus is made up of several different nuclei. These different nuclei supply different parts of the cortex with afferents. As we also saw earlier, the thalamic nuclei provide a relay station for those impulses sent from sensory receptors to the cortex. So, for example, the ventral nucleus of the thalamus receives impulses from the somatosensory receptors and projects to the somatosensory cortex. The lateral geniculate body acts as a relay station for the pathway from the retina to the striate or visual cortex. The medial geniculate body serves a similar function for audition (projecting to the auditory cortex). Other nuclei mediate pathways between the cerebellum and the basal ganglia, and the motor or premotor cortex. The anterior thalamic nucleus receives axons from the mammillary bodies and projects to the cingulate gyrus whereas the mediodorsal thalamic nucleus receives axons from the amygdala and projects to the frontal lobes. The posterior part of the thalamus projects to the posterior parietal cortex. These connections are usually reciprocal, providing 'feedback loops'.

Association areas

Many of the connections made within the cortex are made via association cortices, seen in Figure 3.14.

These cortices do not receive inputs from sensory or motor receptors directly but do receive projections from the primary sensory and motor cortices. The role of the association cortices appears to be to integrate information and to send back information to other parts of the cortex.

For example, the association area found in Areas 5 and 7 of the parietal cortex (the posterior cortex) integrates somatosensory and visual information and sends projections to the premotor and motor area. For this reason, damage to the **parietal**

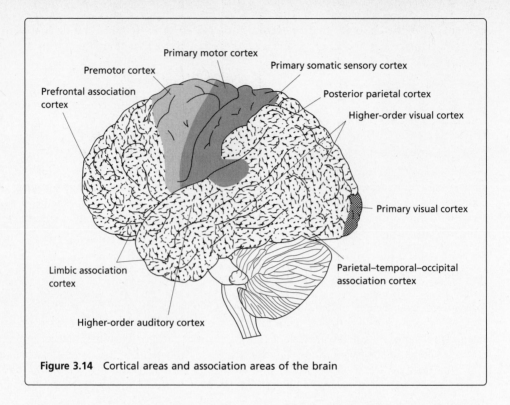

Figure 3.14   Cortical areas and association areas of the brain

association cortex can produce disturbances in voluntary movement, the inability to grasp or manipulate objects in the absence of paralysis (the patient might, for example, pour water from a jug outside the glass rather than into it), a deficit in drawing and copying ability, an inability to use tools correctly and, when damage is to the right hemisphere, neglect of the side of the body contralateral to the lesion (see Chapters 7 and 8).

The association area of the frontal lobes is the prefrontal cortex and is found at the anterior end of the frontal lobe. This is a rather important association area because it receives connections from all sensory modalities and also has connections with areas responsible for mediating emotion. For this reason, the frontal lobes have been described as the brain's 'orchestra leader', a role which is described more fully in Chapter 6.

Finally, the **temporal association area** comprises the superior temporal gyrus (which connects with the primary temporal cortex) and the inferior temporal cortex (which has connections with the extrastriate visual area). The types of deficit which follow temporal association cortex damage include memory loss (amnesia, but only if damage is bilateral), visual agnosia (the inability to recognize objects) and the inability to interpret complex visual stimuli. The basis for these deficits is returned to in Chapters 7 and 8.

■ Cranial nerves

Earlier, we noted that the peripheral nervous system contains major nerves that are necessary for the execution of essential behaviours, such as seeing, hearing, smelling, swallowing, salivating and other behaviours. These nerves convey information from the senses to the brain which, in turn, integrates and tries to make sense of this information. They are also necessary for certain head and trunk movements. These are the twelve **cranial nerves** and they originate or terminate in the brainstem. Their location and projections can be seen in Figure 3.15. They are numbered in the order encountered in the brain, anterior to posterior. The twelve nerves and their function are described in Table 3.3.

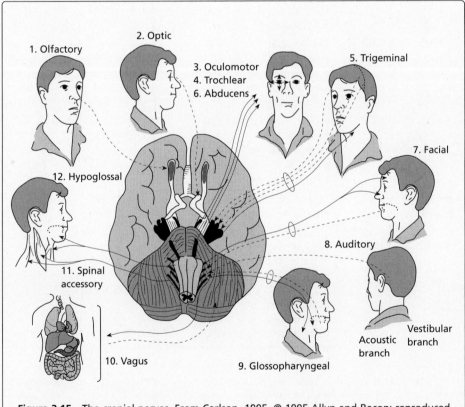

Figure 3.15 The cranial nerves. From Carlson, 1995. © 1995 Allyn and Bacon; reproduced by permission

Table 3.3 The twelve cranial nerves and their functions

Nerve	Function	Damage
12 Hypoglossal	Motor nerve of tongue Swallowing Vomiting	Ipsilateral paralysis of tongue
11 Accessory nerve	Sends fibers to two neck muscles Rotation of shoulder blade	Peripheral paresis; elevation of arm difficult
10 Vagus nerve	Sends projections to neck, thorax and abdomen including heart, trachea, stomach, liver, gall bladder Reduces heart rate, constricts bronchi and controls peristalsis	Impairment in any of the functions listed
9 Glossopharyngeal nerve	Innervation of the tongue, taste buds, mucous membrane and saliva	Impairment in any of the functions listed
8 Vestibulocochlear nerve	Responsible for physical equilibrium Influences ability of eye to keep object stationary when head moves	Impairment in any of the functions listed especially nystagmus (abnormal oscillation of eyes)
7 Facial nerve	Motor nerve of mimetic facial muscles Responsible for facial expression Secretion of tears and saliva	Ipsilateral peripheral facial paralysis
6 Abducent nerve	Responsible for lateral rectus muscle pulling eye so that cornea is lateral-facing	Unilateral lesion produces head turned to the side of lesion. Lateral motion lost
5 Trigeminal nerve	Largest cranial nerve. Sensory nerve of the face Branches into ophthalmic, maxillar and mandibular nerves, all of which innervate parts of the face Reflexes include sneezing, sucking and stretching of masseter muscle	Motor fiber damage results in mastication difficulties Impairment in any of the functions listed
4 Trochlear nerve	Supplies superior oblique muscle which directs gaze downwards and laterally	Impairment in downward gaze

Table 3.3 (*cont.*)

Nerve	Function	Damage
3 Oculomotor nerve	Largest nerve innervating extraocular muscles including those moving eye medially, upwards, downwards and lifting upper eyelid	Abnormal eye positioning (lateral and downward). Double vision. Ptosis (drooping of upper eyelid). Light reflex absent; pupil is large. Accommodation of lens absent resulting in myopia
2 Optic nerve	Actually a brain tract, not a peripheral nerve Part of the visual pathway from eye to optic chiasm	Homonymous hemianopia
1 Olfactory nerve	Responsible for sense of smell	Anosmia (loss of ability to perceive odour)

■ Covering the brain

In addition to hair, scalp and skull, the brain has other layers of protection which directly surround it. These are membranes called **meninges** and there are three of them (these layers also cover the spinal cord). The immediate covering is called the **pia mater**. This covers the brain very closely and covers all sulci and fissures.

The second covering is the **arachnoid mater**. Unlike the pia mater, this covers *over* the sulci. The space between this layer and the pia mater is called the **subarachnoid space** which is found all over the CNS. It is filled mostly with cerebrospinal fluid but also contains thin threads of tissue which connect the two layers. Sometimes, a blood vessel in the brain might rupture, causing **subarachnoid haemorrhage** where the blood mixes with the cerebrospinal fluid. The subarachnoid space is not equal across the cortex: some spaces are larger than others. These spaces are called **cisterns** and the largest of them is found below the cerebellum.

Finally, the third and outer layer of the brain is called the **dura mater** ('hard matter'). There is not much space between the arachnoid and dura mater, but what there is, is called the **subdural space**. The third layer is tough and covers the inside of the skull. It has indentations which limit the movement of the brain. This layer covers all of the CNS including the cauda equina. When it reaches the cauda it forms a sac called the **dural sac**. This region is where a clinician might perform a **lumbar puncture** in order obtain a sample of CSF (the contents of the CSF can give many clues about possible brain dysfunction). The spinal cord would not be damaged because spinal nerve roots are the only fibers in this region.

■ Ventricular system

The cerebrospinal fluid (CSF) is found in the brain's cavities or ventricles illustrated by Figure 3.16.

The canal of the spinal cord extends up to the brainstem where it forms the fourth ventricle. The cerebellar peduncles joining the cerebellum to the brainstem form a tent-like shape which is filled with CSF. The next ventricle is the third ventricle which comprises a narrow space between the two thalami. The first and third ventricles, called **lateral ventricles**, are found in the parietal lobes, just above the thalamus, and extend horns into each of the other lobes. The anterior horn (the largest) extends frontally, the posterior horn extends occipitally, and the inferior horn extends temporally.

Cerebrospinal fluid is made by small vascular tufts called **choroid plexuses** which are attached to the walls of the ventricles by a thin stalk. CSF has the same sodium and potassium concentration as blood but contains two-thirds of blood's glucose content. It contains neurotransmitters, neuropeptides and hormones. The fact that it contains neurotransmitters suggests that obtaining a sample of the CSF will give us a measure of neurotransmitter and other substances' levels in extra-cellular fluid.

About 0.5 litres of CSF is produced each day but only about 150 millilitres is found in the ventricles and subarachnoid space. There is an effective drainage system which removes the excess fluid. The CSF also helps to protect the brain from extreme pressure (such as a blow to the head) because it makes the brain lighter (by about 1300 grams). The brain is made buoyant by this fluid; when a

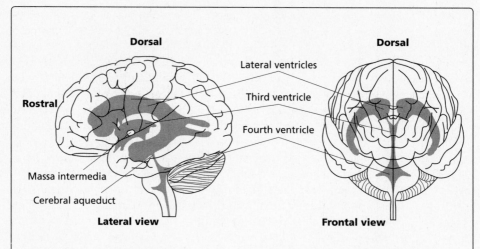

Figure 3.16 The ventricles of the brain. From Carlson, 1995. © 1995 Allyn and Bacon; reproduced by permission

blow is received by the head, this fluid has to be pushed aside before brain hits the skull.

■ Arteries of the brain

The blood supply to the brain is provided by the **internal carotid artery**, which supplies the cortex, and the **vertebral artery**, which supplies the brainstem and cerebellum. The arteries supplying the brain are seen in Figures 3.17 and 3.18.

The carotid artery enters the cavity of the skull and divides into three other arteries: the **ophthalmic artery**, the **anterior cerebral artery** and the **middle cerebral artery** (the largest). Branches extend from these arteries and supply most

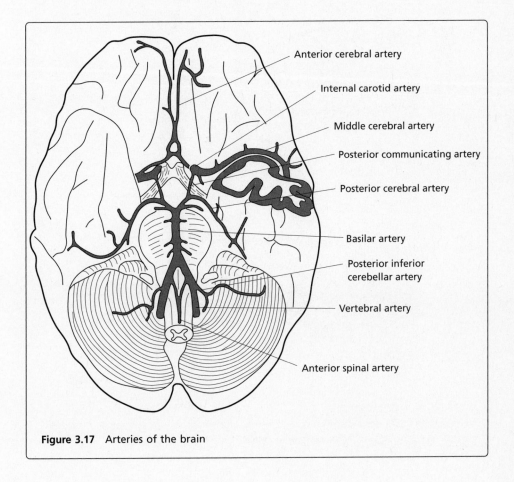

Anterior cerebral artery

Internal carotid artery

Middle cerebral artery

Posterior communicating artery

Posterior cerebral artery

Basilar artery

Posterior inferior cerebellar artery

Vertebral artery

Anterior spinal artery

Figure 3.17   Arteries of the brain

of the cortex, especially the motor and somatosensory cortical areas. The anterior cerebral artery supplies motor and sensory neurons responsible for the legs; the middle cerebral artery supplies the basal ganglia and internal capsule.

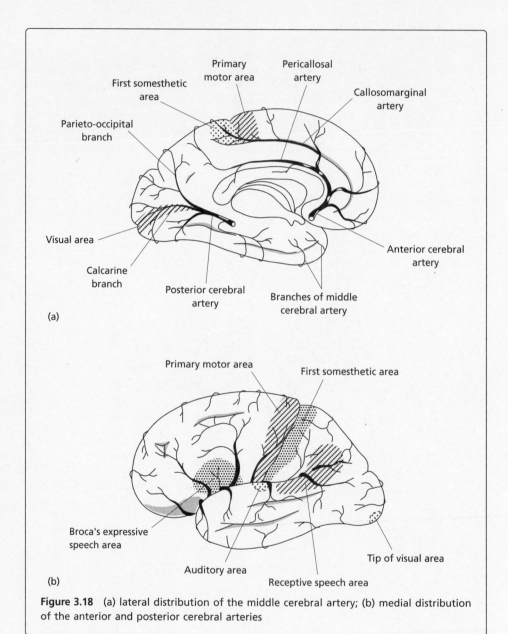

Figure 3.18 (a) lateral distribution of the middle cerebral artery; (b) medial distribution of the anterior and posterior cerebral arteries

The vertebral arteries are found the back of the head. These join at the pons to form the **basilar artery** which sends off branches to the medulla oblongata, the pons, the mesencephalon and the cerebellum. The basilar artery bifurcates at the top of the pons to form the **posterior cerebral arteries**. These supply the visual cortex and inferior temporal lobe with blood. The middle cerebral arteries and the posterior cerebral arteries are connected on the left and right side by another artery called the **posterior communicating artery**. There is also a communicating artery between the anterior cerebral arteries. These three communicating arteries form a circle of arteries called the **circle of Willis**.

The spinal cord is served by an **anterior spinal artery**, which runs along the cord's midline, and **posterior spinal arteries** which run along its side. The spinal arteries begin as branches of the vertebral arteries.

The brain also manifests deep and superficial veins which empty into folds in the dura mater called **venous sinuses**. Veins from the subarachnoid space to the venous sinuses are called bridging veins. These are important because, if torn, the damage will result in a bleeding between the dura mater and arachnoid in the subdural space. This is called a **subdural haematoma**. Unlike bleeding in the subarachnoid space which flows along all the space, bleeding in the subdural space is fairly localized and does not spread. It may be possible, therefore, to predict which functions are likely to be disrupted based on the localization of the haematoma.

▪ Malfunctions of the brain

One of the commonest sources of information in human neuropsychology comes in the form of damage or injury to the brain. The effects of tumour (or its removal), stroke, haemorrhage and other trauma indicate the extent to which the malfunctions of the brain can help to highlight how the organ normally functions. Some of the commonest forms of brain malfunction and their mechanisms are described below.

Closed-head injury

Closed-head injury describes an insult to the head which does not penetrate the skull or any of the meninges. This type of injury has primary consequences such as bleeding or swelling of the brain or damage to the brain's surface following impact with the skull; it also has secondary effects such as cell death. This type of injury contrasts with **penetrating head injury** which, as its name suggests, involves penetration of the skull and/or meninges.

Cerebral edema

An edema (or oedema) is a swelling of part of the brain and its surrounding tissue. There are three types: vasogenic, cytotoxic and interstitial.

Infarction

An infarction is any area of dead tissue resulting from a loss of blood supply.

Ischemia

Ischemia describes the loss of blood flow to the brain due to a narrowing or blockage of an artery. Complete blockage can result in an infarction as well as a confused mental state, memory decline and intellectual deficits. If there are episodic attacks of ischemia, the disorder is called a **transient ischemic attack**.

Thrombosis

Thrombosis describes the blockage of a blood vessel caused by coagulated blood. There may be an itinerant form of thrombosis which may travel down narrow arteries thereby plugging them. This blockage is called an **embolism** and can cause stroke. Embolisms need not always be coagulated blood: they can also be pockets of air, fatty tissue or hardened tissue.

Cerebrovascular accident/stroke

A cerebrovascular accident describes a sudden loss of blood supply to the brain. The commonest form of this is **stroke**. The effects of stroke depend on which artery is involved. For example, the middle cerebral artery, which supplies about 70 per cent of the cortex with blood, supplies many important areas including Broca's area, Wernicke's area, the pre- and postcentral gyri and the temporal and parietal lobes. Thus, deficits might involve weakness, sensory loss and paralysis of the face and arm contralateral to the side of the artery involved. Recovery from stroke may depend on several factors including the age of the individual, the site of the damage and a previous history of cerebrovascular accident.

There are two main types of stroke. **Ischemic strokes** result from a reduction in blood supply causing a lack of oxygen and glucose. They are usually caused by **atherosclerosis**, i.e. a blockage caused by deposits of cholesterol or other materials attached to the artery wall. **Haemorrhagic strokes** result from bleeding into brain tissue (**intracerebral haemorrhage**) or its surface (subdural haemorrhage). These result from three possible problems:

1. A **ruptured aneurysm**. An aneurysm is the ballooning of an artery wall, usually the walls of the circle of Willis in its anterior half. If an aneurysm ruptures, it can cause bleeding which is life-threatening. Alternatively, it may not rupture but could displace part of the cortex near to it or may contain stagnant blood.
2. **Arteriovenous malformation (angioma)**. This is a collection of abnormal blood vessels which produces abnormal blood supply. It is most commonly found in the middle cerebral artery.
3. **Hypertension**. This describes an increase in blood pressure due to the constriction of small blood vessels.

Haemorrhage (subarachnoid)

A subarachnoid haemorrhage describes the bleeding into the subarachnoid space and usually results from a ruptured aneurysm. Less commonly, it is caused by an arteriovenous malformation. Symptoms of this type of haemorrhage include explosive headaches followed by an almost immediate loss of consciousness. When loss of consciousness does not occur, the headache may be accompanied by nausea, vomiting, neck stiffness or fever. Around 40 per cent of the aneurysms giving rise to haemorrhage are formed in the internal carotid artery; 35 per cent in the anterior cerebral artery; 20 per cent in the middle cerebral artery, and 5 per cent in the posterior or vertebral–basilar artery. Sometimes, there may be a danger that a haemorrhage will recur. The most likely period in which this would happen would be one to two weeks after the initial haemorrhage.

Tumour (intracranial)

A tumour is a space-occupying lesion of the brain and surrounding tissue. It comes in many forms and its effects depend on factors such as speed of growth, the degree of pressure it causes, the cortex it displaces. Slower-growing tumours may go unnoticed for some time and it is these that are less likely to have a dramatically harmful effect on intellectual ability and behaviour. Tumours can be **invasive**, where they invade the neural tissue, or **non-invasive**, where they invade supporting tissue, meninges or blood vessels. The pressure they exert can cause regions to be displaced, causing compression of some areas. Symptoms of pressure inside the skull include headache, sickness and disturbed consciousness. There are several types of tumour. The names of the following indicate where the lesion occurs: **astrocytoma, glioma, haematoma, meningioma, angioma/hemangioblastoma** (tumour of the blood vessels) and **adenoma** (tumour of the pituitary gland). Surgery is the most common and effective form of treatment.

Anoxia

Anoxia refers to the loss of oxygen in the blood supplying the brain. A partial loss in this supply is called **hypoxia**. There can be many causes of anoxia including suffocation (mechanical, or gaseous such as from carbon monoxide fumes), strangulation, partial drowning and exposure to high altitudes. The brain, being extremely sensitive to lack of oxygen, can malfunction severely with prolonged oxygen loss. This can produce cell death in all layers of the cortex and in the cerebellum.

Encephalopathy

Encephalopathy describes inflammation of the central nervous system caused by reaction to chemical, toxic or physical agents. It sometimes affects boxers – the pyramidal, extrapyramidal and cerebellar malfunctions and the dementia make individuals look 'punch drunk'. In the severest cases, it results in coma and death.

Encephalitis

Encephalitis is the inflammation of the brain and results from the cells of immune tissues, fluid and protein moving out of the blood vessels. At the turn of the century, it used to be called 'brain fever' and there is still controversy over the use of the term when applied to specific conditions. Inflammation due to bacterial infection around a brain abscess is called **cerebritis**. An inflamed spinal cord is called **encephalomyelitis**. Inflammation involving the grey matter of the brain is called **polioencephalitis**. Viruses can sometimes cause inflammation of the brain and often result in patient fatigue. **Myalgic encephalomyelitis** (ME), also disparagingly known as yuppie flu, however, does not involve brain inflammation.

Hydrocephalus

Hydrocephalus describes the increase in the volume of the cerebral ventricles owing to overproduction of cerebrospinal fluid or blockage of the absorption of fluid by the ventricles. The dilation (enlargement) of the ventricles is called **ventriculomegaly**. The increase in volume causes pressure on the walls of the ventricles, especially the periventricular region. Adult and children's conditions have different causes.

Headache

This commonplace symptom, usually taking the form of a dull throbbing pain in the head, can be an indicator of a more serious underlying condition if it persists. Headaches of abrupt onset can indicate subdural bleeding especially if a stiff neck and vomiting accompany them.

If a headache is continuous, it may indicate a tumour. The pain is described as 'bursting' and may help to localize the tumour because there are pain receptors in the blood vessels and dura. The 'cluster headache' is normally caused by migraine and involves recurrent attacks. It is also known as **migrainous neuralgia** and tends to be unilateral.

Epilepsy

Epilepsy describes recurrent fits and seizures which are caused by abnormal electrical discharges in the grey matter of the brain. It affects mainly the young (around 75 per cent of those likely to develop epilepsy will have done so by the age of eighteen years) and is characterized by **partial seizures** or **generalized seizures**. A partial seizure is restricted to one part of the brain; a generalized seizure spreads to other parts of the brain. Many factors can trigger a fit. In individuals with a low threshold of neuronal excitability, low blood sugar, flickering lights, drowsiness and sleep might trigger a seizure. The inherited form of epilepsy is called **idiopathic epilepsy** or **primary generalized epilepsy**.

There are different types of seizure falling within each of the two general groups. A person suffering a generalized seizure called the **grand mal** will experience a fit involving both sides of the body. The person will fall to the ground unconscious with muscles contracting; arms and legs go straight and rigid, the body becomes taut and the mouth might be clenched. In another phase, the 'clonic' phase, there will be jerking of the body's muscles.

Other generalized seizures include **absence seizure** (**petit mal**) where the patient has a blank period, completely unaware of what is happening and what is going on around him or her. **Drop attacks** involve a sudden loss of consciousness and muscle tone and the person drops to the ground, whereas **myoclonic attacks** involve uncontrollable jerks on one or both sides of the body.

Partial seizures may be **simple** or **complex**. The simple form does not affect consciousness but the complex form does. These seizures normally being with an 'aura' which acts as a warning that a seizure is about to begin. Seizures which begin in the motor cortex are characteristic of **Jacksonian epilepsy**.

▣ Sensory and motor systems

Many of the most unusual and peculiar functional phenomena seen by neuro-psychologists are observed following impairment to the sensory, perceptual or motor systems (see Chapters 7 and 8). An understanding of these deficits requires a fairly sound knowledge of each type of system: sensory and motor. In what follows, the central and peripheral motor systems, together with the visual, auditory, somatosensory, olfactory and gustatory systems are described.

▣ Visual system

The sense which we rely on and prize the most is vision. In evolutionary terms, this sense has become our dominant means of perceiving the world, a status which has probably evolved from our ancestors' ability to raise themselves from the ground and walk on their hindlegs. The reliance on the sense of vision is thought to be one reason why the sense of smell is no longer as important to human beings as it used to be thousands of years ago. Vision is, indeed, a powerful usurper. Given its importance, it is not surprising that studies of the neuropsychology of the senses have been dominated by vision research. This section reviews what we currently understand of the neurophysiology and neuroanatomy of the visual system and describes some of the consequences of damage to this system.

The eye and beyond

The initial structure for sensing the visual environment is the eye. The eye contains the **retina** which itself contains certain cells important for the relay of visual information. These cells are called **ganglion cells** made up of W, X or Y cells. These cells are categorized by size, the areas they project to and the function they serve. W cells have small cell bodies and comprise about 10 per cent of retinal cells; X cells have medium-sized cell bodies and comprise 80 per cent of retinal cells, and Y cells have large cell bodies and comprise the final 10 per cent of cells. Y cells appear to respond to large, moving objects in the visual environment and appear to be involved in the analysis of crude forms and in directing attention to moving objects. X cells, in contrast, respond better to small targets and appear to be involved in the analysis of detailed, high-resolution and colour images. This arrangement illustrates one principle of visual system functioning: that it is involved in the parallel processing of stimuli; one type of cell responds to moving images, another responds to colour, another responds to size and so on, simultaneously.

The cells of the retina have a specific property called a **receptive field**. A receptive field is an area in which stimulation causes excitation or inhibition.

Different parts of the eye have cells with differently sized receptive fields. For example, the receptive fields are larger in the peripheral parts of the retina than in the fovea. The fields also have two types of cell. The **on-centre cells** have a central excitatory area and an inhibitory surround whereas the **off-centre cells** have an excitatory surround and an inhibitory centre. These cells are important because they can detect and appreciate contrasts in the visual environment.

All retinal cells project to the **optic disk** at the back of the eye where they become myelinated and join other axons to form the **optic nerve** (this has over 1 million fibers; compare this with the auditory nerve which has 30 000). The optic disk lies medial to the fovea and is insensitive to light. An intriguing phenomenon in vision is the blindspot: light from the area which reaches both eyes does not hit both optic disks. Eventually, the optic nerve of each eye converges at a point called the **optic chiasm**.

When we see, we see from two visual fields: the right and the left. Visual fields are the areas in which the external world is viewed by the eye without the head moving. The right visual field contains light that is sensed predominantly by the right eye; conversely, the light in the left visual field is sensed primarily by the left eye. Light that goes directly to both eyes (from the middle of the visual fields) occupies the **binocular zone**; light reaching only one eye occupies the **monocular zone**. A term used with regard to visual fields is hemiretina. The part of the retina that is medial to the fovea is called the **nasal hemiretina**; the hemiretina lateral to the fovea is called the **temporal hemiretina** as seen in Figure 3.19. Each half of the hemiretina is divided into dorsal and ventral parts.

The superior half of the visual field projects to the inferior half of the retina; similarly, the inferior half of the visual field projects to the superior half of the retina. This arrangement is dealt with by the brain to enable us to see normally. Light that occupies the binocular zones goes to both retinas: light falls on the temporal hemiretina of the left eye and the nasal hemiretina of the right eye. Only the fibers from the nasal hemiretina of each retina cross at the optic chiasm; the fibers from the temporal hemiretina do not. Fibers that exit the optic tract project to the **lateral geniculate nucleus** of the thalamus, an important relay station in the visual system. From here, axons are sent to the visual cortex.

Light that occupies monocular zones projects to the nasal hemiretina on the same side as the light (the nose prevents light from reaching the other eye). The monocular area of the visual field is called the **temporal crescent**. Light from this region cannot be sensed binocularly.

Lateral geniculate nucleus

The lateral geniculate nucleus (LGN) is found in the posterior thalamus and is important for a number of reasons, not least because the optic tract fibers terminate here and because different axons terminate in specific areas of the LGN. Greater

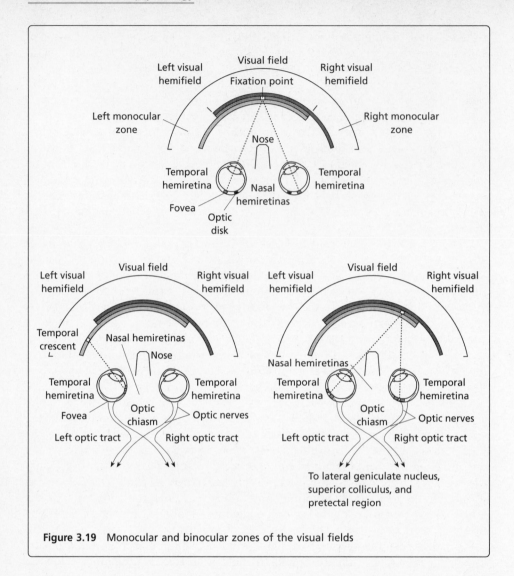

Figure 3.19   Monocular and binocular zones of the visual fields

input is provided from central than from peripheral lines of vision from the retina. In the primate, the LGN has six layers of neurons separated by axons and dendrites. Each layer receives information from one eye only: the contralateral nasal hemiretina projects to layers 6, 4 and 1; the ipsilateral temporal hemiretina projects to layers 5, 3, and 2 (see Figure 3.20).

Layers 1 and 2 (the most ventral layers) are called **magnocellular layers** because they contain large cells. Layers 3 to 6 (the most dorsal layers) are called **parvocellular layers**. Y cells project to the magnocellular layer; X cells to the parvocellular

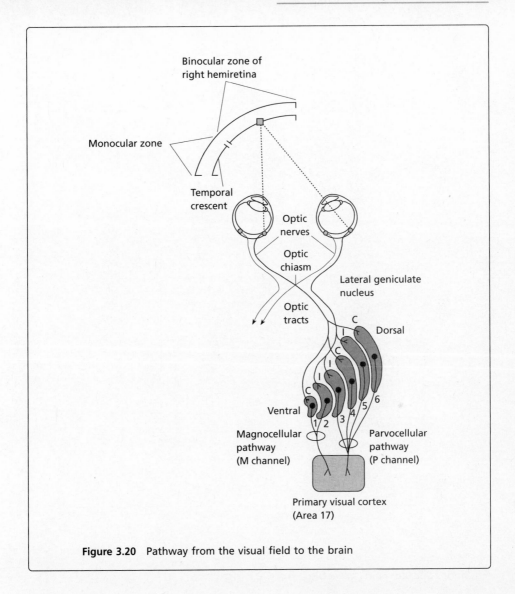

Figure 3.20 Pathway from the visual field to the brain

layer. Because of this projection pattern, the pathways are called **X-parvocellular** and **Y-magnocellular**. These pathways are illustrated in Figure 3.21.

All the cells project to the visual cortex. Retina cells, however, also project to the **superior colliculus**, a structure which is important for the control of eye movement. The types of ganglion cell found in these structures differ. X cells project only to the LGN; Y cells project to those layers of the LGN not receiving X axons and to the superior colliculus; W cells project primarily to the superior colliculus.

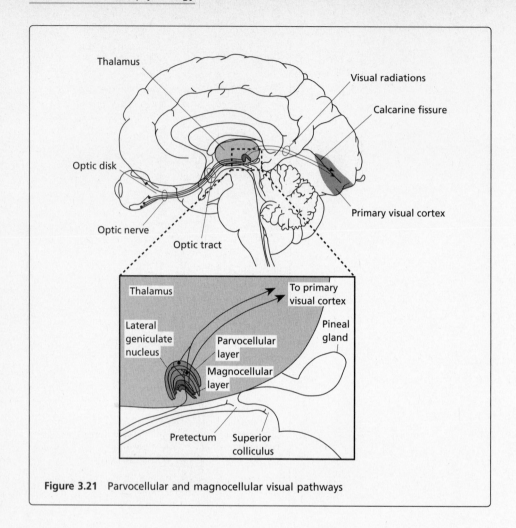

Figure 3.21   Parvocellular and magnocellular visual pathways

Superior colliculus and pretectum

Like the LGN, the superior colliculus has several layers and receives visual input from the retina. Its superficial layers receive visual input; its deepest layers receive somatic, sensory and auditory input. The primary function of the superior colliculus, however, appears to be the orienting of head and eyes towards a visual stimulus and the control of rapid eye movements (called **saccades**). The guidance of the head is done in association with the frontal eye fields of the frontal cortex which receives information from the visual cortex via X cells. The superior colliculus, via the Y cells, is also concerned with movement, visual attention and identifying broad visual outlines. There are also **tectopontine axons** (superior colliculus axons synapsing in the pontine nuclei) which help to relay visual information to the cerebellum.

The pretectum mediates pupillary light reflexes. Light that is picked up by retinal cells stimulates axons which project from the optic nerve to the pretectum which lies rostral to the superior colliculus. The pupillary reflex is an important one because its absence indicates substantial midbrain damage. The reflex usually takes the form of a direct and consensual response. The former describes the constriction of the pupil following light shone directly onto the eye; the latter describes constriction occurring in the other eye at the same time (although it is not directly stimulated).

Damage to the visual pathway

Certain deficits in vision can occur with lesions to the visual pathway. For example, if the optic nerve is lesioned, vision functions only in the intact eye (**monocular blindness**). Damage to the optic nerve can also result in blindness in the temporal crescent on the lesioned side. Damage to the fibers crossing the optic chiasm results in a **bilateral hemianopia**: a loss of vision in the temporal parts of both visual fields. A complete **homonymous hemianopia** can result from a lesion to one optic tract. When this occurs, there is a complete loss of vision in the contralateral visual field. **Quadrantic anopia** occurs when there is partial loss of vision in one visual field. Sometimes, individuals develop 'blind spots' (**scotomas**) which result from isolated lesions of the primary visual cortex. Individuals are aware of what they see and are capable of responding to stimuli because involuntary eye movements are made which cover these blind spots (this is called **nystagmus**). When the eyes move about, the scotoma also moves about. More information in the visual fields thus reaches the brain. If, however, the patient stays still and an object is placed directly in front of the scotoma, the object cannot be seen.

Cortical blindness refers to loss of vision following damage to the primary visual cortex. It results in the inability to distinguish forms and patterns while remaining responsive to light and dark. It has been argued that visual discrimination takes place at the thalamic level, while the cortex is necessary for the conscious experience of visual stimuli (Hecaen and Albert, 1978). In fact, total blindness requires some destruction of the thalamus and the visual cortex and its afferent pathways (Teuber, 1975). In **denial of blindness** (**visual anosagnosia** or **Anton's syndrome**), patients do not acknowledge that they are blind and behave as if sighted. Corticothalamic connections are thought to be disrupted here, as are sensory feedback loops.

Primary visual cortex

The primary visual cortex (PVC) is located in the occipital lobe and is also referred to as the **striate cortex**. It corresponds to Brodmann's Area 17. It was given the name striate because it contains a distinctive stripe of white matter called the **stria of Genari**. The appearance of matter is the result of termination of myelinated axons from the LGN in layer IV. The PVC receives axons, called the **optic radiation**, from the LGN and is about 3 mm thick. It is layered with alternating layers performing different functions. Axons from the LGN terminate in layer IV. In a series of innovative experiments, Hubel and Wiesel (1979) discovered that layer IV was made up of three separate layers (IVa, b and c; IVc can be further subdivided into IVcα and IVcβ). Layer IVc receives input from one or other eye from different layers of the LGN; the output from layer IVc goes to the larger layers above and below it. Layer IVc neurons also send axons to layers II and III which, in turn, connect to layer V. Layer V itself projects to layer VI. Each layer projects to different parts of the cortex. For example, axons from layers II and III project to the medial temporal lobe of Area 18 (the area of higher visual function); layer V projects to the superior colliculus. Layer VI projects back to the LGN thus providing the visual system with a feedback loop. To further illustrate the interconnectedness of the visual system, neurons in layer IV project axons to layers II and III, to the superior colliculus via layer V and back to the LGN via layer VI.

The cells above and below layer IVc have receptive fields that respond to stimuli with linear properties (such as lines or bars). These cells are either simple or complex. The simple cells, the smaller of the two types, are excited by parallel, perpendicular lines. The complex cells are larger and respond to the position and movement of a stimulus.

Like the rest of the neocortex, the visual system's arrangement is both laminar (layered) and columnar. Columns are about 2 mm deep and 30–100 μm wide. The columns appear to represent a shift in orientation and alternate, representing left and right eye movement for binocular and depth perception.

The PVC only receives information from the contralateral hemifield. Information can also be sent to the higher visual function areas, or **extrastriate cortex** (Area 18), which can send information to the medial temporal cortex (Area 19), infero-temporal cortex (Areas 20 and 21) and posterior parietal cortex (Area 7). In a series of pioneering studies involving primates, Zeki (1993) has argued that Area 17 sends four separate projections to Area 18. These four parallel systems represent colour, motion and form (which has two systems). One X pathway projects from the PVC (V1) to area V2, then V3 and V3a, V4 and the inferotemporal cortex. This system is involved in the perception of form and colour. Y cells project from the PVC to V2 and V3 and then to V5 and the posterior parietal cortex. This may be involved in the perception of movement.

The massive complexity of this arrangement has to accommodate lowest-level visual response (e.g. the retina's response to brightness) to the highest level (e.g.

abstracting information and ascribing meaning to the visual images perceived as well as being able to act on what is seen). Lesions to V4 result in **achromatopsia** (colour blindness) in which the world is perceived in shades of grey. Damage to V5 results in **akinetopsia**: the patient cannot see or understand the world in motion. Curiously, when objects are still, they can be seen clearly; when they are moved, they appear to disappear. This occurs even when motion is actually illusory.

Theories of visual system functioning

The dissociable effects of damage to the visual system indicate that certain visual system pathways may be more influential in processing certain types of visual information than others. In 1969, Schneider proposed that visual system functioning was served by two major pathways (Schneider, 1969). One, the geniculostriate pathway, was responsible for the organism's ability to identify stimuli and discriminate between patterns. The other, the retinotectal pathway, was responsible for the organism's ability to locate objects in space. Currently, a similar distinction is made in neuropsychology although the specific proposals of Schneider have been challenged and modified.

What appears to be clear, however, is that object location and identification are dissociable. For example, Ungerleider and Mishkin (1982) have proposed that the visual processing involved in the appreciation of an object's qualities is subserved by the inferior temporal cortex whereas knowledge of spatial location is subserved by the posterior parietal cortex. Furthermore, Ungerleider and Mishkin proposed that these two cortices received independent projections from the striate cortex: the 'ventral stream' projected to the inferotemporal cortex: the 'dorsal stream' projected to the posterior parietal cortex. Lesions to these cortices in experimental animals resulted in object identification and object location difficulties respectively.

Goodale and Milner (1992) have developed the two visual systems theory of visual function in a slightly different direction. Instead of focusing on the input aspect of visual processing, they have proposed a theory of visuomotor function based on the output requirements of the visual system. That is, they suggest that the important distinction is between 'what' and 'how' not 'what' and 'where.' Implicit in this assumption is the notion that parts of the visual system can be put to different uses – specifically, to allow guided grasping and reaching. Before examining Goodale and Milner's hypothesis more closely, it is important to consider some background to parietal cortex damage and visuospatial movement. For example, lesions to the superior parietal cortex can lead to impairments in visually-directed reaching movement. This is called **optic ataxia** and is characterized by inaccurate movements and an erring of movement in the direction ipsilateral to the side of the lesion (Jeannerod, 1986; Perenin and Vighetto, 1988). The duration of the movements takes longer in these patients and velocity of movement in reduced. Commonly, it is found that patients cannot guide their hand to a slit in an object and are sometimes impaired at grasping and manipulating objects (Perenin and Vighetto, 1988).

Patients with **Balint's syndrome** (Balint, 1909) also show bilateral lesions of the inferior parietal cortex. While rare, the disorder is characterized by three principal symptoms: (1) neglect of the left visual field and parts of the right, with attentional gaze directed 35 or 40 degrees to the right; (2) inattention to other objects when the object in the field of vision has been detected, and (3) difficulty in reading under guidance (Jakobson *et al.*, 1991). Apart from these visuospatial impairments, patients do not exhibit cognitive or visual defects.

The most common behavioural deficits following parietal lobe lesions are, as these disorders suggest, difficulties in visuospatial performance. Patients have difficulty perceiving horizontal and vertical axes and in perceiving length, distance and orientation (Von Kraman and Kerkoff, 1993), although they can recognize objects. Jeannerod and colleagues' patient AT, for example, presented with large bilateral occipitoparietal infarction which produced not only optic ataxia but also a severe inability to estimate length of lines and the size of drawn figures. (Jeannerod *et al.*, 1994) AT's ability to reach was fairly normal, but the ability to grasp, especially the ability to grasp small objects, was impaired.

An interesting and associated case was presented by Goodale and his colleagues (Goodale *et al.*, 1994). Patient RV also suffered bilateral occipitoparietal damage, but whereas both RV and AT had damage to Areas 18 and 19, only AT had damage to Areas 7 and 39, the parietal areas. Reaching is also fairly normal in RV and grasping is poor, but unlike AT, the ability to compare shapes is unimpaired. Jeannerod (1997) has interpreted this dissociation following parietal lobe lesions as reflecting a view of brain function in which object-oriented responses are distributed in two cortical visual systems. Dorsal damage results in grasping impairments, ventral damage results in impairments in judging the size of objects.

Based on their and others' data, Goodale and Milner have suggested that there is a dual system for the processing of the form of objects in the ventral system (Goodale and Milner, 1992; Milner and Goodale, 1993). They further suggest that the dorsal system has a greater role in vision: specifically, it mediates visuomotor transformation which allows goal-directed action. Their patient, DF, had suffered a large bilateral occipital lesion destroying Areas 18 and 19 but sparing most of Area 17, following carbon monoxide poisoning (Goodale *et al.*, 1991). Perception of simple forms was quite poor – she performed at chance levels – and the perception of motion was also poor. However, she was able quite accurately to guide her hands and fingers in the directions of the objects she failed to recognize. When presented with similar or different rectangular blocks, she was unable to discriminate between them, even by indicating their width using her index finger and thumb. When asked to pick up one of the blocks, however, she was able to adjust her fingers accordingly and accurately. A similar dissociation was seen when she had to orientate her hand (or describe the orientation of her hand) in the direction of a large slot. When she had to guide her hand through the slot, however, she performed as normal, adjusting her hand to match the orientation of the slot before reaching it.

Goodale and Milner suggest that because other cases of parietal lobe damage show the opposite pattern – patients may recognize objects but are poor at guidance – and because temporal lobe damage is associated with aspects of visuospatial processing, the visual projection system to the parietal cortex represents information about object characteristics and orientation that are related to movement. This represents the dorsal stream. They suggest that disruption to the projections to the inferotemporal cortex may be responsible for the deficits seen in DF. This disruption occurs in the ventral stream.

■ Auditory system

Audition, like vision, is served by a number of distinct structures and neural pathways. A person with normal hearing will be able to detect a soundwave that is between 20 and 20 000 Hz although he or she will be most sensitive to sounds that are between 1000 and 4000 Hz. These soundwaves travel through the air, reach the ear and stimulate the **tympanic membrane** (or **eardrum**). From this point, the impulse if transmitted via three **ossicles** (or bones) called the **malleus, incus** and **stapes** to the **cochlea**. The cochlea is part of a membranous labyrinth which includes the **vestibular apparatus** which is characterized by three **semicircular canals**.

The part of the cochlear that is membranous is called the **cochlear duct** which is about 3 cm long and forms a spiral-shaped structure. The lowest part of this duct is made up of the **basilar membrane** on which rests the **organ of Corti** (see below). The top end is made up of the **vestibular membrane**. Outside the duct are two parallel canals: the **scala tympani**, situated below the basilar membrane, and the **scala vestibuli**, situated above the vestibular membrane. These tympani have windows or openings called **fenestra vestibuli** and **fenestra cochleae** which are closed by different mechanisms. At the end of the scala vestibuli lies the **oval window**; at the end of the scala tympani lies the fenestra cochleae or **round window**.

Audition begins properly with soundwaves reaching the external ear. This is called the **external auditory meatus**. Waves also reach the middle ear and tympanic membrane which is found at the lower end of the auditory meatus.

Connecting the eardrum with the oval windows are small bones. The malleus (or hammer) connects to the incus (or anvil) and the incus is connected to the stapes (or stirrup). These bones are important because they are sensitive to soundwaves which make them vibrate and thus transmit an impulse to the fluid in the cochlea. When the stapes are pressed into the oval window, the scalae vestibuli are closed and the fluid in them (called **perilymph**) is stimulated by movement from the soundwave which stimulated the stapes. The movement caused by the vibration is then transmitted to the fluid (called **endolymph**) in the auditory canal; the movement then travels on to the basilar membrane which transmits an impulse to the fluid in the scala tympani. The movement of the basilar membrane stimulates receptors in the cochlea which have sensory hairs called **stereocilia**. The inner and outer hair cells are separated by large supporting cells called **pillar cells**. Together these form the tunnel of Corti which is part of the organ of Corti, the region where receptors are organized. One of the most interesting features of the basilar membrane is that different frequencies are required to stimulate it at different points along its length. The highest pitches are sensed by hair cells near the oval window (the bottom of the basilar membrane); the lowest pitches are sensed at the anterior part of the cochlea.

From the cochlea, the sound impulse is sent via part of the eighth cranial nerve called the cochlear nerve. These efferents reach a collection of structures called the **superior olivary complex** in the medulla. The superior olive itself is located in the pons (at the bottom end) in the trapezoid body. The cochlear nuclei form a pathway which reaches the inferior colliculi. This ascending pathway is called the **lateral lemniscus**. Other nuclei reach the olivary complex which then project to the inferior colliculi. From the inferior colliculi, fibers are sent to the **medial geniculate body of the thalamus**. The efferents from this part of the thalamus thus finally terminate in specific areas of the auditory cortex, or AI. Like the visual system, there is some crossing of the pathways in the auditory system. Unlike the visual system, however, there is also a considerable number of uncrossed fibers. This means that unilateral damage to the auditory pathway may not result in obvious hearing impairment because there are uncrossed fibers which still allow the transmission of auditory information. Damage to the cochlear nerve, however, does result in deafness in the ear ipsilateral to the lesion. The pathway of the auditory system is seen in Figure 3.22.

The **core projection** of the ascending pathway terminates in the auditory cortex and is so called because it reaches the core area of the cortex responsible for audition. The **belt projection** makes its way from the peripheral inferior colliculi to the areas surrounding AI which are also responsive to other types of stimulus. The belt projection is so called because the projected fibers surround the auditory cortex like a belt. The auditory system also features descending connections from AI to the thalamus and inferior colliculi. The auditory pathways contain many inhibitory interneurons. Given the amount of auditory information that this system receives, this inhibition is perhaps not surprising and is certainly essential for allowing only the most relevant or salient information to be processed. Imagine

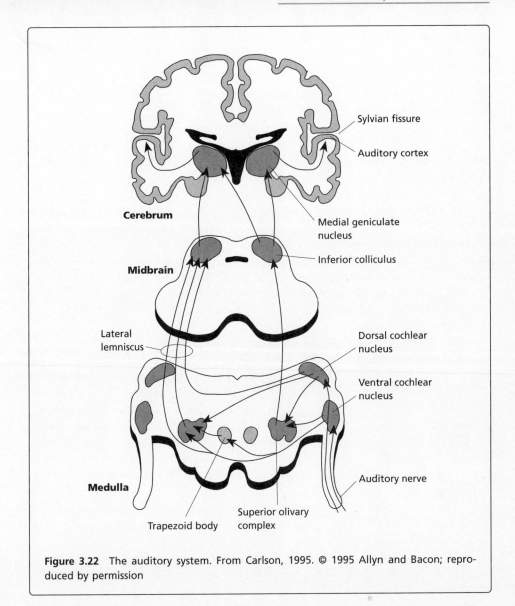

Sylvian fissure

Auditory cortex

Cerebrum

Medial geniculate
nucleus

Midbrain

Inferior colliculus

Lateral
lemniscus

Dorsal cochlear
nucleus

Ventral cochlear
nucleus

Medulla

Auditory nerve

Trapezoid body

Superior olivary
complex

Figure 3.22 The auditory system. From Carlson, 1995. © 1995 Allyn and Bacon; reproduced by permission

how difficult it would otherwise be to attend to a single conversation in a crowded room of several noisy, chattering individuals and the importance of this inhibition becomes clear. Of course, the system not only allows the selective attention to auditory information but also mediates **startle reflexes** (sudden, involuntary behavioural responses prompted by unexpected or loud auditory stimuli) which occur via the reticular formation's links with the association auditory pathways.

■ Somatosensory system

The system which allows us to sense touch, to feel pain, to experience changes in temperature and to ascertain the position of limbs and other parts of the body (**proprioception**) is the somatosensory system, and all of these phenomena are described by the term **somatosensation**. In addition to sensing all the somatosensory input described above, this system also allows us to detect differences in pressure placed on the skin, the usual receptor site of the somatosensory system.

Tactile sensation for most somatosensory functions, except proprioception of the lower extremities and basic forms of tactile stimulation, is undertaken by the **dorsal column–medial lemniscal system**. Pain and crude tactile sensation, on the other hand, are mediated by the **anterolateral system**. Receptors in the skin and subcutaneous tissue send afferents to the spinal cord via the dorsal roots. An axon branch ascends into the dorsal column and synapses in the medulla. Those axons of sensory cells in the dorsal column nuclei then project in the opposite direction. At the midline of the medulla, they cross and pass through the brainstem contralaterally, making synapses with cells in the ventral posterior lateral nucleus of the thalamus, as seen in Figure 3.23.

From here, thalamic projections are sent to the cerebral cortex. This pathway is called the **thalamocortical projection** or **radiation** and runs through the internal capsule, terminating in the **primary somatic sensory cortex (SI)** or **somatosensory cortex** which is found in the precentral gyrus of the parietal lobe. SI can be subdivided into three distinct areas, based on Brodmann's classification: Areas 1, 2, 3a and 3b. This arrangement appears to be important because the thalamic axons terminate primarily in Areas 3a and b. These areas then send projections to Areas 1 and 2. Thalamic fibers also project to nearby cortex called the **secondary somatic sensory cortex (SII)**. SI and SII are distinctive in that SI receives primarily contralateral input, whereas SII receives bilateral input. The next projection stage sees axons being sent from SI to the posterior parietal cortex (Areas 5 and 7).

If lesions are made to different parts of the primary somatosensory cortex in animals, different deficits in somatosensation are observed. If SI is removed, for example, there is an impairment in the ability to discriminate between different types of touch and in proprioception. Deficits in appreciating the texture of stimuli are observed following lesions to Area 3b. Lesions to Area 2 are associated with impairments in the ability to discriminate shapes and sizes in the tactile modality. Damage to SII, however, results in the inability to learn to discriminate between objects of different shapes.

There is further differentiation at the cortical level in relation to the body parts subserved by the somatosensory cortex. For example, electrical stimulation studies, we saw in Chapter 1, have indicated that parts of the somatosensory cortex are more devoted to certain parts of the body than others. The area responsible for the hand (especially the index finger) and face (especially the lips), for example, is

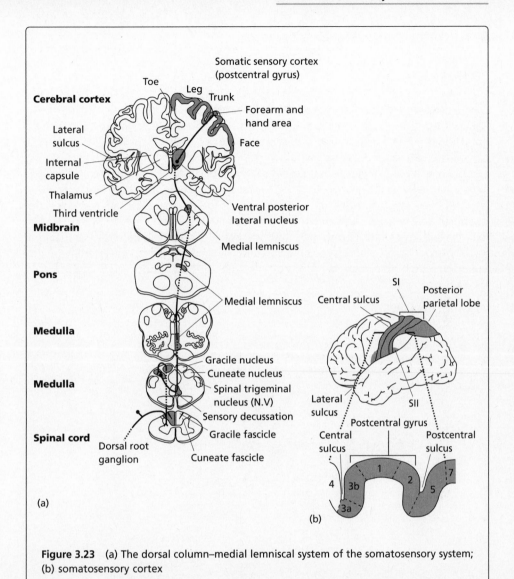

Figure 3.23   (a) The dorsal column–medial lemniscal system of the somatosensory system; (b) somatosensory cortex

larger than that responsible for the big toe. The reason for this is that body parts like the hand and face are involved in finer, more complicated and sophisticated movements than are other parts of the body and require more cortical 'power' to enable them to function at this level.

■ Gustatory and olfactory systems

Gustatory system

The gustatory system is one of the two most important sense organs for the perception of food flavour. Its receptors allow us to distinguish between at least four classes of taste: sourness, bitterness, sweetness and saltiness. There may also be a fifth taste called umami which represents a savoury taste similar to monosodium glutamate. The external receptors for taste are the taste buds which contain epithelial cells that are specialized taste receptors. Each taste bud contains about 50–100 cells and they are found principally on the tongue, although some are also found in the pharynx and palate. The taste buds are innervated by three cranial nerves – the seventh, ninth and tenth – each of which innervates a different collection of taste buds. In primates, these cranial projections terminate in the rostral region of the nucleus of the solitary tract in the medulla (Scott *et al.*, 1986), as seen in Figure 3.24.

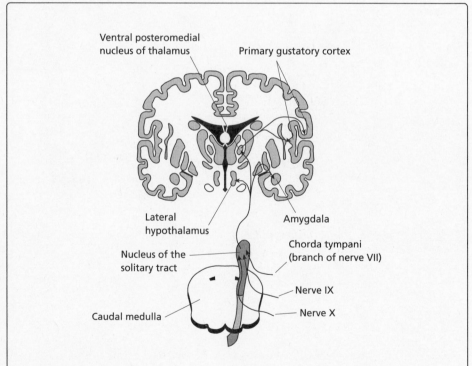

Figure 3.24 The gustatory system. From Carlson, 1995. © 1995 Allyn and Bacon; reproduced by permission

Second-order neurons are then projected to the parvicellular division of the ventroposteromedial thalamic nucleus, or the taste thalamus. Fibers from the taste thalamus project to the cortex, specifically the rostral frontal operculum and insula. These cortices comprise the primary taste cortex (Rolls, 1989).

There may also be a secondary taste cortex in the caudolateral orbitofrontal cortex which lies anterior to the primary taste cortex (Rolls *et al.*, 1989; Rolls and Baylis, 1994). In a novel series of experiments, Rolls and Baylis found evidence to suggest that the orbitofrontal cortex acts as a form of convergence zone for chemosensation because olfactory stimulation produces responses in its medial part, visual stimulation activates an area between the secondary taste cortex and the medial orbitofrontal cortex and, as we have already seen, gustatory inputs stimulate the secondary taste cortex.

Rolls and Baylis found that some neurons were activated by taste and visual stimuli, others by both taste and olfactory stimuli, and others by one type of sensory stimulus. All were in very close proximity to each other, suggesting that this region of the brain might be the first cortical stage of integrating food-related information.

Olfactory system

Like the gustatory system, the olfactory system is important, if not more important, for the perception of food flavour. Unlike the sense of taste, the number of classes of stimuli that the olfactory system can perceive is apparently limitless. We can perceive thousands of different odours but only very few tastes. This is why when individuals have a cold or the 'flu they fail to identify the foods they eat, claiming that the food has lost its taste. What they actually mean is that they cannot perceive the food's smell.

Initial perception in the olfactory system occurs at the back of the nasal cavities in a region called the olfactory neuroepithelium. This contains specialized receptors and three types of cell: olfactory sensory neurons, supporting cells and basal cells. Unlike the neurons in other parts of the central nervous system, the cells of the olfactory system are the only ones which can regenerate. The olfactory neuron extends a dendrite whose cilia extend into a layer of mucus; an axon from each receptor is sent to a structure called the olfactory bulb. There are two of these located beneath the frontal lobes in humans and non-human primates (Buck *et al.*, 1994). The olfactory bulbs are made up of six layers of different types of neuron. One layer is the superficial olfactory nerve layer which terminates in regions called glomeruli. The projection pathway of the olfactory bulbs is ipsilateral and fairly extensive, reaching the primary olfactory cortex (principally the piriform cortex), parts of the amygdaloid nucleus and the lateral part of the entorhinal cortex. All of these regions have reciprocal connections with the olfactory bulb (Kratskin, 1995). See Figure 3.25.

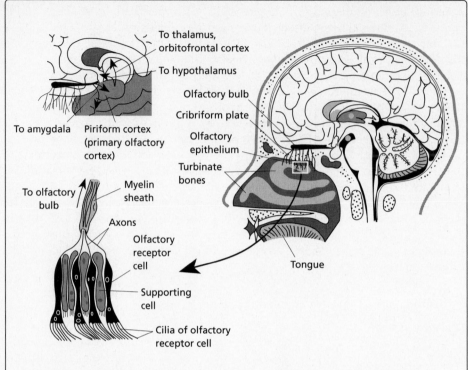

To thalamus, orbitofrontal cortex

To hypothalamus

Olfactory bulb

Cribriform plate

Olfactory epithelium

Turbinate bones

To amygdala

Piriform cortex (primary olfactory cortex)

To olfactory bulb

Myelin sheath

Axons

Olfactory receptor cell

Supporting cell

Cilia of olfactory receptor cell

Tongue

Figure 3.25 The olfactory system. From Carlson, 1995. © 1995 Allyn and Bacon; reproduced by permission

■ Motor system

The motor system is represented by those cells in the CNS which control the skeletal muscles. The general motor system is subserved by two distinct motor systems: one involving the peripheral motor neurons and another involving central motor neurons. Both of these systems are responsible for mediating the responses from muscles to motor centres, such as initiating movement. Other important structures play a part in these systems such as the basal ganglia and the cerebellum which are involved in execution and maintenance of motor behaviour rather than its initiation. The types of behaviour governed by the motor system can be crudely described as automatic and voluntary. Basic, reflexive motor movements, such as withdrawing your hand from fire, are automatic, relying on spinal cord response. Precision grips are voluntary and require control at the cortical level. Walking, however, is neither fully one nor the other, being controlled by the brainstem or the cortex's control of the brainstem.

Peripheral motor system

Peripheral motor neurons send axons to skeletal muscles. Lower motor neurons are found in the ventral horn of the spinal cord and are of two types: **alpha** and **gamma motorneurons**. The axons of these neurons leave the spinal cord and innervate muscle at the trunk and extremities. When axons are damaged, muscle paralysis can result. As we saw in the section on cranial nerves, several of these nerves also innervate various muscles in the body.

Central motor system

The central motor system contains upper motor neurons important for voluntary movement and are found in the brainstem and cortex. The system is roughly divided into neurons of the pyramidal tract (also called the **corticospinal tract**) and the rest (the **extrapyramidal system**). The pyramidal tract is important for the execution of precise, voluntary movement. Most fibers cross over to the opposite side of the body at the point of the medulla; the pyramidal tract is the only pathway making its way directly from the cortex to the spinal cord. Most motor neurons in this system are found in the fifth cortical layer which contains pyramidal cells and many, and the thickest, are found in the precentral gyrus (the primary motor area or MI). Electrically stimulating MI, as we saw in Chapter 1, produces muscle contraction.

Other motor tracts

Other tracts also pass impulses from higher cortical areas to the motor neurons in the spinal cord, as seen in Figure 3.26.

The **rubrospinal tract** sends fibers from the red nucleus to the spinal cord and influences the activity of the cerebellum. The **reticulospinal tract** is composed of the reticular formation which can influence motor neurons and appears to be involved in maintaining posture, orientating to external stimuli and executing stereotypical movements. The **tectospinal tract** represents fibers found in the superior colliculus and is important for controlling the movement of the head and eyes in response to movement in the visual field. Finally, the **vestibulospinal tract** is important for maintaining balance and posture. These ventromedial pathways are illustrated in Figure 3.27.

The cortex and movement

The higher brain areas responsible for the maintenance of voluntary movement are the primary motor cortex (PMC, also known as MI), the premotor area (A6) and the supplementary motor area (SMA), seen in Figure 3.28.

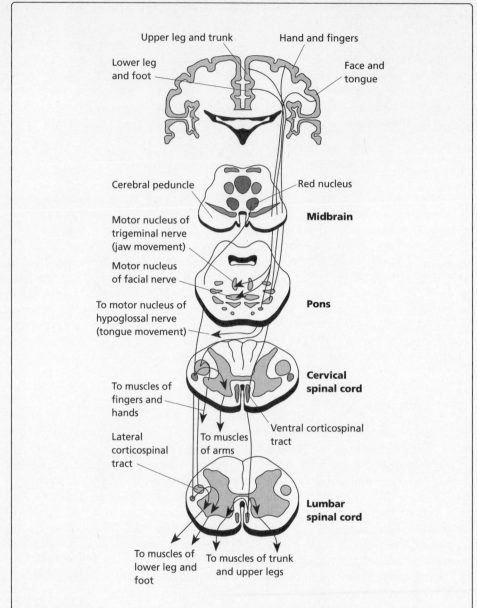

Figure 3.26 Motor tract pathways. From Carlson, 1995. © 1995 Allyn and Bacon; reproduced by permission

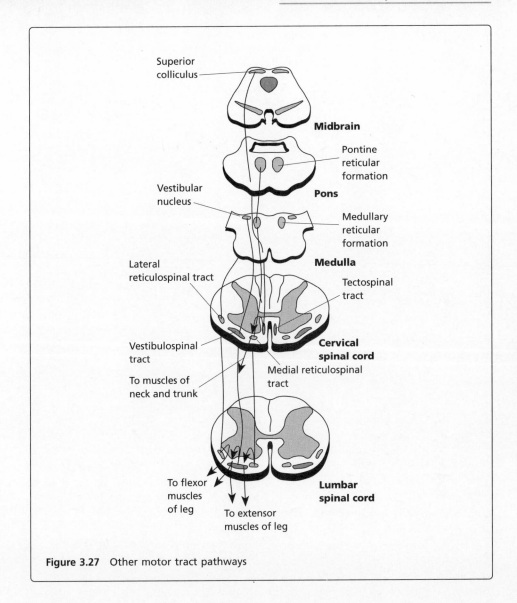

Superior colliculus

Midbrain

Pontine reticular formation

Pons

Vestibular nucleus

Medullary reticular formation

Medulla

Lateral reticulospinal tract

Tectospinal tract

Vestibulospinal tract

Cervical spinal cord

To muscles of neck and trunk

Medial reticulospinal tract

To flexor muscles of leg

Lumbar spinal cord

To extensor muscles of leg

Figure 3.27 Other motor tract pathways

The PMC is the more likely of the three to respond when electrically stimulated, and lesions to this area cause paralysis (damage to any part of the motor system, from motor cortex to motor neuron, can cause paralysis or partial paralysis). Areas 5, 7 and the prefrontal cortex are also important cortical areas for movement.

The PMC receives afferent axons from a variety of areas including Areas 1, 2, 3, 5 and 6 and the ventrolateral nucleus of the thalamus. As we saw in Chapter 1, a large part of the PMC is devoted to hand movement (especially the finger and

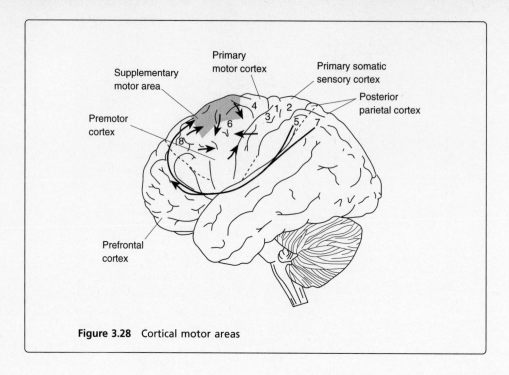

Figure 3.28   Cortical motor areas

thumb), probably owing to the cortical requirements necessary to make precision movements. Stimulation of the PMC elicits movement in other muscles as well, such as the abdomen and back muscle. Unilateral or bilateral stimulation results in movement of these muscles. However, unilateral stimulation of the 'hand area' of the cortex produces movement in the contralateral hand because pyramidal tract fibers are crossed.

The SMA appears to subserve a different type of motor behaviour. Whereas movement of the hand will activate the PMC, sequences of movement will activate the SMA. The ability to imagine also activates this part of the motor cortex and it appears to be involved in motor planning and organization. The premotor area, conversely, is important for the control of visually guided movement such as coordinating hand movement when reaching for an object. The posterior parietal cortex also appears to play a role in movement in that its destruction will produce an inability to execute complex voluntary movements (apraxia). Apraxia and other movement disorders such as hemiparesis, Huntington's chorea, Parkinsonism, Wilson's disease, dyskinesia and upper and lower motor neuron disease are reviewed in Chapter 8.

Summary

- The central nervous system begins as a hollow cylinder called a neural tube. This develops into the foundations of the CNS, neurons and glial cells. As it develops, cavities, called ventricles, begin to form. These are filled with cerebrospinal fluid.

- The spinal cord measures about 4–45 cm long, is as thick as a little finger and is cylindrical. The bone surrounding it is called the vertebral column which has 7 cervical vertebrae, 12 thoracic vertebrae and 5 lumbar vertebrae. Unlike the other vertebrae, the saccral and coccygeal parts of the column are fused. The cord runs through a space inside the column called the spinal foramen. It ends in a collection of spinal roots called the cauda equina.

- The spinal nerves form part of the peripheral nervous system and enter and exit the spinal cord in bundles of axons called rootlets. These unite to form a root, which can be dorsal (containing afferent sensory fibers) or ventral (containing efferent motor fibers). There are 31 pairs of nerves which divide the spinal cord into convenient segments.

- Each segment, when cut transversely, contains white matter on the outside and H-shaped grey matter on the inside. The arms of the H are called the ventral and dorsal horns. The ventral horns send axons from the CNS; dorsal roots receive sensory information. Different types of neuron are found in different parts of the spinal cord segments. The arrangement of cells are called Rexed's laminae. The spinal cord is under the control of the cortex and brainstem.

- The brainstem comprises the medulla oblongata, the pons, the mesencephalon and the diencephalon. Most of the cranial nerves of the brain arise here. The brainstem contains the reticular formation at its core; this is involved in a number of behaviours. The medulla leads to a fissure which leads to the pyramidal tract. It also contains the medial lemniscus which receives sensory information from the skin and surrounding muscle joints. The pons sends projections to the cerebellum and a number of cranial nerves exit here.

- The mesencephalon contains the inferior and superior colliculi (two of each) which are involved in the relay of auditory and visual information respectively. It also contains the substantia nigra, an area involved in movement.

- The diencephalon contains the thalamus and hypothalamus. The thalamus plays a vital role as a relay station for projections coming from various parts of the brain. A Y-shaped band of white matter divides the thalamus into medial thalamic nuclei, lateral thalamic nucleus and the anterior thalamic nucleus. The posterior thalamus comprises the pulvinar (which covers the lateral geniculate body) and the medial ngeniculate body, two relay areas important for vision and audition respectively. The hypothalamus, lying anterior to and beneath the thalamus, is important for a number of autonomic nervous system functions. Finally, the diencephalon contains the mammillary bodies and fornix, two regions thought to play a role in memory.

☐ The cerebellum extends from the pons and controls of the execution of movement and maintenance of balance and posture.

☐ The cerebral cortex is the largest part of the CNS and is made up of six layers of convoluted and grooved neurons and axons. The grooves are called fissures or sulci. Each hemisphere has a lateral (Sylvian) fissure and a central sulcus (Rolandic fissure). The areas between the grooves are called gyri. At the end of each lateral fissure, there are gyri called the insula.

☐ At the general level, the cortex is divided into four lobes: frontal, parietal, temporal and occipital. The temporal lobes are involved in audition, memory and (on the left) speech production; the occipital lobe is specialized for visual functions, the parietal lobe for spatial relations and somatosensation, and the frontal cortex with planning, strategy formation and (on the left) language production.

☐ The basal ganglia are a collection of structures deep inside the cortex and include the caudate nucleus, the globus pallidus and putamen, all of which play an essential role in the regulation of movement. The limbic system is also subcortical and contains the hippocampus (important for memory), the septal nuclei, the amygdala, the cingulate gyrus, the mammillary bodies and the hypothalamus.

☐ The cerebral cortex is organized into six parallel layers, each of which contains distinct types of neurons. Layers 2 and 4 are receiving layers; layers 3, 5 and 6 are sending layers. The cortex is also organized into columns of specific arrangements of neurons.

☐ There are many connections between brain regions: from the thalamus to the cortex and cortex to thalamus (thalamocortical connections) and from the cortex to other parts of the cortex (corticocortical connections). Many

➠

connections are made via association cortices. These do not receive direct motor or sensory inputs but do receive inputs from the primary sensory and motor cortices.

☐ The brain is protected by hair, skin, bone, membranes called meninges and fluid. The brain's immediate covering is the pia mater; the second covering is the arachnoid mater; the third and final meninge is the dura mater.

☐ The fluid found between these meninges and in the brain's four cavities is called cerebrospinal fluid (CSF). The first and third ventricles are called the lateral ventricles. CSF is produced by choroid plexuses attached to the walls of these ventricles. The CSF contains neurotransmitters and hormones; it protects the brain by making it lighter via its immersion in fluid.

☐ There are 12 cranial nerves, each of which serves a specific function.

☐ The brain receives its blood from the internal carotid artery (which supplies the cortex) and the vertebral artery (which supplies the cerebellum and brainstem). The carotid artery branches into the opthalmic artery, anterior cerebral artery and the middle cerebral artery (the largest). The vertebral arteries join at the pons to form the basilar artery. This divides into the posterior cerebral arteries. The middle cerebral arteries and the posterior cerebral arteries are connected on either side by the posterior communicating arteries. This connection forms the circle of Willis. The spinal cord is supplied by the anterior spinal artery and the posterior spinal arteries.

☐ When the brain malfunctions, a number of things can go wrong. There may be a swelling (edema), dead tissue resulting from lack of blood (infarction), loss of blood due to narrowing or blockage of an artery (ischemia), a blockage of a blood vessel caused by coagulated blood (thrombosis), a sudden loss of blood supply to the brain (stroke/cerebrovascular accident), bleeding into the space between the pia mater and arachnoid (subarachnoid haemorrhage), a space-occupying lesion (tumour), a loss of oxygen in the blood supply (anoxia), inflammation (encephalopathy), increased ventricular volume (hydrocephalus), constriction of blood vessels (headache) or abnormal electrical discharges (epilepsy).

Recommended further general and specific reading

Key: (1) = introductory, *(3)* = intermediate, *(5)* = advanced

General

Brandt, T., Caplan, L.R., Dichgans, J., Diener, H.C. and Kennard, C. (1996). *Neurological Disorders: Course and treatment.* New York: Academic Press. *(4)*

Brodal, P. (1991). *The Central Nervous System.* Oxford: Oxford University Press. *(4)*

De Armond, S.J., Fusco, M.M. and Dewey, M.M. (1989). *Structure of the Human Brain: A photographic atlas.* New York: Oxford University Press. *(1)*

England, M.A. and Wakely, J. (1991). *A Colour Atlas of the Brain and Spinal Cord.* Aylesbury: Wolfe. *(1)*

Kandel, E.R., Schwartz, J.H. and Jessell, T.M. (1995). *Essentials of Neural Science and Behaviour.* New Jersey: Prentice Hall. *(3)*

Specific

Andersen, R.A., Snyder, L.H., Bradley, D.C. and Xing, J. (1997). Multimodal representation of space in the posterior parietal cortex and its use in planning movements. *Annual Review of Neuroscience,* **20**, 303–30. *(3)*

Asanuma, H. (1989). *The Motor Cortex.* New York: Raven Press. *(4)*

Buck, L.B., Firestein, S. and Margolskee, R.F. (1994). Olfaction and taste in vertebrates: molecular and organizational strategies underlying chemosensory perception. In G.J. Siegel, B.W. Agranoff, R.W. Albers and P.B. Molinoff (eds), *Basic Neurochemistry.* New York: Raven Press. *(5)*

Crick, F. and Koch, C. (1995). Are we aware of neural activity in primary visual cortex? *Nature,* **375**, 121–3. *(3)*

Edelman, G.M., Gall, W.E. and Cowan, W.M. (1987). *Functions of the Auditory System.* New York: Wiley. *(3)*

Goodale, M.A. and Milner, A.D. (1992). Separate visual pathways for perception and action. *Trends in Neurosciences,* **15**, 20–5. *(3)*

Huebel, D. and Wiesel, T. (1962). Receptive fields, binocular interaction and functional architecture in the cat's visual cortex. *Journal of Physiology,* **160**, 106–54. *(4)*

Jeannerod, M. (1988). *The Neural and Behavioural Organization of Goal-directed Movements.* Oxford: Oxford University Press. *(3)*

Jeannerod, M. (1997). *The Cognitive Neuroscience of Action.* Oxford: Blackwell. *(3)*

Rolls, E.T. and Baylis, L.L. (1994). Gustatory, olfactory and visual convergence within the primate orbitofrontal cortex. *Journal of Neuroscience,* **14**(9), 5437–52. *(4)*

Sakata, H., Kusunoki, M., Murata, A. and Tanaka, Y. (1997). The parietal association cortex in depth perception and visual control of hand action. *Trends in Neurosciences,* **20**(8), 350–7. *(4)*

Teasdale, G.M. (1995). Head injury. *Journal of Neurology, Neurosurgery and Psychiatry,* **58**, 526–39. *(2)*

Tootell, R.B.H., Dale, A.M., Sereno, M.I. and Malach, R. (1996). New images from human visual cortex. *Trends in Neurosciences,* **19**, 481–9. *(2)*

Zeki, S. (1993). *A Vision of the Brain.* Oxford: Blackwell. *(2)*

Chapter Four

Hemispheric localization and lateralization of function

■ Introduction

The brain has millions of connections between its regions and structures, allowing many neurons and groups of neurons to communicate with other groups of neurons. It is also characterized by neuronal specificity, i.e. the cells of each layer of the cortex tend to be different in cytoarchitecture. The brain also exhibits examples of functional specificity. There is a particular brain system for visual sensation and perception, for auditory sensation and perception, and so on. That the brain should exhibit discrete, but often interrelated, neural systems such as these is, perhaps, not surprising. After all, you would not expect the machine that plays your records to play your cassettes and CDs as well: these various components of the stereo system are connected, but they perform entirely different functions. The system is modular: it is made up of semi-independent, self-contained 'modules' that perform discrete functions. The function of the brain has been conceived in the same way (Fodor, 1983) although the history of neuropsychology, especially during its phrenological and functionalist period, indicates that the idea is not that recent.

At a simple level, the stereo metaphor usefully describes the brain's 'modules' or functions: it would be unlikely and unwise for the apparatus that allows us to see to be the same as that which allows us to hear, touch, move, smell or taste. They are entirely different functions, often subserved by different and specific types of neuron, but are interconnected. Each sends and receives input to the other in a vastly complicated arrangement.

As we saw in Chapters 2 and 3, basic functions such as sensation, perception and movement, have each their own brain system. Components of these systems can be localized in fairly specific areas, hence the use of the terms 'auditory cortex', 'visual cortex' and so on. These sensory systems highlight localization of function at the basic sensory or motor level. Localizing complex behaviours such as language, reasoning, visuospatial ability, emotion and so on, however, presents a greater challenge.

To begin with, associations between function and structure or regions of activation, are often vaguely defined. It is not helpful or particularly accurate, for example, to state that one part of the brain is responsible for language because language is a complicated process or behaviour that involves a number of components. It has written, aural and spoken forms. It involves phonology and morphology. It may involve production and comprehension. In the same way that our record player cannot fulfil all our musical wishes, 'one part' of the brain is unlikely to be responsible for all aspects of language. What is possible, however, is to state that some areas may be responsible for specific elements of language, and this can be demonstrated experimentally. A similar problem besets concepts such as 'spatial ability'. Spatial ability can refer to many different functions: the mental rotation of letters or cubes, deciding which of several alternative shapes or patterns fits a space in a pattern, measuring distance and map-reading. As with language, however, it is possible to state that different regions may be responsible for different elements of visuospatial ability.

The above emphasis on language and spatial ability reflects the localization literature's preoccupation with the functions that neuropsychologists have sought to localize. Furthermore, these two functions, perhaps more than others, may be especially important because they are lateralized, i.e. one hemisphere is dominant for these functions. In Chapter 1, this phenomenon was referred to as asymmetry of function, hemispheric asymmetry and laterality. It is also referred to as hemispheric specialization. All of these terms, to all intents and purposes, describe the same phenomenon.

■ Laterality in non-humans

Laterality refers to the preferential use or superior function of one part of the body and was first observed in humans. It was thought to reflect the human central nervous system's development from a simple, symmetrical system into a complex, finely tuned, specialized one (Corballis, 1991). Laterality brought with it a greater flexibility and complexity of function: if some functions could be performed better by one aspect of the side of the body (including the brain), this would free up the other side for other tasks; there would be no unnecessary duplication. One important behavioural example of laterality is handedness. The majority of humans, for example, express a preference for using the right hand (Gilbert and Wysocki, 1992); the right hand also appears to be the 'manipulator' of objects whereas the left is characterized as the 'holder' (in fact, the word 'dextrous' meaning right-handed, is synonymous with skilfulness). Our degree of laterality may be the functional characteristic that makes us unique and separates us, intellectually, from other mammals and higher primates (Corballis, 1991).

There is evidence, however, of lateralization of function even in species such as songbirds, domestic chicks, rats, cats, toads and non-human primates (Hiscock and Kinsbourne, 1995). Songbirds, for example, have left-hemisphere control of song, although parrots appear to have symmetrical control of vocalization. Memory, learning and imprinting have been found to be severely impaired in chicks with lesions of the left intermediate medial hyperstriatum ventrale (Rose, 1992). There appears to be a foot, claw, paw or hand preference in some species, although data are inconsistent and are based on various measures of handedness. Domestic chicks appear to prefer to use their right foot when scratching the ground; some cats preferentially use one paw over another when reaching for food (Warren *et al.*, 1967) and similar right-pawedness has been found in toads (Bisazza *et al.*, 1996). However, consistent asymmetries at the general, population level are difficult to demonstrate.

Some non-human primates do not appear to show a preference in handedness at the general, population level either, but they do show individual examples of hand preference. There are problems with the types of task administered to primates, however, in that not even humans would be expected to show strong laterality effects on them (Hiscock and Kinsbourne, 1995). Tasks which elicit reliable human asymmetries do elicit some degree of primate laterality. For example, in Old World Monkeys, the left hand appears to be the preferred limb for reaching and the right for manipulating objects (Hatta and Koike, 1991). Fine motor skill, on the other hand, appears to involve preferential right hand use (R.D. Morris *et al.*, 1993). When split-brain monkeys are required to distinguish between photographs of two different monkeys showing the same expression and between photographs of the same monkey showing different facial expression, 70 per cent of the monkeys showed right hemisphere superiority (Hamilton and Vermiere, 1983), a finding that is consistent with the human literature on face recognition. Despite findings such as these, however, non-human primates do not appear to exhibit the same degree of laterality as humans.

Laterality in humans

Superficially, we appear to exhibit no obvious physical asymmetries. We have two arms, legs, eyes, ears, nostrils, hands, thumbs and nipples. This symmetry is reflected in internal anatomy: we have two lungs and two kidneys, for example. Women have two ovaries, men have two testicles. We have two cerebral hemispheres. Yet, this appearance belies some subtle, genuine physical and neuro-anatomical asymmetries.

Physical asymmetry

One example of physical asymmetry is the face. A glance at Figure 4.1 quickly illustrates that the left and right sides of the face are not mirror images of each other. In fact, they are quite different.

Furthermore, there is some evidence that the face is asymmetrically expressive, with a more intense expression found on the left side (Levy *et al.*, 1983). Studies in which individuals have rated the attractiveness of both sides of a woman's face

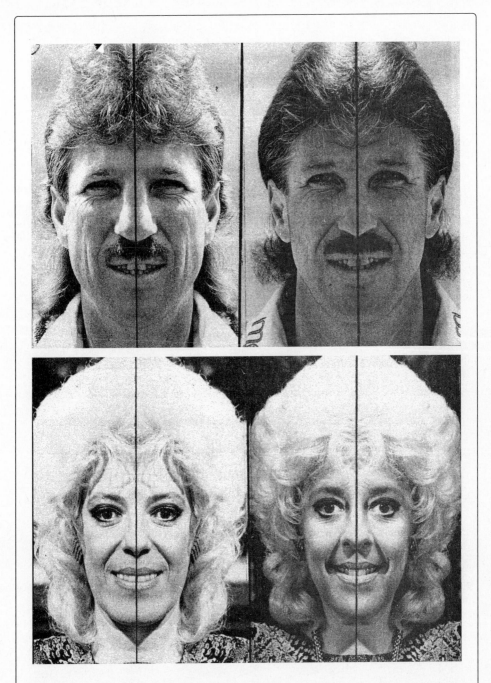

Figure 4.1 Asymmetry of the face revealed by constructing composite faces in which the face is made up of the same two sides

have shown that the right side is significantly more attractive than the left (Zaidel and FitzGerald, 1994; Zaidel *et al.*, 1995).

Neuroanatomical asymmetry

The brain itself, although appearing outwardly symmetrical, exhibits elements of asymmetry. These asymmetries are summarized in Table 4.1.

One of the earliest reports of **cerebral asymmetry** described two transverse gyri on the right and one on the left in the majority of post-mortem human brains (Heschl, 1878). The left gyrus was subsequently found to be more oblique than the right (Galaburda, 1995) and doubled over more on the right (Campain and Minckler, 1976; Chi *et al.*, 1977) although these findings have been contradicted in a smaller set of brains (Rademacher *et al.*, 1993). These gyri, known as Heschl's gyri, represent the primary auditory cortex.

There are several other examples of asymmetry at the neuroanatomical level. The right hemisphere, for example, is thought to be larger and heavier than the left (Heschl, 1878; Schwartz *et al.*, 1985) although this observation has been challenged (Hadziselimovic and Cus, 1966). The left occipital lobe was found to be larger than the right in a study by Cunningham (1892) whereas a larger right than left frontal lobe has been reported (Weinberger *et al.*, 1982).

Pfeifer (1936) reported a larger **planum temporale**, a structure in the Sylvian fissure posterior to the primary auditory cortex, in the left hemisphere than in the

Table 4.1 Summary of neuroanatomical asymmetries in the human brain

Structure/region	Characteristics	Reference
Heschl's gyri	Two in RH; one in LH More oblique in LH	Heschl (1878) Galaburda (1995)
Right hemisphere	Larger/heavier than LH	Heschl (1878); Schwartz *et al.* (1985)
Left occipital lobe	Larger than right	Cunningham (1892)
Right frontal lobe	Larger than left	Weinberger *et al.* (1982)
Planum temporale	Larger in LH	Pfeifer (1936); Geschwind and Levitsky (1968); Wada *et al.* (1975)
Tpt	Larger in LH	Galaburda *et al.* (1978)
Sylvian fissure	Larger in LH	Eberstaller (1890); Cunningham (1892); Yeni-Komishian and Benson (1976)
Pallidum	Larger in LH	Kooistra and Heilman (1988)
Area 44	Larger in LH	Eberstaller (1890); Galaburda (1980)

RH = right hemisphere; LH = left hemisphere

right. Pfeifer's finding was subsequently replicated in 65 per cent of the 100 cases studied by Geschwind and Levitsky (1968) and in 82 per cent of the 100 brains studied by Wada *et al.* (1975). In Geschwind and Levitsky's sample, 11 per cent had a larger right planum temporale whereas 24 per cent had symmetrical plana. These results are also reflected in human foetal brain data: these brains show left-sided planum temporale asymmetry (Teszner *et al.*, 1972; Witelson and Pallie, 1973).

The planum corresponds to Area 22 and has a specific cytoarchitectonic organization called **Tpt** which appears to contain features of the auditory association cortex and parietal higher-order association cortex. In other words, the area is functionally the same as Wernicke's area, the language region responsible for the comprehension of language. Not surprisingly, Tpt has been found to be up to seven times larger in the left than the right hemisphere (Galaburda *et al.*, 1978).

The human brain also has a longer Sylvian (lateral) fissure in the left hemisphere (Yeni-Komishian and Benson, 1976), a finding that dates back to Eberstaller (1890) and Cunningham (1892) who, in addition, observed that the left fissure was more horizontal than the right. In foetuses, the Sylvian fissures appear to be asymmetrical by mid-gestation (Chi *et al.*, 1977).

The importance of neuroanatomical asymmetries lies in their possible relationship with function. If the planum temporale is larger on the left, specifically in that part of the left hemisphere that we know governs aspects of speech, is this physical asymmetry related to functional asymmetry? Demonstrating conclusive relationships of this kind may, however, be impossible: the relationship between anatomical asymmetry and functional significance is far from clear (Beaton, 1997). Galaburda (1995), discussing the significance of the larger left planum temporale, has even argued that leftward asymmetry represents nothing more than the majority situation.

Galaburda (1995) highlights a number of problems associated with studies claiming to demonstrate neuroanatomical asymmetries. These problems include the variability in the description of structures such as the planum temporale, the use of inappropriate methods of localization (such as an MRI scan employing a horizontal plane which is too near to that of the planum temporale), and the fact that the cortex is folded and manifests gyri, fissures and sulci for a reason: to fit inside the skull. It is possible that cortical folding is the result of nothing more grand than the imposition of the skull on the cortex's shape so that asymmetries in folds could reflect functionally meaningless bony asymmetries.

Instead, Galaburda (1995) argues that one possible means of demonstrating clear asymmetries would be to look at neuroanatomy at the morphological level. Area Tpt, for example, has a distinct cytoarchitecture and is positively correlated with planum temporale asymmetry (it may even be responsible for the planum's asymmetry). Furthermore, instead of looking at relative size, perhaps attention should be directed towards the *density* of neurons in a given area. Galaburda has argued that the generation of asymmetry is attributable to the asymmetric production (and subsequent death) of neurons. Galaburda and others' work has involved mainly non-human data. An extensive exploration of data from other species would obviously be valuable.

■ Functional hemispheric asymmetry: some preliminary observations

The conventional view of hemispheric function is that the left hemisphere is rational, verbal, linear and analytic whereas the right hemisphere is emotional, spatial, holistic and intuitive (Bradshaw and Nettleton, 1981; Van Lancker, 1997). The left and right hemispheres have even been characterized as representing 'western' and 'eastern' styles of thinking, respectively (Corballis, 1991).

Underlying this dichotomy is the suggestion that the two hemispheres are qualitatively and quantitatively different. This idea was pursued in the early nineteenth century by the English physician Arthur Wigan in his book *The Duality of Mind*. Wigan (1844) had argued that the two hemispheres were independent entities that required efficient coordination in order to function adequately. This notion of the independence of the hemispheres was given a more vivid spin following reports of split-brain patients who, because the fibers connecting their cerebral hemispheres had been severed to block the path of epileptic seizure, appeared to have 'two brains'. Information available to one hemisphere did not appear to be available to the other. The behaviour of split-brain patients is discussed more fully in the next chapter.

This dichotomy, although crude, is generally accurate. That is, the left hemisphere does appear to be a more effective processor of language; the right hemisphere does appear to be more involved in aspects of visuospatial ability. However, there are complications and ambiguities that cloud these apparently straightforward dichotomies. For example, the right hemisphere is capable of undertaking rudimentary or compensatory language processing and the left hemisphere is capable of undertaking some spatial processing. Individual differences such as sex and handedness further complicate the pattern and development of functional hemispheric asymmetry and these differences are dealt with in a separate section later in the chapter.

■ Functional hemispheric asymmetry: the evidence

There are invasive and non-invasive ways of localizing function. Invasive methods include the Wada procedure, commissurotomy, brain surgery, electrical stimulation and unilateral brain damage. Obviously, none of these can be directly manipulated by an experimenter unless there is a medical reason for doing so.

Consequently, the samples in these sorts of study are, by necessity, clinical and neurologically impaired. The most common, non-invasive method of investigating normal asymmetry in normal individuals is via visual hemifield and dichotic listening techniques. As we saw in Chapter 3, the visual pathways cross over at the optic chiasm so that information to one visual field is relayed to the contralateral hemisphere. A stimulus can be presented very briefly to either side of a fixation spot. Information from one visual field is then processed by the contralateral hemisphere. Auditory stimulation appears to work in a similar way to visual stimulation, although, as we saw in Chapter 3, the cross-over is not as clear; stimuli presented via the left ear may project directly to the right hemisphere, with right-ear stimuli projecting to the left hemisphere. These techniques have been most widely applied to the study of the lateralization of human language. Although this is considered in more detail in Chapter 9, the section below provides a brief introduction to the types of language process that have been localized.

■ Language

Invasive and non-invasive studies of localization have shown left hemisphere dominance for speech and language. Electrical stimulation studies, for example, report impaired speech following left- but not right-sided stimulation. Similarly, the Wada test has shown that injection into the hemisphere dominant for speech (usually the left) results in an almost complete arrest of speech, lasting minutes. Injection into the non-dominant hemisphere also produces speech impairments but these are brief.

Non-invasive, tachistoscopic studies in which words or single-letters are presented to a single hemisphere usually showing a right visual field advantage for the recognition and identification of these stimuli (e.g. Bryden, 1965). Similarly, dichotic listening studies demonstrate a right ear advantage for verbal material (Kimura, 1967; Hugdahl, 1995). This right ear advantage is reversed in patients with right hemisphere speech (Zatorre, 1989).

Modern imaging techniques allow a more direct measure of specific neural areas that may be involved in language processing. Positron emission tomography (PET) studies, for example, show that listening to words is associated with increased activity not only in the auditory cortex but also in Wernicke's and Broca's areas; speaking results in increases in activity in the motor areas representing the mouth (Lassen *et al.*, 1978). Furthermore, phonetic and semantic analysis of language is associated with left hemisphere activation, with selective activation in the frontal, temporal and parietal cortices (Binder *et al.*, 1997).

In a pioneering PET study of single-word processing, Petersen and colleagues reported increased activation in the left posterior temporal cortex during the passive listening of words (Petersen *et al.*, 1988). When subjects had to decide whether pairs of spoken syllables ended in a consonant or not, an increase in blood flow to Broca's area was observed (Zatorre *et al.*, 1992a). Similar left-sided increases have been found during word association tasks, even in left-handers (Markus and Boland, 1992).

Early studies have been supported by later investigations which have examined more specific aspects of linguistic processing. Price and colleagues, for example, have reported greater activity in the left inferior and middle frontal cortices during a lexical decision task whereas increases in the left middle and superior temporal regions were found during reading aloud and silently (Price *et al.*, 1994). Petersen and co-workers also reported left-sided activity during a word recognition task (Petersen *et al.*, 1990). Specifically, silent viewing of words and pseudowords activated the left medial extrastriate cortex but silent viewing of consonant strings did not. They argued that this brain region was associated with visual word recognition and not phonological processing. Increased blood flow was found in the inferior temporal lobe during reading, a finding that was replicated by Nobre and colleagues who found that increased activation in the posterior and anterior fusiform gyrus was found during the presentation of letter-strings (Nobre *et al.*, 1994). Measurement from blood flow studies of the middle cerebral artery has also indicated increased flow to the left hemisphere during a task in which subjects had to chose two words (out of six) that belonged to the same class (Bulla-Hellwig *et al.*, 1996).

However, although there is left hemisphere dominance for language and speech, the right hemisphere does play some part in language processing. There may even be greater activation in the right than in the left hemisphere if the verbal task that the subject undertakes is automatic, e.g. recital of days of the week (Ryding *et al.*, 1985).

The right hemisphere might also play a role in the appreciation of metaphors. Bottini and colleagues reported that sentence comprehension was associated with the typical increased activation in left hemisphere regions such as the prefrontal and basal frontal cortex and the middle and inferior temporal gyri (Bottini *et al.*, 1994). The comprehension of metaphors, however, although associated with similar increases in left hemisphere activity, was also associated with increases in various parts of the right hemisphere including the right prefrontal cortex and the middle temporal gyrus. The reasons for this are complex but may be connected with the ability of the right hemisphere to undertake mental imagery, a process which the authors suggest is necessary for the successful comprehension of metaphors. They draw attention to studies showing that a patient with unilateral visual imagery deficit had right frontal lobe lesions (Guariglia *et al.*, 1993) and another PET study showing increases in the same areas when subjects had to imagine their living-room and how it was furnished (Roland and Friberg, 1985).

Finally, the right hemisphere's involvement in the processing of the affective tone of speech has been widely reported (see, for example, the views by Ross, (1983) and Pell and Baum (1997). This relationship between the right hemisphere and affect is considered in more detail in Chapter 10, as is its involvement in the appreciation of humour.

▦ Visuospatial ability

Visuospatial ability appears to be more reliant on the performance of the right than the left hemisphere (De Renzi, 1982) although not all visuospatial tasks tap the same visuospatial function. A division has been suggested between tests of mental rotation ability which do appear to elicit reliable hemispheric asymmetries and tests involving spatial relations, such as the organization of elements in a stimulus configuration (McGhee, 1979). Kosslyn (1987) has also distinguished between spatial tasks which involve assigning spatial relations to a category such as 'outside of' or 'above' and those which involve making decisions about metric distances between spatial relations. The right hemisphere makes better use of the latter; the left hemisphere makes better use of the former.

One of the more common tasks of visuospatial ability involves spatial transformation such as mental rotation. There are several types of mental rotation task but the most widely used is that of Shepard (Cooper and Shepard, 1973; Shepard and Metzler, 1971). This task involves imagining the rotation of a series of stimuli (cubes, letters, digits) so that their position and orientation match the position and orientation of another set of rotated or unrotated target stimuli (Figures 4.2 and 4.3).

Evidence from a number of sources suggests that mental rotation is largely a function of the right hemisphere, although this is not clear-cut (Corballis, 1997). Right posterior brain damage is associated with mental rotation deficit (Butters *et*

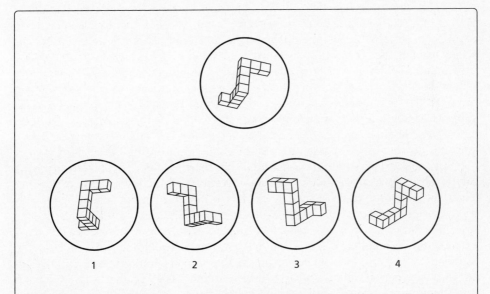

Figure 4.2 A typical rotation task. Which of the four alternatives represents the cubes on top?

Same　　　　　　　　Different

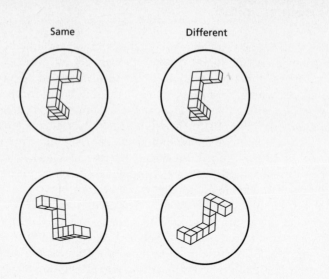

Figure 4.3　Another rotation task. The task is to decide whether each set of cubes is the same or is different

al., 1970) whereas a left visual field advantage is found for mental rotation in healthy individuals (Ditunno and Mann, 1990). Greater rCBF has also been reported in the right hemisphere (Deutsch *et al.*, 1988). Mental rotation produces strong asymmetries, especially in the right parietal cortex (Deutsch *et al.*, 1988).

EEG and ERP studies of language processing and visuospatial ability generally reflect the stereotypical asymmetries found in other studies. For example, Morgan *et al.* (1971) reported lower alpha activity over the right hemisphere in most subjects during the performance of a spatial task, indicating an increase in brain activation. Gevins *et al.* (1979), however, failed to find task-dependent asymmetries but did reported bilateral increases in activation during the performance of cognitive tasks. These authors concluded that there was no evidence to suggest a relationship between asymmetrical EEG activation and the type of task processed. They subsequently made several criticisms of studies purporting to show EEG asymmetries (Gevins *et al.*, 1980). Perhaps one of the more important criticisms was aimed at the type of task used. They argued that in order to observe any clear asymmetry of function, tasks must be psychometrically matched, that is the asymmetry they produce must be due to the variable under investigation (language, visuospatial ability) and not to some other aspect of the task. This is an important point because if tasks are not matched (for motor components, say, or for difficulty) then any asymmetry observed may not be due to the type of processing involved but to some component of the task that is unrelated to whether the task is spatial or verbal. This caveat applies to any study of the brain's activity during cognitive stimulation. However, the expected pattern of asymmetry has been found in other EEG studies using matched tasks (e.g. Davidson *et al.*, 1990a; Miller *et al.*, 1995).

In the event-related potential (ERP) literature, larger ERPs have been reported for the right than for the left hemisphere for the N2 and P3 components during mental rotation (Desrocher *et al.*, 1995). Desrocher and colleagues have suggested that the processes involved in mental rotation can be broken up into separate operations, each of which follows a particular time-course. Thus, stimulus evaluation occurs in the first 200–300 ms of the task; evaluation of the complexity of the stimuli and the selection of strategy occurs between 300 and 400 ms; actual rotation in the 400–800 ms window, and decision-making in the 1000–1200 ms window. The frontal areas are thought to be associated with the first two stages (stimulus evaluation and strategy formation), with centroparietal regions thought to be involved in the final two stages (rotation and decision).

Other visuospatial, right hemisphere functions include the perception and recognition of non-verbal visual stimuli such as faces. In studies where the right hemisphere, especially the temporoparietal cortex, is electrically stimulated, impairments in the identification of facial expression and in short-term memory for faces are found (Ojemann, 1983). Visual field studies also show a right hemisphere advantage for face recognition, i.e. it recognizes facial expressions more quickly than does the left hemisphere (Rizolatti *et al.*, 1971). This impairment in visuo-spatial function extends to other stimuli as well as to faces. Individuals with unilateral right hemisphere damage, for example, have greater difficulty than those with left-sided lesions in differentiating ground from figure (Russo and Vignolo, 1967) and in localizing points in space (Hannay *et al.*, 1976). The right hemisphere appears to be better than the left at matching an arc to a part of a circle at the correct angle, at pattern completion (Nebes, 1972) and at localizing dots (Bryden, 1976). Visual field studies in neurologically healthy individuals have confirmed the right hemisphere's 'superiority' in localizing dots. Kimura (1969), for example, found that memory for the location of dots was significantly better when stimuli were presented in the left visual field, thereby being transferred to the right hemisphere.

Spatial processing is not limited exclusively to the right hemisphere, however. Mehta and Newcombe (1991), for example, have found that left hemisphere lesions were associated with impaired performance on a task in which individuals had to indicate which of ten lines, spaced at equidistant angles up to 180 degrees, were at the same angle as two lines presented in isolation. These subjects also showed deficits on two shape rotation tasks.

Most of the invasive and non-invasive studies reviewed above ascribe a greater role for the right hemisphere in visuospatial processing. Clarification of the type of visuospatial test used, however, is crucial in determining the type of localization. More importantly, lateralization is not absolute: one hemisphere is often able to subsume the function of the hemisphere dominant for that function, even if this ability is at a rudimentary level. The picture is complicated by the function of memory.

■ Memory

Memory and learning are probably the most difficult human functions to localize in the brain because memory is a process and not a single 'entity', and that process is itself a multiple not a unitary process.

James (1890) was one of the earliest psychologists to suggests that memory was made up of different memory systems. He called memory for short-term processing **primary memory**, and that which represented more long-term processing and storage **secondary memory**. In 1958, Broadbent specifically postulated a **short-term** (STM) and **long-term memory** (LTM) process in which items from STM would, via specific mechanisms, make their way into LTM.

Current literature, however, is dominated by dichotomies of memory processes. One dichotomy is represented by **declarative memory** (Cohen and Squire, 1980) which refers to facts that are accessible to conscious recollection (the facts from this book, for example) and **procedural memory** which refers to skills and automatic operations needed to perform a certain function (e.g. the motor skills required for typing a letter or riding a bike). Declarative memory is similar to explicit memory which represents the conscious learning or memorization of material. According to Squire (1994), declarative memory, 'refers to a biologically meaningful category of memory dependent on a specific brain system'. Some forms of memory, however, clearly do not fit the declarative memory description, but neither do they fit the definition of procedural memory particularly well. A broader term, 'non-declarative memory', has been used to describe those abilities not fitting the other description (Squire and Zola-Morgan, 1988). This is similar to Schacter's (1987) **implicit memory**: memory which involves no explicit or conscious intention to learn or memorize; learning is incidental. This, according to Schacter, 'embraces several kinds of memory and depends on multiple brain systems'.

A widely accepted neurobiological theory is that of Hebb (1949) who, in his famous book, *Organization of Behaviour,* proposed that each psychologically important event is conceived as the flow of activity in a given neuronal loop (the interconnections between dendrite, cell body and the synapses on these structures) and proposed that the synapses in a particular path become functionally connected to form a cell assembly. The assumption is that if two neurons are excited together, they become linked functionally. To produce functional changes in synaptic transmission, the cell assembly must be repeatedly activated. After initial sensory input, the assembly will reverberate. Repeated reverberation brings about structural changes. Short-term memory, therefore, is reverberation of the closed loops of the cell assembly; long-term memory is the more structural, lasting change in synaptic connections. This long-term change in structure is thought to reflect **long-term potentiation**, a term which describes the strengthening of neuronal connections via repeated stimulation.

Even organisms with a primitive nervous system such as the sea-slug, *Aplysia*, can learn and show evidence of 'memory'. As memories rely on information received by several sensory systems, this process would suggest that memory has multiple components or is subserved by multiple memory systems. The current view in neuropsychology suggests that this is the case. Based on evidence from brain imaging studies and studies of amnesia and brain damage, it has been argued that different parts of the brain are responsible for mediating the various dichotomies of memory (Squire, 1994).

For example, one study reports differential changes in brain structure metabolism according to the type of amnesia presented and claims that clusters of cerebral areas are associated with primary components of memory function. Periani *et al.* (1993) compared the performance of patients with Alzheimer's disease with that of global amnesiacs and age- and education-matched controls. They found that the best predictors of episodic memory deficit (characteristic of amnesia and Alzheimer's) were the metabolic values from the left and right hippocampus, whereas the best predictors of verbal and spatial memory in amnesic patients were those for the thalamus and cingulate gyrus. In Alzheimer's patients, the best predictors of verbal and spatial memory impairment were the metabolic values for left and right hippocampus and cingulate gyrus. The best predictive variables for verbal STM decline (for Alzheimer's only, no other group showed a decline) were the metabolic values of the left superior temporal, parietal, frontal associative and frontal areas. Spatial STM deficit was predicted by values for right parietal and frontal associative areas. A further PET study of healthy volunteers' activation during the encoding and retrieval of episodic memory (also referred to as autobiographical memory) reported a different pattern of activation for each type of process (Fletcher *et al.*, 1995). Encoding was associated with increased activation in the left prefrontal cortex and part of the cingulate gyrus whereas retrieval was associated with bilateral activation of the precuneus and increased activation in the right prefrontal cortex. Both studies suggest that different forms of memory and different memory processes are subserved by different cortical areas.

Cortical and subcortical influences on memory

Much of the evidence implicating particular regions of the brain in memory is derived from studies of pathological memory. There are three terms normally used to describe memory loss in such cases: **amnesia** refers to the partial or total loss of memory; **retrograde amnesia** refers to a difficulty in recalling events prior to the onset of amnesia and **anterograde amnesia** refers to an inability to remember events subsequent to the onset of amnesia.

Many diseases can produce brain damage and amnesia. These include head trauma, vascular disorders, infections and degenerative illnesses such as Alzheimer's disease (see Chapter 11). Surgical lesions can also bring about an impairment in memory if certain structures (e.g. the hippocampus) are damaged.

Temporal lobes

Damage to the temporal lobe, and especially to the anterior temporal cortex, the amygdala, the hippocampus and the entorhinal cortex, is associated with various degrees of amnesia.

The hippocampal formation itself is composed of two distinct structures: **Ammon's horn** (often referred to as the hippocampus) and the dendate gyrus. Ammon's horn comprises the substructures **CA1**, **CA2** and **CA3**. CA1 is sometimes referred to as **Sommer's sector**. There is also significant hippocampal output to the mammillary body via a tract called the **fornix**. Damage to each of these structures is sometimes associated with memory loss although the evidence for the involvement of the fornix is mixed (see the review in Calabrese *et al.* (1995), for example). One early suggestion was that the hippocampus, the fornix and the mammillary bodies represented the functional system for memory and that any disruption to this system would result in memory impairment (Delay and Brion, 1969). Anterograde amnesia and object discrimination difficulties have been reported with fornix damage (Gaffan *et al.*, 1991; Calabrese *et al.*, 1995) although distinctive patterns of impairment are sometimes not seen (e.g. Gaffan *et al.*, 1991).

The most famous example of hippocampus-related memory impairment is patient HM who has been studied for over 35 years (Scoville and Milner, 1957; B. Milner *et al.*, 1968; Keane, *et al.*, 1995). HM had experienced generalized epileptic seizures which became worse despite considerable medication. On 23 August 1953, Scoville performed a bilateral medial temporal lobe resection in an attempt to stop the seizures. This resulted in intractable and severe anterograde memory impairment. For example, HM is impaired on any test requiring a delay between presentation and recall such as photograph recognition; maze and verbal learning is almost impossible.

The hippocampus itself appears to exhibit functional dissociations. Right hippocampus removal, for example, is associated with impairment in visuospatial learning, whereas damage to the left hippocampus is associated with impaired verbal memory (Trenerry *et al.*, 1993).

Famously, O'Keefe and Nadel (1978) in their book *The Hippocampus as a Cognitive Map*, argued that the hippocampus constructs cognitive maps which animals use to locate memories or to understand spatial locations in the world. At about the same time, Olton and colleagues reported that hippocampal lesions in rats produced deficits in a type of STM called **working memory**, the memory for information kept for immediate processing (Olton *et al.*, 1979). However, the notion that the hippocampus may be disproportionately concerned with spatial memory is not well supported by later evidence (Squire, 1994). Part of the confusion lies in the exact locus of the damage. Humans with hippocampal formation damage do not exhibit disproportionately large spatial memory impairments (Cave and Squire, 1991).

Lesions of the anterior temporal lobe, sparing the hippocampus, result in memory impairments, but not of the global kind seen in HM. Lesions of the right temporal lobe result in impaired non-verbal memory (recall of complex geometric figures, paired-associate learning of nonsense figures, and recognition of nonsense figures, tunes and photographs); left temporal lobe lesions result in impaired verbal memory (recall of previously presented stories, pairs of words, recognition of words, numbers and nonsense syllables). Verbal memory impairments are common following temporal lobe resection (Ivnik *et al.*, 1987).

Diencephalon

The major structures of the diencephalon are the hypothalamus and the thalamus; damage to either causes amnesia. The dorsal medial nucleus of the thalamus and the mammillary body of the hypothalamus appear to be particularly important. The first human case of combined mammillary body and medial thalamic lesions was reported in 1996 (Kapur *et al.*, 1996). These authors found that the patient showed fairly intact retrograde memory but had impaired anterograde memory, especially on a task requiring delayed recall of stories.

Both regions also become degenerated to some extent in chronic alcoholics who exhibit **Korsakoff's syndrome**. Korsakoff's syndrome describes the memory impairments seen following long-term alcoholism. They were first described in 1889 by Sergei Korsakoff, a Russian physician, who noted a severe syndrome of memory impairment following chronic alcoholism. The most marked feature of Korsakoff's syndrome is severe anterograde amnesia. The disorder results from a thiamine (vitamin B1) deficiency caused by alcoholism. Because their diet is primarily made up of alcohol, drinkers get their calories from alcohol and, therefore, receive fewer vitamins. Alcohol also appears to interfere with the intestinal absorption of thiamine. Prognosis is poor, with only about 20 per cent of patients showing much recovery over a year on a B1-enriched diet.

The location of brain damage in Korsakoff's syndrome is unclear since all cases are accompanied by damage to many regions. Current thinking suggests specific damage to the medial thalamus, and possibly the mammillary bodies of the hypothalamus. It was believed that severe memory defects resulted from hypothalamic damage because the mammillary bodies receive hippocampal efferents throughout the fornix. The role of fornix lesions in amnesia is, as we have already seen, controversial.

The importance of parts of the thalamus is highlighted by another of memory's famous case studies. Squire and Moore's patient NA had a focal lesion in the dorsal medial nucleus resulting from an accident in which a fencing foil entered the right nostril and punctured the base of the brain (Squire and Moore, 1979). Severe amnesia followed. PET scans show little activation in NA's right medial temporal lobe which suggests the importance of this structure to memory. However, the relative contribution of other damaged parts of NA's brain to amnesia is unclear.

Basal forebrain

The basal forebrain describes the region in front of and above the optic chiasm. It includes the nucleus accumbens, septal nuclei, anterior hypothalamus, the nucleus of Meynert and the prefrontal cortex, all of which are associated with impairments in memory if damaged. In fact, the prefrontal cortex may be especially important for working memory (Goldman-Rakic, 1995), as we shall see in Chapter 6.

In terms of what we know concerning the neuropsychology of memory, there is much work to be done both at the metabolic and molecular level. Examples of human brain damage indicate the involvement of gross regions and structures in memory processes. Much of the experimental, biochemical evidence we have is derived from animal studies, although conditions such as dementia also allow us to manipulate biochemistry, a point returned to in Chapter 11. Often, such evidence can be of enormous benefit. One example is the construction of animal models of Alzheimer's disease or Parkinson's disease in which the symptoms of the disorders are reproduced. The advantage of such models is that they offer the possibility of manipulating symptoms and experimenting with treatments. One such treatment is neural grafting, which is examined more closely in Chapter 8. What is clear from our current knowledge of memory, however, is that the neurobiology of memory is a system made up of multiple processes: different types of memory process (e.g. learning and retrieval) require different brain systems to mediate them.

▓ Somatosensation

As might be expected from the organization of the somatosensory system, stimulation on one side of the body is associated with increases in contralateral prefrontal brain activation in regional cerebral blood flow (rCBF) studies (Risberg and Prohovnik, 1983). Left hand movement also produces significant changes in the contralateral hemisphere (Halsey *et al.*, 1979). At a behavioural level, asymmetries in somatosensation have been measured using dihaptic techniques. These are similar to the procedure used in dichotic listening except that the stimuli are shapes and the individual has to match a picture of a shape with two shapes presented out of vision simultaneously to each hand. This task produces a left-hand advantage (Bradshaw *et al.*, 1986).

Perception of music

Although the right ear appears to be superior at identifying verbal material, there is evidence to suggest that musical chords and melodies are processed better when presented to the left ear (Kimura, 1964; Bartholomeus, 1974; Gordon, 1980). This has also been reported for harmonies, pitch and timbre.

Trained musicians appear to show left hemisphere superiority in the recognition of melodies whereas untrained subjects show a right hemisphere advantage (Bever and Chiarello, 1974). Similarly, Davidson and Schwartz (1977) found that musicians showed more left hemisphere EEG activation when they whistled than did non-musicians. Both musicians and non-musicians showed left hemisphere activation during the recitation of song lyrics. This evidence lends support to the notion that musicians are inclined to use their more 'analytic' hemisphere (the left) than were non-musicians who performed no such analysis or did not have the ability to do so.

In another study, a larger planum temporale was found in those musicians with perfect pitch than in non-musicians or musicians without perfect pitch (Schlaug *et al.*, 1995), suggesting the further involvement of the left hemisphere in certain music-related abilities. This suggestion is supported by a recent PET study in which left hemisphere activation was greater during tasks involving musical familiarity, pitch and timbre in six musically naive subjects. Further specific activations were found for each task, possibly reflecting the different mental strategies involved in each task (Platel *et al.*, 1997).

There is also evidence to suggest a role for the left hemisphere in rhythm. Although there is no hand difference in tapping in time to a metronome, the right hand appears to be better at tapping out a simple rhythm (Wolff *et al.*, 1977). This finding appears to hold for left- and right-handers, which suggests that the difference is due to hemispheric differences and not to the hand preference of the participant.

Mathematical ability

Difficulties in performing mathematical operations fall into various categories. Individuals may exhibit difficulties in reading numbers (**alexia**) or writing them (**agraphia**). The terms 'alexia' and 'agraphia' have a more general currency in neuropsychology (the former means reading difficulty, the latter difficulty in writing). Therefore, strictly speaking, the disorders encountered in mathematics should be termed alexia and agraphia for numbers. Other mathematical difficulties include problems in representing numerical information spatially by misreading signs, omitting numbers or having problems with decimal places despite preserved number reading and writing skills (**spatial acalulia**), and in retrieving arithmetical information from long-term memory despite preserved number reading and writing and spatial representation of numbers (**anarithmetria**).

Alexia and agraphia for numbers usually occur in the absence of other arithmetical disabilities and are associated with left hemisphere lesions (Hecaen, 1962). Spatial acalulia, on the other hand, is associated with posterior right hemisphere damage (Benson and Weir, 1972; Spiers, 1987; Rourke and Finlayson, 1978), possibly because of the emphasis on visuospatial skills in calculation and arithmetical calculations. In support of this, Hartje (1987) has noted that counters and the manipulation of counters are widely used during children's learning of arithmetical skills. Anarithmetria appears to be a consequence of posterior left hemisphere damage (McCloskey *et al.*, 1991), although there appears to be a dissociation within this disability in that a failure in the retrieval of facts or an inability to carry out arithmetical procedures can be observed. The primary deficit seen in anarithmetria, however, appears to be difficulty in arithmetical fact retrieval (Geary, 1993). The evidence thus appears to confirm the predominant involvement of the right hemisphere in mathematical tasks, possibly because of the spatial nature of some of the tasks involved in mathematics.

▓ Individual differences

Handedness

Handedness refers to the degree to which an individual preferentially uses one hand. On the surface, determining handedness might seem like a simple task, but the classification of handedness is fraught with problems (Peters, 1995). The most widely used classification systems require an individual to rate the frequency of use for each hand for a number of activities such as writing, throwing and catching a ball, threading a needle, unscrewing a jar and so on (Oldfield, 1971; Annett, 1970). Figure 4.4 shows a sample from the Annett Handedness Questionnaire.

If individuals use the right or left hand exclusively to perform these tasks, then there may be no problem in classifying them as right- or left-handed. However, if an individual writes with the left hand and throws a ball with the right or an individual writes with the right hand and throws a ball with the left, how should this person be classified? One solution is to classify according to the degree and strength of handedness (strong/weak hand preference). Even this is problematic, however. Peters (1992), for example, argues that, depending on the length of the questionnaire and the classification method used, the percentage of individuals classified as non-right handers in the same sample can range from 9.4 per cent to 86.7 per cent.

Handedness exerts an important influence on hemispheric asymmetry because of the likelihood that left- and right-handers have their language regions organized differently in the brain. Based on Wada test performance and the language

Name . . . . Age . . . . Sex . . . .

Were you one of twins, triplets at birth or were you single born? . . . .

Please indicate which hand you habitually use for each of the following activities by writing R (for right), L (for left) or E (for either).

Which hand do you use:

1. To write a letter legibly? . . . .

2. To throw a ball to hit a target? . . . .

3. To hold a racket in tennis, squash or badminton? . . . .

4. To hold a match whilst striking it? . . . .

5. To cut with scissors? . . . .

6. To guide a thread through the eye of a needle? . . . .

7. At the top of a broom while sweeping? . . . .

8. At the top of a shovel when moving sand? . . . .

9. To deal playing cards? . . . .

10. To hammer a nail into wood? . . . .

11. To hold a toothbrush while cleaning your teeth? . . . .

12. To unscrew the lid of a jar? . . . .

If you use the left hand for all of these actions, are there any one-handed actions for which you use the right hand? Please record them here

. . . .

. . . .

. . . .

Figure 4.4 The Annett Handedness Questionnaire. From Annett, 1970

performance of those with unilateral brain damage, the majority of right-handers have left hemisphere speech. Most left-handers also have left hemisphere speech but some also have right hemisphere or bilateral represented language (Goodglass and Quadfasel, 1954; Segalowitz and Bryden, 1983). According to Rasmussen and Milner (1977), 96 per cent of their right-handers and 70 per cent of their left-handers showed left hemisphere speech impairment following the injection of sodium Amytal. Four per cent of right-handers had right-hemisphere speech. Segalowitz and Bryden (1983) also estimate that the left hemisphere is language-dominant for 95.3 per cent of right-handers but for only 61.4 per cent of left-handers. This said, however, there appears to be no significant difference between the rate or degree of recovery of language for left- and right-handers with unilateral brain damage.

Left-handers appear to be superior to right-handers on tests of verbal ability as measured by performance on the verbal IQ range of subtests on the Wechsler Adult Intelligence Scale (WAIS) but are inferior to right-handers on tests of visuospatial ability as measured by performance on the performance IQ subtest of the WAIS (Levy, 1969). Levy explained this in terms of a crowding hypothesis. Left-handers, Levy argued, have superior verbal ability because they have more variable language representation and have a greater neural mass devoted to language, hence their superior performance. However, because the right hemisphere is undertaking part of a function (language) considered to be the prerogative of the left hemisphere, it has less neural mass to devote to its own specialization, visuospatial ability. This is an interesting hypothesis, although the inclusion of a very small sample of undergraduates as participants in this study suggests that caution is necessary in interpreting these results.

Whether left/right hand differences are really associated with differences in verbal and spatial ability is not exactly clear. Some studies suggest a difference (Miller, 1971); others have not (Kutas *et al.*, 1975). An early review by Hardyck and Petrinovich (1977) concluded that there was no reliable, systematic difference between left- and right-handers for cognitive ability, although Hicks and Beveridge (1978) point out that this might only apply to tests of crystallized intelligence (knowledge tests). When tests tapping fluid intelligence (problem-solving, creativity) are used, left-handers perform significantly better.

One particular aspect of handedness that may be detrimental to task performance is **familial sinistrality** (**FS**), or a family history of left-handedness. In general, left-handers with FS perform more poorly than right-handers and left-handers with no FS on tests of non-verbal ability but not on tests of verbal ability (Bradshaw *et al.*, 1981). Left-handers with FS also perform more poorly on mathematics tests than do weak left-handers and strongly left-handed individuals with no FS (Searleman *et al.*, 1984). The conclusion from these and other studies is that FS combined with strong left-hand preference has a detrimental effect on visuospatial ability (McKeever, 1986, 1991; O'Boyle and Benbow, 1990) although this conclusion is not entirely accepted. Van Strien and Bouma (1995), for example, found that left-handers with a family history of sinistrality were better at tests of numerical reasoning, verbal reasoning and two visuospatial tasks than were left-handers without a history of sinistrality. Two possible explanations for this might be that (1) there is no detrimental effect of familial sinistrality, or (2) different tests designed to measure the same factor produce inconsistent findings. The authors suggest that the latter cannot be ruled out.

Sex

Sex, like handedness, exerts a significant influence over the degree of type of functional lateralization. Whereas there is some evidence to suggest that verbal ability is less lateralized in right-handed women than right-handed men (McGlone, 1980; Hiscock *et al.*, 1994), the most stereotypical sex difference emerges on tests of visuospatial ability (McKeever, 1991; Van Strien and Bouma, 1995). Some examples of the types of test eliciting sex differences are seen in Figure 4.5.

It has been estimated that 76 per cent of right-handed men and 56 per cent of right-handed women have right hemisphere dominance for spatial ability, with the clearest sex difference found for mental rotation performance (Linn and Petersen, 1985; Deutsch *et al.*, 1988): men are better at it than women. Rugg and Dickens (1982), for example, reported greater right-sided theta activation during a visuo-spatial task only in men. One reason for the male superiority on visuospatial tasks may be gonadal, especially androgen, hormone influence, because less 'masculine' men appear to be better at spatial tasks than are more 'masculine' men (Broverman *et al.*, 1968; Lewis and Diamond, 1995). The evidence, however, is inconclusive (Christiansen and Knussman, 1988).

There is a complex relationship between sex, hand preference and the type of task undertaken by the participant. Early studies, for example, suggested that right-handed men were better at spatial tests than were women and left-handed men, although there was no significant difference in ability between left- and right-handed women (Yen, 1975). Later studies, however, found better performance in right-handed than left-handed women (Sanders *et al.*, 1982). One explanation for this inconsistency is that the differences might be attributable to differences in reasoning ability (Harshman *et al.*, 1983). In other words, individuals with the ability to reason well would produce the pattern seen in Yen's study whereas individuals with less proficient reasoning ability would produce a different pattern.

Coren (1995) has recently reported that left-handed men perform better on a semantic-based divergent thinking test than do right-handed men, although there is no difference between left- and right-handed women. There was, however, a right-hand superiority for an inductive reasoning test regardless of sex, which indicates that left-handedness is an advantage for certain, but not all, types of divergent thinking test.

Psychopathology

There appear to be distinct hemispheric asymmetries associated with certain psychopathological conditions. Flor-Henry (1969), for example, found that in-dividuals with temporal lobe epilepsy with left foci exhibited schizophrenic symptoms whereas those with right foci exhibited manic symptoms. Later evi-dence suggested that the left hemisphere became overactivated (Nachshon, 1980)

Figure 4.5 Two visuospatial tasks on which sex differences are found. In (a) the task is to indicate whether the shape on the card is the same as the stimulus; in (b) the task is to indicate which glove the target glove represents

or dysfunctional (Gur, 1978). Gruzelier and his colleagues proposed that active symptoms (e.g. delusions, overactivity and rapidity of thought) were associated with left hemisphere activation, whereas withdrawal symptoms (e.g. paranoia) are associated with right hemisphere activation (Gruzelier, 1981, 1984; Gruzelier and Hammond, 1980).

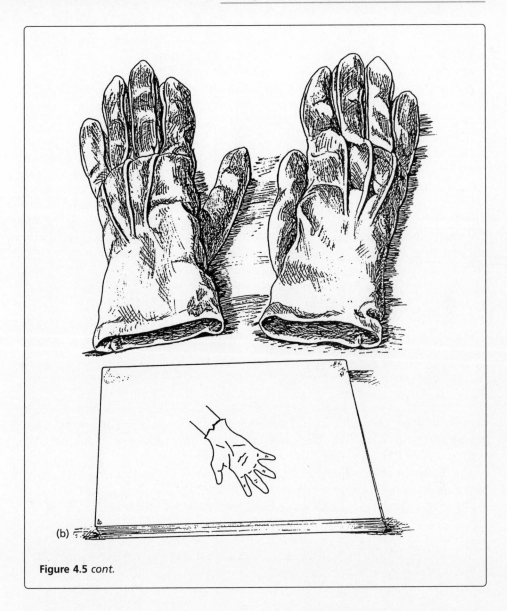

(b)

Figure 4.5 *cont.*

More recent data, however, have implicated more specific regions of the cortex. Crow (1990), for example, suggests that schizophrenia might be associated with disturbances in the left posterior temporal lobe and the superior temporal gyrus, including the planum temporale. Perhaps these findings might explain why schizophrenics show an extremely large right ear advantage in dichotic listening studies (Nachshon, 1980). Overactivation of the language areas might produce this extreme advantage. ERP data and brain imaging evidence also suggest a role for the left temporal lobe (Bruder, 1995). Specifically, ERP studies have shown reduced left P3 amplitude in medicated and unmedicated schizophrenics when compared with controls (McCarley *et al.*, 1991). Furthermore, the P3 recorded from the left temporal region was associated with positive symptoms and a wider left Sylvian fissure. A reduction of the volume in the left posterior superior temporal gyrus has also been significantly correlated with reduced P3 amplitude in the left temporal region (McCarley *et al.*, 1993).

One recent PET study suggests that the frontal lobes play an important part in schizophrenia. This study highlighted the role of the left middle temporal gyrus and supplementary motor area in imagining sentences being spoken by another voice (auditory hallucinations) in hallucinating schizophrenics (McGuire *et al.*, 1995). Activation in these areas was significantly reduced in hallucinating schizophrenics when compared with non-hallucinating schizophrenics and normal subjects, suggesting perhaps that a predisposition to verbal hallucination may be due to a failure to activate those areas of the brain normally activated during the monitoring of inner speech. The role of hemispheric asymmetry in other psychopathologies such as anxiety and depression is considered in Chapter 10.

■ Why is there laterality?

'Everything,' argues Corballis (1991), 'even a billiard ball, is asymmetrical if examined closely enough or with sensitive enough measuring instruments'. This caveat serves as a sensible reminder that asymmetry may not be functionally significant but simply a physical characteristic.

Most theories of laterality focus on the role of the 'dominant' left hemisphere and its role in language production. From this focus, the development of asymmetry is seen as an evolutionary step up from non-human primates. Luria (1973), for example, suggested that the higher the function, the more asymmetric it becomes. Thus, we are more clearly lateralized because we are higher-thinking human beings. We are higher-thinking because we have language. Asymmetry thus reflects a developmental or adaptive trait.

Adaptive significance

However, the question of whether asymmetry serves some adaptive role is not an easy one to answer. What, for example, is the adaptive point of right- or left head-turning? Is bisymmetry itself adaptive? For example, bipedal locomotion (walking on two feet) relies on symmetry – we do not walk about with one foot (Corballis,

1991). The consequences of asymmetry here would clearly serve no adaptive advantage. If this is the case, however, why do humans also exhibit footedness?

Evolution of language

One theory of localization makes use of the fact that the hemisphere dominant for language is also the hemisphere which controls the dominant hand. Thus hemispheric localization of speech is seen as a consequence of the evolution of motor skills and not as symbolic behaviour or analytic ability. On a more general level, it has been suggested that because the cognitive processes used for language and spatial and perceptual functions are entirely different, then these different functions require different hemispheres to undertake them efficiently (Levy, 1974, 1990). The idea behind this hypothesis is that a function is better served by one hemisphere which is specialized for that function than by two hemispheres which have to share a function and which, therefore, engage in unnecessary doubling of function.

Corballis (1989) has suggested that the evolution of flexible, dynamic and rapid delivery of speech developed only recently in evolutionary terms (150 000–200 000 years ago) whereas left hemisphere speech may have been present in our hominid ancestors 2 million years ago. Corballis sees the development of language (and other complex) behaviour as reflecting a process of **generativity**, which is left-hemisphere based (Corballis, 1989, 1991). Generativity refers to the ability to combine aspects of behaviour according to given rules. Combinations could include those of words to make sentences or objects to make tools. This theory is, however, complicated somewhat by the lack of systematic or grossly detrimental differences between the cognitive abilities of individuals with left, right or bilateral hemispheric language and speech.

Geschwind and Galaburda model

A more detailed and complex theory of functional hemispheric asymmetry has been proposed by Geschwind and Galaburda. They argued that the development of cerebral lateralization is influenced by levels of foetal testosterone (Geschwind and Behan, 1982; Geschwind and Galaburda, 1985). These levels influence the anatomical and physiological development of the left hemisphere and, perhaps more controversially, may influence the development of neuropsychological (e.g. dyslexia) and immune (e.g. asthma) disorders.

The theory argues that testosterone levels alter the growth of the left cerebral hemisphere, which in turn produces 'anomalous dominance' (Annett, 1985; Geschwind and Galaburda, 1987). A testosterone-induced delay in left hemisphere development may produce random dominance, that is, the individual could become left- or right-handed. This delay also brings with it an increase in immune disorders and learning difficulties.

Geschwind and Galaburda base their theory on a selection of studies. For example, they found that strongly left-handed individuals and their first- and second-degree relatives were more likely to suffer from a variety of immune disorders than were their right-handed counterparts (Geschwind and Behan, 1982). Left-handers also exhibited a greater degree of learning disabilities such as developmental dyslexia. In an extensive re-evaluation of the evidence for and against the Geschwind–Galaburda model, Bryden *et al.* (1994) conclude that supportive evidence is either ambiguous or sparse. Their conclusions are summarized in Table 4.2.

Many of the studies reviewed by Bryden *et al.* show highly anomalous results. Studies do show a higher incidence of left-handedness and immune disorders in

Table 4.2 Factors for and against the Geschwind, Behan and Galaburda model of lateralization

Item	Rating
Anomalous dominance (AD)	−2
Immune disorders and AD	−1
Immune disorders and giftedness	0
Immune disorders and language disability	+1
AD and language	
Dyslexia	+1
Developmental language disorders	+1
Stuttering	+1
Autism	+1
Tourette syndrome	0
AD and giftedness	
Exceptional talents	−1
Spatial ability	−2
Verbal ability	−2
Language and giftedness	0
Testosterone effects on AD	−1
Testosterone effects on language	−1
Testosterone effects on giftedness	0

−2 = Studies are consistently against; −1 = Evidence is inconsistent but the good studies are against; 0 = Studies not available/seriously flawed/ambiguous; +1 = Consistent evidence for, but alternative explanations available; +2 = Unequivocal support with no better available model to explain the data
Adapted from Bryden *et al.*, 1994

dyslexics, but there is no significant difference between left-handed and right-handed dyslexics, as would be predicted by the model. On the point of handedness, Bishop (1990) has argued that it is not left-handedness that may be related to increased incidence of developmental language disorder but uncertain or ambiguous handedness.

Following the publication of the Bryden *et al.* review, Flannery and Liederman (1995) reported data from a large study in which the relationships among left-handedness, neurodevelopmental disorder, immune disorder and special talent were examined. They found no significant relationship between non-right-handedness and reading disability but did find a relationship between non-right-handedness and general brain damage (cerebral palsy, mental retardation). Immune disorder was not associated with non-right-handedness. The only immune disorder to be significantly associated with neurodevelopmental disorder was asthma (associated with attention deficit disorder). Less than 1 per cent of a sample of 11 578 mother/child pairs had three or four of the traits dictated by the theory. This study, together with the mass of studies reviewed by Bryden *et al.*, indicates that the data supporting the model are highly inconsistent and may be accounted for by alternative explanations.

DISCUSSION POINT

Do left-handers die sooner than right-handers?

One of the more prominent examples of laterality in humans is hand preference. In 1988, Halpern and Coren published a controversial paper in the science journal *Nature* in which they examined the relationship between death rates and hand preference. Using data from *The Baseball Encyclopaedia* which detailed the birthday, date of death, and throwing and batting hand of 2271 players, they found a difference of 8 months between the mean age of death of strong right- and left-handers. This difference favoured the right-handers. A re-analysis of the data to account for statistical irregularities in the data showed that right-handers lived significantly longer than left-handers. More surprisingly, mortality rates were almost identical for the two groups up until the age of 33. From that age onwards, the average number of right-handers surviving was higher than the average number of left-handers. An earlier mailshot survey (Porac and Coren, 1981) of 5147 questionnaires indicated that the proportion of left-handed individuals decreased from approximately 15 per cent among 20–30 year olds to 5 per cent for those in their fifties and 0 per cent for those 80 years or older. A survey of 987 deceased individuals showed that right-handers actually outlived the left-handers by, on average, 8.97 years (Halpern and Coren, 1990).

Why is there such a comparatively low number of left-handers in the elderly population? One explanation suggests that left-handers become less common in elderly samples because they have learned to become right-handed through environmental pressure. This is called the *modification hypothesis*. A second, more controversial explanation argues that left-handedness is not found in older samples because left-handers have 'disappeared'. The most obvious reason for this disappearance, Coren argues, is death. This is called the *elimination hypothesis* and it is this that is the source of the controversy.

In a review of handedness and mortality, Coren and Halpern (1991) argued that there is little evidence for the modification hypothesis but there was considerable empirical support for the elimination hypothesis. Left-handedness may be a marker for increased risk of early mortality or 'reduced survival fitness'. To account for the greater risk in left-handers, they suggest a number of explanations. One is the *right-sided world hypothesis*: left-handers have continually to adjust to right-handed tools and environments. Consequently, they are clumsy and cause accidents.

To test this hypothesis, Coren (1989) asked a sample of 1896 university students to indicate their degree of handedness and the number of accidents they had experienced in the previous two years while (1) using tools or implements, (2) driving, (3) at home or at work, or (4) participating in some sporting activity. He found that left-handers were at increased risk of accidents in all of these categories: in fact, they were twice as likely to have sustained accident-related injuries than were right-handers. All of this evidence appeared to indicate that left-handedness was potentially life-threatening, or life-shortening. Or did it?

In a reply to Coren and Halpern's (1991) review, Harris (1993) questioned many of the assumptions underlying Coren's findings and questioned the quality of the data collected. In Porac and Coren's (1981) study, for example, approximately 20 000 individuals were included in the initial sample yet only 5147 individuals' responses were selected. There were also large differences in the composition of each of the eight age groups: 292 individuals in the 10–20 age group, 3409 in the 20–30 age group, 468 in the 30–40 group, 278 in the 40–50 group, 361 in the 50–60 group, 213 in the 60–70 group, 89 in the 70–80 group and 37 in the 80+ group. The small size of these last two groups indicates that they may not have been representative. Harris suggests that other studies (e.g., Ellis *et al.*, 1988; Lansky *et al.*, 1988) whose return rates were substantially higher (82 per cent returned their questionnaires in Ellis *et al.*'s sample) are a better reflection of population trends. These studies, although showing the same pattern as the Coren data, did not show such large handedness differences. Furthermore, setting aside questions of hand preference measurement, Harris argues that the baseball player study omitted 563 players who changed hands in batting or who had mixed handedness. Furthermore, two other studies using larger samples of baseball players reported contrary results (E.K. Wood, 1988;

➥

Anderson, 1989). The mean difference in the age of death of left- and right-handers in the Wood study was one month. In the Anderson study, there was a right-hand advantage for longevity for players born before 1890 but a left-hand advantage for players born later.

The next-of-kin study has been criticized for the use of post-mortem, subjective assessment of handedness. The accident-related injury indicated that the only category of accident showing a statistically significant difference between right- and left-handers was driving, and this finding was qualified by an interaction between sex and handedness: left-handed men reported more accidents. Beaton *et al.* (1994) found that the incidence of hand injury reported at an accident and emergency hospital unit was slightly higher for left- than for right-handers. It appears that when data from injury reports take ambidexterity (and not simply right- and left-handedness) into account, however, ambidexters report a greater number of accidents than right- or left-handed individuals (Daniel and Yeo, 1991).

Based on the available data, there is no clear answer to the question, do left-handers die sooner than right-handers? There are strong indications that left-handedness becomes less apparent in later years of life but whether this is attributable to mortality or modification is debatable.

Summary

☐ Hemispheric asymmetry refers to the degree to which one hemisphere may be dominant for a specific function such as language. Similar terms used interchangeably to describe the same phenomenon include laterality, hemispheric specialization, functional asymmetry and hemispheric dominance. If a function is said to be the responsibility of one hemisphere, that function is said to be lateralized.

☐ There is some evidence that humans are the only species to show consistent lateralization, neuroanatomically and behaviourally, at the population level. The most well known lateralized behaviour is hand preference.

☐ Human neuroanatomical asymmetries include two gyri (Heschl's gyri) in the right primary auditory cortex and one in the left in the majority of right-handed humans. The right is also doubled-over. The right hemisphere is larger and heavier than the left.

☐ The planum temporale, a structure in the Sylvian fissure posterior to the primary auditory cortex, is larger on the left than on the right. This may be involved in language. The Sylvian fissure is also longer in the left hemisphere. The asymmetries in the planum temporale and Sylvian fissure are present at birth.

☐ Galaburda (1995) has highlighted several problems associated with demonstrating consistent neuroanatomical asymmetry such as variability in the description of the exact position and length of Heschl's gyri and the Sylvian fissure.

☐ The cerebral hemispheres' functions have stereotypically been viewed as a dichotomy. The left hemisphere is verbal, analytic, rational and western-style in thought; the right is emotional, holistic, spatial, more eastern-style in thought. Although crude, the dichotomies are generally accurate.

☐ The most clearly lateralized higher function is language. All lateralization techniques show a left hemisphere superiority for the processing and production of various aspects of language, although the right hemisphere is capable of some linguistic processing and may be necessary for the appreciation of metaphors.

☐ Visuospatial ability is associated with right-hemisphere dominance. Visuospatial tests generally fall into two categories: those requiring spatial transformation (such as mental rotation) and those requiring an understanding of spatial relations. Different forms of the same types of task lead to inconsistencies in findings.

☐ Memory is a complex and dynamic process which is difficult to localize specifically in the human brain. Evidence from brain imaging studies and cases of human brain damage implicate the temporal lobes (especially the hippocampus and entorhinal cortex), the diencephalon (especially the thalamus and mammillary bodies) and the basal forebrain (especially the nucleus basalis of Meynert and the prefrontal cortex) in amnesia, the partial or total loss of memory.

☐ The left hemisphere appears to be more dominant in trained than in untrained musicians and appears to be more involved in processing analytic aspects of music even in musically naive subjects. Also, a larger planum temporale has been reported in musicians with perfect pitch when compared with non-musicians and musicians without perfect pitch.

☐ There are different types of mathematical disability that may follow regional brain lesions. These disorders are alexia for numbers (difficulty in

➠

reading numbers; left hemisphere lesions), agraphia for numbers (difficulty in writing numbers; left hemisphere lesions), spatial acalulia (difficulty in spatially representing numerical information; posterior right hemisphere lesions) and anarithmetria (difficulty in retrieving arithmetical information from long-term memory; posterior left hemisphere lesions).

☐ Individual differences which complicate the pattern of clear asymmetries include handedness and sex. Ninety per cent of the population is estimated to be right-handed. The measurement of handedness is problematic, however, because of the difficulty in constructing appropriate handedness questionnaires and tasks.

☐ Familial sinistrality (a history of left-handedness in the family) appears to be disadvantageous to visuospatial performance. Superiority for visuospatial tasks has been found in left-handers, whereas superiority for verbal tasks has been found in right-handers. Negative results have also been reported indicating that this difference may not be systematic.

☐ Spatial ability may be more lateralized in the right hemisphere in men than women. Men consistently outperform women on tests of mental rotation. Handedness also interacts with sex such that left-handed men may perform differently from right-handed men or left- or right-handed women.

☐ There is evidence of laterality in psychosis, with schizophrenia associated with overactivation, underactivation or dysfunctional left hemisphere activity. One possible neuroanatomical locus of schizophrenic difficulties is the left superior temporal gyrus.

☐ A number of theories have sought to explain why laterality exists. One theory explains the phenomenon in terms of superior evolution: the more sophisticated the task, the greater the hemispheric asymmetry observed. Another suggests that left-hemisphere speech is an extension of the left's motor control of the dominant, contralateral hand.

☐ The Geschwind–Galaburda model suggests that anomalous cerebral development is the result of disproportionate levels of testosterone. These levels influence the development of the left hemisphere. Delayed development, the model argues, results in immune disorders and neurodevelopmental disorders. The evidence for the model is weak, however, with the literature showing contrary or inconsistent findings.

☐ Some evidence suggests that the incidence of left-handedness declines in the population in later years. The reasons for this are unknown.

Recommended further general and specific reading

Key: (1) = introductory, *(3)* = intermediate, *(5)* = advanced

General

Corballis, M. (1991). *The Lopsided Ape.* New York: Oxford University Press. *(2)*

Davidson, R.J. and Hugdahl, K. (1995). *Brain Asymmetry.* Cambridge, MA: MIT Press. *(3)*

Hellige, J.B. (1993). *Hemispheric Asymmetry: What's right and what's left?* Cambridge, MA: Harvard University Press. *(3)*

Hugdahl, K. (1996). Brain laterality – beyond the basics. *European Psychologist*, **1**(3), 206–20. *(2)*

Iaccino, J. (1993). *Left Brain–Right Brain Differences: Inquiries, evidence and new approaches.* Hillsdale, NJ: Lawrence Erlbaum Associates. *(2)*

Springer, S.P. and Deutsch, G. (1993). *Left Brain, Right Brain* (4th edition). New York: Freeman. *(1)*

Specific

Beaton, A.A. (1997). The relation of planum temporale asymmetry and morphology of the corpus callosum to handedness, gender and dyslexia: a review of the evidence. *Brain and Language*, in press. *(3)*

Bishop, D.V.M. (1990). *Handedness and Developmental Disorder.* Oxford: Blackwell. *(3)*

Bottini, G., Corcoran, R., Sterzi, R., Paulesu, E., Schenone, P., Scarpa, P., Frackowiak, R.S.J. and Frith, C.D. (1994). The role of the right hemisphere in the interpretation of figurative aspects of language. *Brain*, **117**, 1241–53. *(3)*

Brain and Language (1997). Special issue. Current studies of right hemisphere function. *Brain and Language*, **57**(1). *(3)*

Bryden, M.P., McManus, I.C. and Bulman-Fleming, M.B. (1994). Evaluating the empirical support for the Geschwind–Behan–Galaburda model of cerebral lateralization. *Brain and Cognition*, **26**, 103–67. *(3)*

Casey, M.B. (1996). A reply to Halpern's commentary: Theory-driven methods for classifying groups can reveal individual differences in spatial ability within females. *Developmental Review*, **16**, 271–83. *(3)*

Geschwind, N. and Galaburda, A.M. (1985). Cerebral lateralization: biological mechanisms, associations and pathology. Parts I, II and III. *Archives of Neurology*, **42**, 428–59, 521–52, 634–54. *(4)*

Gur, R.C., Ragland, D.J., Mozley, L.H., Mozley, P.D., Smith, R., Alavi, A., Bilker, W. and Gur, R.E. (1997). Lateralized changes in regional cerebral blood flow during performance of verbal and facial recognition tasks: correlations with performance and 'effort'. *Brain and Cognition*, **33**, 388–414. *(2)*

Habib, M. (1989). Anatomical asymmetries of the human cerebral cortex. *International Journal of Neuroscience*, **47**, 67–79. *(3)*

Halpern, D.F. (1996). Sex, brains, hands and spatial cognition. *Developmental Review*, **16**, 261–70. *(2)*

Harris, L.J. (1993). Do left-handers die sooner than right-handers? Commentary on Coren and Halpern's (1991) 'Left-handedness: a marker for decreased survival fitness'. *Psychological Bulletin*, **114**(2), 203–34. *(2)*

Hiscock, M., Inch, R., Jacek, C., Hiscock-Kalil, C. and Kalil, K.M. (1994). Is there a sex difference in human laterality? I. An exhausitive survey of auditory laterality studies from six neuropsychological journals. *Journal of Clinical and Experimental Neuro-psychology*, **16**(3), 423–35. *(3)*

Kertesz, A. (1983). Issues in localization. In A. Kertesz (ed.), *Localization in Neuropsychology*. New York: Academic Press. *(3)*

Kimura, D. (1992). Sex differences in the brain. *Scientific American*, **267**(3), 81–95. *(2)*

Callosal syndromes

> Each hemisphere ... has its own ... private sensations, perceptions, thoughts, and ideas all of which are cut off from the corresponding experiences in the opposite hemisphere. Each left and right hemisphere has its own private chain of memories and learning experiences that are inaccessible to recall by the other hemisphere. In many respects each disconnected hemisphere appears to have a separate 'mind of its own.'
>
> (Sperry, 1974)

What is a callosal syndrome?

The direct neural associations between brain regions allow the brain to engage in the active and effective transfer of information from one region directly to another or simultaneously to a number of other sites. If these links are broken or obstructed, certain behavioural problems manifest themselves. Wernicke, for example, found that severing the connections between the posterior and anterior speech areas produced a type of speech disorder called conduction aphasia (for more on aphasia, see Chapter 9). When this happens, a **disconnection** is said to have occurred: the severance of neural connections between two brain areas which does not in itself damage those areas. The behavioural symptoms seen following such disconnections are called **disconnection syndromes**.

The most famous and astonishing example of brain disconnection is produced by **commissurotomy**. Here, the commissures connecting various brain structures are surgically severed for medical reasons. The largest of these commissures is the **corpus callosum** (CC), the mass of fiber connecting the two cerebral hemispheres. When this structure alone is severed, the procedure is called a **callosotomy**. Sometimes there is a partial split where only a certain region of the corpus callosum, for example the anterior half, is lesioned. When other commissural fibers such as the **anterior commissure**, the **dorsal** and **ventral hippocampal commissures** and the **basal telencephalic commissures** are also severed, the process is called **commissurotomy**.

When these commissures are severed, certain irregularities appear in the way that patients process information. These irregularities make up the **callosal syndromes**. The term is in the plural because lesions to different parts of the corpus callosum and damage to specific commissures produce different symptoms (these are reviewed later in the chapter). Although it is the most striking cause of a disconnection syndrome, the commissurotomy is not the only means by which transfer of information can be prevented. Diseases (e.g. thrombosis, tumour) can cause a partial disconnection between brain regions owing to lesions to the corpus callosum.

One of the earliest reported cases of a split-brain was that reported by Dejerine (1892). This patient had a left occipital infarct and a minor lesion to the posterior part of the corpus callosum. Puzzlingly, he could write but could not read and could name objects and numbers but could not name a single letter. This unusual presentation of behaviours is discussed in the section on symptoms. Another fascinating phenomenon is that of **callosal agenesis**, the congenital absence of parts or all of the corpus callosum. More fascinating still, these individuals do not show the same behavioural irregularities as commissurotomized patients.

Commissurotomy: a brief history

Early evidence indicated that epileptic seizures made their way from one hemisphere to the other in monkeys via the corpus callosum (Erickson, 1940). Later that decade, surgical procedures were undertaken to sever the human commissures in order to relieve the symptoms of epilepsy. The outcome, however, was variable, with some patients showing no improvement. Soon after the mixed effects of the surgery became known, the behavioural significance of the corpus callosum was questioned. In fact, McCulloch (1949) mused that the corpus callosum was there to allow the spread of epileptic seizures whereas Lashley (1951), perhaps tongue-in cheek, proposed that the structure existed to prevent the two hemispheres from sagging.

It was the later work of Myers and Sperry and their colleagues in the late 1950s, however, which prompted a re-evaluation of the role of the commissures in behaviour. In their famous experiments with cats, visual information that was presented to one cerebral hemisphere appeared to be unavailable to the other (Myers, 1956; Myers and Sperry, 1958). For example, cats taught a visual discrimination task with one eye covered were able to perform a discrimination task using either eye. When the corpus callosum and optic chiasm were severed, however, the cat trained with one eye open could perform the task with that eye, but when a patch was placed on the open eye and the occluded eye was opened, the cat was unable to do so. The authors concluded that sectioning the corpus callosum had prevented the transfer of information between the two hemispheres. In the 1960s, a series of human split-brain operations was undertaken by Vogel and Joseph Bogen at White Memorial Hospital in Los Angeles, California, in order to alleviate the symptoms of epilepsy. The corpus callosum, the anterior commissure and hippocampal commissure were all severed during surgery. The results of these operations provided an unusual insight into the way that the two cerebral hemispheres processed and integrated information because they appeared to indicate that information made available to one cerebral hemisphere could not be accessed by the other, just as was seen in Sperry's cats. A discussion of this phenomenon and the behavioural effects of split-brain surgery can be found later in this chapter.

▪ Corpus callosum

The corpus callosum is the largest nerve fiber tract connecting neocortical areas and contains around 200 million to 800 million fibers. It seems to appear only in placental mammals, becomes evident only in the fourth month of gestation and myelinates slowly. It is conventionally divided into regions called (from front to back) the **rostrum, genu, body** and **splenium**, illustrated by Figures 5.1 and 5.2.

It is common for callosal fibers to connect homologous regions, that is, regions from one hemisphere are connected to similarly situated regions in the other hemisphere, although connections to non-homologous regions are found. The rostrum and genu make up the anterior end and connect the prefrontal areas (Pandya and Selztzer, 1986). The areas just posterior to the genu connect the superior frontal area and motor area respectively. The posterior midbody of the corpus callosum connects the somatosensory areas. More caudal regions connect the temporal–parietal–occipital areas. Sometimes, however, the somatosensory fibers and the auditory fibers may be intermixed. The splenium, the bulbous posterior one-fifth of the callosum, connects the occipital and anterior temporal regions relevant to vision and has tremendous variability in size and shape. These demarcations have been based on work with macaque monkeys (e.g. Rockland and Pandya, 1986; Pandya and Selztzer, 1986). The picture is slightly different in humans. Axonal diameter, for example, appears to be largest in the middle of the corpus callosum in macaques (Lamantia and Rakic, 1990) whereas in humans, the largest fibers appear more caudally, posterior to the midbody (Aboitiz *et al.*,

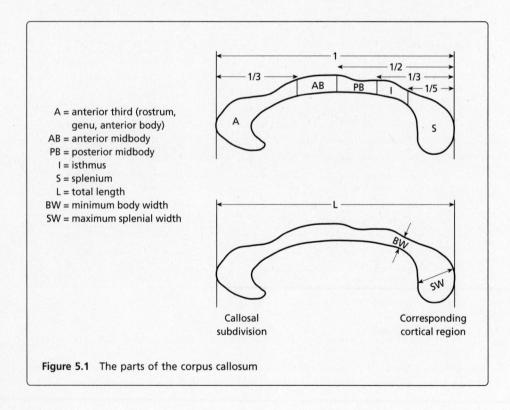

A = anterior third (rostrum, genu, anterior body)
AB = anterior midbody
PB = posterior midbody
I = isthmus
S = splenium
L = total length
BW = minimum body width
SW = maximum splenial width

Callosal subdivision

Corresponding cortical region

Figure 5.1   The parts of the corpus callosum

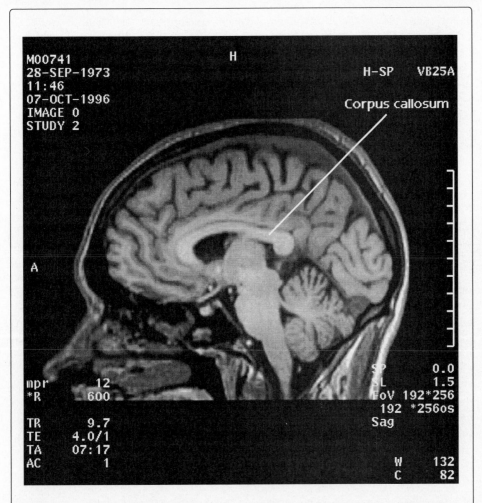

MOO741
28-SEP-1973
11:46
07-OCT-1996
IMAGE 0
STUDY 2

H

H-SP   VB25A

Corpus callosum

A

mpr   12
*R   600

TR   9.7
TE   4.0/1
TA   07:17
AC   1

SP   0.0
SL   1.5
FoV 192*256
192 *256os
Sag

W   132
C   82

Figure 5.2 Sagittal view of an MRI scan of a living human brain showing the white band of fibers called the corpus callosum

1992a). However, the pathways of these general callosal channels are similar in both species.

It appears that the larger the size of the corpus callosum, the larger the number of fibers contained within it (Machiyama *et al.* 1987) although actual callosal connections may be limited (Kennedy *et al.*, 1991). Group differences in the size of the corpus callosum have also been reported. One of the earliest groups to be examined was mixed- and right-handers. Because of the organization of the language areas in these two groups, it was suggested that the corpus callosum was involved in the localization of language in individuals with bilateral language. Early studies found significant differences between the size of the corpus callosum in right- and mixed-handers: Witelson (1985), for example, reported that the corpus callosum was 11 per cent larger in a group of 15 mixed handers than in a group of 17 right-handers, even when cerebral weight and sex had been taken into account. The posterior of the corpus callasum was found to be 19 per cent larger in right-handers (Witelson, 1986). The isthmus, the posterior one-third minus the posterior one fifth, was found to be larger in non-consistent than consistent right-handed men, with no effect of handedness found for women (Witelson, 1989).

Similar findings have been reported elsewhere (Habib *et al.*, 1991). Confusingly, however, other studies have reported contradictory findings. Steinmetz *et al.* (1992), for example, found no interaction between sex and handedness but did find that women had a larger isthmus than men. Perhaps this sex difference is more specific. For example, Aboitiz *et al.* (1992a) reported a significant correlation between (1) a larger number of fibers in the isthmus in men and anterior splenium in women, and (2) smaller planum temporale asymmetries in both men and women, although a separate study by the same group found a correlation but for men only (Aboitiz *et al.*, 1992b). It should be noted that many early studies, which normally used gross volume or size measures, reported no consistent sex differences (e.g. Bean, 1906; Lacoste-Utamsing and Holloway, 1982; Witelson, 1985). At more specific levels, such as the anterior corpus callosum or splenium, differences did emerge, with men having a larger anterior area than women (Bean, 1906; although Witelson's 1985 study found no difference), and women having a significantly wider splenium (Holloway and Lacoste, 1986). Given the variety of findings in the individual differences literature, however, the relative importance of the significant differences cannot be properly assessed. Furthermore, because many of the findings are contradictory, there is always the possibility that significant studies are reporting artefacts and not genuine differences.

■ Characteristics of split-brain patients

Split-brain patients have normal postsurgery intelligence, personality and general behaviour. In the first few days after surgery, however, they appear to have difficulty in following complex multiple commands, although each *individual* command is understood. Patients are often mute (Bogen, 1976) and have difficulty using the left hand or arm in response to a command (the right limb performs fairly normally). The older the subject the more severe these postoperative phenomena (Lasonde *et al.*, 1991). After a few months, patients perform at a normal intellectual and social level but aspects of their behaviour are irregular and patients behave as if each of their hemispheres acts independently of the other when the patient is required to complete tests designed to examine the effectiveness of communication between the two halves of the split brain. In their extensive review of interhemispheric function, Hoptman and Davidson (1994) concluded that 'all the evidence suggests that the corpus callosum plays a significant role in high-level attentional and cognitive functions'. Generally, the patients behave as if some stimuli are inaccessible to one or other hemisphere. The most obvious examples of this are seen in experiments where objects (or names of objects) cannot be named when held by one hand (or seen in a particular hemifield).

Somatosensory effects

One of the clearest examples of the hemispheres' inability to interact effectively occurs when the split-brain patient fails to retrieve with one hand an object handled by another. For example, an unseen object can be held by the right hand and identified; an object handled (or palpated) in the left hand, however, cannot be identified. Yet, when the patient is allowed to select the object from an array of objects, the left hand selects the correct object. This is sometimes called unilateral left tactile anomia or hemialexia and a diagnosis of asterognosis or tactile agnosia (see Chapter 7) has to be ruled out before the behaviour is so described.

Visual effects

The commissurotomized patient is also unable to read or identify stimuli presented in the left visual field but can identify the same stimuli presented in the right visual field. Sometimes the patient reports 'seeing nothing' or having seen a 'flash of light' (Bogen, 1993). This phenomenon is reported after complete callosotomy but can also occur with splenium lesions (Gazzaniga and Freedman, 1973; Damasio et al., 1980a). In a typical experiment, the patient is required to fixate on a black dot while a picture of an object (a cup, for example) is flashed briefly (100–200 ms) to the right of the dot via a tachistoscope. The patient is asked to name the object and is able to do this. The patient then fixates on the dot again while a picture of a different object (a spoon) is flashed to the left of the dot. The patient is asked to identify the object but is unable to and reports seeing 'nothing.' When allowed to select the object just seen, by touch alone, from a selection of objects, the patient's left hand chooses the spoon. When asked to identify the object, the patient replies, 'spoon.'

In a similar experiment, the patient focuses on a fixation spot while a picture of a naked woman is presented to the left of it. She giggles but reports having seen nothing, 'just a flash of light'. These responses were made by a female patient, NG, one of several split-brain patients studied by Sperry and his colleagues (Gazzaniga, et al., 1962; Sperry, 1968; Sperry et al., 1969). Although the patient can see and identify stimuli presented in the right visual field (information going to the left hemisphere), material presented to the left visual field also appears to be 'seen' because the patient giggles when the naked woman is presented and correctly identifies the object presented in the left visual field when allowed to select it from a group of objects. Two possible explanations for this phenomenon might be that the patient may not be able to provide the object with a verbal label or she may not have been consciously aware of the object being presented. This type of anomia is not exclusive to the visual domain and is present even for olfactory stimuli. For example, commissurotomized patients are unable to identify odours presented to the right nostril but can identify those presented to the left nostril, despite having no lesions to the olfactory apparatus (Gordon and Sperry, 1969). The pathway from nostril to hemisphere is ipsilateral (unlike many of the other senses') so that an odour presented to the left nostril is processed by the left hemisphere.

When images of arcs are presented to the right hemisphere and the patient's task is to indicate which differently sized circles would be made up of the arcs, patients perform significantly better than when stimuli are presented to the left hemisphere (Nebes, 1978). This indicates that the perception of part/whole relations appears to be better in the right hemisphere of commissurotomized patients. Similarly, Franco and Sperry (1977) found that the right hemisphere was better at matching touched, unseen objects with geometric shapes presented in free vision: a superiority which increased as the shapes became less geometric and more free-form. The split-brain patient also appears to see whole figures or shapes when there are in fact different or fractured shapes. Patient NG was presented with a chimeric face (where each half of the face is made from a different face) and instructed to name the right as Dick and the left as Tom. When the chimera was presented to her and she was asked which face she saw, she indicated Dick. When asked to identify the face by pointing with either hand to a series of faces, she identified Tom (Levy *et al.*, 1972).

Apraxia

The earliest documented symptom of commissurotomy was the inability to follow commands to move with the left limb. This disorder, regardless of the side affected, is called apraxia and is described in more detail in Chapter 8. Commissurotomized patients have difficulty following commands to make a fist or wriggle fingers with the left hand (the right performs these normally), probably because the ipsilateral control of this limb by the left hemisphere is poor or because the right hemisphere is poor at comprehending the instructions. Therefore, it is important to be able to rule out poor comprehension ability, limb weakness and lack of coordination. There is some variability among individuals concerning the ipsilateral control of the hands. There is sometimes an inability to write with the left hand. This is called agraphia and is described in Chapter 9.

A symptom related to limb apraxia is the inability to copy or draw an image in its entirety. This is called constructional apraxia and is seen in the right hand of the right-handed split-brain patient.

Auditory effects

When split-brain patients undertake a dichotic listening task, there is a massive (almost complete) right ear advantage. It was suggested earlier that a right ear advantage for reporting words presented simultaneously to two ears may be because ipsilateral pathways from the left ear are suppressed by simultaneous but different inputs (Kimura, 1967). In split-brain patients, the pathway conveying information from the left ear to the left and right hemispheres is impaired because the callosal pathway has been severed. However, when patients are repeatedly tested on this task, symmetry is increased, which indicates that the left ear's pathways are capable of some effective transmission of information or that practice is exerting a positive effect on the results.

Intermanual conflict

Sometimes in split-brain patients, the hands appear to behave in a contradictory manner – there is intermanual conflict. For example, one patient was observed doing up the buttons on a shirt with one hand and undoing the buttons with the other (Akelaitis, 1944/45). A similar phenomenon is illustrated by a patient who selected one neck-tie with one hand but a different tie with the other.

Alien hand

A related, but different, symptom is *la main étrangère* or alien hand (Brion and Jedynak, 1972). Here, the patient believes that one of his or her hands (usually the left) is behaving in an odd, uncooperative or alien way. The patient may even castigate the hand for behaving in a peculiar way. One reason why the alien hand phenomenon occurs, suggests Della Salla and his colleagues, is that the inhibition of actions organized elsewhere, but which originates in the frontal cortex, is lost (Della Salla *et al.*, 1991).

Attention

Split-brain patients have difficulty on divided attention tasks in which they are asked to complete concurrent verbal and tapping exercises (Kreuter *et al.*, 1972). They also show poor ability to maintain visual vigilance (Dimond, 1976). The reason for this lack of attention is unclear.

Compensatory actions

In order to try to circumvent the problems brought about by these symptoms, commissurotomized patients sometimes adopt compensatory strategies which help them to perform better. For example, if they are unable to name a handled object such as a comb, they may run their fingers along its teeth which produces a noise picked up by both hemispheres. Smell is another factor which can be used in compensation. There is also evidence of significant recovery in commissurotomized patients. Gazzaniga's patient, JW, for example, was able to identify 25 per cent of stimuli in the left visual field fourteen years after surgery. One year later, this patient was able to identify 60 per cent (Gazzaniga *et al.*, 1996).|Explanations for these types of recovery suggest either that the right hemisphere is gradually acquiring speech or that information may be being conveyed from one hemisphere to another via unsevered commissures| Gazzaniga and Hillyard (1971), however, had an alternative explanation. They argued that patients used whatever cues were available to them in order to identify an object (as in the comb example above). This was called **cross-cueing**. The recovery seen in JW, however, is unlikely to have resulted from cross-cueing and, as the authors suggest, is more likely to be due to some form of transfer of information between the two hemispheres.

■ Interhemispheric transfer: callosal channels?

Although the commissurotomized patient suffers massive loss of tissue connecting the two halves of his or her brain, not all connections between the hemispheres are lost. There are still connections from other brain structures such as the cerebellum, pons and hypothalamus, i.e. the subcortical connections are still intact. Similarly, the split-brain operation sometimes involves a partial split where only parts of the corpus callosum are severed or where some of the other, smaller commissures are spared. This situation raises the possibility that some transfer of information may be possible because of the spared tissue (this is the subject of the discussion point at the end of the chapter). If information is transferred from one hemisphere to another via these commissures, what form of neural organization makes this possible?

It has been argued that what these connections provide is a series of callosal channels which convey specific types of information from one region in one hemisphere to an homologous site in another. For example, when the head of the splenium is lesioned, unilateral left anomia and apraxia occur although the transfer of visual information is fairly normal (Risse *et al.*, 1989). When the splenium and isthmus are spared, no anomia or apraxia occurs. When the splenium is completely lesioned, the transfer of visual information does not occur (Bentin *et al.*, 1984). A patient with posterior sectioning of the corpus callosum was unable to name words presented in the left visual field but was able, with the experimenter's assistance, to make associations to objects presented to the left visual field (Sidtis *et al.*, 1981). Perhaps this performance was regulated by the left hemisphere's access to some semantic network in the right hemisphere which could be accessed via the anterior corpus callosum. It has been found, for example, that there is a significant correlation between verbal fluency and the size of the anterior callosal area in female patients with multiple sclerosis, who had demyelating lesions of the corpus callosum and smaller anterior and posterior callosal areas than did controls (Pozzilli *et al.*, 1991). Negative results have been reported, however, with some studies showing no relationship between the anterior part of the corpus callosum and transfer of semantic information (e.g. Hines *et al.*, 1992).

Lesions to the genu and anterior half in fact result in very few symptoms, although there may be impairments in areas such as hearing and somatosensation. These structures appear to be relatively unimportant for attention because patients with anterior corpus callosum and anterior commissure lesions are able to sustain visual monitoring for up to 30 minutes. A complete commissurotomy, however, is associated with impairments in visual vigilance after only 10 minutes (Dimond, 1976).

Based on these observations, Levy, Trevarthen, Banich and others have proposed that the corpus callosum provides a means whereby information can be transferred either via direct channels or via a hemisphere that assumes the dominant information processing role.

■ Models of interhemispheric transfer

The integration of information from two regions is assumed to occur either directly or indirectly. For example, a **direct transfer** route sends information directly from one region to another. This assumes some form of duplication of information because the information sent by one region is the same as that received by another. An alternative view would be to argue that information received by two or more regions is then sent to a third area. In this way, the two areas do not directly share information but send it to a common source. This has been called **third party convergence** (Goldman-Rakic, 1988). A further alternative would be to suggest that information is sent from two regions but this time is sent on to several different regions. In this model, **non-convergent temporal integration**, there is no grand convergence zone where all projections meet – a very similar phenomenon to that seen in the visual system where there are two distinct, independent neural pathways. There are examples of all of these types of inter- and intra-hemispheric connections in the brain.

Levy and Trevarthen's metacontrol

In an early study of four commissurotomized patients, Levy and Trevarthen (1976) found that the hemisphere that was assumed to be superior for a specific function was not always the hemisphere that undertook that function. More generally, the hemisphere taking control was not always the one with the greatest ability. They called the mechanism underlying this, **metacontrol**: 'the neural mechanisms that determine which hemisphere will attempt to control cognitive operations'. They distinguished between hemispheric ability (the degree of success that a hemisphere showed in performing a task) and hemispheric dominance (the degree to which one hemisphere takes control). This mechanism, argued Levy and Trevarthen, might explain how the two cerebral hemispheres behave when the same information is available to both hemispheres, and suggests that one hemisphere's mode of control will dominate behaviour.

Joseph Hellige, at the University of California, has made an attempt at establishing whether metacontrol may also occur in neurologically intact individuals (Hellige, 1991). In a series of experiments, he and his colleagues found that the left hemisphere was the dominant hemisphere for some but not all tasks when information was available to both hemispheres (Hellige *et al.*, 1989; Hellige and Michimata, 1989). Furthermore, as predicted from Levy and Trevarthen's data, the dominant hemisphere was not always the hemisphere specialized for undertaking the task.

Banich's model of interhemispheric processing

Banich's (1995) model also attempts to explain interhemispheric transfer in terms of metacontrol and proposes that:

1. The transfer of information occurs via channels provided by the corpus callosum and subcortical commissures.
2. The hemispheres interact but that only one assumes a dominant role in this interaction.
3. Callosal channels allow for more efficient processing of complex information than would one hemisphere alone.

The model suggests that two types of information do not require transfer: emotional information and aspects of spatial attention. The findings, including those of Hellige, suggest that the types of interhemispheric transfer possible are many.

For example, in an experiment in which the subject was presented with two numbers either to the left visual field (LVF), the right visual field (RVF) or both and was required to indicate whether either number was less than a previously presented target number, LVF trials showed no significant difference between the speed of responding yes or no (Banich, 1995). However, reaction times for the RVF were significantly different (yes was faster), a finding repeated when the stimuli were presented bilaterally. On some trials, regardless of whether the two numbers were identical (e.g. target of 12 followed by 17, 17) or not (e.g. target of 12 followed by 17, 14), both were larger than the target number. Banich and her colleagues found that bilateral trials were similar to the LVF trials but dissimilar to the RVF trials. Responses were significantly faster in the RVF for the same digit/same decision trials than the different digit/same decision trials. What appears unclear, however, is which factors influence the similarity (or dissimilarity) between interhemispheric processing and single-hemisphere processing.

Cook's model of corpus callosum function

Cook's model of corpus callosum function suggests that the corpus callosum serves to inhibit neural activity topographically (Cook, 1984a,b). That is, inhibition in the corpus callosum suppresses the same pattern of neuronal activity in one hemisphere that had originated in the other. The structure does not, however, inhibit neural activity in surrounding areas (which may relate to the function performed). Thus neurons in the left hemisphere may respond to a specific word (e.g. 'spoon') but inhibition by the corpus callosum prevents the right hemisphere from accessing the information. However, the surrounding excitation allows the transfer of semantic information related to that object. Therefore, information such as eating, fork, soup would still be accessed. Woodward (1988), however, suggests that processing in the left hemisphere relies on connections between strong vertical neuronal columns whereas the right hemisphere relies on weaker, horizontal connections. The corpus callosum inhibits vertical neurons thus allowing horizontal connections to be utilized. There is no evidence of this occurring between the hemispheres, although it is feasible that one type of neuronal circuitry may be more greatly utilized in one hemisphere than the other. Both Woodward's and Cooks models propose some form of inhibition and both suggest that the pattern of activity in one hemisphere is suppressed in the other by the corpus callosum. Evidence for both, however, is weak.

■ Split and intact brains: clues to localization of function?

Split-brain patients provide investigators with an astonishing population of subjects and they have contributed a great deal to our knowledge of functional asymmetry and of the functions of the corpus callosum. These data appear to confirm many of the observations made in the study of localization of normal brains, such as left hemisphere superiority for language, right hemisphere advantage for non-verbal tasks. However, split-brain data, by their nature, are questionable. Patients have, after all, experienced severe neurological problems prior to surgery, a fact that must always be recognized before making inferences about normal brain processes. Models of function such as Levy and Trevarthen's metacontrol, however, are beginning to be applied to the normal, intact brain with some success. Without the extraordinary behavioural phenomena observed in commissurotomized patients, such advances would have been much slower.

DISCUSSION POINT

Can the hemispheres of a split-brain patient still transfer information?

The evidence considered in the chapter so far indicates that interhemispheric transfer of information in split-brain patients is, if not absent, then difficult to achieve. However, we have also seen how cortical lesions do not affect the functioning of subcortical connections. These remaining fibers can still allow one hemisphere to communicate with the other. Trevarthen (1987) suggested that the other hemisphere's access to information was implicit, i.e. unconscious, and not explicit, i.e. conscious.

In a series of extensive studies with split-brain patients, Sergent (1987, 1990, 1991) has suggested that even complex information can be transferred interhemispherically in split-brain patients. For example, she found that when two stimuli were presented to both hemifields and the patient was required to decide whether (1) two lines formed a broken or a single line, (2) the angle made by two arrows was greater or less than 90 degrees when combined, (3) the total number of dots presented bilaterally was odd or even, (4) the sum of two digits was less or greater than ten, or (5) a four-letter string (two letters to each hemifield) formed a word, patients were able to make correct decisions (Sergent, 1987). When asked to describe the arrows or name the letters presented, however, the patients could not make a correct response. A follow-up study demonstrated similar interhemispheric communication ability (Sergent, 1991). In these experiments, patients were required to indicate which of two circles, one presented to each hemifield, was the bigger and to decide which of two oblique lines was closest to a vertical line. In the first task, two out of the three split-brain patients tested gave the correct answer. In the second task, one out of the two patients tested made the correct decision. When the task required both decisions to be made in the same task, none of the patients made a correct answer.

Recently, doubt has been cast on the reliability of Sergent's findings. Corballis and Trudel (1993), for example, found that only one of their two split-brain patients performed above chance level using a larger set of stimuli than Sergent's. Similarly, Seymour *et al.* (1994) have published new data suggesting that the corpus callosum is critical for the transfer of sensory and high-level information. For example, they draw attention to the fact that studies in which a successful transfer of information is reported have done so using a small group of split-brain patients, specifically patients LB and NG. These authors also question of the completeness of the callosal section in one of these patients (LB). This patient showed evidence of small patches of substance in the splenium during the testing undertaken by Sergent (1987) although a more recent MRI scan indicates complete section. Also, this patient's behaviour is similar to that of control subjects (Lambert, 1991). Because of this, Seymour *et al.* argue, LB is not very representative of split-brain patients. In their study, a series of four experiments were undertaken by three patients (JW, VP and DR). These tasks were similar to those used by Sergent, although not all of Seymour *et al.*'s patients participated in each of the experiments. Two of the patients performed below chance levels on these tasks, indicating that no interhemispheric communication occurred. VP, however, who had some sparing of callosal fibers, showed some evidence of interhemispheric transfer.

Based on this evidence, Seymour *et al.* argue that the pattern of behavioural symptoms that characterizes callosal disconnection will emerge if patients have callosal lesions. Sparing of parts of the callosum will produce evidence of interhemispheric transfer (as seen in VP, the patient who had spared fibers in the rostrum and splenium). Also, JW, VP and DR had spared anterior commissures which suggests that this channel may not have been effective in allowing the transmission of information. Given that one of the hypotheses regarding callosal genesis patients' accurate performance on disconnection tests argues that performance occurs because of intact anterior commissures, this is particularly relevant. It must be noted, however, that all split-brain patients show considerable interindividual differences. Patient DR, for example, had her callosum sectioned seven years prior to testing. Both the other patients had undergone callosotomy thirteen years prior to testing. One patient was male (JW), the others were female (DR, VP). Similarly, some of the procedures in Seymour *et al.*'s study showed irregularities. For example, not all patients undertook the same number of trials, and as mentioned above, some experiments included only one participant. As with all split-brain studies, conclusions have to be drawn circumspectly.

Summary

☐ Callosal syndrome is a term used to describe the behavioural symptoms presented following severance of the corpus callosum. The surgical section is normally undertaken to alleviate the symptoms of intractable epilepsy. A disconnection syndrome describes the behavioural symptoms which follow the disconnection of pathways between two brain regions.

☐ Fibers which connect regions of one hemisphere with regions of another are called commissures. When the corpus callosum, a largest commissure connecting the two hemispheres, is severed, the surgery is called a callosotomy. When other commissures as well as the corpus callosum are severed, the procedure is called a commissurotomy. Individuals who have undergone this surgery are commonly described as split-brain patients.

☐ Early studies with animals had suggested that severing the corpus callosum prevented the transfer of information from one hemisphere to another.

☐ The corpus callosum contains around 200 million to 800 million fibers and is made up of four distinct areas: the rostrum, genu, body and splenium.

☐ The rostrum and genu connect homologous regions of the prefrontal cortex; parts posterior to the genu connect the superior frontal area and the motor area; the midbody connects the somatosensory areas; and the splenium connects the temporal and occipital areas.

☐ Differences in the size and weight of these parts have been reported between men and women and between right-, left- and mixed-handers. Evidence is inconsistent and contradictory, however.

☐ Split-brain patients have normal postoperative intelligence and personality. However, they have difficulty following simple commands using the left hand, are mute and demonstrate some unusual behaviours under laboratory conditions. These behaviours are somatosensory, visual, apraxic, auditory, attentional and compensatory in nature.

☐ Patients are unable to name an object held and palpated by the left hand although they can with the right hand. They are unable to read or identify stimuli presented to the left visual field, but can do so when stimuli are presented to the right visual field. There is apraxia in these patients: they are unable to follow simple commands which require the use of the left hand (if the patient is right-handed). Commissurotomized individuals have a massive right ear advantage on dichotic listening tasks. There may ⇒

be intermanual conflict, with one hand performing one action and the other performing a contradictory movement, or the patient may believe that his or her hand is behaving in an alien way. Patients have difficulty on divided attention tasks but show evidence of employing compensatory strategies when faced with difficult tasks. For example, they may use clues from other sensory modalities to identify stimuli. This is called cross-cueing.

☐ The symptoms following commissurotomy suggest that the corpus callosum is the structure which provides channels via which information can be transferred from one hemisphere to the other. Evidence for this comes from studies in which damage to specific areas of the corpus callosum inhibits the transfer of specific types of information (e.g. the lesioning of the splenium results in a failure to transfer visual information).

☐ Transfer of information may occur either directly between one region and another, or indirectly, where two regions project to a common target area. A third possibility is where two areas project to two different areas which project to two other, different areas.

☐ Levy and Trevarthen's notion of metacontrol suggests that the hemisphere that is dominant for a function is not always the hemisphere that undertakes that function. There is some evidence for this from commissurotomized patients and normal individuals.

☐ Although split-brain patients' data provide a unique source of behavioural information, these individuals are not ideal subjects given their neurological condition and their preoperative condition.

☐ Controversy surrounds the idea that split-brain patients can transfer high-level information. Recent studies indicate that commissurotomized patients can perform well on tasks which make bilateral demands on the patients, perhaps owing to spared subcortical commissures. However, studies in which patients with spared subcortical commissures were examined show the typical disconnection syndrome.

Recommended further general and specific reading

Key: (1) = introductory, *(3)* = intermediate, *(5)* = advanced

General
Bogen, J.E. (1993). The callosal syndromes. In K.M. Heilman and E. Valenstein (eds), *Clinical Neuropsychology* (3rd edition). New York: Oxford University Press. *(3)*

Gazzaniga, M.S., Bogen, J.E. and Sperry, R.W. (1962). Some functional effects of sectioning the cerebral commissures in man. *Proceedings of the National Academy of Sciences*, **48**, 1765–9. *(3)*

Lepore, F., Ptito, M. and Jasper, H.H. (1986). *Two Hemispheres – One Brain: Functions of the corpus callosum*. New York: Alan R. Liss. *(3)*

Nebes, R. (1990). *Handbook of Neurology*, volume 4, *The Commissurotomized Brain*. New York: Elsevier. *(3)*

Specific

Banich, M.T. (1995). Interhemispheric processing: theoretical considerations and empirical approaches. In R.J. Davidson and K. Hugdahl (eds), *Brain Asymmetry*. Cambridge, MA: MIT Press. *(4)*

Hellige, J.B. (1991). Cerebral laterality and metacontrol. In F.L. Kitterle (ed.), *Cerebral Laterality: Theory and research*. Hillsdale, NJ: Lawrence Erlbaum Associates. *(3)*

Hoptman, M.J. and Davidson, R.J. (1994). How and why do the two cerebral hemispheres interact? *Psychological Bulletin*, **116**(2), 195–219. *(3)*

Lasonde, M. and Jeeves, M.A. (1994). *Callosal Agenesis: A natural split-brain?* New York: Plenum Press. *(4)*

Liederman, J. (1995). A reinterpretation of the split-brain syndrome: implications for the function of corticocortical fibres. In R.J. Davidson and K. Hugdahl (eds), *Brain Asymmetry*. Cambridge, MA: MIT Press. *(4)*

Sergent, J. (1987). A new look at the human split brain. *Brain*, **110**, 1375–92. *(3)*

Seymour, S.E., Reuter-Lorenz, P.A. and Gazzaniga, M.S. (1994). The disconnection syndrome: basic findings reaffirmed. *Brain*, **117**, 105–15 *(4)*.

Zaidel, E. (1995). Interhemispheric transfer in the split brain: long-term status following complete cerebral commissurotomy. In R.J. Davidson and K. Hugdahl (eds), *Brain Asymmetry*. Cambridge, MA: MIT Press. *(4)*

Chapter Six

The frontal lobes: cognition, social behaviour and personality

■ Frontal lobes: a brief review

No two human brains are exactly alike in structure, yet all normal, healthy human brains share the same gross characteristics. The central sulcus, the lateral sulcus and other major sulci divide the hemispheres into occipital, parietal, temporal and frontal lobes. The conventional demarcation of the brain into four lobes is not based on actual functional or structural characteristics but on the brain's gross appearance, conveniently divided by the sulci, and the area of skull overlying them. Neurogeographically, the frontal lobes occupy the region found above the lateral sulcus and in front of the central sulcus, the parietal lobes occupy the region anterior to the central sulcus and inferior to the lateral fissure, the occipital lobes occupy the area at the back of the brain bordered by the parietal and temporal lobe, and the temporal lobes themselves occupy the area below the lateral sulcus. See Figure 6.1.

Each lobe appears to be responsible for discrete aspects of behaviour. The occipital lobe, as we discussed in Chapter 2, contains Area 17 (the primary visual cortex) and the association visual cortex. The temporal cortex contains the primary auditory cortex and association cortex. The parietal cortex contains the motor cortex (Area 4), and areas concerning aspects of somatosensation, such as touch and temperature. The frontal lobes, however, are the structures which (1) mediate the ability to engage in abstract thought, (2) organize behaviour in logical sequence and in temporal order, and (3) inhibit responses to the environment. In summary, the frontal lobes have been regarded as the cortical locus of 'higher learning' and sometimes, rather mysteriously, as the structures which define the self (K. Goldstein, 1936; Halstead, 1947). The specific portion of the frontal lobes responsible for maintaining these cognitive behaviours is known as the **prefrontal cortex**. According to Luria (1973), the prefrontal cortex is essential for planning, making goals, and regulating and verifying behaviour – processes collectively known as **executive functions**. It also has a part to play in regulating social behaviour and personality.

Studies of the brain and its relation to personality are problematic, however. Changes in personality are often cited after frontal cortex damage, although quantifying personality is more of a problem, despite attempts by neuropsychologists to do so (Stuss et al., 1992). Another important consideration is that many

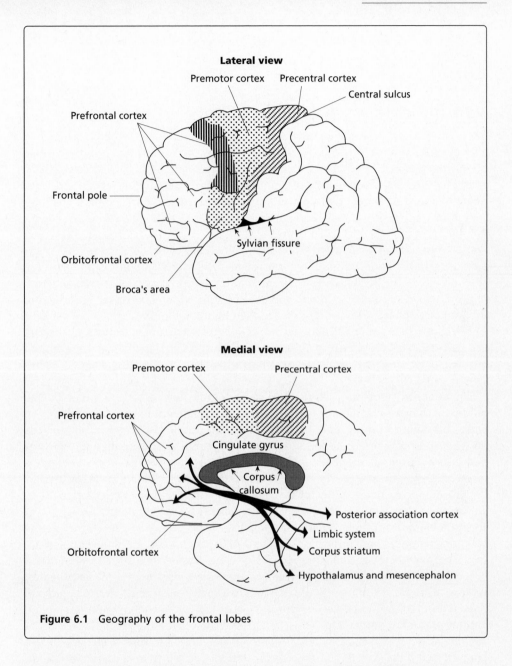

Lateral view

Premotor cortex   Precentral cortex

Central sulcus

Prefrontal cortex

Frontal pole

Sylvian fissure

Orbitofrontal cortex

Broca's area

Medial view

Premotor cortex   Precentral cortex

Prefrontal cortex

Cingulate gyrus

Corpus callosum

Posterior association cortex

Limbic system

Orbitofrontal cortex   Corpus striatum

Hypothalamus and mesencephalon

Figure 6.1   Geography of the frontal lobes

forms of brain damage can and do affect personality, if by personality we mean the cognitions, feelings, movements and perceptions that define ourselves and which are unique to us. The changes brought about by the involvement of the frontal lobes may, therefore, be one of degree and may be related to the architecture of this structure and its connections with a vast number of other important areas of the cortex. This topic is returned to a little later.

▣ Frontal lobes: an anatomical sketch

The frontal lobes are the most recently developed of the four lobes and comprise about one-third of the cerebral cortex (Goldman-Rakic, 1987). Brodmann (1909) identified thirteen anatomically distinct areas in this region and several areas are anatomically and functionally distinguishable within it. They comprise the pre-motor area, including (Area 6 and part of Area 8), the prefrontal area (Areas 9, 10, 45, 46) and the precentral/basomedial area (Areas 9, 10, 11, 12, 13, 24, 32) which contains the motor cortex. Just in front of this area are several other important frontal regions including the premotor region which contains the supplementary motor area or MII (Brinkman and Porter, 1983), the frontal eye field (Area 8) which controls aspects of eye movement, and Broca's area, which controls the production of voluntary speech. The head of the frontal lobes is the prefrontal region, the part of the cortex thought to be involved in the maintenance and execution of abstract thought and reasoning. This is often subdivided into two regions: the orbitofrontal cortex (sometimes used synonymously with ventromedial cortex) and the dorso-lateral region.

The complexity of the frontal lobes is such that they seem to impinge on the whole repertoire of behaviour – from motor movement and movement planning to social behaviour and personality. It is the brain's 'orchestra leader', directing the activity of other sensory, motor and cognitive systems and coordinating inputs to and outputs from all the major association sensory areas of the cortex as well as areas of the limbic system. This involvement of the frontal lobes in many aspects of behaviour is reflected in the region's massive connections with other brain areas. According to Luria (1973), 'the functional organization of the frontal lobes is one of the most complex problems in modern science'. The primary somatosensory cortex (SI), for example, sends projections to the primary motor area (MI), the supplemen-tary motor area, certain gustatory regions near the frontal lobe and the somatosen-sory association cortex (SAI). In turn, SAI is connected to Area 6 in the premotor cortex. Other association cortices such as SAII send projections to various parts of Area 6 and the prefrontal cortex whereas SAIII has connections to the dorsal and ventral prefrontal cortex and Areas 23 and 24 (the cingulate gyrus).

Other sensory systems, especially the visual and auditory systems, do not connect with the frontal lobes directly but do so via association cortices or **convergence zones** where inputs from different sensory systems arrive.

Further connections are found within the limbic system. For example, one part of the cingulate gyrus (Area 24) projects to Areas 8 and 6 of the premotor cortex, MII and the orbitofrontal cortex; another part projects to Areas 46 and 11. The frontal lobes receive inputs from the thalamus and hypothalamus, with the precentral region receiving input from the ventrolateral and ventral posterior thalamic areas, and premotor areas receiving input from the ventromedial nucleus. These connections are reciprocal, in that the frontal lobes may project to these subcortical (and cortical) areas as well as receiving projections from them. Connections are not made in a general fashion with all divisions of the frontal lobes connecting with these structures, but are made selectively. Thus, the orbitofrontal region projects to the temporal pole and related structures more than it does to other regions.

■ Early studies of frontal lobe function

The first comprehensive report of behavioural change following frontal lobe damage appeared 150 years ago (Harlow, 1848, 1868). Later studies demonstrated that damage to the frontal cortex was associated with impaired cognitive and intellectual functioning. Rylander (1939), for example, reported that 21 out of 32 frontal lobe patients scored more poorly on tests of intellectual ability than did healthy controls. This impairment was not damage-general either. Patients with temporal, parietal and occipital lobe resection showed no difficulty with 'abstract thinking, the power of combination, and acts involving judgement' (Rylander, 1943). Further support for the role of the frontal lobes in intelligence came later with studies showing poorer ability to sort items according to a given rule in these patients than in non-frontal patients (Halstead, 1940).

These early studies, however, did not go unchallenged. Hebb (1939, 1941, 1945), for example, argued that there was no real significant difference between frontal and posterior damage patients on tests of intellectual ability (IQ tests). Although he did not argue that the frontal lobes had no part to play in intellectual behaviour, Hebb concluded that there was little evidence to suggest that these areas were more involved than others. One reason for the inconsistency may have been the small sample sizes and the likelihood that the intelligence tests used were not particularly sensitive measures.

■ Tests used to measure frontal lobe dys/function

The problem of measurement is a recurrent one in frontal lobe and neuropsychological research. Tests of frontal lobe function normally, but not always, measure the ability of the patient (1) to sequence events logically and temporally, (2) to reason abstractly, and (3) to behave spontaneously.

The most commonly used test in frontal cortex injury is verbal fluency, usually measured by the Controlled Oral Word Association test from the Multilingual Aphasia Examination (Benton and Hamsher, 1978). This test requires the patient to name as many items as possible beginning with a given letter. Frontal lobe patients perform poorly, naming significantly fewer words than do controls and patients with brain lesions other than frontal.

The earliest tests of abstract reasoning were sorting tests involving cards printed with different designs (Goldstein and Scheerer, 1941). In one of these tests, two packs of 64 cards featured designs that differed in shape, colour or number and the patient was required to sort them according to some principle decided by the experimenter (Weigl, 1941; Grant and Berg, 1948). Without warning, the experimenter would then change the sorting principle and the patient would have to shift his or her sorting strategy accordingly. The current version of the test is the Wisconsin Card Sorting Test (Milner, 1964).

In Milner's (1963) version of the card-sorting task, four cards whose faces have one red triangle, two green stars, three yellow crosses and four blue circles are placed before the patient. Patients are given 128 cards (comprising two sets of 64 cards) and are required to sort them according to a fixed criterion: colour, form or number. The examiner informs the subject whether a decision was right or wrong. Turning over a card with two yellow crosses could go with the two green stars (based on number) or three yellow crosses (based on colour). Therefore, more than one sorting must be undertaken in order to determine the correct strategy. If the examiner chooses colour and the patient makes ten consecutive correct responses, the criterion is, without the patient's knowledge, changed to number (or shape). Following ten consecutive correct answers, the criterion is changed again. Two measures of performance are (1) the number of categories obtained – four correct sorts by category indicates successful performance – and (2) the number of perseverative errors committed, i.e. the number of times that the patient responds using the criterion set in the previous sort.

Some frontal lobe patients perform poorly on this task, making significantly more perseverative errors and failing to complete sorts. Similar sorting tasks in which some frontal lobe patients also have problems are ones that involve sorting six cards into two piles of three cards based on some feature of the design on the cards (Delis et al., 1992) or sorting blocks according to colour, shape, width or height (the Modified Vygotsky Concept Formation Test).

Another popular test is Shallice's (1982) Tower of London task. This task involves moving blocks into a given position in as few moves as possible, as seen in Figure 6.2. The outcome on the task is measured by the number of problems solved without error in 60 seconds.

Shallice has also devised two, more 'realistic' tests of frontal lobe function in which the ability of the patient to undertake sequences of events in real life is measured. Shallice and Burgess's (1991) Six Elements Test, for example, requires the subject to undertake six open-ended tasks in a fixed time period, as seen in Table 6.1. The Multiple Errands Task involves the completion of a number of

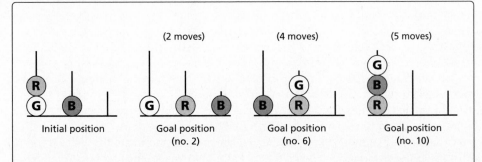

Figure 6.2 Problems encountered in the Tower of London task. The arrangement on the left is the starting point. The other three positions must be reached from this starting point. The second arrangement can be achieved in a minimum of two moves, the third in a minimum of four and the last one in a minimum of five. Adapted from Shallice, 1982

Table 6.1 Shallice and Burgess's Six Elements Test

Participant's tasks
1   Dictation of a brief account of the participant's journey to the testing place
2   Dictation of a brief account of the participant's intended journey from there
3   Writing the names of as many pictures from one set of pictures
4   Writing the names of as many pictures from another set of pictures
5   Solving as many arithmetical problems as possible from one set of problems
6   Solving as many arithmetical problems as possible from another set of problems

everyday errands such as shopping in an unfamiliar street according to a given set of rules. For example, the patient might have to buy specific items or send the experimenter a postcard on which he should have detailed four pieces of information, including the coldest place in Britain on the previous day. Frontal lobe patients show impairments on both tests.

■ The symptoms: an introduction

The neuropsychological consequences of frontal lobe injury have been characterized as a 'syndrome', i.e. brain injury is associated with a cluster of behavioural symptoms that reliably appear. However, there is considerable variation in the types of symptom seen in frontal lobe patients. Changes in social behaviour and personality can tend towards the depressive or manic end of the affective spectrum. Test performance between individuals with frontal damage can differ significantly, and the picture is further complicated by the specific region and hemisphere of the prefrontal cortex damaged. These findings cast doubt over the use of the blanket description 'syndrome' for the behavioural sequelae of frontal lobe damage. The sections below describe some of the symptoms that often, but not always, accompany frontal lobe damage. These symptoms are classed as motor, where damage is to the precentral or motor strip, or cognitive, where damage is prefrontal. What is more, specific deficits can be localized to subdivisions of these regions: thus, personality changes and emotional disorders are associated with orbitofrontal lesions whereas some cognitive and memory disorders are associated with dorsolateral damage.

▨ Motor (precentral) symptoms

One characteristic symptom of frontal cortex damage is impairment in organization and planning. This symptom involves not only abstract planning such as thinking ahead but also voluntary motor behaviour itself (Passingham, 1995). For example, a patient may not be able to undertake a behaviour or response in a particular order (Luria, 1966). Luria described this impairment as a disintegration in learned sequential actions in the sense that learned behaviours had become 'series of isolated fragments'. This impairment is evident even when copying simple gestures. Kolb and Milner (1981), for example, found that patients with left and right frontal lobe damage were poor at copying a series of facial (but not arm) movements, making more errors of sequence than did controls and other patients.

Removal of the supplementary motor cortex results in a brief impairment in all voluntary movements with the only long-lasting impairment occurring in the patient's inability to make rapid alternating hand and finger movements. On the basis of blood flow and lesions studies, Roland *et al.* (1980) have suggested that the supplementary motor areas are 'programming areas for motor subroutes' where fast, independent movement is programmed. This is returned to in the section on apraxia in Chapter 8.

Given that the frontal lobes contain the frontal eye fields, it is not surprising that frontal damage causes oculomotor disturbances. Guitton *et al.* (1982) reported that frontal lobe patients had difficulty in making a voluntary eye movement in a direction opposite to that of the visual field in which a stimulus cue was presented. The normal response is to make a saccade – a quick eye movement – towards the stimulus, yet corrective responses are impaired in frontal lobe patients.

Finally, one other oculomotor deficit seen in frontal patients is impaired corollary discharge. This refers to the transmission of information from one brain region to the other so that the one informs the other of its intended action. If you push your eyeball, the world appears to move; when you move your eyes, the world stays still. There is a signal to indicate that the eyes are moving and that, therefore, the world is still; there is no signal when the eyeball is pushed mechanically. Thus, voluntary actions require a corollary discharge from the frontal lobe to the parietal and temporal association cortex that primes the sensory system to anticipate movement. Frontal lobe patients seem to have an impaired corollary discharge (Teuber and Mishkin, 1954).

▓ Cognitive (prefrontal) symptoms

The types of symptom seen in patients following prefrontal lobe damage can be grouped broadly along the following lines: impairments in spontaneous behaviour, planning and strategy formation, attention, utilization behaviour, memory and olfactory function.

Spontaneous behaviour

Some frontal lobe patients are characterized by lack of spontaneity in that they appear quite lethargic and speak very little, or they may perform badly on formal tests of verbal spontaneity, such as a verbal fluency task (Benton *et al.*, 1994), or the alternative uses test in which patients generate as many uses for a common object as possible. On tests of spontaneity, different frontal regions appear to be required for different types of task. Patients with anterior brain damage, for example, perform significantly worse on this task than do patients with posterior lesions or undamaged control subjects (Eslinger and Grattan, 1993). Patients with bilateral or left unilateral frontal impairment produce significantly fewer words on the word fluency test than do control subjects whereas right frontal patients show no significant impairment (Janowsky *et al.*, 1989a). Eslinger and Grattan (1993) have described this impairment as a failure in 'cognitive flexibility'. This impairment also has a non-verbal form. Patients with right frontal damage, for example, complete fewer drawings using four lines than do those with left frontal damage or control subjects (Jones-Gotman and Milner, 1977).

The absence of 'formal' spontaneity is not always seen in frontal lobe patients, however. There are some patients with considerable frontal lobe damage who perform extremely well on verbal fluency tests and other 'frontal lobe' tests, which suggests caution in describing the symptom as characteristic of frontal lobe damage (Eslinger and Damasio, 1985; L.H. Goldstein *et al.*, 1993). In fact, 'normal' performance on these tests is not uncommon, yet the individual exhibits marked impairments in the planning and organization of his or her day. One well known example of this is Eslinger and Damasio's patient, EVR (see case study).

Case study: EVR

EVR was a well-liked and efficient accountant who, at the age of 35, developed a large orbitofrontal meningioma (a cerebral tumour). Although surgical removal of the tumour alleviated the symptoms of the trauma, EVR's behaviour changed markedly for the worse. His progress has been extensively followed by Paul Eslinger and Antonio Damasio of the Department of Neurology, University of Iowa (Eslinger and Damasio, 1985; A.R. Damasio et al., 1990) and his behaviour has been contrasted with that of other frontal lobe patients. The reason for the attention paid to EVR, and others like him, is that he performs well on standard neuropsychological and frontal tests but his capacity for planning and organizing his own life and his conduct of relations with others are severely impaired. A brief bibliographical sketch will help to fill in the details.

EVR was the eldest of five children. He appeared to have had an unremarkable childhood: he was free of developmental illnesses and reached the normal developmental milestones. An excellent student with many friends, he married after college and worked to pay for his two years' training in accounting. At the age of 25, he had become the father of two children, was involved in church activities and was an accountant with a firm of home builders. By 29, he had been promoted to chief accountant, and by 32, had become comptroller. He was regarded as a paragon: his sister looked on him as a role model; his brother described him as someone people looked up to. At 35, after experiencing the personality changes and impaired vision that accompany a tumour, he was diagnosed as having the orbitofrontal meningioma. This was removed and he was discharged from hospital two weeks later. It is at this point that EVR's life began to change.

Three months after the operation, he became an accountant for a small home construction business. Against the advice of his friends and family, he invested all his savings in setting up a home building partnership with a former co-worker described by Eslinger and Damasio as having a 'questionable reputation'. The business failed and EVR became a bankrupt. Following this incident, he attempted, and failed, to hold down a number of other jobs including warehouse labourer, a buildings manager, and accountant for a car-spares company. He was described by his employers as tardy and disorganized although his skills, manners and temperament were acceptable. His marriage broke up (after 17 years) and, unable to keep a job or a family, EVR moved in with his parents.

Two years after the operation, EVR's difficulties continued. He worked for a while as a tax-returns officer but his employment was terminated. He was fired from another job that he had to drive 100 miles to get to – he was fired for lack of punctuality. He remarried after his divorce but this marriage ended after two years. He would take an inappropriately long time to make the simplest of decisions, take two hours to get ready for work and spend an inordinately long time shaving and grooming. He would spend hours deciding on a restaurant in which to dine, poring

▶

over the restaurant's seating arrangements, the menu plan and the atmosphere. He would drive to restaurants to see how busy they were, but could not decide which one to choose. Even buying the most insignificant of items was tortuous: he would need to know the exact price of the item, a comparison of prices and the best method of purchase. He also began to hoard, refusing to part with dead house-plants, old telephone directories, six broken fans, three empty orange juice cartons and fifteen cigarette lighters amongst other detritus.

Two years and six years after the operation, his cognitive ability was evaluated on a range of tests. Two years after the injury, his verbal IQ was superior, his perform-ance IQ average, his memory IQ above average and his personality showed no deviation from the norm. Six years after surgery, his IQ still placed him in the average to superior category.

At this point, he was referred to the neurology unit after a series of failed psychotherapeutic interventions. He was alert, cooperative, articulate and showed no impaired performance on frontal lobe tests. On the Wisconsin Card Sorting Test (WCST), he achieved criterion for 6 out of 7 categories in 70 sorts. At the beginning of the fifth category, he remarked, 'Oh, it's designs now.' He was knowledgeable about national and international affairs and would answer rapidly and competently when given a social judgement task (solving moral dilemmas). He was described as showing a cynical attitude.

CAT and MRI slices of EVR's brain indicated that his entire orbital cortex on the right and part of the orbitofrontal cortex on the left had been removed by surgery. On the right, Areas 11, 12 and 25 were damaged, and on the left, Areas 11 and 12 were partially damaged, with Area 25 remaining intact. Right mesial damage involved Areas 32, 10, 8, 9, 24 and the posterior of Area 6; left mesial damage involved Areas 8 and 9. Lesions also affected Areas 8, 9 and 46 of the right prefrontal cortex (the dorsolateral cortex), with the left remaining intact. White matter sub-jacent to the premotor area was also damaged in the right.

Perhaps the most remarkable aspect of EVR's behaviour, apart from the marked postoperative change, is the dissociation between average-to-superior performance on standardized tests and a failure to demonstrate the same, efficient cognitive strategies in his own life. Eslinger and Damasio (1985) hypothesized that this dissociation could be for a number of reasons. It is possible that EVR was unable to analyze or integrate the premises of real-life problems. In standard tests, these premises are presented to the subject. Alternatively, EVR may have been unable to execute planned behaviour, despite having knowledge of the skills and principles necessary to do so and despite having the ability to analyze and integrate the premises of real life. Yet, he could perform well on the WCST and did express and conceive *inappropriate* plans which he did carry out. Eslinger and Damasio suggest that the most likely explanation is that EVR had a defect of analysis and integration of real-life stimuli which may be attributable to an impairment in accessing

➡

previously learned strategies. This explanation is persuasive. Shallice and Burgess (1991), for example, have argued that the design of neuropsychological tests makes finding frontal-cognitive impairments especially difficult because the patient is normally presented with a single, well defined problem which has to be solved in a short period of time, often prompted by the examiner. This is very different from the planning and cognition necessary in day-to-day life. Tests devised to take in the multiple demands on the patient in everyday life show that frontal patients have extreme difficulty in performing on these tasks (Shallice and Burgess, 1991; L.H. Goldstein *et al.*, 1993).

EVR continues to be monitored and assessed and provides modern neuropsychology with one of its classic case studies. Perhaps EVR's greatest contributions to frontal lobe understanding are the realization that dissociations do exist between test and real-life performance, and that not all frontal patients are the same.

Planning/strategy formation

The card-sorting tasks described in the section on frontal lobe tests (pages 191–3) are tasks which involve the patient engaging in planning or forming strategies. Both Milner (1963) and Heaton (1981) found that fewer correct sorts were obtained by dorsofrontal than by non-frontal patients. In Milner's research these patients also made more perseverative errors: dorsolateral patients made 57, outpatients made 11 and the cortical non-frontals made 16, a pattern repeated in Heaton's data.

From these findings, Milner (1964) argued that 'the ability to shift from one mode of solution to another on a sorting task is more impaired by frontal than by posterior cerebral injury'. Some evidence, however, casts doubt on the usefulness of the Wisconsin Card Sorting Test (WCST) as a measure of frontal lobe function. In one study, no significant difference in severity of impairment was found between frontals and non-frontals on this task (Grafman *et al.*, Salazar, 1990). Similarly, no significant difference in the number of correct categories achieved or perseverative errors made was found in another study of 49 frontal patients and 24 non-frontal (temporal, parietal, occipital, thalamic, basal ganglia) patients (Anderson *et al.*, 1991) – some patients even performed better than average on the test. However, a recent PET study in which the brain activation of normal, healthy volunteers was monitored while the subjects participated in a modified version of the WCST reported significant increases in activation in left or bilateral dorso-lateral prefrontal cortex (Nagahama *et al.*, 1996). This finding, however, may be complicated by the strictness of the statistical test used. For example, Van Horn and co-workers sought to investiagate possible functional lateralization of frontal lobe task performance using PET in fourteen healthy volunteers (Van Horn *et al.*,

1996). They found neither significant interaction between hemisphere and region nor any significant increase in activation in the prefrontal cortex during completion of the WCST, a delayed response alternation task and a spatial delayed task. With more liberal statistical comparisons, however, a significant increase in right superior frontal gyrus activation was observed during the WCST and the spatial delayed response task. Both studies highlight the importance of paying close attention to the ways in which data are analyzed.

A shortened form of the WCST has also been developed (Nelson, 1976) but appears to be performed no better by non-frontal than frontal patients (Van den Broek *et al.*, 1993). The WCST, therefore, appears to be an adequate test of general brain dysfunction, i.e. it can discriminate between patients with brain damage and those with no damage, but its usefulness as a specific test of frontal lobe dysfunction is questionable.

Although the WCST is thought to tap into the individual's ability to form strategies, there are other tests which tap similar qualities. Maze tests, such as the Porteus Maze Test, are thought to measure the individual's forward planning capacity. Porteus (1965) argued that planning was a prerequisite to every intelligent act and noted that lobotomized patients performed poorly on this maze test. Other studies had found that posterior and superior lesions produced more consistent deficits than did lesions at other sites (Lewis *et al.*, 1956). Right frontal lobe damage, especially, is associated with poor performance on finger- and stylus-maze tests. If a subject enters a wrong alley on this test, a bell rings which indicates that an error has been made. Controls commit about 100 of these errors, yet even when told of their errors, frontal lobe patients make the same errors again. Right, but not left frontal lobe patients may make up to 350 errors with no further success.

Another spatial test with frontal lobe associations is Koh's Block Design Task in which subjects are asked to recreate a design using patterned blocks. Frontal lobe patients may not correct their errors or may attend to only a small area of the design or may not be able to plan such a reconstruction. In a single photon emission computed tomography study, Rezai and colleagues found significant blood flow increases in healthy subjects' frontal regions during performance of the WCST and the Continuous Performance Test (in which subjects are instructed to respond only when a blue M follows a red H), but not the Porteus Maze Test (Rezai *et al.*, 1993). The findings suggest that three out of the four standard frontal tests produced activation in the relevant brain regions, although such crude frontal measures cannot lead us to localize functions in these areas. This is an important study because, as the authors state, brain lesion studies 'only assess the absence of function, leaving the localization of the function as a matter of inference'. More recently, Baker and colleagues have noted increases in rCBF in the bilateral prefrontal cortex, anterior cingulate gyrus, supplementary motor cortex and dorsolateral prefrontal cortex during performance of the Tower of London task (Baker *et al.*, 1996). There was also parietal activation and a decrease in activation at the bilateral superior temporal cortex, bilateral superior frontal cortex and bilateral sensorimotor cortex. In a comparison of hard and easy versions of the task, the authors found that the difficult version was associated with significant increases in the prefrontal and premotor areas. This study is interesting because the areas activated are also associated with activation during visuospatial working memory performance, and perhaps reflect the executive, planning areas of the brain. This association between working memory and frontal lobe function is returned to later in the chapter.

Sequencing is perhaps the behaviour which may be most clearly affected in frontal lobe patients (Sirigu *et al.*, 1995). Ultimately, sequencing – the organization of stimuli in the correct, logical or learned order – is a function of rule-learning. We learn to do things in a certain way in order to make them work, e.g. writing a letter on a computer entails enacting a sequence of behaviours such as plugging in the computer and switching on the hard disk and monitor, opening up the word processing application, opening a folder and file and starting to write. Deficits of this kind were seen clearly in the behaviour of a 51 year old man studied by L.H. Goldstein *et al.* (1993), who had suffered from a surgically removed frontal lobe tumour. See Figure 6.3.

Despite having been employed as a senior manager in an international company, two years after surgery the patient worked from home, was lethargic and had difficulty in making decisions. On one occasion, he took two weeks to decide which slides to show at a professional presentation. He never made the decision in the end. Yet, his performance on a variety of frontal and neuropsychological tests was normal or above average. In order to determine the effect of the brain damage on the patient's everyday organizational behaviour, Goldstein *et al.* administered Shallice and Burgess's (1991) Six Elements Test and Multiple Errands Task. In comparison with Shallice and Burgess's control group, Goldstein *et al.*'s patient performed badly. For example, he would have to return to a shop to buy additional items; he would misinterpret instructions such as placing the stamp on the wrong card and would not complete tasks. He made these mistakes despite being able to explain his errors and recite the rules of the test. This disregard of instructions or task requirements despite having full knowledge and understanding of them has been termed **goal neglect** (J. Duncan, 1995).

Similarly, Della Malva and colleagues required thirteen patients with anterior brain damage and thirteen patients with posterior brain damage to complete verbal and visual sequencing tasks (Della Malva *et al.*, 1993). A series of cards featuring a single word or picture was presented to the patient. The patients' task was to arrange the cards to make a meaningful or logical sequence, but the stimuli also included 'capture' sequences. These sequences were two words or two pictures that went together logically but which had to be broken up in order for the sentence or visual sequence to make sense. Thus, a verbal capture sequence would include 'of/full/the/was/*coffee*/*cup*'. The correct order, 'the cup was full of coffee', would entail breaking up the coffee/cup pair. Similar pairings were made for the visual stimuli. Della Malva *et al.* found that frontal patients had significantly greater difficulty in sequencing stimuli with capture sequences than did the

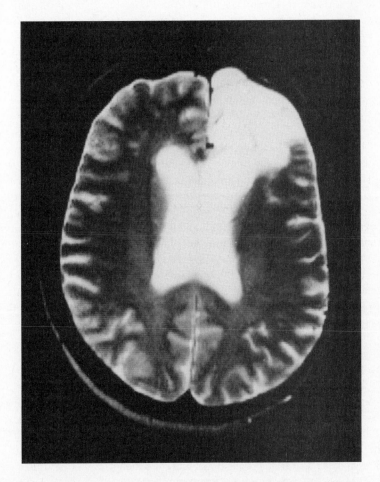

Figure 6.3 The MRI scan of Goldstein *et al.*'s patient. Note the large lesion in the left frontal cortex (MRI scans are read backwards: left is right and right is left)

posterior patients. Their patients were not *less able* than the posterior group to break the capture pair but made more *errors in sequencing* when capture sequences were present.

Attention

A number of the neuropsychological impairments that follow brain injury have been attributed to a failure in selective attention. Attention requires that an individual perceives and analyzes data from one source of information while excluding other, irrelevant or interfering sources of information. Frontal lobe patients appear to have impaired attentional capacity in that they show poor concentration and are highly distractible (Mesulam, 1986; Janowsky *et al.*, 1989a). This evidence, however, is not consistent (Godefroy *et al.*, 1994; Brazzelli *et al.* 1994).

Godefroy and Rousseaux (1996) have measured the reaction times of eleven prefrontal patients in tasks requiring divided or focused attention and found that these patients showed significantly greater distraction to irrelevant items than did controls. Duncan (1995) has suggested that this attentional deficit in frontal lobe patients may be related to impaired general intelligence, a suggestion that is explored in 'Do the frontal lobes mediate intelligence?' on page 204.

The primate literature also implicates the prefrontal cortex in attention. Dias *et al.* (1996), for example, found that monkeys whose lateral prefrontal cortex (Area 9) had been damaged failed to shift their attention to a different dimension of a discrimination task, but that monkeys who had received orbitofrontal lesions were able to do this. There are similar findings from the human literature. Godefroy *et al.* (1996), for example, found impaired performance on the go/no go task in frontal patients and noted that the impairments in focused and divided attention were more prominent when the lesion was localized in the left dorsolateral prefrontal cortex and caudate nucleus.

Utilization behaviour

Utilization behaviour (UB) describes a behavioural disturbance in which the patient uses objects, prompted or unprompted, in his or her environment. Two types of UB have been identified (Shallice *et al.*, 1989). 'Induced' UB describes a behaviour where the experimenter's comportment appears to prompt the use of objects (Lhermitte, 1983) whereas incidental UB describes behaviour where the patient uses objects nearby when performing other tasks. According to Lhermitte *et al.* (1986), frontal lobe patients may also exhibit imitation behaviour (IB), i.e. they imitate the examiner's gestures even though they are instructed not to. This behaviour precedes UB. In their study, UB and/or IB was present in 96 per cent of 29 patients with frontal lobe lesions. The exact reasons for this are unknown. At the behaviour level, both types of patient are thought to be abnormally dependent on the environment. As Lhermitte *et al.* (1986) have argued, 'the sight of the movement is perceived in the patient's mind as an order to imitate; the sight of an object implies the order to use it.' At the cortical level, Lhermitte (1983) suggests that UB is the result of impaired inhibitory action of the frontal lobe on the parietal lobe. In normal individuals, the parietal lobe integrates sensory information from the environment while the frontal lobe inhibits some of the parietal lobe's activity. This relationship ensures the relative dependence on or independence from the external environment, making sure that the quality of external stimuli is examined.

Frontal lobe patients are thought to have 'released' parietal lobe activity which leaves the patient exposed to all external stimuli.

Memory

Memory is a concept so vague and broad that no behaviour can be said to be uninfluenced by it. It is essential for thinking, reasoning, even for 'constructing' oneself. A person with no memory of his or her past relinquishes the criterion that make him or herself unique. We have seen that frontal lobe patients are sometimes poor at sequencing, ordering, planning and verbal fluency, all of which involve some memorial component. These patients also exhibit memory deficits on tasks of free recall, interference, metamemory, temporal memory and working memory. Working memory describes the online supervision of information which has yet to be stored, and the concept is closely related to short-term memory (Baddeley, 1986). This is considered in more detail in the section on theories of frontal lobe function (page 209).

Free recall

Although patients with frontal cortex damage tend to perform without significant impairment on tests where they have to learn new information, they do perform poorly on tests which involve the unprompted recall of as many words as possible following the presentation and removal of a list of words (free recall). However, their recognition memory – the ability to recognize previously presented stimuli – appears intact. They can recognize the words they saw if presented with a list of those words and distractor words, even after one week's interval (Della Rocchetta, 1986; Janowsky et al., 1989a). Similarly, Brazzelli et al.'s (1994) patient, PG, was unable to find three objects that had been hidden in front of her five minutes earlier. It is clear from these deficits that the patient has difficulties in retrieving the material rather than in processing it since recall is poor and recognition is intact. Frontal lobe patients may also be highly susceptible to **proactive inter-ference**, i.e. their old memories interfere with the learning of new ones (Shima-mura, 1995).

Metamemory

Metamemory refers to our knowledge about what we remember. In a test context, this would be evaluated by having the subject recall a list of previously presented words after a delay (delayed recall). If the subject cannot recall a word correctly, he or she is asked to rate how likely it is that he or she would be able to recognize the word from a list of other words. Thus the test provides a measure of 'feeling of knowing'. Apparently, frontal lobe patients show impaired feeling of knowing (Janowsky et al., 1989b).

Temporal memory

Temporal organization of memory refers to the organization of events in the correct temporal order, i.e. the order in which they happened. Part of temporal organization might also involve recency memory, the memory for recent events. For example, frontal lobe patients appear unable to indicate which of two stimuli was the most recently presented (Milner *et al.*, 1991).

Olfactory function

Damage to the right orbitofrontal cortex has been associated with significant impairments in human olfactory perception, discrimination and identification (Jones-Gotman and Zatorre, 1993). Bilateral orbitofrontal and mesial cortex removal can produce bilateral **anosmia**: the inability to detect an odour presented to either nostril (Eslinger *et al.*, 1982). One PET study has shown that a simple odour-sniffing exercise unilaterally activated the right orbitofrontal cortex (Zatorre *et al.*, 1992b).

Do the frontal lobes mediate intelligence?

Since Hebb's (1939, 1941, 1945) devastating reviews of the role of the frontal lobes in intelligence – he concluded that there was not much of one – frontal lobe function and conventional intelligence have not been strongly associated. Warrington *et al.* (1986), for example, administered the Wechsler Adult Intelligence Scale (WAIS) battery to 656 patients with either unilateral parietal, temporal, occipital or frontal lobe damage and reported similar scores for each patient group. As we have seen in the preceding sections, some frontal lobe patients perform very well on standard 'intelligence' tests.

However, Duncan and his colleagues (Duncan, 1995; Duncan *et al.*, 1995) propose that frontal lobe function is related to intelligence but not to conventional, *general* intelligence, or *g*. Instead, Duncan proposes that the frontal lobes might be involved in the execution of tests of **fluid intelligence** that is, tests that do not require the subject to use prior information explicitly. (Those tests tapping *g*, such as tests measuring **crystallized intelligence**, do require such use, e.g. tests of vocabulary and general knowledge). Duncan found that three of the frontal lobe patients he studied performed well on the WAIS but were poor on the Multiple Errands Task. However, on tests of fluid intelligence, such as Cattell's Culture–Fair Test, the patients' IQ scores were 22–28 points lower than their WAIS IQs.

Furthermore, their Culture–Fair IQs were 23–60 points lower than those of normal controls. This study suggests that when *g* is measured by tests of fluid intelligence, frontal lobe integrity is important for successful performance. If tests are tapping crystallized intelligence, the frontal lobes appear to be no more or less involved than other lobes.

■ Social behaviour and personality

In the report of their patient, PG, Brazzelli *et al.* (1994) suggest that 'one of the possible consequences of severe "frontal" derangement is social inadequacy' (p.45). One of the most striking cases of frontal lobe damage associated with emotional and personality disturbance was reported by Harlow in 1848. This is the case of Phineas Gage, whose accident has been excellently summarized by H. Damasio *et al.* (1994):

> On 13 September 1848, Phineas P. Gage, a 25-year old construction foreman for the Rutland and Burlington Railroad in New England, became a victim of a bizarre accident. In order to lay new rail tracks across Vermont, it was necessary to level the uneven terrain by controlled blasting. Among other tasks, Gage was in charge of the detonations, which involved drilling holes in the stone, partially filling the holes with explosive powder, covering the powder with sand, and using a fuse and a tamping iron to trigger an explosion into the rock. On the fateful day, a momentary distraction let Gage begin tamping directly over the powder before his assistant had a chance to cover it with sand. The result was a powerful explosion away from the rock and toward Gage. The fine-pointed, 3-cm thick, 109-cm-long tamping iron was hurled, rocket-like, through his face, skull, brain, and then into the sky. Gage was momentarily stunned but regained full consciousness immediately thereafter. He was able to talk and even walk with the help of his men. The iron landed many yards away. (p.1102)

When John Harlow, the physician who treated Gage and wrote up the case study, arrived at the scene of the incident, he observed that Gage 'bore his sufferings with the most heroic firmness' and wrote:

> From their appearance, the fragments of bone being uplifted and the brain protruding, it was evident that the fracture was occasioned by some force acting from below upward ... I passed an index finger in its [the scalp's] whole length, without the least resistance, in the direction of the wound in the cheek, which received the other finger in like manner. [The tamping iron had cracked the floor of the orbit of the left eye] entered the cranium, passing through the anterior left lobe of the cerebrum, and made its exit in the median line, lacerating the longitudinal fissures, fracturing the parietal and frontal bones extensively, breaking up considerable portions of the brain, and protruding the globe of the left eye from its socket, by nearly one half of its diameter. (Harlow, 1848, pp. 20,21)

Gage made a good physical recovery and many of his cognitive abilities remained intact. However, during and after convalescence, his personality appeared to change. He became profane, irreverent, capricious, lost all sense of responsibility, lost his job and thought nothing of contravening social niceties. His acquaintances remarked that he was 'no longer Gage'. As Harlow (1868) observed, 'the

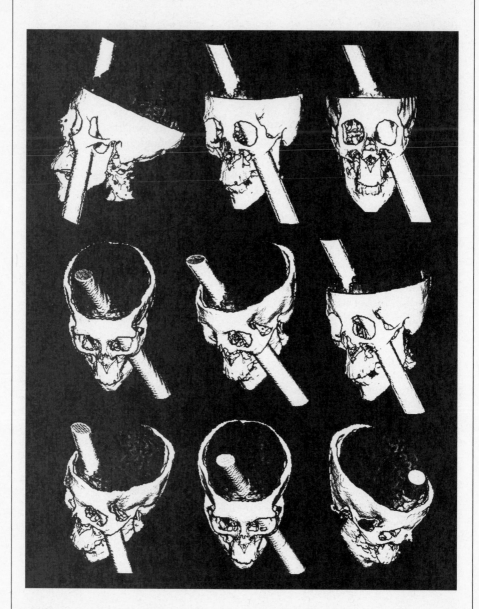

Figure 6.4 Examples of the reconstruction of the trajectory of the iron rod that shot through Phineas Gage's head

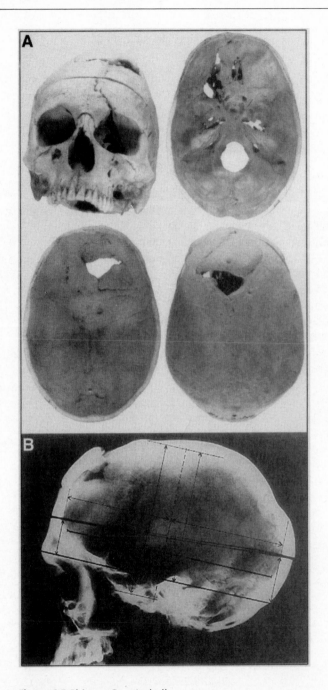

Figure 6.5 Phineas Gage's skull

equilibrium between his intellectual faculty and animal propensities had disappeared.

Gage died in 1861, in San Francisco. Little neuropsychological interest was prompted by Harlow's report, perhaps surprising given the implicit observation that damaged frontal cortex was associated with impaired planning and execution of social behaviour (Damasio *et al.* 1994). Harlow (1848) himself remarked, that 'the injury has been seriously questioned by many medical men for whom I entertain a very high respect.' As there was no autopsy, no clear description of the lesion could be obtained post-mortem. Harlow did retrieve Gage's skull, however, and both this and the tamping iron now belong to the Warren Anatomical Medical Museum at Harvard University.

Based on the dimensions of the skull, Damasio *et al.* (1994) remarkably plotted the trajectory of the tamping iron to ascertain the precise anatomical path of the object, as seen in Figures 6.4 and 6.5.

They concluded that the tamping iron must have produced lesions in the anterior half of the left orbitofrontal cortex (Areas 11 and 12), the left polar and anterior mesial frontal cortex (Areas 8, 9, 10 and 32) and the most anterior part of the anterior cingulate gyrus (Area 24). The supplementary motor area was apparently spared as was the frontal operculum (which contains Broca's area). There were lesions to the right anterior and mesial orbital region (Area 12), the right mesial and polar frontal cortices (Areas 8, 9, 10 and 32) and the right anterior part of the anterior cingulate gyrus (Area 24). The supplementary motor cortex was also spared on the right. No damage occurred outside the frontal lobes.

Damasio and his colleagues' reconstruction of the iron's trajectory gives a more precise picture of the brain structures damaged after the accident. These structures are part of what is known as the ventromedial or orbitofrontal cortex. Since Harlow's report, a number of studies of frontal cortex damage suggest that damage to various parts of the cortex produce disturbances in personality (Stuss and Benson, 1986). For example, Table 6.2 highlights those personality changes that have been found to accompany frontal cortex damage (Stuss *et al.*, 1992).

The first observation one can make of the list is that these features could characterize many friends and colleagues, yet it is unlikely that they are suffering from lesions to the frontal cortex. The second is that the list appears to represent

Table 6.2 Reported emotional changes following frontal cortex damage in humans

Exhilaration	Childish behaviour	Lack of restraint
Depression	Anxiety	Restlessness
Decreased concern with social propriety	Social withdrawal	Purposelessness
	Irritability	Slowness in thinking
Apathy and indifference	Inertia	Decreased self-concern
Lack of judgement	Lack of ambition	Impulsivity
Lack of reliability	Indifference to the opinions of others	Distractibility
Facetiousness		Egocentricity

a dichotomy in that some symptoms are clearly 'active' whereas others are 'inactive'. Thus, damage can cause euphoria, listlessness, restlessness, distractibility and so on, but also social withdrawal, indifference, lack of ambition, inertia and depression. Blumer and Benson (1975) noted that two distinct behaviours could be seen following frontal lobe damage: **pseudodepression** and **pseudopsychopathy**. Pseudodepression is characterized by lack of drive, interest, motivation and verbal spontaneity and often accompanies dorsal frontal lesions. Pseudopsychopathy, on the other hand, is characterized by impulsiveness, immaturity, lack of restraint, foul-mouthedness and sexual promiscuity and is often associated with orbitofrontal lesions. Depression is more severe with left anterior lesions than with left posterior or right hemisphere lesions. Right frontal lesions are also likely to produce greater depression than right posterior damage (Ross and Rush, 1981). Depression is, however, common with bilateral frontal lesions. There is also the problem of possible involvement of subcortical structures and subcortical damage. As Stuss *et al.* (1992) conclude, 'disturbances in drive, mood and affect probably involve pathology beyond the strict confines of the frontal lobes.' Some alternatives are considered in Chapter 10.

▒ Theories of frontal lobe function

Major theories of frontal lobe function include Luria's classical view, Norman and Shallice's supervisory system, Rolls's theory of orbitofrontal function, Damasio's model, and the working memory model proposed by Baddeley and Goldman-Rakic.

Luria's theory: the classical view

Luria (1973) regarded the frontal lobes as the third principal brain unit responsible for programming, regulating and verifying human behaviour, and the prefrontal cortex as the region which controlled the general state of the cortex and basic human mental activity.

Luria characterized the frontal lobes as a **tertiary zone** which regulated the organism's state of activity when it carried out a mental process. One of the most important functions of the frontal lobes was 'the disturbance of the operation of comparing the result of an action with its original intention, or disintegration of the "action acceptor" function'. This is, perhaps, the most obvious manifestation of frontal cortex damage. Luria went on to emphasize that the prefrontal zones were important for forming plans and for acting on the consequences of these plans. When complex programmes of activity are disrupted by frontal cortex damage, simpler, more basic forms of behaviour might replace them or they might be replaced by stereotypical behaviour that is either irrelevant to the situation or illogical. A number of subsequent theories have incorporated Luria's ideas in some form.

Luria also noted that damage to the lateral portion of the frontal lobes caused disruption to motor behaviour because this region was connected to the motor structures. Damage to regions linked to the limbic system and reticular formation led to disinhibition and changes in affect.

The notion that prefrontal lobe patients have difficulty in disregarding or inhibiting irrelevant information, i.e. their online cognitive processes are disrupted, has been incorporated into a theory of frontal lobe function that suggests that the prefrontal cortex modulates activity by means of a dynamic 'filtering' or 'gating' mechanism (Shimamura, 1995). This filtering or gating inhibits irrelevant information. The reason why different symptoms follow damage to different parts of the prefrontal cortex, the theory argues, is not because each region is responsible for the disrupted function but because different connections within the prefrontal cortex are filtering different aspects of cognition. This mechanism should inhibit irrelevant search strategies when trying to remember the temporal order of events, for example, but would be disrupted in prefrontal patients. The theory receives some backing from physiological evidence indicating that the frontal lobes have an inhibitory effect on posterior brain regions (as we saw with corollary discharge and utilization behaviour). Frith *et al.* (1991), for example, noted that in their PET study, increases in the dorsolateral prefrontal cortex were related to decreases in the posterior cortical regions. Based on this evidence, it is possible that different prefrontal symptoms arise because different areas of the cortex are inhibiting different posterior cortical areas. Thus, attention problems become a failure to inhibit irrelevant stimulus information; memory impairments become a failure to inhibit previous memories; and problem-solving difficulties become a failure to inhibit irrelevant or incorrect search strategies. This is an idea that deserves further investigation.

Norman and Shallice's supervisory attentional system

Norman and Shallice's (1986) theory of frontal lobe function and dysfunction is based on a similar idea to that of Luria: that the frontal lobes programme, regulate and verify activity. The theory assumes that the processes involved in the cognitive control of action and thought can be divided into two systems: **contention scheduling** and a **supervisory attentional system (SAS)**. Contention scheduling controls the execution of ordered or routine actions or skills. So, action schemata (plans of action) or well defined sets of responses associated with specific environmental stimuli or triggers are selected when a threshold specific to that schema is activated. The SAS, on the other hand, provides the conscious attentional control needed to modulate performance and may be employed in non-routine operations.

The inhibitory control scheduling prevents two competing schemata requiring the same resource from being selected. It is the job of the SAS to influence the probability of a schema being selected by contention scheduling. Furthermore, the SAS is required for situations (1) involving planning/decision-making, (2) involving error-correction, (3) requiring responses that are neither well learned nor familiar, (4) considered to be dangerous or difficult, and (5) requiring the organism to ignore strong habitual responses. Supervisory processes thus involve responsibility for formulating or modulating plans, creating markers or triggering, evaluating and articulating goals. It is a breakdown in one or more of these processes that may occur with frontal damage. As a result, the SAS is probably not a unitary system but a fractionated one.

One instance where there is clearly inadequate control by the frontal systems over behaviour is utilization behaviour (UB). According to the Norman and Shallice model, when no strong schema exists, then actions would be triggered by irrelevant environmental cues which is what appears to happen in UB. There is some strong support for Norman and Shallice's system and, as we see below, the model is closely related to the 'central executive' of working memory.

Rolls's theory of orbitofrontal function: stimulus–reward

Rolls's (1990, 1995) theory of frontal lobe function is directed more at explaining the neural basis of emotion than cognition, hence the emphasis on the orbitofrontal cortex. Rolls regards emotions as states produced by instrumental reinforcing stimuli. Some stimuli are unlearned reinforcers (pain, taste of food); other stimuli become reinforcers because of their association with primary reinforcers and are thus called secondary reinforcers. Thus, types of learning result from stimulus–reinforcement associations. A positive reinforcer is a reward and a negative reinforcer is punishment or the omission or termination of a positive reinforcer.

This theory argues that frontal lobe damage results in a failure to react normally to non-reward in different contexts. Thus, inappropriate responses to stimuli will appear when those responses are not rewarded. For example, both monkeys and humans with frontal cortex damage may show impairment at the go/no go task (Iversen and Mishkin, 1970) whereas monkeys may either make an incorrect response to an object because that object was previously rewarded with food or may fail to realize that a response will not provide them with a reward (Butter, 1969). This latter task illustrates the concept of extinction: a response is extinguished because it is not reinforced or rewarded.

Rolls argues that the orbitofrontal cortex is involved in correcting responses made to stimuli that were previously associated with reinforcement. Support for this comes from studies in which some neurons responded during the extinction task while others responded in the reversal task. These responses are thought to reflect information that the expected reward has not been made. This information is essential for the primate's ability to change behaviour if a response is contingent on changes in the environment. Neurons also selectively respond to different sensory stimuli and may also respond if responses to these stimuli had previously been rewarded. Finally, the orbitofrontal cortex is thought to evaluate whether a reward is expected and generates a mismatch (as seen in the firing of non-reward cells) if an expected reward is not obtained. The orbitofrontal cortex corrects stimulus–reinforcement associations when they become inappropriate. Rolls's model is based almost exclusively on animal work although the human literature suggests that the alteration of inappropriate responses is impaired following frontal cortex damage.

Damasio's somatic marker hypothesis

Damasio's model of frontal lobe function attempts to explain the role of the frontal cortex in emotion and social behaviour. The case of Phineas Gage suggested that emotion and the neural mechanisms responsible for emotion may be implicated in making social decisions. As the damage to Phineas Gage's brain involved the ventromedial (orbito-) frontal cortex, emotion and its neural machinery's participation in making decisions in a social context depend on an intact ventromedial system (H. Damasio et al., 1994). The involvement of emotion is further suggested by the ventromedial cortex's links, via the mediodorsal nucleus of the thalamus, with the amygdala and hypothalamus, two collections of subcortical nuclei heavily implicated in emotional processing. Furthermore, dorsolateral lesions which do disrupt the ability to perceive extrapersonal space/objects and to produce language do not impair emotional behaviour.

Damasio (1995) has suggested a **somatic marker** hypothesis to account for the emotional changes seen after orbitofrontal cortex damage (A. Damasio, 1995). This states that although the patient may be able to understand the implications of inappropriate social behaviour, EVR-type patients (see case study on page 196) are unable to mark these implications with a signal that automatically distinguishes between appropriate and inappropriate actions. EVR's deficit may be attributable to the inability to choose a course of appropriate action or to implement it.

This deficit results, according to the theory, from a failure to activate certain specific **somatic states** (visceral and skeletal) that were activated or evoked at the time of social learning. In other words, social learning is derived from punishment or reward associations. These associations modify somatic states and these modifications, in turn, are despatched to other brain areas such as the sensory and limbic association cortices. This signalling enables the consequences of reward or punishment to be experienced as 'feelings' and 'emotions'. This hypothesis is partly supported by Damasio's recent study of risk-taking in frontal lobe patients (Bechera et al., 1997). In this experiment, healthy individuals and patients with bilateral ventromedial prefrontal cortex damage participated in a task which required them to turn the cards from four decks of cards. In two decks, turning up certain cards was rewarded with $100; in the other two the reward was lower

($50). In the high-reward condition, however, there was a higher penalty for turning over specific cards, compared with the low-reward deck. Damasio and his colleagues found that although the healthy controls had, by card 50, realized that the high-reward deck was also a lot riskier and generated anticipatory skin conductance response (SCR) when considering choosing a card from those decks, this 'hunch' and the anticipatory SCR was absent in the frontal patients. Three patients could correctly identify the 'bad' decks but continued to make disadvantageous choices; they also did not exhibit the normal anticipatory autonomic response. Damasio interprets this as indicating that autonomic response reflects a process of 'non-conscious signalling' which represents access to records of previous events and behaviours related to reward and punishment.

This theory has parallels with Rolls's orbitofrontal cortex theory in that they both attribute the experience of emotion to stimulus–response associations and both emphasize the role of the ventromedial, and not the dorsolateral, cortex in the formation of these associations.

Working memory

Baddeley (1986) has characterized frontal (specifically, prefrontal) dysfunction as a **'dysexecutive' syndrome** involving the disruption of **working memory**. The relationship between working memory and frontal lobe function has been made quite explicit in a series of recent reviews (Roberts *et al.*, 1996). Working memory represents the mental process of 'moment-to-moment awareness and instant retrieval of archived information' (Goldman-Rakic, 1992, 1996) and has been called 'the blackboard of the mind' because it allows the online supervision of information. The most important part of working memory is the **central executive** which is thought to control resources and monitor information processing. It is served by two other processes, the **phonological loop** which stores and rehearses verbal information, and the **visuospatial sketchpad** which is concerned with visuospatial information and imagery. An example of the type of operation carried out by working memory is finding a number in the telephone directory and holding it in mental space until the number is dialled. Another is carrying over numbers in a mental arithmetic task: this involves storing one string of numbers while carrying out the next calculation.

Baddeley explained the central executive component of working memory in terms of Norman and Shallice's supervisory attentional system (SAS). The SAS and the central executive are, according to Baddeley (1986), the same. Thus, the impairments seen after frontal damage are malfunctions of the central executive. The central executive cannot be a unitary system, however, because performance on the Wisconsin Card Sorting Test correlates with tests of working memory, but performance on other tests of executive function does not (Lehto, 1996).

A large part of the evidence for the role of the prefrontal cortex in working memory has come from primate studies in which monkeys perform a delayed-response task. These tasks require the retention of information for later use while simultaneously performing another mental operation. For example, in a fairly standard version of the task, a visual or auditory stimulus is presented to the monkey. After a delay of a few seconds, the animal is signalled to indicate where the stimulus had appeared. A correct answer is rewarded, usually with food or drink (Goldman-Rakic, 1992). Neurons in the prefrontal cortex during the performance of this task appear to respond selectively to the period during the delayed-response task. Some become active during the presentation of the information, others become active during the delay, while others become active when the animal makes a motor movement to indicate the location of the stimulus. Neurons capable of 'remembering' that a stimulus had appeared were organized in a specific region of the prefrontal cortex. It is thought that these represent the prefrontal cortex's spatial working memory system. Disruption of these neurons causes failure on the delayed-response task.

Based on this and related evidence, Goldman-Rakic (1992) has argued that the prefrontal cortex is divided into multiple memory domains where each domain is responsible for a different aspect of memory: one is responsible for the location of objects, another for features of objects and others for semantic and mathematical knowledge. Furthermore, the prefrontal cortex, like other parts of the cortex, operates by inhibiting or exciting other parts of the cortex. These inhibitory or excitatory commands might be issued via neurotransmitters such as the catecholamines, especially dopamine (the prefrontal cortex is rich in these neurotransmitters). When levels of these chemicals are reduced, the types of working memory impairment seen on the delayed-response task in brain-damaged monkeys are apparent. Restoring the level of these chemicals restores performance.

While speculative, this evidence is complemented by a recent brain imaging study in which an increase in left or bilateral prefrontal cortex activation was found during the performance of a working memory task (E. Salmon et al., 1996). A study of frontal lesion patients, temporal lesion patients and patients with amygdalo-hippocampectomy also found that while frontal lobe patients were poor at undertaking even the least challenging aspects of a spatial working memory task, the other patients only showed difficulties at the most challenging level of the task (Owen et al., 1996). This finding was attributed to inefficient use of a particular searching strategy on the part of the frontal lobe patients. Two recent fMRI studies have also demonstrated the involvement of the prefrontal cortex in the maintenance of information that is characteristic of working memory (D.C. Cohen et al., 1997; Courtney et al., 1997).

While not one of the more widely adopted models of frontal lobe function – because of its functional specificity – the working memory model does provide a testable explanation of the role of the frontal cortex in working memory and executive functioning and, as we have seen, has support from the animal and human literature.

DISCUSSION POINT

Are psychopathy and frontal lobe damage related?

The frontal lobe literature suggests that these regions of the brain are intrinsically linked to the psychopathology of emotion. Some patients show quite clear impairments in affective response after frontal lobe damage, becoming depressed or euphoric or obscene or listless and so on. In the past fifteen years, a small body of evidence has suggested that not only might the frontal lobes be involved in emotional disturbance but also, more controversially, they might be implicated in the development of psychopathy and antisocial behaviour (Raine, 1993).

This controversial suggestion has been based largely on psychopaths' and antisocial individuals' frontal lobe test performance and the activity or structure of their brains as measured by CAT, MRI, PET or EEG. For example, Volkow and Tancredi (1987) found hypofrontality and left temporal dysfunction in a small number of violent psychiatric inpatients although temporal dysfunction was more common than the hypofrontality. In one PET control-matched study of 22 murderers, Raine and co-workers reported that these subjects were characterized by significant prefrontal dysfunction (Raine et al., 1993). Significantly lower glucose metabolism was found at the anterior medial prefrontal cortex of murderers compared with normal controls whereas activity at other areas, such as the medial prefrontal cortex, did not distinguish between the two groups.

In his review of the current literature on the brain imaging of aggressive/murdering/antisocial individuals, Raine (1993) concludes that only eight of the fourteen studies reviewed at that time showed evidence of differences between psychopathic and control subjects. The eight that did indicate significant findings localized differences in the anterior and temporal area. Interestingly, the CAT literature, when it does find an anatomical difference, almost unanimously indicates temporal lobe deficits and not frontal ones although one reason for this finding may be because the CAT scan is not sensitive to frontal abnormalities. A point to note in these studies, however, is the heterogeneity of the samples used. These have ranged from murderers to aggressive individuals to sadists to child molesters. It is wise to distinguish between the violent offender and the psychopath. The literature on psychophysiology and psychopathy, for example, is highly inconsistent on this point (Hare, 1978). Syndulko's review of the literature concluded that only six studies showed abnormal EEGs in psychopaths, four studies did not (Syndulko, 1978).

Neuropsychological tests appear to show frontal dysfunction in violent adult criminals (Yeudall et al., 1979) although a direct comparison of violent and nonviolent delinquents on neuropsychological tests has shown no frontal group differences (Yeudall et al., 1982). Results from other neuropsychological test batteries (e.g. the Luria–Nebraska Neuropsychological Battery) suggest that differences exist on tests of temporal lobe function (Brickman et al., 1984).

⬛⬛⬛➡

What would be informative is the measurement of these individuals' performance on tests supposedly tapping frontal lobe function. Psychopaths actually perform badly on some 'frontal lobe' tests including the Porteus Maze Test (Schalling and Rosen, 1968), a remunerated card-sorting task (Newman *et al.*, 1987) and the WCST (Gorenstein, 1982). These results, however, are by no means consistent with other studies reporting no differences between psychopathic and non-psychopathic individuals (Hare, 1984; Hoffman *et al.*, 1987; Sutker and Allain, 1983).

One study has provided more support for the hypothesis that psychopaths have specific, frontal dysfunction. Lapierre and colleagues compared the performance of thirty psychopathic and non-psychopathic individuals on what they described as 'orbitofrontal' and 'ventromedial' tasks (go/no go task; Porteus Maze; anosmia), 'frontodorsolateral measures' (the WCST) and 'posteriorolandic measures' (mental rotation). While there was no significant difference between the groups on the WCST and mental rotation, there was a significant difference on all three ventromedial tasks. In each test, the psychopaths were significantly impaired, even in the test requiring olfactory identification (Lapierre *et al.*, 1995).

These results suggest that group differences, where such differences exist, are likely to be found on tests of orbitofrontal ability (go/no go task) rather than dorsolateral ability (WCST). EVR, you will recall from the case study, had ventromedial lesions and a sparing of the dorsolateral cortex: his social behaviour was disrupted and yet he could perform well on 'frontal lobe' tests. L. H. Goldstein *et al.*'s (1993) patient also exhibited extreme antisocial behaviour following orbitofrontal damage while performing well on neuropsychological tests (see page 200). Furthermore, this dissociation highlights the socially disruptive and potentially violent characteristics of the psychopath. Psychopaths, it should be remembered, although certainly having the capacity for extreme violence and expressing this capacity, can be non-violent. Raine (1993) concludes that the available evidence suggests that prefrontal dysfunction indicates a predisposition to crime although, as we have seen, the term 'prefrontal' is a broad term and is probably inappropriate in this context. Frontal dysfunction could have a role to play in antisocial behaviour in general but it does not appear to be tied exclusively to psychopathy.

Summary

- [ ] The frontal lobes comprise about one-third of the human neocortex and are the most recently developed part of the cerebrum. Their principal roles appear to be the regulation of ongoing behaviour and the planning and maintenance of goals. These are called executive functions. The frontal lobes are also thought to regulate social behaviour and, because they contain the premotor cortex, regulate and plan voluntary movement.

- [ ] Anatomically and neurophysiologically, the frontal lobes have complex interconnections with other parts of the brain. These lobes are sometimes divided into the premotor area (which contains the visual eye fields and Broca's area), the prefrontal area and the precentral area. Another common distinction is between dorsolateral and orbitofrontal regions which appear to serve different psychological functions.

- [ ] The frontal lobes are a great integrator of neural information. The sensory systems do not make direct connections with the frontal lobes but do so via association cortices. There are also selective connections with the limbic system.

- [ ] The earliest studies of the consequences of frontal lobe damage suggested that these structures were important for 'intelligence'. Although not strictly true, these lobes do appear to be important for the integrity of fluid intelligence, i.e. that intelligence not requiring previous familiar information.

- [ ] Several tests are used to measure frontal lobe dysfunction. The commonest type of test is the controlled oral word association test. Other tests include the Wisconsin Card Sorting Test, the Tower of London task, go/no go tasks and the Porteus Maze. Not all frontal lobe patients perform poorly on these tests: some, such as EVR, perform well, which casts doubt on the validity of these tests as 'frontal lobe' tests.

- [ ] Frontal lobe damage produces motor/precentral symptoms and cognitive/prefrontal symptoms. Not all frontal lobe patients exhibit the same or all of these symptoms.

- [ ] Motor symptoms include an inability to make voluntary motor movement (with the limbs) or voluntary eye movement.

- [ ] Prefrontal symptoms include an inability to behave spontaneously, as evidenced by performance on verbal fluency tasks, the inability to plan, form strategies and execute these strategies effectively, an inability to shift response strategy, a failure to maintain attention, the unprompted utilization of objects in the environment, poor free memory recall and impaired working memory.

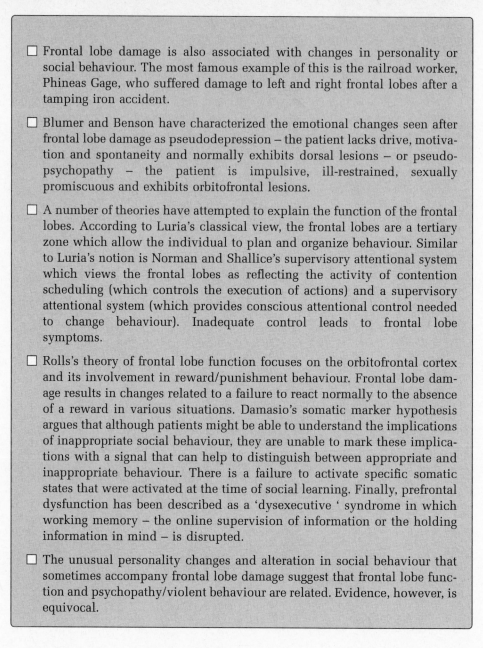

☐ Frontal lobe damage is also associated with changes in personality or social behaviour. The most famous example of this is the railroad worker, Phineas Gage, who suffered damage to left and right frontal lobes after a tamping iron accident.

☐ Blumer and Benson have characterized the emotional changes seen after frontal lobe damage as pseudodepression – the patient lacks drive, motivation and spontaneity and normally exhibits dorsal lesions – or pseudopsychopathy – the patient is impulsive, ill-restrained, sexually promiscuous and exhibits orbitofrontal lesions.

☐ A number of theories have attempted to explain the function of the frontal lobes. According to Luria's classical view, the frontal lobes are a tertiary zone which allow the individual to plan and organize behaviour. Similar to Luria's notion is Norman and Shallice's supervisory attentional system which views the frontal lobes as reflecting the activity of contention scheduling (which controls the execution of actions) and a supervisory attentional system (which provides conscious attentional control needed to change behaviour). Inadequate control leads to frontal lobe symptoms.

☐ Rolls's theory of frontal lobe function focuses on the orbitofrontal cortex and its involvement in reward/punishment behaviour. Frontal lobe damage results in changes related to a failure to react normally to the absence of a reward in various situations. Damasio's somatic marker hypothesis argues that although patients might be able to understand the implications of inappropriate social behaviour, they are unable to mark these implications with a signal that can help to distinguish between appropriate and inappropriate behaviour. There is a failure to activate specific somatic states that were activated at the time of social learning. Finally, prefrontal dysfunction has been described as a 'dysexecutive ' syndrome in which working memory – the online supervision of information or the holding information in mind – is disrupted.

☐ The unusual personality changes and alteration in social behaviour that sometimes accompany frontal lobe damage suggest that frontal lobe function and psychopathy/violent behaviour are related. Evidence, however, is equivocal.

Recommended further general and specific reading

Key: (1) = introductory, *(3)* = intermediate, *(5)* = advanced

General

Damasio, A.R. and Anderson, S.W. (1993). The frontal lobes. In K.M. Heilman and E. Valenstein (eds), *Clinical Neuropsychology* (3rd edition). New York: Oxford University Press. *(3)*

Hebb, D.O. (1945). Man's frontal lobes: a critical review. *Archives of Neurology and Psychiatry*, **54**, 10–24. *(3)*

Levin, H.S., Eisenberg, H.M. and Benton, A.L. (1992). *Frontal Lobe Function and Dysfunction*. New York: Grune and Stratton. *(3)*

Rabbitt, P. (1997). *Methodology of Frontal and Executive Function*. Hove, UK: The Psychology Press. *(3)*

Stuss, D.T., Gow, C.A. and Hetherington, C.R. (1992). 'No longer Gage': frontal lobe dysfunction and emotional changes. *Journal of Consulting and Clinical Psychology*, **60**(3), 349–359. *(3)*

Stuss, D.T., Eskes, G.A. and Foster, J.K. (1994). Experimental neuropsychological studies on frontal lobe functions. In F. Boller and H. Splinner (eds), *Handbook of Neuropsychology*, volume IX. Amsterdam: Elsevier. *(4)*

Specific

Bechera, A., Tranel, D., Damasio, H. and Damasio, A.R. (1996). Failure to respond autonomically to anticipated future outcomes following damage to prefrontal cortex. *Cerebral Cortex*, **6**, 215–25. *(3)*

Bechera, A., Damasio, H., Tranel, D. and Damasio, A.R. (1997). Deciding advantageously before knowing the advantageous strategy. *Science*, **275**, 1293–5. *(2)*

Blumer, D. and Benson, D.F. (1975). Personality changes with frontal and temporal lesions. In D.F. Benson and F. Blumer (eds), *Psychiatric Aspects of Neurologic Disease*. New York: Grune and Stratton. *(2)*

Damasio, H., Grabowski, T., Frank, R., Galaburda, A.M. and Damasio, A.R. (1994). The return of Phineas Gage: clues about the brain from the skull of a famous patient. *Science*, **264**, 1102–5. *(2)*

Darrell, J., Horn, V., Berman, K.F. and Weinberger, D.R. (1996). Functional lateralization of the prefrontal cortex during traditional frontal lobe tasks. *Biological Psychiatry*, **39**, 389–99. *(2)*

Deary, I.J. and Caryl, P.G. (1997). Neuroscience and human intelligence differences. *Trends in Neurosciences*, **20**(8), 365–71. *(3)*

Duncan, J., Emslie, H., Williams, P., Johnson, R. and Freer, C. (1996). Intelligence and the frontal lobe: the organization of goal-directed behavior. *Cognitive Psychology*, **30**, 257–303. *(3)*

Eslinger, P.J. and Damasio, A.R. (1985). Severe disturbance of higher cognition after bilateral frontal ablation: patient EVR. *Neurology*, **35**, 1731–41. *(3)*

Gershberg, F.B. (1997). Implicit and explicit conceptual memory following frontal lobe damage. *Journal of Cognitive Neuroscience*, **9**, 105–16. *(3)*

Harlow, J.M. (1868). Recovery from the passage of an iron rod through the head. *Boston Medicine and Surgery Journal*, **39**, 389–93. *(2)*

Passingham, R.E. (1995). *The Frontal Lobes and Voluntary Action*. Oxford: Oxford University Press. *(4)*

Prigatano, G.P. (1992). Personality disturbances associated with traumatic brain injury. *Journal of Consulting and Clinical Psychology*, **60**(3), 360–8. *(4)*

Rolls, E.T. (1990). A theory of emotion, and its application to understanding the neural basis of emotion. *Cognition and Emotion*, **4**(3), 161–90. *(4)*

Rushton, J.P. (1997). Race, intelligence and the brain: the errors and omissions of the 'revised' edition of S.J. Gould's *The Mismeasure of Man*. *Personality and Individual Differences*, **23**(1), 169–80. *(1)*

Schore, A.N. (1996). The experience-dependent maturation of a regulatory system in the orbital prefrontal cortex and the origin of developmental psychopathology. *Development and Psychopathology*, **8**, 59–87. *(4)*

Shimamura, A.P. (1995). Memory and frontal lobe function. In M.S. Gazzaniga (ed.), *The Cognitive Neurosciences*. Cambridge, MA: MIT Press. *(3)*

Wheeler, M.A., Stuss, D.T. and Tulving, E. (1997). Toward a theory of episodic memory: the frontal lobes and autonoetic consciousness. *Psychological Bulletin*, **121**(3), 331–54. *(3)*

Chapter Seven

Agnosias and other perceptual disorders

▇ Introduction

In previous chapters we examined some of the cognitive and social consequences of brain damage and brain surgery. Localization of function is sometimes possible at the crude level (hemispheric) or at a more specific level (structural or neural). This is more clearly and straightforwardly seen in the sensory and motor systems, where damage to certain brain regions is associated with predictable and explicable sensory or motor deficits. However, from a neuropsychological point of view there are other disorders related to the sensory systems which are arguably more interesting, not least because of the unusual problems they present. These disorders are principally disorders of perception: brain damage has resulted in a clear deficit in perception despite adequate sensation and relatively unimpaired language ability. The most well documented of the perceptual disorders is **agnosia** (literally, without knowledge), a condition in which a patient is unable to recognize objects in a particular sensory modality. For example, a patient may not be able to recognize an object by sight (visual agnosia) or sound (auditory agnosia) or touch (tactile agnosia), despite having unimpaired language and sensation. This phenomenon, and others like it, is examined in this chapter.

▇ Blindsight

Patients with agnosia typically have relatively intact sensation. There are other patients, however, who have a recognized sensory impairment such as cortical blindness but who present a more unusual problem: they are able to make simple perceptual decisions despite being unaware of the perceived stimuli and despite the absence of the part of the brain responsible for higher visual functioning, the striate cortex. This phenomenon is called **blindsight**. (There are similar phenomena in the somatosensory and auditory systems called numbsense/blindtouch and deaf hearing, respectively.)

The earliest cases of blindsight were reported at the beginning of this century (Holmes, 1918; Riddoch, 1917). Holmes' patients, for example, could identify objects but were unable to notice them when in visual range. They were also unable to follow a moving object with their eyes. Riddoch reported patients who were apparently blind but could grasp moving objects or indicate the direction of movement despite reporting being unable to see the objects.

The blindness in these patients need not necessarily be complete. Damage to the striatal cortex can produce areas of complete blindness called **scotomas**. Blindsight patients can discriminate some stimuli in these areas but report being unaware of the stimuli presented. One of the most celebrated cases of blindsight is that of patient DB whose behaviour has been extensively reported by Oxford psychologist Larry Weiskrantz (1986). DB required surgery to remove an arteriovenous malformation in his right occipital lobe. The removal of the right striatal cortex resulted in a left visual field scotoma, specifically in the lower left quadrant of his visual field. Although appearing unaware of stimuli presented in his blind field of vision, DB performed well above chance on a number of simple perceptual tasks. These included indicating whether a stick was horizontal or vertical, detecting the location of a stimulus by pointing at it, being able to detect the presence or absence of a stimulus and distinguishing between certain shapes (such as a cross from a circle). On other tasks he performed poorly. For example, he was unable to distinguish a triangle from a cross or a curved triangle from a normal one. More importantly, however, was his lack of awareness of any stimuli presented to him. According to DB, he 'couldn't see anything' when the test stimuli were presented in his impaired visual field, a phenomenon which suggests that the processes of being able to see and being aware of what is seen are, possibly, dissociable.

A number of hypotheses have sought to try to explain blindsight. Campion *et al.* (1983), for example, suggest that perceptual tasks can be completed successfully, at above chance levels, because stray light emitted by stimuli makes its way from the intact field of vision to the scotoma. The stray light hypothesis, however, appears to be an unlikely explanation because DB is able to make perceptual decisions in the presence of strong ambient light which reduces the amount of stray light emitted by stimuli. More to the point, this theory does not explain how DB can still make decisions based on the spatial dimensions of objects. An alternative hypothesis suggests that the residual perceptual abilities of patients such as DB are attributable to the degrading of normal vision, possibly due to the presence of some residual striatal cortex. Implicit in this hypothesis is the notion that residual abilities are not attributable to the functioning of another visual system pathway. As we saw in Chapter 3, there appear to be two distinct pathways in the visual system which mediate different aspects of vision. The visual location of objects, for example is thought to be a function of a system which includes the superior colliculus, the posterior thalamus and Areas 20 and 21, whereas the analysis of visual form, pattern or colour is thought to be a function of the geniculostriate system which sends projections from the retina to the lateral geniculate nucleus, then to Areas 17, 18 and 19, and then to Areas 20 and 21. Blindsight could, therefore, conceivably be due to a disconnection between these two systems. Again, there are arguments against this hypothesis. Primates with their striate cortex removed exhibit blindsight. DB also showed variable performance depending on the area of the scotoma that the stimuli were presented in. For example, he was better at distinguishing a blank stimulus from a grating than at discriminating between a cross and a triangle in one region of the scotoma, but exhibited the opposite pattern when the stimuli were presented in a different region.

What seems intuitively correct, but for which there is no hard evidence, is the hypothesis that what is at work in blindsight is a primitive, early visual system that is not dependent on the striate cortex. A note of caution should be struck, however. Blythe *et al.* (1987), for example, found only 5 cases of blindsight in a sample of 25 patients; Marzi *et al.* (1986) found a similar ratio (4 patients out of 20) in their sample. The degree of variability in the appearance of blindsight following striatal removal, therefore, suggests some restraint in extrapolating from individual cases. An interesting discussion and review of the role of the striate cortex in blindsight can be found in Stoerig and Cowey (1997).

Agnosia

According to Bauer (1993), agnosia is classically defined as a 'failure of recognition that cannot be attributed to elementary sensory defects, mental deterioration, attentional disturbances, aphasic misnaming, or unfamiliarity with sensorially presented stimuli.' Sometimes, brain damage can affect aspects of sensation such as determining the presence or absence of light, detecting changes in contrast (**acuity**), discriminating between shapes (**shape discrimination**) or perceiving colour. Patients unable to perceive colour exhibit **achromatopsia** and describe the world as being drained of colour or grey. The classical diagnosis of agnosia dictates that these sensory deficits are absent.

The most commonly studied of the agnosias are **visual agnosia**, **auditory agnosia** and **tactile agnosia** and clear modality specificity is normally observed, i.e. a person unable to recognize an object by sight will be able to name the object if allowed to palpate it. The principal agnosias are summarized in Table 7.1.

Visual agnosia

In visual agnosia, there is a severe inability to recognize visual stimuli despite intact sensory abilities. According to Lissauer (1890), agnosia manifested itself in two distinct forms: **apperceptive agnosia** and **associative agnosia** (Lissauer originally termed them **apperceptive mindblindness** and **associative mindblindness**). For example, apperceptive agnosia described an inability to recognize visual objects owing to some deficit in perceptual processing. Associative agnosia,

Table 7.1 The principal agnosias and their neural basis

Agnosia	Locus of damage
Apperceptive visual agnosia	RH parietal or temporal lesions
Associative visual agnosia	LH posterior lesions
Optic aphasia	LH parieto-occipital lesions
Colour agnosia	
Central achromatopsia	Unilateral inferior occipital lesion
	Lingual/fusiform gyri lesions
Prosopagnosia	RH posterior lesions
	Possible parahippocampal gyrus, lingual/fusiform gyri and splenium lesions
Auditory agnosia	
Pure word deafness	Bilateral, symmetrical cortico-subcortical lesions of the anterior temporal gyri
Auditory sound agnosia	Parietel lobe lesions
	Temporal and angular gyri lesions
Somatosensory agnosia	
Tactile agnosia	Contralateral postcentral gyrus and motor cortex hand area lesions

RH = right hemisphere; LH = left hemisphere

however, described a disorder in which perception was relatively normal but the process of associating an object's percepts with its meaning was impaired. It was Freud (1891) who introduced the term agnosia, arguing that the deficits seen in mindblindness could be considered not only sensory disorders but also impairments in existing knowledge of objects. Agnosia was the inability to bring together visual elements into a complete, recognizable whole. The visual agnosic is unable to identify or recognize visually presented material. The deficit is present despite unimpaired language (so, anomia is excluded as an explanation) and it can appear in a number of guises.

These two general distinctions (apperceptive vs associative) exist in the literature to this day although researchers have delineated more specific types of agnosia falling under each category. There is, however, controversy surrounding the use of these two terms. It has been suggested, for example, that apperceptive agnosia has 'fuzzy boundaries' that make it less distinguishable from associative agnosia (De Renzi and Lucchelli, 1993). Farah (1991) suggests that the difference between the deficits symptomatic of the two disorders is one of level of processing. That is, the description of absence or presence of symptoms as a means of distinguishing between the two types is not practicable. She draws this conclusion on the basis of studies which suggest that even associative agnosia may be reflective of subtle perceptual impairments, specifically the inability to see the whole of an object simultaneously. These studies and others like them are reviewed in the remainder of the chapter.

Apperceptive visual agnosia

Apperceptive agnosia (or visual object agnosia) refers to the inability to recognize objects owing to a deficit in forming stable representations or percepts of a visual stimulus. It commonly results from carbon monoxide or mercury poisoning, cardiac arrest, stroke or bilateral posterior cortical atrophy. Apperceptive agnosics are unable to copy drawings or match objects although they are able to identify objects and drawings. Persons with visual agnosia have intact visual acuity, which distinguishes them from patients with **Anton's syndrome** which is characterized by a denial of blindness. Degraded or incomplete objects, pictures or letters are difficult to identify. On the Gollin's test (Gollin, 1960) which requires the identification of a drawn object whose features are successively revealed, patients require a more complete picture than do controls before being able to identify the object (Warrington and Taylor, 1973). Alterations in the lighting conditions make tasks difficult for these patients. Shadows cast by objects, for example, make the stimuli more unidentifiable (Warrington, 1982). Patients also have greater difficulty in identifying objects from 'unusual' perspectives, performing more poorly than controls (Warrington and Taylor, 1973). These impairments are associated with right inferior parietal lobe lesions. Stimuli that involve complex shape and pattern present the most difficulty, however. Usually, the patient is unable even to point to a named object. Interestingly, these recognition deficits may be alleviated if stimuli are moved while identification is attempted.

This impairment in complex shape and pattern identification highlights one of the controversial issues in agnosia. According to Warrington, any deficit in shape discrimination or even colour discrimination is a defect in sensory processing and does not, therefore, constitute an agnosia. Mr S, a patient studied by Efron (1968), had developed cortical blindness following carbon monoxide poisoning. His symptoms included an inability to identify pictures, objects and people. Efron attributed these deficits to one of shape discrimination (this patient also had more formal shape discrimination difficulties such as being unable to differentiate a square from a rectangle). This notion is controversial because there are some authors (e.g. Humphreys and Riddoch, 1987a) who argue that agnosia does represent the inability to perceive form and have termed the inability to discriminate between shapes, **shape agnosia**. They describe the deficits in patients who misperceive foreshortened or ambiguously presented objects as showing **transformational agnosia**, a disorder considered in the section below on theories of agnosia. They also propose a third, distinct type of agnosia which describes an inability to integrate elements of a stimulus to create a recognizable whole. This they describe as **integrative agnosia**, a disorder exhibited by their patient, HJA (Humphreys and Riddoch, 1987a,b).

Integrative agnosia: patient HJA

Patient HJA was a businessman who had suffered a bilateral stroke. He appeared to show some visual deficits although his ability to discriminate line length and position were normal. He is able to copy drawings but he is not an associative agnosic. Humphreys and Riddoch have described HJA's case in some detail, especially his painstaking process of drawing. In one instance, he took six hours to complete a drawing he was then unable to name. The unusual feature of HJA's deficit appears to be the inability to bring together elements of a stimulus into a meaningful unit. One or two minor elements of an object will be used as a basis for attempting to identify the object. Humphreys and Riddoch chose the expression integrative agnosia to describe this phenomenon as a means of distinguishing it from another disorder, simultanagnosia, which is similar but has a more precise symptomatology.

The mechanism underlying HJA's disorder is unclear, but Humphreys and Riddoch have suggested that one of two processes necessary for visual processing is defective. They argue that visual perception involves (1) the establishment of the global form of a stimulus and (2) a process whereby individual features of a stimulus are perceived and are 'bound' together. HJA's problem appears to be an inability to appreciate 'integrative local grouping cues'. The distinction between global and local processing is supported by a small number of cases in the literature. For example, Butter and Trobe's patient can name globally processed stimuli such as silhouettes better than he does stimuli which feature many local visual cues, such as line drawings (Butter and Trobe, 1994). Grailet *et al.*'s patient, HG, also exhibits symptoms similar to those of HJA (Grailet *et al.*, 1990).

Farah's classification of agnosia

In addition to the distinct disorders outlined by other authors, Farah (1990) has argued that apperceptive agnosia can be further subdivided into four categories she describes as **narrow apperceptive agnosia, dorsal simultanagnosia, ventral simultanagnosia** and **perceptual categorization deficit**.

Narrow apperceptive agnosia refers to the inability to recognize, match, copy or discriminate between elementary visual forms despite adequate visual function, whereas dorsal simultanagnosia describes an inability to appreciate a whole stimulus despite adequate recognition of its parts (Wolpert, 1924). Whether subjects actually do recognize these parts individually, however, is open to question. Luria (1959) defined the disorder as an inability to see or attend to more than one object simultaneously. The locus of damage in most patients is bilateral, affecting the parieto-occipital area (especially the superior occipital and the inferior parietal lobes). The underlying deficit appears to be a failure to undertake feature-by-feature analysis of stimuli. The disorder is similar to **Balint's syndrome** in which patients with bilateral parietal damage have paralysis of fixation, difficulty in viewing objects voluntarily in peripheral vision and are unable to respond to visual stimuli manually. A patient with Balint's syndrome might focus quite narrowly on the tip of a cigarette in his or her mouth and be unable to see a match offered a short distance away.

Ventral simultanagnosia describes a condition that is not as severe as the dorsal version: patients can negotiate the environment and can perform tasks such as dot-counting significantly better than patients with the dorsal form. The locus of damage appears to be the left occiptotemporal junction although it is debatable whether this is a separate disorder or whether it simply differs in degree from dorsal simultanagnosia.

Farah's final category, perceptual categorization deficit, describes an impairment in experimentally induced recognition with apparently unimpaired real-life recognition. That is, in experiments, patients show recognition impairment but this impairment does not affect their daily life. The best known of these experiments requires the subject to identify several two- and three-dimensional objects placed at various angles (De Renzi *et al.*, 1969; Warrington and James, 1986). Patients normally have right-sided parietal lesions (De Renzi *et al.*, 1969) although impairments have been noted following right temporal lobe injury (B. Milner, 1958).

In summary, apperceptive agnosia is probably the most controversial agnosia because its existence as a distinct disorder not involving underlying visual disturbance has been challenged (Bay, 1953). Some have argued, for example, that the disorder is a combination of visual sensory disturbance, ocular fixation problems, inattention and dementia (Bender and Feldman, 1972). Others have argued that the precise anatomical basis for this disorder is virtually impossible to determine because of the variability in attention, memory, perception and occulomotor behaviour seen in these patients (Bauer, 1993). Despite these objections, the term continues to be used. An awareness of the controversy surrounding its use, however, is important.

Associative visual agnosia

Patients exhibiting associative visual agnosia are also characterized by poor object recognition, but this deficit does not involve faulty perception. Instead, the patient appears to have problems making meaningful associations to stimuli presented visually. The disorder is usually modality-specific in that patients are able to match objects with those presented in a different sensory modality. They are also able to point at objects named by the examiner. There appear to be degrees of severity associated with the disorder. For example, identification of line drawings is more difficult than identification of real-life objects and pictures of objects whereas pictures are more difficult to identify than real-life objects. In general, however, the more complex the stimulus, the greater the number of semantic errors that the associative agnosic patient makes.

An unusual example of associative visual agnosia was reported by Rubens and Benson (1971). Their patient was a physician with superior verbal skills but impaired visual object identification. He was able to identify objects by touch, but when asked to identify his stethoscope visually would reply that it was a 'long cord with a round thing at the end'. He could copy drawings and draw well (a characteristic of patients with this disorder), but identified his drawings incorrectly. Often, patients are slow at the copying task and perform the exercise painstakingly, taking time over small detail and features. Humphreys and Riddoch's patient, HJA, for example, took six hours to complete an accurate drawing that he was unable to identify. Strictly speaking, however, as we have already noted, HJA may not be a true associative agnosic.

The disorder is associated with a right homonymous hemianopia usually resulting from posterior, left hemisphere lesions (Warrington, 1985; Geschwind, 1965), bilateral occipital lobe lesions (M.P. Alexander and Albert, 1983) or, it has been reported, right occipital lesions (Levine, 1978). The variability in the locus of these lesions might explain the variability of symptoms seen in associative visual agnosia. Lissauer's original case presented lesions of the left hemisphere at the occipital–temporal junction (Lissauer, 1890). Hecaen and his colleagues have also reported left occipital lobe lesions (Hecaen and Ajuriaguerra, 1956; Hecaen et al., 1974), as have McCarthy and Warrington (1986) using MRI in one case study. Posterior left hemisphere lesions appear to be reliably associated with this deficit (Warrington and Taylor, 1973).

Associative agnosia is rare and is sometimes seen in combination with other agnosias (such as the inability to identify faces or colours) but its existence has been challenged (Teuber, 1965). Hecaen and Angelergues (1963), for example, found that only 4 patients out of 415 presented this deficit. Patients may not be completely unable to assign meaning to objects because they are able to assign objects to a superordinate class such as mammal, insect and bird (McCarthy and Warrington, 1986; Bubb et al., 1988). There is also the potential difficulty of ruling out the presence of any perceptual deficits in these patients. It is also possible that patients showing this type of agnosia may, in fact, be exhibiting optic aphasia.

Optic aphasia

Optic aphasia is a disorder in which the naming, but not recognition, of visual stimuli is impaired. The disorder is different from anomia, the inability to name objects, because correct identification is possible in other sensory modalities. The earliest case of **optic aphasia** was reported by Freund (1889) whose patient suffered a right homonymous hemianopia owing to a parieto-occipital tumour. The relative independence of these two disorders, associative agnosia and optic aphasia, has, however, been questioned. It is possible that optic aphasia is a milder form of associative agnosia or that the types of impairment seen in patients fall at some point along a continuum from associative agnosia to optic aphasia. De Renzi and Saetti (1997), for example, argue that both disorders reflect an impaired ability to access structured representations in the semantic, left hemisphere. The disorders differ in the degree of semantic compensation that the right hemisphere provides. The right hemisphere's semantic capacity, therefore, plays a significant role in the appearance of these disorders, according to De Renzi and Saetti's hypothesis.

Colour agnosia

Colour agnosia refers to an inability to name colours despite the ability to discriminate between them. Patients may be unable to sort differently coloured patches into groups of the same colour or may be unable to colour-in pictures appropriately (Sittig, 1921; De Renzi and Spinnler, 1967). Pointing to a colour named by the examiner is not possible nor is naming the colour that the examiner points to. Three colour agnosia syndromes include **central achromatopsia (dys-chromatopsia), colour anomia** and **specific colour aphasia**.

Central achromatopsia (Green and Lessell, 1977) involves a loss of colour vision owing to a lesion to the visual system pathways (the optic nerve, the optic chiasm or both) although it can occur with unilateral inferior occipital lobe lesions. Oddly, this damage can affect one colour more than another. Patients commonly observe that the world is drained of colour and is either black and white, grainy, or grey. Although unable to identify colours, patients can, however, perform verbal tasks that are colour-related (e.g. answer correctly when asked what is the colour of blood). Damage to the lingual and fusiform gyri has been implicated in the disorder. It is possible that these regions represent the area in humans that corresponds to that in rhesus monkeys responsible for responding to wavelengths of light (Damasio *et al.*, 1980b).

Colour anomia is the literal inability to name colours despite being able to answer verbal questions about colour. Finally, specific colour aphasia describes a condition in which even verbal questions about colour cannot be answered.

▤ Theories of visual agnosia

The models developed to explain visual agnosia tend to fall into distinct camps. For example, Bauer (1993) lists four such models: stage models, disconnection models, computational models and cognitive neuropsychological models.

An example of a stage model is that of Lissauer (1880) who proposed that recognition comprised two stages of processing: apperception and association. Disconnection models, such as those of Geschwind (1965), argue that agnosia results from a disconnection between two processes, such as visual and verbal processes.

Computational models such as Marr's (1982) suggest that the variation in the perceptual world with which we are presented every day is made possible by three types of representation: a primal sketch, a viewer-centred or $2\frac{1}{2}$-D sketch, and an object-centred 3-D sketch. The first representation does not depend on an individual's point of view (it is viewpoint-independent); the second, however, is viewer-centred and, therefore, viewer-dependent. An extension of this computational model to include neurology has been proposed by A. Damasio (1989). He argues that the varieties of perceptual experience stimulate representative neural areas corresponding with each type of experience. The features of the object are then combined to form a 'convergence zone', where the whole can be constructed. Recognition, the model argues, depends on the activation of the neural pattern which defines a particular object.

Finally, cognitive neuropsychological models take a slightly different view and are inclined to regard any neuropsychological disorder in terms of components or modules. These models view the various cognitive and emotional operations as dissociable and are reviewed in the following sections.

Apperceptive agnosia

Much of the controversy in visual agnosia research is generated by two problems. (1) Are apperceptive and associative agnosias dissociable? (2) Are visual, sensory deficits necessary or unnecessary for a diagnosis of agnosia? Lissauer's model clearly separates the two process of apperception and association. Warrington also suggests a dichotomy in which perceptual classification is separate from semantic classification (and perhaps reflects Lissauer's dichotomy in a more specific, neuropsychologically driven way). As we have already seen, Warrington argues strongly for the absence of lower-level visual deficits before a diagnosis of agnosia can be made, describing such disorders involving lower-level disruption as pseudoagnosia. Humphreys and Riddoch, however, dismiss the notion of pseudoagnosia, arguing that shape discrimination deficits do reflect recognition difficulties and not specifically sensory ones.

One computational theory of apperceptive agnosia which has gained some favour in those quarters represented by Warrington is based on the concept of axis transformation (Marr, 1982). Marr's theory suggests that a three-dimensional representation of an object is obtained by determining the object's minor and major axes. Seeing a tennis racket from the side, for example, supplies information from the major axis (its length) which we can then use to make inferences about other aspects of the racket (such as the width of the handle). A task in which the subject is required to identify objects from unusual perspectives is difficult, Marr argued, because a major axis has been obscured or foreshortened. Based on this reasoning, Humphreys and Riddoch (1987a) attributed apperceptive agnosia to a deficit in axis transformation and, as we saw earlier, termed it transformational agnosia.

An alternative theory, the distinctive-features model of object recognition (Warrington and James, 1986), suggests that sets of distinctive features identify an object's structure. The determinants of object recognition, therefore, would not be axis rotation but how many features were made available at a specific angle. One objection to the theory is that object perception deficits are not homogeneous, i.e. there seem to be dissociations between classes of stimuli (McCarthy and Warrington, 1990). Unless the model suggests a stimulus-specific feature-specific deficit, it cannot account for these dissociations.

A final model suggested by Rudge and Warrington (1990) is based on data from patients with splenium lesions who perform poorly on the unusual views task but are normal at recognizing perceptually simple pictures, i.e. there is no visual agnosia. This 'optional resource' hypothesis suggests that information may be processed in parallel: object meaning is derived from both visual information processing that is sensory in nature and the functioning of the right hemisphere and splenium, but only if a task requires the analysis of an ambiguous or difficult object structure.

Associative agnosia

One theory of associative agnosia argues that there is one system responsible for mediating the meaning of all stimuli. This is called the **shared-systems theory**. Agnosia, therefore, is a problem of connecting the output of perceptual analysis with the patient's general store of knowledge. Riddoch *et al.* (1988) suggest that problems occur because of a breakdown in the transmission of information from the perceptual to semantic systems, i.e. there is a disconnection. This theory does not appear to account fully for the disorder, however, because the literature features great variability in symptoms.

For example, a second approach, the **independent-systems theory**, suggests that processes such as visual object recognition are independent of other processes such as those required for speech production or comprehension of words. Evidence for this approach comes from studies in which impairments in visual processing do not accompany verbal impairments, and vice versa (McCarthy and Warrington, 1988). What the theory suggests is a form of modularity in which some psychological processes are dissociable and independent of each other (Fodor, 1983). Further evidence for this model comes from data showing that an ability to recognize common objects may be impaired but the ability to recognize complex shapes is not. Furthermore, based on an extensive review of the literature reporting cases of alexia (A), visual object agnosia (VOA) and prosopagnosia (P, face recognition impairment), Farah (1990, 1991) has suggested that object recognition is subserved by two independent but parallel processes. One process concerns the perception of the whole pattern of stimuli; the other concerns the perception of constituent elements of an object. Farah drew this conclusion from literature which showed that although all of the following combinations were possible:

A, VOA and P
A and VOA
VOA and P

no case of alexia with face recognition impairment but without visual object agnosia had been reported. This suggested two systems: one which recognized wholes (e.g. faces) and another which recognized constituents (e.g. words). Visual object recognition depended on both processes. The logical extension of this thinking dictates that the apperceptive/associative distinction becomes unnecessary. Humphreys and Riddoch (1993), however, have argued against such a view, citing evidence from patients who are unable to recognize objects but are able to make decisions based on the properties of objects. That said, their patient HJA, although being poor at face recognition, was better at identifying silhouettes than line drawings which perhaps indicates the operation of some 'holistic' process.

▓ Category-specific visual agnosia

Some agnosic patients appear to be poorer at recognizing some visual stimuli than others (Newcombe *et al.*, 1994). In neuropsychology, one category of stimuli – faces – stands out, and this is considered in the next section. However, other dissociations in recognition have been reported. Warrington and Shallice's patient, JBR, for example, is apparently unable to name living things or musical instruments but can name non-living things and parts of the body (Warrington and Shallice, 1984). This case appears to confirm similar disorders reported in the literature. Reports of patients who are unable to recognize living things (Nielsen, 1937) or animals (McCrae and Trolle, 1956) have been documented. Does this evidence suggest that different regions of the brain process different categories of stimuli? In an illuminating PET study, Alex Martin and his colleagues compared brain activation in healthy individuals as they named drawings of tools or animals (Martin *et al.*, 1996). They found that although both tasks bilaterally activated the ventral temporal lobes and Broca's area, the naming only of animals activated the left medial occipital lobe. The naming of tools only was associated with activation of the left premotor area and middle temporal gyrus, areas that are known to be activated during hand movement and generation of 'action' words, respectively. This study suggests that an object's identity is processed by different regions of the brain, depending on the meaning assigned to that object, and might go some way towards explaining the dissociations seen in associative agnosia.

Or does it? It is possible that these dissociations in neuropsychological patients are not the result of genuine inability to recognize specific categories of object but are the consequence of stimulus artefact. For example, the stimuli used in experiments in which dissociations have been reported may not be entirely appropriate. Consider the perception and a drawing of a cup and a drawing of a fly, for example. Critics have argued that the former is a lot less detailed than the latter and would, therefore, be recognized and identified more easily. A dissociation, therefore, can be attributed to stimulus complexity or familiarity rather than to specific categories of object. In similar vein, some written words may be more familar than drawings of the objects they are meant to represent. In addition, the usual picture database used to examine recognition itself contains fewer *familiar* living than non-living things. The dissociation between impaired animate and inanimate object recognition, therefore, becomes questionable because the results can be attributed to factors unrelated to stimulus category. Stewart and his colleagues have found that when controls are in place to account for these artefacts, the dissociations disappear (Stewart *et al.*, 1992). Even JBR's deficit disappears when all stimuli are made equally familiar. This said, there are patients who continue to show dissociations despite being examined under well controlled conditions (e.g. Sheridan and Humphreys, 1993) so that artifacts may not explain away the dissociations completely.

Prosopagnosia

The best known and most reliable category-specific recognition disorder is **prosopagnosia**. In 1947, Bodamer reported three patients who had difficulty recognizing faces but who could recognize objects normally (Bodamer, 1947). He termed this phenomenon prosopagnosia ('loss of knowledge of faces') and regarded it as a distinct neurological deficit. Later, Hecaen and Angelergues (1962) reported 22 cases of prosopagnosia who failed to recognize the faces of even old acquaintances (in some cases, even themselves). One patient remarked when looking at his wedding photograph, 'Two people . . . one of them could be my wife because of the silhouette . . . if it is my wife, the other person could be me.' Despite the inability to identify faces, patients are able to identify individuals by their voice, clothing or marks on other parts of the body. Sometimes, faces are described as having a distorted, warped or flat appearance. Patients can, however, recognize a face as being a face and can discriminate between faces. The problem lies in being unable to identify individual faces. One of the more famous examples of prosopagnosia was reported by Sacks (1985). Dr P, 'the man who mistook his wife for a hat', had severe prosopagnosia. According to Sacks, 'he saw faces when there were no faces to see: genially, Magoo-like, when in the street, he might pat the heads of water-hydrants and parking meters, taking these to be the heads of children; he would amiably address carved knobs on the furniture, and be astounded when they did not answer.' There are many other unusual examples of prosopagnosics' behaviour, such as the man who had wondered why a diner in the same restaurant had been staring at him intently for some time only to discover from the waiter that he was staring at his own reflection in the mirror (Pallis, 1955).

In experiments, prosopagnosia is demonstrated by administering a number of facial recognition tests. One is the same/different task and requires patients to determine whether two photographs are of the same individual when the pairs could be two different views of the same person, or two different but similar-looking people. Another task might require the patient to match a frontal view of a person with one of six stimuli which may be a three-quarter view of the same face or the same face under different lighting conditions (Benton and Van Allen, 1968). A slightly more unusual but sensitive test requires subjects to rank quadruplets of faces by age (De Renzi *et al.*, 1989). However, there is evidence that prosopagnosic patients can distinguish between faces based on the criteria of expression, age and sex (Tranel *et al.*, 1988).

There is evidence to suggest that some patients might be sensitive to particular features of the face. Gloning and Quatember (1966), for example, found that prosopagnosic patients were worse at matching eyes to whole pictures than they were at matching mouths, although the reasons for this are unclear. The accurate perception of facial expression may be impaired (De Kosky *et al.*, 1980), but this is complicated by the inability to identify *emotional* facial expression (Etkoff, 1984).

Sometimes, patients may have difficulty recognizing famous people (Warrington and James, 1967) or very familiar people like spouses (De Renzi, 1986a,b). One patient, a 73 year old public notary, studied by De Renzi, once remarked to his wife, 'Are you . . .? I guess you are my wife because there are no other women at home, but I want to be reassured.' His face perception evaluated on sensitive tests was normal.

In an interesting study by Bruyer *et al.* (1983), one patient had difficulty recognizing all but very familiar faces. When taught to associate names with the faces, he was able to do so but he was much slower at associating the names when they were false ones, which suggests some unconscious knowledge of the faces' names. Prosopagnosia has, to date, never occurred in pure form, i.e. without associated perceptual deficits.

Explaining prosopagnosic deficits, however, presents neuropsychology with one of its most interesting challenges. Is it a form of object visual agnosia or is it a form that is specific to faces? Or perhaps it is an inability to identify individuality in a class of objects? This last question has been addressed in a small number of studies in which prosopagnosics were unable to identify specific chairs (Faust, 1955) or cars (Lhermitte and Pillon, 1975). Bornstein *et al.* (1969) reported two patients, one a farmer, the other a birdwatcher, who were unable to identify specific cows and birds respectively. Of course, the inability to name faces has led to the suggestion that prosopagnosia may be an impairment of memory. Impaired familiar face perception often indicates amnesia, for example, and prosopagnosics are poor at learning new faces (as are amnesiacs). This relationship is not, however, reciprocal. It is rare, for example, for an amnesic to be prosopagnosic. Alternatively, it has been suggested that a visual categorization defect and a material-specific defect are necessary for prosopagnosia to occur (A. Damasio *et al.*, 1982). What Damasio and his colleagues suggest is that a 'visual trigger' cannot prompt the retrieval of 'multimodal memories' although the context of learning has been processed. This is known because individuals can be identified by voice or clothing.

The locus of brain damage in prosopagnosia tends to be right-hemisphere based, although the disorder does occur with bilateral damage to white matter and cortex in the occipitotemporal gyrus. However, cases have been reported where proso-pagnosia was found without lesion to this junction (A. Damasio *et al.*, 1982). These authors also report bilateral damage associated with the disorder, suggesting that unilateral right hemisphere lesions may be necessary but not sufficient for proso-pagnosia to occur. Unilateral right hemisphere lesions are common (De Renzi *et al.*, 1994; Landis *et al.*, 1986). Studies of perception and recognition of facial expression have also associated deficits with unilateral right hemisphere damage (Bowers *et al.*, 1985). De Renzi *et al.* (1994), in a review of the literature, noted 27 cases where neuroimaging data demonstrated right hemisphere damage with prosopagnosia. Lesions in the parahippocampal gyrus and lingual and fusiform gyri are also considered necessary for prosopagnosia (Meadows, 1974; De Renzi, 1986a) as is damage to the splenium (Benton, 1990).

Interestingly, two recent electrophysiological studies have associated right parietotemporal cortex involvement with face perception in normal, healthy individuals. In an evoked potential study, Bentin *et al.* (1996) reported a negative potential occurring at about 172 ms in response to face stimuli but not to other animate stimuli or inanimate, non-face stimuli. Exposure to eyes alone was associated with smaller N170 than was exposure to the whole face, whereas latency was longer during exposure to noses and lips. Face perception was associated with largest EPs at right temporoparietal regions. In similar vein, Burgess and Gruzelier (1997) noted that face recognition was associated with attenuation of alpha, beta1 and beta2 in right temporoparietal regions. Both clinical and normal data, therefore, appear to localize face recognition in the same general cortical region.

Covert recognition in prosopagnosia

Despite the apparent inability of prosopagnosics to identify faces, there is evidence that some patients may be able to do this covertly. For example, Bauer (1984) measured galvanic skin response (GSR) while his patient, LF, viewed a familiar face then listened to five names read aloud. When the name associated with the face was read, there was a greater change in galvanic skin response than when the other names were heard. Yet, when asked to identify the name associated with the picture, performance was at chance level. Bauer's explanation for this phenom-enon was that overt recognition and orientating to emotional stimuli involve two pathways: a ventral route which allows overt recognition but which is damaged in prosopagnosia and a dorsal route which is spared and allows emotional sig-nificance to be attached to faces.

In a conceptually simple experiment, Tranel and Damasio (1985) presented a prosopagnosic patient with a series of famous and unfamiliar faces. GSR changed significantly during exposure to the familiar faces. One of their patients also demonstrated an inability to recognize faces after illness, what Tranel and Damasio called 'anterograde prosopagnosia'. What appears to be lost is not complete recognition, but an awareness of recognition (Young, 1994a). Despite these studies, however, it should be borne in mind that evidence of covert recognition in prosopagnosics is not always found.

■ Amygdala and face processing

Any discussion of the neural substrates of face processing must, for two reasons, include the amygdala. First, damage to this structure has been associated with impaired memory for faces, and secondly, there are cells in the amygdala which respond selectively to faces in primates (Rolls, 1984; Leonard *et al.*, 1985) and humans (Seeck *et al.*, 1993). Rolls (1990), for example, has argued that these neurons receive inputs from the superior temporal sulcus which responds to features of faces and that this part of the amygdala is thought to be especially involved in the emotional and social response to a face.

Human data have, however, been limited to studies of memory for faces and not of performance over a range of face processing tasks. Jacobson (1986), in one case, found poor learning of new faces, borderline abnormalities in the matching of unfamiliar faces, and impaired recognition of familiar faces (especially in naming faces). Young *et al.*'s study of DR, a 51 year old woman whose amygdala had been partially but bilaterally removed, reported that she was able to recognize pre-operative, familiar faces but was impaired at naming faces and recognizing faces learned postoperatively (Young *et al.*, 1995). Matching unfamiliar faces was unimpaired, but the matching and identification of emotional facial expressions was poor.

■ A model of face processing

Given the data provided by studies of prosopagnosia, it may be possible to construct a model of face processing that explains which systems mediate which aspects of face perception and recognition. A well known model is that of Bruce and Young (1986). This model proposes that the processing of facial expressions, the recognition of familiar faces and the matching of unfamiliar faces involve different cognitive abilities (see Figure 7.1).

Facial expression analysis is thought to be 'dependent on view-centred descriptions created at the structural encoding stage', familiar face recognition is dependent on access to 'face recognition units' via expression-independent descriptions, and unfamiliar face matching is dependent on both view-centred and expression-independent descriptions. Therefore the pathway needed for each function differs.

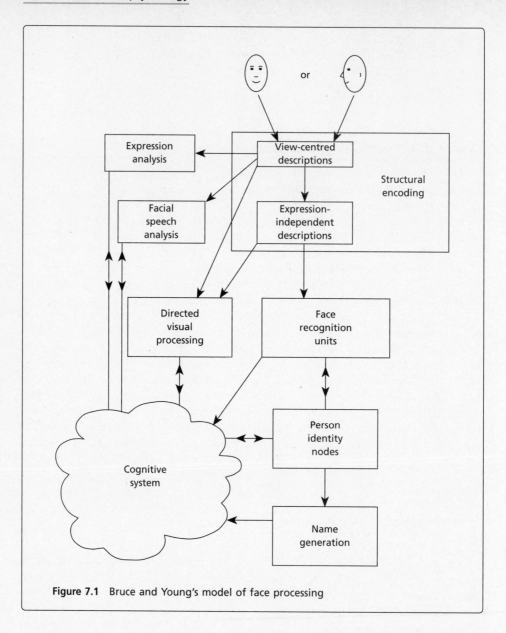

Figure 7.1   Bruce and Young's model of face processing

There is some evidence for the model. Patients with facial identity problems, for example, can readily identify facial expression (Tranel *et al.*, 1988). Evidence from prosopagnosic patients also lends supports to the model (Benton and Van Allen, 1968; Warrington and James, 1967). The discussion point at the end of the chapter takes up this theme.

◼ Auditory agnosia

Auditory agnosia refers to the inability to recognize or identify sounds despite an intact auditory system. Agnosia may be for general speech and non-speech sounds or may be specific to non-speech sounds. Within each of the two types of disorder there are a number of more specific disorders (Bauer, 1993). Into the general category fall **auditory sound agnosia**, **auditory verbal agnosia** and a disorder involving both of these. Into the second, narrower category fall **pure word deafness** (an impairment in the ability to recognize speech sounds) and **auditory agnosia** (an impairment in the ability to recognize non-speech sounds). There are also related disorders such as **cortical deafness**, where patients are unaware of any type of sound although their tone threshold is normal, and **receptive amusia**, the inability to appreciate features of aural music.

Pure word deafness

Pure word deafness, which is also known as auditory agnosia for speech or auditory verbal agnosia, is the inability to comprehend spoken speech despite having unimpaired speech, writing and reading. Comprehension of non-verbal sounds is spared. It is described as 'pure' because the characteristics of aphasia common to that disorder are usually absent. Patients remark that sounds are muffled or sound like a foreign language (Albert and Bear, 1974). The neuro-anatomical basis of the disorder is thought to involve bilateral, symmetrical corticosubcortical lesions of the anterior temporal gyri. Cases of unilateral sub-cortical lesions in the temporal cortex of the language-dominant hemisphere have been reported, however. There may also be some specificity within the disorder, with some patients presenting impaired auditory comprehension of abstract but not concrete words (Franklin *et al.*, 1994).

Auditory sound agnosia

Auditory sound agnosia, or auditory agnosia for non-speech sounds, is rare and has been divided into two specific types (Vignolo, 1969). The first results from right hemisphere lesions and involves a deficit in perceptual discrimination of non-speech sounds. The loci of the damage appear to involve the parietal lobe, specifically the superior temporal and angular gyri, and the inferior and middle frontal cortex and the insula. The second type is associated with left hemisphere lesions and involves a disruption in semantic processing such as mistaking the sound of an object for that of another (e.g. mistaking a man whistling for bird-song, a train for a motor engine, and so on).

Receptive amusia

Receptive amusia, or sensory receptive amusia, is found in cases of auditory sound agnosia, most aphasias and pure word deafness. It is one of the more difficult disorders to diagnose, however, because a diagnosis relies on a knowledge of the patients' previous ability to appreciate characteristics of heard music and this is not always obtainable.

■ Somatosensory agnosia

The final class of agnosias discussed in this chapter are those involving somato-sensation and are probably the least well understood of the agnosias. Early classification divided the somatosensory agnosias into **amorphognosia** (an inability to recognize an object's size or shape), **ahylognosia** (an inability to determine an object's weight, texture or temperature) and **tactile asymboly** (an inability to identify objects when amorphognosia and ahylognosia are absent) (Delay, 1935). The terms **tactile agnosia** and **astereognosis** are the most commonly employed today.

Tactile agnosia describes the inability to identify an object by touch despite having adequate sensory, intellectual and linguistic ability. Astereognosis describes the inability to distinguish three-dimensional forms or to discriminate between objects based on size or shape. Tactile agnosia and astereognosis are sometimes used interchangeably, although they are most likely to be dissociable. When there is an inability to identify objects by touch in the presence of sensory impairment, the disorder is called **steroanaesthesia**.

The neural basis of the disorder is usually damage to the contralateral post-central gyrus (SI) and hand area of the motor cortex. It has been suggested that unilateral damage to SI causes contralateral impairment, but unilateral damage to SII results in less severe impairments affecting both hands (Corkin, 1978). Like most of the agnosias, the reality of the disorder has been questioned, with tactile agnosia being interpreted as a basic somatosensory dysfunction, a modality-specific anomia, or a disorder in spatial perception. The first interpretation receives some support from a study in which those patients with CNS and PNS disorders who had somatosensory deficits also had greater tactile object recognition problems when unilateral damage was found in the parietotemporal cortices (Caselli, 1991). A recent case study, however, indicates that tactile shape perception can be dissociated from tactile spatial ability, shape exploration and perception of length (Reed *et al.*, 1996). Reed *et al.*'s patient, EC, had sustained a left inferior parietal infarction involving Areas 39, 40, 17, 18 and 36 which affected her ability to identify objects by touch. Despite intact tactile sensation, this patient manifested unilateral tactile agnosia.

■ Unilateral spatial neglect

The disorder unilateral spatial neglect (often referred to as simply **spatial neglect, spatial hemineglect** or **hemi-inattention**) is a failure to report, or respond or attend to, stimuli or events in the hemifield contralateral to brain injury (usually temporo-parietal) despite adequate elementary sensory or motor function (Heilman *et al.*, 1994). Patients appear to 'see' only half of the world, and the neglect of stimuli can occur for months and even years after the lesion. A neglect of stimuli on the left following right hemisphere damage is more common, although right neglect following left hemisphere lesion is also observed but is usually not as severe.

The disorder can manifest itself in any modality but usually involves a neglect of personal or body space, neglect of space that is within reach of the patient (**peripersonal space**) or neglect of space that is within walking distance (**extrapersonal space**). There is evidence that neglect is dissociable, in that patients may have impaired perception of peripersonal space, for example, but not of extrapersonal space (Halligan and Marshall, 1991). This is an important observation because, even until the mid 1980s, the existence of the disorder was not widely known, was poorly characterized and had no real taxonomy (Halligan and Marshall, 1994). It is clear that spatial neglect is not unitary: some aspects are impaired while others are spared. Heilman *et al.* (1994), for example, suggest that different types of neglect can be defined by the mechanism underlying them: inattention underlies sensory/perceptual neglect; disorders of action and intention underlie motor neglect; and representation underlies the neglect of visual/mental images.

Most spatial neglect deficits are characterized by an apparent unawareness of information or stimuli presented in one hemifield. The neglect is not for stimuli presented to one or other side of the midline of the body, but for stimuli found on either side of a fixation point on which the patient must focus. Behavioural examples of spatial neglect include difficulty in reading the time from a clock, missing food on the left side of the plate, dressing one side of the body, failing to read words on the left-hand side of a newspaper and believing that items in the left visual field have been 'lost' (Halligan and Cockburn, 1993). Often, patients appear to be unaware of the deficit (**anosagnosia**) until it is pointed out to them that they are neglecting the left half of their visual field. This lack of awareness can persist and presents a problem for any programme of rehabilitation.

Spatial neglect can be measured in different ways although there are four standard, clinical tasks which tap the disorder. These are line bisection, a cancellation test, copying and spontaneous drawing, and imagery tasks.

▧ Tests of spatial neglect

Line bisection

In the line bisection task, the patient is required to indicate the midline of a straight line by placing a mark at its centre. Normally, the line is horizontal, although vertical and oblique lines have been employed. Typically, the neglect patient errs to the right or, if the lines are vertical or oblique, to the upper end of the line or away from the body, respectively. See Figure 7.2.

The longer this line is, the bigger the error made (Butter, Mark and Heilman, 1988). An increase in the number of errors is seen if the line is placed in the neglected hemispace or if the patient's attention is drawn towards the ipsilateral side (Riddoch and Humphreys, 1983).

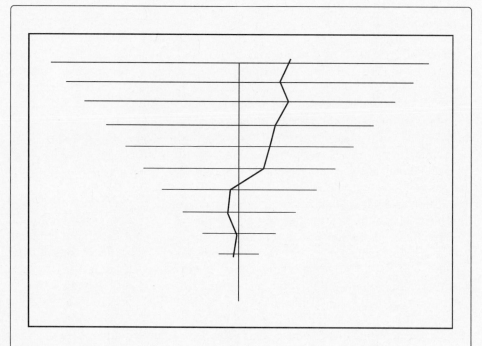

Figure 7.2   A spatial neglect patient's performance on the line bisection task

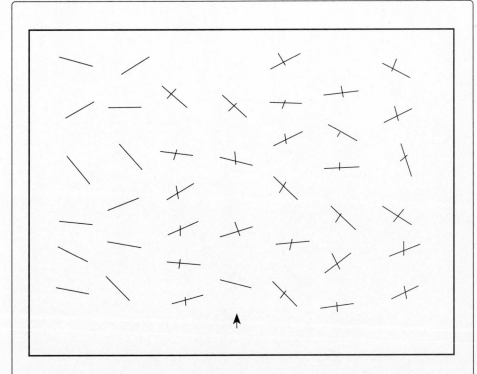

Figure 7.3 A spatial neglect patient's performance on a line cancellation test

Cancellation

In the cancellation test, the patient is presented with an array of identical targets on a sheet of paper and has to cross out as many stimuli as possible. Neglect patients fail to cross off those stimuli appearing on the side opposite to their brain lesion, as seen in Figure 7.3 for a patient with a right hemisphere lesion.

Spontaneous drawing or copying

The neglect patient, when copying or drawing an object, might omit the entire side of the object that is contralateral to the lesion. See Figure 7.4.

Perhaps the most famous example of this is clock-drawing, where a patient might place all the numbers of the clock face into the right-hand side, leaving the left side blank, as seen in Figure 7.5.

Despite the clearly failed attempt at drawing, the patient might indicate that the drawing is, in fact, an accurate representation. Some objects are better copied than

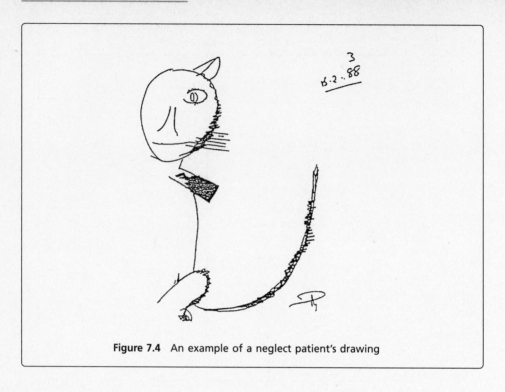

Figure 7.4 An example of a neglect patient's drawing

others. Asymmetrical, nonsense objects, for example, tend to be more poorly copied than meaningful, symmetrical ones (Heilman *et al.*, 1994). There are degrees of impairment, however. For example, neglect patients may be able to copy the blades of grass on the left side of a picture of a daisy but may neglect the left petals (Ishai *et al.*, 1989). Marshall and Halligan's (1988) patient was unable to distinguish between two drawings of a house, one of which had a fire raging on its left side, but when asked which one he would like to live in, chose the one without the fire. This suggests that there may be some covert processing of information in the left hemifield.

Sometimes, the patient may show a degree of contrapositioning, that is the patient transfers elements of the stimuli on the left side to drawings of stimuli on the right side (Halligan *et al.*, 1992). For example, the numbers on the left-hand side of a clock may be transposed to the right hand side. This phenomenon is called **allesthesia** or **allochiria** (Meador *et al.*, 1991). The reasons for this are unclear although one explanation is that information on the left side is partially processed but, because the processing of the image is incomplete, features may be incorporated into the good, right side. These partially processed features may be stored in the intact part of some form of visual buffer or may be incorrectly transcribed from this buffer (Halligan *et al.*, 1992).

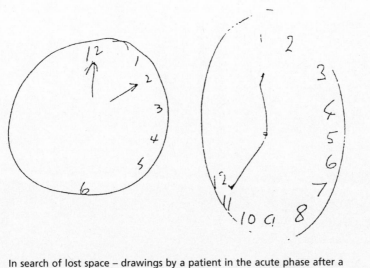

In search of lost space – drawings by a patient in the acute phase after a stroke (omission of the numbers on the left of the clockface) and the chronic phase (transposition of the numbers on the left to the right)

Figure 7.5   The well known asymmetric clockface drawn by neglect patients

Mental imagery

Mental imagery tasks are designed to tap the patient's representation of a stimulus. One of the controversies in spatial neglect concerns whether the disorder is one of inattention or impaired representation. For example, in one study of patients by Bisiach and Luzzatti (1978), neglect patients were asked to describe, without any cues, the Piazza del Duomo in Milan. When asked to describe the features of the piazza from a viewpoint where their back was to the front door of the cathedral, patients reported more details from the right than from the left side. Yet, when asked to describe the piazza from the other side (facing the cathedral), they again supplied more information about the right than the left side, despite the fact that the right side was the same as the left side that they had failed to report from the previous viewpoint. A different phenomenon, however, was reported by Guariglia *et al.* (1993). Their 59 year old patient had suffered an ischemic attack involving the right frontal lobe and performed adequately on tests of personal, peripersonal and extrapersonal space. However, he was unable to undertake visual imagery of stimuli in the left visual field. These stimuli involved geographical features of Italian piazzas similar to those employed by Bisiach and Luzzatti (see Figure 7.6).

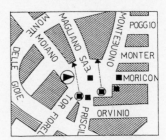
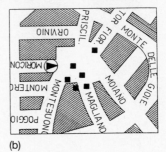
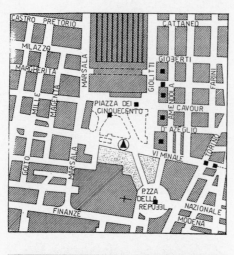

(b)

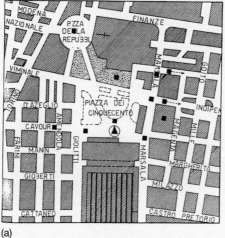

(a)

Figure 7.6 Maps of the familiar piazzas used in mental imagery tests. The circle containing an arrow indicates the subject's vantage point: the task is to describe what is in front of that vantage point. The black squares indicate those places recalled from mental imagery by neglect patients. They show the typical left neglect

Guariglia *et al.*'s study is unusual because no patient before this report had manifested neglect for visual images without accompanying neglect for visual space, possibly because of the involvement of the right frontal lobe in this patient.

■ Reducing spatial neglect

Recovery from neglect can be slow and the disorder can persist for 18 months (Kinsella and Ford, 1985), 12 years (Zarit and Kahn, 1974) or indefinitely (Heilman and Valenstein, 1979). Several strategies can reduce the degree of spatial neglect seen in patients, however. For example, flashing a red light to the left as the patient is reading, copying or cancelling can reduce neglect, as can requesting that the patient pay more attention to one side of an imagined scene in an imaginary task (Bisiach *et al.*, 1981). If stimuli on the right-hand side are made less salient, neglect may also be reduced (Mark *et al.*, 1988).

Vibrating the left posterior neck muscles lessens neglect (Karnath *et al.*, 1993). This is thought to work by stimulation of the neck muscles that contribute to the neural generation of an egocentric, body-centred frame – the vibration corrects a previously displaced body-centred frame. Caloric vestibular stimulation is one of the more unusual remedial procedures. This procedure involves eliciting a vestibular ocular reflex which may produce eye movement in the direction opposite to the attentional bias (Rubens, 1985). Using this technique, Rubens noted that 17 out of 18 stroke patients improved on a battery of spatial neglect tests although this improvement was short-term – a shortcoming noted by others (Cappa *et al.*, 1990). Optokinetic stimulation which also acts to improve voluntary eye gaze direction, appears too to be partially successful (Bisiach *et al.*, 1996). What these procedures appear to be rectifying is the patient's inability to (*automatically*) shift attention to the neglected side. A excellent review of spatial neglect can be found in Robertson *et al.* (1993).

■ Location of lesions in spatial neglect

The lesions found in most neglect patients tend to be focused in the right parietotemporal cortex. The precise locus for sensory neglect is thought to be Areas 39/40, the inferior parietal lobe (Heilman *et al.*, 1994). The frontal eye fields and cingulate gyrus may also be damaged because these structures have connections with the pulvinar nucleus and the head of the caudate nucleus, both of which, when damaged, are associated with neglect. According to Heilman *et al.* (1994), the presentation of a stimulus activates two pathways: one determines the location of a stimulus, i.e. its spatial position, the other determines what it is. The inferior temporal lobe is thought to mediate the latter, the parietal cortex the former.

■ Explanations for spatial neglect

As noted earlier, most discussions of why neglect occurs revolve around the notions of attention or representation. There are several theories to account for neglect – and most of the salient ones are summarized in Halligan and Marshall (1994) – but most evoke the concepts of attention, intention, representation or all. For example, neglect has been characterized as a disorder of space awareness (Berti and Rizzolatti, 1994), automatic orienting (Posner, 1980; Gainotti, 1994), hypo- or hyperattention (Ladavas, 1994), attention along the left–right axis (Kinsbourne, 1987), the distribution of global and local attentional resources (Robertson and Lamb, 1991), and norepinephrine system dysfunction (Posner, 1993).

One idea suggests that neglect may involve a disturbance in perceptuomotor cortical and subcortical 'pragmatic maps' which, when simultaneously activated, allow space awareness. Each map, which has different mechanisms responsible for head, arm and leg movements, has its own 'neural space representation' (Berti and Rizzolatti, 1994). Damage to a map will result in neglect in some aspect of space. Karnath (1994), on the other hand, suggests that a process of central transformation converts coordinates from sensory input (from the eye, skin and muscle) into an egocentric, body-centred coordinate system. An error in this system means that spatial reference has deviated horizontally across to the ipsilateral (intact) field. Patients may be either hypoattentional, weakly orientating to the affected side, or hyperattentional, overattending to the right (Ladavas, 1994). Heilman and Valenstein (1979) have cautioned that patients may also suffer from directional hypokinesia, a slowness in initiating movement in the direction contralateral to the brain lesion, which might contribute to the symptoms of neglect manifested in the line bisection task.

According to Marshall and Halligan (1994), hypotheses which attempt to explain neglect wholly in terms of impaired attention are questionable. They cite studies in which patients are unable to bisect lines accurately but are able to place a dot in the middle of a square (Tegner and Levander, 1991) or place marks in four corners of a page, as evidence against an exclusive attentional hypothesis. Instead, they suggest that what appears to be impaired is the global processing ability of the right hemisphere. Focal processing and global processing of visual images appear to be left and right hemisphere functions, respectively (Fink *et al.*, 1996). In neglect patients, the right hemisphere injury brings about this impairment in global processing, reducing visual attention to an 'attentional spotlight', which highlights only part of an image. The authors suggest, however, that an impaired attentional mechanism underlies many cases of neglect (Marshall and Halligan, 1996). What this impaired mechanism does not explain is some of the dissociable symptoms presented by neglect patients.

In a recent case study, an interesting series of neglect dissociations was seen in a 72 year old patient with right brain damage and left neglect (Cubelli and Simoncini, 1997). On standard neglect tests she performed as expected, erring to the right. However, when asked to copy or read words, she showed the typical neglect only for the reading aloud task. The ability to copy, and to name letters, was relatively spared. The principal error in the reading task was the deletion of initial letters. This error worsened when the space between letters was widened. Increasing the distance between letters did not affect the copying task. Cubelli and

Simoncini suggest that this dissociation is attributable to differences in word processing. That is, the manifestation of the disorder depends on whether the word is processed at the letter or the string level. When reading aloud, the patient processes the word as a letter string; when copying she processes the word letter by letter. This hypothesis is similar to those proposed above by Humphreys and Riddoch (1987b) and Halligan and Marshall (1994), both of which emphasize the difference between local or 'within object' representation or processing and global or 'between object' representation or processing.

The fragmentary nature of spatial hemineglect suggests that more than one model may be needed to account for all the symptoms subsumed under spatial neglect. Any general model, therefore, will need to recognize these differences.

DISCUSSION POINT

What does prosopagnosia tell us about the way in which the brain perceives faces?

An adequate explanation of prosopagnosia ultimately hinges on whether it is a specific disorder separate from other disorders or whether it reflects an inability to attend to certain features of faces.

To explore the possibility that familiar face identification, unfamiliar face matching and expression analysis were independent of each other and, therefore, activated different brain regions, Young and his colleagues studied ex-servicemen who had unilateral missile wound lesions in posterior left and right hemispheres (Young et al., 1993). Two tests each of face identification, matching unfamiliar faces and analyzing facial expression were used, and accuracy as well as latency (the time taken to complete the tasks) were measured. If the three components of perception studied were independent, the authors hypothesized, then selective impairment would be expected on both tasks measuring the same function but not on the four others. In fact, there was evidence for selective impairment for all three tasks.

One patient with right hemisphere lesions performed badly at identifying familiar faces only, another was selectively impaired in accuracy when matching unfamiliar faces; and a number of men with left hemisphere lesions had impairments on facial expression analysis only. There was no evidence of selective impairment of identification and unfamiliar face matching when latency data were considered.

Interestingly, an earlier study by Tranel et al. (1988) found that three out of four prosopagnosic patients were unable to identify faces yet were able to distinguish between facial expressions, the sex of the faces and the ages of the faces. One patient had impairments in all four tasks. The authors argued that different processing levels are necessary for different types of recognition. These types of recognition are subserved by different neural areas; specifically, the inability to categorize faces appears to be linked to bilateral damage to the subcalcarine association cortices.

Recently, lesions to the right lingual and fusiform gyri have been associated with prosopagnosia (Takahashi *et al.*, 1995). Three of the four patients studied had deficits in face perception and impairments in familiar face memory tasks. One, however, showed no abnormality in face perception and could recall familiar faces. All patients showed deficits in the ability to memorize new faces.

Of course, all of these data come from brain-damaged individuals. Sergent *et al.* (1992) have argued that because most of what we know about the neural substrates of face processing has come from neurologically impaired subjects, this presents a difficulty in understanding normal face perception. Sites associated with prosopagnosia may be different from the cortical areas associated with normal face perception. In their study, PET was used to examine metabolic activity in seven healthy adult men as they perceived objects and faces. Activity resulting from object recognition and face recognition was compared. Subjects were also required to identify famous people and to identify the sex of individuals from photographs.

Both the ventromedial cortex and the anterior temporal lobe of the left and right hemispheres appeared to be significantly activated during face perception. Compared with a control condition, the sex discrimination task resulted in differences in activation at the right extrastriate cortex, the face identity condition was associated with changes at the fusiform gyrus and anterior temporal cortex of both hemispheres, and high levels of activation at the right parahippocampal gyrus, and object recognition was associated with activation in the left occipitotemporal cortex but not in the right hemisphere. The results, they argue, 'provide the first empirical evidence from normal subjects regarding the crucial role of the ventromedial region of the right hemisphere in face recognition.' These results are also in keeping with the model of face processing suggested by Bruce and Young: that is, different brain areas appear to be activated depending on the type of facial recognition task undertaken.

Summary

☐ Agnosia is a perceptual disorder which refers to the inability to recognize objects in any sensory modality despite intact sensory apparatus.

☐ Blindsight describes the ability of patients with striatal cortex damage, and who are therefore cortically blind, to complete perceptual tasks successfully despite self-reports of being unaware of stimuli being presented. Patient DB performs well on several perceptual tasks but reports having seen nothing when test stimuli are presented. Some authors suggest that this ability is due to stray light from the intact field making

➠

making its way to the impaired visual field. Others suggest that degraded vision is made possible by existing striatal cortex. A third approach suggests that the residual ability reflects the functioning of a primitive visual system. Blindsight is rare, even in patients with striatal damage, which suggests caution in interpreting the meaning of its symptoms.

☐ Lissauer characterized visual agnosia as representing two processes: apperception and association. Apperceptive mindblindness was characterized by impairments in sensory discrimination and perception whereas associative mindblindness referred to the inability to interpret sensory or perceptual events.

☐ The two distinctions continue in the current literature but are called apperceptive agnosia and associative agnosia. The classic diagnosis of visual agnosia dictates that the patient must be free of sensory impairment. This, together with the terms used to describe the various visual agnosias, is controversial.

☐ Apperceptive visual agnosia or visual object agnosia refers to a rare impairment in object perception and is attributable to right-sided parietal lesions.

☐ Farah has divided this disorder into four subtypes: (1) an impairment in recognizing, copying or matching simple shapes (narrow apperceptive agnosia); (2) an inability to see objects as wholes (dorsal simultanagnosia); (3) a less severe form of dorsal simultanagnosia (ventral simultanagnosia); and (4) an experimentally induced impairment in recognition despite normal day-to-day recognition ability.

☐ Associative visual agnosia is a rare disorder which describes an inability to assign meaning to objects despite normal vision and is associated with posterior, left hemisphere lesions. There may be dissociations evident in that some classes of object may be recognized and identified and others not.

☐ Humphreys and Riddoch's patient, HJA, is able to reproduce drawings in painstaking detail but is unable to name the object represented by the drawing. The authors have described his disorder as an integrative agnosia – the inability to integrate elements of a stimulus to create a recognizable whole, and suggest that the mechanism involves an inability to utilize one of the two processes necessary for visual processing: the perception and integration of local grouping cues.

☐ Optic aphasia describes an inability to name objects presented visually despite unimpaired ability to describe the object's function. It may be a mild form of associative agnosia. Alternatively, associative agnosics may actually be optic aphasics.

☐ Colour agnosia refers to the inability to name colours despite being able to discriminate between them.

☐ Marr's theory suggests that apperceptive agnosia results from a failure to determine the major and minor axes of a three-dimensional image. An alternative model suggests that there may be a deficit in recognizing distinctive features.

☐ Associative agnosia may result from an impairment in connecting the output of perceptual analysis with the patient's knowledge. This theory argues that one system is responsible for mediating all recognition. An alternative suggests that independent systems exist which mediate different forms of recognition. There is evidence for this based on Farah's review of the literature which reported cases of alexia, visual object agnosia and prosopagnosia. No case of alexia with prosopagnosia but without visual object agnosia was found. Farah suggests that visual object recognition depends on the functioning of two processes: the perception of wholes and constituents.

☐ There may be category-specific dissociations in visual recognition ability. For example, patient JBR is unable to name living things but can name non-living things. However, the stimuli used in such dissociation studies have been criticized. For example, drawings of living things are more detailed and complex than drawings of non-living things. Written words may be more familiar than the objects they represent. When these factors are controlled, the dissociations seem to disappear.

☐ Prosopagnosia refers to the inability to recognize individual faces although the perception of facial expression and of the age and sex of a face is spared. Damage is usually to the right hemisphere and unilateral although bilateral lesions have been reported. There is evidence that some prosopagnosic patients may be able to recognize individual faces covertly.

☐ The amygdala is an important subcortical structure for face perception. Damage to it results in impaired memory for faces, and neurons within it respond selectively to faces. Bruce and Young have proposed a model of face processing which suggests that the analysis of facial expression, the recognition of familiar faces and the ability to match unfamiliar faces are dissociable functions. Evidence from PET studies of healthy individuals and from studies of brain injury supports this model.

➡

☐ Auditory agnosia refers to the inability to recognize or identify sounds despite an intact auditory system. Pure word deafness (auditory agnosia for speech or auditory verbal agnosia) describes the inability to comprehend spoken speech despite normal language ability. Auditory sound agnosia describes disorders where non-speech sounds cannot be discriminated or where semantic processing of sound is impaired.

☐ Somatosensory agnosia is the most poorly understood of the agnosias and refers to an inability to recognize objects by touch alone. This is more specifically known as tactile agnosia. The contralateral postcentral gyrus and hand area of the motor cortex are usually affected.

☐ Unilateral spatial neglect describes an inability to attend to stimuli in one hemifield (usually left). Damage to the right parietotemporal area results in left neglect (the more common and more severe); damage to the homologous left area results in right neglect. It is not a unitary disorder.

☐ Tests of hemispatial neglect include line bisection, line cancellation, copying/drawing and mental imagery. Neglect can be reduced by making stimuli on the neglected side more salient or by vibrating the vestibular apparatus. The principal failure in spatial neglect appears to be the inability to attend voluntarily and automatically to stimuli on the neglected side.

Recommended further general and specific reading

Key: (1) = introductory, *(3)* = intermediate, *(5)* = advanced

General

Bauer, R.M. (1993). Agnosia. In K.M. Heilman and E. Valenstein (eds), *Clinical Neuropsychology* (3rd edition). New York: Oxford University Press. *(3)*

De Renzi, E. (1982). *Disorders of Space Exploration and Cognition.* New York: Wiley. *(4)*

Farah, M.J. (1990). *Visual Agnosia: Disorders of object vision and what they tell us about normal vision.* Cambridge, MA: MIT Press. *(3)*

Farah, M.J. and Ratcliff, G. (1994). *The Neuropsychology of High-level Vision.* Hove, UK: Lawrence Erlbaum Associates. *(3)*

Grusser, O-J. and Landis, T. (1991). *Visual Agnosias and Other Disturbances of Visual Perception.* London: Macmillan. *(3)*

Halligan, P.W. and Marshall, J.C. (1994). *Spatial Neglect: Position papers on theory and practice.* Hove, UK: Lawrence Erlbaum Associates. *(3)*

Heilman, K.M., Watson, R.T. and Valenstein, E. (1993). Neglect and related disorders. In K.M. Heilman and E. Valenstein (eds), *Clinical Neuropsychology* (3rd edition). New York: Oxford University Press. *(3)*

Milner, A.D. and Goodale, M.A. (1996). *The Visual Brain in Action*. Oxford: Oxford University Press. *(3)*

Robertson, I.H. and Marshall, J.C. (1993). *Unilateral Neglect: Clinical and experimental studies*. Hove, UK: Lawrence Erlbaum Associates. *(3)*

Ullman, S. (1996). *High-level Vision: Object recognition and visual cognition*. Cambridge, MA: MIT Press *(4)*

Specific

Bentin, S., Allison, T., Puce, A., Perez, E. and McCarthy, G. (1996). Electrophysiological studies of face perception in humans. *Journal of Cognitive Neuroscience*, **8**(6), 551–65. *(3)*

Bisiach, E. (1993). Mental representation in unilateral neglect and related disorders: the twentieth Bartlett Memorial Lecture. *Quarterly Journal of Experimental Psychology*, **46A**(3), 435–61. *(4)*

Bruce, V. and Humphreys, G.W. (1994). Recognizing objects and faces. *Visual Cognition*, **1**, 141–80. *(3)*

Coslett, H.B. (1997). Neglect in vision and visual imagery: a double dissociation. *Brain*, **120**, 1163–71. *(3)*

Farah, M.J. (1991). Patterns of co-occurrence among the associative agnosias: implications for visual object representation. *Cognitive Neuropsychology*, **8**, 1–19. *(3)*

Farah, M.J., Mayer, M.M., McMullen, P.A. (1996). The living/nonliving dissociation is not an artifact: giving an *a priori* implausible hypothesis a strong test. *Cognitive Neuropsychology*, **13**, 137–54. *(3)*

Fink, G.R., Marshall, J.C., Halligan, P.W., Frith, C.D., Frackowiak, R.S.J. and Dolan, R.J. (1997). Hemispheric specialization for global and local processing: the effect of stimulus category. *Proceedings of the Royal Society of London*, **264**, 487–94. *(3)*

Goodale, M.A. and Milner, A.D. (1992). Separate visual pathways for perception and action. *Trends in Neurosciences*, **15**, 20–5. *(4)*

Grossman, M., Galetta, S. and D'Esposito, M. (1997). Object recognition difficulty in visual apperceptive agnosia. *Brain and Cognition*, **33**, 306–42. *(3)*

Guariglia, C., Padovani, A., Pantano, P. and Pizzamiglio, L. (1993). Unilateral neglect restricted to visual imagery. *Nature*, **364**, 235–7. *(3)*

Halligan, P.W. and Marshall, J.C. (1991). Left neglect for near but not far space in man. *Nature*, **350**, 498–500. *(3)*

Kentridge, R.W., Heywood, C.A. and Weiskrantz, L. (1997). Residual vision in multiple retinal locations within a scotoma: implications for blindsight. *Journal of Cognitive Neuroscience* **9**(2), 191–202. *(3)*

Martin, A., Wiggs, C.L., Ungerleider, L.G. and Haxby, J.V. (1996). Neural correlates of category-specific knowledge. *Nature*, **379**, 649–52. *(2)*

Mozer, M.C., Halligan, P.W. and Marshall, J.C. (1997). The end of the line for a brain-damaged model of unilateral neglect. *Journal of Cognitive Neuroscience*, **9**(2), 171–90. *(4)*

Rafal, R.D. (1997). Balint syndrome. In T.E. Feinberg and M.J. Farah (eds), *Behavioral Neurology and Neuropsychology*. New York: McGraw-Hill. *(2)*

Reed, C.L., Caselli, R.J. and Farah, M.J. (1996). Tactile agnosia. *Brain*, **119**, 875–88. *(4)*

Robertson, I.H. and Halligan, P.W. (1997). *Spatial Neglect: A clinical handbook for diagnosis and treatment*. Hove, UK: The Psychology Press. *(3)*

Rumiati, R.I., Humphreys, G.W., Riddoch, M.J. and Bateman, A. (1994). Visual object agnosia without prosopagnosia or alexia: evidence for hierarchical theories of visual recognition. *Visual Cognition*, **1**(2/3), 181–225. *(4)*

Schweinberger, S.R., Klos, T. and Sommer, W. (1995). Covert face recognition in prosopagnosia: a dissociable function? *Cortex*, **31**, 517–29. *(4)*

Stoerig, P. (1996). Varieties of vision: from blind responses to conscious recognition. *Trends in Neuroscience*, **19**(9), 401–6. *(3)*

Stoerig, P. and Cowey, A. (1997). Blindsight in man and monkey. *Brain*, **120**, 535–59. *(4)*

Tranel, D., Damasio, A.R. and Damasio, H. (1988). Intact recognition of facial expression, gender, and age in patients with impaired recognition of face identity. *Neurology*, **38**(5), 690–6. *(2)*

Warrington, E.K. and James, M. (1988). Visual apperceptive agnosia: a clinico-anatomical study of three cases. *Cortex*, **24**, 13–32. *(3)*

Weiskrantz, L. (1986). *Blindsight: A case study and implications*. Oxford: Oxford University Press. *(2)*

Young, A.W., Newcombe, F., de Haan, E.H.F., Small, M. and Hay, D.C. (1993). Face perception after brain injury. *Brain*, **116**, 941–59. *(3)*

Young, A.W., Aggleton, J.P., Hellawell, D.J., Johnson, M., Broks, P. and Hanley, J.R. (1995). Face processing impairments after amygdalotomy. *Brain*, **118**, 15–24. *(3)*

Chapter Eight

Apraxias and other motor system disorders

■ Some disorders of the human motor system

Disorders of the human motor system come in many forms. Some disorders result from degeneration of neurons in deep, subcortical structures; others from lesions to the cortex itself. These cortical lesions produce less fatal but psychologically unusual consequences. The subcortical structures most often involved in motor dysfunction are the basal ganglia. These, as we saw in Chapter 3, are a collection of structures in the forebrain which include the caudate nucleus, putamen and globus pallidus. Disorders involving these nuclei are called **extrapyramidal disorders**, and involve either excessive motor activity (such as that seen in **Huntington's chorea**, **Wilson's disease** and **Gilles de la Tourette syndrome**) or restricted movement (such as that seen in **parkinsonism**). This chapter begins with a description of the extrapyramidal disorders.

■ Parkinsonism and Parkinson's disease

Parkinson's disease was first described by James Parkinson in 1817. The motor features of the disease are known collectively as parkinsonism. Its classical features include **akinesia** (general loss of movement), **rigidity** (resisting passive movement) and **tremor at rest**. Tremor at rest arises from alternating agonist and antagonist contraction in distal muscles of the arm. The most common manifestation of this is 'pill-rolling', where the fingers appear to imitate the rolling of a pill. There is usually no tremor of the lip, neck or tongue. Although exacerbated by stress, tremors are reduced during sleep and voluntary movement. Akinesia can take the form of slowness of movement (**bradykinesia**), reduction of movement (**hypokinesia**) or lack of spontaneous and automatic voluntary movement (akinesia itself). **Axial akinesia** refers to impaired movement of the trunk or proximal muscles; this makes turning difficult for the parkinsonian patient. There may also be stooped posture, speech difficulties, excessive sweating, incontinence and/or constipation.

The early symptoms appear as disturbed fine motor control in the hand: this makes activities such as writing or doing up buttons difficult. Speech becomes hoarse, the swing of the arm might be reduced, and making two simultaneous movements becomes problematic. The posture difficulties (such as falling over following a period of hesitation or 'freezing') tend to be resistant to therapy.

The most common form of parkinsonism occurs with idiopathic Parkinson's disease (PD for short) where the aetiology of the disorder is unknown. Parkinsonism can also occur secondary to other degenerative diseases. A history of stroke or hydrocephalus is symptomatic of parkinsonism.

Clinical features

A clinical diagnosis of PD involves confirming the presence of two of the three classic symptoms outlined above. Diagnosis is probable if onset of the motor disturbance is asymmetrical, there is rest tremor, the patient is responsive to the standard drug treatment and if the fluctuations in symptoms following the administration of this drug are present. There appear to be three distinct syndromes of PD. One is characterized by akinesia, tremor and rigidity (mixed type), one by akinesia and rigidity with minimal or absent tremor (akinetic-rigid type), and another by tremor with almost total absence of akinesia or rigidity (tremor-dominant type).

The mean age of onset of the disease is about 60 years. It affects approximately 0.15 per cent of the world's population, a figure which increases to 0.5 per cent in those over 50 years old. The incidence has been given at 5 in 100 000 for individuals under 54; 32 in 100 000 for individuals between 55 and 64; 113 in 100 000 for individuals between 65 and 74; and 254 in 100 000 in individuals between 75 and 84 (Rajput *et al.*, 1984). It is a progressive disease with no clear evidence of genetic transmission. The common causes of death are cardiovascular disease, tumour, cerebrovascular disease and bronchopneumonia. The underlying causes are unknown although many explanations have been given (see below).

Neuropathology

The most prominent neuropathological feature of PD is a loss of the striatal dopamine pathway which runs from the substantia nigra to the neostriatum (caudate nucleus and putamen) and globus pallidus. There is degeneration of the ventrolateral layer of the substantia nigra projecting to the striatum (Fearnley and Lees, 1991). Material called Lewy bodies is also found in the substantia nigra and locus coeruleus which may be a diagnostic marker for the disease (although other diseases with parkinsonian symptoms also show evidence of these Lewy bodies and Lewy bodies are also found in other parts of the brain such as the cortex and raphe nuclei).

Neurotransmission

Dopamine and dopamine's metabolite, bolite homovanille, have been found to be depleted in the caudate nucleus, putamen, substantia nigra and globus pallidus in patients with PD, with greater loss in the putamen (the loss is about 70–90 per cent) than in the caudate nucleus (Kish *et al.*, 1988). The residual striatal neurons may compensate for the loss of dopamine by increasing their activity, increasing dopamine or increasing dopamine's release. These compensatory measures mean that clinical symptoms do not present themselves until dopamine levels have declined by approximately 80 per cent, the 'threshold' for PD (Strange, 1992). Levels of postsynaptic striatal D1 and D2 dopamine receptors have been found to be greater in PD patients who had not received L-DOPA prior to death, whereas normal levels were found in those patients who had received L-DOPA (Seeman and Niznik, 1990). Levels, overall, were found to be extremely variable, however. There is also a reduction in GABA and 5-hydroxytryptamine (5-HT) in the striatum and substantia nigra (where these two transmitters predominantly exist). The serotonin reduction may be due to the effects of drug therapy (Levodopa) which reduces 5-HT.

The complex picture of neurotransmission involvement in parkinsonism has in part been accounted for by a model of basal ganglia circuitry which suggests a complex arrangement of indirect and direct striatal outputs (Alexander *et al.*, 1990). The indirect pathway is thought to be overstimulated in PD by an increase in glutamate release. This is normally inhibited by D2 receptors but the outer globus pallidus becomes overactivated. Meanwhile, the internal part becomes overstimulated as does the pathway leading to the thalamus. This pallidothalamic projection is inhibitory but it is overactive; therefore, it has an overinhibitory effect on thalamic neurons. The direct pathway represents the inhibitory neurons of the striatopallidal pathway to the internal globus pallidus. This is excited by dopamine but the pathway is underactive. Both pathways increase the activity of the internal globus pallidus.

Treatment

A summary of the psychopharmacological therapies for PD are listed Table 8.1.

Levodopa (L-DOPA), the precursor of dopamine and the first dopaminergic therapy for PD, reduces the symptoms of PD significantly (Cotzias *et al.*, 1967). L-DOPA is taken up by nigrostriatal nerve endings where it is decarboxylated and

Table 8.1 Some psychopharmacological treatments for parkinsonism

Substance	Generic name	Example
L-dopa	L-DOPA	Levadopa, Brocadopa
AADC inhibitors	L-DOPA, benserazide, co-beneldopa	Madopar
	L-DOPA, carbidopa, co-careldopa	Cronomet, Sinemet
Dopamine receptor agonists	Apomorphine	Britaject
	Bromocriptine	Bagren, Bromocriptin, Parlodel
	alpha-dihydroergocryptine	Alminid
	Lisuride	Revanil, Permax
	Piribedil	Trivastal
MAOB inhibitors	Selegiline (deprenyl)	Eldepryl, Depreynl
Adamantanamine	Amantadine HCl, memantine HCl	Mantadine, Symmetrel, Tregor
Anticholinergics	Benztropine	Cogentin, Cotulate
	Biperiden HCl	Akineton
	Biperiden lactate	Akineton lactate
	Bornaprin	Sormorden
	Metixen	Mexitil, Tremonil
	Orphenadrine HCl	Biophen, Disipal
	Orphenadrine dihydrogencitrate	Norflex
	Procyclidine	Arpicolin, Kemadrin
	Trihexphenidyl	Artane, Bentex, Broflex
Antiemetics	Domperidone	Motilium

dopamine is released. Since striatal dopamine loss is characteristic of PD, increasing levels of dopamine might seem a sensible treatment. L-DOPA is used instead of dopamine itself because L-DOPA can penetrate the blood/brain barrier (and is converted into dopamine) whereas orally administered dopamine cannot. One early problem was that a high dosage of L-DOPA led to its peripheral decarboxylation before reaching the brain. One gram per day-1 of L-DOPA plus the administration of a peripheral decarboxylase inhibitor (PDI, 100 mg per day-1) reduces many PD symptoms although there are side-effects such as dyskinesia (movement disturbance, see section below) and psychiatric disturbances. The normal dosage of L-DOPA is about 2–8 grams per day but is reduced if taken with the PDIs: the combination of these two has been described as the 'gold standard' of PD drug treatment (Oertel and Quinn, 1996). About 15 per cent of patients are unresponsive to treatment but these are not likely to have PD. After chronic treatment, improvement may also be seen to wane, with motor oscillations occurring either because the drug is 'wearing off' or because of the fluctuating clinical state of the subject.

Other drugs used include dopamine agonists acting on pre- and postsynaptic receptors but they are not as effective as L-DOPA and there are gastrointestinal side-effects. However, they have a low incidence of response fluctuation. Examples include bromocriptine and lisuride. The most potent is apomorphine (an agonist for certain types of dopamine receptor – D1, D2 and D3). Monamine B inhibitors, such as selegiline (deprenyl), are sometimes used. These are thought to reduce the breakdown of dopamine thus producing a greater dopamine lifespan. Although it does enhance the effect of L-DOPA and enables a reduction in L-DOPA administration to take place, the drug on its own is not as effective as L-DOPA. Antiviral agents such as amantadine have been used to combat parkinsonism and are thought to increase dopamine synthesis via dopamine reuptake blockage. This can delay the need for L-DOPA in young cases but there are rare side-effects (epileptic seizures). Finally, anticholinergic drugs which reduce rigidity and rest tremor have been used although they do cause side-effects such as urinary constipation and blurred vision. The search for new drug treatments, especially treatment for debilitating illnesses such as PD is ongoing, and new, experimental drugs such as the dopamine agonist corbergoline and the weak MOAB inhibitor budipine are both currently being systematically studied for their long-term effects.

There are two other radical forms of treatment which may be appropriate for PD: surgery and transplantation. Surgery is used for reducing drug-resistant tremor and sometimes takes the form of a unilateral **thalamotomy** (also called **stereotactic coagulation**), removal of one side of the thalamus. This reduces rest tremor in 80–90 per cent of patients operated on. A less destructive method is to stimulate the nucleus ventralis and intermedialis of the thalamus. This, too, is effective. Tremors and rigidity are also alleviated by pallidotomy, as is akinesia when the internal pallidus is lesioned (Svennilson *et al.*, 1960). Pallidotomies appear to have quite long-lasting beneficial effects on bradykinesia and rigidity (Laitinen *et al.*, 1992).

Transplantation of intracerebral dopamine-synthesizing tissue perhaps holds the most remarkable possibilities for reducing PD symptoms. Originally, the rationale for transplantation was based on primate models of parkinsonism. Dopamine-synthesizing cells are transplanted into the putamen or caudate nucleus which may then begin releasing dopamine or may restore the depleted neuronal circuitry. Studies are currently only at rudimentary stages. Work with animal models of parkinsonism (and dementia), together with early trials with humans, however, show promising signs. (This is discussed in Chapter 11 in relation to recovery of function.)

Aetiology

There has been some attempt to link environmental agents with the appearance of PD. Factory workers exposed to manganese or carbon disulphide for long periods may, for example, exhibit symptoms very much like parkinsonism (akinesia and rigidity). Parkinsonism also appears secondary to other disorders. Carbon monoxide poisoning and some antipsychotic drugs are associated with parkinsonian symptoms. Strangely, a high incidence of three degenerative diseases – amyotrophic lateral sclerosis, parkinsonian syndrome and senile dementia – has been reported on the island of Guam (Garruto and Yase, 1986), a finding thought to be associated with water supplies having low magnesium and calcium but high aluminium content, or with the consumption of cycad seed (the B-N-methylamino alanine in the seed is thought to be a neurotoxin). As the neurotoxin is likely to have been taken out of the seed, however, another candidate seems more likely (Strange, 1992).

The substance, 1-methyl-4-phenyl-1,2,3,6-tetrahydropyridine (MPTP), a byproduct of the synthesis of meperidine, a synthetic heroin substitute, and erroneously sold to heroin addicts in California in 1982, has been found to produce symptoms similar to those found in PD (Langston, 1985; Singer et al., 1987). These addicts also showed degeneration of the striatal dopamine pathway. The likely toxin would appear to be the MPP^+ produced by monoamine oxidase B activity and taken up by dopamine cells. Other substances containing MPP^+ include certain foods and pesticides (paraquat). There is evidence of a high incidence of PD in Canadian agricultural regions where the use of pesticides is high. Although there is little evidence to suggest a genetic component to PD, a report of a large kindred with inherited PD has been published (Golbe et al., 1990).

Strange (1992) has proposed a theory whereby PD is thought to result from an abnormal loss of mesostriatal cells which are found in addition to the loss of these cells occurring normally with age. When the threshold for the loss is reached, Strange argues, the symptoms of parkinsonism emerge.

Given the detailed documentation available regarding the neuropathology, it is disappointing that studies have not yet been able to identify the cause of this neuropathology in parkinsonism. Current treatment is dominated by L-DOPA although promising alternatives, such as surgery and, more controversially, grafting, are being investigated.

■ Huntington's chorea

Another well known degenerative motor disorder is Huntington's chorea (HC), first described by George Huntington who studied the incidence of chorea (jerky, dance-like movements) in families in Long Island, New York. The disease is inherited, autosomal-dominant and appears to involve a mutation of a gene on the arm of chromosome 4. The result is degeneration of small- and medium-sized neurons in the striatum, particularly GABAergic neurons, which project to the globus pallidus. The disorder can be traced back many years in a person's history and because of its inherited status, can be traced back many centuries. Historically, it has been thought that the infamous witches of Salem may have suffered from HC.

Clinical features

HC is rare and affects approximately 0.01% of the world population (the prevalence is 2 to 7 individuals per 100 000). Age of onset is usually around 40–50 years and the average duration of the disorder is 19 years. A small percentage of patients have earlier onset (i.e. before 20 years). This is the juvenile version of the disorder and physical decline is most common in this group. It is a progressive disorder and death can follow between 15 and 20 years after onset.

The most prominent feature of HC is involuntary, **choreiform** (dance-like) movement and dementia. Less frequently, there may be akinesia, rigidity and disturbances in personality. Movements appear out of control and jerky, and the patient may also have difficulty speaking and standing. The first signs of the disease might manifest themselves in changes in personality or in gradual clumsiness or unsteadiness. Early motor signs include restlessness in the fingers, toes and face. There is a variant of HC called the akinetic–rigid type (which as the name suggests involves akinesia and rigidity), in which all striatal neurons become degenerated. In common HC, interneurons projecting to the lateral globus pallidus degenerate. In the late stages of the disorder, patients may be bedridden and in a vegetative state and often die of complications related to their immobility or difficulties in swallowing.

Because the disease is inherited and is an autosomal-dominant one, the child of an HC parent has a 50 per cent chance of developing the disease. If the gene is present, it will be expressed. This poses a problem since those at risk will have had children by the time of onset. The children of these parents may make a decision not to have any children, which would terminate the line of the disease. Gene probes using markers on chromosome 4 can predict the disorder's appearance, but not its time of onset. The application of this test, however, presents a hellish dilemma. If the test indicates that the individual is free of the disease, all well and good. If, on the other hand, the test is positive and indicates that the individual will develop HC, then the individual is resigned to the fact that the disease will later develop. Given the absence of effective treatment, this is not a pleasant scenario.

Neuropathology

There is normally a reduction in brain size of up to 20 per cent in HC patients at post-mortem. Neuronal loss is found in the neostriatum, globus pallidus, cerebellum and the cortex. Earliest loss is seen in the striatum, where up to 95 per cent of neurons may be lost in advanced cases. Glucose metabolism is reduced in the striatum (especially the caudate nucleus) which suggests that this altered metabolism may be associated with neuronal loss in the neostriatum (Carter et al., 1989).

Treatment

There are hardly any long-term, successful treatments for HC. Current treatment involves the use of dopamine antagonists (e.g. sulpiride, tetrabenazine, perphenazine) which bring relief of acute symptoms but still leave bradykinesia. The notion behind most pharmacological interventions is to restore the balance of neurotransmitters in the basal ganglia.

Aetiology

The cause of the degeneration in HC is unknown although speculation has revolved around the action of a possible toxin which affects cell degeneration. Three of these toxins may be kainic acid, quinolinic acid and glutamic acid. The idea is that these toxins overstimulate cells which results in the cells' death.

▩ Sydenham's chorea

Sydenham's chorea is a childhood disorder involving the gradual appearance of chorea between the ages of 7 and 12 years which subsides between 1 and 4 months after onset. This disorder is associated with streptococcal infection, which can precede the disorder by up to 6 months.

▩ Dyskinesia

Dyskinesia describes a sustained, involuntary contraction of muscles which results in twisting, repetitive movements and abnormal posture. Examples of this type of disorder are the **dystonias**, motor disorders in which distorted trunk or limbs occur as a result of excessive muscle tone. **Generalized dystonia** may involve lesions to the basal ganglia, especially the putamen, and is treated by anticholinergic drugs. **Focal dystonia**, as the name suggests, indicates a motor abnormality specific to a particular part of the body (or a small group of muscles) and is treated with botulinum toxin (BTX). **Blepharospasms** describe the intermittent or sustained closure of both eyes because of contractions of the orbicularis occuli muscles surrounding the eye. BTX is again a successful treatment. **Cranial dystonia** (Meige's syndrome) is a motor disorder of the masticatory, lower facial and tongue muscles in which there is difficulty in opening and closing the jaw. **Cervical dystonia** describes the directionless deviation of the head often leading to a fixed head posture. Neck muscles are the focal muscles affected and the disorder worsens when the patient walks. **Hand cramps**, such as those seen in writer's/musician's cramp, result only from the execution of precise, well rehearsed fine motor movements with the hand. Symptoms are a tight grip and abnormal finger position. **Hemifacial spasm** describes a dysfunction of the seventh cranial nerve and involves unilateral twitching/spasms in muscles innervated by this nerve. The cause appears to be compression of the nerve by blood vessels.

▨ Gilles de la Tourette syndrome

Gilles de la Tourette syndrome is a disorder in which motor and phonic tics occur despite otherwise normal behaviour. The first case was described by Gilles de la Tourette in 1885. It has its onset usually in childhood (before 15 years) and early symptoms include blinking, grimacing, head jerking and shrugging of the shoulders (Janowic, 1993). Phonic tics include sniffing, snorting, the repetition of words (palilalia), echolalia and the uttering of obscenities (coprolalia). The disorder has been associated with reduced left basal ganglia volume and is more often seen in boys than in girls. The disorder is normally treated with the drug haloperidol.

▨ Wilson's disease

Wilson's disease, also known as hepatolenticular degeneration, is a genetic disorder in which disturbed copper metabolism leads to build-up of excessive intracellular copper, causing cell death. Characteristics of the disease are increased copper in the liver, kidney, brain and cornea, atrophy of the striatum, and increased sponginess of the white matter. Most neuronal loss is seen in the striatum and globus pallidus. The behavioural symptoms are very similar to those of parkinsonism, which means that Wilson's disease must be ruled out before a clinical diagnosis of PD can be made. These symptoms include tremor, akinesia, dystonia, chorea and walking difficulties. About half of patients develop liver disease; the other half show these symptoms. One useful diagnostic measure is the detection of the Kayser–Fleischer ring of the cornea of the eye. This is brownish, appears at the innermost layer of the cornea and is symptomatic of Wilson's disease. Wilson's disease tends to affect about 3 in 100 000. Treatment is aimed at reducing the build-up of intracellular copper.

▨ Motor neuron damage

Examples of motor disorders involving a dysfunction of the motor neurons include muscular paralysis and atrophy such as **poliomyelitis** which is caused by a viral infection of the motor neurons of the spinal cord, limb weakness, especially lower limbs or arms, resulting from loss of myelin in motor and sensory tracts such as

multiple sclerosis, paralysis of both lower limbs resulting from complete transection of the spinal cord (**paraplegia**) and paralysis in all four limbs (**quadriplegia**). **Cerebral palsy** describes motor dysfunction resulting from foetal brain damage.

Myoclonus

Myoclonus describes brief, sudden, involuntary movements originating from any point in the CNS. Perhaps the most well known, and least disruptive example of myoclonus is the hiccup. Another well known and not too disruptive example is the orgasm.

Ataxia

Ataxia refers to uncoordinated, involuntary movement associated with cerebellar lesions. Patients may fail to reach an object they are reaching for (**dysmetria**), or may oscillate near the object or might exhibit tremor during any movement. Patients may overshoot when reaching for an object (**hypermetria**) or may undershoot and fail to reach (**hypometria**). A well known example of ataxia is **gait ataxia** in which the legs walk in a very broad-based fashion often giving the impression that the person is drunk. Damage is usually to the medial zone of the cerebellum. Arms are affected by lateral cerebellar lesions. There is also a disorder known as thalamic syndrome in which unilateral thalamic damage causes contralateral ataxia. Another ataxia, **optic ataxia** (inability to perform coordinated voluntary lateral eye movements), is also known as Balint's syndrome, referred to in Chapter 7. Finally, **Friedreich's ataxia** describes a rare, inherited disorder which involves degeneration of the spinocerebellar tracts. In addition to the ataxia, patients often also exhibit weakness and abnormal reflexes.

Apraxia

According to Heilman (1979), apraxia is a motor disorder 'defined by exclusion'. It is a 'disorder of skilled movement not caused by weakness, akinesia, deafferentiation, abnormal tone/posture or movement disorder.' Complex disorders of voluntary action are called apraxia (literally, no action). The term was coined by Steinthal (1871) who used it to describe the inability to make a voluntary action related to object use in the absence of paralysis. Meynert made the distinction between object recognition deficits and deficits affecting action by referring to the former as 'sensory asymbolia' and the later as 'motor asymbolia' (impaired memory for images of movement). Apraxia nowadays describes skilled movement deficits such as omitting actions or making inappropriate ones in the absence of primary motor system impairment or comprehension impairment. It is complicated by aphasia, which often accompanies apraxia: an inability to follow a command or instruction may be owing to language impairment and not to a disorder of voluntary movement. Patients are usually anosognosic and will attribute their motor problems to clumsiness.

Liepmann (1900) was one of the first to publish a report of a genuinely apraxic patient, MT. This patient was an 'ambidextrous syphilitic' councillor who was unable to imitate hand position or pantomime with his right hand but could make spontaneous hand movements and was less impaired with his left hand. Liepmann argued that not only could impairments in voluntary action be distinguished from language impairment and paralysis, but also that the disorder was not unitary. His theory argued that apraxia was associated with left hemisphere or callosal damage and that damage to different left hemisphere regions produced different types of apraxia (Liepmann, 1920). In most patients, the non-dominant hand is more impaired than the dominant hand. This theory is discussed with other theories a little later on.

Tests of apraxia

Some of the tests used to determine apraxia are listed in Table 8.2. The instructions in these tests normally take the form of oral commands from the experimenter. Included in these are tasks involving **gesture to command**, where the patient is required to mime tool use and show the experimenter how to use an object, and tasks involving the performance of emblem gestures such as waving goodbye. Both hands are tested. Patients may also be required to imitate behaviour: some patients are able to follow commands but are unable to imitate. Other tests involve requiring the patient to mime the use of a tool on seeing it or to mime the use of the tool which works on a seen object. For example, if the patient sees a nail, he or she will be required to mime the use of a hammer). Actual tool use is tested, as is the comprehension of tool use, i.e. the experimenter will ask the patient what tool is being used in the experimenter's mime.

Types of apraxia

As one might expect from a disorder involving motor behaviour, different parts of the body may be affected in apraxia. Thus, disorders are named after the motor behaviour or body part most affected (e.g. construction, gait, buccofacial).

Table 8.2 Some of the tests used to detect apraxic symptoms

Intransitive limb gestures	Waving goodbye Hitchhiking Saluting Beckoning 'come here' Indicating 'stop' Indicating 'go'
Transitive limb gestures	Opening a door with a key Flipping a coin Opening a screw-top bottle Using a screwdriver Using a hammer Using a pair of scissors
Intransitive buccofacial gestures	Sticking out the tongue Blowing a kiss
Transitive buccofacial gestures	Blowing out a match Sucking on a straw
Sequential movement	Cleaning a pipe, putting tobacco in it and lighting it Folding a letter, putting it in an envelope, sealing the envelope and stamping it

Adapted from Heilman and Rothi, 1993

Limb apraxia

Limb apraxia (or **limb-kinetic apraxia**) refers to impaired fine movements of precision. Finger tapping presents extreme difficulty for limb apraxia patients, as does making single repetitive movements, e.g. tapping a stylus alternately on two sides of a line (Wyke, 1967) or flipping a coin (Heilman, 1975). Making bilateral hand movements which require coordination is also difficult: patients cannot make a fist in one hand and a palm with the other or alternate fist and flat-hand movements (Luria, 1966). Imitating meaningless hand positions is difficult (Piec-zuro and Vignolo, 1967) as is imitating novel hand postures (Lehmkuhl *et al.*, 1983).

Ideational apraxia

Ideational apraxia refers to the inability to undertake a series of movements involving some ideational or planning component. Objects may be inappropriately used: a patient might try to light a candle by striking a match on it (Pick, 1905). Interestingly, De Renzi *et al.* (1968) found a dissociation between the use of the object in the experiment and the use of the object in a natural context. Their patient was unable to use a toothbrush appropriately in the experiment yet was able to use it normally at home. Sequencing errors are manifested in several contexts. For example, when asked to open a can of soup with a can opener, patients have been found to beat the side of the can with the opener (Poeck and Lehmkuhl, 1980). These inappropriate movements were termed 'parapraxic'. De Renzi and Lucchelli (1988) also found that patients would make omissions in series of actions, e.g. pouring water from a sealed bottle.

Ideomotor apraxia

Ideomotor apraxia refers to an inability to mime the use of an object (pantomiming) despite normal dexterity (Hecaen, 1978) and is the most commonly reported apraxia (Pramstaller and Marsden, 1996). Patients might use their body parts as objects despite given repeated instructions not to. There appears to be a double dissociation between miming when given the name of the object orally and miming when shown a picture of the object (De Renzi *et al.*, 1982).

Gait apraxia

Gait apraxia refers to a difficulty in walking or making any voluntary movement with the legs.

Oral (buccofacial) apraxia

Oral apraxia refers to impaired ability to make oral and guttural movements and was first reported by Hughlings-Jackson (1870). Hughlings-Jackson's patient was unable to cough or stick out her tongue when asked to but was able to do so when eating normally.

Constructional apraxia

Constructional apraxia refers to an impairment in the organization of complex spatial actions such as piecing together a jigsaw, drawing a clock face, copying designs and simple/complex geometrical shapes and building bridges or towers with blocks. Understandably, interpreting the results of such tasks is difficult because there are individual differences in people's constructional skills.

■ Cerebral basis of apraxia

The earliest suggestion of cortical involvement in apraxia was made by Liepmann (1900; Liepmann and Maas, 1907). Liepmann's hypothesis argued that the left hemisphere's language area had been disconnected from the motor area of the right hemisphere that controls fine movement in the left hemisphere (remember that the cerebral control of movement is contralateral). This disconnection was the result of a callosal lesion. The theory suggested that the left hemisphere contained hand 'movement formulas' which were responsible for controlling purposeful movements and which were disconnected from the right movement areas after callosal lesions. The evidence for this hypothesis is fairly mixed: Gazzaniga *et al.* (1967) found no evidence for the theory, although Watson and Heilman's (1983) patient failed to imitate and use objects. Heilman and Rothi (1993) suggest that the difference may have been due to variability in brain organization. As we saw in Chapter 5, the types of symptom that occur after callosal lesions depend very much on how many and how much of the commissures have been lesioned.

Almost all cases of apraxia in right-handed patients involve left hemisphere damage (Geschwind, 1965), which might explain the incidence of language difficulty in apraxia. Wyke (1967) found that bilateral impairment on the tapping test was associated with left hemisphere lesions. Lesions to the supplementary motor cortex or frontal lobes are associated with bimanual hand movement impairment (Laplane *et al.*, 1977).

Left frontal and parietal lobe lesions have also been associated with impaired performance on unfamiliar sequence tasks (Kimura, 1982; De Renzi *et al.*, 1987) with left parietal lesions associated with impairments in producing meaningful gestures (Hecaen and Rondot, 1985). Gait apraxia has been associated with bilateral frontal lesions. Damage to the anterior left hemisphere, especially the left central opperculum and insula, has been found in cases of oral apraxia (Tognola and Vignolo, 1980). Constructional apraxia appears to be a right-hemisphere, especially right parietal, disorder although there are task-differences. Left-lesioned patients oversimplify the shape of a cube, for example, whereas right-lesioned patients do not (Arrigoni and De Renzi, 1964). Perhaps constructional apraxia has two dissociable elements – the right hemisphere shows impairment in the processing of spatial relationships whereas the left hemisphere shows deficits in the organization of actions needed to draw.

Although characterized as a cortical disorder, apraxia might be associated with lesions to the basal ganglia and the thalamus to a greater degree than was previously thought. In an extensive review of the involvement of basal ganglia and thalamic involvement in apraxia, Pramstaller and Marsden (1996) found that lesions confined to the basal ganglia rarely caused apraxia (8 out of 82 cases). However, apraxia was found to result after lesions in the putamen and associated white matter (58 out of 72 cases) and occurred with thalamic damage in 26 cases and minor thalamic lesions in 8 cases. The authors conclude that although apraxia cannot result from exclusive lesioning of the basal ganglia, it can result from basal ganglia damage and associated white matter lesions.

■ Theories of apraxia

Liepmann's theory of apraxia argues that the left parietal cortex (Area 40) is the brain region mediating complex movement and proposes that a connection runs from the left parietal cortex to the left frontal cortex via the corpus callosum (Liepmann, 1905). This connection, if disrupted, will result in apraxia.

Geschwind's disconnection hypothesis expanded on Liepmann's model by proposing that apraxia resulted from disconnections between motor association pathways (Geschwind, 1965). A disconnection between posterior language areas from motor association areas important for implementing motor programmes resulted from lesions to the arcuate fasciculus. However, patients with lesions to this area should still be able to imitate and the damage does not explain why some patients are gauche in their object use.

Heilman's representational hypothesis argues that the nervous system, because it stores knowledge of motor skills, does not construct a programme for carrying out those skills from scratch (Heilman, 1979). Patients with parietal lesions exhibit apraxic symptoms because their 'learned time–space movement representations' or praxicons (the skills to be retrieved) are stored there. These praxicons programme the motor association cortex which implement the programme by activating the motor cortex. Based on this theory, Heilman and his colleagues (e.g. Heilman *et al.*, 1982) have suggested that there may be two forms of ideomotor apraxia. The first is the result of praxicon loss in the supramarginal or angular gyrus. The second results from lesions anterior to these areas which disconnect the praxicons from the premotor and motor association areas or damage the premotor cortex. One model of the command apparatus of the parietal lobe is illustrated by Figure 8.1.

■ Hemiplegia

Hemiplegia refers to a loss of voluntary motor control on the side of the body contralateral to the damaged side of the brain. Damage is done to the cortex, cerebrospinal fibers and basal ganglia normally as a result of cerebral palsy (in infants), aneurysm, tumour or head insult (in young adults) and brain haemorrhage (especially in the middle-aged, the group most likely to be affected). The locus of the disease is usually the middle cerebral artery (which supplies blood to the motor area). Once voluntary movement is lost, patients often exhibit muscular spasticity which results in posture and lower limb movement problems.

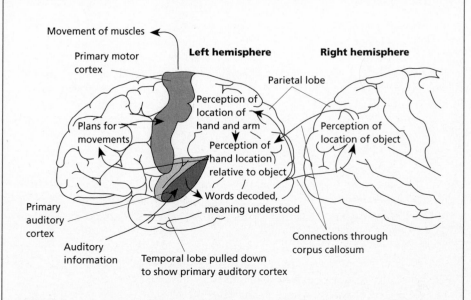

Movement of muscles

Primary motor
cortex

Left hemisphere

Right hemisphere

Parietal lobe

Perception of
location of
hand and arm

Plans for
movements

Perception of
hand location
relative to object

Perception of
location of object

Words decoded,
meaning understood

Primary
auditory
cortex

Connections through
corpus callosum

Auditory
information

Temporal lobe pulled down
to show primary auditory cortex

Figure 8.1   An illustration of the possible command apparatus of the parietal lobe. From Carlson, 1995. © 1995 Allyn and Bacon; reproduced by permission

---

DISCUSSION POINT

Discussion point: Can neural transplants abolish the symptoms of Parkinson's disease?

The primary neuropathological characteristic of Parkinson's disease is a reduction in dopamine. Levodopa, the drug treatment of choice for parkinsonism, aims to combat this reduction via replacement. What if, instead of replacing the drug chemically, it were possible to replace the degenerated neural tissue that was responsible for supplying the dopamine?

This treatment strategy has become a possibility in recent years, based largely on work on animals. Two recent reviews have provided an excellent summary of our current knowledge of the effects of neural transplants on cognition in animals (Stein and Glaser, 1995; Sinden et al., 1995). Sinden et al., for example, describe a large number of experiments in which neural tissue from one animal is transplanted into the brain of another whose tissue has been lesioned to produce cognitive symptoms similar to those seen in Parkinson's disease, Alzheimer's disease and memory disorder.

These experiments have focused on replacing damaged ascending forebrain cholinergic projections (which degenerate in Alzheimer's disease) or hippocampal formation tissue (which is important for memory). It has been found that transplants of cholinergic tissue into the terminal cortical and hippocampal regions in the receiving brain restores performance on particular memory tasks. Non-cholinergic transplants do not result in improvement, indicating that the neural grafts must be of a specific type before behaviour is changed. Recovery is seen within seven to nine weeks after transplantation.

Animal work has prompted trials with human participants, particularly patients with Parkinson's disease (PD). In fact, the transplantation of neural tissue in PD patients should produce better results than those for Alzheimer's disease because the neural locus of impairment is more specific. In PD, dopamine-producing nigrostriatal neurons are lost; in Alzheimer's disease, there is more widespread neuronal degeneration.

The tissue used is normally foetal tissue obtained from voluntarily or spontaneously aborted foetuses. Like normal tissue, it can send electrical signals and synthesize and release dopamine spontaneously (Olanow et al., 1996). One of the earliest studies of the effects of neural grafts in PD patients was undertaken by Lindvall and his colleagues (Lindvall et al., 1989). In this study, two PD patients received ventral mesencephalic grafts transplanted into the caudate nucleus and anterior putamen. After six months, there was a small but significant improvement during the 'off' period of the drug treatment. In a second experiment with two other PD patients, younger neural tissue was transplanted into the posterior and anterior putamen. This time, an improvement was seen after six to twelve weeks and behaviour improved over three years. Bradykinesia was reduced bilaterally and the reduction in rigidity was more apparent on the side of the body contralateral to the side of the transplant.

Several other studies have shown positive results following foetal neural transplants, although it is often difficult to compare studies because of differences in grafting techniques, the site of the graft, how much tissue is replaced, the lateralization of the graft, patient variability and inconsistencies in follow-up studies. Freed and his colleagues, for example, transplanted unilateral nigral grafts into the caudate and putamen of two patients and bilateral transplants in the remaining five (Freed et al., 1992). Substantial improvement was seen after twelve months, with patients achieving 39 per cent reduction in their drug treatment. Spencer et al. (1992), however, found improvement in patients receiving right caudate grafts but only when compared with their preoperative condition; patients did not perform better than a control group. Greater improvement appears to result from grafts given to patients whose parkinsonism has been induced by MPTP (Widner et al., 1992). In this study, bilateral caudate and putamen grafts in two patients were associated with improvements in motor function three to four months after the transplant.

⫸

In their review of neural transplant studies in PD, Olanow *et al.* (1996) suggest that a number of factors can influence the successful outcome of a neural graft. These are summarized in Table 8.3.

These factors include the age of the donor graft, the number of donors, the amount of tissue grafted, the distribution of the graft, the site of the graft and the type of patient operated on. For example, the optimal age for graft donation is $5\frac{1}{2}$–9 weeks. An older donor is likely to be ineffective. About 500 000 dopamine-containing cells exist in the human substantia nigra and about 25 000 of these project to the putamen. The PD patient loses approximately 60–80 per cent of striatal dopamine, which suggests that a graft which replaces the complete number of dopamine-containing cells is unnecessary. In addition, a graft often contains other neurons which may be irrelevant to the process that the graft is trying to improve. For human transplants, striatal grafts innervate an area of about 2–5 mm radius. The site of the graft is important because different regions will project to other, different regions. The best sites for grafts in PD are the putamen and caudate.

Why do grafts work? What is the mechanism for recovery? These are important questions because different types of graft will show very different outcomes. Animal work, for example, has found that hippocampal grafts in the basal ganglia do not produce an improvement in cognition whereas cholinergic grafts do. One possible mechanism is that the graft releases a missing neurotransmitter (in PD's case, dopamine). In this sense, grafts provide a 'drug-delivery system' (Sinden *et al.*, 1995). Alternatively, the grafts could form reciprocal connections with other regions in a fairly normal manner. A test of this hypothesis would be the transplantation of grafts that secrete the same neurotransmitter but function differently. However, the grafts themselves might secrete the neurotransmitter differently. Finally, it is possible that the grafts secrete growth factors which help to repair the damaged tissue (Sinden *et al.*, 1995). At present, it is unclear which of these mechanisms (or others) are responsible for the improvement in cognitive and motor behaviour seen after transplantation.

Parkinson's disease, perhaps more than Alzheimer's disease, is the degenerative disorder most likely to benefit from neural transplants because the system affected is fairly specific and the deficits can be mimicked in animal studies more effectively than can Alzheimer's symptoms. This form of treatment, however, is likely to provoke a number of ethical arguments.

Table 8.3 Some conclusions from studies of human foetal transplantation undertaken to alleviate Parkinson's disease

Study	No. of patients	Follow-up period	Donor age	Site	Benefit	Decrease levodopa %
Lindvall et al. (1989)	2	6 months	7–9 weeks	Anterior P & C	Mild	0
Lindvall et al. (1990, 1992)	2	5 and 14 months	6–7 weeks	P	Moderate	0
Lindvall et al. (1994)	2	36 months	6–7 weeks	P	Moderate	100
Freed et al. (1990)	2	12–33 months	5–6 weeks	P & C	1 = nil; 1 = moderate	39
Freed et al. (1992)	5	12–33 months	5–6 weeks	P	Mild to moderate	
Spencer et al. (1992)	4	4–18 months	5–9 months	C	1 = nil; 3 = mild	24
Perchanski et al. (1994)	2	10 and 17 months	6–8 weeks	P & C	Moderate	0, 19
Widner et al. (1992)	2	12 and 24 months	6–8 weeks	P/C & P	Moderate	0–70
Freeman et al. (1995)	4	6 months	6½–9 weeks	Posterior P	Moderate	0

P = putamen; C = caudate nucleus
Adapted from Olanow et al., 1996

Summary

☐ Basal ganglia disorders, also referred to as extrapyramidal disorders, involve symptoms of excessive or restricted motor activity.

☐ Parkinson's disease (PD), first described by James Parkinson in 1817, is a motor disorder characterized by loss of movement (akinesia), resisting passive movement (rigidity) and tremor at rest. Early symptoms of the disorder include disturbed fine motor control by the hand. Symptoms of PD are called parkinsonism.

☐ Idiopathic PD is of unknown aetiology; secondary parkinsonism occurs secondary to another disorder.

☐ PD affects 0.15 per cent of the population in general, affecting 0.5 per cent of individuals over the age of 50 years. The prominent neuropathology is the loss of the striatal dopamine pathway which runs from the substantia nigra to the caudate nucleus, putamen and globus pallidus. Dopamine is depleted in the basal ganglia and GABA is reduced in the striatum and substantia nigra.

☐ PD is treated effectively by levodopa (L-DOPA) which makes more dopamine available to nigrostriatal nerve endings. Other drugs used to treat parkinsonian symptoms include dopamine agonists, antiviral agents and anticholinergic drugs. Severe parkinsonism may be alleviated by surgery. Grafting of foetal neural tissue into the parkinsonian brain is a form of treatment that is currently being assessed in the long term.

☐ Huntington's chorea is an inherited motor disorder characterized by involuntary, dance-like, jerky movement. It is associated with a mutation of the gene on the arm of chromosome 4. Neuronal loss occurs in the basal ganglia, cerebellum and cortex but is most severe in the striatum. Dopamine agonists are the most commonly recommended treatment but there is currently no long-term successful treatment.

☐ Sydenham's chorea is a childhood disorder characterized by the gradual appearance of chorea.

☐ Dyskinesia describes sustained, involuntary contraction of muscles resulting in twisting, repetitive movements and abnormal posture. Examples include the dystonias which involve distortion of the trunk or limbs owing to excessive muscle tone.

☐ Gilles de la Tourette syndrome describes motor and phonic tics which occur despite otherwise normal motor behaviour. Symptoms include blinking, grimacing, head jerking, sniffing, snorting, repetition of words and uttering obscenities.

➠

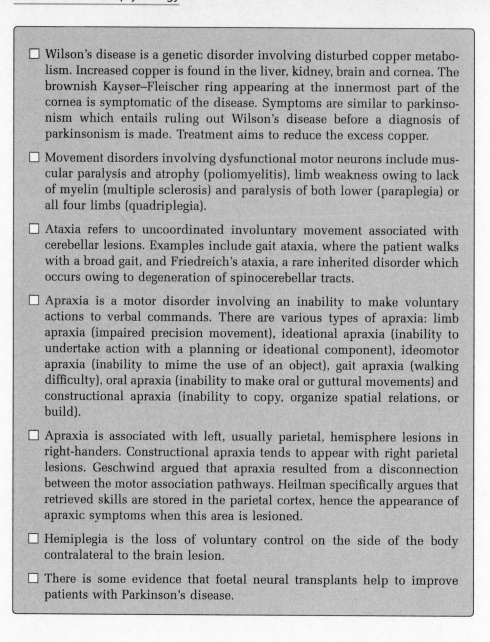

☐ Wilson's disease is a genetic disorder involving disturbed copper metabolism. Increased copper is found in the liver, kidney, brain and cornea. The brownish Kayser–Fleischer ring appearing at the innermost part of the cornea is symptomatic of the disease. Symptoms are similar to parkinsonism which entails ruling out Wilson's disease before a diagnosis of parkinsonism is made. Treatment aims to reduce the excess copper.

☐ Movement disorders involving dysfunctional motor neurons include muscular paralysis and atrophy (poliomyelitis), limb weakness owing to lack of myelin (multiple sclerosis) and paralysis of both lower (paraplegia) or all four limbs (quadriplegia).

☐ Ataxia refers to uncoordinated involuntary movement associated with cerebellar lesions. Examples include gait ataxia, where the patient walks with a broad gait, and Friedreich's ataxia, a rare inherited disorder which occurs owing to degeneration of spinocerebellar tracts.

☐ Apraxia is a motor disorder involving an inability to make voluntary actions to verbal commands. There are various types of apraxia: limb apraxia (impaired precision movement), ideational apraxia (inability to undertake action with a planning or ideational component), ideomotor apraxia (inability to mime the use of an object), gait apraxia (walking difficulty), oral apraxia (inability to make oral or guttural movements) and constructional apraxia (inability to copy, organize spatial relations, or build).

☐ Apraxia is associated with left, usually parietal, hemisphere lesions in right-handers. Constructional apraxia tends to appear with right parietal lesions. Geschwind argued that apraxia resulted from a disconnection between the motor association pathways. Heilman specifically argues that retrieved skills are stored in the parietal cortex, hence the appearance of apraxic symptoms when this area is lesioned.

☐ Hemiplegia is the loss of voluntary control on the side of the body contralateral to the brain lesion.

☐ There is some evidence that foetal neural transplants help to improve patients with Parkinson's disease.

Recommended further general and specific reading

Key: (1) = introductory, *(3)* = intermediate, *(5)* = advanced

General

Jeannerod, M. (1997). *The Cognitive Neuroscience of Action*. Oxford: Blackwell. *(4)*

Marsden. C.D. and Fahn, S. (1982). *Movement Disorders*. London: Butterworth Scientific. *(3)*

Moses, J.A. (1996). Motor skill disorders. In J. G. Beaumont, P.M. Kenealy and M.J.C. Rogers (eds), *Blackwell Dictionary of Neuropsychology*. Oxford: Blackwell. *(2)*

Roy, E.A. (1985). *Neuropsychological Studies of Apraxia and Related Disorders*. New York: North-Holland. *(3)*

Strange, P.G. (1992). *Brain Biochemistry and Brain Disorders*. New York: Oxford University Press. *(2)*

Specific

Batiste, L. (1996). Parkinson's disease. *Advances of Neurology*, volume 69. New York: Lippincott-Raven. *(4)*

Bhatia, K.P. and Marsden, C.D. (1994). The behavioural and motor consequences of focal lesions of the basal ganglia in man. *Brain*, **117**, 859–76. *(4)*

Chesselet, M-F. and Delfs, J.M. (1996). Basal ganglia and movement disorders: an update. *Trends in Neuroscience*, **19**(10), 417–22. *(3)*

De Long, M.R. and Wichmann, T. (1993). Basal ganglia–thalamocortical circuits in parkinsonian signs. *Clinical Neuroscience*, **1**, 18–26. *(4)*

Dunnett, S.B. and Bjorklund, A. (1994). *Functional Neural Transplantation*. New York: Raven Press. *(4)*

Heilman, K.M. and Rothi, L.J.G. (1993). Apraxia. In K.M. Heilman and E. Valenstein (eds), *Clinical Neuropsychology* (3rd edition). New York: Oxford University Press. *(3)*

Marsden, C.D. and J.A. Obeso (1994). The functions of the basal ganglia and the paradox of stereotaxic surgery in Parkinson's disease. *Brain*, **117**, 877–97. *(4)*

Oertel, W.H. and Dodel, R.C. (1995). International guide to drugs for Parkinson's disease. *Movement Disorders*, **10**, 121–31. *(3)*

Oertel, W.H. and Quinn, N.P. (1996). Parkinsonism. In T. Brandt, L.R. Caplan, J. Dichgans, H.C. Diener and C. Kennard (eds), *Neurological Disorders: Course and treatment*. New York: Academic Press. *(4)*

Pramstaller, P.P. and Marsden, C.D. (1996). The basal ganglia and apraxia. *Brain*, **119**, 319–40. *(4)*

Sandor, P. (1995). Clinical management of Tourette's syndrome and associated disorders. *Canadian Journal of Psychiatry*, **40**, 577–83. *(4)*

Schnider, A., Hanlon, R.E., Alexander, D.N. and Benson, D.F. (1997). Ideomotor apraxia: behavioural dimensions and neuroanatomical basis. *Brain and Language*, **58**, 125–36. *(3)*

Shoulson, I.D. (1986). Huntington's disease. In A. Ashbury, G.M. McKhann and W.I. McDonald (eds), *Diseases of the Nervous System: Clinical neurobiology*. Philadelphia: Saunders. *(3)*

Simpson, S.A. and Harding, A.E. (1993). Predictive testing for Huntington's disease: after the gene. *Journal of Medical Genetics*, **30**, 1036–38. *(3)*

Strange, P.G. (1993). Dopamine receptors in the basal ganglia: relevance to parkinson's disease. *Movement Disorders*, **8**(3), 263–70. *(4)*

Youdim, M.B.H. and Rieder, P. (1997). Understanding Parkinson's disease. *Scientific American*, January, 38–45. *(1)*

Chapter Nine

The neuropsychology language and language disorders

NICKY BRUNSWICK

This chapter was contributed by Nicky Brunswick, Wellcome Department of Cognitive Neurology, Institute of Neurology, London.

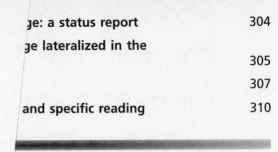

nguage: an introduction

U........................ of language presents neuropsychology with one
of its perennial challenges. Those who take up this challenge generally
approach it from one of a number of standpoints: they may study language
function in individuals with normal cortical development, in individuals who
have suffered some form of cerebral insult or in individuals with abnormal or
unexpected language development. By drawing together the findings from these
different strands of research it might be possible to make sense of the neuropsychology of normal and abnormal spoken and written language.

The earliest scientific studies of the localization of language were reported in the
mid-nineteenth century. The French neurologists Pierre Paul Broca (1861) and
Marc Dax (1865) both observed that damage to the frontal region of a patient's left
hemisphere resulted in an inability to produce fluent speech. Most famously, this
was seen in Broca's patient Leborgne. This patient became known as Tan because
this was the only word he was able to produce effortlessly. Comprehension of
language, however, was spared. Autopsy revealed that Tan had lesions of the
frontal operculum in the frontal lobe. This area subsequently became known as the
brain area responsible for language *production* and is called **Broca's area**. Although this language disorder is called Broca's aphasia, Broca originally described
the disorder as 'aphemia'. Further investigations by Carl Wernicke (1874) demonstrated that damage to posterior regions of the left hemisphere resulted in an
inability to comprehend speech, despite unimpaired speech production. Wernicke's area, as this region was termed, became known as the area responsible for
language *comprehension*. As both of these language disorders resulted from
damage to the left hemisphere it was initially thought that the right hemisphere
played no part in linguistic processing. As we saw in Chapter 4, this led to the
dichotomizing of hemispheric functions, with the left side characterized as mediating verbal, sequential, analytical, rational processing, and the right side as
mediating non-verbal and visuospatial tasks. The view that the right hemisphere
plays no part in language, however, is erroneous although in the majority of people
its role is not as great as that of the left hemisphere.

Mapping of the speech regions

Electrical stimulation

A major advance in the modern approach to understanding the neuropsychology of language was mapping the language areas of the neocortex via electrical stimulation in patients due to undergo surgery for the treatment of epilepsy. This work was pioneered by Penfield and his colleagues. They observed that, depending on the particular region stimulated, a total arrest of speech, slurring and hesitant speech, an inability to name objects or count in sequence, misnaming objects and the production of distorted speech sounds could result (Penfield and Jasper, 1954; Penfield and Roberts, 1959; Penfield and Perot, 1963). On the basis of these studies, three cortical language regions were identified as having some responsibility for language: the anterior language area (corresponding to Broca's area), the posterior language area (corresponding to Wernicke's area) and the supplementary language area (more specifically, the supplementary motor area). The regions of primary interest for language processing are illustrated in Figure 9.1.

Other electrical stimulation studies have also implicated the temporal lobe of the dominant hemisphere in language processing (Nielsen, 1946; De Renzi *et al.*, 1987). For example, Luders and colleagues found that certain types of language production disorder such as global, productive and sensory aphasia (see below) were elicited following electrical stimulation of the fusiform (occipitotemporal) gyrus of the dominant temporal lobe (Lesser *et al.*, 1986; Luders *et al.*, 1985). Electrical stimulation of the basal temporal region resulted in language comprehension deficits that are almost identical to those produced by stimulation of Wernicke's area. The impaired language ability of patients with posterior-inferior temporal gyrus lesions of the dominant hemisphere suggests that this area may be the brain's 'naming centre' or 'language formulation area' (Penfield and Roberts, 1959). In other words, this region mediates the integration of the auditory representations of words and their meanings retrieved from the sensory association cortex.

Subcortical structures are also involved in language processing, a finding first reported by the British neurologist, John Hughlings-Jackson. Penfield and Roberts (1959), for example, suggested that the thalamus played a role in the coordination of the activity of the cortical speech regions. More recently, it has been shown that stimulation of the left ventrolateral and pulvinar nuclei of the thalamus produces aphasic symptoms including total arrest of speech, naming difficulties, slowed speech and perseveration (Ojemann, 1982). Similar speech disturbances are also reported following lesions of the left ventrolateral thalamus. The involvement of the thalamus in speech production appears unquestionable although the extent of its involvement is unknown.

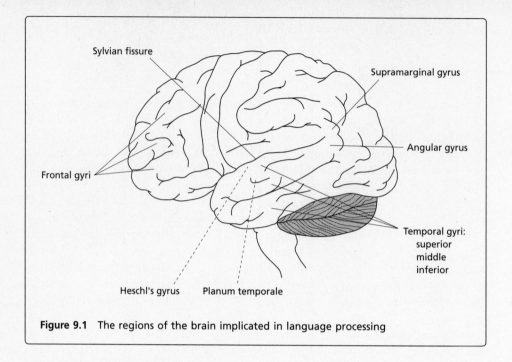

Figure 9.1   The regions of the brain implicated in language processing

Regional cerebral blood flow (rCBF)

Electrical stimulation studies of language have their limitations. Perhaps the most important is that they cannot be used in studies of healthy individuals. Furthermore, the individuals who can be assessed using these techniques are already in a state of ill health. Alternative, non-invasive techniques have been developed which overcome some of these limitations, brain imaging techniques being among these methods. As we saw in Chapter 4, the brain imaging literature has highlighted the role of particular cortical and subcortical regions in the production and comprehension of speech. In a pioneering study, Petersen *et al.* (1988) reported a bilateral increase in blood flow in the primary and secondary sensory areas during the passive perception of words but bilateral activation in the sensory and motor face areas and supplementary speech regions when speech was produced.

Others have observed increased blood flow in the left inferior and middle frontal cortices during performance of a lexical decision task and in the temporal region of the left hemisphere during reading (Price *et al.*, 1994; Wood *et al.*, 1991; Flowers *et al.*, 1991). There is also increased activation in the left frontal cortex during the passive perception of real words but not pseudowords (Petersen *et al.*, 1990).

The ability to localize the brain region responsible for putting together sounds to form meaningful words, a process called **phonological processing**, has presented imaging studies with problems. Studies have shown increased activation in the left frontal cortex near Broca's area, for example, when subjects were required to perform a number of tasks including (1) discriminating between spoken words on the basis of phonetic structure (Fiez *et al.*, 1995), (2) monitoring phonemes and discriminating between consonants (Zatorre *et al.*, 1996), and (3) making phonological similarity (rhyme) judgements and undertaking phonological short-term memory tasks (Paulesu *et al.*, 1996). Zatorre and colleagues have argued that these findings illustrate the importance of Broca's area to the extraction and manipulation of the phonetic segments of speech (Zatorre *et al.*, 1992a).

Frontal activation has not been a consistent finding, however. Others have reported increased blood flow in the left temporal lobe during reading. Nobre *et al.* (1994), for example, observed activation in the posterior fusiform gyrus of the inferior temporal lobe during the reading of words and pseudowords while the anterior fusiform gyrus was active when the semantic context in which the words and pseudowords were presented had to be considered. Similarly, Gur *et al.* (1994) found increased blood flow in the left hemisphere's angular gyrus during the detection of verbal analogies. In this paradigm, subjects are presented with a target word followed by two alternative words one of which is associated in some way with the target; the task is to identify the analogous word. On the basis of this evidence, it has been argued that activation of Broca's area occurs when phonetic manipulations of language are required but that activation of the posterior temporal cortex occurs when speech has to be analyzed perceptually (Zatorre *et al.*, 1996). Support for this suggestion comes from studies in which activation in both frontal regions (Broca's area) and temporal regions (Wernicke's area) of the left hemisphere are observed in normal readers during the performance of rhyming and short-term memory tasks (Paulesu *et al.*, 1996).

One problem with positron emission tomography (PET), however, is that it can only be used to study brain activation in adults, not children. PET requires the introduction of a radioactive isotope into the bloodstream, and although these isotopes are short-lived, and relatively non-hazardous, the technique is nonetheless invasive and provokes anxiety in children. Charting the cortical development of language is, therefore, virtually impossible using these techniques. A second inhibiting factor is the timescale involved. The half-life of radioactive isotopes is typically in the realm of minutes, which means that the images are fairly slow to obtain and would require a great deal of patience from the child, or even the adult, as illustrated by the discussion point in Chapter 1. Perhaps the greatest problem with the use of the PET technique, however, is the means by which the positrons are detected. This requires the patient's head to remain perfectly still inside a scanner. Given the stress that this might cause a child and given the inevitable restlessness, PET imaging has been considered impracticable in the study of child language. Similarly, functional magnetic resonance imaging (fMRI) presents problems by requiring the volunteer's head to be restrained within the scanner for an extended period of time. Electroencephalographic (EEG) measures offer a workable alternative. EEG and ERP recordings are non-invasive, relatively naturalistic (the subject can perform a variety of tasks during the recording) and record the brain's electrical activity in real time. ERP techniques are advantageous in that they allow the measurement of both adults' and children's brain electrical activity. This measurement sometimes highlights the lateralization of language or, in the case of dyslexic individuals, the lack of it.

Event-related potentials

Event-related potential (ERP) studies have also implicated the left hemisphere in the processing of language (Segalowitz and Berge, 1995). For example, studies in which subjects were required to articulate a series of letter strings covertly report larger N100 and P200 amplitudes over the left than over the right hemisphere (Papanicolaou et al., 1983). The N100 and P200 are potentials thought to reflect early sensory processing. Similar asymmetries have been observed during the perception of nonsense words (Segalowitz et al., 1992) and consonant–vowel (C–V) phonemes (Wood et al., 1971; Brunswick and Rippon, 1994), the detection of target words in a series of phonetically different distractor words (Brunswick and Rippon, 1995), and performance on a phonological task in which the subject is required to name letters that rhyme with 'v' (Taylor, 1993).

Lateralized effects have also been observed for the P300, the ERP component thought to reflect cognitive processing. There is evidence, for example, that greater left than right hemisphere involvement is found during reading (Johnstone et al., 1984), during the rhyme task described above (Taylor, 1993) and during the discrimination of letters beginning with stop consonants, e.g. /b/, from those that do not, e.g. /d/ (Taylor and Keenan, 1990).

Finally, one other late, negative ERP component, the N400, has been found to be associated with 'receptive language function', that is, the process of attributing meaning to sentences (Connolly and Phillips, 1994; Nobre and McCarthy, 1994, 1995). Studies have localized semantic processing in the frontal and frontocentral regions of the brain during the passive perception of auditorily presented sentences. Connolly and Phillips (1994), for example, presented subjects with spoken sentences in which the final words were either semantically appropriate (e.g. at night the old woman locked the door) or semantically inappropriate (e.g. the dog chased our cat up the queen). They observed an N400 wave, especially at frontocentral regions, only in response to the semantically inappropriate sentences, not to those sentences with semantically appropriate endings. In this context it is suggested that the N400 reflects a disturbance in the individual's 'online and continuous' processing of speech that bestows it with coherent meaning.

Individual differences: sex and handedness

While neuropsychological studies provide some indication of which regions of the brain mediate the comprehension and production of speech, there is still considerable between-subject variation in terms of the precise regions involved. Two variables which are considered to be important in influencing the precise pattern of the hemispheric localization of language are handedness and sex, as noted in Chapter 4. A vast amount of neuropsychological evidence suggests that men are more lateralized for language than are women (McGlone, 1980; Bryden, 1982). In the performance of a vocabulary test, for example, women are detrimentally affected by damage to either hemisphere, whereas men are affected only by damage to the left hemisphere (Kimura, 1983). The incidence of language production and comprehension disturbances is up to three times higher in men than in women following damage to the left hemisphere (McGlone and Davidson, 1973; McGlone and Kertesz, 1973).

More recently, Shaywitz *et al.* (1995) have employed functional magnetic resonance imaging to investigate sex differences in the functional organization of the brain for language. Individuals performing a rhyme (phonological) judgement task showed predominantly left-hemisphere (inferior frontal gyrus) activation in men whereas the women displayed a more diffuse pattern of activation, with both the left and right inferior frontal gyri becoming activated. These data have been interpreted as indicating clear sex differences in the localization of language functions in male and female brains. It is possible, however, that this sex difference in language asymmetry reflects the subject's approach to the task rather than revealing anything about underlying physiological differences. Women, for example, may tend to use verbal strategies in the performance of tasks, whether the tasks be verbal or visuospatial. This would obviously generate a 'false' laterality effect that has little to do with differences in cerebral organization between the sexes.

Neurophysiological evidence, however, appears to challenge this possibility. The male brain is reported to be structurally more asymmetrical than the female brain. A great deal of this evidence derives from work by Geschwind and Galaburda (1987) who, as noted in Chapter 4, suggested that the presence of prenatal androgens (male sex hormones such as testosterone) may suppress left hemisphere development in boys, with a concomitant increase in the functional potency of the right hemisphere. In fact, in humans (as well as in rats) the right cerebral hemisphere has been found to be larger than the left in males but not in females (Lacoste-Utamsing and Holloway, 1982). This suppression of the left hemisphere development during a critical growth phase might explain the higher incidence of language disorders in males than in females.

The evidence is not quite so clear cut, however. Inglis and Lawson (1981), reviewing sixteen studies of the effects of lateralized lesions on the cognitive performance of men and women, concluded that while left or right hemisphere lesions depress

➡

verbal or performance IQ respectively in men, left but not right hemisphere lesions in women were found to impair both verbal and performance IQ equally. Right hemisphere lesions failed to impair either. Interestingly, there is no higher incidence of language production or comprehension difficulties in women than in men with right hemisphere damage, as would be expected if women relied on both hemispheres for language processing (Hier and Kaplan, 1980; De Renzi, 1980; Kimura, 1983).

The neuropsychology of language disorders

Normal language processing is the result of a complex interaction of sensory, motor and memory processes. Impairments in any of these processes can lead to language disorders such as **aphasia** (a disturbance in the comprehension or production of speech), **dysgraphia** (impaired writing) or **dyslexia** (disordered reading). The focus of the remainder of the chapter will be on these three disorders.

Aphasia

The term aphasia, although literally meaning 'complete loss of language', may be more accurately labelled **dysphasia** (meaning a 'partial lack of language') because patients with aphasia-producing brain damage generally retain some degree of linguistic ability. Despite the misnomer, however, the term aphasia remains that most widely used to describe the loss of language function.

Specifically, aphasia refers to disturbance in the comprehension or production of spoken, written or signed language. It is estimated that approximately 85 per cent of cases of aphasia are the result of cerebrovascular accidents (strokes) in the language areas of the brain. Other causes include tumours, organic brain disease and head injuries. A diagnosis of aphasia is made only in the absence of sensory impairments (poor vision or hearing), perceptual impairments (agnosia), impaired movement (apraxia) or thought disturbances (autism, dementia or schizophrenia, for example). This condition is thought to represent a breakdown in the link between thought and language (Mesulam, 1990).

A number of attempts have been made to classify the different features of aphasia by associating the symptoms displayed with the locus of the cerebral lesion. This has proved difficult for three reasons: (1) few patients have been studied in any great detail; (2) lesions are rarely found in identical locations or restricted to discrete regions in every individual, and (3) the production and comprehension of language depends on a complex and dynamic interaction between numerous regions of the brain, sometimes extending over vast areas of the cortex and the subcortex. Attempts to localize aphasic symptoms to particular regions of the brain are, therefore, problematic. As Hughlings-Jackson noted in 1874: 'to locate the damage which destroys speech and to locate speech are two different things'.

In spite of such problems, however, numerous subtypes of aphasia have been described, each with its own specific cluster of symptoms and each produced by damage to a particular cortical region. These regions are generally found in left hemisphere and are usually perisylvian, i.e. near the Sylvian fissure. Structures including Broca's area, Wernicke's area, Heschl's gyrus, the planum temporale, the supramarginal, angular and temporal gyri and the frontal gyri have all been implicated in the processing of language. These regions are illustrated in Figures 9.1 and 9.2.

The symptoms and regions of damage of the main types of aphasia (sensory, production, conduction, deep, transcortical sensory, transcortical motor and global) are summarized in Table 9.1 and are described more fully below.

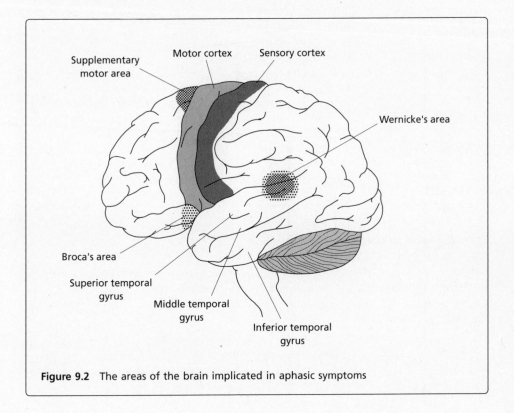

Figure 9.2 The areas of the brain implicated in aphasic symptoms

Table 9.1 Types of aphasia, their primary symptoms and the possible site of the associated brain lesion

Type of aphasia	Primary symptoms	Brain lesion to
Sensory (Wernicke's) aphasia	General comprehension deficits, neologisms, word retrieval deficits, semantic paraphasias	Posterior perisylvian region: posterosuperior temporal, opercular supramarginal, angular and posterior insular gyri; planum temporale
Production (Broca's) aphasia	Speech production deficits, abnormal prosody, impaired syntactic comprehension	Posterior part of the inferior frontal and precentral convolutions of the left hemisphere
Conduction aphasia	Naming deficits and impaired ability to repeat non-meaningful single words and word strings	Arcuate fasciculus; posterior parietal and temporal regions; left auditory complex; insula; supramarginal gyrus
Deep dysphasia	Word repetition deficits: verbal (semantic) paraphasia	Temporal lobe, especially regions which mediate phonological processing
Transcortical sensory aphasia	Impaired comprehension, naming, reading and writing; semantic irrelevancies in speech	Temporoparieto-occipital junction of the left hemisphere
Transcortical motor aphasia	Transient mutism and telegrammatic, dysprosodic speech	Connection between Broca's area and the supplementary motor area; medial frontal lobe; regions anterolateral to the left hemisphere's frontal horn
Global aphasia	Generalized deficits in comprehension, repetition, naming and speech production	Left perisylvian region, white matter, basal ganglia and thalamus

Sensory (Wernicke's) aphasia

Sensory or Wernicke's aphasia is a general inability to comprehend speech produced by other people or oneself. While language production is generally fluent, with no articulatory problems, the words produced are typically jargon-like. For example:

Doctor: What kind of work did you do before you came into the hospital?

Patient: Never, now mista oyge I wanna tell you this happened when happened when he rent. His – his kell come down here and is – he got ren something. It happened. In these ropiers were with him for hi – is friend

– like was. And it just happened so I don't know, he did not bring around anything. And he did not pay it. And he roden all o these arranjen from the pedis on from iss pescid. In these floors now and so. He hadn't had em round here.

(Kertesz, 1981)

This exchange illustrates the common observation that although the patient's speech is syntactically and prosodically correct, neologisms, word retrieval deficits and semantic paraphasias are rife. The failure of Wernicke's aphasics to comprehend their own speech typically renders them unaware of their language processing problems and they will continue to participate in conversations, nodding in the appropriate places and taking turns to speak, blissfully unaware of their disorder.

Wernicke's aphasia is associated with lesions to the first and posterior part of the second convolutions of the superior temporal gyrus adjacent to Heschl's gyrus (part of the auditory association cortex), and the planum temporale in the left hemisphere (Naeser *et al.*, 1981; Zatorre *et al.*, 1992a). This region has been suggested as the locus of memory for the constituent sounds of speech and is thought to mediate the linking of the auditory representations of words with their meanings. The clinical findings are complemented by imaging studies which show increases in activation in Wernicke's area during the performance of language tasks with a semantic component (Petersen *et al.*, 1988; Price *et al.*, 1994) while object naming is associated with a spread of neural activity from Wernicke's area to the frontal motor systems responsible for activation of the muscles in the production of speech (Damasio and Damasio, 1992).

While the problems experienced by Wernicke's aphasics are essentially sensory, involving 'semantic-lexical' aspects of linguistic processing, problems at the more elemental 'syntactic-articulatory' (Bradshaw and Mattingly, 1995) level of linguistic processing are characteristic of patients with Broca's aphasia.

Production (Broca's) aphasia

Production or Broca's aphasia is also called **fluent aphasia, expressive aphasia** or **motor aphasia** and describes difficulty in the production of language. This ranges from a complete inability to speak to the ability to produce speech only with considerable effort. Speech, when it is produced, is typically non-fluent, slow and laboured, although language comprehension at a simple level remains fairly normal. For example:

Doctor: Why did you come to the hospital?

Patient: Ah . . . Monday . . . ah dad and Paul . . . and Dad . . . hospital. Two . . . ah doctors . . . and ah . . . thirty minutes . . . and yes . . . ah hospital. And er Wednesday . . . nine o'clock . . . doctors. Two doctors . . . and ah . . . teeth. Yeah . . . fine.

(Goodglass, 1976)

This example shows that the speech of the Broca's aphasic is characterized by extreme verbal economy, by an omission of prepositions and definite articles, by little grammatical construction – it is 'telegrammatic' – and by abnormal prosody. While patients have unimpaired semantic comprehension, their understanding may be impaired by syntactic ambiguities. The sentence 'The dog ate the bone' would cause a Broca's aphasic no problem, for example: the bone can be eaten by the dog, but the dog cannot be eaten by the bone. A more syntactically ambiguous sentence, such as 'The dog chased the cat', may not be so easily understood: the cat can chase the dog as easily as the dog can chase the cat. Unfortunately for Broca's aphasics, insight into their linguistic abilities is preserved: they know that they make mistakes, but they cannot correct them.

Neurological examination of Broca's aphasics reveals atrophy of the posterior part of the third frontal with the adjacent part of the second frontal and precentral convolutions of the left hemisphere (Benson, 1967; Mazzocchi and Vignolo, 1979). This region, which is anterior to the motor cortex, specifically the region of the motor cortex responsible for facial movements, is labelled Broca's area. Ironically, however, it was Wernicke (1874) who explained the association between the cortical damage of Broca's aphasics and their symptoms. He suggested that sensory experiences are stored in the cortical regions adjacent to the areas responsible for those functions. As Broca's area is situated adjacent to the region of the motor cortex responsible for the movements of the mouth, damage to this region will result in destruction of the memory traces of the movements required to produce speech.

The severity of the articulatory disturbances following damage to Broca's area is far more variable than that of the language disturbances which result from lesions to Wernicke's area. While lesions to Broca's area produce transient impairments in speech production, subcortical damage is necessary before a persistent deficit in speech production emerges (Mohr *et al.*, 1978).

A wealth of evidence indicates that the production and comprehension of language are mediated by a complex interaction of processes residing in different cerebral regions. Evidence from neural imaging studies has shown that numerous regions are activated simultaneously during language processing. It may be expected, therefore, that damage to the pathways connecting these regions would impair an individual's ability to repeat verbally presented words. In fact, this suggestion was first proposed by Wernicke in 1874. Such a deficit is called **conduction aphasia**.

Conduction aphasia

Patients with conduction aphasia display apparently normal speech comprehension and production, but impaired naming ability and deficits in the repetition of non-meaningful words and word sequences. The ability to repeat colloquialisms and stock phrases, however, may be preserved (Goodglass, 1993). Consider, for example, this exchange between doctor and patient where the patient's task is to repeat what the doctor is saying (Margolin and Walker, 1981):

Doctor: Bicycle.
Patient: Bicycle.
Doctor: Hippopotamus.
Patient: Hippopotamus.
Doctor: Blaynge.
Patient: I didn't get it.
Doctor: Up and down.
Patient: Up and down.
Doctor: Yellow, big, south.
Patient: Yellen . . . Can't get it.

(Carlson, 1986)

As with patients exhibiting Broca's aphasia, patients with conduction aphasia are aware of their language problems and will often make attempts to correct their errors. If presented with alternative pronunciations, patients are generally able to reject obviously inappropriate alternatives and will often accept the correct ones; this is taken as indicating that the phonological processing skills of these patients are intact and that the problem is confined to the process of retrieval (Goodglass, 1993).

Once again it was Wernicke (1874) who offered an explanation for this disorder by suggesting that disconnection of the arcuate fasciculus, the bundle of fibers which connects Broca's and Wernicke's areas, would impair the ability to repeat heard words. Support for this hypothesis comes from Damasio and Damasio's study in which conduction aphasics were found to have damage to the association fibers of the inferior parietal lobe which normally connect Wernicke's and Broca's areas (Damasio and Damasio, 1980). This type of aphasia is also found in patients with lesions of the posterior parietal and temporal regions and sometimes the second transverse gyrus (Hoeft, 1957).

Geschwind (1965) has suggested that when a conduction aphasic hears a word (e.g. bicycle), the patient produces a mental representation of the object described by the word. Information concerning this image is then sent from the visual association cortex to Broca's area (thus bypassing the damaged arcuate fasciculus) in order to initiate the movements necessary to produce the sounds which constitute the word. Such a strategy is only effective for the repetition of meaningful words and phrases, however. If the perception of a non-word fails to produce a visual image the patient is unable to reproduce the word.

Deep dysphasia

A rarer form of dysphasia, deep dysphasia, is characterized by the replacement of verbally presented target words by semantically related words. For example, when asked to repeat the words 'kite' or 'shell', the deep dysphasic may respond with 'balloon' or 'kernel' (Goodglass, 1993). The accuracy of the repetition depends on the class of word used. Concrete nouns are more likely to be repeated correctly than are abstract words; nouns are repeated with greater accuracy than verbs; and non-words are rarely repeated correctly.

Deep dysphasia may result from lesions to the temporal lobe. As discussed above, the temporal lobe is strongly implicated in the processing of language and in phonological memory. It is this latter role which may account for the impairments of deep dysphasics. Patients often report that they have forgotten the actual word presented although they retain the general meaning. This may be used to guess, often incorrectly, the target word.

Transcortical sensory aphasia

Transcortical sensory aphasia describes the inability to comprehend, name, read and write despite the unimpaired recitation of previously learned passages (e.g. poems or prayers) and repetition. Speech is spontaneous and fluent but semantically irrelevant, as in Wernicke's aphasia. The difference between Wernicke's aphasics and transcortical sensory aphasics is that transcortical sensory aphasics can repeat words and non-words spoken to them and can correct grammatical errors in spoken phrases. It is suggested that this preserved repetition ability is phonologically rather than lexically based, i.e. words and non-words to be repeated are treated as a collection of sounds (phonological elements) rather than as meaningful wholes (Kertesz et al., 1982).

This type of aphasia can result from destruction of the temporoparieto-occipital junction in the dominant hemisphere. This disconnection of Wernicke's area from the remaining parietal association areas weakens the control of the auditory regions over those mediating speech production, although the arcuate fasciculus may remain intact. The effective isolation of the sensory language areas from the remaining cortex of the dominant hemisphere prevents the transfer of information from the non-language regions to Wernicke's area for encoding into their verbal representations (Kertesz et al., 1982).

Transcortical motor aphasia

Transcortical motor aphasia, the motoric counterpart of transcortical sensory aphasia, results from the disconnection of Broca's area from the adjacent supplementary motor area. Aphasia-producing lesions have been reported in the left hemisphere regions anterolateral to the frontal horn (Damasio, 1981) and in the medial frontal lobe, including the supplementary motor area (Freedman et al., 1984). Symptoms are similar to those seen in Broca's aphasia – transient mutism followed by non-fluent, dysprosodic, telegrammatic speech. Repetition, object naming and comprehension are spared (see Berthier *et al.*, 1991) but right-sided motor impairments may also be seen (Benson, 1993).

Global aphasia

Perhaps the most debilitating form of aphasia, global aphasia describes a generalized inability to (1) comprehend or repeat heard speech, (2) produce speech, or (3) name objects. The production and comprehension of automatic phrases and word sequences such as days of the week, expletives and greetings may, however, be spared. Global aphasia results from extensive lesioning of the brain, including the left hemisphere's perisylvian region, white matter, the basal ganglia and the thalamus. Damage to these regions also produces right-sided sensory and motor impairments.

Recovery from aphasia

It may be hard to imagine the debilitating effect that aphasia can have on the individual's day-to-day life. Intensive speech therapy is frequently employed to redevelop the language processing skills lost in aphasia, and many patients are able to recover to some extent (Kertesz, 1993). Aetiology of the aphasia, time of onset, initial severity and size and location of the lesion are the most important factors in prognosis. The likelihood of recovery from aphasia following cerebral trauma is greater than following stroke; severe production, sensory and global aphasias generally improve very little, while dissociative speech disorders tend to improve rapidly and often completely (Adams and Victor, 1993). Approximately one-third of aphasic patients recover fully within the first three months; thereafter the possibility of full recovery diminishes such that complete recovery of language is unlikely after six months (Kertesz, 1995). Exactly how recovery is achieved is not fully understood, however. One possibility is that cells in the regions adjoining the damaged parts of the brain may regain some of their linguistic processing abilities; alternatively it is possible that unaffected regions of the brain (possibly corresponding regions within the right hemisphere) may gradually learn to compensate for the affected regions (Blumstein, 1981). Some of the variables affecting the recovery of function are discussed in Chapter 12.

Dyslexia

As with aphasia, the generic label 'dyslexia' (indicating 'impaired reading') encompasses many subdivisions although these fall under two main headings: the acquired dyslexias and the developmental dyslexias. The primary characteristics of each are summarized in Table 9.2.

Table 9.2 The dyslexias

Type of dyslexia	Primary symptoms	Brain regions implicated
Acquired dyslexia		
Visual word form dyslexia	Impaired sight reading; some decoding is possible	Disconnection between the angular gyrus of the dominant hemisphere and the visual input system
Phonological dyslexia	Deficits in reading pseudowords and non-words	Temporal lobe of the dominant hemisphere?
Surface dyslexia	Tendency to produce regularization errors in the reading of irregular words	?
Deep dyslexia	Semantic substitutions; impaired reading of abstract words, inability to read non-words	Extensive damage to the dominant hemisphere
Developmental dyslexia	Impaired reading and spelling of words/non-words/pseudowords; poor phonological processing skills, sequencing and short-term memory; some visuoperceptual defects	Temporoparietal regions of the dominant hemisphere

Acquired dyslexia

Acquired dyslexia, as its name implies, describes a reading impairment that follows brain damage in individuals with previously normal levels of reading ability. Again, this disorder has various subdivisions. The four principal classes are described below.

Visual word form dyslexia

Individuals with visual word form dyslexia are unable to recognize words immediately but are able to read words when given time to name the individual letters of the word (Warrington and Shallice, 1980). Severest forms result in poor recognition of individual letters: a visual word form dyslexic may respond with 'c, a, t . . . cat' when presented with the word 'mat'. The individual reads on the basis of the letters that they perceive rather than the letters which are actually printed.

Speedie *et al.* (1982) have suggested that visual word form dyslexia is the result of a disconnection between the angular gyrus of the left hemisphere, which normally mediates the recognition of word forms, and the visual input system. In order to compensate for this disconnection, patients rely on the visual and perceptual functions of the intact right hemisphere. Once the right hemisphere has identified the letters, this information is sent via the corpus callosum to the speech areas of the left hemisphere, the letter sounds are accessed, the patient 'hears' the word spelled out and is able to recognize it.

Phonological dyslexia

Phonological dyslexia describes an impaired ability to read pseudowords and non-words. These words cannot be read via the direct lexical access route ('reading by eye') from print to sound. This route represents the process whereby readers recognize known words visually, as familiar letter strings. Repeated encounters with a word result in the formation of a 'visual word recognition unit' which serves to access the word's meaning (semantic representation) in the mental lexicon. Obviously, lexical entries do not exist for words which have never been seen. Reading, therefore, relies on grapheme–phoneme translation. The grapheme–phoneme route from print to sound ('reading by ear') may be conceptualized as the 'sounding out' of words on the basis of their spelling–sound correspondences. On the basis of the resulting acoustic representations, the individual's auditory word recognition system may recognize the word as if it had been heard rather than read. Following this route, it may be possible to read words or non-words regardless of whether they have been encountered before.

Although phonological processing impairments are a characteristic feature of developmental dyslexia (see below), acquired phonological dyslexia is relatively rare. Little is known about the cortical involvement in the disorder although studies of the phonological impairments in developmental dyslexia suggest the abnormal development of the temporal region of the left hemisphere (Rosenberger, 1990; Wood *et al.*, 1991; Galaburda *et al.*, 1994).

Surface dyslexia

Surface dyslexia is the inability to recognize words on the basis of their physical appearance, i.e. by the direct lexical access route. However, the ability to decode words by applying grapheme–phoneme correspondence rules is spared. Patients are able to read regular words and non-words but have specific difficulties with irregular words (e.g. 'yacht' which would be read as 'yatcht'). The exact location of damage responsible for this disorder is unknown.

Deep dyslexia

Deep dyslexia describes a severe impairment in the ability to read. Concrete nouns can be read although they are frequently replaced by semantically related words. For example, attempting to read the word 'dream', the patient may say 'sleep' (Coltheart *et al.*, 1980). Abstract words are very rarely read successfully and the apparent inability to apply grapheme–phoneme correspondence rules renders deep dyslexics unable to read pronounceable non-words (Patterson and Marcel, 1977).

Deep dyslexia is usually associated with extensive damage to the left hemisphere. Because the damage generally results in global language impairments, localizing the precise cortical area producing the deep dyslexia is problematic. The similarities between the symptoms of deep dyslexia and conduction aphasia have led to the suggestion that these specific reading deficits may result from (1) lesions to cerebral areas responsible for phonological decoding, and (2) a disconnection of the mechanisms responsible for the visual perception of words and those responsible for speech production.

Developmental dyslexia

One definition of developmental dyslexia, supplied by the World Federation of Neurology (Critchley, 1973), suggests that it is a difficulty in learning to read despite adequate intelligence and appropriate educational opportunities. The children, most commonly boys, may be bright and articulate and even excel in other areas of achievement, but they show severe delays in learning to read.

More recently, attempts have been made to identify subgroups in the developmental dyslexic population in line with the acquired dyslexias. These subgroups are generally formed either on the basis of clustering observations of functional impairment (Fletcher and Satz, 1985; Bakker, 1990), or by drawing analogies between the impairments seen in developmental dyslexics and those seen in acquired dyslexics (Seymour, 1986; Castles and Coltheart, 1993). The resultant classifications have generally involved distinguishing between two types of developmental dyslexia. One is characterized by a primary deficit in the 'sounding out' of words (applying grapheme–phoneme translation rules), the other by an impaired ability to identify words on the basis of their visual forms. These two syndromes have variously been labelled dysphonetic and dyseidetic dyslexia (Boder, 1973; Fried *et al.*, 1981), phonological and surface/morphemic dyslexia (Temple and Marshall, 1983; Seymour and MacGregor, 1984) and P- (perceptual) type and L- (lingual) type dyslexia (Bakker, 1986, 1992).

In spite of these various attempts to fractionate developmental dyslexia, a vast amount of evidence consistently indicates that a particularly salient and enduring characteristic of developmental dyslexia is poor phonological awareness (Stahl and Murray, 1994). Dyslexics perform poorly on tests measuring rhyme awareness (MacLean *et al.*, 1987), rhyme production ability (Lundberg *et al.*, 1980), the ability to segment words into their individual sounds (Snowling *et al.*, 1986), awareness of alliteration (Bryant *et al.*, 1990), verbal repetition (Brady *et al.*, 1989) and verbal naming (Katz *et al.*, 1981; Snowling *et al.*, 1988).

A complementary aspect of phonological processing in dyslexia is impaired verbal memory. The acquisition of proficient literacy skills is dependent, to a considerable extent, on the child's memory (Gathercole *et al.*, 1991). Memory is strongly implicated not only in the ability to link the sounds and visual forms of letters (Hulme, 1988), but also in the development of spoken vocabulary and general language skills (Ellis and Large, 1988). Phonological memory has been considered as another source of impairment in developmental dyslexia (Snowling and Hulme, 1989). Dyslexics demonstrate reduced memory span, relative to good readers, for letter strings (Holligan and Johnston, 1988), unrelated word strings (Beech and Awaida, 1992), words in a sentence (Wiig and Semel, 1976) and strings of digits (Spring, 1976). These memory deficiencies are not restricted to printed stimuli but they are language-dependent: unfamiliar faces, abstract designs or visual patterns fail to elicit similar memory impairments (Liberman *et al.*, 1982).

However, memory deficits may not be enough to explain 'severe and intransigent reading difficulties' (Hulme and Roodenrys, 1995). Phonological memory skill is one aspect of the individual's cognitive armoury. Visual perception, the ability to process and discriminate between visually presented forms is another cognitive skill important for normal reading development. Dyslexics have shown impaired ability to copy complex figures (Satz and Sparrow, 1970; Eden *et al.*, 1993), to match visual figures (Eden *et al.*, 1993), to retain visual images in memory (Johnson and Blalock, 1987) and to orient visually (Johnson and Grant, 1989). Poor visual direction sense, binocular convergence and visual fixation have also been suggested as factors leading to delays in learning to read (Stein, 1991).

Studies have highlighted the importance of more fundamental aspects of visual processing. Vision is mediated by two parallel systems (cell layers) in the dorsal lateral geniculate nucleus: the magnocellular system and the parvocellular system. The parvocellular system is involved with the processing of colour and fine detail while the more primitive magnocellular system includes cells specialized for the detection of orientation, movement, direction and depth perception (Dautrich, 1993). It is this latter system which has been implicated in dyslexia. Research has shown, for example, that specific occulomotor difficulties, such as poor binocular convergence, impaired ability to track a left-to-right moving target visually and poor eye stability in visual fixation, may lead to problems in learning to read (Willows *et al.*, 1993; Eden *et al.*, 1994). The functioning of the cortical target for the magnocellular pathway, Area V5, discriminates between dyslexic and control readers. The perception of random, moving dots activates this area bilaterally in competent readers but little activation is found in V5 in either hemisphere in dyslexics (Eden *et al.*, 1996). Taken together, these data indicate that dyslexics perform worse than normal readers on tasks that require fast, sequential processing. In summary, it is suggested that although only a minority of dyslexics experience reading problems purely related to deficient visual processing abilities

(Seymour, 1986; Felton and Wood, 1989), the evidence indicates that a large number of dyslexics may suffer impairments in the processing of visual information at some level.

Neurophysiological studies have made an association between developmental reading problems and reduced or delayed left hemisphere specialization for the processing of language (Galaburda *et al.*, 1994). For example, dyslexics are more likely than normal readers to display symmetry of the planum temporale (Kusch *et al.*, 1993; Galaburda *et al.*, 1994) and in the posterior regions of the brain across the posterior tip of the splenium (Tallal and Katz, 1989; Hynd and Semrud-Clikeman, 1989). They are also more likely to display reversed asymmetry in the parieto-occipital region (Rosenberger and Hier, 1980). It is possible that these findings may indicate a reduction in the normal left hemisphere superiority for the processing of verbal information in dyslexics (Hynd *et al.*, 1990). There is evidence from MRI studies, for example, that a reduction in the normal asymmetry of the planum temporale is found in adult dyslexics whose chief characteristic was poor phonological processing (Larsen *et al.*, 1990).

Post-mortem examinations have also revealed structural differences between the brains of good and impaired readers. High concentrations of **microdysgenesis** ('disorganized islands of cortex') have been observed in the left temporoparietal regions of dyslexics' brains. Once again, this concentration is notable in the region of the planum temporale (Galaburda *et al.*, 1985; Kaufman and Galaburda, 1989; Duane, 1989). Although these clusters are not unknown in the brains of normal readers, they are rare and generally occur in the right anterior temporal cortex (Kaufmann and Galaburda, 1989). These microdysgeneses seriously disturb the normal pattern of architecture in the brains of the dyslexics and remove the asymmetry normally observed between the enlarged language areas of the left temporoparietal region and the smaller, homologous areas of the right hemisphere (Galaburda *et al.*, 1985). In humans, the capacity for language is generally correlated with a significant development in the magnitude of the left temporoparietal region and an attrition of neurons in the right hemisphere. These neuronal casualties are part of 'programmed cell death' (Brown *et al.*, 1994). This combination produces the observed asymmetry between corresponding areas in the left and right hemispheres (Geschwind and Levitsky, 1968). The relative symmetry in the dyslexics' brains might reflect, therefore, their impaired linguistic development.

In view of the linguistic impairments and the cortical symmetry which characterize dyslexia, it is arguable that cognitive impairments are the result of a developmental failure of the left hemisphere. This is not necessarily true, however. Physiological symmetries observed in dyslexics' brains may not be the result of smaller than expected left hemisphere regions but of abnormally large cortical regions in the right hemisphere (Galaburda *et al.*, 1985; Kaufman and Galaburda, 1989). It has been suggested that this symmetry may be due to the unexpected survival of neurons in the right hemisphere – a failure of the 'programmed cell death'. The surviving right-hemisphere neurons support the left hemisphere's language processing functions (Hermann and Zeevi, 1991). Alternatively, both phenomena could be the result of reduced intrahemispheric specialization in dyslexics, i.e. dyslexics' brains may display less differentiation between the hemispheres in terms of the type of processing which they mediate. Neither hemisphere is, therefore, dominant for the processing of language (Porac and Coren, 1981; Galaburda *et al.*, 1985).

Over the years, reading disabilities have been associated with strong sinistrality (Geschwind and Behan, 1982, 1984; Annett and Manning, 1990), with mixed handedness (Orton, 1937; Harris, 1957), with strong dextrality (Annett and Kilshaw, 1984; Annett and Manning, 1990), with a lack of strong right-handedness (Schachter *et al.*, 1987) and with no particular lateralized preference (Neils and Aram, 1986; Bishop, 1990).

Mirroring this apparent inconsistency in handedness research, dichotic listening studies have variously produced verbal right ear advantages (REAs) for both impaired readers and chronological-age-matched normal readers (Tzavaras *et al.*, 1993; Kershner *et al.*, 1984), REAs for normals but not for dyslexics (Obrzut *et al.*, 1989) and no REA for either group (Zurif and Carson, 1970) under different recall conditions. These patterns may suggest that both normal and impaired readers are lateralized as expected (with left hemisphere mediation of language and a moderate degree of dextrality), that dyslexics are less lateralized than normal readers, or that both good and poor readers display inconsistent lateralization.

ERP studies examining interhemispheric differences between good and poor readers in response to visual and auditory linguistic stimuli, for example, have reported evidence of greater symmetry in ERP amplitude (J. Cohen and Breslin, 1984; Brunswick and Rippon, 1994) and latency (Sutton *et al.*, 1986) in poor readers than in controls. An example of this can be seen in Figure 9.3.

This greater symmetry in ERP amplitude may indicate a lesser degree of hemispheric specialization in the dyslexics. Different patterns of asymmetry have also been found in the two groups, with dyslexics showing less involvement of the left hemisphere in linguistic processing (Landwehrmeyer *et al.*, 1990). The general failure to find hemispheric differentiation amongst the poor readers suggests some support for the hypotheses linking dyslexia with reduced or delayed left hemisphere specialization for the processing of linguistic stimuli.

■ Dysgraphia/agraphia

The ability to process word sounds and the possession of a knowledge of syntax and grammar are crucial to support the production, perception and interpretation of written language. **Agraphia** is the loss of the ability to produce written language, secondary to a CNS disorder. **Dysgraphia** describes an impairment of this ability, although the terms agraphia and dysgraphia are used interchangeably (Weekes and Coltheart, 1996). The disorder often accompanies dyslexia although it is sometimes seen in the absence of other language impairments (Thomas-Anterion *et al.*, 1994). Dysgraphic difficulties are not motor problems because the individual

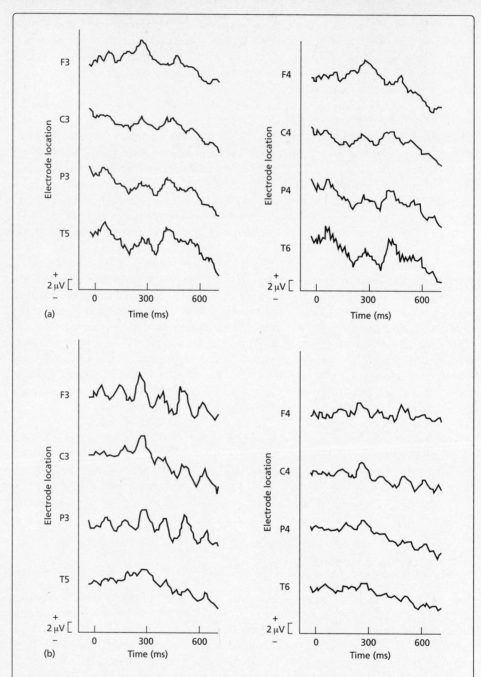

Figure 9.3 (a) ERPs from dyslexic readers undertaking a phonological task; (b) ERPs from reading-age-matched controls during performance of the same task

Table 9.3 Types of agraphia, their primary symptoms and the brain regions associated with them

Type of agraphia	Primary symptoms	Brain regions implicated
Phonological agraphia	Deficient spelling of non-words; real words are spelled 'visually'	Superior temporal lobe
Orthographic (surface) agraphia	Impaired spelling of irregular words; regular words and non-words are spelled phonetically	Inferior parietal lobe
Deep agraphia	Inability to spell phonetically; tendency to make semantic substitutions	Extensive left hemisphere damage

typically retains the ability to produce the movements necessary for writing. Instead, they are seen as spelling impairments – the inability to translate spoken words into their written form.

Articulating sounds or scanning the visual form of the word is important for spelling, as demonstrated by an attempt at writing a word such as 'anthropological' whilst repeating the word 'the' subvocally. Rather than relying on phonological processes, spelling may still be achieved by visualizing the word to be spelled. Even when a word has been spelled phonetically, visual processes may still be employed in the case of ambiguous spellings, to check that the word 'looks right'. As with the dyslexias, there are distinctive and discrete syndromes: these are outlined in Table 9.3.

Phonological dysgraphia

Phonological dysgraphia describes the inability to spell phonetically. Individuals retain the ability to employ visual strategies to mediate their spelling of real words, although spelling of pseudowords is not possible (Shallice, 1981). As with phonological dyslexia, phonological dysgraphia is associated with damage to the superior temporal lobe (Benson and Geschwind, 1985).

Orthographic (surface) dysgraphia

Conversely, individuals who lose the ability to spell via visual processes have great difficulty in spelling irregular words such as 'yacht' or 'enough'. However, they are able to invoke phonological strategies to facilitate the spelling of regular words and nonsense words (Beauvois and Derouesne, 1981). This is called orthographic or surface dysgraphia. Indeed, people with this type of dysgraphia seem to be overly dependent on grapheme–phoneme conversion and show impairment in the ability to spell at the level of the whole word. Orthographic (surface) dysgraphia is seen in individuals with damage to the inferior parietal lobe (Benson and Geschwind, 1985).

Deep dysgraphia

An alternative form of dysgraphia, deep dysgraphia, mirrors deep dyslexia in that it involves a loss of the ability to spell phonetically and the tendency to replace dictated real words with semantically related words, e.g. writing 'cake' in response to the word 'bun' (Newcombe and Marshall, 1980). If asked to spell a dictated non-word, a deep dysgraphic would typically produce a real word that is similar in sound to a semantically related real word, producing 'flower', for example, in response to the dictated non-word 'blom', possibly via the word 'bloom' (Bub and Kertesz, 1982). The ability to recognize orally spelled words is also lost although, somewhat surprisingly, deep dysgraphics retain the ability to read and repeat words and non-words which they can no longer spell (Cipolotti and Warrington, 1996). As with deep dyslexia, deep dysgraphia is associated with extensive damage to the dominant hemisphere (Cossu *et al.*, 1995; Cipolotti and Warrington, 1996).

■ The neuropsychology of language: a status report

Beaumont (1982) suggested that, 'a psychology without any reference to physiology can hardly be complete. The operation of the brain is relevant to human conduct, and the understanding of how the brain relates to behaviour may make a significant contribution to understanding how . . . psychological factors operate in directing behaviour' (p.4). Attempts to relate different aspects of linguistic processing with underlying physiology have a long history, as we have seen, although traditionally these investigations were driven by the study of individuals whose language processing skills had been impaired or lost as a result of accident or disease of the brain. Over the years, however, the development of increasingly sophisticated brain imaging techniques has facilitated investigation of the relationship between psychology and neurophysiology in normal, intact subjects. Such studies have generally implicated regions of the left cerebral hemisphere of normal adults in the processing of auditorily and visually presented language (Price *et al.*, 1994; Segalowitz and Berge, 1995).

Of course, these techniques also help increase our knowledge of the neuropsychology of language disorders, enabling the localization of brain lesions with relative accuracy without the need for invasive surgery. Electrophysiological research has supported behavioural findings, providing more direct evidence of reduced or delayed left hemisphere specialization for the processing of language in dyslexic samples (Voeller *et al.*, 1983). Yet, given the extreme complexity of spoken and written language mechanisms, it must be acknowledged that much remains unknown about the neuropsychology underlying normal and abnormal human language processes.

DISCUSSION POINT

Is sign language lateralized in the prelingually deaf?

Evidence from brain imaging studies indicates that the left cerebral hemisphere is 'hardwired' or 'prededicated' for linguistic, sequential processing while the right hemisphere is committed to non-linguistic information in 90 per cent of 'neurologically intact' individuals (Leonard *et al.*, 1996). How does this traditional view of hemispheric lateralization relate to individuals who have never encountered spoken language? Does similar 'cerebral preprogramming' exist for sign language in the congenitally deaf?

Of course, these questions assume an absolute definition of language and assume that language processes are localized in parts of the left hemisphere. Goldberg has suggested that instead of referring to language *per se*, we should adopt the more general term 'descriptive systems' (Goldberg, 1989). Under this umbrella he includes various cognitive systems ('superstructures') which are normally employed to assemble the 'codes' received via the elementary 'feature detection' systems such as the visual and auditory cortices. Language, as traditionally defined, is one such system. Others include mathematical or computational languages and musical notation. Early encounters with these systems are characteristically tentative, but gradual familiarity develops into automatic processing.

According to Goldberg and Costa's model of hemispheric specialization (Goldberg and Costa, 1981), the left cerebral hemisphere is specialized for automatic, routinized processing, whereas the right hemisphere is specialized for the processing of novel and complex information, 'when no task-relevant descriptive system or code is immediately available in the child's cognitive repertoire' (Dool *et al.*, 1993). In the early stages of acquiring a novel skill, the right hemisphere is critically involved in the acquisition of the 'descriptive system' needed to support the skill. With increasing competence, however, the descriptive system is established and a shift in hemispheric superiority occurs as the left hemisphere takes over the application of the now routinized codes. This process may be conceptualized in physiological terms as reflecting 'adaptive pruning' of superfluous neurons (Brown *et al.*, 1994). So, novel skills whether verbal or non-verbal, are initially mediated to a large extent by the right hemisphere. It is only at a later stage of skill development that the skill becomes routinized as a left hemisphere function.

The importance of the individual's experience (linguistic or non-linguistic) during development is crucial. Lenneberg (1967) famously argued for a 'critical period' for language acquisition and for the establishment of hemispheric dominance (language acquisition is best before, and cerebral dominance is established by, puberty). As long as a child has acquired language by the age of 7, he suggested, the left cerebral hemisphere would assume dominance for the mediation of linguistic processing. Any disturbance in the acquisition of language by this age retards the development of the left hemisphere and impedes the establishment of hemispheric lateralization.

One such disturbance would be congenital deafness. Schlesinger (1988) has observed a specific inability in some deaf children to manipulate the linguistic code, i.e. they experience difficulty in understanding questions, they are unable to formulate hypotheses, they have difficulty in conceptualizing superordinate categories, and they appear to exist in a 'preconceptual, perceptual world'. In short, these people display precisely the syntactic and semantic deficits associated with isolated right hemisphere speech in those who have experienced left hemisphere damage in later life. Perhaps these deficits are caused by a shift from an initial stage of right hemisphere language to mature left hemisphere language. Neville (1989), for example, has found that only deaf people with a perfect grasp of English grammar displayed 'normal' left hemisphere specialization, concluding that both in the deaf and in those with normal hearing, grammatical competence is necessary and sufficient for left hemisphere specialization if it occurs early. Early competence in spoken or signed language brings about this development of the left hemisphere and bestows an advantage on the right side of perceptual space, i.e. the right visual field and the right ear, via the dominant contralateral sensory pathways. Obviously, this perceptual advantage is grossly impaired following left hemisphere damage.

Unfortunately, this early exposure to signed language which brings about the shift of language functions to the left hemisphere is not always available to deaf children. Evidence has shown that hearing children of deaf parents and deaf children of deaf parents acquire sign language in infancy as a primary language and tend to show the shift to left hemisphere mediation of language (Grossi et al., 1996). Many deaf children of hearing parents, however, have only restricted exposure to sign language during the critical period of development, a privation which may lead to a total arrest or delay, depending on the degree of deficiency of the linguistic experience, of cerebral maturation. In this situation, the child would continue to display signs of predominantly right hemisphere language as predicted in the absence of a shift to left hemisphere dominance.

A famous, if tragic, example of right hemisphere language (preserved right hemisphere dominance for the mediation of linguistic functions) was that of Genie. Genie was a girl of 13 who had been found in conditions of extreme isolation. She had been severely deprived of social contact and linguistic experience during childhood and only learned to talk following her discovery by the authorities. Although her subsequent language development followed the normal pattern she never attained normal proficiency. Her vocabulary was fairly rich although her syntax and grammar remained poor (Curtiss, 1977). Dichotic listening tests suggested that Genie's language was mediated by the right hemisphere. After the sensitive period for language acquisition has passed, the left hemisphere had lost the ability to assume control of the acquisition of language. Genie's linguistic development is considered in more detail in Chapter 12.

Despite being essentially a visuospatial skill, sign language will develop into a left-hemisphere-mediated skill just as any other analytical skill such as understanding music, communicating in Morse code or developing complex mathematical concepts. These require a representational system that is functionally similar to language. None of these skills develops spontaneously but each requires prolonged exposure to, and experience of, the codes which underlie them. As Sacks (1991) has observed, 'if language, a linguistic code, can be introduced by puberty, the form of the code (speech or sign) does not seem to matter; it matters only that it be good enough to allow internal manipulation – then the normal shift to left hemisphere predominance can occur.'

Summary

☐ Clinical and brain imaging data suggest that speech production and comprehension are mediated by two different regions within the left hemisphere. The anterior language region (Broca's area), next to the motor cortex in the left hemisphere, is thought to be responsible for the mediation of language production. The posterior language region (Wernicke's area), located above the temporal gyrus and the planum temporale in the left hemisphere, mediates language comprehension.

☐ At a subcortical level, the left ventrolateral and pulvinar nuclei of the thalamus have been implicated in coordination of the activity of the cortical language regions.

☐ Studies suggest that (1) semantic processing may be mediated by the left frontal cortex, (2) the discrimination of orthographically legal letter strings from orthographically illegal letter strings is mediated by the left posterior extrastriate cortex, and (3) phonological processing – the ability to manipulate the component sounds within words – is mediated by the posterior temporal cortex of the left hemisphere and Broca's area.

☐ ERP studies report greater amplitude and shorter latency peaks (N100, P200 and P300) in the left hemisphere than in the right hemisphere in 'normal' subjects performing language tasks. The N400 has been found to show signs of *intra*hemispheric, rather than *inter*hemispheric, localization, showing a bilateral appearance in the frontocentral regions of the brain.

☐ Individuals with age-appropriate reading skills display greater asymmetry (favouring the left hemisphere) in both amplitude and latency than do dyslexic readers. Evidence of reduced left-hemisphere involvement in language in dyslexics supports hypotheses linking dyslexia with reduced/ delayed specialization of this hemisphere for the processing of linguistic stimuli.

☐ Men's brains appear to be more structurally asymmetric than women's, with men more strongly lateralized for language than women. However, it has been suggested that rather than differing interhemispherically, men and women differ intrahemispherically: women are more likely than men to exhibit aphasia following left hemisphere frontal damage whereas men are more likely to become aphasic following damage to more posterior regions.

☐ Aphasia describes the inability to produce or comprehend language. Subtypes of aphasia are characterized by deficits in comprehension and word retrieval with preserved language production abilities (sensory aphasia); telegrammatic speech with abnormal prosody and syntactic ambiguities but normal comprehension (production aphasia); normal comprehension and production but impaired naming of objects and repetition of non-words (conduction aphasia); the tendency to replace visually presented words with semantic associates (deep aphasia); impaired comprehension, naming, reading and writing (transcortical sensory aphasia); periods of transient mutism interspersed with telegrammatic, dysprosodic speech (transcortical motor aphasia) and generalized comprehension, repetition, speech production and naming deficits (global aphasia).

☐ Each type of aphasia is associated with specific regions of neural damage. Sensory aphasia follows damage to the region of Wernicke's area. Production aphasia is associated with atrophy of frontal regions of the left hemisphere, specifically surrounding Broca's area. Damage to the arcuate fasciculus which connects Broca's and Wernicke's areas leads to conduction aphasia. Deep dysphasia is associated with lesions to regions of the temporal lobe which mediate verbal auditory representations. Damage to a specific region of the left hemisphere's temporal lobe, the temporoparieto-occipital junction, is associated with transcortical sensory aphasia while transcortical motor aphasia results from lesions in the medial frontal lobe of the left hemisphere, in the region of Broca's area and the supplementary motor area. The most severe form of aphasia, global aphasia, is the result of extensive lesioning of the left hemisphere, especially in the perisylvian region.

☐ Dyslexia refers to an impairment in the ability to read. There are two principal subdivisions: acquired dyslexia, the loss of previously normal reading skills following brain damage, and developmental dyslexia, a difficulty experienced in learning to read with a presumed neurological basis. Each type has its own subtypes. Types of acquired dyslexias include visual word form dyslexia (an impairment in sight reading although some decoding of words is possible), phonological dyslexia (an impairment in the reading of pseudowords and non-words), surface dyslexia (impaired ability to read words 'visually' and over-reliance on decoding strategies which leads to frequent regularization errors), and deep dyslexia (severe inability to read non-words and abstract words and the tendency to replace seen words with semantically related associates. The question of subtypes in developmental dyslexia is still a matter of controversy but similar categories have been suggested.

☐ Visual word form dyslexia is found in individuals with damage to the connections between the left hemisphere's angular gyrus and the visual input system. Lesions of the dominant temporal lobe may underlie acquired phonological dyslexia, just as abnormal development of the temporoparietal region of the left hemisphere is implicated in developmental dyslexia. The precise locus of damage associated with deep dyslexia is not yet clearly defined, although the damage appears to be extensive in the dominant hemisphere. Little is known about the lesions responsible for surface dyslexia.

☐ Dysgraphia or agraphia describes various specific impairments in the production of written language (generally spelling deficits) in the absence of motor problems. Forms of dysgraphia include phonological dysgraphia (the reliance on visual spelling strategies in the absence of phonetic spelling skills), orthographic dysgraphia (dependence on phonetic

➠

spelling following a loss of the ability to invoke visual spelling strategies), and deep dysgraphia (a loss of the ability to spell phonetically and the tendency to make semantic substitutions when spelling to dictation).

☐ Phonological dysgraphia has been linked with damage to the superior temporal lobe of the language hemisphere; orthographic dysgraphia is associated with lesions in the inferior parietal lobe; deep dysgraphia appears in individuals with extensive damage to the dominant hemisphere.

☐ Evidence indicates that early competence in language, whether spoken or signed, is sufficient to engender a shift of language functions to the left hemisphere and to bestow a perceptual advantage on the right side of space, i.e. the right visual field and the right ear. Children who fail to develop sufficient competence in the grammatical subtleties of language at an early age, possibly by the age of 7 years, are liable to forgo this shift to left hemisphere mediation of language and will continue to produce syntactic and semantic deficits characteristic of right hemisphere language.

Recommended further general and specific reading

Key: (1) = introductory, *(3)* = intermediate, *(5)* = advanced

General

Bellugi, U., Poizner, H. and Klima, E.S. (1989). Language, modality and the brain. *Trends in Neurosciences*, **10**, 380–8. *(4)*

Caramazza, A. (1989). *Cognitive Neuropsychology and Neurolinguistics: Advances in models of cognitive function and impairment.* Hillsdale, NJ: Lawrence Erlbaum Associates. *(4)*

Coltheart, M, Sartori, G. and Job, R. (1987). *The Cognitive Neuropsychology of Language.* Hove, UK: Lawrence Erlbaum Associates. *(3)*

Henderson, L. (1984). *Orthographies and Reading: Perspectives from cognitive psychology, neuropsychology, and linguistics.* Hove, UK: Lawrence Erlbaum Associates. *(4)*

Luzzatti, C. and Whitaker, H. (1996). Clinical and anatomical observations in the prehistory of neurolinguistics and neuropsychology. *Journal of Linguistics*, **9**(3), 157–64. *(3)*

Stromswold, K. (1995). The cognitive and neural bases of language acquisition. In M. Gazzaniga (ed.), *The Cognitive Neurosciences.* Cambridge, MA: MIT Press. *(4)*

Studdert-Kennedy, M. (1983). *Psychobiology of Language.* Cambridge, MA: MIT Press. *(3)*

Specific

Binder, J.R., Rao, S.M., Hammeke, T.A., Frost, J.A., Bandettini, P.A., Jesmanowicz, A. and Hyde, J.S. (1995). Lateralized human brain language systems demonstrated by task subtraction functional magnetic resonance imaging. *Archives of Neurology*, **52**, 593–601. *(3)*

Binder, J.R., Frost, J.A., Hammeke, T.A., Cox, R.W., Rao, S.M. and Prieto, T. (1997). Human brain language areas identified by functional magnetic resonance imaging. *Journal of Neuroscience*, **17**(1), 353–62. *(3)*

Bishop, D.V.M. (1997). Listening out for subtle deficits. *Nature*, 129–30. *(2)*

Damasio, H., Grabowski, T.J., Tranel, D., Hichwa, R.D. and Damasio, A.R. (1996). A neural basis for lexical retrieval. *Nature*, **380**, 499–505. *(4)*

Demonet, J.F., Fiez, J.A., Paulesu, E., Petersen, S.E. and Zatorre, R.J. (1996). PET studies of phonological processing: a critical reply to Poeppel. *Brain and Language*, **55**, 352–79. *(3)*

Duchowny, M., Jayakar, P., Harvey, A.S., Resnick, T., Alvarez, L. Dean, P. and Levin, B. (1996). Language cortex representation: effects of developmental versus acquired pathology. *Annals of Neurology*, **40**(1) 31–8. *(4)*

Eden, G.F., Van Meter, J.W., Rumsey, J.M., Maisog, J.N., Woods, R.P. and Zeffiro, T.A. (1996). Abnormal processing of visual motion in dyslexia revealed by functional brain imaging. *Nature*, **382**, 66–9. *(3)*

Emmorey, K. and Kosslyn, S.M. (1996). Enhanced image generation abilities in deaf signers: a right hemisphere effect. *Brain and Cognition*, **32**, 28–44. *(4)*

Langfitt, J.T. and Rausch, R. (1996). Word-finding deficits persist after left anterotemporal lobectomy. *Archives of Neurology*, **53**, 72–6. *(3)*

Manning, L. and Warrington, E.K. (1996). Two routes to naming: a case study. *Neuropsychologia*, **34**(8), 809–17. *(3)*

Maratsos, M. and Matheny, L. (1994). Language specificity and elasticity: brain and clinical syndrome studies. *Annual Review of Psychology*, **45**, 487–516. *(3)*

Muller, R-A. (1996). Innateness, autonomy, universality? Neurobiological approaches to language. *Behavioral and Brain Sciences*, **19**, 611–75. *(3)*

Ogden, J.A. (1996). Phonological dyslexia and phonological dysgraphia following left and right hemispherectomy. *Neuropsychologia*, **34**(9), 905–18. *(3)*

Paulesu, E., Frith, U., Snowling, M., Gallagher, A., Morton, J., Frackowiak, R.S.J. and Frith, C.D. (1996). Is developmental dyslexia a disconnection syndrome? Evidence from PET scanning. *Brain*, **119**, 143–57. *(3)*

Petersen, S.E., Fox, P.T., Posner, M.I., Mintun, M. and Raichle, M.E. (1988). Positron emission tomographic studies of the cortical anatomy of single-word processing. *Nature*, **331**, 585–9. *(3)*

Poeppel, D. (1996). A critical review of PET studies of phonological processing. *Brain and Language*, **55**, 317–51. *(3)*

Poeppel, D. (1996). Some remaining questions about studying phonological processing with PET: response to Demonet, Fiez, Paulesu, Petersen and Zatorre (1996). *Brain and Language*, **55**, 380–5. *(3)*

Price, C.J., Wise, R.J.S., Warburton, E.A., Moore, C.J., Howard, D., Patterson, K., Frackowiak, R.S.J. and Friston, K.J. (1996). Hearing and saying: the functional neuroanatomy of auditory word processing. *Brain*, **119**, 919–31. *(3)*

Pulvermuller, F. (1996). Hebb's concept of cell assemblies and the psychophysiology of word processing. *Psychophysiology*, **33**, 317–33. *(3)*

Shaywitz, B.A., Shaywitz, S.E., Pugh, K.R., Constable, R.T., Skudlarski, P., Fulbright, R.K., Bronen, R.A., Fletcher, J.M., Shankweiler, D.P., Katz, L. and Gore, J.C. (1995). Sex differences in the functional organization of the brain for language. *Nature*, **373**, 607–9. *(3)*

Sim, K.H.S., Relkin, N.R., Lee, K-M. and Hirsch, J. (1997). Distinct cortical areas associated with native and second language. *Nature*, **388**, 171–4. *(3)*

Slaghuis, W.L., Twell, A.J. and Kingston, K.R. (1996). Visual and language processing disorders are concurrent in dyslexia and continue into adulthood. *Cortex*, **32**, 413–38. *(4)*

Wright, B.A., Lombardino, L.J., King, W.M., Puranik, C.S., Leonard, C.M. and Merzenich, M.M. (1997). Deficits in auditory temporal and spectral resolution in language-impaired children. *Nature*, 176–8. *(4)*

Chapter Ten

Emotion – normal and abnormal aspects

NORMAL ASPECTS OF EMOTION

■ What is an emotion?

Neuropsychology has long had an active if ululating interest in the biology and psychology of emotion. One rather fundamental problem encountered early on in evaluating any physiological basis of human emotion, however, is achieving a satisfactory definition and characterization of emotion. In short, what exactly is an emotion? One study has listed 223 terms representing emotion (Conte, 1975) while another has found that 556 descriptive words and phrases were generated by students asked to name emotion-related words (Davitz, 1970). Similarly, Kleinginna and Kleinginna (1981; cited in Plutchik, 1994), in a review of dictionaries, textbooks and other materials, identified 92 different definitions of emotion. In view of all this heterogeneity and ambiguity, it is not surprising that emotion has 'proved to be a slippery concept for both psychologists and neuroscientists' (LeDoux, 1995a).

Scientists have made several attempts at defining emotion. Its literal Latin translation is 'to move' or 'to stir up'. One of the earliest, modern definitions was proposed by William James (1884). James had argued that emotion was our feeling of bodily changes when 'the bodily changes follow directly the perception of the exciting fact.' A century later, Stuss and Benson (1983), noted that emotion is 'a broader term that brings together a sizeable number of behavioural responses linking bodily and mental activities with the underlying feeling tone.' Other definitions have included 'reactions to an appropriately evocative stimulus involving cognitive appraisal/perception, subjectively experienced feeling, autonomic and neural arousal, expressive behaviour, and goal-directed activity' (Borod, 1992) or as a term 'referring to a group of interrelated brain functions – emotional expression and emotional experience' (LeDoux, 1987). Others have regarded emotion in more behaviouristic terms. Watson (1924), for example, saw emotion as 'an hereditary "pattern-reaction" involving profound changes of the bodily mechanisms as a whole, but particularly of the visceral and glandular systems', whereas Rolls (1990) suggests that 'emotions can be usefully defined as states produced by instrumental reinforcing stimuli'. Instrumental reinforcers are defined as 'stimuli which if their occurrence, termination or omission is made contingent upon the making of a response, alter the probability of the future emission of that response'. As we saw in Chapter 6 on frontal lobe function, Rolls has suggested that emotions are mediated by connections between the orbitofrontal cortex and other subcortical structures. Our experience of emotion is the result of the activation of these connections by reward and punishment. Not surprisingly, this behaviourist view of emotion is derived largely from animal studies in which fear and anxiety (as well as immediate and delayed reward) can be carefully manipulated.

One distinction which is almost unanimously accepted in the literature, however, is that emotion is different from 'mood' and 'affect'. Affect, as Brewin (1988) notes, is a broad term and subsumes many behaviours including mood, feeling, attitude, preferences and evaluations. It has been described as the expression of emotion (Stuss et al., 1992). Mood sometimes refers to the frame of mind or 'emotional state' of a person, which is defined by the individual's internal state and not external behaviour. Emotions are thought to be briefer, more spontaneous and detectable from the appearance of the organism.

The notion of frame of mind is important given that the most frequently debated issue in the psychology of emotion is the question of whether cognition is a necessary precursor of emotion or whether emotions may occur without any cognitive precursor. This issue in essence revolves around the definition of cognition (LeDoux, 1995). If sensory and perceptual input constitute cognitive processes (such as appraisal), then emotion clearly has cognitive determinants. Put very crudely, a person at the edge of a cliff, blindfolded and unaware that he is at the edge of a cliff will not experience as much anxiety as an individual who has had the blindfold removed. The sight of the drop and the rocks below (visual input) combined with the sight and sound (auditory input) of the sea act as sensory cognitive cues. They are the stimuli which the individual associates with fear. Thus, arguably an emotion cannot occur without perception and the appraisal of the perceptual world.

Lazarus (1966), for example, has suggested that emotions arise from 'how a person construes the outcome, actual or anticipated, of a transaction or a bit of commerce with the environment', i.e. a certain amount of appraisal must take place before the individual can experience what is thought to be an 'emotion'. This views appraisal as information processing. Weiner (1985) has similarly argued that human emotion depends on cognitive operations such as attributions and appraisals. Both of these approaches argue that cognition is a necessary precursor of emotional experience and expression.

The alternative view, that cognition is unnecessary for emotion, has been most famously argued by Zajonc (1980). He suggested that affect is more than a post-cognitive emission and that cognition is not a necessary precursor of emotional response. Ekman (1984), in a form of halfway house, suggests that affect and cognition involve separate biological systems which interact in a Cartesian way. This argument over the necessary precursors of emotion has been fought for decades and, although interesting, the cognition–affect controversy will not be considered any further here. Interested readers are directed to Plutchik (1994) or Oatley and Jenkins (1996) for further discussion.

Given that the definition of an emotion, in psychological terms, is complicated, it might be more beneficial to describe what an emotion should be and make prescriptive judgements. For example, we may not be able to define emotions, but we know that happiness and sadness are two of them. According to Ekman (1973), for example, there are six 'basic' emotional reactions and other emotions are made up of these. These emotions are happiness, anger, fear, sadness, disgust and surprise. While the first five might appear to be intuitively correct, the last may be itself surprising. This last emotion, in fact, was included in Ekman's list based on the assumption that the facial expression associated with this emotion should be recognized cross-culturally.

There have been objections to this list of basic emotions and of the use of the term basic (Russell, 1994). Ortony and Turner (1990), for example, have argued that we 'cannot find basic emotions' since 'we do not have and probably cannot have, a satisfactory criterion of basicness.' Thus, there is conflicting opinion not only regarding the definition of emotion but also of what constitutes a basic emotional response, a point worth bearing in mind when considering the findings from emotion studies.

One way out of this quagmire of contradictions, objections and ambiguities might be to outline particular neural features of emotions which might distinguish one from the other. If happiness is an emotion then it must produce certain brain activity that distinguishes it from sadness or fear or anxiety. In fact, there is evidence from animal and human studies not only that certain neural pathways are implicated in the expression of particular emotions but also that particular brain structures and regions are also involved. In animal studies, much work has revolved around the amygdala and thalamus. In humans, the cortex (especially the orbitofrontal cortex) have been suggested as regions important for the expression of emotion. It is important to note that these areas may be involved in the experience or expression of emotion. There may be other systems and mechanisms which regulate emotional perception, i.e. recognizing an emotion.

▨ Subcortical structures and emotion

The brain has evolved from the brainstem into a complicated mass of circuitry. The most basic structures of the brainstem regulate the autonomic and endocrine systems, two systems which are important to emotion. The development of the limbic system, the later differentiation of the paralimbic region arising from regions around the limbic system, and the extension of the paralimbic region to neocortical areas, afforded the brain greater flexibility in the expression and interpretation of emotions.

Descending connections are made from the neocortex to the subcortex ('top-down' connections); ascending connections from lower brain regions to the neocortex are also found, such as the regulatory projections from the brainstem and limbic system to the cortex, and the pathways conveying information from the musculature and viscera ('bottom-up' connections). As this organization might suggest, emotion cannot be localized exclusively to a specific area of the brain, but specific areas of the brain may be involved in the perception or experience of an emotion. The principal subcortical structures thought to be involved in the regulation of emotion are the brainstem, the hippocampal system and the amygdala.

Hippocampal system

The hippocampal system includes the entorhinal cortex on the input side and the subiculum and lateral septum on the output side. Perhaps the most famous model of hippocampal function as related to emotion is that proposed by Gray (1982). In this model, a neuropsychological model of anxiety, the 'septohippocampal system' is thought to respond to innate fear signals, signals which predict punishment and those which predict non-reward. Once a stimulus is detected, the hippocampus inhibits motor behaviour, adjusts autonomic responses, arouses the cortex and allows the organism to focus on the relevant parts of the environment. Those individuals with highly reactive systems will be sensitive to aversive signals and exhibit a more introvert personality and be more prone to anxiety and depression. Gray's model is revisited in the section on abnormal emotion.

The hypothalamus appears to be relatively uninvolved in the regulation of emotion. In a recent study of patients with third ventricle damage, Wedell (1994) found that hypothalamic damage was associated with the induction of appetitive disorders without affecting emotional function. Lesions in the right medial temporal region resulted in impaired emotional recognition. Frontal and basal ganglia damage was associated with impaired emotional facial expression.

Amygdala

Described by Aggleton and Mishkin (1986) as the sensory gateway to the emotions, the amygdala is a collection of subnuclei in the anterior temporal lobe thought to be heavily involved in the learning and maintenance of fear, anxiety and other emotions (Aggleton, 1992). The amygdala, together with the hippocampus, septum, fornix and olfactory bulb, is considered part of the limbic system, a collective name for subcortical structures near the thalamus. It was thought that emotional expression was the result of the activity of these interconnecting structures, the so-called Papez circuit (Papez, 1937) illustrated by Figure 10.1.

If the anterior temporal lobes were damaged or removed in monkeys (which means that the amygdala is removed or damaged too), inappropriate emotional behaviour was elicited. For example, they might indiscriminately consume anything that is edible, become highly sexually active and mount sexually inappropriate objects, explore repeatedly familiar objects and exhibit tameness and lack of fear. This has been termed the Kluver–Bucy syndrome (Kluver and Bucy, 1939). In humans, however, the same behaviours are not elicited.

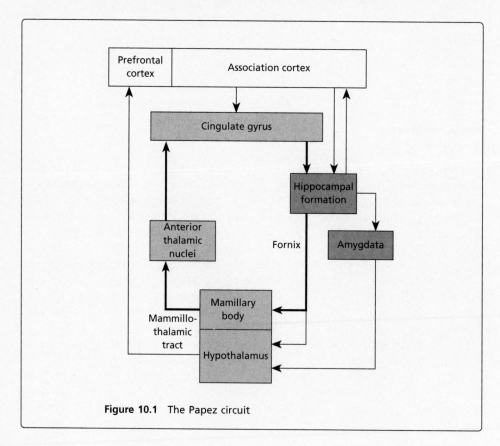

Figure 10.1 The Papez circuit

According to Halgren (1992), the amygdala 'has all of the right connections with the cognitive neocortex and visceral brainstem to provide the link between them that is central to emotion.' It has connections with the neocortex, hypothalamus, the septum, the thalamus, the hippocampus and the reticular formation. Inputs from the sensory systems normally arrive in the amygdala. The amygdala and hippocampal system also project to regions controlling endocrine, autonomic and motor activity. In his review of the neural basis of emotion, LeDoux (1995b) describes some of the pathways to and from various brain structures, but especially the amygdala and thalamus, that are involved in the conditioning of fear. Fear is a 'good' emotion to study in a laboratory since procedures for eliciting fear within a classical conditioning framework are relatively easy to control and undertake with animal subjects.

In animal studies, the fear conditioning procedure may occur as follows. The organism is exposed to a tone or flash of light (the conditioned stimulus, CS), followed by a brief electric shock (the unconditioned stimulus, US). If the US is intense enough, then pairing the CS with the US will result in rapid conditioning of the fear response. This conditioning is measured by freezing responses, endocrine activity, autonomic activity, reflexes (eyeblink) or the degree to which the CS interferes with the organism's routine behaviour.

Using neuroanatomical staining and lesioning techniques, the pathway of an acoustic stimulus, for example (the CS), can be traced from the auditory system outwards after conditioning has taken place. In fact, lesioning the midbrain and thalamus along this pathway prevents conditioning but lesioning the auditory cortex does not (LeDoux et al., 1984). Furthermore, the auditory thalamus projects to the auditory cortex and the amygdala. Lesioning the connections between the auditory thalamus and the amygdala interferes with conditioning. LeDoux and his colleagues observed that the lateral nucleus of the amygdala was the region responsible for receiving information about the auditory stimulus (LeDoux et al., 1990). Cells in this area are particularly responsive to stimuli similar to auditory CS stimuli.

It has been found that the direct thalamic pathway to the amygdala is direct and fast but carries few auditory impulses; the link to the amygdala from the thalamic pathway via corticocortical connections is slower but carries greater auditory impulses. Thus emotional responses associated with simple stimuli might be mediated by the first route; responses associated with complex sets of stimuli may be mediated via the second route. It is thought that the lateral nucleus acts as the place where these two systems meet and possibly integrates information from the two parallel systems (LeDoux, 1995b). See Figure 10.2.

The output region of the amygdala is considered to be the central nucleus. Lesioning the central nucleus affects the expression of emotion. The expression of particular emotional behaviours may also be impaired if certain areas to which the central nucleus projects are lesioned. For example, freezing responses are inhibited by lesions to the central grey area; neuroendocrine responses are affected by lesions to projections to the bed nucleus of the stria terminalis. To illustrate the

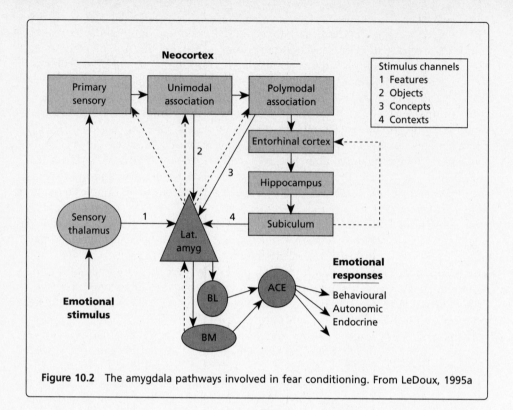

Figure 10.2 The amygdala pathways involved in fear conditioning. From LeDoux, 1995a

extent of the amygdala's involvement in the acquisition and maintenance of fear-learning, lesioning of the structure, even after extensive training, produces deficits in fear conditioning (Kim and Davis, 1993). Similar pathways and circuitry are involved in the conditioning of fear to visual stimuli. The origin of the US's pathway to the amygdala, however, is unknown.

Conditioning of fear appears to be a better protocol for examining the neural basis of emotion than is passive avoidance conditioning. However, as LeDoux notes (1995b), whether the mechanisms of fear conditioning outlined from these studies are the same as those that mediate other forms of fear specific to humans (e.g. fear of authority, heights, social situations) is unclear. LeDoux's protocol is also highly experimental and based on animal data. There is some evidence from the human literature, however, for a role for the amygdala in the perception of fearful or fear-related stimuli. In a case study of a 30 year old woman who had sustained complete bilateral destruction of the amygdala (sparing the hippocampus and cortex), the patient was unable to recognize fear but could recognize happiness, surprise, anger, disgust and sadness in facial expressions. Neither could she could recognize multiple emotions in a single facial expression (Adolphs et al., 1994). Adolphs and co-workers have also reported data showing that unilateral but

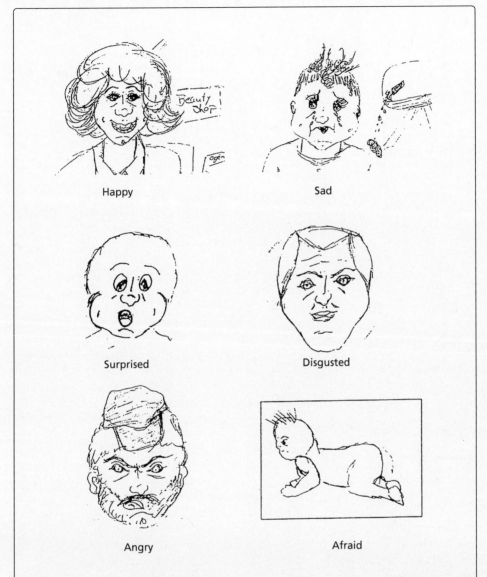

Figure 10.3 Patient SM-046's drawings of various emotional states. Note that she was unable to draw the fear expression

not bilateral damage to the amygdala impairs the recognition of fearful facial expressions (Adolphs *et al.*, 1995). In Figure 10.3, drawings from a patient with almost complete bilateral amygdala damage indicated an inability to draw a fearful facial expression from memory while being able to draw other types of emotional facial expression.

Finally, Morris and his colleagues have published data indicating activation of the left side of the amygdala in five individuals in response to photographs of individuals with fearful facial expressions; this activation increased with the intensity of the fearfulness of the expression (J.S. Morris *et al.*, 1996).

Frontal lobes

The ventromedial lobe damage of Phineas Gage and others (encountered in Chapter 6) has suggested a strong role for the frontal lobes in the regulation of emotion. Later studies have supported the notion that these structures, and especially the orbitofrontal cortex, are responsible for mediating or regulating some forms of emotional expression.

In one early study, for example, Kolodny (1929) described two consequences of frontal lobe lesion: mood alteration (exaltation or depression) and changes in the social aspects of personality. This study was not unique, with Holmes (1931) later arguing that frontal brain damage could result in increased indifference, depression or exuberance/euphoria. Closed-head injury patients with frontal damage have been found to exhibit symptoms of depression and withdrawal (Levin *et al.*, 1979). Frontal patients are also found to be irritable or indifferent to the rules of social engagement (Stuss and Richard, 1982). These typographies are very similar to those proposed by Blumer and Benson (1975), discussed in Chapter 6. It is the peculiar and striking change in personality which partly informed the movement towards lobectomy for the removal of psychotic symptoms in the 1940s and 1950s. About 100 000 people underwent the frontal brain lesioning procedure in this period. The earliest reports of lobectomy indicated that the main postoperative symptoms were inertia, lack of ambition, indifference and poor judgement (Freeman *et al.*, 1942). Two problems associated with these studies, however, were that there was no formal testing of emotional perception or expression, and premorbid levels of emotional processing were not considered.

Later attention focused on the orbitofrontal cortex. Kleist (1934) suggested that this region was important to a unified sense of personality and that damage would result in deviant behaviour, puerility and euphoria. In fact, damage to this region is commonly associated with these behaviours (Blumer and Benson, 1975; Stuss and Benson, 1986).

There are other sources of evidence indicating the frontal lobes' neural involvement in emotion. Nauta (1971, 1973) has emphasized the prefrontal cortex's connections with the limbic system, arguing that it might regulate emotion by integrating sensory input from the external environment with information about the internal environment that is derived from the hypothalamus and other limbic structures. Rolls (1990, 1995) has similarly argued that the orbitofrontal cortex is an important structure in the disconnection of stimulus–reinforcement associations, the processes which Rolls believes make up our experience of emotions. The amygdala, Rolls suggests, may elicit learned emotional responses while the orbitofrontal cortex may be involved in the correction 'or adjustment of these emotional responses as the reinforcing value of environmental stimuli alters'. Much of Rolls's evidence is derived from animal work. Human data, however, appear to confirm the frontal cortex's involvement in the perception and expression of emotion. More interestingly, these data indicate that the left and right frontal cortices may have different parts to play in emotion.

■ Hemispheric functional asymmetry and emotion

Early studies of emotion and the human brain focused on affective disturbances following head injury. A common finding amongst these and later studies was that left-sided lesions tended to be associated with depressive, negative symptomatology (such as crying, low self-esteem, misery) whereas lesions to the right hemisphere were associated with increased elevation and euphoria (Alford, 1933; Goldstein, 1939; Robinson and Benson, 1981; Sackheim et al., 1982).

The right-for-emotion hypothesis, as couched in neuropsychological terms, was based on early anecdotal studies of patients with unilateral right hemisphere lesions (Hecaen and Angelergues, 1962). The involvement of the left hemisphere, however, suggested interhemispheric differences in emotional expression. Furthermore, there might also have been intrahemispheric differences, i.e. differences in activation within different regions of the same hemisphere. In emotion research, these brain regions are sometimes divided into anterior (pre-Rolandic fissure structures – the frontal lobes) and posterior regions (post-Rolandic fissure structures – parietal, temporal and occipital lobes).

On the basis of the evidence implicating the right hemisphere in emotion, Ross (1981, 1985) has suggested that the right hemisphere contains an emotional processor and that the production of emotion is associated with anterior regions while comprehension is associated with posterior regions. It is important to note, however, that there is a difference in the type of emotional processing that can occur. The difference lies in the distinction drawn between emotional perception and emotional expression. It is this difference which has given rise to conflicting evidence regarding the lateralization of emotion in the human brain and it is important to treat each process separately.

Emotional perception

The ability to perceive or recognize emotions is thought to be a right hemisphere function. If subjects are asked (1) whether two emotionally toned sentences are the same or different, (2) to identify or discriminate between emotional facial expressions, or (3) to process neutral and emotional words, there is usually a left ear and left visual field advantage in these tasks indicating the involvement of the right hemisphere. A left hemifield superiority for recognizing emotional versus neutral faces has been found (Bryden and Ley, 1983) as has a left visual field advantage in the identification of facial emotional expressions with photographic, line-drawing, chimeric and cartoon stimuli (Strauss and Moscovitch, 1981). Dichotic listening experiments generally indicate a left ear superiority for processing the affective tone of natural speech, non-verbal vocalization and music in non-musicians.

Findings from brain-lesioned individuals point to the same degree of lateralization. Borod *et al.* (1986a) and Etkoff (1984), for example, found that an impairment in the perception of facial expression was associated more with right than left hemisphere damage. In one study where subjects were required to rate the intensity of emotional facial expression after having received an injection of intacarotid sodium Amytal, ratings of the intensity of the facial expressions were lower than baseline when the non-dominant hemisphere, usually the right, was anaesthetized (Ahern *et al.*, 1991). There was no difference in rating when the dominant hemisphere was anaesthetized.

Interestingly, in a single case study of a split-brain patient (JW), the ability to distinguish between two different facial expressions was better when material was presented to the right hemisphere but the left hemisphere's ability to perform the task improved if the facial expressions were associated with verbal labels (Stone *et al.*, 1996).

Recent studies have reaffirmed the importance of the right hemisphere in the perception of emotion in facial and prosodic stimuli (e.g. Schmitt *et al.*, 1997). There may also be a specific role for the right hemisphere in the perception of fear although the perception of this emotion might also involve the amygdala (Schmitt *et al.* 1997; Adolphs *et al.*, 1996).

Emotional experience

EEG studies

The spontaneous expression of emotion is most commonly associated with left hemisphere activity (Wyler *et al.*, 1987), although an absence of asymmetry has been reported (Hager and Ekman, 1985). In an intriguing set of EEG studies by Richard Davidson and his colleagues, hemispheric asymmetries have been found in response to the experience of pleasant and unpleasant emotional visual stimuli (Davidson, 1992; Davidson and Sutton, 1995). The affective stimuli used in these studies were self-contained film clips, pre-rated for positive and negative affect (more naturalistic materials have been used elsewhere, e.g. Schelleberg *et al.*, 1993).

Early EEG studies (e.g Harman and Ray, 1977) had suggested that affective response could be characterized by asymmetrical patterns of EEG activity. Specifically, increases in left hemisphere power were obtained during generation of positive memories, with decreases accompanying the generation of negative memories. Davidson and his colleagues later found greater relative left frontal hemisphere activation in the alpha frequency to positive film clips and greater right frontal hemisphere activation to negatively rated film clips (Davidson *et al.*, 1979).

In a later study, Davidson and colleagues recorded EEG activity from frontal and anterior temporal regions of 11 right-handed women as they watched standardized video clips designed to elicit positive or negative emotions (Davidson *et al.*, 1990b). In the positive condition, subjects watched clips of either puppies playing with flowers or monkeys playing or a gorilla taking a bath. In the negative condition, subjects saw clips of a leg amputation and third-degree burns. Davidson *et al.* found greater alpha power (more activation) in the right frontal and anterior temporal regions during the negative ('disgust') than the positive ('happiness') condition. The positive condition was associated with greater left-sided activation in the anterior temporal regions than was the negative condition.

In a follow up study, Ekman *et al.* (1990) reported more left-sided anterior temporal and parietal activation when subjects exhibited the Duchenne smiles (the 'natural' smile which involves the movement of the zygomatic muscles and orbicularis muscles) than other smiles. It is important to note that in all of these studies, subjects were women. It is unclear whether this should have any effect on the generalizability of the results but the restricted sample should raise appropriate questions about the applicability of these findings.

On a related note, H.D. Cohen *et al.* (1976) reported increased theta activity in the right hemisphere during sexual orgasm, although the quality of the recording in such a condition would make one doubtful of its integrity. A recent PET study has found decreased activity in every brain area of right-handed men during orgasm except the right prefrontal cortex (Tiihonen *et al.*, 1994)

Muscle contraction

A small group of studies also suggests that the side of the body in which muscle contraction occurs can be associated with changed affect. Bernard Schiff and his colleagues (Schiff and Lamon, 1989, 1994; Schiff and Gagliese, 1994) found that contraction of various right- and left-sided muscles in healthy, right-handed subjects resulted in feelings of positive and negative emotion, respectively. In keeping with the EEG studies, the side of the contraction was consistently associated with one type of emotion, indicating that negative feelings to left-sided contraction were consistent with contralateral right hemisphere activation, and vice versa. Subjects making right-sided facial contractions reported a more positive emotional state

➠

whereas those making left-sided facial contractions experienced less positive, sadder emotional states, possibly because of the association between the side of the contraction and the contralateral hemisphere activated (Schiff and Lamon 1989, 1994; see Figure 10.4).

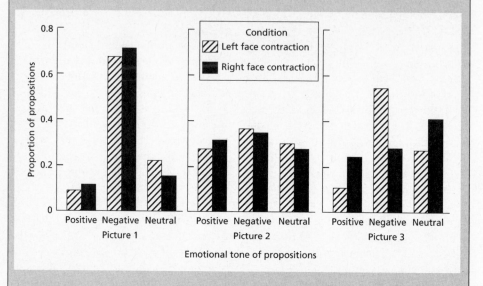

Figure 10.4 The proportion of negative, positive and neutral stories told in response to two practice and one target picture after left and right facial contraction

In one of these experiments individuals were required to tolerate pain by placing either their left or their right hand in a bucket of iced water (Schiff and Gagliese, 1994). This test (the cold-pressor test) is a measure of pain tolerance. Subjects kept their right hand in the water, i.e. could tolerate greater pain, significantly longer than they did their left hand.

Although perhaps suggesting that left hemisphere control of the right hand resulted in greater pain tolerance, the possibility cannot be ruled out that the right hand was more tolerant owing to use and desensitization: all subjects in the experiment were right-handed and would thus have used their right hand for most activities, especially those requiring force and power. The authors repeated this experiment using a between-subjects design in which the left and right hands belonged to different subjects; in the previous experiment, the same individual's left and right hands were monitored. The results of this study were negative: although the right hand was kept longer in the water than was the left, this difference was not statistically significant. In contrast, Schiff and Lamon (1994) found that when subjects contracted their left hands (by squeezing a rubber ball) and had to generate stories to a neutral picture, these stories were more negative than when they had to generate stories following contraction of the right hand. There appears to be some evidence, therefore, for laterality of different types of emotion in healthy individuals, although the methodology used to obtain these asymmetries is sometimes questionable (cf. Schiff and Gagliese, 1994). These difficulties sometimes highlight the problems in lateralizing human emotional processing.

Brain damage

Evidence from brain-damaged individuals indicates similar, but qualified, findings. Patients with damage to the right hemisphere as a result of a stroke have been found to be poorer at posing accurate spontaneous emotional expression than those with left lesions (Borod et al., 1986b). However, this picture is not that clear. In a study of patients with tumour and vascular complaints, for example, Mammucari et al. (1988) found no difference between left and right lesioned patients in their ability to make spontaneous emotional expression although both clinical groups differed from controls. Weddell et al. (1990), however, found that anterior right- and left-lesioned patients were significantly more impaired than controls and posterior lesioned patients when required to make accurate negative and positive emotion poses.

The general finding in these studies, however, is that emotional perception is better when undertaken by the right hemisphere whereas emotional expression implicates both hemispheres in the region of the frontal cortex. The question then arises, why should asymmetry exist for these two apparently discrete functions? Some models of laterality that might answer this question are discussed below.

The neuropsychology of humour

One emotional response which is frequently overlooked in discussions of emotion is mirth. Most studies of emotional expression have used affective indices, such as happiness, anger, disgust and so on, and sometimes have included types of smile as variables. Laughter, and the brain regions responsible for it, are not usually considered. Perhaps this neglect is owing to the complexity of the behaviour subsumed under the term 'laughter'. Motor, sensory and cognitive systems interact to produce laughter. This means that, in order to determine the brain mechanism which prompts laughter after sensory stimulation, the sensory, perceptual, motor and cognitive processes involved must be separated. Despite its complexity, however, there is some evidence to indicate that this area might be a fruitful one for emotion research.

Humour is associated with increased activity of the sympathetic nervous system (Sternbach, 1962), increased heart rate (Averill, 1969), increased skin conductance (J.H. Goldstein et al., 1975), increased muscle tension (Chapman, 1976), and altered respiratory (Svebak, 1975, 1977) and altered EEG patterns (Svebak, 1982). Schachter and Wheeler (1962) reported that an injection of epinephrine increased laughter in subjects watching a humorous film.

At an anatomical level, right hemisphere damage appears to be consistently associated with irregularities in laughter, perception of humour and enjoyment of it. For example, right hemisphere damage has been associated with outbursts of spontaneous laughter (Sackheim et al., 1982) whereas anaesthetizing the right hemisphere also increases laughter (Perria et al., 1961). In a well known study, Gardner et al. (1975) found that right hemisphere patients showed greater variability in their laughter (i.e. too much or too little) than did left hemisphere patients.

Right hemisphere patients also appear to have greater difficulty than controls in placing correct punchlines to cartoons, where the captions were classed as 'joking', 'non sequitur', 'straightforward-neutral' and 'straightforward-sad' (Wapner et al., 1981). They placed the greatest number of non sequiturs as punchlines to the cartoons, an appropriate choice (it made the cartoon funny) but it made the cartoon lack coherent meaning. Right hemisphere patients also showed differences in humour differentiation with a tendency to give higher ratings to unfunny items. Winner and Gardner (1977) found that both left hemisphere patients and controls laughed at literal pictorial representations of metaphors but right hemisphere patients did not. Interestingly, Brazzelli et al. (1994) reported a single-case study of a woman with bilateral frontal lobe damage who was unable to caption cartoons properly but did show signs of amusement and surprise when, after lifting a series of boxes and finding they were empty, lifted the final box and discovered that it was heavier than the others.

These studies indicate that the right hemisphere may be important in the understanding of humour, although very few studies have systematically examined the neuroanatomical basis of laughter and the response to humour (see discussion in Martin and Gray, 1996).

■ Models of human emotional expression: neuropsychological perspectives

Two general models of the neuropsychology of emotional expression and perception have been proposed (although there are several more detailed ones, e.g. Rinn, 1984). The **right hemisphere hypothesis** states that the right hemisphere is dominant for emotional perception and expression regardless of whether the emotion is positive or negative (Borod *et al.*, 1983). The **valence hypothesis** argues that there is right-hemisphere dominance for negative emotions and left hemisphere dominance for positive emotions (Silberman and Weingartner, 1986; Davidson, 1992). This hypothesis is divided into two other hypotheses: one states that the valence hypothesis applies to both the perception and expression of emotion; the other states that the expression of emotion may be lateralized but there is right hemisphere dominance for perception of emotion regardless of valence.

The evidence reviewed thus far indicates that the right hemisphere hypothesis does not adequately explain all the data currently available in neuropsychological studies of emotion. The number of studies demonstrating right hemisphere superiority for emotional perception and left hemisphere superiority for emotional experience suggests that this is too crude a model to account for the existing data. The evidence, at the cortical level, appears to support the second model, specifically that positive emotional expression is confined to the left hemisphere and negative emotional expression is confined to the right hemisphere.

Davidson, for example, has interpreted the affective EEG findings in terms of approach and withdrawal behaviour (Davidson, 1984, 1992). This hypothesis argues that affective differences between the two sides of the brain reflect different motivational tendencies (Ehrlichman, 1987): an approachable stimulus will evoke positive emotional experience; an unapproachable stimulus (one provoking withdrawal) will evoke negative emotional experience. The evidence for the hypothesis has been obtained in EEG studies both from normal subjects and from individuals scoring high on depression inventories. Schaffer *et al.* (1983), for example, found that depressed subjects showed less left frontal baseline activation than non-depressed subjects. Right frontal hemisphere EEG variability has also been reported in depressive patients (Perris *et al.*, 1978). However, studies employing different experimental conditions such as induction of euphoric/depressive states or self-generated depression/sexual arousal have reported alpha symmetry or no left-sided activation (Tucker *et al.*, 1981). It could be argued that these latter studies contain an element of motor and perceptual activity that is not present when viewing a film and rating it for its emotional content. The studies using film clips may, therefore, be more reliable in terms of the methods they employ. It should be noted, however, that Harman and Ray (1977) also requested subjects to generate emotional memories and reported increased left hemisphere power during positive affect when compared with negative affect.

Evoked potential measures have produced similar results to those of Davidson. Significantly greater right frontal hemisphere lateralization in individuals scoring highly on depression have been reported (Biondi *et al.*, 1993). The latency of the P300 in these individuals was also shorter at right hemisphere sites.

It has been suggested that increased left frontal activation may be an index of the individual's capacity to respond to an emotional stimulus. Wheeler *et al.* (1993), for example, report that increased left frontal activation and decreased right frontal activation predicted greater affective response to positive films whereas Tomarken *et al.* (1990) report that baseline asymmetry at frontal electrodes significantly predicted global negative affect. Taken together with the reports of decreased left frontal activation in depressed subjects, these findings suggest a **diathesis model** of affective response. This means that the asymmetrical activation represents a predisposition to respond to emotional stimuli in a particular way. As Davidson (1988) notes, 'right frontal activation may be necessary but not sufficient for the experience of negative emotion. Its presence may mark a vulnerability for negative affect, given an appropriate elicitor.' Elsewhere he argues, 'individual differences in frontal activation asymmetry [represent] a diathesis, which in combination with the requisite situational or contextual factors, will result in the predicted type of emotional response. Frontal asymmetry is thought to be neither sufficient nor necessary for the experience of approach-related positive and withdrawal-related negative emotion. Rather, frontal asymmetry is regarded as a contributory cause of such emotional states.' (Wheeler *et al.*, 1993).

Intriguingly, studies of infant response to separation from their mothers support the model. In one study, greater baseline right-sided frontal EEG activation was found to differentiate between those ten-month old infants who became distressed (criers) when separated from their mother and those who did not (non-criers) (Davidson and Fox, 1989).

More recently, Fox *et al.* (1995), in a study of the EEG response of 48 four-year-old children, found that those children monitored during a free-play session who made several 'social initiations' and displayed positive affect exhibited greater left hemisphere frontal activation at a later EEG recording session. Those characterized as socially withdrawn during play exhibited greater relative right hemisphere frontal activation. This finding, they suggest, indicates that individual differences in EEG activation may reflect 'in part, their pattern of affective responsivity and consequent social competence' although the effects of the initial play experience cannot be ruled out as a confounding variable. The explanation may be *ad hoc*. A better test of the model would be, as Tomarken *et al.* (1990) have done with adults, to group the children according to individual EEG differences and see if these EEG-based groupings predict behaviour. This might also help to clarify the relative contribution of experience and physiology to individual differences and social behaviour. Does experience influence the individual differences in EEG or does the EEG activation influence behaviour? A longitudinal study, as the authors themselves suggest, might partly answer this question.

Finally, as we saw in Chapter 6, Damasio has proposed a theory of emotion based on somatic markers and more detail on this can be found in that chapter and in the further reading suggestions.

DISCUSSION POINT

Does the human brain show asymmetrical activation to all types of emotional stimuli?

In an earlier section, we saw that some types of affective visual stimuli produced changes in different sides and areas of the brain. According to one theory, the cerebral asymmetry is characterized by increased right frontal hemisphere activation during the expression of negative emotion and increased left frontal activation during the expression of positive emotion. This asymmetry, the theory suggests, reflects more basic 'approach' and 'withdrawal' behaviour. This model is based on studies employing visual stimuli. If the model is correct, however, and asymmetrical activation is characteristic of emotional experience, one might expect similar asymmetries to occur in response to emotional stimuli from other sensory modalities. If similar asymmetries are not obtained in other senses, perhaps the EEG findings are **modality-specific**.

In a recent series of experiments, Martin (1995a,b) sought to discover whether the findings above could be replicated with a different sensory stimulus, smell. In these experiments, spontaneous EEG activity was recorded from subjects as they smelled the pleasant and unpleasant odours of synthetic and real foods. Following the recording of the baseline EEG, the odours, which included strawberry, spearmint, almond, chocolate (all four pleasant-synthetic), baked beans, coffee (both pleasant-real), cumin, garlic and onion (both unpleasant-synthetic) and rotting pork (unpleasant-real) were presented consecutively, with a minute separating the presentation of each odour. When real odours of cooked foods were presented, hot water was also used as a stimulus for fear that the results obtained would be due to trigeminal stimulation by the steam emitted by these foods. EEG was recorded from frontal, central, parietal and occipital sites in the alpha and theta wavebands (theta is highly responsive to olfactory stimulation). Subjects then rated the odours for various psychometric properties such as pleasantness, familiarity, strength and so on.

In the experiment where synthetic odours were used, the odour of spearmint was rated as being the most pleasant and the odour of garlic and onion rated as being the least pleasant. However, there was no significant difference between the degree of activation seen in either hemisphere for these odours in the alpha or the theta frequency. This, of course, was problematic because it does not confirm the earlier results with video clips.

However, there was the possibility that the odours were not sufficiently relevant or salient to produce the predicted EEG asymmetries. Subjects may have been aware of the odour's synthetic quality, for example, or the odours may not have been sufficiently pleasant or unpleasant. In a second experiment using real food odours, the odour of baked beans was rated the most pleasant, with the odour of rotting meat rated as the least pleasant. This time, greater left hemisphere temporal than frontal alpha activation was found for the more pleasant odour. Furthermore, greater left-sided frontal activity was apparent for baked beans than for rotting meat in the theta frequency, as seen in Figure 10.5.

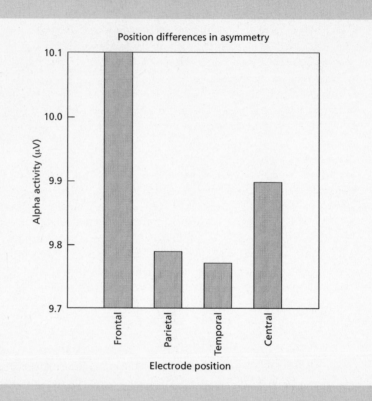

Figure 10.5   Greater frontal activity in alpha observed in response to a pleasant odour

   The finding in theta is interesting because this frequency, more than alpha, appears to be affected by olfactory stimulation. Changes in this waveband have also been related to the degree of attention paid to stimuli and degree of involvement in cognitive tasks. If theta is the primary channel for the processing of olfactory information, it may reflect changes in attention brought about by exposure to odour (Martin, 1996). Why were temporal, not frontal, areas activated during perception of the most pleasant odour? Is the left-sided increase in theta activity seen in response to the pleasant odour the olfactory analogue of increased left frontal activation to pleasant experiences elicited by visual stimuli? Does this suggest that the brain processes emotional experiences from different sensory modalities differently? Does it also suggest that the brain may not be processing the 'emotional' parts of a stimulus, but its 'cognitive' or 'perceptual' parts? Like most research in emotion, the findings prompt just as many questions as answers.

Summary – normal aspects of emotion

☐ There is ambiguity concerning what 'emotion' actually is although there is some evidence from neuroscience that some emotions may be differentiated (1) on the basis of neural pathways, and (2) on the basis of gross measures of regional activity. Data from animal studies have highlighted the importance of the amygdala, brainstem and hippocampal system in fear conditioning. Whether the highly stylized tasks used in animal studies make good analogues of human fear and anxiety is open to question.

☐ Based on his animal work and evidence from the human frontal lobe literature, Rolls proposes a theory of emotion in which the subcortical nuclei and orbitofrontal cortex form a stimulus–reward mechanism where associations between a response and whether it is rewarded or punished represent our feeling of emotion.

☐ Studies of brain injury indicate that different areas of the neocortex are involved in the perception and expression of emotion. The left hemisphere appears to be superior for the experience or expression of emotion whereas the right hemisphere is superior for the recognition and perception of emotion.

☐ Evidence suggests that activation of the left frontal cortex is associated with positive emotional expression whereas activation of the right frontal cortex is associated with negative emotional expression. These patterns are thought to reflect approach–withdrawal behaviour: some individuals exhibit a predisposition to respond positively (approach) or negatively (withdrawal) to emotional stimuli.

☐ The majority of studies to date have focused on the emotions elicited by visual stimuli. The problem with extending to other sensory modalities is that the brain regions involved would 'mask' the regions involved in perception. This may not be an insurmountable problem since vision also has its own system and brain regions which mediate it. Cross-modality studies would be a first step in determining the generality of emotion-based brain systems.

ABNORMAL ASPECTS OF EMOTION

▓ What is an abnormal emotion?

The majority of the studies reviewed in the previous section were concerned with the measurement of normal emotion: whether brain activity can distinguish between the individual's happy response and disgusted response, for example. Studies such as these can indicate some of those brain regions and mechanisms that govern our responses to stimuli which move us, either positively or negatively. Certain emotional responses, however, go beyond the normal experience of happiness and sadness into the realm of the clinical. Clinical emotional disorders, so-called **affective disorders**, are distinguished from normal emotional or mood changes in a number of ways. The *Diagnostic and Statistical Manual* (American Psychiatric Association, 1994) lists a number of criteria that a patient must meet before he or she is considered to be clinically depressed or anxious, for example. Most of us will experience mood changes occasionally: elation at having got a better-paid job, achieving a high grade in an exam, becoming a parent, winning the lottery. We might experience sadness at the death of a friend or relative, at failing to win an important business order or at failing exams. However, while upsetting, these experiences are not normally long-lasting and do not usually impair an individual's way of life permanently. Clinical emotional disturbances, if they go untreated, are long-lasting and do impair the individual's normal way of life.

The most common disorders of mood and affect are **depression** and **mania**. There are other emotional disorders classed as anxiety disorders and include **phobias**, **generalized anxiety disorder** and **obsessive–compulsive disorder**. These disorders involve an extreme emotional response – clinical anxiety or depression. Whereas normal mood shifts can disappear relatively easily, clinical mood changes are normally alterable only by medication or intensive behavioural or cognitive therapy. In this chapter, the neuropsychological basis of these two types of disorder – depression and anxiety – are considered.

▓ Depression: a description

Although swings in everyday mood are normal, a more persistent and continuous mood change indicates a clinical problem. The symptoms of depression depend on the degree of depression experienced. Thus, some individuals will be miserable and show little interest in normally interesting activities (moderate depressive disorder). They might be pessimistic about the present, past and future and feel helpless. Other individuals might experience the same thoughts and feelings but at a greater intensity (severe depressive disorder). At the other end of the scale, individuals might experience bouts of mania which alternate with depressive episodes. Individuals exhibiting mania are overactive, erratic, disinhibited, hyper-sexual, highly frustrated, demanding, flirtatious, insomniac and irritable. When manic episodes alternate with depressive episodes, the condition is described as a **bipolar disorder**. When depressive episodes alone are observed, the condition is described as **unipolar**. This unipolar/bipolar distinction is widely used.

Unipolar, or major, depression is characterized by depressive symptoms which have spanned at least two weeks. It is twice as common in women as in men (bipolar disorder shows no sex difference) and symptoms tend to be worse in the morning. According to DSM-IV, a major depressive syndrome is defined as one which has at least five of the manual's stated symptoms experienced within a two-week period. Mean age of onset for bipolar disorder tends towards adolescence/young adulthood; unipolar disorder has a later onset. There is some suggestion that those individuals with severe bipolar illness are born in winter months.

The classification of depression into further subcategories is problematic. A number of these fractionated classifications have been suggested. For example, a distinction has been made between **primary** and **secondary depression** where the latter occurs with another, primary illness. Mild depressive disorders have been classed as **neurotic depression** whereas severe depressive disorders have been classed as **psychotic depression**. Whether these disorders are discrete and inde-pendent or represent a continuum is unclear. The term **reactive depression** has been used to describe a response to an external cause whereas **endogenous depression** describes a disorder that cannot readily be attributed to an external cause. Although a popular distinction, there is evidence that depressive symp-tomatology is not that simple, with adverse life events preceding depressive episodes, whether the depression is endogenous or reactive (Bebbington *et al.*, 1988).

There is some evidence for a genetic influence in affective disorder. Con-cordance rates of 50–70 per cent have been found in monozygotic twins where one twin has a severe affective disorder; for dizygotic twins the concordance rate is 13–20 per cent. The rates are paralleled in a limited number of studies of separated and adopted twins. The genetic influence appears to be greater for bipolar than for unipolar disorder. Linking the genetic influence to a chromosome marker has not been entirely successful. Predisposing factors for affective disorder are many, although the actual influence they have is open to question. Candidates have included maternal deprivation and parental relationships (the evidence for this is inconsistent), personality disturbance (likely), adverse life events such as bereave-ment or separation (again, likely), the vulnerability of the individual to life events (i.e. the individual may be predisposed to the disorder but the disorder needs a major event to trigger it off), and season of birth.

▨ Neuropathology of depression

Neuropathological post-mortem studies of depressives' brains are not particularly common. The available evidence shows cortical cell loss in temporal and frontal regions (Bowen *et al.*, 1989). CT scans show larger ventricles in 10–30 per cent of patients with affective disorders when compared with controls. The difference between the two groups is quite small and there also exists the possibility that the patients' drug regime was responsible for the finding. A reduction in glucose metabolism has also been found in the left frontal lobe of depressed patients (Baxter *et al.*, 1989) and, as noted in the section on normal emotion, left frontal-temporal and right posterior lesions have been associated with subsequent depression.

A number of studies have reported reduced metabolic activity in frontal regions (Baxter *et al.*, 1985, 1989; Austin *et al.*, 1992; Bench *et al.*, 1993) and in the basal ganglia (Austin *et al.*, 1992; Post *et al.*, 1987). In a slightly different study, Nobler *et al.* (1994) assessed regional cerebral blood flow (rCBF) in depressed patients before ECT (electroconvulsive therapy – the passing of an electrical current through the brain), 30 minutes before and 50 minutes after a single treatment and during the week following ECT. ECT effects were also observed for a small group of manic patients. Depressed patients who were responsive to ECT showed markedly reduced rCBF in the acute period following treatment. Compared with non-responders, responders were characterized by this global reduction in rCBF, and especially by anterior cortical reduction. A similar pattern was also observed in the responsive manic patients during the acute period.

Depression has been associated with increased right hemisphere activity relative to the left hemisphere (Otto *et al.*, 1987). Right hemisphere tests are performed poorly by some depressed patients (S.G. Goldstein *et al.*, 1977) and an improvement in performance is seen following ECT (Kronfol *et al.*, 1978). As noted in the section on normal emotion, higher pain thresholds have been reported for the right hand than the left (Haslam, 1970), and patients with right hemisphere lesions have been found to tolerate pain for longer than do controls or left hemisphere lesion patients (Cubelli *et al.*, 1984; Neri *et al.*, 1985). On the basis of this evidence, Otto *et al.* (1987) propose that the right hemisphere is activated in response to negative emotional stimuli and that this activation will lead to the perception of subsequent stimuli as more negative. Along similar lines, Davidson and his colleagues have found less frontal activation both in individuals selected on the basis of their Beck Depression Inventory scores and in clinically depressed patients (Schaffer *et al.*, 1983; Henriques and Davidson, 1991).

▨ Neurochemistry of depression

Neurochemical changes in depressed patients (usually seen as a change in neuro-transmitter level and function, and neurotransmitter metabolite and receptor function) have been observed from four principal sources: the patient's blood plasma, urine, cerebrospinal fluid (CSF) and post-mortem brain. The first three sources are not particularly informative since it is not known to what extent the level of neurotransmitter in these fluids is reflective of their level in the brain. The principal chemicals studied have been the monoamines dopamine, noradrenaline, 5-hydroxytryptamine (5-HT or serotonin) and their metabolites. Reduced levels of the dopamine metabolite homovanillic acid have been found in the cerebrospinal fluid of depressed patients. No change in levels of noradrenaline has been found but levels of 5-hydroxyindoleacetic acid are reduced in some patients. However, this reduction is present after recovery, suggesting that it is not a distinctive neurochemical characteristic of depression. It is also far more consistent in patients attempting suicide. Post-mortem brain studies of depressed individuals have normally focused on suicides, although whether all patients were depressed before committing suicide is unclear. No dopamine or noradrenaline changes have been observed in these brains.

There is inconsistent evidence that the number of beta-adrenergic receptors and certain serotonin receptors (5-HT1 and 5-HT2) is increased in depressed subjects (Arora and Meltzer, 1989) sometimes in the prefrontal cortex (Arango *et al.*, 1990). Some studies have suggested that depression is associated with a dysfunction in the serotonin system, with a decreased level of serotonin neurotransmission (Malone and Mann, 1993). Early theories argued that presynaptic function in 5-HT neurons was decreased, although the absence of decreased levels of 5-HT argued for the hypothesis that postsynaptic neurons were not responsive to normal levels of 5-HT. There is no conclusive evidence either way. Some studies report lower plasma tryptophan levels, reduced CSF 5-hydroxyindoleacetic acid levels and decreased 5-HT platelet 5-HT reuptake; others report increased 5-HT receptors in the brains of suicides (Malone and Mann, 1993).

In a recent study to determine the effects of reducing tryptophan, a precursor of serotonin synthesis, in depressed patients, Delgado and his colleagues depleted the tryptophan levels in 43 untreated depressed patients who later received antidepressant medication (Delgado *et al.*, 1994). This depletion reduces brain 5-HT function. If the presynaptic hypothesis is correct, decreasing 5-HT levels should exacerbate depression; if the postsynaptic hypothesis is correct, decreasing 5-HT levels should not have a significant effect because postsynaptic cells are not particularly responsive in the first place. In their patients, there was no self-reported mood change on the day of depletion but there was the following day: 37 per cent had 10-point or greater decrease in the Hamilton Depression Rating Scale, while 23 per cent had a 10-point or greater increase. The authors argue that the findings indicate that serotonin function is not linearly related to the level of depression; reduced serotonin function is a predisposing factor or is due to 'a postsynaptic deficit in the utilization of serotonin.'

Pharmacological treatments of the disorder, however, act on a number of neurotransmission systems.

■ Pharmacological treatment of depression

The most well known pharmacological treatments for depression are the mono-amine oxidase inhibitors (MOIs, e.g. phenelzine, iproniazid, tranylcypromine, brofaromine, moclobemide) and tricyclic antidepressants (e.g. desipramine, imipramine, clomipramine). Monoamine oxidase (MO) A and B are important for the metabolism of dopamine, noradrenaline and 5-HT. The principal pharmacological treatments for depression are listed in Table 10.1.

Drugs which inhibit MO tend to have antidepressant effects in mild but not severe depression (an inhibition of 80 per cent of MO must be observed before antidepressant effects are observed). One major side-effect of MOIs is the 'tyramine-cheese reaction', a hypertension resulting from the high concentration of tyramine in certain foods consumed, such as cheese, beer, chocolate and pickles. As the monoamine oxidase no longer metabolizes tyramine, the tyramine displaces noradrenaline from adrenergic nerve endings. The behavioural result is that the patient might develop occipital headaches and begin vomiting, experience chest pain and become restless. Although a short-term reaction, it could lead to intracranial bleeding. If this occurs, it could be fatal.

Table 10.1 Some of the drugs used to treat depression

Substance	Generic name	Example
Norepinephrine-reuptake inhibitors (Tertiary amine tricyclics)	Amitriptyline	Elavil
	Clomipramine	Anafranil
	Doxepin	Adapin, Sinequa
	Imipramine	Tofranil
	Trimipramine	Surmontil
Norepinephrine-reuptake inhibitors (Secondary amine tricyclics)	Amoxapine	Asendin
	Desipramine	Norpramin, Pertofrane
	Maprotiline	Ludiomil
	Nortriptyline	Pamelor
	Protriptyline	Vivactil
Serotonin-reuptake inhibitors	Fluoxetine	Prozac
	Fluvoxamine	Luvox
	Paroxetine	Paxil
	Sertraline	Zoloft
	Venlafaxine	Effexor
Atypical antidepressants	Bupropion	Wellbutrin
	Nefazodone	Serzone
	Trazodone	Desyrel
Monoamine oxidase inhibitors	Phenelzine	Nardil
	Tranylcypromine	Parnate
	Selegiline	Eldepryl

From Baldessarini, 1996a

Earlier MO inhibitors such as phenelzine, iproniazid and tranylcypromine inhibited forms A and B of MO and inhibited the enzyme irreversibly. It now appears that the A type is important in exerting antidepressant effects. Newer drugs such as brofaromine and moclobemide have reversible effects. It is not known precisely which monoamine's inhibition is likely to be more important. Also, it is puzzling why acute inhibition occurs a few days following drug administration but the antidepressant effect is not seen until about three weeks later. It has been suggested that the inhibition leads to subsequent long-term change (Strange, 1992).

Tricyclic antidepressants are the most popular antidepressant drugs. So called because of their common three-ring structure, tricyclics, like MOIs, take a few weeks to reach maximum effect and are thought to inhibit the reuptake of monoamines in the nerve terminal, resulting in an increased level of monoamine at the synapse. Side-effects of the drugs include blurred vision, dry mouth (an anticholinergic response), postural hypotension (an antiadrenergic response) and drowsiness (an antihistamine response). The different tricyclic drugs also inhibit reuptake of the three monoamines selectively, with one drug inhibiting one monoamine better than it would another.

Another group of drugs, so-called **second generation drugs**, have been modelled on the presumed pharmacological action of previous antidepressants. The original antidepressants (MOIs and tricyclics) were not designed specifically as anti-depressants but were found to have antidepressant effects. The new drugs such as maprotiline and fluoxetine (Prozac) inhibit the reuptake of noradrenaline and 5-HT respectively. The drugs are effective and have few of the tricyclics' side-effects. Oddly, although these drugs selectively inhibit reuptake and have effective anti-depressant effects, cocaine (which inhibits noradrenaline uptake) is a poor antidepressant.

Other 'biological' treatments have included L-tryptophan, an amino acid, which appears to work via an increase in levels of 5-HT. Taken with MOIs, L-tryptophan has been found to be an effective antidepressant, perhaps enhancing MOI action. Electroconvulsive therapy (ECT) may be an effective antidepressant for patients with severe, endogenous depression who do not respond to tricyclics (Kendell, 1981). However, effects are not long-lasting and relapses are high. Lithium carbon-ate is an effective drug treatment for mania and recurrent unipolar affective disorder but has a slow onset (Schou, 1989).

▓ Neurochemical hypotheses of depression

As the most effective biological treatment of clinical depression involves some form of pharmacological action, it is unsurprising that biological theories of the aetiology of depression have focused on neurochemical systems and changes.

Cholinergic hypothesis

The cholinergic hypothesis was one of the earliest neurochemical theories of depression and suggested that an imbalance between the cholinergic and catecholamine systems led to an alteration in mood (Janowsky *et al.*, 1972). More cholinergic activity was thought to produce depression; more relative catecholaminergic activity was thought to produce mania. However, there is little evidence to suggest the involvement of cholinergic systems in depression and the hypothesis is an informational slave to the period of its formulation, i.e. we have more information about antidepressant neurochemistry today.

Monoamine hypothesis

This is the most influential neurochemical hypothesis of depression, based on the effects of two drugs administered to patients in the 1950s when a drug (reserpine) used to alleviate hypertension became associated with depressive symptoms in some patients. Animal studies indicated that it reduced levels of dopamine, noradrenaline and 5-HT in rats. Two others drugs which inhibited MO and were used to combat tuberculosis – iproniazid and isoniazid – appeared to produce a lightening of the depression experienced by tubercular patients. These two separate findings suggested that depression was produced by a reduction in monoamine neurotransmitter and that returning monoamine levels to normal would lead to a removal of the depression. Tricyclic drugs, as discussed above, inhibit monoamine reuptake thus potentially increasing synaptic levels of the monoamines. The important monoamine candidates are considered to be noradrenaline and 5-HT. Interestingly, patients with seasonal affective disorder have disturbed 5-HT metabolism (Wurtman and Wurtman, 1989).

There are a number of problems with the hypothesis, however. First, it is unclear whether antidepressant drugs increase the levels of synaptic monoamines. Secondly, the newer drugs selectively inhibit monoamines thus indicating that linking a specific neurochemical monoamine change with mood change is difficult. Furthermore, antidepressant drugs such as iprindole do not alter levels of synaptic monoamine. Finally, why do the tricyclics and MOIs take neurochemical effect almost immediately but take behavioural effect up to six weeks later?

Specific monoamine hypotheses

Newer theories, such as the **noradrenergic hypothesis**, attempt to account for some of these shortcomings. The noradrenergic hypothesis states that changes in the efficiency of synapses are due to presynaptic alpha 2-adrenergic receptors altering the synapses' control of neurotransmitter release. Chronic administration of antidepressants increases synaptic efficacy. Because all of this is a slow process, it might explain the delay in the behavioural action of the drugs. However, as yet, there is no human evidence that depression results from highly sensitive pre-synaptic alpha 2-adrenergic receptors which in turn lead to reduced noradrenaline release.

An alternative hypothesis argues that postsynaptic beta-adrenergic receptors are increased in depressed patients and that antidepressants return the numbers to their normal level. Giving a patient a receptor agonist, therefore, should exacerbate the depression. There is no evidence that this happens either.

One final hypothesis, the 5-HT hypothesis, argues that depression results from reduced 5-HT (as noted above) and that antidepressants increase the efficacy of 5-HT systems. Thus, the behavioural delay in symptom alleviation is accounted for by the fact that the drugs produce a slow increase in the efficacy of 5-HT synapses.

■ Anxiety: a description

The term anxiety describes a number of disorders characterized by danger, distress or fear. In 1984, approximately 8 per cent of the British population took an antianxiety drug (Dunbar *et al.*, 1989). This finding is a sound reflection of the estimate that 10 per cent of the population will experience anxiety severe enough to require medical help. The two bestselling drugs in Great Britain in 1990 were both for the treatment of gastric ulcer, an anxiety-related condition.

Three specific neurotic syndromes are described by the term anxiety. These are generalized anxiety disorder (GAD) which represents feelings of anxiety and somatic sensations occurring in the absence of an identifiable stimulus; phobic anxiety disorders which involve the same symptoms as GAD but occur only in response to specific events or objects (agoraphobics, who are anxious in crowds or in places other than the home, may experience panic attacks and a fear of fainting or losing control); and obsessive–compulsive disorder which involves experiencing obsessional thoughts and impulses or obsessively performing behavioural rituals such as excessive washing of hands. Common to all, to some extent, are awareness of threat, tension, difficulty in concentration, fear, restlessness, sleep disturbance, increased muscle tension, gastrointestinal alteration such as dry mouth, nausea and diarrhoea, difficulty in respiration and increased sweating. The incidence of GAD is about 3–6 per cent; the lifetime risk for phobia is 10 per cent, for panic disorder 1 per cent, and for obsessive compulsive disorder 2–3 per cent. A 40 per cent concordance rate for anxiety disorder is seen in monozygotic twins whereas 15 per cent or less is found for dizygotic twins (Mahmood *et al.*, 1983; Marks, 1986).

■ Neuropathology of anxiety

Cerebral blood flow studies suggest a role for the temporal lobe in anxiety. Reiman *et al.* (1986) found changes in rCBF at the polar temporal cortex in patients during a panic attack. Asymmetric rCBF activation in the parahippocampal gyrus was found in these patients before the attack (Reiman *et al.* 1986). Temporal lobe abnormalities have also been found in MRI studies of patients with panic disorder (Fontaine *et al.*, 1990). In a follow-on study, Reiman *et al.* (1989) observed rCBF changes in the polar temporal cortex in patients experiencing anticipatory anxiety. A problem with characterizing anxiety neurochemically and neuropathologically is that the state is often a normal response to an event, object, person or situation. However, some indicator of the neurochemical substrates of the state may be gleaned from pharmacological treatment of the disorder (see below).

In a recent study, Tomarken and Davidson (1994) recorded EEG activity from 90 subjects who were characterized by a repressed or non-repressed coping style. Repressors exhibited significantly greater left frontal activation than did low-anxiety and high-anxiety subjects as classified by State Trait Anxiety Inventory; results were similar for repressed depressed subjects when compared with high-depressive and low-depressive subjects, as measured by Beck Depression Inventory. The authors argue, on the basis of this and other evidence, that the results 'support the notion that resting left frontal activation may index decreased risk for psychopathology.' However, they note that all subjects were women (and therefore not ideally representative), and that the EEG may not be the most sensitive measure of brain activity in this context.

■ Pharmacological treatment of anxiety

Antianxiety drugs are called **anxiolytics** and a number of compounds are used to alleviate the disorder, including barbiturates, benzodiazepines and antidepressant drugs. Some of these are listed in Table 10.2.

Table 10.2 Some of the drugs used to treat anxiety

Substance	Generic name	Example
Benzodiazepines	Alprazolam	Xanax
	Chlordiazepoxide	Librium
	Clonazepam	Klonopin
	Clorazepate	Tranxene
	Diazepam	Valium
	Halazepam	Paxipam
	Lorazepam	Ativan
	Oxazepam	Serax, Zaxopam
	Prazepam	Centrax
Atypical agent	Buspirone	Buspar

From Baldessarini, 1996b

Barbiturates

Barbiturates, derivatives of barbituric acid, are sedative drugs and include barbital and Phenobarbital. Once a popular anxiolytic, their toxicity and their potential for fostering physiological and 'psychological' dependence led to a gradual reduction in their use. Since the effects of withdrawal were severe, the possibility of death with overdose was a possibility, and since other new drugs such as the benzodiazepines became available, barbiturate prescription has become uncommon.

Benzodiazepines

These sedative and anticonvulsant compounds are the most frequently prescribed drugs in medicine and the most widely used anxiolytics. The most common of them are chlordiazepoxide (Librium) and diazepam (Valium) and all are low in toxicity. Side-effects may be produced if the drug is taken for a long period, however, and these include sedation and impaired memory/concentration. Depression and outbursts of violence may also be seen. It has been estimated that one in five women and one in ten men are prescribed benzodiazepines, with 30 million prescriptions issued in Great Britain in 1981 (Dunbar *et al.*, 1989). After about four weeks, however, the body becomes tolerant to benzodiazepines and the drug becomes ineffective (Lader and File, 1987). Withdrawal symptoms are marked after chronic administration and approximately 40 per cent of patients on long-term prescription experience them (the anxiety tends to be intensified postadministration). The tolerance to benzodiazepines and the withdrawal symptoms after their removal suggest the selective use of the drug, i.e in the short-term alleviation of distress or in response to a stressful situation.

Antidepressant drugs

Some of these, such as the tricyclics, tend to be effective in alleviating GAD and some panic disorders. The way in which they do this neurochemically, however, is unknown.

5-HT receptor-sensitive compounds

Compounds such as buspirone which act as agonists at 5-HT receptors have anti-anxiety effects and do not produce the sedation seen with benzodiazepines (File, 1987).

Alcohol

Unsurprisingly, this is the most widely used psychoactive substance in the world. At low doses, it has anxiolytic effects, although the response to the dosage is dependent on the responsiveness of the individual. Its disadvantages are many and it has no long-term benefit.

Beta-blockers

Beta-blockers (e.g. propranolol) are beta-adrenergic receptor antagonists and are normally taken to alleviate extreme forms of stress. Angina patients are particularly prone to emotional upset, resulting in increased heart rate; together with a deficient coronary artery blood supply, this produces anginal pain. The accelerated beating of the heart is produced by stimulation of nerve endings called beta-receptors. Beta-blockers, as the name suggests, act by blocking these receptors and eliminating excessive stimulation of the heart. They also prevent the same kind of stimulation occurring during exercise: less blood is pumped out of the heart and less oxygen is consumed.

DISCUSSION POINT

Can Gray's model help to explain human anxiety?

There are a number of psychological models to explain the psychology of anxiety. Some were mentioned earlier in this chapter, e.g. the theories of Lazarus and Weiner. Few provide an explanation of anxiety at the neuropsychological level. One model, however, does (Gray, 1982). Based on a substantial review of animal data and the effects of anxiolytics in humans, Gray has argued that anxiety is evoked by signals of punishment, signals of lack of reward, novel stimuli and innate fear stimuli. A behavioural inhibition system (BIS), the brain system responsible, detects the threat and generates anxiety. Anxiety thus reflects the activity of the BIS. See Figure 10.6.

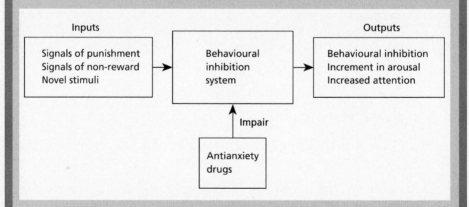

Figure 10.6 The behavioural inhibition system

This system allows the organism to evaluate the environment for threat or possible threat, and is thought to be represented by the septum and hippocampal formation, or septohippocampal system, which comprises a number of interacting brain structures, as seen in Figure 10.7.

Evidence for the involvement of this system comes from animal lesion studies, rCBF studies implicating the parahippocampal gyrus in panic attacks, and electrical stimulation studies in which stimulation of the polar temporal cortex, the parahippocampal gyrus and the amygdala are associated with anxiety. Information about the state of the organism is obtained via the parahippocampal gyrus and information about possible outcomes from the prefrontal cortex. The subiculum is thought to be the structure which compares the actual and predicted outcome.

Gray also suggests that noradrenergic pathways linking the locus coeruleus to the septohippocampal system and 5-HT pathways linking the raphe to it may control some of the BIS's activity. Threats activate these pathways which, in turn, affect the septohippocampal system.

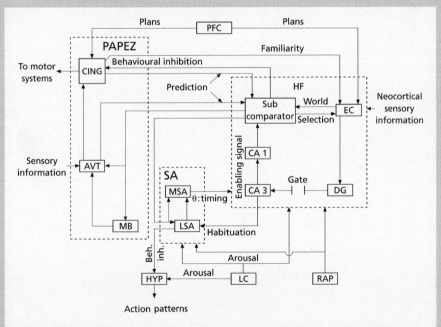

Key: HF=hippocampal formation; EC=entorhinal cortex; DG=dendate gyrus; SUB=subicular area; SA=septal area; MSA=medial septal area; LSA=lateral septal area; MB=mammillary bodies; AVT=anteroventral thalamus; CING=cingulate gyrus; HYP=hypothalamus; LC=locus coeruleus; RAP=raphe nuclei: PFC=prefrontal cortex

Figure 10.7 The septohippocampal system

However, there are other structures beyond those of the septohippocampal system which may mediate anxiety responses. Electrical stimulation of the amygdala, for example, may provoke anxiety or fear in laboratory animals. This structure may be important in the detection of threat from the environment, as LeDoux's experiments have demonstrated. Also important is the periaqueductal grey region which also results in fear/anxiety when electrically stimulated. Both the amygdala and peri-aqeductal grey region are innervated by 5-HT systems. These structures are important because, as Gray (1995) himself admits, the mechanism that one postulates for the mediation of anxiety depends on which system one uses as a starting point. LeDoux's work on the amygdala, for example, concerns the formation of conditioned responses which are not significantly affected by anxiolytic drugs. The responses elicited by conditioned stimuli, however, can be alleviated by these drugs and this is the focus of Gray's model.

There is some evidence that drugs do affect the septohippocampal system. GABA$_A$ receptor modulators (such as the benzodiazepines) increase the inhibitory action of GABA. Noradrenergic neurons innervating the septohippocampal system are also inhibited in activating the septohippocampal system under the administration of these drugs.

The important question is, however, can the model explain human anxiety, bearing in mind that the postulated systems have been derived largely from extensive animal work? Does the BIS reflect the anxiety of the agoraphobic or the social phobic? According to Gray, it is possible to make such associations. For example, he suggests that the behavioural symptoms of anxiety reflect the behavioural inhibition of the BIS. This inhibition results in a phobic avoidance when the individual responds to a threatening stimulus. Symbolic or linguistic threats, such as fear of failure in an exam, may be mediated by the pathway which links the cortical language areas to the prefrontal cortex and from there onto the motor programming circuits of the basal ganglia. From here, the pathway leads to the hippocampal formation via the entorhinal cortex. The inclusion of the basal ganglia here emphasizes the importance of movement-related systems in anxiety. Both the basal ganglia and the limbic system are, according to Gray, responsible for the attainment of goals: sensory aspects are governed by the limbic system; motor aspects are governed by the basal ganglia. The maintenance and the monitoring of goals would be accomplished by the septohippocampal system.

Gray's model provides a testable and sound basis on which one can attempt to explain the feeling of anxiety. Unlike LeDoux's model, its emphasis is on the response to a conditioned stimulus rather than on the conditioning of the response *per se*. A number of influential theorists in fields such as schizophrenia (e.g. Frith, 1992) have adopted many of the postulates of Gray's theory in their own formulations. The advantage of the model is that it makes precise predictions about what happens during the experience of anxiety. Because of this, much of its detail can be supported or disputed. Currently, it stands as one of the most effective models of anxiety in neuropsychology.

Summary – abnormal aspects of emotion

☐ Emotional disorders are principally of two types: those involving disturbances in affect and those involving extreme responses to threat and stressors.

☐ Depression can be unipolar (periods of acute depression followed by normal periods) or bipolar (depression alternates with mania). Brain imaging techniques have implicated reductions in metabolic activity in the frontal regions of depressives' brains and limited post-mortem studies indicate cell loss in frontal and temporal regions.

☐ The most widely accepted pharmacological theory of depression argues that depression is produced by a reduction in monoamine neurotransmitters (serotonin, noradrenaline, dopamine).

☐ More specific hypotheses have sought to account for the monoamine hypothesis' shortcomings. The two most frequently prescribed drugs for depression are monoamine oxidase inhibitors (drugs which inhibit the enzyme monoamine oxidase) and tricyclic antidepressants (drugs which inhibit reuptake of monoamines in the nerve terminals). The mechanism by which these drugs work is far from clear.

☐ Anxiety, as a clinical term, may refer to generalized anxiety, phobia or obsessive–compulsive disorder.

☐ The neuropathology of anxiety is difficult to characterize accurately because anxiety is generally a result of some specific event or stimulus and is state-bound. Abnormalities in temporal cortex functioning may be partly involved.

☐ The most widely used drugs to alleviate anxiety symptoms are the benzodiazepines (Librium, Valium) which involve modulation of GABAergic systems.

☐ Gray has proposed that a behavioural inhibition system, mediated by the septum and hippocampal formation, is responsible for detecting and responding to threat. Anxiety reflects the activity of this behavioural inhibition system.

Recommended further general and specific reading

Key: (1) = introductory, *(3)* = intermediate, *(5)* = advanced

Normal emotion – general

Davidson, R.J. and Sutton, S.K. (1995). Affective neuroscience: the emergence of a discipline. *Current Opinion in Neurobiology*, **5**, 217–24. *(2)*

Ekman, P. and Davidson, R.J. (1995). *The Nature of Emotion*. New York: Oxford University Press. *(2)*

LeDoux, J. (1995). Emotion: clues from the brain. *Annual Review of Psychology*, **46**, 209–35. *(3)*

LeDoux, J. (1996). *The Emotional Brain*. Englewood Cliffs, NJ: Simon and Schuster. *(3)*

Lewis, M. and Haviland, J.M. (1993). *Handbook of Emotions*. New York: Guilford Press. *(3)*

McNaughton, N. (1989). *Biology and Emotion*. Cambridge: Cambridge University Press. *(2)*

Oatley, K. and Jenkins, J.M. (1995). *Understanding Emotions*. Oxford: Blackwell. *(1)*

Plutchick, R. (1994). *The Psychology and Biology of Emotion*. London: Harper Collins. *(2)*

Normal emotion – specific

Adolphs, R., Tranel, D., Damasio, H. and Damasio, A.R. (1995). Fear and the human amygdala. *Journal of Neuroscience*, **15**(9), 5879–91. *(3)*

Adolphs, R., Damasio, H., Tranel, D. and Damasio, A.R. (1997). Cortical systems for the recognition of emotion in facial expressions. *Journal of Neuroscience*, **16**(23), 7678–87. *(3)*

Aggleton, J.P. (1992). *The Amygdala: Neurobiological aspects of emotion, memory and mental dysfunction*. New York: Wiley/Liss. *(4)*

Aromory, J.L., Servan-Schreiber, D., Cohen, J.D. and LeDoux, J.E. (1997). Computational modeling of emotion: explorations through the anatomy and physiology of fear conditioning. *Trends in Cognitive Sciences*, **1**(1), 28–34. *(4)*

Bechera, A., Damasio, H., Tranel, D. and Damasio, A.R. (1997). Deciding advantageously before knowing the advantageous strategy. *Science*, **275**, 1293–5. *(2)*

Borod, J.C. (1992). Interhemispheric and intrahemispheric control of emotion: a focus on unilateral brain damage. *Journal of Consulting and Clinical Psychology*, **60**(3), 339–48. *(3)*

Damasio, A.R. (1995). Toward a neurobiology of emotion and feeling: operational concepts and hypotheses. *The Neuroscientist*, **1**(1), 19–25. *(4)*

Davidson, R.J. (1992). Anterior cerebral asymmetry and the nature of emotion. *Brain and Cognition*, **20**, 125–151. *(3)*

LeDoux, J.E. (1995). In search of an emotional system in the brain: leaping from fear to emotion and consciousness. In M.S. Gazzaniga (ed.), *The Cognitive Neurosciences*. Cambridge, MA: MIT Press. *(5)*

Miller, G.A. (1996). How we think about cognition, emotion and biology in psychopathology. *Psychophysiology*, **33**, 615–28. *(3)*

Rolls, E.T. (1995). A theory of emotion and consciousness, and its application to understanding the neural basis of emotion. In M.S. Gazzaniga (ed.), *The Cognitive Neurosciences*. Cambridge, MA: MIT Press. *(5)*

Scott, S.K., Young, A.W., Calder, A.J., Hellawell, D.J., Aggleton, J.P. and Johnson, M. (1997). Impaired auditory recognition of fear and anger following bilateral amygdala lesions. *Nature*, **385**, 254–7. *(2)*

Stuss, D.T., Gow, C.A. and Hetherington, C.R. (1992). 'No longer Gage': frontal lobe dysfunction and emotional changes. *Journal of Consulting and Clinical Psychology*, **60**(3), 349–59. *(3)*

Abnormal emotion – general

Gray, J.A. (1982). *The Neuropsychology of Anxiety: An enquiry into the functions of the septo-hippocampal system*. Oxford: Oxford University Press. *(4)*

Gray, J.A. (1993). The neuropsychology of the emotions: framework for a taxonomy of psychiatric disorders. In S. van Goozen (ed.), *Emotions: Essays on emotion theory*. Hillsdale, NJ: Lawrence Erlbaum Associates. *(3)*

Mann, J.J. and Kupfer, D.J. (1993). *Biology of Depressive Disorders: Part A. A Systems Perspective*. New York: Plenum. *(4)*

Strange, P.G. (1992). *Brain Biochemistry and Brain Disorders*. New York: Oxford University Press. *(3)*

Abnormal emotion – specific

Drevets, W.C. and Raichle, M.E. (1995). Positron emission tomographic imaging studies of human emotional disorders. In M.S. Gazzaniga (ed.), *The Cognitive Neurosciences*. Cambridge, MA: MIT Press. *(2)*

Drevets, W.C., Price, J.L., Simpson, J.R., Todd, R.D., Reich, T., Vannier, M. and Raichle, M.E. (1997). Subgenual prefrontal cortex abnormalities in mood disorders. *Nature*, **386**, 824–7. *(2)*

Gershon, E.S. and Rieder, R.O. (1992). Major disorders of mind and brain. *Scientific American*, **267**(3), 89–95. *(2)*

Gray, J.A. (1995). A model of the limbic system and basal ganglia: applications to anxiety and schizophrenia. In M.S. Gazzaniga (ed.), *The Cognitive Neurosciences*. Cambridge, MA: MIT Press. *(4)*

Harmon-Jones, E. and Allen, J.J.B. (1997). Behavioral activation sensitivity and resting frontal EEG asymmetry: covariation of putative indicators related to risk for mood disorders. *Journal of Abnormal Psychology*, **106**(1), 159–63. *(2)*

Heilman, K.M., Bowers, D. and Valenstein, E. (1993). Emotional disorders associated with neurological diseases. In K.M. Heilman and E. Valenstein (eds), *Clinical Neuropsychology* (3rd edition). New York: Oxford University Press. *(3)*

Heller, W., Etienne, M.A. and Miller, G.A. (1995). Patterns of asymmetry in depression and anxiety: implications for neuropsychological models of emotion and psychopathology. *Journal of Abnormal Psychology*, **104**, 327–33. *(3)*

Sackheim. H.A. and Prohovnik, I. (1993). Brain imaging studies of depressive disorders. In J.J. Mann and D.J. Kupfer (eds), *Biology of Depressive Disorders: Part A. A Systems Perspective*. New York: Plenum. *(3)*

Tucker, D.M. (1984). Lateral brain function in normal and disordered emotion: interpreting electroencephalographic evidence. *Biological Psychology*, **19**, 219–235. *(4)*

Chapter Eleven

The dementias

▓ Dementia

Dementia describes a condition in which there is a gradual, insidious and relentless loss of cognitive function. There are several different types of dementia presenting different symptoms. This variability sometimes makes it difficult for the clinician to make a diagnosis of specific dementia (Stuss and Levine, 1996). There is also the added problem of cognitive decline with increasing age. Frequently, normal cognitive decline may mask the early appearance of dementia because memory impairment, difficulty in name-finding and increased reaction times occur among the healthy aged. The degree of intellectual competence in the elderly population is itself varied, which can lead to the misdiagnosis of dementia in individuals of poor intelligence (Gurland, 1981).

A diagnosis of dementia is decided on the basis of a set of key clinical, histopathological and localization factors. The *Diagnostic and Statistical Manual* (American Psychiatric Association, 1994), for example, lists the main clinical and behavioural symptoms that should appear in order to confirm a diagnosis of dementia. According to DSM-IV, the diagnostic criteria for dementia are: a demonstrable impairment in short- and long-term memory; the ability of memory/ cognitive impairment to interfere with work, social activities and relationships; evidence of an organic factor which is 'aetiologically related' to the disturbance, and at least one of the following: abstract thinking impairment; impaired judgement; higher cortical function disturbance (aphasia, apraxia, agnosia) or personality change. The ability of memory/cognitive impairment to interfere with work, social activities and relationships; evidence of an organic factor which is 'aetiologically related' to the disturbance.

Further differentiation of diagnosis can be made by considering the site and the histology of the dementia (these two factors help to determine what type of dementia the patient is exhibiting). Histopathology is probably the criterion that is least susceptible to interpretation because the molecular and biochemical evidence is clear-cut. Because of this, the only certain confirmation of a diagnosis of dementia can be made by autopsy or biopsy (McKhann, *et al.*, 1984).

Different types of dementia affect different brain systems and present slightly different clinical symptoms. The degenerative disease, **Alzheimer's disease (AD)**, is the most common cause of dementia, occurring in approximately 45 per cent of demented patients in the USA (Cummings and Benson, 1992) and with an estimated prevalence of 3.75 million worldwide (Stuss and Levine, 1996). The disease was named after Alois Alzheimer who, in 1907, reported the case of a 56 year old patient with abnormal formations called **presenile plaques** and **tangles** in her brain. She exhibited an obvious form of presenile **dementia**, to which Alzheimer gave his name. This dementia is referred to as **dementia of the Alzheimer type** or **DAT**. Other types of dementia occur with Parkinson's disease, Huntington's chorea, **Pick's disease** and other pathologies which are discussed later.

Dementia of the Alzheimer type

Although there are no completely accurate figures, it is estimated that between 5 per cent and 10 per cent of individuals over 65 years of age will develop Alzheimer's disease (Rocca *et al.*, 1986) with the percentage quadrupling in the over-80s. The disease can occur sporadically or in a genetic form called familial Alzheimer's disease. The familial form is thought to be autosomal-dominant with the gene carried on chromosome 21 and, possibly, chromosome 19. The gene expresses itself by producing the amyloid precursor protein from which the protein associated with the senile plaques is formed.

In addition to a genetic factor, there are other risk factors associated with the disease. For example, a family history of Down's syndrome (Rocca *et al.*, 1986) and exposure to aluminium have been suggested. The former is based on evidence showing a similarity in the degeneration of the AD brain with that of a developing Down's syndrome brain. The latter suggestion, as we see later on, is controversial.

Clinical features

The major cognitive impairment in AD is loss of memory. This impairment is gradual and occurs in the presence of a normal level of consciousness but in the absence of any other CNS disease that might account for the symptoms. Specific memory impairments include impaired short-term memory and poor explicit memory. Implicit memory is not as severely affected, neither is memory for remote events. In two recent experiments, however, Greene and Hodges found significant impairment on all components of remote memory tests such as naming, identifying and recognizing famous faces in 33 patients with dementia of the Alzheimer type (Greene and Hodges, 1996a). More interesting, however, was a further study in which Greene and Hodges compared public memory (such as the ability to identify famous faces and names) and autobiographical memory (reporting events that occurred in childhood) in 24 patients with Alzheimer's dementia during the course of one year (Greene and Hodges, 1996b). They report that although both public (famous face and name processing) and autobiographical memories were impaired in Alzheimer patients, only public memory deteriorated longitudinally. This, the authors argue, indicates the fractionation of remote memory. It would be intriguing to read the results from a study in which an autobiographical version of the famous faces exercise was used.

Language deficits which accompany AD include impairments in comprehension and naming and an inability to utter speech with coherent or semantically accurate content. Both semantic knowledge and concept formation are poor in AD patients. Learning of new information is difficult, and reduced visual memory span has been reported (Albert and Moss, 1983). Demented patients will recognize and correct syntactic errors but mildly demented patients have difficulty correcting semantic errors. In the early stages, conversational speech is relatively normal with few solecisms. Speech content, however, is abnormal with anomia present and a reliance on stock phrases occurring. Reading ability is preserved but reading comprehension is poor. Patients also exhibit deficits in drawing, copying, constructional ability, left–right topographical orientation and perceptual discrimination.

In the first stage of AD (within two years), memory for recent events is impaired. Spatial perception declines, disorientation in time and place occur and concentration is impaired. The patient feels fatigued and restless. In the second stage (within two to three years), memory failure progresses and parietal lobe dysfunction such as dyspraxia and agnosia occur. Judgement and the capacity for abstract thought disappear. In the third and final stage, all intellectual function breaks down. Gross emotional disinhibition occurs and the former personality is lost. Patients reach the stage where they cannot recognize relatives, or even recognize themselves in a mirror.

Neuropathological features

Post-mortem brains of AD patients show a shrinkage of primarily frontal and temporal gyri (up to 20 per cent) and ventricle enlargement, although there is the possibility that the shrinkage is due to normal aging because not all AD patients exhibit shrinkage. There is neuronal loss in the cortex, hippocampus, amygdala, basal forebrain, the locus coeruleus, raphe nuclei and nucleus basalis of Meynert. There is some evidence to suggest that the loss of cortical columns of cells is greater than that found during normal aging (Coleman and Flood, 1987).

The classic pathological symptoms of AD are: (1) neurofibrillary tangles, (2) senile plaques, (3) granulovacuolar degeneration, and (4) Hirano bodies. There are abnormal **amyloid protein deposits** in both intracellular and extracellular sites in the demented individual's brain (Muller-Hill and Beyreuther, 1989). Neurofibrillary tangles are straight or paired helical filaments which collect intracellularly and are made up of special proteins. Tangles normally consist of a pair of helical filaments found in the cytoplasm of cortical and hippocampal pyramidal cells. Ubiquitin, the protein marker for cell degeneration, has been localized in tangles (Gallo and Anderton, 1989) and the amyloid B-protein that they contain may be responsible for the formation of the senile plaques (Anderton, 1987). Temporal, parietal and frontal areas are especially affected by tangles. The tangles do not appear with normal aging, although they are found in other dementias. Senile plaques are spherical and are made up of glia and abnormal nerve cell processes; these surround the extracellular amyloid proteins (usually B-amyloid, an amino acid peptide). Senile plaques in the cortex are more pronounced in AD patients than in age-matched controls. They are 15–20 μm in diameter and have an outer rim of abnormal neuronal processes called neurites. There are also glial cell processes (astrocytes) which surround amyloid protein and are made up of fibrils that are 6–10 nm in diameter. The formation of plaques precedes neuronal loss. Some patients exhibit tangles but not plaques. Granuovacuolar degeneration occurs primarily in the hippocampus and, as the name suggests, results in neuronal tissue becoming full of holes. Finally, Hirano bodies are rod-shaped material which intrude on neurons.

Brain imaging studies indicate parietal lobe dysfunction, with extensive degeneration in this region and at temporal sites (Friedland *et al.*, 1985; Najlerahim and Bowen, 1988a,b; Esiri *et al.*, 1990). Wilcock *et al.* (1988) have suggested that parietal involvement occurs with early onset and temporal lobe involvement occurs with later onset of the dementia. There is evidence of hypermetabolism in AD patients (Procter *et al.*, 1988) as well as early, asymmetric glucose metabolism reduction in frontal, parietal and temporal regions (Haxby *et al.*, 1990). Areas of metabolic reduction tend to be positively correlated with neuronal degeneration (Najlerahim and Bowen, 1988a,b).

Neurochemical features

There is a loss of synapses in the AD brain which appears to correlate with the loss in intellectual function (Terry *et al.*, 1991). It is known that certain neurotransmitter receptors are lost in AD these include cortical acetylcholine, acetylcholinetransferase and nicotinic receptors. In the mid 1970s it was found that a loss of up to 70 per cent of choline acetyltransferase, the cholinergic marker enzyme which synthesizes acetylcholine (ACL), occurs in the temporal and parietal cortices of AD patients. This acetylcholine synthesis impairment is correlated with the severity of the dementia, and the loss of choline acetyltransferase is correlated with the number of senile plaques and the degree of dementia (Perry *et al.*, 1978). The cholinergic pathways linking the nucleus basalis of Meynert to the cerebral cortex, and those linking the septum to the hippocampus are both lost in AD, a finding which has given rise to the possibility that grafting neural tissue to replace the loss of connection might produce an alleviation of cognitive decline (Sinden *et al.*, 1995). This role of the cholinergic system in memory was encouraged by studies in which **scopolamine**, a cholinergic agonist, produced amnesia in healthy individuals. Scopolamine was normally administered with analgesia during surgery; women in labour would report not being able to recall events during the delivery when they were given scopolamine (Thal, 1992). Experiments with healthy individuals indicated impaired non-verbal IQ but not verbal IQ following administration of scopolamine (Drachmann and Leavitt, 1974).

Based on the effects of scopolamine both on neurochemistry and cognition, work began into developing pharmacological treatment which would prolong the action of acetylcholine. One such drug, **physostigmine** appeared to have a significant positive effect on verbal and non-verbal memory when given intravenously (Christie *et al.*, 1981). Oral administration was not as successful (Thal, 1992). A second drug, **tetrahydroaminoacridine**, also appears to produce improvements in verbal memory (Kaye *et al.*, 1982). However, the response to these and other drugs is variable. Thal (1992) suggests that this variability and the lack of success of agents in increasing ACh are owing to a number of factors, among them the fact that some agents are poorly absorbed, do not cross the blood/brain barrier and have severe side-effects. In short, because our understanding of the psychopharmacology of the cholinergic system and of these drugs is poor, psychopharmacological interventions in AD have not been uniformly successful.

In addition to the cholinergic system, other neurotransmitter systems have been implicated in AD. For example 5-HT and noradrenaline neuron markers have been found to be reduced in the cortex of AD patients (Mann *et al.*, 1982), a reduction possibly due to the loss of projections from the dorsal raphe and locus coeruleus to the cortex. Reductions in the concentrations of cortical noradrenaline and the metabolite 3-methoxy-4-hydroxy-phenylglycol have been found in AD patients, especially in the cingulate gyrus. Similarly, amounts of 5-HT and the metabolite 5-hydroxyindoleacic acid have been found to be reduced in AD brains in a large number of other studies (e.g. Gottfries, 1990; Cross *et al.*, 1984). Levels of the neuropeptide somatostatin are reduced in the cortex, although there is little evidence to indicate the loss of other neurotransmitters such as GABA. There is some evidence that markers for glutamate in the frontal and temporal cortices are lost (Cowburn *et al.*, 1990).

◼ Aetiology of Alzheimer's disease

A number of factors are thought to contribute to the cause of AD. These include genetic, environmental, transmissible, metabolic and viral factors.

Environmental agents

Environmental hypotheses argue that the manifestation of AD is the result of some environmental toxin. Aluminium has been thought to be one such toxin because evidence from animal studies suggests that the administration of aluminium results in structures that are similar to the helical filaments of AD tangles. Aluminium has also been found in the tangles and plaques of some AD patients (in the form of aluminosilicates) and the level of aluminium in drinking water has also been associated with AD (Martyn *et al.*, 1989). However, the link is far from clear and other studies have not confirmed its involvement (Markesbery *et al.*, 1981).

Transmissible agents

Transmission models suggest that AD appears because of the transfer of some agent from one organism to another. Diseases such as **Creuzfeldt–Jakob disease**, Gerstmann–Straussler syndrome (a familial disease) and the animal diseases scrapie (sheep and goat disease), milk encephalopathy and bovine spongiform encephalopathy (BSE) are all transmissible diseases. Neuropathological features of these diseases include spongiform brain tissue (due to vacuolation of nerve cells), tangles and plaques and, in humans, dementia. At present, however, there is no evidence for the transmission hypothesis of the aetiology of AD.

Disturbed metabolism

PET studies, as noted above, have shown a reduction in glucose metabolism in frontal, parietal and temporal brain regions in early AD, which may suggest the beginning of neuronal degeneration. Whether the altered metabolism is indicative of neuronal degeneration or whether neuronal degeneration is indicative of altered metabolism, however, is unclear.

Nasal infection

Although most sensory and motor systems are not particularly affected by AD, the olfactory system is an exception. Plaques and tangles are seen in the olfactory bulb and anterior olfactory nucleus (Averback, 1983) and choline acetyltransferase is reduced in the olfactory tubercles of AD patients (Simpson *et al.*, 1984). It has been suggested that the toxic agent may make its way transneuronally along inter-connections from the olfactory bulb to structures such as the amygdala and hippocampus, two structures that are severely affected in AD; the hippocampus is isolated from its inputs and outputs (Strange, 1992). AD patients exhibit marked deficits in olfactory identification and detection (Serby *et al.*, 1992), an impairment which may act as an early diagnostic marker for the disease (see the review by Duncan and Smith, 1995).

It is apparent from these competing models that an understanding of the causes of AD are far from clear. It has been suggested that AD symptoms appear when a threshold of cell death is reached (Roth, 1986). This threshold is reached via a brain insult (leading to cell death) or via accelerated cell death – the most likely scenario (Strange, 1992). One general model of the aetiology of AD is represented in Figure 11.1.

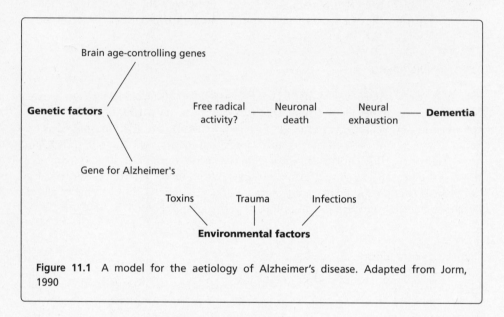

Figure 11.1   A model for the aetiology of Alzheimer's disease. Adapted from Jorm, 1990

Treatment of Alzheimer's disease

No current treatment is able to halt the progress of AD. Those treatments that have been attempted have focused on alleviating the memory impairments in DAT. **Hydergine**, for example, a mixture of ergot alkaloids which alters neurotransmitters, oxygen consumption and blood flow, produces minor improvements in cognitive functioning (Thompson *et al.*, 1990).

Based on the mechanism suggested by the cholinergic hypothesis, **anticholinesterases** which may increase ACh levels (e.g. choline or lecithin) have been used to combat DAT symptoms with, as we have seen, limited success. Nicotine administration also appears to improve attention and information processing but not memory performance (Sahakian *et al.*, 1989). In view of the fact that the cholinergic system is not the only system affected in AD, the lack of success of the 'cholinergic' treatments is not surprising. Perhaps the loss of cortical pyramidal cells is the more important abnormality, a neuropathology which may be alleviated by neural grafts. Current models of neuropathology based on neural grafts are incomplete, largely because experiments have been based on animal models of diseases and partly because degeneration in AD tends to be more widespread than that seen in dementia accompanying other degenerative diseases such as Parkinson's disease. Future studies will help to highlight the long-term value of such grafts, however, and new systematic studies are awaited.

▨ Vascular dementia

Vascular dementia is the second most common form of dementia, accounting for 15–20 per cent of all cases of dementia (Mirsen and Hachinski, 1988).

Neuropathologically, the dementia can arise from ischemia and haemorrhage or from cerebral injury caused by cardiac arrest. **Multi-infarct dementia** results from many small cortical and subcortical infarcts, although the reason for their appearance is unclear. Symptoms have abrupt onset and are a risk factor for vascular diseases. The term multi-infarct dementia has been superseded by the term vascular dementia; both are used synonymously. Features include anterograde and retrograde amnesia, general intellectual decline, evidence of cerebrovascular disease and a fluctuating and stepwise course of symptoms. There is some evidence to indicate that patients with vascular dementia are slower on tests of motor and cognitive speed than are patients with Alzheimer's disease (Almkvist *et al.*, 1993). Infarcts to different regions of the cortex and subcortex are associated with different cognitive symptoms. Treatment of vascular dementia is normally aimed at treating the cause, i.e. stroke. Ticlopidine appears to help prevent cerebrovascular accident and improve the symptoms of dementia (McPherson and Cummings, 1996).

▨ Pick's disease

Pick's disease is characterized by a more insidious onset than AD and an earlier, different symptomatology involving disruption in social behaviour and personality. The effects of the disease have an onset occurring at around late middle life and death occurs 3–12 years following onset. There is no effective treatment.

Typically, the patient displays the ventromedial 'frontal lobe symptoms' described in Chapter 6, hence the alteration in social behaviour and personality. Social disinhibition may occur with a loss of drive as the disease progresses. This is largely attributable to frontal cortex degeneration. Temporal cortex degeneration may also occur in the later stages although the parietal cortex is relatively unimpaired. The frontal lobe symptoms might lead to a misdiagnosis of the disorder as frontal lobe dementia and other dementias with a frontal cortex component. Histologically, however, the disease is characterized by a collection of Pick bodies intracellularly (A.F. Wechsler *et al.*, 1982). Pick bodies, named after their discoverer, are agyrophylic inclusions in abnormal, balloon-shaped neural cells. There is also a proliferation of astrocytes and cell loss. These histological symptoms confirm the diagnosis of Pick's disease.

Behaviourally, however, it is sometimes difficult to distinguish between AD and Pick's disease because, as Pick's disease worsens, the cognitive degeneration is similar. Differences between the two dementias exist, however. Personality and social behaviour alterations are seen first in Pick's disease whereas the initial symptoms of AD are cognitive and memory impairments. Also, parietal functions are impaired in AD but not in Pick's disease. If the patient exhibits the classic frontal lobe characteristics, has asymmetrical frontal or temporal atrophy but normal EEG, Pick's disease is the more likely diagnosis (Whitehouse et al., 1993).

■ Frontal lobe dementia

A separate dementia has been suggested based on frontal lobe degeneration that is unrelated to AD (Brun, 1987). Like Pick's disease, there is temporal or frontal atrophy but frontal lobe dementia is more common than Pick's and has distinct features (Neary and Snowden, 1996). These include disorganized personality and adaptive behaviour which precede cognitive symptoms, deficits in planning and flexibility and memory impairments reflected in poor learning strategy (Sungaila and Crockett, 1993). These patients are also more susceptible to interference, find maintaining sustained attention difficult (Mayes, 1988) and show decreased rCBF in the right and left frontolateral regions which is correlated with global impairment on neuropsychological tests (Elfgren et al., 1996).

■ Lewy body dementia

Lewy body dementia (LBD) or **diffuse Lewy body disease** is characterized, neuropathologically, by the senile plaques and neurofibrillary tangles seen in Alzheimer's disease plus the presence of Lewy bodies. The neuropathological associations with Alzheimer's had led to the dementia being seen as variant of AD (Hansen et al., 1990). The picture is further complicated by the similarities between the neuropsychological symptoms of AD and Lewy body dementia. Both diseases are insidious and progressive and both are characterized by progressive cognitive impairment and early memory loss (D.P. Salmon et al., 1996). This similarity had led to patients with the Lewy body variant of dementia being diagnosed as having AD. However, there is evidence that the two dementias are dissociable.

For example, unlike AD patients, those with Lewy body dementia exhibit extrapyramidal parkinsonian symptoms such as rigidity and bradykinesia, and hallucinations (Perry et al., 1990). Patients also present cognitive symptoms that are not normally seen in AD patients. For example, patients with Lewy body disease have greater impairment in fluency, concentration and visuospatial ability. In a recent study, these patients were compared with AD patients and those with the Lewy body variant of AD (Galasko *et al.*, 1996). Initially, all demented groups showed similar cognitive decline with no significant group differences found for attention, verbal and non-verbal episodic memory and problem-solving. However, greater parkinsonian signs and hallucinations were seen in the Lewy body groups. Furthermore, the Lewy body group performed significantly more poorly than AD patients on tests of visuospatial ability, psychomotor speed and verbal fluency. There is the possibility that the visuospatial deficit is attributable to psychomotor performance rather than visuospatial ability, however, because the nature of these tasks (copy a block, copy a cube, block design) makes demands on manual and motor functions which are already impaired in Lewy body patients.

■ Parkinson's disease and Huntington's chorea

These two motor disorders also result in progressive, demented symptomatology. Parkinsonian patients exhibit memory and visuospatial impairments as well as attentional difficulties. Patients with Huntington's chorea have an impaired ability to maintain attention and concentration and show deficits in executive functioning. Storage and retrieval of memory are difficult and retrograde memory is poor.

■ Subcortical dementia

The term subcortical dementia is a general term reflecting a subcortical cause of dementia. Originally, the dementia was referred to as **progressive supranuclear palsy**. It has symptomatology similar to Parkinson's disease but brainstem degeneration is also involved and its neurofibrillary tangles are short rather than paired and helical (as they are in AD). The disease shares many features with frontal lobe pathology and so may sometimes be referred to as frontosubcortical dementia. In comparison with AD patients, those with subcortical dementia do not exhibit as severe a decline in intellectual function. For example, their recognition memory is better than those with DAT and they can retain information better than DAT patients over long intervals (Helkala *et al.*, 1988).

■ Alcoholic dementia

Alcoholic dementia describes a demented symptomatology resulting from chronic alcoholism and is apparent even after detoxification (Ryan and Butters, 1980). Visuospatial skills are poor but not as poor as verbal skills. Memory, problem-solving and concept formation may also be severely impaired with particularly severe rapid memory loss over time (Salmon *et al.*, 1993).

■ Korsakoff's psychosis

A distinct disorder, separate from alcoholism, is Korsakoff's psychosis or **Korsakoff's syndrome** (Korsakoff, 1889a,b). Korsakoff's psychosis is an alcohol-related organic disorder in which alcohol has been a large source of caloric intake for many years. As we saw in Chapter 4, it is a rare disorder and is caused by thiamine (vitamin B1) deficiency. Damage to the medial diencephalon is common, especially in the dorsomedial nucleus of the thalamus and the mammillary bodies.

The first scientific description of alcohol abuse linked with amnesia was made by Lawson (1878). Lawson described cases of severe loss of recent memory which was sometimes, but not always, associated with alcohol consumption. Korsakoff (1889a,b) reported memory loss in 30 cases of chronic alcohol abuse as well as in 16 patients who had developed a behavioural syndrome for other reasons. In Korsakoff's syndrome, 'the memory of recent events . . . is chiefly disturbed . . . everything that happened during the illness and a short time before' (Korsakoff, 1889a). Recent as well as past memories may be affected. Korsakoff noted that the severity of the deficits varied, with mild cases showing an ability to remember recent memories, if only vaguely. Patients also invented fictions and repeated them. Although different forms of brain pathology may lead to amnesic syndromes, the term Korsakoff's syndrome is used to refer to cases of specific memory impairment which have a specific neuropathology (see below) and results from thiamine deficiency.

Clinical features

Clinical features of the dementia include an inability to encode new information and retain it in long-term memory (Ryan and Butters, 1980; Butters and Cermak, 1980). This impairment affects mainly declarative memory; non-declarative memory is relatively spared (Shimamura *et al.*, 1987; Tulving and Schacter, 1990; Frith *et al.*, 1992). Recognition memory is poor, as is memory for events occurring 20–30 years prior to the disorder (Butters and Stuss, 1989). A point of ambiguity here is whether this information had been lost or was not encoded in the first place. Information lost or unable to be retrieved includes those memories related to public events and autobiographical facts. This and the anterograde amnesia have been attributed to the development of lesions in the dorsomedial nucleus of the thalamus. Victor *et al.* (1971) found extensive atrophy of the dorsomedial nucleus in 38 out of 43 brains they studied.

Performance on span tests is relatively preserved (Kopelman, 1991). Although semantic memory is intact, patients are impaired on verbal fluency tests (Kopelman, 1995), digit/symbol substitution tasks (Glosser *et al.*, 1977; Jacobson *et al.*, 1990), embedded figures tests (Kapur and Butters, 1977) and on tasks requiring the shifting of problem-solving strategies (Oscar-Berman, 1973). These impairments have been attributed to association cortex atrophy (Squire, 1982). There are also impairments in concept formation tests such as the Wisconsin Card Sorting Test (Leng and Parkin, 1988).

Neuropathological features

Arendt *et al.* (1983) reported a reduction of 47 per cent in the nucleus basalis of Meynert (NbM) of patients with Korsakoff's psychosis (compared with 70 per cent loss in AD). No significant loss was noted for chronic alcoholics, schizophrenics or patients with Huntington's chorea. Perhaps the thiamine deficiency combined with heavy alcohol consumption results in the death of cells in the NbM (Butters, 1985). Support for this hypothesis comes from animal studies of thiamine deficiency in which the nutritional deficit results in consistent damage to the dorsomedial nucleus of the thalamus (Irle and Markowitsch, 1982). Further evidence was obtained by Witt and Goldman-Rakic (1983a,b) who observed lesions in the basal ganglia, cerebellum and brainstem nuclei of monkeys with thiamine deficiency.

Other neuropathological features include an enlargement of the third ventricle and widening of the Sylvian fissures and left frontal sulci in Korsakoff patients relative to controls (Shimamura *et al.*, 1988). Chronic alcoholics had structures measuring midway between the Korsakoff patients and controls. Enlarged third ventricles have also been reported by Jacobson and Lishman (1987, 1990). In their study, a comparison of 38 Korsakoff patients with non-Korsakoff alcoholics and controls, larger lateral ventricles and wider interhemispheric fissures were found in Korsakoff patients. Anterior commissure enlargement was correlated with general intellectual decline whereas the third ventricle enlargement was correlated with memory impairment. MRI and PET studies have been largely inconsistent, owing mainly to mixed samples. Some show blood flow reduction in the hypothalamus and basal forebrain (Hata *et al.*, 1987) whereas others show metabolic disruption within anterior brain regions and right posterior white matter (Martin *et al.*, 1992).

Given that some cholinergic disruption may underlie both AD and Korsakoff's psychosis, a similar pattern of memory deficit should be seen in both. Butters *et al.* (1983) reported that although patients with Huntington's chorea (HC) could use language to improve their picture-context recognition memory, AD and Korsakoff patients could not. Furthermore, AD and Korsakoff patients made more perseveration errors than did the patients with Huntington's chorea. On a letter fluency task, patients from each of the clinical groups performed more poorly than controls, but HC patients performed most poorly. The AD and Korsakoff patients, however, were more likely to commit intrusion errors, i.e. including detail that was not in the original passage, during the recall of a passage of prose.

There are other marked differences between the groups in terms of cognitive decline. AD patients may develop constructional apraxia in the early stage of the disease, whereas Korsakoff patients show mild to moderately severe constructional ability. There is little evidence of general language dysfunction in Korsakoff psychosis. Although Korsakoff and AD patients may be equally poor at retrieving episodic memory (learning unrelated words), AD patients are significantly more impaired than Korsakoff patients at retrieving semantic memory (Weingartner *et al.*, 1983).

Dementia associated with infection

Viral dementia

Viral infections such as herpes simplex can cause severe inflammation of brain regions, damaging neurons in the hippocampus and the temporal lobe in particular. Accompanying this inflammation is a mild dementia.

Postinfectious encephalomyelitis

Patients who have suffered from measles, rubella and associated viral infections may show symptoms of dementia which are subsumed under this term. An impaired autoimmune system is thought to be responsible for the underlying neuropathology.

Human immunodeficiency virus type I encephalopathy

HIV infection is associated with gradual cognitive decline and the eventual onset of dementia. Figures vary, but between 20 per cent and 60 per cent of AIDS patients will exhibit dementia by the time they die. Encephalopathy associated with HIV appears in the later stages of AIDS and appears to be responsible for the decline in intellectual performance.

Creutzfeldt–Jakob disease

Creutzfeldt–Jakob disease (CJD) is a rare degenerative disorder affecting one individual in a million per year (Brown, 1980). Recent controversy in the UK regarding the transmissibility of CJD from animals to humans has been fuelled by the increased incidence of the disease in the human population. Clinical features of CJD include a progressive and rapid dementia. Initial symptoms are quite subtle but, once they appear, the progress of the dementia is rapid and unrelenting. The cause of the disorder is neuronal loss and vacuoles in the cytoplasm of neurons and astrocytes. According to Prusiner (1987), this spongiform encephalopathy is caused by prions (infectious particles of protein) which arise from mutations in the prion protein gene.

Miscellaneous causes of dementia

Other diseases and disorders causing dementia include hydrocephalus, which produces confusional states as well as dementia, demyelinating lesions such as those seen in multiple sclerosis, head trauma such as that developed following repeated blows to the head giving rise to post-traumatic dementia (Smith and Kiloh, 1981), neoplasms, and (in very rare cases) epilepsy.

DISCUSSION POINT

Normal and abnormal cognitive decline – the problem of aging

The symptoms of dementia of the Alzheimer type (DAT) can pose problems for diagnosticians because the aging population also exhibits deficits in some aspects in cognitive functioning as well as showing degeneration of some parts of the brain. It might be useful, therefore, to find a way to more clearly describe the differences between the effects of normal aging and the effects of dementia.

By the time that individuals reach 70 years of age, it has been estimated that brain volume is 6 per cent less than that of younger adults (Haug and Eggers, 1991). This reduction is greatest in the frontal cortex (10–17 per cent loss) and striatum (8 per cent loss). The characteristic of this reduction appears to be a shrinkage in neuron size rather than a loss of actual neurons. Again, this reduction in size is more apparent in the prefrontal cortex (West, 1996). Why this should occur is outside the scope of this section, but some researchers have argued that neurons degenerate with age and that dendritic processes become fewer, making the functioning of cell bodies ineffective (Scheibel et al., 1975). As a result, the number of synapses, receptor sites and amounts of neurotransmitters present in the brain declines (Suhara et al. 1991; Goldman-Rakic and Brown, 1981). Perhaps of greater relevance to dementia is the presence of senile plaques in the aging brain (Kubanis and Zornetzer, 1981). These are greatest in the temporal and frontal cortex, which contrasts with the main sites affected in Alzheimer's disease which are the hippo-

⬛➡

campus, locus coeruleus and nucleus basalis and association cortices (Horvath and Davis, 1990).

Further neurophysiological changes with aging are found in rCBF studies. These show that the brain's use of oxygen, as measured by rCBF, declines by up to 27 per cent in some areas in aging individuals (Melamed *et al.*, 1980). Whereas hyper-frontality (increase in frontal rCBF) is characteristic of young and middle-aged individuals, hypofrontality (decline in frontal rCBF) is characteristic of older in-dividuals. It is strange to note that although these changes are seen when the individual is resting, few changes are seen between age groups when individuals perform particular arithmetical, verbal and visuospatial tasks (Gur *et al.*, 1987).

Strange, because decline in cognition is probably the most obvious psychological characteristic of aging. This said, one study has compared young subjects' (26 years old on average) and old subjects' (70 years on average) brain activation during the encoding, recognition and recall of word pairs (Cabeza *et al.*, 1997). It was found that during encoding, young subjects showed greater activation than did the old subjects in the left prefrontal and occipitotemporal region whereas they showed greater right prefrontal and parietal activation during retrieval. In old subjects, there was greater activation in the insula during encoding, the cuneus and precuneus during recognition and the left prefrontal region during recall. Although young subjects showed left frontal activation during encoding and right activation during recall, old subjects showed little frontal activation during encoding and more bilateral activation during recall. The authors suggest that what is happening is the inefficient processing of stimuli, as evidenced by decreases in activation, and overcompensation for this inefficiency, as evidenced by age-related increases in activation.

The focus on memory is important because its impairment may be confused with the symptoms of DAT. There appears to be no decline in sensory memory, short-term memory and remote memory in the elderly, but recall and recognition in long-term memory are significantly impaired (Poon, 1985; Light, 1991). This decline is illustrated in Figure 11.2. The dissociation between deficits on tests of explicit and implicit memory provides further evidence for a multiple systems model of human memory, as discussed in Chapter 4.

Specific deficits have been found in the ability to recall words that were previously presented (Davis *et al.*, 1990). In Davis *et al.*'s study, the over-50s recalled significantly fewer words than did individuals in their 40s or younger. When there was a delay between presentation and recall of stimuli, the over-50s were significantly poorer than they were when recall was immediate. Deficits are also seen on tasks in which individuals have to acquire cognitive skill. For example, with practice, most in-dividuals can learn to complete the Tower of Hanoi task. This task is similar to the Tower of London task described in Chapter 6. In this exercise, individuals must move a series of differently sized rings from one peg to another so that the second set of pegs remains in the same order as the first. Only one ring can be moved at a time and

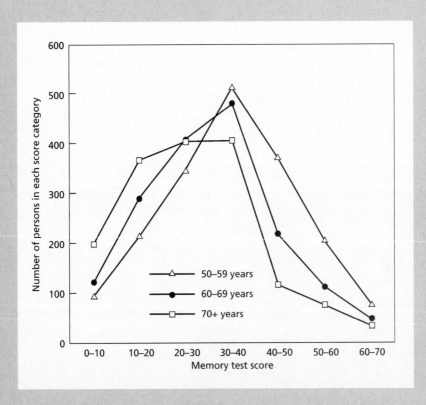

Figure 11.2 Memory test scores for three groups of individuals

a larger ring cannot be placed on a smaller one. The minimum number of moves necessary to complete the task successfully is 31. Older individuals perform significantly more poorly on this task than do the under-40s (Davis and Bernstein, 1992). Individuals in their 70s and 80s make significantly more moves than do those in their 20s and 40s.

However, not all tasks show a decline with aging. Vocabulary, for example, appears to be quite resistant to the effects of advancing age (Rabbitt, 1993), as seen in Figure 11.3. According to Horn and Cattell (1967), this preservation is owing to the fact that vocabulary requires the constant acquisition and continued use of information and is an example of crystallized intelligence which is stable. Tests on which elderly individuals perform poorly are characteristic of fluid intelligence which declines with age. The correlation between vocabulary scores and scores on other cognitive tests tends to decline with age.

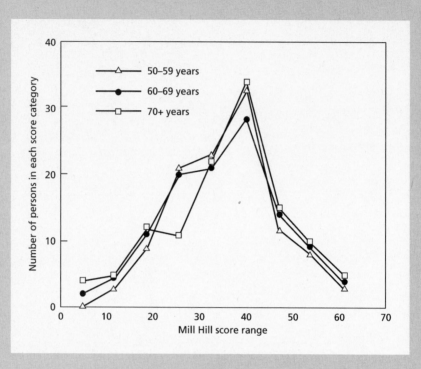

Figure 11.3   Vocabulary scores for three groups of individuals

Are these functional and neural deficits seen in both degenerating and aging brains related? It is known that temporal, parietal and frontal degeneration, especially the association cortices, occurs in AD. The types of deficit seen in AD might result from parietal and temporal association cortex degeneration because these regions integrate sensory information from several modalities. Furthermore, the cognitive and memorial decline seen in AD can be related to the loss of cholinergic cells innervating the cortex and hippocampus. Anticholinergic drugs such as scopolamine bring about deficits in short-term memory in humans; disruption of cholinergic pathways in animals results in deficits in memory tests. Perhaps the cholinergic pathways and their connections allow the formation and retention of new memories.

What is obvious is that the relationships between normal aging and Alzheimer's disease, and cognitive and neural decline are complex. There do, however, appear to be cognitive dissociations between normal and clinical degeneration.

Summary

- [ ] Dementia is a term used to describe a gradual and insidious decline in cognitive function. The diagnosis is complicated by cognitive decline that occurs during normal aging.

- [ ] According to DSM-IV, a diagnosis of dementia requires the patient to exhibit impairment in short- and long-term memory, memory/cognitive impairment that interferes with work, social activities and relationships, and at least one of the following: abstract thinking impairment, impaired judgement, higher cortical function disturbance (aphasia, apraxia, agnosia) or personality change.

- [ ] Alzheimer's disease (AD) is the commonest cause of dementia, and dementia of the Alzheimer type (DAT) is the commonest form of dementia, occurring in approximately 45 per cent of demented patients.

- [ ] There is a familial form of Alzheimer's disease which is autosomal-dominant. The gene is thought to be carried on chromosome 21.

- [ ] The major cognitive symptom of AD is memory loss, especially impaired explicit memory. There is some impairment in remote memory, with evidence that public but not autobiographical memory declines longitudinally. There may be deficits in speech content and comprehension, despite normal reading ability. Reduced visual memory span is common, as are deficits in constructional and drawing ability.

- [ ] There is evidence of shrinkage of the frontal and temporal gyri in AD and there is neuronal loss from the cortex, hippocampus, amygdala, basal forebrain, the locus coeruleus, raphe nuclei and nucleus basalis of Meynert. PET studies indicate parietal and temporal lobe abnormalities.

- [ ] The hallmark characteristics of AD are neurofibrillary tangles, senile plaques, granulovacuolar degeneration and Hirano bodies in various parts of the brain.

- [ ] Loss of synapses appears to be correlated with decline in intellectual function in AD. Particularly important is the loss in cortical acetylcholine, acetylcholinetransferase and nicotinic receptors. Cholinergic pathways linking the nucleus basalis of Meynert with the cortex are lost.

- [ ] Scopolamine, a cholinergic agonist, produces memory loss when administered to healthy individuals. Pharmacological interventions have thus focused on prolonging the action of acetylcholine. Results of this treatment are mixed. Other neurotransmitter systems involved include the serotonin and noradrenaline neurotransmitter systems.

⇒

□ The causes of AD are unknown. Possible causes have included environmental toxins such as aluminium, some transmissible agent, disturbed metabolism and nasal infection.

□ Other major causes of dementia include Pick's disease, frontal lobe dysfunction, diffuse Lewy body disease, Parkinson's disease, Huntington's chorea, subcortical dysfunction, alcoholism, Korsakoff's psychosis, cerebrovascular accident, infection, Creutzfeldt–Jakob disease and various neurological complaints.

□ Pick's disease is characterized by marked changes in social behaviour and personality although cognitive symptoms are similar to those seen in AD. Frontal lobe dementia is characterized neuropathologically by temporal and frontal atrophy and behaviourally by poor planning ability and adaptation. Diffuse Lewy body disease has initial symptoms similar to AD but is also characterized by parkinsonian signs, hallucinations and deficits in verbal fluency and, possibly, visuospatial ability. Subcortical dementia, previously known as progressive supranuclear palsy, has symptoms similar to Parkinson's disease and shares many features of frontal lobe dementia. It is thus sometimes referred to as frontosubcortical dementia.

□ Distinct from alcoholic dementia, Korsakoff's dementia is an alcohol-related disorder characterized by thiamine deficiency and lesions to the medial diencephalon, especially the dorsomedial nucleus of the thalamus, the mammillary bodies and nucleus basalis of Meynert. Various memory impairments are seen, especially in declarative memory. Recognition memory is poor, as is memory for events occurring 20–30 years prior to the onset of the disorder.

□ Vascular dementia is the second most common form of dementia and results from some cerebrovascular accident. One example is multi-infarct dementia which is characterized by anterograde and retrograde amnesia and a fluctuating course of symptoms.

□ Aging is accompanied by many changes in neurophysiology and cognition, including a reduction in the size of neurons, especially in the prefrontal cortex, a decline in the brain's oxygen use and an impairment in explicit memory. The brain areas affected in aging appear to be different from those affected in AD.

Recommended further general and specific reading

Key: (1) = introductory, (3) = intermediate, (5) = advanced

General

Jorm, A.F. (1990). *The Epidemiology of Alzheimer's Disease and Related Disorders*. London: Chapman and Hall. *(3)*

Miller, E. and Morris, R.G. (1993). *The Psychology of Dementia*. Chichester: Wiley. *(3)*

Parks, R.W., Zec, R.F. and Wilson, R.S. (1993). *Neuropsychology of Alzheimer's Disease and Other Dementias*. Oxford: Oxford University Press. *(3)*

Sagar, H.J. and Ackermann, H. (1996). Dementia. In T. Brandt, L.R. Caplan, J. Dichgans, H.C. Diener and C. Kennard (eds), *Neurological Disorders: Course and treatment*. New York: Academic Press. *(3)*

Whitehouse, P.J., Lerner, A. and Hedera, P. (1993). Dementia. In K.M. Heilman and E. Valenstein (eds), *Clinical Neuropsychology* (3rd edition). New York: Oxford University Press. *(3)*

Specific

Black, S.E. (1996). Focal cortical atrophy syndromes. *Brain and Cognition*, **31**, 188–229. *(3)*

Darvesh, S. and Freedman, M. (1996). Subcortical dementia: a neurobehavioural approach. *Brain and Cognition*, **31**, 230–49. *(3)*

Forstl, H., Besthorn, C., Hentschel, F., Geiger-Kabisch, C., Sattel, H. and Schreiter-Gasse, U. (1996). *Dementia*, **7**, 27–34. *(3)*

Galasko, D., Katzman, R., Salmon, D.P. and Hansen, L. (1996). Clinical and neuropathological findings in Lewy body dementias. *Brain and Cognition*, **31**, 166–75. *(3)*

Greene, J.D.W. and Hodges, J.R. (1996). Identification of famous faces and famous names in early Alzheimer's disease. *Brain*, **119**, 111–28. *(3)*

Greene, J.D.W. and Hodges, J.R. (1996). Identification of remote memory: evidence from a longitudinal study of dementia of Alzheimer type. *Brain*, **119**, 129–42. *(3)*

Hardy, J. (1997). Amyloid, the resenilins and Alzheimer's disease. *Trends in Neurosciences*, **20**(4), 154–9. *(5)*

Iyo, M., Namba, H., Fukushi, K., Shinotoh, H., Nagatsuka, S., Suhara, T., Sudo, Y., Suzuki, K. and Irie, T. (1997). Measurement of acetylcholinesterase by positron emission tomography in the brains of healthy controls and patients with Alzheimer's disease. *Lancet*, **349**, 1805–9. *(4)*

Katzman, R. and Jackson, J.E. (1991). Alzheimer's disease: basic and clinical advances. *Journal of the American Geriatrics Society*, **39**, 516–25. *(4)*

Kopelman, M.D. (1995). The Korsakoff syndrome. *British Journal of Psychiatry*, **166**, 154–73. *(3)*

Kramer, J.H. and Duffy, J.M. (1996). Aphasia, apraxia and agnosia in the diagnosis of dementia. *Dementia*, **7**, 23–6. *(3)*

McPherson, S.E. and Cummings, J.L. (1996). Neuropsychological aspects of vascular dementia. *Brain and Cognition*, **31**, 269–82. (3)

Murdoch, B.E., Chenery, H.J., Wilks, V. and Boyle, R.S. (1987). Language disorders in dementia of the Alzheimer type. *Brain and Language*, **31**, 122–37. *(3)*

Rabbitt, P. (1993). Does it all go together when it goes? *Quarterly Journal of Experimental Psychology*, **46A**(3), 385–434. *(2)*

Rasmusson, D.X., Carson, K.A., Brookmeyer, R., Kawas, C. and Brandt, J. (1996). Predicting rate of cognitive decline in probable Alzheimer's disease. *Brain and Cognition*, **31**, 133–47. *(3)*

Sano, M., Ernesto, C., Thomas, R.G., Klauber, M.R., Scafer, K., Grundman, M., Woodbury, P., Growdon, J., Cotman, C.W., Pfeiffer, E., Schneider, L.S. and Thal, L.J. (1997). A controlled trial of selegiline, alpha-tocopherol, or both as treatment for Alzheimer's disease. *New England Journal of Medicine*, 24 April, 1216–22. *(4)*

Stuss, D.T. and Levine, B. (1996). The dementias: nosological and clinical factors related to diagnosis. *Brain and Cognition*, **31**, 99–113. *(2)*

Van Hoesen, G.W. (1990). The dissection by Alzheimer's disease of cortical and limbic neural systems relevant to memory. In J.L. McGeogh, N.M. Weinberger and G. Lynch (eds), *Brain Organization and Memory*. New York: Oxford University Press. *(4)*

West, R.L. (1996). An application of prefrontal cortex function theory to cognitive aging. *Psychological Bulletin*, **120**(2), 272–92. *(3)*

Chapter Twelve

Development and recovery of function

■ Development and recovery: an introduction

One of the most intriguing questions in neuropsychology concerns whether the young damaged brain recovers its function better than the adult damaged brain. Tied to this conundrum is the question of how function develops and how this functional development is related to changes in the brain's structure and activity. There are several problems encountered in attempting to solve these problems. The principal problem is that immature brains and adult brains are functionally incomparable. Because adult brains will already have been exposed to a multitude of environmental influences, from visual stimuli to speech, they are already functioning at a fairly sophisticated level. This incomparability in function suggests that the effect of damage seen in children and adults may not be comparable (St James-Roberts, 1981). The young child's brain is also a developing brain and there is evidence of a series of brain **growth spurts** which makes comparing recovery even of children of different ages problematic. According to Epstein (1978), these spurts do not develop in a linear fashion but fairly inter-mittently at between 3–10 months and 18 months, 2 and 4 years, 6 and 8 years, 10 and 12 years, and 14 and 16 years.

Brain damage may go unnoticed in the immature brain because other brain areas may compensate for the damaged region. Furthermore, as Kertesz (1987) notes, aphasia in children is normally due to trauma or infection, whereas aphasia in adults commonly results from stroke. There are, therefore, problems in clearly quantifying the developmental effects of brain damage. This chapter considers some of these problems in the context of the mechanisms of brain growth in children and adults and of the development of function. Recovery of function is also an important neuropsychological topic, as is the implementation of a pro-gramme of treatment that will facilitate that recovery. Both of these topics are considered in later sections.

■ Neural characteristics of development

The human neonatal brain weighs about 350 grams. By the time it reaches young adulthood, this weight has increased to around 1200–1400 grams. By the age of 2 years, the brain will have reached approximately 75 per cent of its adult weight (Carmichael, 1990). See Figure 12.1.

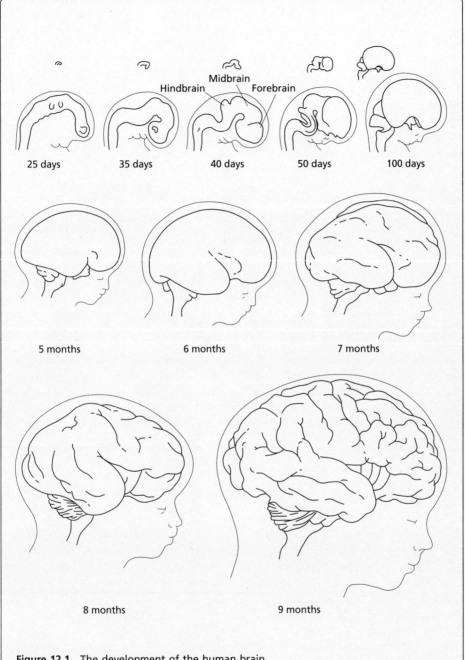

Figure 12.1 The development of the human brain

This increase in weight occurs despite the fact that humans are born with all the neurons they will ever get. The growth that is seen in the first two decades of life after birth is attributable to the growth of neurons, the development of inter-connections between them and the extensive development of glial cells and the myelination of axons, as seen in Figures 12.2 and 12.3.

The growth of neurons is particularly important because, as we saw in Chapter 11, aging is associated with the shrinkage in the cell bodies of neurons, a finding which might be correlated with reduced cognitive and motor functioning in elderly individuals. In addition to neuron growth in the early stages of develop-ment, the brain is also thought to undergo some removal of its connective tissue. Processes such as dendrites, for example, may die or reduce in number. This is called **pruning**. This pruning may also be related to a reduction in connections between cells. One theory argues that we develop an excess of synapses which are pruned with age because we utilize only some of them; others are redundant. This has been referred to as 'neural Darwinism', the notion that the fittest of synapses will survive whereas the superfluous and unnecessary disappear (Edelman, 1989).

The brain exhibits some fairly reliable characteristics of growth during its development. These include **cell migration**, **axonal growth**, **dendrite formation**, **synaptic formation** and **myelination**. As neurons migrate to their respective destinations, their axons sprout in a particular direction. The growing end of the axon is called the growth cone and can traverse large distances in the brain in order to reach its desired target. The mechanism responsible for this process is unknown. Axonal growth and extension can be disrupted by blockage resulting from head trauma, poisoning, malnutrition, axonal damage or other factors. When axons are damaged, they might degenerate or move to an inappropriate target. If they do reach inappropriate targets, then the function subsumed by the invaded area may be disrupted.

The formation of dendrites begins in earnest after cells have migrated and settled and is timed so that dendrites meet the axons innervating them. Prenatally, there are few dendritic spines; postnatally, they burgeon. It is, in fact, the loss of these abundant dendrites and their dendritic branches which represents the pruning referred to above. In cases of mental retardation, dendrites may be thinner than normal and have fewer spines or have small spines with short stalks. Complement-ing the dendritic pruning is **synaptic shedding**. Up to the age of 2 years there is a steady increase in the number of synapses in the young brain. By the time that the brain reaches adulthood, however, up to 50 per cent of these synapses may have been shed. Synapses are made in specific cells in a region – a process which may be genetically engineered or which may be due to the orientation of cells or by the timing of the arrival of axons.

Successful myelination, as we saw in Chapter 3, indicates successful structural maturation of the brain. Myelin insulates certain nerve fibers, particularly axons, and neurons are thought to reach maturity when myelination is complete. The process of myelination is thought to begin postnatally, continues to 15 years and

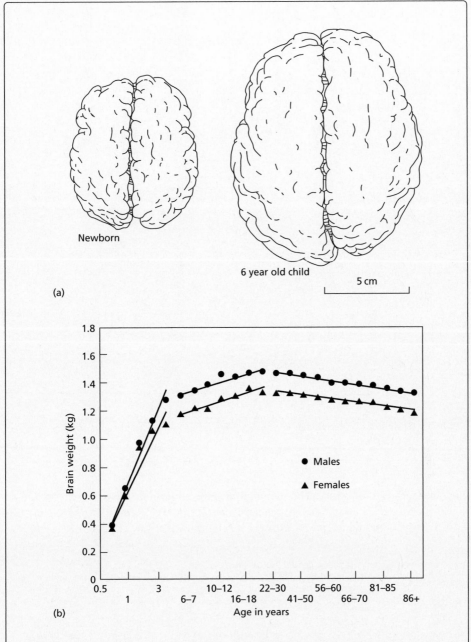

Figure 12.2 Comparison of the size (a) and weight (b) of the human brain during development

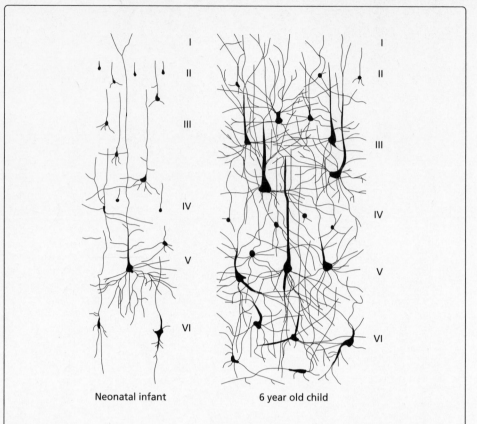

Neonatal infant   6 year old child

Figure 12.3 The burgeoning of connections between neurons and their processes from birth to 6 years

may extend up to 60 years. The primary sensory and motor areas, however, appear to be partly myelinated during prenatal development. More information on this and the mechanisms of neural growth can be found in Levitt (1995).

Structural development: MRI evidence

Recent MRI studies have described some of the structural asymmetries that appear during development. In one study, 85 normal children and adolescents whose ages ranged from 5 to 17 years of age showed clear age and sex differences in brain asymmetry (Reiss *et al.*, 1996). For example, the total brain volume for boys was found to be 10 per cent larger than that for girls, a finding that was attributable to

⟫

increased cortical grey matter in boys. The degree of structural asymmetry, however, was similar for boys and girls. Both showed a rightward asymmetry for cortical and subcortical grey matter and left asymmetry for cerebrospinal fluid. These authors also found a significant positive correlation between total brain volume, especially the amount of grey matter in the prefrontal cortex, and IQ.

Similar findings have been reported by Giedd et al. (1996). Larger cerebral volume as well as cerebellar volume was found in boys than girls. Their sample of 104 healthy 4–18 years olds also showed a larger globus pallidus and putamen in boys and a larger caudate nucleus in girls. The size of the putamen decreased with age. In both sexes, the left lateral ventricles and putamen were larger than the right, which is compatible with the left, asymmetrical CSF volume in seen in Reiss et al.'s (1996) study. In general, the right hemisphere was larger than the left, although there was considerable variability in the data. This final observation invokes a cautionary warning and one that was mentioned in Chapter 1 when the advantages and disadvantages of brain imaging techniques were discussed: no two brains are exactly alike; positioning of structures shows tremendous variability between individuals even though gross position can be described quite efficiently. However, it is important to acknowledge this degree of variability. Both studies are valuable, however, because studies of cerebral development in children are rarely undertaken. Giedd et al. draw attention to the fact that of the 483 brains in the Yakolev brain collection housed in Washington DC, only 12 are from individuals who were aged between 4 and 18 years.

■ Effect of environment on brain development

The nervous system is governed by the environment in which it functions. Stimuli from the external environment help to shape the development of the brain and can help to alter the efficiency of synaptic machinery. This modulation and stimulation of neuronal growth is an important characteristic of brain development. Much of the work in this area has involved depriving animals of environmental stimulation in the first few days of life and examining the effects of this deprivation on subsequent behaviour and brain development. In one non-experimental human study, Skeels (1966) reported that children removed from orphanages and placed in mental institutions developed normal intelligence whereas those remaining showed evidence of intellectual retardation. The explanation for this difference was that those who had been removed had been exposed to a more intellectually rich environment that would stimulate brain activity. The precise mechanism by which the stimulation works, however, is unclear. Several alternative explanations are available: (1) the brain can develop autonomously but requires environmental stimulation to function at an efficient level; (2) the brain develops autonomously until it reaches a point at which it requires stimulation for further development or, (3) the nervous system does not develop all that autonomously but must receive continued stimulation. All these hypotheses are based on the concept of **functional validation**, the notion that the nervous system requires stimulation during its development in order to become fully functional.

Animal studies suggest that the more enriched the environment during brain development, the greater the brain size, especially the neocortex and occipital neocortex (Kolb and Whishaw, 1989). Exposure to an enriched environment is also associated with an increase in glial cells, synaptic spines and synapse size. These changes occur more readily early in life although similar but less dramatic changes may be seen with later stimulation.

One of the most well researched areas of brain development in animals has been the development of the visual system. When animals are visually and binocularly deprived by being reared in the dark or having both eyelids sutured, 70 per cent of the visual cortex cells have disturbed protein synthesis and fewer/shorter dendrites, whereas deprivation later in development does not produce cell abnormalities. **Monocular deprivation**, in which a sutured eye will in effect be blind in the few weeks after opening, has long-term effects on normal vision. The earlier the deprivation, the shorter the time needed to bring about the visual abnormalities and the more severe these abnormalities become. There may also be a degree of competition between functioning eyes. An animal with one eye visually deprived for 5 months will show 31 per cent cell response rate when the normal eye is removed, but only 6 per cent when the normal eye is present (Kratz *et al.*, 1976).

■ Development of functional asymmetry

The MRI evidence above suggests that the brain develops in an asymmetrical fashion during childhood. There is also evidence to suggest that specific psychological functions are also characterized by milestones in the child's life: functional asymmetry only develops up to, and is complete before, a particular age. In 1967, Lenneberg in his well known book, *The Biological Foundations of Language*, argued that functional lateralization of language begins at the same time as the child begins to acquire language and is complete at puberty. This conclusion was based on an earlier study showing that in half a sample of children with right or left brain lesions, language was delayed if the lesion occurred in the first two years of life. The other half of the sample developed language normally (Basser, 1962). In adults and adolescents, language difficulties were associated with left hemisphere lesions whereas mild language difficulties were associated with right hemisphere lesions. Lenneberg thus argued that there was a sensitive period during which language should be acquired and lateralization would develop.

These lateralization milestones, however, were challenged by Krashen (1973) who argued that the hemispheres of the brain are equipotential at birth, that is, each hemisphere is capable of undertaking the function for which the other becomes specialized. According to Krashen, the critical period for lateralization is complete by the age of 5 or 6 years. If lesions to the right hemisphere occur before the age of 5, the child will show aphasic symptoms. If damage occurs after the age of 5, no deficits in speech arise, suggesting that the normal left-for-language functional asymmetry had developed and was relatively complete. Krashen was also involved in the study of an unusual case in which a young girl had been deprived of auditory stimulation and failed to develop normal language. This case is returned to in the discussion point.

The brain lesion and development literature tends to favour one of these hypotheses. In a series of famous experiments, Dennis and Whitaker (1977) and Woods (1980) found that the incidence of aphasia following right hemisphere lesions was greater during infancy than if the lesions had occurred later in life. A more specific timeframe was suggested by Riva and Cazzamiga (1986) who found that language difficulties arose if damage occurred before the age of 1 year regardless of the hemisphere damaged, but only left hemisphere damage was associated with these difficulties if lesions occurred after the age of 1 year. Other authors suggest that left hemisphere lesions would produce the greatest deficits in language and speech if they occurred after the age of 5 or 6 years (Vargha-Khadem et al., 1985).

Another source of data suggesting a critical period for the development of asymmetry is found in studies of hemispherectomy, where one hemisphere is removed for medical reasons, usually because of the growth of a large tumour. In adults, left hemispherectomies are reliably associated with aphasia which is frequently severe (Gott, 1973; Searleman, 1977). Left hemispherectomies in children, however, are associated with almost complete recovery of language function (Searleman, 1977). Non-invasive studies indicate similar developmental patterns of functional asymmetry. For example, dichotic listening studies have shown that the typical right ear advantage for words increases with increasing age (Bryden and Allard, 1978), especially between the ages of 5 and 13 years (Berlin et al., 1973). There also appears to be a difference in the development of asymmetry for different types of auditory stimulus so that a right ear advantage for the sounds of digits are seen from the age of 4 years (Kimura, 1963) whereas the typical left ear advantage for the perception of the emotional intonation of sounds becomes apparent at the age of 5 years (Saxby and Bryden, 1984). The superior right visual field perception of verbal stimuli also occurs at around the age of 4 or 5, with the usual left visual field superiority for facial expression appearing at between the ages of 5 and 8 years (Broman, 1978; Witelson, 1977). ERPs on the left are also larger than those on the right when children process language (Segalowitz and Berge, 1995).

Given that this evidence suggests that the development of functional asymmetry is fairly complete by the age of 5 or 6 years – supporting Krashen's hypothesis –

what can we make of the development of other asymmetries that are non-linguistic in nature? Is there evidence of functional lateralization at birth? This question has been prompted and partly answered by a series of different studies in which babies were found to turn their heads more to the right (Turkewitz, 1988). Infants were also more likely to reach with the left hand and grasp with the right, the typical hand asymmetry seen in right-handed adults (Ramsay, 1980). This asymmetry has been seen in infants as young as 2 months (Caplan and Kinsbourne, 1976). An unusual interaction exists between the child's and mother's behavioural asymmetry: it appears that mothers prefer to cradle their babies in the left arm (Sieratzki and Woll, 1996), a finding that the authors attribute to the mother's preference for perceiving the baby's emotional expression via input to the left visual field. This information, the theory argues, is relayed to the right hemisphere, the hemisphere specialized for the perception of emotion. This explanation has not gone unchallenged, however, and lively discussions can be found in Zaidel (1996) and Turnbull and Matheson (1996).

Age also plays a significant role in the development of concept formation, a function commonly characterized as a frontal lobe specialization. There are complicated developmental issues involved in the improvement (or deterioration) of performance in frontal lobe patients because these regions develop slowly, although they are probably functional by puberty (Luria, 1973). Levin et al. (1991) compared performance of children of various ages on 'frontal lobe tests', such as the Wisconsin Card Sorting Test (WCST), word fluency, the Tower of London task, the Delayed Alternation task and a go/no go task. The latter task involves responding with a button when one sees a particular set of stimuli (red squares) but inhibiting a response when confronted with a different set (blue squares). The Delayed Alternation task involves identifying in which of two drawers the examiner has hidden a coin (Freedman and Oscar-Berman, 1986). If the subject identifies the correct drawer the examiner moves the coin to the other drawer and the task recommences. The coin remains in the same drawer if the subject makes an incorrect response.

Levin et al. tested three groups of children: 8–9 year olds, 9–12 year olds and 13–15 year olds. Apart from the Delayed Alternation task, developmental changes were seen in all neuropsychological tests. The most marked improvements were seen between the ages of 7–8 and 9–12 years for the WCST and the go/no go task, confirming previous studies' findings of improvement on the WCST within approximately the same age band (Chelune and Baer, 1986). Improvements up to the age of 15 were found for the Tower of London task. The authors conclude that damage to the frontal cortex in children older than 8 years will lead to impairment on frontal lobe tests, i.e. those measuring concept formation, planning and strategy-shifting.

> ### Does bilingualism develop asymmetrically?
>
> Just as the development of a first language is thought to be left-hemisphere based, so similar suggestions have been made regarding the development of a second language. However, the right hemisphere appears to be more important in the development of a second language because it may undertake the function of pattern recognition (Obler, 1979). This may be one reason why bilinguals with right hemisphere lesions show a greater degree of aphasia than do bilinguals with left hemisphere lesions (Hakuta, 1986).
>
> To determine whether a critical period exists for the development of a second language, Johnson and Newport (1989) compared the English proficiency achieved by Korean and Chinese speakers who had arrived in the USA between the ages of 3 and 39 years and had lived in that country between the ages of 3 and 26. The proficiency of these individuals was correlated with time of arrival and was correlated with age before puberty. Those arriving early clearly showed greater proficiency than those who had arrived later. This correlation between age at arrival and performance was evidenced on every measure of English proficiency administered and suggests that the critical period for the acquisition of a second language is similar to that for a first language.

Maturational gradient

According to Best (1988), functional asymmetries such as those reviewed above develop because brain development occurs in a particular gradient, from anterior to posterior. The effect of this development is that the right frontal lobe will develop sooner than the left frontal lobe. We saw in the Chapter 4 that some neuroanatomical asymmetries are observed even in the foetal brain. Best argues that because the major fissures in the right hemisphere develop at least two weeks before those in the left, then right hemisphere function should be first to be clearly observed. This hypothesis is based on data indicating that left ear advantage for music occurs earlier than the right ear advantage for language (Best *et al.*, 1982). This is not surprising, Best argues, because emotional intonation tends to occur before the production of meaningful speech in babies.

A similar but different maturational gradient model has been suggested by Corballis and Morgan (1978). These authors argue that this gradient shows a left hemisphere advantage. The issues surrounding the asymmetrical development of the brain and function are complicated and these hypotheses generate very general statements regarding the direction in which development occurs. It seems likely that the newer, non-invasive brain imaging techniques such as functional magnetic resonance imaging (fMRI) might shed greater illumination on this problem, thus complementing the early invasive studies of brain lesions in infants and children.

■ Processes involved in recovery

According to Kertesz (1993), recovery following brain injury comprises two stages. In the first stage, the brain recovers from the effects of metabolic and membrane failure, neurotransmission impairments, haemorrhage and edema (swelling of tissue following injury). Management of the damage is directed towards controlling the edema. There is also a certain degree of axonal regeneration occurring immediately after the injury, with new connections developing to replace the old.

The second stage occurs months and even years later, as the brain reorganizes itself: axons regrow, new collaterals sprout, other regions compensate for the loss of the damaged region, areas surrounding the damage as well as subcortical structures connected to the damaged region help to compensate for the loss. It is this second stage which reflects the patient's functional recovery.

■ Recovery from aphasia

The most widely studied example of recovery following cerebral injury is recovery from aphasia. Recovery of function is dependent on a large number of variables including the type of insult giving rise to the aphasia, the age of the patient, the extent of the lesion, the type of aphasia elicited and patient characteristics such as personality. Most jargon and global aphasia, for example, appears to result from ruptured middle cerebral artery aneurysms (Kertesz, 1993). Broca's aphasia or expressive aphasia appears to show the best recovery of all the aphasias (Kertesz and McCabe, 1977). In one study, the recovery rates of different types of aphasia were compared (Kertesz and Poole, 1974). Global aphasics continued to show severe impairment at follow-up; Wernicke's aphasics continued to use jargon and were characterized by anomia; Broca's aphasics showed a fair to good recovery, whereas conduction and transcortical aphasics showed the most complete recovery. After a period of one year, 40 per cent of the 47 aphasics had made a good recovery, with 19 per cent showing a fair recovery.

■ Variables affecting recovery from aphasia

The time course for recovery of function is thought to begin in the first two weeks following injury. Greatest recovery is seen in the first few months with little significant recovery seen after six months and no spontaneous recovery occurring after one year (Kertesz and McCabe, 1977). It has been hypothesized that recovery from brain lesions will be better if the patient is young, left-handed, female and intelligent since any or all of these variables may affect the result of brain damage.

Age is the variable that has drawn most attention, not least because of evidence from the studies reviewed above.

Age

The general assumption in developmental neuropsychology has been that the younger the patient, the better the recovery following brain damage (Vignolo, 1964). Recovery from aphasia is superior in children if the brain damage occurs before the age of 10–12 years (Hecaen, 1976). The conventional view of recovery suggests that there are three important periods in recovery: before 1 year of age, 1–5 years, and over 5 years. Lesions before 5 years allow recovery of language function, for example, but those after 5 years do not. Alajouanine and Lhermitte (1965) reported difficulties in reading, writing and speaking in half of a sample of thirty-two 6–15 year old children with aphasia. One-third of the sample recovered spontaneous language six months after recovery although others also improved slightly. One year following the onset of damage, 24 out of 32 had normal or fairly normal language whereas 14 continued to show evidence of dysgraphia. Similarly, Woods and Carey (1979) examined the recovery of function in 27 patients who sustained left hemisphere lesions before 1 year of age or at a later age (a mean age of 6 years). Patients were examined ten years or more after injury. Of the eight language tests administered to the patients, only one test (spelling) was impaired in the early lesion patients (compared with normal controls). For later lesion patients, six out of the eight tests (including sentence completion and picture naming) were poorly performed. The two groups showed a similar verbal IQ which indicates that the general level of intelligence of the two groups did not account for the language impairments.

In an older sample of soldiers who had sustained brain damage, lesions occurring at 17–20 years of age were associated with better functional recovery than those occurring at 21–25 years (Teuber, 1975). The latter group, in turn, recovered better than did a group comprising those aged 26 or older. Patients in their 40s and over did not recover as well from posterior temporal speech zone damage as did their younger counterparts.

In an extensive study of 50 patients with pre- or postnatal, left or right hemisphere brain damage, Woods and Teuber (1978) concluded that language survives left-sided damage and argued that this was attributable to right hemisphere compensation. This compensation may occur at the expense of the right hemisphere's visuospatial ability (right-sided lesions produced similar deficits in childhood and adulthood). Woods (1987) has also reported that some functions do not recover. There are deficits in speech-shadowing after left and right lesions in childhood and in adulthood, although speech is spared considerably after early left hemisphere lesions. Younger, however, is not always better, as witnessed in experiments in which rats given frontal cortex lesions at 1 day and 5 days after birth were retarded in task performance in adulthood. Rats with the cortex removed at 10 days performed within the range of control animals (Kolb and Whishaw, 1989). These results, however, seem inconsistent with the human literature.

Handedness

Handedness is thought to be an important variable in recovery of function because left-handers recover more efficiently from brain lesions than do right-handers (Subirana, 1969). Presumably, this is because left-handers' language functions are not as clearly or as conventionally lateralized as those of right-handers. There is also evidence to suggest that left-handers are more likely to exhibit aphasia regardless of the hemisphere damaged (Gloning et al., 1969). Global aphasics who do not have the typical asymmetry of language function also appear to recover better than those with typical asymmetry (Pieniadz et al., 1983) although these results have not been confirmed (Kertesz, 1988).

Severity of aphasia

The severity of the initial impairment is sometimes overlooked in studies of recovery. It is certainly an important variable because if groups of patients are to be compared, they must be initially matched for the severity of their impairment. Severity is a good predictor of later recovery, with severe deficits predicting poor recovery and mild deficits predicting almost complete recovery (Gloning et al., 1976).

Type of language function

Different types of language function are likely to recover at different rates and to a different degree than others. For example, impairments in naming, oral imitation and comprehension of nouns appear to be the most long-lasting (Kreindler and Fradis, 1968). Comprehension, however, recovers more efficiently than expressive speech in Broca's aphasia (Kenin and Swisher, 1972). Other studies have shown better recovery of grammar and sentence production (Ludlow, 1977).

Lesion site

The degree of functional recovery seen following brain injury depends on the part of the brain that is damaged and the extent of this damage (Knopman et al., 1983). Language is a function that is subserved by many different structures, for example, so that damage to one part may not produce the protracted recovery observed following damage to several parts (Kertesz, 1988). In Wernicke's aphasia, the second temporal gyrus, insula and the supramarginal gyrus which surrounds the superior temporal region are important regions which, if damaged singly, do not affect languages as severely as when they are all damaged (Kertesz *et al.*, 1989).

Other variables

Other variables thought to influence recovery are the level of the individual's preinjury intelligence, health and social status (Darley, 1972). Some studies, however, show no effect of these factors on recovery (Keenan and Brassel, 1974). Studies of recovery following head injury have been criticized on methodological grounds. Oddy (1993), for example, argues that a major problem in studies of recovery is the lack of well designed, well controlled follow-up studies. In a review of head injury recovery in children, he concludes that children with mild to moderate injuries make excellent recovery with few detrimental long-term behavioural consequences. However, he cautions that some cognitive and person-ality changes may have gone unnoticed owing to design faults in previous studies.

▪ Recovery from other disorders: spatial neglect, visual agnosia and memory impairment

Unilateral spatial neglect can occur up to three to six months and even years after the brain injury that was associated with it (Campbell and Oxbury, 1976). Some-times the neglect disappears but visuospatial deficits remain. Prognosis is often poor and is compounded by the patient's anosagnosia. The recovery of visual agnosics is also variable (Kertesz, 1979). Memory deficits are probably the most persistent deficits of amnesia which has followed brain damage. Recovery of function is impossible in patients with Korsakoff's psychosis and Alzheimer's disease. Persistent amnesia is also seen following bilateral posterior cerebral artery.

▪ Sparing of function: some mechanisms

In the above sections we reviewed how damage to the brain early in life can produce severe deficits in linguistic function if lesions occurred after a certain age. If lesions occurred before that time, language developed normally. Earliest system-atic, experimental studies of the recovery of function date back to the beginning of the century and the pioneering studies of Margaret Kennard. Kennard observed that unilateral motor cortex lesions in monkeys produced much more severe abnormalities in adults than in infants (Kennard, 1936, 1940, 1942). This **sparing** of function in youth became known as the **Kennard principle**. This principle encapsulates the general belief that early damage is better than late damage. However, in certain examples, early damage results in severe problems. Speech, for example, may survive early damage but aspects of language processing such as syntax may not.

Recovery of function following brain damage can present problems for an advocate of localization of function because if an unrelated area of the brain can compensate for a damaged area, then surely this argues against localization of function? Flourens (1824) and later Lashley (1938), for example, argued that it was not the specific area of the cortex that was damaged that was important to loss of function, it was the amount of cortex damaged. Some areas, however, would need to remain intact for function to be adequate and an example of this type of cortex would be the primary visual area.

The theory of equipotentiality may explain why early damage to either hemisphere (if it is not too severe) produces no severe long-term consequence in language ability but it does not explain why damage in young adulthood and beyond produces such severe impairments in language. An alternative view argues that there are redundant parts of the cortex which can be summoned for use if another part is damaged. This is called **vicarious functioning** (Fritsch and Hitzig, 1870; Munk, 1881), so called because the undamaged cortex subserves the lost function vicariously. In an excellent test of this hypothesis, Bucy (1934) performed a series of reverse ablations, destroying those regions that were thought to undertake the function of a damaged part of the cortex. He found that these lesions resulted in no lasting impairment, indicating that these regions were not essential for normal functioning. Other theories of recovery of function are considered below.

Three basic hypotheses explain the sparing of function observed following early brain damage. The **invariance hypothesis** argues that the left hemisphere shows language specialization at birth and that the right must take over responsibility for language function if the language areas of the left hemisphere are damaged. The second hypothesis, the **maturation hypothesis**, argues that both hemispheres are involved in language and non-language functions at an early stage but that the left becomes dominant for language. Lenneberg (1967) argued that lateralization of function develops relatively quickly between the ages of 2 and 3–5 years and continues to develop until puberty at which point lateralization is almost complete. He cites the evidence reviewed above which suggests that aphasia between the ages of 3 and 10 years is recoverable because the hemispheres are still not fully lateralized. One hemisphere may then still undertake the function of the other. After the age of 10, recovery would be difficult and after 14, would be poor.

Evidence against right hemisphere acquisition of language ability was reported by Rasmussen and Milner (1975). They found that left hemisphere lesions after the age of 5 years did not change speech. They argued that after the age of 6, language

ability does not transfer to the right hemisphere but is reorganized intrahemispherically with undamaged left hemisphere areas undertaking the function impaired by damage to another left hemisphere region. Woods (1980) similarly
reported that left hemisphere lesions before the age of 1 year were associated with
impairments in verbal and performance IQ, although lesions after year 1 year of
age were associated with no significant impairment on either measure. Right
hemisphere lesions at any age lower only non-verbal IQ. Furthermore, Woods and
Teuber (1978) argue that aphasia rarely results from right hemisphere damage,
despite earlier evidence that this form of **crossed aphasia** did (Basser, 1962).

If the invariance hypothesis is correct, one might expect complete removal of
either left or right cortex to result in complete immediate impairment in the ability
undertaken by the respective cortex. In a well known analysis of function following right and left hemisphere damage, Kohn and Dennis (1974) found that
unilateral hemidecortication (a surgical procedure undertaken to alleviate intractable epilepsy and hemiplegia) resulted in a severe impairment in the function
mediated by the removed cortex, although both hemispheres appeared to show
some evidence of taking over each other's function. However, it is possible that two
of the five left-sided patients could understand reversible passive sentences and
one was too young to perform the tasks administered (Bishop, 1983). After left
hemidecortication, simple language tasks are performed normally but complex
language tasks are not (Dennis and Whitaker, 1976). Both hemispheres can
produce lists of objects and identify an object from a photograph or description
although the left is better at generating words that rhyme with others. Left
hemisphere superiority was found for reading and spelling unfamiliar words, for
fluent reading of prose passages and for detecting syntactic errors (Dennis, 1980;
Dennis et al., 1981). Right hemidecortication produced no severe impairment in
simple visuospatial performance such as drawing but was associated with complex
visuospatial performance impairment such as that found on maze negotiation or
map-reading.

The third hypothesis, the parallel-development hypothesis, states that the left
hemisphere is specialized for language functions and the right for non-language
functions. This argues that lateralization of cognitive function (high-level behaviour), such as it is, develops from low-level behaviours which are located in one or
other hemisphere.

■ Some problems with recovery

In their review of mass action and equipotentiality as mechanisms for recovery,
Kolb and Whishaw (1987) distinguish between getting better and actual recovery.
They propose three criteria for evaluating recovery from cortical damage:

1. Cortical removal should be accompanied by the removal of behaviour thought
   to be mediated by that part of the cortex. Thus, recovery of function following

decortication is not recovery in this sense since the recovery may be subcortical.

2. The recovered behaviour is the same behaviour that is lost. For example, if a cortical lesion abolishes orientation by disrupting eye movement, then recovery owing to the substitution of a head movement is not recovery.

3. If treatment produces recovery, then recovery must be attributable to that treatment and would not have occurred without it.

As we have already seen, recovery of function following brain damage is dependent on a large number of variables. Those thought *to promote* recovery include early lesions, serial lesions, type of pharmacological intervention, environmental treatments and grafts. Apart from the ability of the brain to initiate repair, factors which can *influence the rate* of recovery include type of lesion, locus of lesion, the extent of the lesion, the age at which the lesion occurred, individual differences in brain organization, social support, the individual's outlook, and degree of rehabilitation. As a result, the variation in the rate and degree of recovery from brain damage is wide. Levin *et al.* (1982) report that of 1285 patients who sustained closed-head injury and underwent six hours in a coma, 40 per cent died. Most of the remaining patients made an adequate to normal recovery. Less than 50 per cent of those who did recover returned to work.

According to Miller (1984), a number of assumptions underlie recovery of function. These assumptions are that the recovery curve is consistent and regular, that lesions in younger patients lead to less behavioural disruption than lesions in adults, that overlearned and older skills are less likely to be disrupted by brain damage (logically, therefore, newly learned skills will be more disrupted; this is known as **Ribot's law**), that more severe lesions will result in a slower rate of recovery, that slowly progressive lesions will present less severe deficits and better recovery, that experience after injury affects recovery and that intervention or rehabilitation will be more effective the closer it occurs to the time of the injury. These assumptions may be met with qualification.

Recovery normally follows a slow process of a gradual return to function, beginning with the return of low-level behaviour in the early stages and the return of normal function in the later stages. Kertesz (1979), in an analysis of recovery from aphasia, notes that recovery of language after stroke is poor whereas recovery in head-injured patients is the most complete and rapid. He also found that most of the recovery occurred in the first three months. After six months, very little recovery occurred. As expected, there was evidence to suggest that the younger the patient at the time of injury, the better the recovery. Finally, the aspects of language ability which were fairly resistant to brain damage were naming, oral imitation, noun comprehension and yes/no responses. The sparing of these functions suggests the possibility that perhaps tests of these functions may indicate the patient's level of premorbid intelligence, i.e. will enable clinicians to determine the patient's normal level of intelligence regardless of the brain injury suffered. The problems associated with determining the individual's normal level of functioning before damage are considered in the next chapter on neuropsychological assessment.

Measures of recovery

Although the foregoing evidence indicates the plasticity of the brain and its potential for recovery, little information is available on long-term recovery. One factor which might affect long-term recovery, however, is **behavioural compensation**. For example, Dresser *et al.* (1973) reported that gainful employment was an effective measure of recovery, with 80 per cent of their war veterans becoming employed. Oddy and Humphrey (1980), however, argue that employment is not a good measure of recovery: 48 of their 54 closed-head patients were employed two weeks following injury but many did not believe that they were working at their best and felt that their activities were restricted.

Often, recovery is measured on batteries of intellectual ability tests and many of these are described in more detail in the next chapter. Behavioural and sensory/perceptual tests are also used. Teuber's (1975) head-injured war veterans whose test results in the first week after injury were compared with their test performance twenty years after, recovered some behavioural functions but not others. Over half did not make any recovery. Forty per cent made some motor recovery, 30 per cent made some somatosensory recovery and 40 per cent made some visual recovery. More than 75 per cent did not recover from dysphasia.

Explanations for recovery

Theories to account for recovery have been grouped into three classes: **artifact theories**, **anatomical reorganization theories** and **functional adaptation theories** (Miller, 1984) although all three may contain elements of overlap. Artifact theories assume that brain damage results in a primary deficit – a lesion destroys those cells responsible for a particular function and disrupts the function subserved by those cells – and secondary behavioural deficits, seen in a disturbance of functioning of other parts of the brain not involved in the primary deficit. Many physiological changes accompany brain damage including shock, edema and reduced blood flow and glucose uptake. Edema, for example, impairs the functioning of the affected tissue and results in behavioural abnormalities.

The most well known artifact theory was proposed by Von Monakow (1914) who suggested that when a brain region is lesioned, shock can occur elsewhere either adjacent to the lesion site or at some distance from it. This shock was termed **diaschisis** and referred to the prevention of innervation by tissue surrounding the damaged region. Accordingly, slow and fast lesions gave rise to serial lesion effects in which sudden lesions would produce more severe deficits than would slow ones such as those produced by slow-growing tumours.

A similar but alternative explanation was proposed by Luria (1963) who suggested the idea of inhibition in which primary injury causes an inhibition of other parts of the brain (as seen in synaptic acetylcholine reduction). LeVere (1980), on the other hand, has suggested that one of the effects of brain damage is to move the responsibility of function from the damaged region to an undamaged region. This form of recovery is sometimes referred to as regional or **hemispheric compensation**. The degree of residual impairment is seen in the difference between the original, damaged system's normal function and the new, compensatory system's attempt at functioning. The basis of such recovery is anatomical reorganization: the function of a damaged region may be undertaken by others. It is a rather vague and general principle. Munk (1878), for example, argued that brain regions not remotely connected with the damaged region might take over a disrupted function. This suggests, however, that there are brain regions which are not in constant use: an assumption that may not be plausible.

The third group of theories, functional adaptation theories, is also based on a general principle: that lesioned individuals may relearn impaired functions by means other than that originally employed (Luria et al., 1969). According to Luria (1970), this relearning was capable of enhancing the reorganization of the nervous system. Because this explanation of recovery of function is based on behavioural rather than neuroanatomical mechanisms, psychological factors such as motivation may be important. For example, there is evidence that positive reinforcement helps to alleviate the symptoms of aphasia (Stoicheff, 1960).

As a real example of the kind of adaptation that might occur, Miller (1984) cites the knotting of a tie. To begin, one needs to look in a mirror to give visual cues which guide the motor behaviour of actually knotting a tie. With experience, tactile and proprioceptive cues will suffice, without the need of visual cues. In one study of the adaptive competence of 86 children with closed injury, Papero et al. (1993) found that severity of injury had no significant general effect on adaptive behaviour. However, severity significantly affected adaptive (especially social) competence in boys but not girls.

Neuropsychological rehabilitation

One of the important clinical undertakings following the measurement of the effects of head injury is the rehabilitation of the individual's intellectual function. McLellan (1991) has defined rehabilitation as 'an active process whereby people who are disabled by injury or disease work together with professional staff, relatives and members of the wider community to achieve their optimum physical, psychological, social and vocational well-being' (p.785). One of the most important aspects of care after brain damage is the encouragement of this rehabilitation (Van den Broek *et al.*, 1995). Given the correct programme of treatment or therapy, it is anticipated that the patients' functions will be restored more speedily than they would be by spontaneous recovery alone. According to B.A. Wilson (1995), the aims of therapy in the rehabilitation of cognitive function are: (1) to restore function via anatomical reorganization or restructuring of the environment, (2) to find other ways of helping the patient to achieve a goal, and (3) to encourage the patient to use residual skills effectively. Rehabilitation programmes are especially common for language dysfunction and memory impairment.

Rehabilitation of language function

One of the more standardized and well documented rehabilitation exercises concentrates on alleviating the symptoms of language dysfunction, most commonly aphasia (Kertesz, 1993). One of the earliest, systematic studies of the rehabilitation of language noted that the use of oral drills and cues was associated with improvements in language six months after the initial injury (Butfield and Zangwill, 1946). A problem with many of the early rehabilitation studies, however, is that they did not appear to consider the possibility of spontaneous recovery (Kertesz, 1993). Other studies indicated similar results to those of Butfield and Zangwill. Vignolo (1964), for example, found that therapy was effective two to six months postinjury. Hagen (1973) also found that better speech production, reading comprehension and spelling were associated with therapy. If the therapy is implemented as soon as is practicable, oral expression improves well with treatment, although if the aphasia has been allowed to continue for some time, the therapy is less effective (Basso *et al.*, 1975).

Various types of rehabilitation programme can improve language. These involve either structured exercises or less formal and more relaxed procedures. An example of the latter might be the stimulation of the patients' emotional or cognitive functions by encouraging them to talk to others, to form group activities and a good, professional relationship with their therapist, or to reinforce responses rather than correcting errors. Programmed instruction involves specific tasks or steps that the patient must complete as part of the rehabilitation programme (Shewan and Bandur, 1986). The materials used are similar to those used during the learning of a second language (Kertesz, 1993). Other techniques include cueing or priming target words or phrases via structurally or semantically similar words or cues (Huber *et al.*, 1991) and encouraging the patient to circumlocute if exact responses are not forthcoming. The idea behind this is that the existing, residual communication ability is enhanced. A similar idea lies behind the therapy called PACE (Promoting Aphasics' Communicative Effectiveness), developed by Davis and Wilcox (1981). In this programme, the aphasic patient is encouraged to communicate via any verbal or non-verbal means. A specific example would be requesting the patient to describe a picture or photograph that the therapist has not seen.

A recent development in rehabilitation has been the use of computer-assisted therapy. Robertson (1990) has reviewed the effectiveness of computerized cognitive rehabilitation and concluded that specific computerized language programmes and those designed to improve attention assisted rehabilitation, although many programmes did not help the rehabilitation of other functions such as memory. Whether these programmes can appropriately encourage normal function in everyday life, however, is questionable. The benefits of computerization are that it is labour-nonintensive and encourages the patient to behave independently. Face-to-face contact with the therapist, however, seems likely to enhance conversational language ability and interpersonal skills. More detail on the language therapies used to reduce aphasia can be found in Berndt and Mitchum (1995) and Holland and Forbes (1993).

Rehabilitation of memory

Memory is probably one of the most difficult functions to restore and is probably impossible to restore to any normal level of function if the amnesia is severe (B.A. Wilson, 1991). The principal problems of amnesia involve an inability to learn or retain new information. The principal problems of rehabilitation are devising programmes that the patient will follow and encouraging patients to use memory strategies spontaneously. Sometimes, these programmes involve very simple measures such as painting the doors to different rooms in different colours and teaching the patient to associate the different rooms with the different coloured doors (Harris, 1980). Other practical steps might be the drawing of lines from one room to another to enable the amnesic patient to get from one place to another. The use of notebooks, diaries and personal organizers often helps the patient to remember previous events or to organize future ones (Sohlberg and Mateer, 1989; B.A. Wilson, 1992). The use of alarms and timers has also been suggested to remind the patient that they should be doing a particular function or should be at a particular place when the alarm sounds (Wilson and Moffat, 1992). Visual imagery might also be employed, as might other mnemonic strategies. As one might expect, however, practical measures to help amnesiacs are problematic in that patients may not remember to use these mnemonics or external cues.

Can a language-deprived child develop normal language after puberty? The case of Genie

On 7 November 1970, the *Los Angeles Times* carried a headline that astonished most of its readers. 'Girl, 13,' it read, 'prisoner since infancy, deputies charged; parents jailed'. The story went on to reveal that the girl's father had harnessed her to a potty in a room in the back of the family house since she was about 20 months old. She slept in a crib which had wire mesh on its sides and which was also covered with wire mesh. Her father was intolerant of noise and would beat her whenever she made any sound. Her mother fed her a diet of baby food, cereals and, occasionally, boiled eggs.

That the child should have been relieved of this horror occurred only by chance. The girl's mother was partially blind and after a particularly violent fight with her husband, went with her mother and daughter to the section of the department of social services that dealt with the blind. By accident, she found herself in the social services welfare department. The social worker's supervisor clearly observed abnormalities in the young girl's behaviour, thinking that she was 6 years old and exhibiting autistic characteristics. The girl was $4\frac{1}{2}$ feet tall and weighed 4 stone. She could not eat solid food and had nearly two complete sets of teeth. She was 13 years and 9 months old.

Apart from her malnutrition and appearance, the most remarkable feature of the young girl's behaviour was her almost complete lack of language. She could not talk and had a vocabulary of about twenty words (she could understand concepts such as red, blue, green). Her speech production was limited to 'nomore', 'stopit' and other negatives. Following her discovery, she was admitted to the Children's Hospital in Los Angeles for treatment.

A young graduate student at the University of California at Los Angeles, Susan Curtiss, was one of the small number of scientists who were able to study the young girl, who was known by the pseudonym Genie, over the next few years. As a linguist, Curtiss was interested in how handicapped Genie's language had become and what possible recovery could be made from such gross linguistic impairment (Fromkin *et al.*, 1972/73; Curtiss, 1977). Such cases in which one can directly observe the effects of linguistic deprivation rarely occur. Ethically, no experimenter can attempt this. There have been isolated instances of 'accidental' cases such as Victor, the 'wild boy of Aveyron'. Victor had been found in 1800, lurking naked in front of a cottage in the Languedoc region of France. He had spent his twelve years from infancy living in the woods, surviving on a diet of acorns and potatoes. He had his throat cut as a toddler and had been left to die. He was subsequently studied and cared for by a young physician, Jean-Marc-Gaspard Itard. Victor had no language, and while he never learned to speak, he achieved a rudimentary ability to spell.

⟫

Genie, although not having suffered these misfortunes, had nonetheless suffered misfortunes great enough to make her virtually mute and unable to communicate with others when first discovered. As more became known of Genie's childhood, the more her behaviour became explicable. Her father would not allow a television in the house and would abhor conversation. Genie's room had two windows, both of which were covered. One was kept open a few inches. Genie's malnourishment was remedied and the girl did not show evidence of brain damage. A year after she was discovered, Genie's language ability underwent marked improvement. Her ability to structure according to rules was the equivalent of a 20 year old's and her spatial ability placed her in the adult ability category. She could tell the difference between singular and plural words and positive and negative sentences and could understand some prepositions. Her speech was limited to one- or-two-word sentences, however, eventually becoming very descriptive and concrete ('big rectangular pillow', 'very, very, very dark-green box'). The 'explosion' of language, normally expected after such dramatic improvements never materialized.

What does the story of Genie tell us about the critical period of language? It tells us a certain amount but deprives us of much. It became clear that Genie could develop new but basic language skills. She made a dramatic recovery from the time of her discovery to the time when the scientists had to abandon their studies. Yet, her language never fully recovered, remaining steadfastly descriptive, almost at the level one would expect primates to achieve with intensive language training. Her study showed, however, the remarkable, devastating effects of language and auditory deprivation on the development of language ability.

Latest accounts indicate that Genie is still alive and living in a home for retarded adults after her mother had been awarded custody of her. Despite an injunction preventing her from disallowing access to Genie for scientific study, Genie's mother has consistently violated the injunction. Many of the scientists who studied her in the 1970s do not know where she lives and do not know how well she is doing today. Of all the case histories in psychology and in this book, that of Genie is probably one of most tragic, remarkable and, yet, informative.

Summary

☐ The human brain undergoes considerable development from birth on-wards. At birth, the brain weighs approximately 350 grams. By the time it reaches adulthood, it will have quadrupled in weight. The reason for the increase is an expansion of neuron size and connective processes. We are born with all the neurons we will ever have.

➠

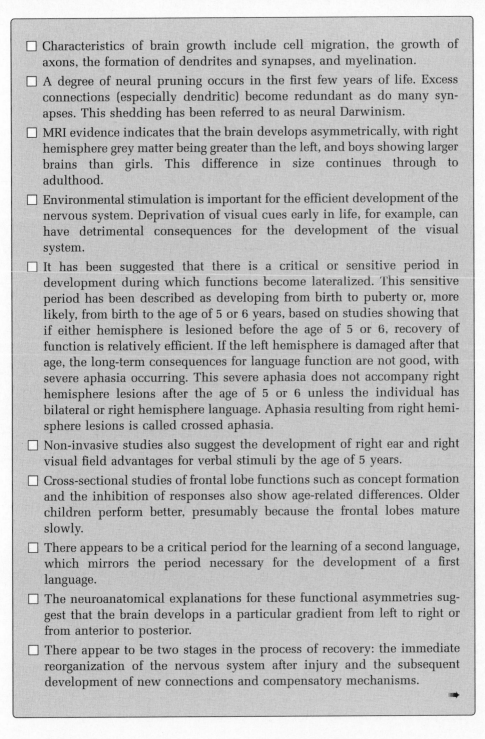

☐ Characteristics of brain growth include cell migration, the growth of axons, the formation of dendrites and synapses, and myelination.

☐ A degree of neural pruning occurs in the first few years of life. Excess connections (especially dendritic) become redundant as do many synapses. This shedding has been referred to as neural Darwinism.

☐ MRI evidence indicates that the brain develops asymmetrically, with right hemisphere grey matter being greater than the left, and boys showing larger brains than girls. This difference in size continues through to adulthood.

☐ Environmental stimulation is important for the efficient development of the nervous system. Deprivation of visual cues early in life, for example, can have detrimental consequences for the development of the visual system.

☐ It has been suggested that there is a critical or sensitive period in development during which functions become lateralized. This sensitive period has been described as developing from birth to puberty or, more likely, from birth to the age of 5 or 6 years, based on studies showing that if either hemisphere is lesioned before the age of 5 or 6, recovery of function is relatively efficient. If the left hemisphere is damaged after that age, the long-term consequences for language function are not good, with severe aphasia occurring. This severe aphasia does not accompany right hemisphere lesions after the age of 5 or 6 unless the individual has bilateral or right hemisphere language. Aphasia resulting from right hemisphere lesions is called crossed aphasia.

☐ Non-invasive studies also suggest the development of right ear and right visual field advantages for verbal stimuli by the age of 5 years.

☐ Cross-sectional studies of frontal lobe functions such as concept formation and the inhibition of responses also show age-related differences. Older children perform better, presumably because the frontal lobes mature slowly.

☐ There appears to be a critical period for the learning of a second language, which mirrors the period necessary for the development of a first language.

☐ The neuroanatomical explanations for these functional asymmetries suggest that the brain develops in a particular gradient from left to right or from anterior to posterior.

☐ There appear to be two stages in the process of recovery: the immediate reorganization of the nervous system after injury and the subsequent development of new connections and compensatory mechanisms.

☐ Recovery from aphasia, the most common neuropsychological disorder observed following brain injury, is reasonably good if the patient is young, left-handed, does not exhibit severe aphasia, and the lesion is not extensive and does not involve many important, language-related structures. The age of the patient, the site of the lesion, the type of language function observed and the severity of the aphasia all influence the rate and degree of recovery from aphasia. An important point to remember is that many studies may not be comparable owing to differences in these measures.

☐ The sparing of function that appears to accompany early brain damage is an example of the Kennard principle: function may be spared if the lesion is made early in life but may be impaired otherwise. The invariance hypothesis suggests that there is left hemisphere specialization of language at birth and that the right hemisphere takes over this function if the left is damaged. The maturation hypothesis argues that both hemispheres are involved in verbal and non-verbal functions from birth, but that the left hemisphere becomes specialized. The parallel-development hypothesis states that the left hemisphere is dominant for verbal functions and the right hemisphere is dominant for non-verbal functions from birth. The evidence would tend to favour the maturation hypothesis.

☐ Recovery is measured in many ways, including performance on neuropsychological tests. One common measure of recovery is employment, although the reliability of this measure has been challenged.

☐ Theories of recovery argue that: (1) damage to one part of the brain can affect the functions of other parts of the brain or that damage to one part might inhibit the activity of another part (artifact theories), (2) undamaged regions not specialized for the function compensate for the impaired function (anatomical reorganization theories), or (3) recovery relies on the adoption of different behavioural strategies to restore function (functional adaptation theories).

☐ Rehabilitation refers to the process whereby treatment or therapy encourages the patient to achieve functioning as near to normal as possible. Different rehabilitation techniques are available for language and memory disorders. Therapy for aphasia can be structured – where the patient is rehabilitated in formal stages – or unstructured. There is evidence that language therapy is successful provided the programme is implemented in the early stages of the aphasia. Memory techniques have their own problems, including ensuring that patients follow their programme of rehabilitation and use the memory strategies they are taught, spontaneously.

☐ The experience of Genie highlights the importance of early exposure to, and encouragement of, language during childhood. It also indicates that some language ability can be taught after puberty.

Recommended further general and specific reading

Key: (1) = introductory, *(3)* = intermediate, *(5)* = advanced

General
Good, D.C. and Couch, J.R. (1994). *Handbook of Neurorehabilitation*. New York: Marcel Dekker. *(4)*

Finger, S., LeVere, T.E., Almli, C.R. and Stein, D.G. (1987). *Brain Injury and Recovery: Theoretical and controversial issues*. New York: Plenum. *(3)*

Finlayson, M.A.J. and Garner, S.H. (1994). *Brain Injury Rehabilitation*. Baltimore: Williams and Wilkins. *(3)*

Greenwood, R., Barnes, M.P., McMillan, T.M. and Ward, C.D. (1993). *Neurological Rehabilitation*. Hove, UK: The Psychology Press *(4)*.

Kertesz, A. (1993). Recovery and treatment. In K.M. Heilman and E. Valenstein (eds), *Clinical Neuropsychology* (3rd edition). New York: Oxford University Press. *(2)*

Ponsford, J., Sloan, S. and Snow, P. (1995). *Traumatic Brain Injury*. Hove, UK: The Psychology Press. *(2)*

Prigatano, G.P. (1993). *Issues in Neuropsychological Rehabilitation of Children with Brain Dysfunction*. Hove, UK: Lawrence Erlbaum Associates. *(3)*

Purves, D. (1994). *Neural Activity and the Growth of the Brain*. Cambridge: Cambridge University Press. *(2)*

Reese, H.W. and Franzen, M.D. (1997). *Biological and Neuropsychological Mechanisms: Life span developmental psychology*. Hillsdale: Lawrence Erlbaum Associates. *(4)*

Rose, F.D. and Johnson, D.A. (1996). *Brain Injury and After*. Chichester: Wiley. *(2)*

Rosenthal, M., Griffith, E.R., Bond, M.R. and Miller, J.D. (1990). *Rehabilitation of the Adult and Child with Traumatic Brain Injury* (2nd edition). USA: F.A. Davis. *(3)*

Shatz, C.J. (1992). The developing brain. *Scientific American*, **267**(3), 34–41. *(2)*

Temple, C. (1997). *Developmental Cognitive Neuropsychology*. Hove, UK: The Psychology Press. *(3)*

Specific
Berndt, R.S. and Mitchum, R.S. (1995). *Cognitive Neuropsychological Approaches to the Treatment of Language Disorders*. Hove, UK: Lawrence Erlbaum Associates. *(3)*

Cappa, S.F., Perani, D., Grassi, F., Bressl, S., Alberoni, M., Franceschi, M., Bettinardi, V., Todde, S. and Fazio, F. (1997). A PET follow-up study of recovery after stroke in acute aphasics. *Brain and Language*, **56**, 55–67. *(4)*

Dennis, M. and Whitaker, H.A. (1976). Language acquisition following hemidecortication: linguistic superiority of the left over the right hemisphere. *Brain and Language*, **3**, 404–33. *(3)*

Giedd, J.N., Snell, J.W., Lange, N., Rajapakse, J.C., Casey, B.J., Kozuch, P.L., Vaituzis, A.C., Vauss, Y.C., Hamburger, S.D., Kaysen, D. and Rapoport, J.L. (1996). Quantitative magnetic resonance imaging of human brain development: ages 4–18. *Cerebral Cortex*, **6**, 551–60. *(3)*

Grattan, L.M. and Eslinger, P.J. (1991). Frontal lobe damage in children and adults: a comparative review. *Developmental Neuropsychology*, **7**(3), 283–326. *(2)*

Kolb, B. and Whishaw, I.Q. (1989). Plasticity in the neocortex: mechanisms underlying recovery from early brain damage. *Progress in Neurobiology*, **32**, 235–76. *(4)*

Ludlow, C.L., Rosenberg, J., Fair, C., Buck, D., Schesselman, S. and Salazar, A. (1986). Brain lesions associated with nonfluent aphasia fifteen years following penetrating head injury. *Brain*, **109**, 55–80. *(3)*

Mehler, J. and Christophe, A. (1995). Maturation and learning of language in the first year of life. In M.S. Gazzaniga (ed.), *The Cognitive Neurosciences*. Cambridge, MA: MIT Press. *(4)*

Oddy, M. (1993). Head injury during childhood. *Neuropsychological Rehabilitation*, **3**(4), 301–20. *(3)*

Patterson, K. (1994). Reading, writing and rehabilitation: a reckoning. In M.J. Riddoch and G. Humphreys (eds), *Cognitive Neuropsychology and Cognitive Rehabilitation*. Hove, UK: Lawrence Erlbaum Associates. *(2)*

Prigatano, G.P., O'Brien, K.P. and Klonoff, P.S. (1993). Neuropsychological rehabilitation of young adults who suffer brain injury in childhood: clinical observations. *Neuropsychological Rehabilitation*, **3**(4), 411–21. *(3)*

Reiss, A.L., Abrams, M.T., Singer, H.S., Ross, J.L. and Denckla, M.B. (1996). Brain development, gender and IQ in children. *Brain*, **119**, 1763–74. *(3)*

Rymer, R. (1993). *Genie: Escape from a silent childhood*. London: Michael Joseph. *(1)*

Teasdale, G.M. (1995). Head injury. *Journal of Neurology, Neurosurgery and Psychiatry*, **58**, 526–39. *(3)*

Webb, C., Rose, F.D., Johnson, D.A. and Attree, E.A. (1996). Age and recovery from brain injury: clinical opinions and experimental evidence. *Brain Injury*, **10**(4), 303–10. *(3)*

Wilson, B.A. and Powell, G.E. (1994). Neurological problems: treatment and rehabilitation. In S.J.E. Lindsey and G.E. Powell (eds), *Handbook of Clinical Adult Psychology*. London: Routledge. *(1)*

Chapter Thirteen

Neuropsychological assessment

What is neuropsychological assessment?

In order to understand and quantify the effects of brain damage on intellectual, motor or emotional function, a clinician administers a set of tests that is designed to measure these effects. This procedure is called **neuropsychological assessment** and often complements the **neurological examination** which assesses the patient's central nervous system function and is undertaken by a neurologist. If the neurologist suspects that a patient is exhibiting an impairment in cognitive functioning, he or she might refer the patient to the clinical neuropsychologist for assessment. To observe neuropsychological assessment is to observe neuropsychology 'in action'.

For example, neuropsychological assessment might help to determine whether intellectual deficits in an elderly sample are due to progressive dementia or to normal aging. They might determine whether a patient has visuospatial problems or is aphasic. Apart from providing information about the patient's cognitive ability, the results from neuropsychological examinations can also show the severity and extent of the brain damage and the regions of the brain likely to be damaged. The results of neuropsychological assessment are also used to help plan the individual's rehabilitation. As we saw in Chapter 12, this is a process whereby the individual is helped to achieve a level of functioning as near to normal as is possible via a specified systematic regime of therapy or remediation.

Neuropsychological assessment dates back to the late nineteenth and early twentieth century, when methods for determining the mental capacities of patients with brain disease were developed. Often, these examinations were undertaken in asylums using patients suffering from 'psychiatric' conditions. Later, newly developed intelligence tests began to be applied to patients with brain injury. This work formed the background for the neuropsychological procedures devised after the Second World War. Many of the tests used by neuropsychologists in practice are, therefore, not designed specifically for neurological patients but for the normal population. This does present something of a problem for neuropsychologists – and is returned to later – but there are tests available that are designed specifically for neuropsychological patients. These are evaluated later in the chapter.

Before neuropsychology: the neurological examination

Before the neuropsychological examination, neurological patients undergo a more basic investigation, the neurological examination. The function of the neurological examination is to determine, identify and localize malfunction of the central nervous system (CNS). The process normally begins before the neurologist sees the patient. Usually, a full clinical history of the patient is prepared. This history documents any CNS and behavioural irregularities in the patient's life from the prenatal period to the present. This information can often be found in medical records but is also obtained from relatives or witnesses. According to Barrett

(1993), the clinical history provides 'the most important evidence of malfunction of the CNS'. There are several reasons for CNS malfunction. For example, it may be attributable to genetic (e.g. inherited disorders, chromosomal defects), intrauterine (e.g. infections, toxins, malnutrition), perinatal (e.g. premature birth), developmental (e.g. malnutrition, deprivation, learning disabilities) or adult (e.g. autoimmune degeneration, vascular complications, infection, trauma) problems.

History-taking involves the collection of information concerning the patient's family background, such as noting the health of parents or siblings, and life (if there were any delays in literacy; if the patient was exposed to any occupational hazards, e.g. toxins). A history of drug and alcohol use would be considered, as would details of the patient's sexual behaviour and orientation. Finally, details of the patient's medical history and presenting problems such as the duration of the disorder, mode of onset, factors affecting the problem and symptoms associated with the problem, would be obtained.

The types of CNS malfunction likely to appear in the neurological examination range from the simple to the complex. There may be problems with lower-order systems involving sensory or motor impairments or higher-order systems involving impaired cognition and attention. Lower CNS functions include voluntary movement, facial and limb movement, coordination, muscle tone, power, reflexes, sensation and cranial nerve function. Some of these are described below; a more detailed treatment can be found in Barrett (1993).

Voluntary movement can be assessed by first observing the patient. For example, is the patient's gait disordered or power reduced? Is the patient ataxic, i.e. unsteady, as he or she walks into the examination room? Is the patient shuffling, stiff-legged or limping? More specific procedures include a test of tandem-gait where the patient is asked to walk toe-to-heel. This determines whether the patient falls to one side or another or whether arm movements are excessive. While the patient is sitting, the examiner might observe asymmetry in facial expression or involuntary movement of the head, mouth, neck, tongue and limbs. Tremor or chorea, for example, are easy to observe under these conditions. The shooting out of limbs (**hemiballisms**) may also be noted.

Problems with coordination may be largely due to malfunction of the cerebellum. For example, when the patient is required to touch the clinician's outstretched vertical but moving finger and then his or her own nose, 'past-pointing' may occur, i.e. the patient will miss the finger. Power might be assessed by requiring the patient to hold his or her arms at right-angles so that the arms and shoulders each form an inverted L shape. If the patient is asked to resist when the clinician pushes down on the patient's shoulders but shows no resistance, this may be a sign of motor disturbance. Reflexes may also be tested in a simple way. If the patient's lips are tapped with a vertically held pen and the behaviour elicits a pout reflex this indicates frontal damage and is considered to be a release sign.

During the neurological examination, the clinician might test for sensory neglect and tactile discrimination in several ways. For example, the clinician might touch the outer side of one or both of the patient's feet or may touch the back of the patient's calves or thighs simultaneously or separately. A mild or developing sensory neglect is indicated if the patient can detect the single touch but not the simultaneous touch. Sensory discrimination can be examined by pressing a blunt or sharp instrument into the skin.

Examination of the cranial nerves might involve the examination of all twelve or a selection of these nerves. Optic nerve malfunction may be examined by moving a vertical finger to the left and right of the midline of the patient's face from a distance of about two feet. A failure of the eyes to track the finger indicates an optic nerve malfunction. A relatively simple test is the examination of pupil size – both pupils should be identical – and their reactivity to light. Hearing can be examined by whispering a digit two feet away from one ear while the second ear is auditorily distracted by an unrelated stimulus, e.g. rubbing of the fingers. Perhaps the most important cranial nerve functions involve the integrity of the visual eye fields and eye movement. These always form part of the neurological examination.

■ Principles of neuropsychological assessment

According to Levin and Benton (1986), neuropsychological assessment has six aims:

1. To identify the presence and type of early or mild disturbance in cognitive function when other diagnostic examinations (e.g. an interview) have failed or their results are ambiguous.
2. To differentiate between brain disease or injury and other factors as causes of cognitive impairment. Depression, for example, can mask the effects of brain damage or may be misconstrued for it if test performance is bad.
3. To evaluate deficits and preserved functions in patients with neurological diseases or injury and to assist in the planning of rehabilitation, e.g. deciding on degree of speech therapy for patients with aphasia.
4. To evaluate the effects of surgical intervention and psychopharmacological treatment, e.g. antidementia drugs for Alzheimer's disease and drugs for combating cognitive deterioration in AIDS.
5. To evaluate scholastic problems and developmental delay in children, e.g. to differentiate between mental subnormality, emotional disturbance and specific learning difficulties. This is most often undertaken by educational psychologists, however, not neuropsychologists.
6. To provide objective data for research.

As one might gather from the groups normally tested by neuropsychologists and clinical psychologists, there are problems and important practical issues involved in neuropsychological assessment. These include the choice of test, the reliability and validity of the test, the estimation of premorbid intelligence and method of administration. Some of these problems, together with some solutions, are considered in a later section.

▓ Fixed battery vs flexible testing

The selection of a test in neuropsychological assessment may follow two principal routes: the neuropsychologist may either (1) administer a **fixed battery** of tests where the same comprehensive series of tests (e.g. the Halstead–Reitan Battery, Wechsler Adult Intelligence Scale – Revised, Luria–Nebraska Neuropsychological Battery) is given to all patients, or (2) make a **flexible selection** of tests depending on the reason for neuropsychological assessment. Some of principal tests used in neuropsychological assessment are presented in Table 13.1.

A neuropsychological test battery has been described variously as 'a group of related tests combined to yield a single total score that is of maximal efficiency in measuring for a specific purpose or ability or trait' (English and English, 1958) and as 'a diagnostic set of tests having comparable norms and usually organised in an easily administered series with uniform style' (Cronbach, 1949). Often, a battery is administered together with selected components of other tests. One of the advantages of a standardized battery is that one test should be directly comparable with another (Russell, 1982). A disadvantage, however, is that some batteries do not test some cognitive components, e.g types of memory. They might also be unnecessarily time-consuming because they involve the administration of tests which may be irrelevant to the problem being examined and can take up to two hours to complete in full. A particular advantage of test batteries, however, is that there is normally a large normative database, a 'population norm', which provides a standard with which one can compare an individual patient's performance. A normative database comprises the statistical features of test performance from a large number of people. The aim is to find the 'normal' performance level for each test, hence 'normative'. The Halstead–Reitan and Wechsler Adult Intelligence Scale – Revised (WAIS-R) batteries, for example, have large databases of test performance scores for different target populations.

One disadvantage of normative databases, however, is that individuals may not fall within the normal pattern of performance prior to brain damage. In this instance, any subsequent comparison with the 'norm' after brain injury is not likely to be informative. In these cases, an estimate of premorbid intelligence, i.e. the individual's intellectual capacity before the injury, is required. There are some fairly reliable tests of premorbid intelligence for certain groups of patients, and the most effective is described below.

A further disadvantage is that batteries might not take into account what Lezak (1995) describes as **contextual factors** – the patient's social history, present life circumstances, medical history and circumstances surrounding the examination. This is a criticism which might also be levelled at some individual tests.

Table 13.1 Some common neuropsychological tests and their uses

Function	Test
General intelligence	Wechsler Adult Intelligence Scale – Revised Halstead–Reitan Battery National Adult Reading Test Raven's Progressive Matrices
Premorbid intelligence	Verbal IQ scale of the WAIS-R National Adult Reading Test
Language (general)	Boston Diagnostic Aphasia Battery Multilingual Aphasia Examination Western Aphasia Battery Aphasia screening test of the Halstead–Reitan Battery Verbal IQ scale of the WAIS-R Mill Hill Vocabulary Scale
Language (comprehension)	Token Test Comprehension subtest of WAIS-R verbal IQ
Memory	Wechsler Memory Scale – Revised Memory Assessment Scale Randt Memory Test Warrington Recognition Memory Test Rey–Osteirreith Figure Test Rey Auditory Verbal Learning Test
Attention	Arithmetic, digit symbol and digit span subtests of the WAIS-R Seashore Rhythm Test Speech Sounds Perception Test Continuous Performance Test Paced Auditory Serial Addition Test
Visuospatial ability	Benton and Allen's Facial Recognition Test Benton Visual Retention Test Visual Object and Space Perception Battery Raven's Progressive Matrices Ambiguous Angles test
Reasoning/concept formation	Wisconsin Card Sorting Test Halstead–Reitan Category Test Porteus Maze Test Tower of London task
Handedness	Pegboard task Annett Handedness Questionnaire Edinburgh Handedness Inventory

The three main neuropsychological test batteries are the Wechsler Adult Intelligence Scale – Revised, the Halstead–Reitan Battery and the Luria–Nebraska Neuropsychological Battery.

▓ The neuropsychological battery

Wechsler Adult Intelligence Scale (WAIS) and Wechsler Adult Intelligence Scale – Revised (WAIS-R)

The WAIS-R (D. Wechsler, 1981) has been described as the 'workhorse of neuropsychological assessment' (Lezak, 1988). It is the single most utilized component of the neuropsychological repertory and is the most commonly used test of adult 'intelligence'. There is a children's version called the Wechsler Intelligence Scale for Children (WISC). The latest version of the WISC is the WISC-III.

Both the adult and children's versions comprise two major scales: verbal IQ (VIQ) and performance IQ (PIQ). Each major scale has various subscales (or subtests). For example, subtests of the verbal scale include tests of:

- information
- comprehension (practical reasoning/interpretation of proverbs)
- similarities (abstraction and verbalization of properties common to objects)
- arithmetic reasoning
- digit span (repetition and reversal of numbers presented aurally)
- vocabulary (definitions)

Subtests of the performance scale include:

- digit symbols
- picture completion (identification of missing features from line drawings)
- picture arrangement (arrangement of cartoon pictures in a meaningful order)
- block designs (block construction from a given design)
- object assembly (timed construction of puzzles)

The performance scale relies less on the retention of previously acquired information than does the verbal scale. As such, it is less dependent on formal education but is more vulnerable to aging and conditions which impair perceptual and motor skills and speed (Rao, 1986). Age-corrected scores are available for each subtest, however.

The earlier version of the battery (WAIS) has been replaced by the WAIS-R. This was standardized on a representative sample of 1880 Americans between 1976 and

1980. The revised version is similar to the original version (D. Wechsler, 1955) but about 20 per cent of the content has been updated. A UK version of the WAIS-R is available (Lea, 1986) as are versions for the Irish and Scottish populations. The biggest difference between the WAIS and WAIS-R is the level of difficulty. The WAIS-R yields IQ scores approximately one-half of a standard deviation lower than those of the WAIS (Mishra and Brown, 1983; Wechsler, 1981). This presents a practical problem because the relationship between test performance on the WAIS and other tests may no longer be relevant. For example, the National Adult Reading Test (NART), a test of premorbid intelligence, was standardized against the WAIS not the WAIS-R. This is important because the premorbid estimate provided by the NART is compared with the patient's obtained IQ. If the test was originally compared with an easier version, this comparison may lead to an inaccurate assessment of impaired functioning.

The most obvious neuropsychological drawback of the WAIS-R is that it is not intended to assess cognitive impairment associated with brain injury. Neither does it take into account factors such as cultural deprivation or emotional disturbance. There are no parallel forms: in order to examine test/retest reliability, i.e. the ability of the test to elicit similar scores on two different occasions, the same tests must be used at the second and first testing sessions. One solution might be to administer the WAIS at the first session and the WAIS-R at the second, but this may be inappropriate because the WAIS-R is more difficult. Administration of the same test on two occasions also has its problems because practice effects have been observed for the performance scale, i.e. performance improves with practice (Wechsler, 1981).

This said, however, the WAIS-R continues to be widely used. It is a relatively well standardized test and results are, in general, reliable. Such standardization allows the construction of IQ bands within which certain percentages of the population perform. Thus, 68 per cent of the population will score between 85 and 115 (within one standard deviation of the mean), and 95 per cent of the population will have an IQ between 70 and 130 (within two standard deviations of the mean). There is further discussion of the use and validity of the WAIS and WAIS-R in Crawford (1992), Levin and Benton (1986) and Reitan and Woolfson (1990).

Halstead–Reitan Battery

The Halstead–Reitan Battery has a longer history than the WAIS. It originally comprised a series of cognitive ability tests chosen by Ward Halstead of the University of Chicago in the 1930s to examine the cognitive effects of brain injury. Ralph Reitan applied the tests to psychiatric populations in the 1950s in order to determine any brain damage or 'organicity'.

The battery includes six tests:

- Category Test (a test of abstract reasoning/hypothesis testing)

- Tactual Performance Test (the arrangement of variously shaped blocks into holes, without the aid of visual cues)

- Seashore Rhythm Test (the detection of similarities and differences between rhythms)

- Speech Sounds Perception Test (identification of spoken nonsense syllables from four visually presented ones)

- Finger-tapping Test (motor speed test; subject taps a counter with index finger at maximum speed for 10 seconds)

- Trail-making

Tests added to the existing ones include the aphasia screening test, sensory-perceptual examination and grip strength. Performance on these tests is ultimately illustrated by the Halstead Impairment Index, a measure of the proportion of the six original tests passed or failed. Although capable of differentiating between neurologically intact and brain-damaged individuals, its ability to discriminate between psychiatric and neurologic patients is unimpressive. Individual tests from the battery continue to be used in neuropsychological practice, however.

Luria–Nebraska Neuropsychological Battery

The Luria–Nebraska Neuropsychological Battery was derived from Christensen's (1979) text and manual which were themselves derived from techniques employed by Luria. Tests measure motor, rhythm, tactile, visuospatial, receptive and expressive speech, writing, reading, arithmetic and intellectual performance (Golden et al., 1978, 1980). Problems with this battery include inadequate documentation of aetiology, site and extent of brain damage in the standardization data and the confounding effects of abilities not directly tested by the scales, i.e. tests make demands on other abilities so that it is unclear what ability the test is actually measuring.

More recently, Reitan and Wolfson (1996) examined whether 'specific' neuropsychological tests were more sensitive measures of cerebral damage than were general tests. Fifty subjects with various forms of brain damage, and fifty control subjects completed a finger-tapping speed test (specific motor function test), tactual performance test (the general test) and two tests of tactile sensation (one specific, one general). They found that the general (complex) tests differentiated between control and brain-damaged subjects better than did the specific (simple) tests although the very small number of tests and functions examined should be borne in mind.

■ Individual tests

In addition to test batteries, neuropsychologists can use a large selection of individual tests tailored to suit a particular behaviour. These are tests of discrete and specialized function and include tests of memory, attention, visuospatial ability, verbal ability and premorbid intelligence, amongst others.

Brief cognitive tests

In view of the time-consuming administration involved in battery testing, attempts have been made to construct brief, 10–30 minute tests that assess mental competence. These have been devised largely to assess functioning in the elderly (e.g. Mini Mental State Examination) and to provide a measure of the severity of dementia (e.g. Mattis Dementia Rating Scale). There is only a moderate correlation between Mini Mental State scores and WAIS IQ in neurologic patients, however, although the Mini Mental State test continues to be widely used. Items from this test are presented in Table 13.2.

Table 13.2 Examples of the type of item seen on the Mini Mental State Examination

Function tested	Item
Orientation	What is the year?
	What is the season?
	What is the date?
	What is the day of the week?
	What is the month?
	What city are we in?
	What floor of the building are we on?
Repetition of the names of three objects spoken by the examiner	
Attention	Subtraction of 7 from 100 and successive subtraction of 7 from the number remaining
	Spelling of word backwards
Recall	Naming the three objects uttered by the experimenter earlier
Language	Patient is asked to name objects pointed at by the examiner (e.g. a watch, pencil)
	Repetition of phrases
	Following a simple written command
	Copying a design on paper
	Writing a sentence

Tests of premorbid intelligence

Although test batteries have standardized, normative scores which may be used for comparison with an individual's score, there is substantial variation in cognitive ability within populations. If individual difference is great, then a comparison of an individual's performance with the population norm will be unhelpful. An **individualized comparison standard** is, therefore, required (Lezak, 1994). One method of devising such a standard is to use test scores obtained before the brain disease or damage and compare them with scores obtained after the injury. However, this information is rarely available for the simple reason that most individuals will not have been neuropsychologically tested before their injury.

An alternative method is to devise a standard which estimates the patient's expected or **premorbid** level of performance (see O'Carroll, 1995, for review). The assumption behind this approach is that a score on one cognitive test will allow the estimation of performance on another. The second assumption is that some tests will be affected by cerebral damage but others will not. One approach is to take the best performance of the individual, i.e. the best score from a series of subtests and to use this as the best index of premorbid intellectual functioning (Lezak, 1995). However, some subscales of the WAIS-R correlate poorly, e.g. digit symbol and digit span, making the scores derived from these subscales a poor reflection of general premorbid ability.

A solution to this problem is to use a test specifically designed to estimate premorbid intelligence. The most widely used is the **National Adult Reading Test** (Nelson, 1982). This allows a comparison with the individual's obtained Wechsler IQ. There is a short version which requires subjects to complete the first half of the test only. This version has variable success in predicting full-length NART performance (Beardsall and Brayne, 1990; Crawford et al., 1991).

The test itself is a single-word, oral-reading test of 50 items. The words are mostly short, legally spelled but irregular, i.e. they do not follow the normal grapheme–phoneme correspondence rules. The test begins with the easier items such as debt, debris and aisle, and increases in difficulty to items such as demesne, epergne, drachm and talipes. The short length of the word means that the subject does not have to analyze complex visual stimuli; the irregularity of the words precludes any guesswork. Nelson and O'Connell (1978) have suggested that successful performance on the NART requires previous familiarity with the words but that the test itself makes minimal demands on current cognitive capacity. However, to be an adequate test of premorbid ability, the NART must be reliable, correlate highly with IQ in the normal population and be largely resistant to the effects of neurological and psychiatric disorder.

The NART has been found to have a fairly high degree of reliability. It has split-half reliability, inter-rater reliability and test/retest reliability (see Crawford, 1992) and loads heavily on factor 'g' in factor analytic studies which suggests that it is a useful measure of general intelligence (Crawford et al., 1989c). It has been found to predict 55 per cent, 60 per cent and 32 per cent of the variance in WAIS full-scale, verbal IQ and performance IQ respectively (Crawford *et al.*, 1989a).

The first NART study by Nelson and O'Connell (1978) found that a group of 40 patients with cortical atrophy were severely impaired on the WAIS in comparison with a standardized group but were no different on the NART. Demographic information was not considered, however. Subsequently, NART performance has been used to compare clinical and healthy subjects matched for demographic variables. Before the development of NART, the verbal subtest of the WAIS was the most commonly used index of premorbid intelligence. The NART, however, is the more resistant of the two to brain damage. It has also been assessed longitudinally. O'Carroll *et al.* (1987), for example, found that severity of dementia and physical disability had worsened in a demented sample a year after initial testing, but NART performance had not. The NART manual provides equations for estimating premorbid WAIS IQ from the NART and Schonell Graded Word Reading Test (Schonell, 1942).

In clinical settings, NART performance is compared with current WAIS-R IQ in order to derive an estimate of premorbid ability and has been found to be resistant to deterioration in a number of conditions. The NART, however, cannot be used with dyslexic samples or patients with articulation problems (anarthria), for obvious reasons. Also, the NART has been found to decline with cerebral dysfunction but this decline is overshadowed by an obvious and gross reduction in overall cognitive functioning.

NART appears to be a better predictor of IQ test performance than are demographic factors such as age, sex, level of education, etc. Although there is little difference in their abilities to predict performance IQ – both methods are poor – NART is better at predicting WAIS and WAIS-R full scale IQ and verbal IQ (Blair and Spreen, 1989; Crawford, 1990). The advantage of demographic variables, however, is that they are independent of the individual's current cognitive state and may be used in groups where NART would be inappropriate, e.g. dyslexic samples.

Ideally, the best test of the NART's ability to estimate premorbid IQ would be in a context where the patient's premorbid IQ was available. NART performance could then be compared with this premorbid score to assess the test's validity. Moss and Dowd (1991) presented such data from a 29 year old man, KB, who had sustained severe closed-head injury in a car accident. Fortunately, at the time of follow-up neuropsychological assessment five years after the accident, KB's WISC-R scores were obtained from his old school. Although the NART was standardized against the WAIS and not the WAIS-R (the WAIS yields higher IQs so that NART should overestimate WAIS-R IQs), the results from KB indicated that the NART estimates were very similar to the WISC-R scores.

Reasoning and concept formation

Perhaps the most common test of abstract reasoning and cognitive flexibility is the Wisconsin Card Sorting Test (WCST) described in Chapter 6. Milner (1963) found consistently poorer performance in patients with frontal dorsolateral excisions than in non-frontal patients. The relationship between frontal lobe damage and WCST performance is ambiguous, however. Some frontal patients perform more poorly than non-frontal patients, others do not (Drewe, 1974; Heaton, 1981). Other studies have indicated no significant difference in performance between frontal and non-frontal patients (Grafman *et al.*, 1990; Anderson *et al.*, 1991).

Frontal lobe patients have been found to fail on the Porteus Maze Test which taps the capacity to inhibit immediate responses in favour of deliberation. Patients are normally impulsive and break rules. It is sometimes the case that frontal lobe patients will perform at a normal level on other tests but show failure on the Porteus Maze Test.

Memory

Tests of memory assess both long-term and short-term components. Visual short-term memory may be assessed by requesting the patient to draw previously seen designs that are subsequently removed from view. This test is more sensitive to the effects of brain damage than is recall of digits.

The Wechsler Memory Scale, a collection of subtests, is widely used as a memory test and yields a Wechsler Memory Quotient (WMQ). Included in the subtests are measures of logical memory, such as the examination of prose recall, and visual reproduction, such as the test described in the preceding paragraph. The early version of this scale did present problems, among which were the absence of standardization for some subtests, a failure to examine the retention of information over time and the inclusion of tests that were not direct tests of memory (e.g. orientation). A revision of the scale was published in 1987 and included separate measures of immediate and delayed, verbal and non-verbal recall plus new visual subtests (Hermann and Wyler, 1988). The measures derived from this test are general memory, verbal memory, visual memory, delayed recall and attention/concentration scales. This test is undergoing further revision.

Another widely used test of memory is the Memory Assessment Scale. This is a standardized series of tests which gives measures of general memory, verbal memory and visual memory. A review of the use of memory tests in neuropsychology can be found in Butters *et al.* (1995)

Attention and vigilance

As we saw in the section on neurological examination, attention may affect performance on tests which do not directly examine it. This is important to consider because, as noted above, a patient unable to pay attention to a task will perform badly on almost any other test that the neuropsychologist administers. Learning and memory tasks, for example, may be particularly affected by attention deficits. There is no battery of tests to examine attention explicitly and the tests used in the neurological examination are fairly simple. As a result, neuropsychologists have administered tests that were designed for other purposes: tests such as the arithmetic, digit symbol and digit span subtests of the WAIS-R. The Seashore Rhythm Test and Speech Sounds Perception Test from the Halstead–Reitan Battery are also thought to be adequate measures of attentional deficit.

The Continuous Performance Test is one of the few tests explicitly assessing degree of attention. This test requires the patient to respond only if a particular letter is present in a series of letters or if a letter follows another specific letter. Performance on reaction time tasks may also be a useful measure of attention if the neuropsychologist requires an assessment of the patient's ability to return to a workplace that demands constant alertness from the subject. Another test which measures sustained attention is the Paced Auditory Serial Addition Test. For this test, the subject is required to add a series of sequentially presented numbers. For example, a 3 followed by 6 becomes 9, followed by 5 becomes 14 and so on.

Recently, a specific test of attention, the Test of Everyday Attention, has been developed with quite good validity and reliability (Robertson et al., 1994, 1996; Crawford et al., 1997).

Language function

The most common language difficulty in neurologic patients is anomia. A popular measure of anomia is the Boston Naming Test (Kaplan et al., 1983). Other standardized aphasia test batteries measure such aspects of language function as fluency and repetition. These include the Boston Diagnostic Aphasia battery, the Multilingual Aphasia Examination, the Western Aphasia Battery and the Aphasia Screening Test of the Halstead–Reitan Battery.

Comprehension impairment can be measured on a token test. A number of tokens varying in size, shape and colour are presented to the patient who is then asked to perform a series of tasks: Would you point to the blue token? Would you place the small round token on top of the large round token? Aphasic patients and even left-hemisphere patients who are not clinically aphasic have difficulties with this test. Variations of it form part of several aphasia batteries.

Visuospatial ability

Visuospatial function can be assessed in a variety of ways. There are tests of complex visual discrimination, meaningful integration of visual information, discrimination of background and foreground, and identification of objects that are at odd or ambiguous angles. Individuals with right temporal lobe lesions, for example, perform poorly on visual form discrimination tests, whereas right hemisphere/bilateral lesions are associated with impaired discrimination of familiar faces (Benton and Van Allen, 1968). Tests of facial recognition include those of Benton and his colleagues (1983). In the full form of the test, the subject has to

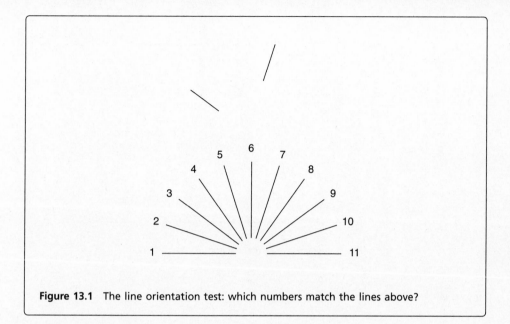

Figure 13.1 The line orientation test: which numbers match the lines above?

identify a target face from photographs of (1) six face-forward faces, or (2) six three-quarter faces, or (3) six faces under different lighting conditions.

Progressive matrices (usually known as Raven's Progressive Matrices) require the patient to indicate which stimulus from a selection of stimuli would correctly complete an incomplete pattern. The matrices are called progressive because this task becomes progressively more difficult with each subsequent pattern. Posterior lesions of either hemisphere are associated with deficits on this task. Performance on the progressive matrices test has been used as an estimate of intellectual ability although the modest correlation with the WAIS suggests caution.

Examples of visuospatial test items can be seen in Figures 13.1 and 13.2.

▧ Practical issues in neuropsychological assessment

Apart from the methodological problems that may beset neuropsychological assessment, there are also practical issues that the neuropsychologist needs to address. These include the choice of test, the effects of assessor–patient interaction, patient compliance, malingering, faults in conducting or reporting the assessment, and methods of test administration. There are also ethical issues to consider. Although outside the remit of this book, this last topic is an important one. Every published study of neuropsychological interest that has employed patients or healthy individuals (and even animals) should have received permission from the author's institution's ethical committee. Although neuropsychological assessment is used to determine a patient's intellectual ability in a very

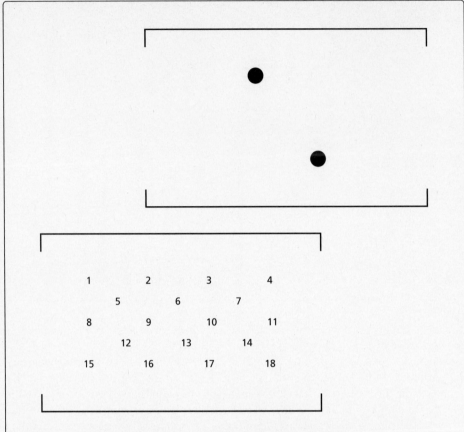

Figure 13.2   The dot localization task: which numbers represent the positions of the dots? Adapted from the Visual Object and Space Perception Battery

practical sense, it is also used to accrue information about the validity of the test itself and of the effects of brain damage on test performance. Scientists are conscious of this fact when writing up their studies and some authors will personally acknowledge the important contribution and cooperation of the patients themselves, especially if the study reported is a case study.

Choice of test

The decision whether to use a battery of tests or a selection of individual tests is largely governed by time and the assessor's hypothesis-testing strategy. If the assessor has a specific hypothesis which can be tested, then individual tests may be more appropriate than a battery which measures a wide range of abilities. Choice of test is also important because it is assumed that the results of test performance reflect the behaviour measured by the test. This, however, may not always be the case, and the assessor may make false inferences. For example, a patient with a motor disorder may perform poorly on a task which requires motor movement but, in fact, the purpose of the test was to examine a cognitive function unrelated to movement. A specific example of this might be performance on the Benton Visual Retention Test, which tests memory for designs by having the patient draw a pattern from memory. Deficits on this tasks are sometimes described as visual memory deficits or taken as evidence of poor visual memory 'suggesting the impairment of the right hemisphere [or] the right temporal region' (Walsh, 1991). However, as the test involves drawing, the deficit may not be cognitive but executive, praxic or graphic. If the assessor suggested that this motor-impaired individual had impaired visuospatial ability, he or she would be making a false inference, an erroneous conclusion based on misinterpreted data. A means of obviating this problem might be to utilize a version of the task with no motor component, e.g. the multiple choice version of the test which requires patients to select the memorized pattern from a choice of four different ones.

Assessor–patient interaction

In a careful neuropsychological examination, instructions and remarks to the patient are standardized and, in a sense, scripted. This scripting is in place to eliminate the obvious problem of inter-tester variability. One tester may be significantly more positive or negative in his reinforcement than another. This biased interaction might be reflected in the patient's performance. To circumvent this problem, tests are accompanied by administration manuals that include specific scripts with instructions and comments to be made by the tester which must not be deviated from. Other personal factors such as the *social* interaction between the patient and tester may also be a problem, and overfamiliarity should be avoided, as should overformality.

Patient compliance

The state of the subject is an important factor to consider before neuropsycho-logical testing commences. Apart from neurological abnormality, deficits on tests may result from inadequate patient cooperation and effort, deliberate exaggeration of disability, disorders of mood, hostility and mistrust (Benton, 1994). Depression, for example, is one of the more prominent patient factors that are considered, and a neuropsychologist might be asked to assess the extent of mood disorder on performance. The level of depression, whether diagnosed clinically or on the basis of inventory, is high in brain-injured patients (Starkstein and Robinson, 1991).

Malingering

A patient with strong negative motivation (not wanting to do well) is, legally, a serious problem since dissembling on tests may support a defence of mental incompetence or a claim for industrial compensation in court proceedings (Larrabee, 1990). A careful consideration of the patient's history and character is, therefore, important. One method of combating this simulation or exaggeration on tests is to administer tests that are so easy that even the brain-damaged may succeed at them (Rey, 1941, 1964). A second approach is to note whether the patient's performance conforms to expectations based on his brain injury. If performance is below expectation, simulation may be inferred (Benton and Spreen, 1961). The relative success and failure of these malingerer tests is considered in the discussion point at the end of the chapter.

Faults in conducting and reporting the results of neuropsychological assessment

During the course of neuropsychological assessment, there may be faults in the conduct of the examination. These may include a failure to consider events close to the time of the injury or a failure to assess the rate and degree of improvement over time. Deficits which are not apparent until some time after the event may not be neurological in origin (Walsh, 1991). Also, it may be appropriate to consider behaviour outside the prescriptive context of the testing situation. Walsh (1991) describes this as 'coffee-break testing'. This refers to the non-deliberate assessment of the patient during a break in testing when the patient is seen to relax and perform quite differently from when observed in a formal setting. For example, patients performing poorly on certain aspects of aphasia tests may show no difficulty with the same linguistic constructions during the break but repeat the failures when the testing recommences. Patients may also indicate difficulty understanding test instructions but understand equally complex syntactic structures in normal conversation. It is important, therefore, to bear in mind the formal nature of the testing and the possible intellectual intimidation that may arise. This also highlights the importance of having test instructions that are unambiguous: instructions should be comprehensible to patients of high, intermediate and low intellectual ability.

Faults in reporting the examination are sometimes found in medicolegal reports of neuropsychological cases. Problems may involve the inadequate reporting of facts from which deductions are made, such as using terms like 'average score' and 'superior'. Instead, the neuropsychologist should present quantitative, 'hard' data, not simply impressions or overgeneralizations. Reports might often compare an individual's performance against the 'norm', a procedure which, as we have seen above, is problematic. The report might also not consider possible reasons for failure on a test. The sin of summation could also be committed where scores from a number of tests are summed to produce one general score. If a test has easy and difficult items, an average such as this will not indicate whether the individual had specific difficulty on the easy, moderately easy or hard items. Alternatively, individuals may have performed badly on early items but performed well at more advanced levels. This sometimes happens.

Computer-based assessment

In recent years, attempts have been made to eliminate the problem of tester-influence by developing methods of computer-based assessment. A computerized method of administration has many advantages: it presents all information in a standardized and consistent manner, a computer does not get bored, angry or tired, inadvertent prompting is avoided, responses may be accurately recorded, complex analysis and scoring may be undertaken quickly, results may be made available almost immediately after testing and data may be saved directly onto a disk drive (S.L. Wilson and McMillan, 1991). Up to 60 per cent of testing time can be saved (French and Beaumont, 1987).

One series of neuropsychological tests is the Cambridge Neuropsychological Test Automated Battery (CANTAB) developed by Trevor Robbins and his colleagues at Cambridge University. This series, a collection of different batteries, evaluates visual memory, attention, working memory and planning via computerized tests and has been used to evaluate deterioration in Alzheimer's disease, Parkinson's disease, depression, multiple sclerosis, schizophrenia, autism and the dementia that accompanies AIDS (R.G. Morris *et al.*, 1986; Sahakian and Owen, 1992; Robbins and Sahakian, 1994).

French and Beaumont (1987) reported that of eight tests administered to psychiatric patients, none was reported to be more enjoyable in its standard, non-computerized form. There are also reports of successful use with elderly patients (Carr *et al.*, 1982; R.G. Morris *et al.*, 1988). More pertinently, various keyboard manipulations are available for physically disabled people.

There are limitations to this method of test administration, however. For example, the type of material that computer packages can present is limited. Questionnaires with easy scoring systems, such as yes/no or multiple choice questions, are relatively easy to present and score on computer. Questionnaires with open answers, such as comprehension questions, are more difficult to score. As a result, current computer-based tests tend to be in multiple choice format. The display of graphical information may be compromised owing to poor resolution, especially if the image is complex. Finally, whereas a battery such as the WAIS-R may be taken outside the hospital setting and is easy to carry around, moving a large computer is a problem. Of course, a more obvious disadvantage is that a computer might not be able to gain information about a person's behaviour, such as the patient's mood and comportment, outside test administration.

DISCUSSION POINT

How to identify a patient malingering on a neuropsychological test

From legal, scientific and clinical points of view, it is important to ensure that a patient sitting a test gives answers that reflect the best of his or her current ability. Clinically, low scores indicate some profound underlying abnormality. Legally, significantly low scores have implications for the patient's financial wellbeing. For example, the ability to receive financial compensation may rest on the patient's significantly impaired functioning following an industrial accident or exposure to hazardous materials. For this reason, assessors are conscious of deliberate low-scoring on neuropsychological tests.

A small number of tests thought to detect extremely abnormally low scores have been developed. One simple sign of malingering is poor performance entirely out of keeping with the extent of the patient's brain damage and which only the most severely brain damaged would achieve. One study, for example, examined the performance of identified malingerers and non-malingerers using a collection of tests, including the Halstead–Reitan and WAIS-R (Trueblood and Schmidt, 1993). They identified seven 'invalidity indicators' on which cutoff points could identify malingerers. Cutoff points for two or more of these indicators were able to identify most of the suspected malingerers.

An alternative and early method of identifying malingerers was the administration of an extended intellectual ability test. Malingerers would often exaggerate their deficits, performing even more poorly than *bona fide* patients. However, malingerers have been able to mimic successfully levels of intellectual impairment seen in genuinely brain-damaged individuals. What appears to be important is the pattern of performance on tests (Tenhula and Sweet, 1996). For example, digit span test performance tends to be lower relative to scores on other tests on the WAIS-R for malingerers (Mittenberg *et al.*, 1995). Similarly, low scores on aspects of some tests (e.g. Weschler Memory Scales) can distinguish the genuine from the disingenuous patient. Performance on the figural memory scale of the Weschler Memory Scale is poorer in malingerers than in brain-damaged patients (Bernard, 1990). Wiggins and Brand (1988) have suggested that whereas the genuinely brain damaged have relatively intact recognition memory but impaired recall, the malingerers may show the opposite pattern (see below). The tests which typically distinguish malingerers from non-malingerers are tests on which brain-damaged individuals should not show remarkable deficits because they are relatively simple tests. From studies such as these, extremely simple tests have been constructed to identify malingerers, e.g. Symptom Validity Testing. These tests may take the form of forced-recognition exercises whereby a string of digits might be presented to the subject. After the string disappears and a delay of thirty seconds has occurred, the subject is presented with two other strings and is asked to decide which of two was the one previously presented. The results are not completely malingerer-proof although it has been suggested that the malingerer might find it difficult to score within chance levels with repeated testing (Lezak, 1995).

One test which may be of benefit in distinguishing the malingerer from the non-malingerer is Halstead and Reitan's Category Test (CT) which examines the patient's ability to engage in abstract reasoning. The test contains easy and difficult questions in the form of multiple choice alternatives. If, as is suspected, malingerers exaggerate performance regardless of the actual difficulty of the test, their performance should identify them. Eighteen of the items on this test are almost never failed by genuine patients. If a patient gets two or more of these wrong, he or she ought to be treated with suspicion. Even this criterion, however, is questionable. One study has shown no significant difference between malingerers and non-malingerers (Trueblood and Schmidt, 1993) while another has actually found poorer performance on the CT in patients with genuine damage.

Tenhula and Sweet (1996) attempted to standardize a test of malingering based on the validity of the CT, using brain-damaged individuals, normal controls and individuals requested to simulate brain injury. Optimal cutoff points correctly classified each group in 64.1–91.5 per cent of cases. The best index of discrimination was performance on subtests I and II which correctly identified 92.2 per cent of subjects with no false positives. The authors argue that the test should not be administered in isolation if the detection of malingering is the aim.

Perhaps the problem of identifying malingerers is most prominent in cases of amnesia (Brandt, 1992; Leng and Parkin, 1995). Suspected malingerers will not admit their deceit even when their deficits are so gross that they are utterly incompatible with true-amnesic syndrome. One approach to sorting out the truly amnesic from the feigned is to obtain scores on tests from individuals who are instructed to simulate amnesia, i.e. they perform as they imagine an amnesiac would. The assumption behind this approach is that simulators and malingerers have similar ideas about the effects of memory impairment. These views may contradict actual findings from the amnesiacs themselves. In one such experiment, a group of normal controls, amnesiacs and simulators were required to answer set of fourteen autobiographical questions in a structured interview (Wiggins and Brandt, 1988). Although all controls and amnesiacs could give their name, date of birth, home address, mother's maiden name and father's first name, a substantial percentage of simulators failed to answer these questions. Twenty-four hours after the initial interview, simulators were better than real amnesiacs at answering the questions, 'what is my [the experimenter's] name?' and 'what did you have for dinner last night?' Although the interview does discriminate between the feigned and real amnesiacs on a number of items, the percentage actually feigning for each item is not large. The highest percentage of incorrect or false answers given by simulators was 48 per cent. This ⟫

was in response to the question, 'what is your social security number'? – 4 per cent of controls and 38 per cent of amnesic patients were unable to answer this question.

There is probably no test that is guaranteed to detected exaggerated, deliberate and misleading poor intellectual performance. All the tests reviewed above, however, have some practical validity when employed with other measures.

Summary

☐ Neuropsychological assessment refers to the testing of a neurological patient's motor, cognitive and emotional function. Assessment has several aims, perhaps the most important of them being (1) the identification of the presence of cognitive impairment, (2) the differentiation between brain injury and other factors as causes of cognitive impairment, and (3) the facilitation of the patient's rehabilitation or recovery of function.

☐ The neurological examination aims to establish deficits in lower- and higher-order CNS function and to localize these deficits. This is normally conducted by a neurologist.

☐ Neuropsychological assessment may utilize a standardized collection of tests measuring various intellectual functions, called a fixed battery, or a flexible selection of tests. The choice is largely governed by time, the examiner's hypothesis-testing strategy and the availability of the test.

☐ The most commonly used intellectual test battery is the Wechsler Adult Intelligence Scale – Revised (WAIS-R). This comprises two scales: verbal IQ and performance IQ. The two other major test batteries are the Halstead–Reitan Neuropsychological Battery and the Luria–Nebraska Neuropsychological Battery, although these are not as widely used now as once they were. The Luria–Nebraska, in particular, has problems of methodology and standardization.

☐ Tests of individual function can be used to measure general cognitive ability, premorbid intelligence, reasoning and concept formation, memory, attention and vigilance, language ability and visuospatial function. The variety of tests available means that the neuropsychologist can select the one that he or she thinks is the most appropriate. To examine aphasia, for example, the neuropsychologists might choose from the Boston Diagnostic Aphasia Battery, the Multilingual Aphasia Examination, the Western Aphasia Battery or the aphasia screening test of the Halstead–Reitan Battery.

☐ Premorbid measure of intelligence refers to some estimate of how intellectually capable the patient was before brain injury. This is important in, for example, trying to assess the person's general intelligence when the brain injury produces impairments on various other cognitive tests. One of the more widely used and validated tests of premorbid intellectual function is the National Adult Reading Test which is robust and relatively immune to the effects of brain damage. It can be used to predict IQ successfully. It cannot be used with dyslexic or anarthic patients.

☐ One reason for estimating premorbid intelligence is to obtain an individualized standard of comparison. This is important because test batteries have normative scores with which patients' individual scores are compared. This comparison may not be helpful if the individual did not perform within the norm to begin with.

☐ Practical issues to consider in the administration of neuropsychological tests include: (1) whether to administer fixed batteries or individual tests, (2) avoiding false inferences, (3) ensuring clarity and lack of ambiguity in test instructions, (4) taking into account the patient's behaviour in an informal context as well as in the formal testing context ('coffee-break testing'), (5) noting the mood, behaviour and cooperativeness of the patient, (6) ensuring clarity in the description of the quantitative results of the assessment, and (7) the application of computer-based neuropsychological assessment tests.

☐ One important legal and psychological problem in neuropsychological testing is deliberate faking of poor performance. Tests have been devised that are so easy that even the severely brain damaged can perform adequately on them. People falling below this cutoff point, therefore, should be treated with suspicion. Halstead and Reitan's Category Test has been shown to discriminate between genuine and malingering patients reasonably well if used in conjunction with similar tests. Wiggins and Brandt's (1988) structured autobiographical questionnaire may also be able to distinguish malingering amnesiacs from genuine patients.

Recommended further general and specific reading

Key: (1) = introductory, *(3)* = intermediate, *(5)* = advanced

General

Barrett, K. (1993). Neurological examination and neurological syndromes. In G. Morgan and S. Butler (eds), *Seminars in Basic Neurosciences*. London: Royal College of Psychiatrists. *(3)*

Benton, A.L. (1994). Neuropsychological assessment. *Annual Review of Psychology*, **45**, 1–23. *(2)*

Cipolotti, L. and Warrington, E.K. (1995). Neuropsychological assessment. *Journal of Neurology, Neurosurgery and Psychiatry*, **58**, 655–64. *(2)*

Crawford, J.R., Parker, D.M., and McKinlay, M.M. (1992). *A Handbook of Neuropsychological Assessment*. Hove, UK: Lawrence Erlbaum Associates. *(2)*

Lezak, M.D. (1995). *Neuropsychological Assessment* (3rd edition). New York: Oxford University Press. *(2)*

Spreen, O. and Strauss, E. (1991). *A Compendium of Neuropsychological Tests*. New York: Oxford University Press. *(2)*

Walsh, K.W. (1991). *Understanding Brain Damage: A primer of neuropsychological evaluation*. Edingburgh: Churchill Livingstone. *(2)*

Specific

Callahan, C.D., Schopp, L. and Johnstone, B. (1997). Clinical utility of a seven subtest WAIS-R short form in the neuropsychological assessment of traumatic brain injury. *Archives of Clinical Neuropsychology*, **12**(2), 133–8. *(3)*

Goodglass, H. and Kaplan, E. (1972). *Assessment of Aphasia and Related Disorders*. Philadelphia: Lea and Febiger. *(3)*

Hayward, L., Hall, W., Hunt, M. and Zubrick, S.R. (1987). Can localized brain impairment be simulated on neuropsychological test profiles? *Australian and New Zeland Journal of Psychiatry*, **21**, 87–93. *(3)*

Johnstone, B., Hexum, C.L. and Ashkanazi, G. (1995). Extent of cognitive decline in traumatic brain injury based on estimates of premorbid intelligence. *Brain Injury*, **9**(4), 377–84. *(3)*

Leng, N.R.C. and Parkin, A.J. (1995). The detection of exaggerated or simulated memory disorder by neuropsychological methods. *Journal of Psychosomatic Research*, **39**(6), 767–76. *(3)*

Little, A.J., Templer, D.I., Persel, C.S. and Ashley, M.J. (1996). Feasibility of the neuropsychological spectrum in prediction of outcome following head injury. *Journal of Clinical Psychology*, **52**(4), 455–60. *(3)*

Moses, J.A., Pritchard, D.A. and Adams, R.L. (1997). Neuropsychological information in the Wechsler Adult Intelligence Scale – Revised. *Archives of Clinical Neuropsychology*, **12**(2), 97–109. *(3)*

O'Carroll, R. (1995). The assessment of premorbid ability: a critical review. *Neurocase*, **1**, 83–9. *(3)*

Rogers, R. (1988). *Clinical Assessment of Malingering and Deception*. New York: Guilford Press. *(3)*

Tenhula, W.N. and Sweet, J.J. (1996). Double cross-validation of the booklet Category Test in detecting malingered traumatic brain injury. *The Clinical Neuropsychologist*, **10**(1), 104–116. *(3)*

Ward, L.C. and Ryan, J.J. (1997). Validity of quick short forms of the Wechsler Adult Intelligence Scale–Revised with brain-damaged patients. *Archives of Clinical Neuropsychology*, **12**(1), 63–9. *(3)*

Appendix

Resources for neuropsychology students

Sources of information

A number of important resources are available to students of neuropsychology to help them to get to grips with the subject. The best and obvious source is reading material, particularly refereed journals which carry important or interesting empirical research or literature reviews in human neuropsychology. Another source of information is computer software. There has been a recent increase in the number of computer software packages that either help you run/or participate in a neuropsychological/psychophysiological experiment or give you tours of the brain and its function. Most are interactive in that they incorporate puzzles to test your knowledge of the subject. Perhaps the most advanced resource available to any student is the Internet. While a lot of what you find on the Internet is quirky or, frankly, rubbish, there are sites that you can visit which offer excellent written and visual resources to any student interested in neuropsychology.

This chapter is designed to give you a fairly comprehensive account of the types of resource available in human neuropsychology which will help you, as a student, gain better understanding of the subject.

Journals

Visit any journal section in any university library and it will seem as if there is a journal covering almost every academic topic imaginable. Publishers have become keen to publish new and more specialized journals, which has resulted in an increase in the number of potential outlets for publishing results and disseminating information. General journals continue to flourish and for good reason: these tend to be the journals that most researchers would like to publish their findings in. Examples include *Nature, Science, Brain, Journal of Neuroscience, Neuropsychologia*. The advantage of specificity, however, is that the journal reaches a particular readership and those workers at the cutting edge of their area of research. *Neuropsychologia*, for example, includes papers on topics ranging from olfactory lateralization in chicks, to frontal lobe dysfunction, to impaired face recognition. Journals such as *Laterality* and *Visual Neuroscience*, on the other hand, limit their coverage to those two aspects of neuropsychology. Often, these specialized journals become leaders in their field.

Below is a list of the more prominent or relevant journals in human neuropsychology. Not every library is going to stock all of them (there are over eighty), but any good library should stock a selection. You should consult the latest issues of these journals regularly. This will allow you to keep up to date with fresh findings in the area.

Aging, Neuropsychology and Cognition
Annals of Neurology

Aphasiology
Applied Neurophysiology
Archives of Clinical Neuropsychology
Archives of Neurology
Behaviour and Brain Research
The Behavioural and Brain Sciences
Behavioural Neurology
Behavioural Neuroscience
Biological Psychiatry
Biological Psychology
Brain
Brain and Cognition
Brain and Language
Brain, Behaviour and Immunity
Brain Injury
Brain Pathology
Brain Research Bulletin
Canadian Journal of Neurological Science
Cerebral Cortex
Child Neuropsychology
The Clinical Neuropsychologist
Cognition and Emotion
Cognitive Brain Research
Cognitive Neuropsychiatry
Cognitive Neuropsychology
Cortex
Current Opinion in Neurobiology
Developmental Brain Research
Developmental Medicine and Child Neurology
Developmental Neuropsychology
Developmental Psychobiology
Electroencephalography and Clinical Neurophysiology
European Journal of Neuroscience
Experimental Brain Research
Experimental Neurology
Human Brain Mapping
International Journal of Clinical Neuropsychology
International Journal of Developmental Neuroscience
International Journal of Neuroscience
International Journal of Psychophysiology
Italian Journal of Neurological Sciences
Journal of Cerebral Blood Flow and Metabolism
Journal of Clinical and Experimental Neuropsychology
Journal of Cognitive Neuroscience

Journal of Cognitive Rehabilitation
Journal of Head Trauma Rehabilitation
Journal of Nervous and Mental Disorders
Journal of Neurobiology
Journal of Neurology, Neurosurgery and Psychiatry
Journal of Neuroimaging
Journal of Neurophysiology
Journal of Neuroscience
Journal of Psychophysiology
Journal of Speech and Hearing Research
Journal of the History of the Neurosciences
Journal of the International Neuropsychological Society
Journal of the Neurological Sciences
Laterality
Movement Disorders
Nature
Neurobiology of Learning and Memory
Neurocase
Neuroimage
Neurology
Neuron
Neuropsychobiology
Neuropsychologia
Neuropsychological Rehabilitation
Neuropsychology
Neuropsychology, Development and Cognition
Neuropsychology Review
Neuropsychopharmacology
Neurorehabilitation
Neuroreport
Neuroscience and Behavioural Physiology
Neuroscience and Behavioural Reviews
Neuroscience Letters
The Neuroscientist
Progress in Brain Research
Psychiatric Research Neuroimaging
Psychobiology
Psychophysiology
Science
Trends in Cognitive Sciences
Trends in Neurosciences
Vision Research
Visual Neuroscience

◼ Computer software

The computer software available to neuropsychologists and neuropsychology students allows you to examine your knowledge of neuropsychology after familiarization with the basic concepts, to interact with the software package by completing the tests it supplies for you, to run an experiment or to undertake neuropsychological assessment. Below are just some of the software packages available.

Neurophysiology

A/DVANCE
Author: McKellar Designs
Available from: McKellar Designs, email: rdouglas@mckellar.com
Compatible with: Apple Mac
Content: Acquisition and analysis of data from neurophysiological experiments involving measurement of electrical potentials. This software is free

Biology Tutorial Series 1.0
Author: P. Stephens
Available from: Intellimation, PO Box 1922, Santa Barbara, CA 93116–1922, USA; fax: 1 805 968 8899
Compatible with: Apple Mac
Content: Tutorials involving neurophysiology such as the action potential and synapses

Brain Browser
Author: F. Bloom
Available from: Academic Press, Harcourt Brace Jovanovich, 1250 Sixth Avenue, San Diego, CA 92101–9665, USA; fax: 1 619 699 6596
Compatible with: Apple Mac
Content: Large package concerning neuroscience, based on rat brain data

Electrophysiology of the Neuron
Authors: J. Huguenard and D.A. McCormick
Available from: Oxford University Press, 198 Madison Avenue, New York, NY 10016, USA; email: eat@oup-usa.org
Compatible with: Apple Mac, IBM PC
Content: Companion to Shepherd's *Neurobiology* in which action potentials, synapses and other aspects of neurophysiology can be explored

The Graphic Brain
Author: T. Teyler
Available from: International Thomson Publishing, Berkshire House, 168–173 High Holborn, London WC1V 7AA; fax: 44 171 497 1426; email: itpuk@itps.co.uk (orders) or info@itpuk.co.uk (information)
Compatible with: Apple Mac, IBM PC
Content: Animation material about neurophysiology

Mapping the Visual Field
Authors: C.M. Levy and G. Levy
Available from: Life Science Associates, 1 Fenimore Road, Bayport, NY 11705–2115, USA; fax: 1 516 472 8146; email: franklsa@aol.com
Compatible with: IBM PC
Content: Recording of cortical neurons from the cat's visual apparatus in a simulated laboratory

Neurosim
Author: W.J. Heitler
Available from: Biosoft, 49 Bateman Street, Cambridge CB2 1LR; fax: 44 1223 312873; email: ab47@cityscape.co.uk
Compatible with: IBM PC
Content: Simulation of various neural functions

Vance's Brain
Author: V. Lemmon
Available from: Vance Lemmon; email: vxl@po.cwru.edu
Compatible with: Apple Mac
Content: Synaptic transmission. This software is free

Psychophysiology

Life Sciences Consortium Neurophysiology Practical – EEG/Evoked Potentials
Author: Dr Malcolm George
Available from: Dr Malcolm George, Dept of Physiology, Queen Mary and Westfield College, Mile End Road, London E1 4NS; fax: 44 171 983 0467; email: m.j.george@qmw.ac.uk
Compatible with: IBM PC
Content: Introduction to various electroencephalographic techniques including EEG and sensory evoked potentials

Neuroanatomy

Brainiac
Authors: Medical Multimedia Systems
Available from: Medical Multimedia Systems, 1247 East 70th Street, Brooklyn, NY
  11234, USA; email: MedMult@AOL.com
Compatible with: IBM PC
Content: Tutorial package presenting large number of brain sections

Brainscape
Authors: J. Wilson and L. Ostergren
Available from: J. Wilson, Dept of Psychological Sciences, Indiana University-
  Purdue, Fort Wayne, IN 46805–1499, USA;
  email: wilsonj@stmplink.ipfw.indiana.edu
Compatible with: IBM PC
Content: Adventure game allowing the user to explore neuroanatomy via problem-
  solving. Free if disk and postage are supplied to the author

Clinical Neuropsychology
Author: J.M. Williams
Available from: Cool Spring Software, PO Box 130, Woodsboro, MD 21798, USA;
  fax: 1 301 845 8422; email: coolspring@aol.com
Compatible with: Apple Mac, IBM PC
Content: Colour and grey images of neuroanatomy and accompanying descriptions
  of various neuropsychological disorders

Interactive Brain Atlas
Authors: Health Sciences Center for Educational Resources
Available from: Health Sciences Center for Educational Resources, University of
  Washington, T-252, Health Sciences Building, SB-56, Seattle, WA 98195, USA;
  fax: 1 206 543 8051; email: center@u.washington.edu
Compatible with: Apple Mac
Content: 3-D and 2-D images of whole and sectioned brains and MRI scans

NeuroABC
Authors: R. Ilmoniemi and M. Perko
Available from: Risto Ilmoniemi, Dept of Neurophysics, Biomag laboratory, Hel-
  sinki University, Central Hospital, Stenbackinkatug 00290, Helsinki, Finland;
  fax: 358 0 4712090; email: rji@oliivi.pc.helsinki.fi
Compatible with: Apple Mac
Content: Tutorial cards on neuroanatomy and neurophysiology

Neuroanatomy Foundations: Academic Version 1.2.1
Author: J.M. Williams

Available from: Intellimation, PO Box 1922, Santa Barbara, CA 93116–1922, USA;
  fax: 1 805 968 8899
Compatible with: Apple Mac
Content: Neuroanatomical brain atlas with 3-D sections of the human brain

Neurological Illness
Author: J.M. Williams
Available from: Cool Spring Software, PO Box 130, Woodsboro, MD 21798, USA;
  fax: 1 301 845 8422; email: coolspring@aol.com
Compatible with: Apple Mac, IBM PC
Content: Text and images relating to neurological disorders

Neuro-Sys
Authors: Biosoft
Available from: Biosoft, 49 Bateman Street, Cambridge CB2 1LR;
  fax: 44 1223 312873; email: ab47@cityscape.co.uk
Compatible with: IBM PC
Content: Tutorial package involving neuroanatomical techniques such as tracing
  and staining

Slice of Brain
Authors: Health Sciences Center for Educational Resources
Available from: Health Sciences Center for Educational Resources, University of
  Washington, T-252, Health Sciences Building, SB-56, Seattle, WA 98195, USA;
  fax: 1 206 543 8051; email: center@u.washington.edu
Compatible with: Apple Mac, IBM PC
Content: Large encyclopaedic package with over 20 000 stills and motion slides of
  neuroanatomy

Neuropsychological assessment

Brain Games 1.1
Authors: J. Epstein and R. Deysach
Available from: Intellimation, PO Box 1922, Santa Barbara, CA 93116–1922, USA;
  fax: 1 805 968 8899
Compatible with: Apple Mac
Content: Neuropsychological assessment presented in the form of seven games for
  students of neuropsychology

Cogrehab, vol. 1
Author: R. Gianutsos
Available from: Life Science Associates, 1 Fenimore Road, Bayport, NY
  11705–2115, USA; fax: 1 516 472 8146; email: franklsa@aol.com
Compatible with: IBM PC
Content: Various cognitive tasks on disk which also stores patient's data

Cogrehab, vol. 2
Authors: R. Gianutsos, G. Vroman and P. Matheson
Available from: Life Science Associates, 1 Fenimore Road, Bayport, NY
   11705–2115, USA; fax: 1 516 472 8146; email: franklsa@aol.com
Compatible with: IBM PC
Content: Tasks of perceptual ability

Cogrehab, vol. 3
Author: R. Gianutsos
Available from: Life Science Associates, 1 Fenimore Road, Bayport, NY
   11705–2115, USA; fax: 1 516 472 8146; email: franklsa@aol.com
Compatible with: IBM PC
Content: Tasks of memory for brain-injured individuals

Cogrehab, vol. 4
Author: L. Laatsch
Available from: Life Science Associates, 1 Fenimore Road, Bayport, NY
   11705–2115, USA; fax: 1 516 472 8146; email: franklsa@aol.com
Compatible with: IBM PC
Content: Tasks based on Luria's model of cognitive functioning

Cogrehab, vol. 5
Author: R. Gianutsos
Available from: Life Science Associates, 1 Fenimore Road, Bayport, NY
   11705–2115, USA; fax: 1 516 472 8146; email: franklsa@aol.com
Compatible with: IBM PC
Content: Evaluation and rehabilitation of individuals who have survived coma

Colorado Malingering Tests 2.0
Authors: H.P. Davis, G.M. Bajszar, G.M. and L.R. Squire
Available from: Colorado Neuropsychological Tests, 102 East Jefferson, Colorado
   Springs, CO 80907, USA
Compatible with: IBM PC
Content: Battery used in the detection of malingering on memory tests

Colorado Neuropsychology Tests 2.0
Authors: H.P. Davis, G.M. Bajszar, G.M. and L.R. Squire
Available from: Colorado Neuropsychological Tests, 102 East Jefferson, Colorado
   Springs, CO 80907, USA
Compatible with: IBM PC
Content: Battery of tests examining explicit memory, implicit memory and
   problem-solving

Microcog: Assessment of Cognitive Functioning
Authors: The Psychological Corporation

Available from: The Psychological Corporation Ltd, 24–28 Oval Road, London
NW1 7DX; fax: 0171 485 4752
Compatible with: IBM PC
Content: Battery of tests examining various cognitive skills

Neuropsych History
Authors: P. Malloy and J.M. Williams
Available from: Available from: Cool Spring Software, PO Box 130, Woodsboro,
MD 21798, USA; fax: 1 301 845 8422; email: coolspring@aol.com
Compatible with: Apple Mac, IBM PC
Content: Checklist of questions concerning the patient's neuropsychological his-
tory and ability to use the computer

Wisconsin Card Sorting Test
Authors: Cybermetrics Testing Services
Available from: Cybermetrics Testing Services, 7921 Ruxway Road, Baltimore, MD
21204–3515, USA; fax: 1 410 821 5618; email: allen@atieninh.sph.jhu.edu
Compatible with: IBM PC
Content: Computer version of the WCST

■ The Internet

What is it?

The Internet is a massive, global, electronic means of communication and distribution of information. If you are studying at university, you should be able to access
the Internet from your university's computer system. If, on the other hand, you do
not have such access, you will need a computer, modem and telephone line which
links you to the Internet. Academics have known about and used the Internet since
its infancy in the early 1980s. Its biggest advantage is its ability both to allow you
to communicate with others who share the same interests as you as well as to
provide information about almost every conceivable topic immediately. Once
hooked up to the Internet, you can visit millions of Web sites. These are pages
which contain information, goods or entertainment which you can search for by
instructing your computer to select sites that are relevant to your topic of interest.
Once accessed, the material you obtain can be downloaded onto your computer or
printed out directly via your printer. The number of Web sites is enormous and you
can find sites devoted to matters as diverse as burrito fillings, designer clothing,
stock exchange performance, psychology, the weather and television programmes.
There is even an electronic, refereed journal for psychologists on the Internet
called *Psycoloquy*.

Your computer will have a navigator that you can use to find your way around
the Internet. The best known navigators are Netscape Navigator and Microsoft

Explorer: the merits and demerits of each are exhaustively debated. These navigators have search engines, software programs that allow you to key in a term or phrase which will enable them to locate a Web site, or many Web sites, relevant to your keyword. Obviously, the more general the keyword, the greater the number of sites the search engine will find. Thus, searching for sites related to 'psychology' will, depending on the search engine, produce a large number of possible sites of interests, but a more specific keyword, e.g. frontal lobes, will produce a much shorter list.

Neuropsychology Web sites

The Web sites listed below are those which provide excellent written and visual material for any person interested in neuropsychology. These sites provide information about neuropsychological subjects, addresses of important societies and research groups, links to neuropsychology journals and books, news about forthcoming conferences and much else besides. Because the Internet is of the moment, continually evolving and regularly updated, some sites become out of date or obsolete very quickly. Sites are normally constructed and maintained by one person whom you should be able to contact with suggestions or queries via his or her email address on the page.

The sites below have been highlighted, based on the prediction that they will still be in operation by the time that you read this. An important feature of these sites is that they provide you with links to other Web pages of interest. In this sense, the Internet is a bit like opening one door to reveal a series of doors. Enter one of these, and another series of doors awaits you. It is not difficult to understand why some individuals become addicted to the Internet.

Neuropsychology Central
Address: www.premier.net/~cogito/neuropsy.html
Content: This is the best neuropsychology site I have been able to find. It has
   information about all strands of neuropsychology as well as links to
   organizations, newsgroups, jobs, assessment procedures and free
   neuropsychology software

World Wide Web Virtual Library for Neuroscience
Address: neuro.med.cornell.edu/VL/
Content: A collection of neuroscience references

Cognitive Neuroscience Resources
Address: www.cs.cmu.edu/Web/Groups/CNBC
Content: A list of links providing resources for the cognitive neuroscientist

Neuroscience on the Internet
Address: www.lm.com/~nab/

Content: A list of links of interest to neuroscientists

Neurosciences on the Net
Address: www.lm.com/~nab/neuroimg.html/non.html
Content: A wide range of links to neuropsychology-related sites

Neuroscience Search Engine
Address: www.acsiom.org/nsr/neuro.html
Content: This is a search engine that will allow you to find Web sites relevant to your keyword search

Yahoo Neuroscience
Address: www.yahoo.com/Health/Medicine/Neuroscience
Content: Yahoo is one of the Internet's premier search engines – this is the result of its best Web site matches for neuroscience

Brain Collection Resources
Address: www.neurophys.wisc.edu/brain/othercollec.html
Content: Large number of sites with brain atlases, including the two described immediately below

Wisconsin/Michigan State Brain Collection
Address: www.neurophys.wisc.edu/brain/
Content: A collection of images of mammalian brain sections

The Whole Brain Atlas
Address: www.med.Harvard.edu/AANHB/home.html
Content: An impressive collection of human brain sections and MRI/PET ages, normal and abnormal

Human Neuroanatomy and Neuropathology
Address: www.lm.com/~nab/neuroimg_l.html/human_neuroanatomy
Content: A collection of images from human neuroanatomy, normal and abnormal

The Harvard Brain
Address: hcs.harvard.edu/~husn/BRAIN/index.html
Content: An impressive Internet magazine on the brain, designed and written by Harvard neuroscience undergraduates

The author
Address: www.mdx.ac.uk/www/psychology/
Content: The author's page can be found at this link

■ Societies

A small number of learned and scientific societies exist to promote and discuss neuropsychology. Two divisions of the American Psychological Association, for example, are devoted to behavioural neuroscience. There is an international society as well as several smaller, national societies. There may also be other societies devoted to particular aspects of neuropsychology such as language or Alzheimer's disease, and these are many. The societies listed below are general societies. Many of these have strict membership application rules so that undergraduates may join only on graduation or applicants must have a PhD or work/ research in human neuropsychology. These may still be useful because you may be able to get onto their mailing list (for a small fee). In return, you will receive news of the society, its members and any forthcoming conferences. Other societies, however, do not impose such membership restrictions. Below is a short list of societies you might contact for further information, especially if you decide to become involved in human neuropsychology in a research or clinical capacity.

American Psychological Association Divisions 6 and 40
Membership information available from Dr Thomas Scott, Office of the Dean, 201 Elliott Hall, University of Delaware, Newark, DE 19716, USA

British Neuropsychological Society
Membership is open to anyone who 'can demonstrate a commitment to neuro-psychology', which limits it to graduates and professionals. However, keen students interested in pursuing neuropsychology at graduate level should, when the time is right, make enquiries with the BNS Secretariat, Russell Cairns Unit, The Radcliffe Infirmary, Oxford OX2 6HE

British Psychophysiology Society
A student membership category exists which provides students with the benefits of full membership but at a discounted price. Fee includes a subscription to the *Journal of Psychophysiology* and *The British Psychophysiology Society Quarterly*. The BPPS Web site can be found at: www.geocities.com/CapeCanaveral/Labs/3839 (this address is case-sensitive, so be careful when typing it). For details contact the author at School of Psychology, Middlesex University, Enfield EN3 4SF, UK or email him on: n.martin@mdx.ac.uk

International Neuropsychological Society
This has over 3300 members and a subscription will also bring you the society's journal, *Journal of the International Neuropsychological Society*. Information about the society can be obtained from: INS, 700 Ackerman Road, Suite 550 Columbus, OH 43202–1559; email: osu ins@postboc.acs.ohio-state.edu

National Academy of Neuropsychology
For details of the academy, contact: NAN, 2600 South Parker Road, Building 1, Suite 215, Aurora, CO 80014. Subscription comes with the *Archives of Clinical Neuropsychology*. The academy runs an Internet shop which sells interesting mugs. You can access the shop via the academy's Web site at: www.nan. drexel.edu

Society for Psychophysiological Research
This is the largest society for psychophysiological research and offers student membership. A subscription to the journal *Psychophysiology* is included in the price of subscription. Write to: SPR, 1010 Vermont Avenue, Suite 1100, Washington DC 20005–4907, USA

References

Aboitiz, F., Scheibel, A.B., Fisher, R.S. and Zaidel, E. (1992a). Fiber composition of the human corpus callosum. *Brain Research*, **598**, 143–53.

Aboitiz, F., Scheibel, A.B. and Zaidel, E. (1992b). Morphometry of the Sylvian fissure and the corpus callosum with emphasis on sex differences. *Brain*, **115**, 1521–41.

Adams, R.D. and Victor, M. (1993). *Principles of Neurology* (5th edition). New York: McGraw-Hill.

Adolphs, R., Tranel, D., Damasio, H. and Damasio, A. (1994). Impaired recognition of emotion in facial expressions following bilateral damage to the human amygdala. *Nature*, **372**, 669–72.

Adolphs, R., Tranel, D., Damasio, H. and Damasio, A. (1995). Fear and the human amygdala. *Journal of Neuroscience*, **15**(9), 5879–91.

Adolphs, R., Damasio, H., Tranel, D. and Damasio, A.R. (1996). Cortical systems for the recognition of emotion in facial expressions. *Journal of Neuroscience*, **16**(23), 7678–7687.

Adrian, E.D. and Mathews, B.H.C. (1934). Berger rhythm: potential changes from the occipital lobes of man. *Brain*, **57**, 355–85.

Aggleton, J.P. (1992). *The Amygdala: Neurobiological aspects of emotion, memory and mental dysfunction*. New York: Wiley/Liss.

Aggleton, J.P. and Mishkin, M. (1986). The amygdala: sensory gateway to the emotions. In R. Plutchik and H. Kellerman (eds), *Biological Foundations of Emotion*, volume 3. New York: Academic Press.

Ahern, G.L., Schomer, D.L., Kleefield, J., Blume, H., Cosgrove, G.R., Weintraub, S. and Mesulam, M.M. (1991). Right hemisphere advantage for evaluating emotional facial expressions. *Cortex*, **27**, 193–202.

Akelaitis, A.J. (1944/45). Studies on the corpus callosum IV: diagnostic dyspraxia in epileptics following partial and complete section of the corpus callosum. *American Journal of Psychiatry*, **101**, 594–9.

Alajouanine, T. and Lhermitte, F. (1965). Acquired aphasia in children. *Brain*, **88**, 653–62.

Albert, M. and Bear, D. (1974). Time to understand: a case study of word deafness with reference to the role of time in auditory comprehension. *Brain*, **97**, 373–84.

Albert, M. and Moss, M. (1983). The assessment of memory disorders in patients with Alzheimer's disease. In N. Butters and L.R. Squire (eds), *Neuropsychology of Memory*. New York: Guilford Press.

Alexander, G.E., DeLong, M.R. and Strick, P.L. (1986). Parallel organization of functionally segregated motor circuits linking basal ganglia and cortex. *Annual Review of Neuroscience*, **9**, 357–81.

Alexander, G.E., Crutcher, M.D. and DeLong, M.R. (1990). Basal ganglia – thalamocortical circuits: parallel substrates for motor, oculomotor, 'prefrontal' and 'limbic' functions. *Progress in Brain Research*, **85**, 119–46.

Alexander, M.P. and Albert, M.L. (1983). The anatomical basis of visual agnosia. In A. Kertesz (ed.), *Localization in Neuropsychology*. New York: Academic Press.

Alford, L.B. (1933). Localization of consciousness and emotion. *American Journal of Psychiatry*, **12**, 789–99.

Almkvist, O., Backman, L., Basun, H. and Wahlund, L-O. (1993). Patterns of neuropsychological performance in Alzheimer's disease and vascular dementia. *Cortex*, **29**, 661-73.

American Psychiatric Association (1994). *Diagnostic and Statistical Manual of Mental Disorders* (4th edition). Washington, DC: American Psychiatric Association.

Anderson, M.G. (1989). Lateral preference and longevity. *Nature*, **341**, 112.

Anderson, S.W., Damasio, H., Jones, R.D. and Tranel, D. (1991). Wisconsin Card Sorting Test performance as a measure of frontal lobe damage. *Journal of Clinical and Experimental Neuropsychology*, **13**, 909–22.

Anderton, B.H. (1987). Alzheimer's disease: progress in molecular pathology. *Nature*, **325**, 648–9.

Annett, M. (1970). A classification of hand preference by association analysis. *British Journal of Psychology*, **63**, 343–58.

Annett, M. (1985). *Left, Right, Hand and Brain: The right shift theory*. Hove, UK: Lawrence Erlbaum Associates.

Annett, M. and Kilshaw, D. (1982). Mathematical ability and lateral asymmetry. *Cortex*, **18**, 547–568.

Annett, M. and Kilshaw, D. (1984). Lateral preference and skill in dyslexics: implications of the right shift theory. *Journal of Child Psychology and Psychiatry*, **25**(3), 357–77.

Annett, M. and Manning, M. (1990). Reading and a balanced polymorphism for laterality and ability, *Journal of Child Psychology and Psychiatry*, **31**(4), 511–29.

Annett, M. and Turner, A. (1974). Laterality and the growth of intellectual abilities. *British Journal of Educational Psychology*, **44**, 37–46.

Arango, V., Ernsberger, P., Marzuk, P.M., Chen, J.S., Tierney, H., Stanley, M., Reis, D.J. and Mann, J.J. (1990). Autoradiographic demonstration of increased serotonin 5-HT2 and beta-adrenergic receptor binding sites in the brain of suicide victims. *Archives of General Psychiatry*, **47**, 1038–47.

Arendt, T., Bigl, V., Arendt, A. and Tennstedt, A. (1983). Loss of neurons in the nucleus basalis of Meynert in Alzheimer's Disease, paralysis agitans and Korsakoff's Disease. *Acta Neuropathologica*, **61**, 101–8.

Arora, R.C. and Meltzer, H.Y. (1989). Serotonergic measures in the brains of suicide victims: 5-HT2 binding sites in the frontal cortex of suicide victims and control subjects. *American Journal of Psychiatry*, **146**, 730–6.

Arrigoni, G. and De Renzi, E. (1964). Constructional apraxia and hemispheric locus of lesion. *Cortex*, **1**, 170–97.

Austin, M.P., Dougall, N., Ross, M., Murray, C., O'Carroll, R.E., Moffoot, A., Ebmeier, K.P. and Goodwin, G.M. (1992). Single photon emission tomography with 99m Tc-exametazime in major depression and the pattern of brain activity underlying the psychotic/neurotic continuum. *Journal of Affective Disorders*, **26**, 31–43.

Averback, P. (1983). Two new lesions in Alzheimer's disease. *Lancet*, **2**, 1203.

Averill, J.R. (1969). Autonomic response patterns during sadness and mirth. *Psychophysiology*, **5**, 399–414.

Baddeley, A.D. (1986). *Working Memory*. Oxford: Oxford University Press.

Bakan, P. (1969). Hypnotizability, laterality of eye movement and functional brain asymmetry. *Perceptual and Motor Skills*, **28**, 927–32.

Baker, S.C., Rogers, R.D., Owen, A.M., Frith, C.D., Dolan, R.J., Frackowiak, R.S.J. and Robbins, T.W. (1996). Neural systems engaged by planning: a PET study of the Tower of London task. *Neuropsychologia*, **34**(6), 515–26.

Bakker, D.J. (1986). Electrophysiological validation of L- and P-type dyslexia, *Journal of Clinical and Experimental Neuropsychology*, **8**, 133.

Bakker, D.J. (1990). Alleviation of dyslexia by stimulation of the brain. In G.Th. Pavlidis (ed.), *Perspectives on Dyslexia*, volume 2. Chichester: Wiley.

Bakker, D.J. (1992). Neuropsychological classification and treatment of dyslexia, *Journal of Learning Disabilities*, **25**(2), 102–9.

Baldessarini, R.J. (1996a). Drugs and the treatment of psychiatric disorders: depression and mania. In J.G. Hardman and Limbird, L.E. (eds), *Goodman and Gilman's The Pharmacological Basis of Therapeutics* (9th edition). New York: McGraw-Hill.

Baldessarini, R.J. (1996b). Drugs and the treatment of psychiatric disorders: psychosis and anxiety. In J.G. Hardman and Limbird, L.E. (eds), *Goodman and Gilman's The Pharmacological Basis of Therapeutics* (9th edition). New York: McGraw-Hill.

Balint, R. (1909). Seelenhammung des 'Schauens', optische Ataxie, raumliche Storungen des Aufmersamkeit. *Monastchrift für Psychiatrie und Neurologie*, **25**, 51–81.

Bandettini, P.A., Wong, E.C., Hinks, R.S., Tikofsky, R.S. and Hyde, J.S. (1992). Time course EPI of human brain function during task activation. *Magnetic Resonance in Medicine*, **25**, 390–97.

Banich, M.T. (1995). Interhemispheric processing: theoretical considerations and empirical approaches. In R.J. Davidson and K. Hugdahl (eds), *Brain Asymmetry*. Cambridge, MA: MIT Press.

Banich, M.T. and Belger, A. (1990). Interhemispheric interaction: how do the hemispheres divide and conquer a task? *Cortex*, **26**, 77–94.

Barrett, K. (1993). In G. Morgan and S. Butler (eds), *Seminars in Basic Neurosciences*. London: Royal College of Psychiatrists.

Bartholomeus, B. (1974). Effects of task requirements on ear superiority for sung speech. *Cortex*, **10**, 215–223.

Basser, L. (1962). Hemiplegia of early onset and the faculty of speech with special reference to the effects of hemispherectomy. *Brain*, **85**, 427–60.

Basso, A., Faglioni, P. and Vignolo, L.A. (1975). Etude controlée de la reeducation de language dans l'aphasie: comparaison entre aphasiques traites et non-traitée. *Revue Neurologie*, **131**, 607–14.

Bauer, R.M. (1984). Autonomic recognition of names and faces in prosopagnosia: a neuropsychological application of the guilty knowledge test. *Neuropsychologia*, **22**, 457–69.

Bauer, R.M. (1993). Agnosia. In K.M. Heilman and E. Valenstein (eds), *Clinical Neuropsychology* (3rd edition). New York: Oxford University Press.

Baxter, L.R., Phelps, M., Mazziotta, J., Guze, B.H., Schwartz, J., Gerner, R., and Selin, C. (1985). Cerebral metabolic rates for glucose in mood disorders. *Archives of General Psychiatry*, **42**, 441–7.

Baxter, L.R., Schwartz, J.M., Phelps, M.E., Mazziotta, J.C., Guze, B.H., Selin, C.E., Gerner, R.H. and Sumida, R.M. (1989). Reduction of prefrontal cortex glucose metabolism common to three types of depression. *Archives of General Psychiatry*, **46**, 243–50.

Bay, E. (1953). Disturbances of visual perception and their examination. *Brain*, **76**, 515–50.

Bean, R.B. (1906). Some racial peculiarities of the negro brain. *American Journal of Anatomy*, 5, 353–432.

Beardsall, L. and Brayne, C. (1990). Estimation of verbal intelligence in an elderly community: a prediction analysis using a shortened NART. *British Journal of Clinical Psychology*, **29**, 83–90.

Beaton, A.A. (1997). The relation of planum temporale asymmetry and morphology of the corpus callosum to handedness, gender and dyslexia: a review of the evidence. *Brain and Language*, in press.

Beaton, A.A., Williams, L. and Moseley, L.G. (1994). Handedness and hand injuries. *British Journal of Hand Surgery*, **19B**, 158–61.

Beaumont, J.G. (1982). *Introduction to Neuropsychology*. Oxford: Blackwell Scientific.

Beaumont, J.G. (1996a). Neuropsychology. In J. G. Beaumont, P.M. Kenealy and M.J.C. Rogers (eds), *Blackwell Dictionary of Neuropsychology*. Oxford: Blackwell.

Beaumont, J.G. (1996b). Lateral eye movement. In J. G. Beaumont, P.M. Kenealy and M.J.C. Rogers (eds), *Blackwell Dictionary of Neuropsychology*. Oxford: Blackwell.

Beauvois, M.F. and Derouesne, J. (1981). Lexical or orthographic agraphia, *Brain*, **104**, 21–49.

Bebbington, P., Brugha, T., MacCarthy, B., Potter, J., Sturt, E., Wykes, T., Katz, R. and McGuffin, P. (1988). The Camberwell collaborative depression study I. Depressed probands: adversity and the form of depression. *British Journal of Psychiatry*, **152**, 754–65.

Bechara, A., Damasio, H., Tranel, D. and Damasio, A.R. (1997). Deciding advantageously before knowing the advantageous strategy. *Science*, **275**, 1293–95.

Beech, J.R. and Awaida, M. (1992). Lexical and non-lexical routes: a comparison between normally achieving and poor readers. *Journal of Learning Disabilities*, **25**(3), 196–206.

Benbow, C.P. (1988). Sex differences in mathematical reasoning ability in intellectually talented preadolescents: their nature, effects, and possible causes. *Brain and Behavioural Sciences*, **11**, 169–232.

Bench, C.J., Friston, K.J., Brown, R.G., Frackowiak, R.S.J. and Dolan, R.J. (1993). Regional cerebral blood flow in depression measured by positron emission tomography: the relationship with clinical dimensions. *Psychological Medicine*, **23**, 579–90.

Bender, M.D. and Feldman, M. (1972). The so-called 'visual agnosias'. *Brain*, **95**, 173–186.

Benson, D.F. (1967). Fluency in aphasia. *Cortex*, **3**, 373–94.

Benson, D.F. (1993). Aphasia. In K.M. Heilman and E. Valenstein (eds), *Clinical Neuropsychology*. New York: Oxford University Press.

Benson, D.F. and Geschwind, N. (1985). The aphasias and related disturbances. In A.B. Baker and R.J. Joynt (eds), *Clinical Neurology*. New York: Harper and Row.

Benson, D.F. and Weir, W.F. (1972). Acalulia: acquired anarithmetria. *Cortex*, **8**, 465–72.

Bentin, S., Sahar, A. and Moscovitch, M. (1984). Intermanual information transfer in patients with lesions in the trunk of the corpus callosum. *Neuropsychologia*, **22**, 601–11.

Bentin, S., Allison, T., Puce, A., Perez, E. and McCarthy, G. (1996). Electrophysiological studies of face perception in humans. *Journal of Cognitive Neuroscience*, **8**(6), 551–65.

Benton, A.L. (1962). The Visual Retention Test as a constructional praxis test. *Confina Neurologica*, **6**, 53–60.

Benton, A.L. (1968). Differential behavioural effects of frontal lobe disease. *Neuropsychologia*, **6**, 53–60.

Benton, A.L. (1990). Face recognition 1990. *Cortex*, **26**, 491–9.

Benton, A.L. (1994). Neuropsychological assessment. *Annual Review of Psychology*, **45**, 1–23.

Benton, A.L. and Hamsher, K. (1978). *The Multilingual Aphasia Examination*. Iowa City: University of Iowa Press.

Benton, A.L. and Spreen, O. (1961). Visual memory test: the simulation of mental incompetence. *Archives of General Psychiatry*, **4**, 79–83.

Benton, A.L. and Van Allen, M.W. (1968). Impairment in facial recognition in patients with cerebral disease. *Cortex*, **4**, 344–58.

Benton, A.L., Hamsher, K., Varney, N.R. and Spreen, O. (1983). *Contributions to Neuropsychological Assessment*. New York: Oxford University Press.

Berger, H. (1929). Über das elektrenkephalogramm des Menschen. *Arch. Psychiat. Nerv-Krankh.*, **87**, 527–70.

Berlin, C.I., Hughes, L.F., Lowe-Bell, S.S. and Berlin, H.L. (1973). Dichotic right ear advantage in children 5 to 13. *Cortex*, **9**, 394–402.

Bernard, L.C. (1990). Prospects for faking believable memory deficits on neuropsychological tests and the use of incentives in stimulation. *Journal of Clinical and Experimental Neuropsychology*, **12**, 715–28.

Berndt, R.S. and Mitchum, R.S. (1995). *Cognitive Neuropsychological Approaches to the Treatment of Language Disorders*. Hove, UK: Lawrence Erlbaum Associates.

Berthier, M.L., Starkstein, S.E., Leiguarda, R., Ruiz, A., Mayberg, H.S., Wagner, H., Price, T.R. and Robinson, R.G. (1991). Transcortical aphasia. Importance of the nonspeech dominant hemisphere in language repetition. *Brain*, **114**, 1409–27.

Berti, A. and Rizzolatti, G. (1994). Is neglect a theoretically coherent unit? In P.W. Halligan and J.C. Marshall (eds), *Spatial Neglect: Position papers on theory and practice*. Hove, UK: Lawrence Erlbaum Associates.

Best, C.T. (1988). The emergence of cerebral asymmetries in early human development: A literature and a neuroembryological model. In D.L. Molfese and S.J. Segalowitz (eds), *Brain Lateralization in Children: Developmental implications*. New York: Guilford.

Best, C.T., Hoffman, H. and Glanville, B.B. (1982). Development of intact ear asymmetries for speech and music. *Perception and Psychophysics*, **31**, 75–85.

Bever, T.G. and Chiarello, R.J. (1974). Cerebral dominance in musicians and nonmusicians. *Science*, **185**, 137–9.

Binder, J.R., Frost, J.A., Hammeke, T.A., Cox, R.W., Rao, S.M. and Prieto, T. (1997). Human brain language areas identified by fucntional magnetic resonance imaging. *Journal of Neuroscience*, **17** (1), 353–62.

Biondi, M., Parise, P., Venturi, P., Riccio, L., Brunetti, G. and Pancheri, P. (1993). Frontal hemisphere lateralization and depressive personality traits. *Perceptual and Motor Skills*, **77**, 1035–42.

Bisazza, A., Cantalupo, C., Robins, A., Rogers, L.J. and Vallortigara, G. (1996). Right-pawedness in toads. *Nature*, **379**, 408.

Bishop, D.V.M. (1983). Linguistic impairment after hemidecortication for infantile hemiplegia? A reappraisal. *Brain*, **85**, 427–60.

Bishop, D.V.M. (1990). *Handedness and Developmental Disorder*. Hove, UK: Lawrence Erlbaum Associates.

Bisiach, E. and Luzzatti, C. (1978). Unilateral neglect of representational space. *Cortex*, **14**, 129–33.

Bisiach, E., Capitani, E., Luzzatti, C. and Perani, D. (1981). Brain and conscious representation of outside reality. *Neuropsychologia*, **19**, 543–51.

Bisiach, E., Pizzamiglio, L., Nico, D. and Antonucci, G. (1996). Beyond unilateral neglect. *Brain*, **119**, 851–57.

Blair, J.R. and Spreen, O. (1989). Predicting premorbid IQ: a revision of the National Adult Reading Test. *The Clinical Neuropsychologist*, **3**, 129–36.

Blakemore, C. and Mitchell, D.E. (1973). Environmental modification of the visual cortex and the neural basis of learning and memory. *Nature*, **241**, 467–8.

Blumer, D. and Benson, D.F. (1975). Personality changes with frontal and temporal lobe lesions. In D.F. Benson and D. Blumer (eds), *Psychiatric Aspects of Neurologic Disease*. New York: Grune and Stratton.

Blumstein, S. (1981). Neurolinguistic disorders: language – brain relationships. In S. Filskov and T. Boll (eds), *Handbook of Clinical Neuropsychology*. New York: Wiley.

Blythe, I.M., Kennard, C. and Ruddock, K.H. (1987). Residual vision in patients with retinogeniculate lesions of the visual path. *Brain*, **110**, 887–905.

Bodamer, J. (1947). Die prosapagnosie. Archiv für Psychiatrie und Zeitschrift für Neurologie, **179**, 6–54.

Boder, E. (1973). Developmental dyslexia: a diagnostic approach based on three atypical reading – spelling patterns. *Developmental Medicine and Child Neurology*, **15**, 663–87.

Bogen, J.E. (1976). Language function in the short term following cerebral commissurotomy. In H. Avakian-Whitaker and H.A. Whitaker (eds), *Current Trends in Neurolinguistics*. New York: Academic Press.

Bogen, J.E. (1993). The callosal syndromes. In K.M. Heilman and E. Valenstein (eds), *Clinical Neuropsychology*. New York: Oxford University Press.

Bornstein, B., Sroka, H. and Munitz, H. (1969). Prosopagnosia with animal face agnosia. *Cortex*, **5**, 164–9.

Borod, J.C. (1992). Interhemispheric and intrahemispheric control of emotion: a focus on unilateral brain damage. *Journal of Consulting and Clinical Psychology*, **60**(3), 339–48.

Borod, J.C., Koff, E. and Caron, H. (1983). Right hemispheric specialisation for the expression and appreciation of emotion: a focus on the face. In E. Perecman (ed.), *Cognitive processing in the Right Hemisphere*. New York: Academic Press.

Borod, J.C., Koff, E. and Buck, R. (1986a). The neuropsychology of facial expression in normal and brain-damaged subjects. In P. Blanck, R. Buck and R. Rosenthal (eds), *Nonverbal Communication in the Clinical Context*. University Park: Pennsylvania State University Press.

Borod, J.C., Koff, E., Lorch, M.P. and Nicholas, M. (1986b). The expression and perception of facial emotion in brain-damaged patients. *Neuropsychologia*, **24**, 345–8.

Bottini, G., Corcoran, R., Sterzi, R., Paulesu, E., Schenone, P., Scarpa, P., Frackowiak, R.S.J. and Frith, C.D. (1994). The role of the right hemisphere in the interpretation of figurative aspects of language. *Brain*, **117**, 1241–53.

Bowen, D.M., Najlerahaim, A., Procter, A.W., Francis, P.T. and Murphy, E. (1989). Circumscribed changes in the cerebral cortex in neuropsychiatric disorders of later life. *Proceedings of the National Academy of Sciences of the USA*, **86**, 9504–8.

Bowers, D., Bauer, R.M., Coslett, H.B. and Heilman, K.M. (1985). Processing of faces by patients with unilateral hemisphere lesions. I: Dissociation between judgements of facial affect and facial identity. *Brain and Cognition*, **4**, 258–72.

Bradshaw J.L. and Mattingley J.B. (1995). *Clinical Neuropsychology: Behavioural and brain science*. London: Academic Press.

Bradshaw, J.L. and Nettleton, N.C. (1981). The nature of hemispheric specialization in man. *Behavioural and Brain Sciences*, **4**, 51–63.

Bradshaw, J.L., Nettleton, N.C. and Taylor, M.J. (1981). Right hemisphere language and cognitive deficit in sinistrals? *Neuropsychologia*, **19**, 113–32.

Bradshaw J.L., Burden, V. and Nettleton, N.C. (1986). Dichotic and dichaptic techniques. *Neuropsychologia*, **24**(1), 79–90.

Brady, S., Poggie, E. and Rapala, M.M. (1989). Speech repetition abilities in children who differ in reading skill. *Language and Speech*, **32**(2), 109–122.

Brandt, J. (1992). Detecting amnesia's impostors. In L.R. Squire and N. Butters (eds), *Neuropsychology of Memory*. New York: Guilford.

Brazzelli, M., Colombo, N., Della Salla, S. and Spinnler, H. (1994). Spared and impaired cognitive abilities after bilateral frontal damage. *Cortex*, **30**, 27–51.

Breasted, J.H. (1930). *The Edwin Smith Surgical Papyrus*. Chicago: University of Chicago Press.

Brewin, C.R. (1988). *Cognitive Foundations of Clinical Psychology*. Hove, UK: Lawrence Erlbaum Associates.

Brickman, A.S., McManus, M., Grapetine, W.L. and Alessi, N.E. (1984). Neuropsychological assessment of seriously delinquent adolescents. *Journal of the American Academy of Child Psychiatry*, **23**, 453–7.

Brinkman, C. and Porter, R. (1983). Supplementary motor area and the premotor area of monkey cerebral cortex: functional organization and activities of single neurons during performance of learned movement. In J.E. Desmedt (ed.), *Motor Control Mechanisms in Health and Disease*. New York: Raven Press.

Brion, S. and Jedynak, C.P. (1972). Troubles du transfert interhemispherique a propos de 3 observations de tumeurs du corps calleux: la seigne de la main étrangère. *Revue Neurologie*, **126**, 257–66.

Broadbent, D.E. (1958). *Perception and Communication*. London: Pergamon.

Broca, P.P. (1861) Remarques sur le siege de la faculté du langage articule, suivies d'une observation d'aphemie. *Bulletin de la Société Anatomique*, **36**, 330–57.

Brodal, P. (1992). *The Central Nervous System: Structure and function*. Oxford: Oxford University Press.

Brodmann, K. (1909). *Vergleichende lokalisationlehr der grosshirnrinde in ihren prinzipien dargestellt auf grund des zelenbaues*. Leipzig: Barth.

Broman, M. (1978). Reaction time differences between the left and right hemispheres for face and letter discrimination in children and adults. *Cortex*, **14**, 578–91.

Broverman, D.M., Klaiber, E., Kobyashi, Y. and Vogel, W. (1968). Roles of activation and inhibition in sex differences in cognitive abilities. *Psychological Review*, **75**, 23–50.

Brown, G.D.A., Hulme, C., Hyland, P.D. and Mitchell, I.J. (1994). Cell suicide in the developing nervous system: a functional neural network model. *Cognitive Brain Research*, **2**, 71–5.

Brown, P. (1980). An epidemiologic critique of Creutzfedlt–Jakob disease. *Epidemiology Review*, **2**, 113–35.

Bruce, V. and Young, A. (1986). Understanding face recognition. *British Journal of Psychology*, **77**, 305–27.

Bruder, G.E. (1995). Cerebral laterality and psychopathology: perceptual and event-related potential asymmetries in affective and schizophrenic disorders. In R.J. Davidson and K. Hugdahl (eds), *Brain Asymmetry*. Cambridge, MA: MIT Press.

Brun, A. (1987). Frontal lobe degeneration of non-Alzheimer type. I: Neuropathology. *Archives of Gerontology and Geriatrics*, **6**, 193–208.

Brunswick, N. and Rippon, G. (1994). Auditory event-related potentials, dichotic listening performance and handedness as indices of lateralisation in dyslexic and normal readers. *International Journal of Psychophysiology*, **18**, 265–75.

Brunswick, N. and Rippon, G. (1995). Dyslexic brains: how do they differ from those of normal readers? *Proceedings of the British Psychological Society*, **3**, 1.

Bruyer, R., Laterre, C., Seron, X., Feyereisen, P., Strypstein, E., Pierrard, E. and Rectem, D. (1983). A case of prosopagnosia with some preserved covert remembrance of familiar faces. *Brain and Cognition*, **2**, 257–89.

Bryant, P.E., MacLean, M., Bradley, L.L. and Crossland, J. (1990). Rhyme and alliteration, phoneme detection, and learning to read. *Developmental Psychology*, **26**(3), 429–38.

Bryden, M.P. (1965). Tachistoscopic recognition, handedness and cerebral dominance. *Neuropsychologia*, **3**, 1–8.

Bryden, M.P. (1976). Responsible bias and hemispheric differences in dot localization. *Perception and Psychophysics*, **19**, 23–28.

Bryden, M.P. (1982) *Laterality: Functional asymmetry in the intact brain*. New York: Academic Press.

Bryden, M.P. and Allard, F.A. (1978). Dichotic listening and the development of linguistic processes. In M. Kinsbourne (ed.), *Asymmetrical Function of the Brain*. New York: Cambridge University Press.

Bryden, M.P. and Lee, R.G. (1983). Right hemisphere involvement in imagery and affect. In Perecman (ed.), *Cognitive Processing in the Right Hemisphere*. New York: Academic Press.

Bryden, M.P., McManus, I.C. and Bulman-Fleming, M.B. (1994). Evaluating the empirical support for the Geschwind–Behan–Galaburda model of cerebral lateralization. *Brain and Cognition*, **26**, 103–67.

Bub, D. and Kertesz, A. (1982). Deep agraphia. *Brain and Language*, **17**(1), 146–65.

Bub, D., Black, S., Hampson, E. and Kertesz, A. (1988). Semantic encoding of pictures and words: some neuropsychological observations. *Cognitive Neuropsychology*, **5**, 27–66.

Buck, L.B., Firestein, S. and Margolskee, R.F. (1994). Olfaction and taste in vertebrates: molecular and organizational strategies underlying chemosensory perception. In G.J. Siegel, B.W. Agranoff, R.W. Albers and P.B. Molinoff (eds), *Basic Neurochemistry*. New York: Raven Press.

Bucy, P.C. (1934). The relation of the premotor cortex to motor activity. *Journal of Nervous and Mental Disorders*, **79**, 621–30.

Bulla-Hellwig, M., Vollmer, J., Gotzen, A., Skreczek, W. and Hartje, W. (1996). Hemispheric asymmetry of arterial blood flow velocity changes during verbal and visuospatial tasks. *Neuropsychologia*, **43**(10), 987–91.

Burgess, A.P. and Gruzelier, J.H. (1997). Localization of word and face recognition memory using topographical EEG. *Psychophysiology*, **34**, 7–16.

Butfield, E. and Zangwill, O.L. (1946). Re-education in aphasia: a review of 70 cases. *Journal of Neurology Neurosurgery and Psychiatry*, **9**, 75–79.

Butter, C.M. (1969). Perseveration in extinction and in discrimination reversal tasks following selective prefrontal ablations in Macaca mulatta. *Physiology and Behaviour*, **4**, 163–71.

Butter, C.M. and Trobe, J.D. (1994). Integrative agnosia following progressive multifocal leukoencephalopathy. *Cortex*, **30**, 145–58.

Butter, C.M., Mark, V.W. and Heilman, K.M. (1988). An experimental analysis of factors underlying neglect in line bisection. *Journal of Neurology, Neurosurgery and Psychiatry*, **51**, 1581–3.

Butters, N. (1985). Alcoholic Korsakoff's syndrome: some unresolved issues concerning etiology, neuropathology and cognitive deficits. *Journal of Clinical and Experimental Neuropsychology* **7**(2), 181–210.

Butters, N. and Cermak, L.S. (1980). *Alcoholic Korsakoff's Syndrome: An information processing approach to amnesia.* New York: Academic Press.

Butters, N. and Stuss, D.T. (1989). Diencephalic amnesia. In F. Boller and J. Grafman (eds), *Handbook of Neuropsychology.* Amsterdam: Elsevier.

Butters, N., Barton, M. and Brody, B.A. (1970). Role of the right parietal lobe in the mediation of cross-modal associations and reversible operations in space. *Cortex*, **49**, 174–90.

Butters, N., Albert, M., Sax, D., Miliotis, P., Nagode, J. and Sterste, A. (1983). Effect of verbal mediators on the pictorial memory of brain-damaged patients. *Neuropsychologia*, **21**, 307–23.

Butters, N., Delis, D.C. and Lucas, J.A. (1995). Clinical assessment of memory disorders in amnesia and dementia. *Annual Review of Psychology*, **46**, 493–523.

Cabeza, R., Grady, C.L., Nyberg, L., McIntosh, A.R., Tulving, E., Kapur, S., Jennings, J.M., Houle, S. and Craik, F.I.M. (1997). Age-related differences in neural activity during memory encoding and retrieval: a positron emission tomography study. *Journal of Neuroscience*, **17**(1), 391–400.

Calabrese, P., Markowitsch, H.J., Harders, A.G., Scholz, M. and Gehlen, W. (1995). Fornix damage and memory: a case report. *Cortex*, **31**, 555–64.

Campain, R. and Minckler, J. (1976). A note on the gross configurations of the human auditory cortex. *Brain and Language*, **3**, 318–23.

Campbell, D.C. and Oxbury, J.M. (1976). Recovery from unilateral visuospatial neglect. *Cortex*, **12**, 303–12.

Campion, J., Latto, R. and Smith, Y.M. (1983). Is blindsight an effect of scattered light, spared cortex, and near-threshold vision? *Behavioural and Brain Science*, **6**, 423–8.

Caplan, P.J. and Kinsbourne, M. (1976). Baby drops the rattle: asymmetry of duration of grasp by infants. *Child Development*, **47**, 532–4.

Cappa, S.F., Sterzi, R., Vallar, G. and Bisiach, E. (1987). Remission of hemineglect and anosognosia during vestibular stimulation. *Neuropsychologia*, **25**, 775.

Caramazza, A. (1992). Is cognitive neuropsychology possible? *Journal of Cognitive Neuroscience*, **4**(1), 80–95.

Carlson, N.G. (1986). *Physiology of Behavior* (3rd edition). Boston: Allyn and Bacon.

Carlson, N.R. (1995). *Foundations of Physiological Psychology* (3rd edition). Boston: Allyn and Bacon.

Carmichael, A. (1990). Physical development and biological influences. In B. Tonge, G.D. Burrows and J.S. Werry (eds), *Handbook of Studies in Child Psychiatry.* Amsterdam: Elsevier.

Carr, A.C., Wilson, S.L., Ancill, R.J., Ghosh, A. and Woods, R.T. (1982). Automated testing of geriatric patients using a micro-computer-based system. *International Journal of Man – Machine Studies*, **17**(3), 297–300.

Carter, C.J., Benavides, J. and Dubois, A. (1989). The biochemistry of Huntington's Chorea. In N.P. Quinn and P.G. Jenner (eds), *Disorders of Movement.* New York: Academic Press.

Caselli, R.J. (1991). Bilateral impairment of somesthetically mediated object recognition in humans. *Mayo Clinical Proceedings*, **66**, 357–64.

Castles, A. and Coltheart, M. (1993). Varieties of developmental dyslexia. *Cognition*, **47**, 149–80.

Cave, C.B. and Squire, L.B. (1991). Equivalent impairment of spatial and nonspatial memory following damage to the human hippocampus. *Hippocampus*, **1**, 329–40.

Channon, S., Daum, I. and Gray, J.A. (1993). Operant conditioning after temporal lobe lesions in man: conditional and simple discrimination learning. *Cortex*, **29**, 315–24.

Chapman, A.J. (1976). Social aspects of humorous laughter. In A.J. Chapman and H.C. Foot (eds), *Humour and Laughter: Theory, research and applications*. Chichester: Wiley .

Chelune, G.J. and Baer, R.A. (1986). Developmental norms for the Wisconsin Card Sorting Test. *Journal of Clinical Experimental Neuropsychology*, **8**, 219–28.

Chi, J.G., Dooling, E.C. and Gilles, F.H. (1977). Gyri development of the human brain. *Annals of Neurology*, **1**, 86–93.

Christensen, A-L. (1979). *Luria's Neuropsychological Investigation* (2nd edition). Copenhagen: Ejnar Munksgaards Vorlag.

Christiansen, K. and Knussman, R. (1988). Sex hormones and cognitive functioning in men. *Neuropsychobiology*, **18**, 27–36.

Christie, J., Shering, A., Ferguson, J. and Glen, A.I.M. (1981). Physostigimine and arecoline: effects of intravenous infusions in Alzheimer's presenile dementia. *British Journal of Psychiatry*, **138**, 46–50.

Cipolotti, L. and Warrington, E.K. (1996). Does recognising orally spelled words depend on reading – an investigation into a case of better written than oral spelling. *Neuropsychologia*, **34**(5), 427–40.

Clements, J.D. (1996). Transmitter timecourse in the synaptic cleft: its role in central synaptic function. *Trends in Neuroscience*, **19**(5), 163–71.

Cohen, D.C., Noll, D.S. and Schneider, W. (1993). Functional magnetic resonance imaging: overview and methods for psychological research. *Behaviour Research Methods, Instruments and Computers*, **25**(2), 101–13.

Cohen, D.C., Peristein, W.M., Braver, T.S., Nystrom, L.E., Noll, D.C., Jonides, J. and Smith, E.E. (1997). Temporal dynamics of brain activation during a working memory task. *Nature*, **386**, 604–8.

Cohen, H.D., Rosen, R.C. and Goldstein, I. (1976). Electroencephalographic laterality changes during human sexual orgasm. *Archives of Behaviour*, **5**(3), 189–99.

Cohen, J. and Breslin, P.W. (1984). Visual evoked-responses in dyslexic children. *Annals of the New York Academy of Sciences*, **425**, 338–43.

Cohen, M.S. and Bookheimer, S.Y. (1994). Localization of brain function using magnetic resonance imaging. *Trends in Neurosciences*, **17**(7), 268–77.

Cohen, N.J. and Squire, L.R. (1980). Preserved learning and retention of pattern analysing skill in amnesia: dissociation of knowing how and knowing that. *Science*, **210**, 207–9.

Coleman, P.D. and Flood, D.G. (1987). Neuron numbers and dendritic extent in normal ageing and in Alzheimer's disease. *Neurobiology of Ageing*, **8**, 521–45.

Coltheart, M., Patterson, K. and Marshall, J.C. (1980). *Deep Dyslexia*. London: Routledge and Kegan Paul.

Connolly, J.F. and Phillips, N. (1994). Event-related potential components reflect phonological and semantic processing of the terminal word of spoken sentences. *Journal of Cognitive Neuroscience*, **6**(3), 256–66.

Conte, H.R. (1975). A circumplex model for personality traits. PhD dissertation, New York University.

Cook, N.D. (1984a). The transmission of information in natural systems. *Journal of Theoretical Biology*, **108**, 349–67.

Cook, N.D. (1984b). Callosal inhibition: the key to the brain code. *Behavioural Science*, **29**, 98–110.

Cooper, L.A. and Shepard, R.N. (1973). Chronometric studies of the rotation of mental images. In W.G. Chase (ed.), *Visual Information Processing*. New York: Academic Press.

Corballis, M.C. (1989). Laterality and human evolution. *Psychological Review*, **77**, 451–64.

Corballis, M.C. (1991). *The Lop-sided Ape*. New York: Oxford University Press.

Corballis, M.C. (1997). Mental rotation and the right hemisphere. *Brain and Language*, **57**, 100–21.

Corballis, M.C. and Morgan, M.J. (1978). On the biological basis of human laterality I: evidence for a maturational left–right gradient. *Behavioural and Brain Sciences*, **2**, 261–336.

Corballis, M.C. and Trudel, C.I. (1993). Role of the forebrain commissures in interhemispheric integration. *Neuropsychologia*, **7**, 306–24.

Coren, S. (1989). Left handedness and accident-related risk. *American Journal of Public Health*, **79**, 1040–1.

Coren, S. (1995). Differences in divergent thinking as a function of handedness and sex. *American Journal of Psychology*, **108**(3), 311–25.

Coren, S. and Halpern, D. (1991). Left-handedness: a marker for decreased survival fitness. *Psychological Bulletin*, **109**(1), 90–106.

Corkin, S. (1978). The role of different cerebral structures in somesthetic perception. In C.E. Carterette and M.P. Friedman (eds), *Handbook of Perception*, volume VIB. New York: Academic Press.

Cormack. A.M. (1963). Reconstruction of densities from their projections, with applications in radiological physics. *Physics, Medicine and Biology*, **18**, 195–207.

Cossu, G., Daprati, E. and Marshall, J.C. (1995). Deep dyslexia and the right hemisphere hypothesis – spoken and written language after extensive left hemisphere lesion in a 12 year old boy. *Cognitive Neuropsychology*, **12**(4), 391–407.

Cotzias, G.C., Papavisiliou, P.S. and Gellene, R. (1967). L-Dopa in Parkinson's syndrome. *New England Journal of Medicine*, **281**, 272–8.

Courtney, S.M., Ungerleider, L.G., Keil, K. and Haxby, J.V. (1997). Transient and sustained activity in a distributed neural system for human working memory. *Nature*, **386**, 608–11.

Cowburn, R.F., Hardy, J.A. and Roberts, P.J. (1990). Glutamatergic neurotransmission in Alzheimer's disease. *Biochemical Society Transactions*, **18**, 390–2.

Crawford, J.R. (1990). The estimation of premorbid intelligence. PhD thesis, University of Aberdeen.

Crawford, J.R. (1992). Current and premorbid intelligence measures in neuropsychological assessment. In J.R. Crawford, D.M. Parker, and M.M. McKinlay (eds), *A Handbook of Neuropsychological Assessment*. Hove: Lawrence Erlbaum Associates.

Crawford, J.R., Parker, D.M., Stewart, L.E., Besson, J.A.O. and DeLacey, G. (1989a). Prediction of WAIS IQ with the National Adult Reading Test: cross-validation and extension. *British Journal of Clinical Psychology*, **28**, 267–83.

Crawford, J.R., Stewart, L.E., Cochrane, R.H.B., Foulds, J.A., Besson, J.A.O. and Parker, D.M. (1989b). Estimating premorbid IQ from demographic variables: regression equations derived from a UK sample. *British Journal of Clinical Psychology*, **28**, 275–278.

Crawford, J.R., Stewart, L.E., Cochrane, R.H.B., Parker, D.M. and Besson, J.A.O. (1989c). Construct validity of the National Adult Reading Test: a factor analytic study. *Personality and Individual Differences*, **10**, 585–87.

Crawford, J.R., Allan, K.M., Besson, J.A.O., Cochrane, R.H.B. and Stewart, L.E. (1990a). A comparison of the WAIS and WAIS-R in matched UK samples. *British Journal of Clinical Psychology*, **29**, 105–9.

Crawford, J.R., Allan, K.M., Cochrane, R.H.B. and Parker, D.M. (1990b). Assessing the validity of NART estimated IQs in the individual case. *British Journal of Clinical Psychology*, **29**, 435–6.

Crawford, J.R., Allan, K.M, Jack, A.M., Morrison, F.M. and Parker, D.M. (1991). The short NART: cross-validation, relationship to IQ and some practical considerations. *British Journal of Clinical Psychology*, **30**, 223–9.

Crawford, J.R., Sommerville, J. and Robertson, I.H. (1997). Assessing the reliability and abnormality of subtest differences on the Test of Everyday Attention. *British Journal of Clinical Psychology*, **36**, 609–18.

Critchley, M. (1973) *The Dyslexic Child* (2nd edition). London: Heinemann.

Cronbach, L.J. (1949). *Essentials of Psychological Testing*. New York: Harper and Row.

Cross, A.J., Crow, T.J., Johnson, J.A., Perry, E.K., Perry, R.H., Blessed, G. and Tomlinson, B.E. (1984). Studies on neurotransmitter receptor systems in neocortex and hippocampus in senile dementia of the Alzheimer type. *Journal of Neurological Sciences*, **64**, 109–17.

Crow, T.J. (1990). Temporal lobe asymmetries as the key to the etiology of schizophrenia. *Schizophrenia Bulletin*, **16**, 433–43.

Cubelli, R. and Simoncini, L. (1997). Dissociation between word reading and word copying in a patient with left visual neglect. *Cortex*, **33**, 177–85.

Cubelli, R., Caselli, M. and Neri, N. (1984). Pain and unilateral cerebral lesions. *Cortex*, **20**, 369-75.

Cummings, J.L. and Benson, D.F. (1992). *Dementia: A clinical approach*. Boston: Butterworth.

Cunningham, D.J. (1892). *Contributions to the Surface Anatomy of the Cerebral Hemispheres: Cunningham memoires*, volume 7. Dublin: Royal Irish Academy.

Curtiss, S. (1977). *Genie: A psycholinguistic study of a modern day 'wild child'*. New York: Academic Press.

Damasio, A.R. (1989). Time-locked multiregional coactivation: a systems-level proposal for the neural substrates of recall and recognition. *Cognition*, **33**, 25–62.

Damasio, A.R. (1995). Toward a neurobiology of emotion and feeling: operational concepts and hypotheses. *The Neuroscientist*, **1**(1), 19–25.

Damasio, A.R. and Damasio, H. (1992). Brain and language. *Scientific American*, **267**(3), 62–71.

Damasio, A.R., Chui, H.C., Corbett, J. and Kassel, N. (1980a). Posterior callosal section in a non-epileptic patient. *Journal of Neurology, Neurosurgery and Psychiatry*, **43**, 351–6.

Damasio, A.R., Yamada, T., Damasio, H., Corbett, J. and McKee, J. (1980b). Central achromatopsia: behavioural, anatomic and physiologic aspects. *Neurology*, **30**, 1064–71.

Damasio, A.R., Damasio, H. and Van Hoesen, G.W. (1982). Prosopagnosia: anatomical basis and behavioural mechanisms. *Neurology*, **32**, 331–41.

Damasio, A.R., Tranel, D. and Damasio, H. (1990). Individuals with sociopathic behaviour caused by frontal damage fail to respond autonomically to social stimuli. *Behavioural Brain Research*, **41**, 81–94.

Damasio, H. (1981). Cerebral localisation of the aphasias. In M.T. Sarno (ed.), *Acquired Aphasia*. New York: Academic Press.

Damasio, H. and Damasio, A. (1980) The anatomical basis of conduction aphasia. *Brain*, **103**, 337–50.

Damasio, H., Grabowski, T., Frank, R., Galaburda, A.M. and Damasio, A.R. (1994). The return of Phineas Gage: clues about the brain from the skull of a famous patient. *Science*, **264**, 1102–5.

Daniel, W.F. and Yeo, R.A. (1991). Handedness and accident proneness. *American Journal of Public Health*, **81**, 1346.

Darley, F.L. (1972). The efficacy of language rehabilitation in aphasia. *Journal of Speech and Hearing Disorders*, **30**, 3–22.

Dautrich, B.R. (1993). Visual perceptual differences in the dyslexic reader: evidence of greater visual peripheral sensitivity to color and letter stimuli. *Perceptual and Motor Skills*, **76**, 755–64.

Davidson, R.J. (1984). Affect, cognition, and hemispheric specialization. In C.E. Izard, J. Kagan and R. Zajonc (eds), *Emotion, Cognition and Behaviour*. New York: Cambridge University Press.

Davidson, R.J. (1988). EEG measures of cerebral asymmetry: conceptual and methodological issues. *International Journal of Neuroscience*, **39**, 71–89.

Davidson, R.J. (1992). Anterior cerebral asymmetry and the nature of emotion. *Brain and Cognition*, **20**, 125–51.

Davidson, R.J. and Fox, N.A. (1989). Frontal brain asymmetry predicts infants' response to maternal separation. *Journal of Abnormal Psychology*, **98**(2), 127–31.

Davidson, R.J. and Schwartz, G.E. (1977). The influence of musical training on patterns of EEG asymmetry during musical and non-musical self-generation tasks. *Psychophysiology*, **14**, 58–63.

Davidson, R.J. and Sutton, S.K. (1995). Affective neuroscience: the emergence of a discipline. *Current Opinion in Neurobiology*, **5**(2), 217–24.

Davidson, R.J., Schwartz, G.E., Saron, C., Bennett, J. and Goleman, D.J. (1979). Frontal versus parietal EEG asymmetry during positive and negative affect. *Psychophysiology*, **16**(2), 202–3.

Davidson, R.J., Chapman, J.P., Chapman, L.J. and Henriques, J.B. (1990a) Asymmetrical brain electrical activity discriminates between psychometrically-matched verbal and spatial cognitive tasks. *Psychophysiology*, **27**(5), 528–43.

Davidson, R.J., Ekman, P., Saron, C.D., Senulis, J.A.. and Friesen, W.V. (1990b). Approach–withdrawal and cerebral asymmetry: emotional expression and brain physiology I, *Journal of Personality and Social Psychology*, **58**(2), 330–41.

Davis, G.A. and Wilcox, M.J. (1981). Incorporating parameters of natural conversation aphasia treatment. In R. Chapey (ed.), *Language Intervention Strategies in Adult Aphasia*. Baltimore: Williams and Wilkins.

Davis, H.P. and Bernstein, P.A. (1992). Age-related changes in explicit and implicit memory. In L.R. Squire and N. Butters (eds), *Neuropsychology of Memory*. New York: Guilford.

Davis, H.P., Cohen, A., Gandy, M., Columbo, P., Van Dusseldorp, G., Simolke, N. and Romano, J. (1990). Lexical priming deficits as a function of age. *Behavioural Neuroscience*, **104**, 288–97.

Davitz, J.R. (1970). A dictionary and grammar of emotion. In M. Arnold (ed.), *Feelings and Emotions: The Loyola Symposium*. New York: Academic Press.

Dax, M. (1865) Lesion de la moitie gauche de l'encephale coincidant avec l'oubli des signes de la pensée. *Gaz. hebd*, **2**, 259–260.

Day, M.E. (1964). An eye movement phenomenon relating to attention, thought and anxiety. *Perceptual and Motor Skills*, **19**, 443–6.

Dejerine, J. (1892). Contributions a l'étude anatomo-pathologique et clinique des différentes variétés de cécité verbale. *Comptes rendus des séances et memoires de la Société de Biologie*, **44**(9), 61–90.

De Kosky, S.T., Heilman, K.M., Bowers, M.D. and Valenstein, E. (1980). Recognition and discrimination of emotional faces and pictures. *Brain and Language*, **9**, 206–14.

Delay, J. (1935). *Les astereognosies: pathologie due toucher*. Paris: Masson.

Delay, J. and Brion, S. (1969). *Le syndrome de Korsakoff*. Paris: Masson.

Delgado, P.L., Price, L.H., Miller, H.L., Salomon, R.M., Aghajanian, G.K., Heninger, G.R. and Charney, D.S. (1994). Serotonin and the neurobiology of depression. *Archives of General Psychiatry*, **51**, 865–73.

Delis, D.C., Squire, L.R., Bihrle, A. and Massman, P. (1992). Componential analysis of problem-solving ability: performance of patients with frontal lobe damage and amnesic patients on a new sorting task. *Neuropsychologia*, **30**, 683–97.

Della Malva, C.L., Stuss, D.T., D'Alton, J. and Willmer, J. (1993). Capture errors and sequencing after frontal brain lesions. *Neuropsychologia*, **31**(4), 363–72.

Della Rocchetta, A.I. (1986). Classification and recall of pictures after unilateral frontal or temporal lobectomy. *Cortex*, **22**, 189–211.

Della Salla, S., Marchetti, S. and Spinnler, H. (1991). Right-sided anarchic (alien) hand: a longitudinal study. *Neuropsychologia*, **29**, 1113–27.

Dennis, M. (1980). Capacity and strategy for syntactic comprehension after left or right hemidecortication. *Brain and Language*, **10**, 287–317.

Dennis, M., Lovett, M. and Wiegel-Crump, C.A. (1981). Written language acquisition after left or right hemidecortication in infancy. *Brain and Language*, **12**, 54–91.

Dennis, M. and Whitaker, H.A. (1976). Language acquisition following hemidecortication: linguistic superiority of the left over the right hemisphere. *Brain and Language*, **3**, 404–33.

Dennis, M. and Whitaker, H.A. (1977). Hemispheric equipotentiality and language acquisition. In S.J. Segalowitz and F.A. Gruber (eds), *Language Development and Neurological Theory*. New York: Academic Press.

De Renzi, E. (1980) The influence of sex and age on the incidence and type of aphasia. *Cortex*, **16**, 627–30.

De Renzi, E. (1982). *Disorders of Space Exploration and Cognition*. Chichester: Wiley.

De Renzi, E. (1986a). Prosopagnosia in two patients with CT scan evidence of damage confined to the right hemisphere. *Neuropsychologia*, **24**, 385–9.

De Renzi, E. (1986b). Current issues in prosopagnosia. In H.D. Ellis, M.A. Jeeves, K.F. Newcombe and A. Young (eds), *Aspects of Face Processing*. Dordrecht, Holland: Martinus Nijhoff.

De Renzi, E. and Lucchelli, F. (1988). Ideational apraxia. *Brain*, **111**, 1173–88.

De Renzi, E. and Lucchelli, F. (1993). The fuzzy boundaries of apperceptive agnosia. *Cortex*, **29**, 187–215.

De Renzi, E. and Saetti, M.C. (1997). Associative agnosia and optic aphasia: qualitative or quantitative difference? *Cortex*, **33**, 115–30.

De Renzi, E. and Spinnler, H. (1967). Impaired performance on color tasks in patients with hemispheric damage. *Cortex*, **3**, 194–216.

De Renzi, E., Pieczuro, A. and Vignolo, L.A. (1968). Ideational apraxia: a quantitative study. *Neuropsychologia*, **6**, 41–52.

De Renzi, E., Scotti, G. and Spinnler, H. (1969). Perceptual and associative disorders of visual recognition. *Neurology*, **19**, 634–42.

De Renzi, E., Faglioni, P. and Sorgato, P. (1982). Modality specific and supramodal mechanisms of apraxia. *Brain*, **105**, 301–12.

De Renzi, E., Zambolin, A. and Crisi, G. (1987) The pattern of neuropsychological impairment associated with left posterior cerebral artery infarcts. *Brain*, **110**, 1099–116.

De Renzi, E., Bonacini, M.G. and Faglioni, P. (1989). Right posterior brain damaged patients are poor at assessing the age of a face. *Neuropsychologia*, **27**, 839–48.

De Renzi, E., Periani, D., Carlesimo, G.A., Silveri, M.C. and Fazio, F. (1994). Prosopagnosia can be associated with damage confined to the right hemisphere: an MRI and PET study and a review of the literature. *Neuropsychologia*, **35** (8), 893–902.

Desrocher, M.E., Smith, M.L. and Taylor, M.J. (1995). Stimulus and sex differences in performance of mental rotation: evidence from event-related potentials. *Brain and Cognition*, **28**, 14–38.

Deutsch, G., Bourbon, W.T., Papanicolaou, A.C. and Eisenberg, H.M. (1988). Visuospatial tasks compared via activation of regional cerebral blood flow. *Neuropsychologia*, **26**, 445–52.

Dias, R., Robbins, T.W. and Roberts, A.C. (1996). Dissociations in prefrontal cortex of affective shifts. *Nature*, **380**, 69–72.

Dimond, S.J. (1976). Depletion of attentional capacity after total commissurotomy in man. *Brain*, **99**, 347–56.

Ditunno, P.L. and Mann, V.A. (1990). Right hemisphere specialization for mental rotation in normals and brain damaged subjects. *Cortex*, **26**, 177–88.

Donchin, E. and Coles, M.G.H. (1988). Is the P300 component a manifestation of context updating? *Behavioural and Brain Sciences*, **11**, 357–74.

Dool, C.B., Stelmack, R.M. and Rourke, B.P. (1993). Event-related potentials in children with learning disabilities. *Journal of Clinical Child Psychology*, **22**(3), 387–94.

Drachman, D.A. and Leavitt, J. (1974). Human memory and the cholinergic system: a relationship to aging? *Archives of Neurology*, **25**, 450–9.

Dresser, A.C., Meirowsky, A.M., Weiss, G.H., McNeel, M.L., Simon, A.G. and Caveness, W.F. (1973). Gainful employment following head injury. *Archives of Neurology*, **29**, 111–16.

Drewe, E.A. (1974). The effect of type and area of brain lesion on Wisconsin Card Sorting Test performance. *Cortex*, **10**, 159–70.

Duane, D.D. (1989). Commentary on dyslexia and neurodevelopmental pathology. *Journal of Learning Disabilities*, **22**, 219–20.

Duffy, F.H. (1986). Brain Electrical Activity Mapping: issues and answers. In F.H. Duffy (ed.), *Topographic Mapping of Brain Electrical Activity*. London: Butterworths.

Duffy, F.H., McAnulty, G.B. and Schachter, S.C. (1984). Brain electrical activity mapping. In N. Geschwind and A.M. Galaburda (eds), *Cerebral Dominance: The biological foundation*. Harvard: Harvard University Press.

Dunbar, G.C., Perera, M.H. and Jenner, F.A. (1989). Patterns of benzodiazepine use in Great Britain measured by a general population survey. *British Journal of Psychiatry*, **155**, 836–41.

Duncan, J. (1995). Attention, intelligence and the frontal lobes. In M.S. Gazzaniga (ed.), *The Cognitive Neurosciences*. Cambridge, MA: MIT Press.

Duncan, J., Burgess, P. and Emslie, H. (1995). Fluid intelligence after frontal lobe lesions. *Neuropsychologia*, **33**(3), 261–8.

Duncan, H.J. and Smith, D.V. (1995). Clinical disorders of olfaction: a review. In R.L. Doty (ed.), *Handbook of Olfaction and Gustation*. New York: Marcel Dekker.

Eberstaller, O. (1890). Zur Oberflachenanatomie der Grosshirnhemispharen. *Wien. Med. Blatter*, **7**, 479–82, 542–82, 644–6.

Edelman, G.M. (1989). *Neural Darwinism*. Oxford: Oxford University Press.

Eden, G.F., Stein, J.F. and Wood, F.B. (1993). Visuospatial ability and language processing in reading disabled and normal children. In S.F. Wright and R. Groner (eds), *Facets of Dyslexia and its Remediation*. Amsterdam: Elsevier.

Eden, G.F., Stein, J.F., Wood, H.M. and Wood, F.B. (1994). Differences in eye movements and reading problems in dyslexic and normal children. *Vision Research*, **34**(10), 1345–58.

Eden, G.F., VanMeter, J.W., Rumsey, J.M., Maisog, J.M., Woods, R.P. and Zeffiro, T.A. (1996). Abnormal processing of visual motion in dyslexia revealed by functional brain imaging. *Nature*, **382**, 66–9.

Efron, R. (1968). *What is Perception?* New York: Humanities Press.

Ehrlichman, H. (1987). Hemispheric asymmetry and positive–negative affect. In D. Ottoson (ed.), *Duality and Unity of the Brain*. London: Macmillan.

Ekman, P. (1973). Cross-cultural studies of facial expression. In P. Ekman (ed.), *Darwin and Facial Expression: A century of research in review*. New York: Academic Press.

Ekman, P. (1984). Expression and the nature of emotion. In K.R. Scherer and P. Ekman (eds), *Approaches to Emotion*. Hillsdale, NJ: Lawrence Erlbaum Associates.

Ekman, P., Davidson, R.J. and Friesen, W.V. (1990). The Duchenne smile: emotional expression and brain physiology II. *Journal of Personality and Social Psychology*, **58**(2), 342–53.

Elfgren, C.I., Ryding, E. and Passant, U. (1996). Performance on neuropsychological tests related to single photon emission computerised tomography findings in frontotemporal dementia. *British Journal of Psychiatry*, **169**, 416–22.

Ellis, A.W. and Young, A.W. (1996). *Human Cognitive Neuropsychology*. Hove, UK: Lawrence Erlbaum Associates.

Ellis, N. and Large, B. (1988). The early stages of reading – a longitudinal study. *Applied Cognitive Psychology*, **2**(1), 47–76.

Ellis, S.J., Ellis, P.J. and Marshall, E. (1988). Hand preference in a normal population. *Cortex*, **24**, 157–63.

English, H.B. and English, A.C. (1958). *Comprehensive Dictionary of Psychological and Psychoanalytical Terms*. New York: Longmans Green.

Epstein, H.T. (1978). Growth spurts during brain development: implications for educational policy and practice. In J.S. Chard and A.F. Mirsky (eds), *Education and the Brain*. Chicago: University of Chicago Press.

Erickson, T.C. (1940). Spread of epileptic discharge. *Archives of Neurology and Psychiatry*, **43**, 429–52.

Esiri, M.M., Pearson, R.C.A., Steele, J.E., Bowen, D.M. and Powell, T.P.S. (1990). A quantitative study of the neurofibrillary tangles and the choline acetyltransferase activity in the cerebral cortex and amygdala in Alzheimer's disease. *Journal of Neurology, Neurosurgery and Psychiatry*, **53**, 161–5.

Eslinger, P.J. and Damasio, A.R. (1985). Severe disturbance of higher cognition after bilateral frontal ablation: patient EVR. *Neurology*, **35**, 1731–41.

Eslinger, P.J. and Grattan, L.M. (1993). Frontal lobe and frontal – striatal substrates for different forms of human cognitive flexibility. *Neuropsychologia*, **31**(1), 17–28.

Eslinger, P.J., Damasio, A.R. and Van Hoesen, G.W. (1982). Olfactory dysfunction in man: anatomical and behavioural aspects. *Brain and Cognition*, **1**, 259–85.

Etkoff, N.K.L. (1984). Selective attention to facial identity and facial emotion. *Neuropsychologia*, **22**, 281–295.

Farah, M.J. (1990). *Visual Agnosia: Disorders of object vision and what they tell us about normal vision*. Cambridge, MA: MIT Press.

Farah, M.J. (1991). Patterns of co-occurrence among the associative agnosias: implications for visual object representation. *Cognitive Neuropsychology*, **8**, 1–19.

Faust, C. (1955). *Die zerebralen Herderscheinungen bei Hinterhauptverletzungen und ihre Beurteiling*. Stuttgart: Thieme Verlag.

Fearnley, J.M. and Lees, A. (1991). Ageing and Parkinson's disease: substantia nigra regional selectivity. *Brain*, **114**, 2283–301.

Felton, R.H. and Wood, F.B. (1989). Cognitive deficits in reading disability and attention deficit disorder. *Journal of Learning Disabilities*, **1**, 3–13.

Fiez, J.A., Raichle, M.E., Miezin, F.M., Petersen, S.E., Tallal, P. And Katz, W.F. (1995). PET studies of auditory and phonological processing: effects of stimulus characteristics and task demands. *Journal of Cognitive Neuroscience*, **7**(3), 357–75.

File, S.E. (1987). The search for novel anxiolytics. *Trends in Neurosciences*, **10**, 461–3.

Fink, G.R., Halligan, P.W., Marshall, J.C., Frith, C.D., Frackowiak, R.S.J. and Dolan, R.J. (1996). Where in the brain does visual attention select the forest and the trees? *Nature*, **382**, 626–8.

Flannery, K.A. and Liederman, J. (1995). Is there really a syndrome involving the co-occurrence of neurodevelopmental disorder, talent, non-right handedness and immune disorder among children? *Cortex*, **31**, 503–15.

Fletcher, J.M. and Satz, P. (1985). Cluster analysis and the search for learning disability subtypes. In B. Rourke (ed.), *Neuropsychology of Learning Disabilities*. New York: Guilford Press.

Fletcher, P.C., Frith, C.D., Grasby, P.M., Shallice, T., Frackowiak, R.S.J. and Dolan, R.J. (1995). Brain systems for encoding and retrieval of auditory – verbal memory. *Brain*, **118**, 401–16.

Flor-Henry, P. (1969). Psychoses and temporal lobe epilepsy: a controlled investigation. *Epilepsia*, **10**, 363–95.

Flourens, P. (1824). *Récherches Experimentales sur les Propriétés et les Fonctions du Système Nerveux dans les Animaux vertèbres*. Paris: Cervot.

Flowers, D.L., Wood, F.B. and Naylor, C.E. (1991). Regional cerebral blood flow correlates of language processes in reading disability. *Archives of Neurology*, **48**, 637–43.

Fodor, J. (1983). *The Modularity of Mind*. Cambridge, MA: MIT Press.

Fontaine, R., Breton, G., Dery, R., Fontaine, S. and Elie, R. (1990). Temporal lobe abnormalities in panic disorder: an MRI study. *Biological Psychiatry*, **27**, 304–10.

Fox, N.A., Rubin, K.H., Calkins, S.D., Marshall, T.R., Coplan, R.J., Porges, S.W., Long, J.M. and Stewart, S. (1995). Frontal activation asymmetry and social competence at four years of age. *Child Development*, **66**, 1770–84.

Franco, L. and Sperry, R.W. (1977). Hemisphere lateralization for cognitive processing of geometry. *Neuropsychologia*, **15**, 107–11.

Franklin, S., Howard, D. and Patterson, K. (1994). Abstract word meaning deafness. *Cognitive Neuropsychology*, **11**, 1–34.

Freed, C.R., Breeze, R.E., Rosenberg, N.L., Schneck, S.A., Kriek, E., Qi, J-X., Lone, T., Zhang, Y-B., Snyder, J.A., Wells, T.H., Ramig, L., Thompson, L., Mazziotta, J.C., Huang, S.C., Grafton, S.T., Brooks, D., Sawle, G., Schroter, G. and Ansari, A.A. (1992). Survival of implanted fetal dopamine cells and neurologic improvement 12 to 46 months after transplantation for Parkinson's disease. *New England Journal of Medicine*, **327**, 1549–55.

Freedman, M. and Oscar-Berman, M. (1986). Frontal lobe disease and selective delayed response deficits in humans. *Behavioural Neuroscience*, **100**, 337–42.

Freedman, M., Alexander, M.P. and Naeser, M.A. (1984). Anatomic basis of transcortical motor aphasia. *Neurology*, **34**, 409–17.

Freeman, W., Watts, J.W. and Hunt, T. (1942). *Psychosurgery*. Baltimore: Thomas.

French, C.C. and Beaumont, J.G. (1987). The reaction of psychiatric patients to computerised assessment. *British Journal of Clinical Psychology*, **26**, 267–78.

Freud, S. (1891). *Zur Aufassung der Aphasien*. Wien: Deuticke.

Freund, D.C. (1889). Ueber optische Aphasie und Seelenblindheit. *Arch. Psychiatr. Nervenkr*, **20**, 276–97.

Fried, I., Tanguay, P.E., Boder, E., Doubleday, C. and Greensite, M. (1981). Developmental dyslexia: electrophysiological evidence of clinical subgroups. *Brain and Language*, **12**, 14–22.

Friedland, R.P., Brun, A. and Budinger, T.F. (1985). Pathological and positron emission tomographic correlations in Alzheimer's disease. *Lancet*, **i**, 228.

Frith, C.D. (1992). *The Cognitive Neuropsychology of Schizophrenia*. Hillsdale, NJ: Lawrence Erlbaum Associates.

Frith, C.D., Friston, K.J., Liddle, P.F. and Frackowiak, R.S.J. (1991). A PET study of word finding. *Neuropsychologia*, **29**, 1137–48.

Frith, C.D., Cahill, C., Ridley, R.M., Baker, H.F. (1992). Memory for what it is and memory for what it means: a single case of Korsakoff's amnesia. *Cortex*, **28**, 53–67.

Fritsch, G. and Hitzig, E. (1870). Über die elektrische Erregbarkeit des Grosshirns. *Archiv für Anatomie, Physiologie und wissenschaftliche Medizin*, **37**, 300–32.

Fromkin, V., Krashen, S., Curtiss, S., Rigler, S. and Rigler, M. (1972/73). The development of language in Genie: a case of language acquisition beyond the 'critical period'. *Brain and Language*, **1**, 81–107.

Fry, W.F. (1994). The biology of humor. *Humor*, **7**(2), 111–26.

Fulton, J.F. (1928). Observations upon the vascularity of the human occipital lobe during visual activity. *Brain*, **51**, 310–20.

Gaffan, E.A., Gaffan, D. and Hodges, J.R. (1991). Amnesia following damage to the left fornix and to other sites. *Brain*, **114**, 1297–313.

Gainotti, G. (1994). The dilemma of unilateral spatial neglect. In P.W. Halligan and J.C. Marshall (eds), *Spatial Neglect: Position papers on theory and practice*. Hove, UK: Lawrence Erlbaum Associates.

Galaburda, A.M. (1995). Anatomic basis of cerebral dominance. In R.J. Davidson and K. Hugdahl (eds), *Brain Asymmetry*. Cambridge, MA: MIT Press.

Galaburda, A.M., Sanides, F. and Geschwind, N. (1978). Human brain: cytoarchitectonic left–right asymmetries in the temporal speech region. *Archives of Neurology*, **35**, 812–17.

Galaburda, A.M., Sherman, G.F., Rosen, G.D., Aboitiz, F. and Geschwind, N. (1985) Developmental dyslexia: 4 consecutive patients with cortical anomalies. *Annals of Neurology*, **18**(2), 222-33.

Galaburda, A.M., Menard, M.T. and Rosen, G.D. (1994). Evidence for aberrant anatomy in developmental dyslexia. *Proceedings of the National Academy of Sciences*, **91**, 8010–13.

Galasko, D., Katzman, R., Salmon, D.P. and Hansen, L. (1996). Clinical and neuropathological findings in Lewy body dementias. *Brain and Cognition*, **31**, 166–75.

Gallo, J.M. and Anderton, B.H. (1989). Ubiquitous variations in nerves. *Nature*, **337**, 1–14.

Gardner, H., Ling, P.K., Flamm, L. and Silverman, J. (1975). Comprehension and appreciation of humorous material following brain damage. *Brain*, **98**, 399–412.

Garruto, R.M. and Yase, Y. (1986). Neurodegenerative disorders of the Western Pacific: the search for the mechanism of pathogenesis. *Trends in Neurosciences*, **9**, 368–74.

Gathercole, S.E., Willis, C. and Baddeley, A.D. (1991). Differentiating phonological memory and awareness of rhyme: reading and vocabulary development in children. *British Journal of Psychology*, **82**, 387–406.

Gazzaniga, M.S. and Freedman, H. (1973). Observations on visual processes after posterior callosal section. *Neurology*, **23**, 1126–30.

Gazzaniga, M.S. and Hillyard, S.A. (1971). Language and speech capacity of the right hemisphere. *Neuropsychologia*, **9**, 273–280.

Gazzaniga, M.S., Bogen, J.E. and Sperry, R.W. (1962). Some functional effects of sectioning the cerebral commissures in man. *Proceedings of the National Academy of Sciences*, **48**, 1765–9.

Gazzaniga, M.S., Bogen, J.E. and Sperry, R.W. (1967). Dyspraxia following diversion of the cerebral commissures. *Archives of Neurology*, **16**, 606–12.

Gazzaniga, M.S., Eliassen, J.C., Nisenson, L., Wessinger, C.M., Fendrich, R. and Baynes, K. (1996). Collaboration between the hemispheres of a callosotomy patient. *Brain*, **119**, 1255–62.

Geary, D.C. (1993). Mathematical disabilities: cognitive, neuropsychological and genetic components. *Psychological Bulletin*, **114**(2), 345–62.

Geschwind, N. (1965) Disconnexion syndromes in animals and man. *Brain*, **88**, 237–94.

Geschwind, N. and Behan, P. (1982). Left handedness: association with immune disease, migraine and developmental learning disorders. *Proceedings of the National Academy of Science*, **79**, 5097–100.

Geschwind, N. and Behan, P. (1984). Laterality, hormones and immunity. In N. Geschwind and A.M. Galaburda (eds), *Cerebral Dominance*. Cambridge, MA Harvard University Press.

Geschwind, N. and Galaburda, A.M. (1985). Cerebral lateralization: biological mechanisms, associations, and pathology. Parts I, II and III. *Archives of Neurology*, **42**, 428–459, 521–552, 634–654.

Geschwind, N. and Galaburda, A.M. (1987). *Cerebral Lateralization*. Cambridge, MA: MIT Press.

Geschwind, N. and Levitsky, W. (1968) Left–right asymmetries in temporal speech region. *Science*, **161**, 186–7.

Gevins, A.S., Zeitlin, G.M., Doyle, J.C., Yingling, C.D., Schaffer, R.E., Callaway, E. and Yeager, C.L. (1979). EEG correlates of higher function. *Science*, **203**, 665–8.

Gevins, A.S., Doyle, J.C., Schaffer, R.E., Callaway, E. and Yeager, C. (1980). Lateralized cognitive processes and the EEG. *Science*, **207**, 1005–7.

Giedd, J.N., Snell, J.W., Lange, N., Rajapakse, J.C., Casey, B.J., Kozuch, P.L., Vaituzis, A.C., Vauss, Y.C., Hamburger, S.D., Kaysen, D. and Rapoport, J.L. (1996). Quantitative magnetic resonance imaging of human brain development: ages 4–18. *Cerebral Cortex*, **6**, 551–60.

Gilbert, A.N. and Wysocki, C.J. (1992). Hand preference and age in the United States. *Neuropsychologia*, **30**, 601–8.

Gloning, I. and Quatember, R. (1966). Methodischer Beitrag zur Untersuchung der Prosapagnosie. *Neuropsychologia*, **4**, 133–44.

Gloning, I., Gloning, K., Haub, G. and Quatember, R. (1969). Comparison of verbal behaviour in right-handed and non-right handed patients with anatomically verified lesion of one hemisphere. *Cortex*, **5**, 43–52.

Gloning, I., Trappl, R., Heiss, W.D. and Quatember, R. (1976). *Prognosis and Speech Therapy in Aphasia in Neurolinguistics*, volume 4, *Recovery in Aphasics*. Amsterdam: Swets and Zeitlinger.

Glosser, G., Butters, N. and Kaplan, E. (1977). Visuoperceptual processes in brain-damaged patients on the digit–symbol substitution test. *International Journal of Neuroscience*, **7**, 59–66.

Godefroy, O. and Rousseaux, M. (1996). Divided and focused attention in patients with lesion of the prefrontal cortex. *Brain and Cognition*, **30**, 155–74.

Godefroy, O., Cabaret, N. and Rousseaux, M. (1994). Vigilance and effects of fatigability, practice and motivation on simple reaction time tests in patients with lesions of the frontal lobe. *Neuropsychologia*, **32**, 983–90.

Godefroy, O., Lhullier, C. and Rousseaux, M. (1996). Non-spatial attention disorders in patients with frontal or posterior brain damage. *Brain*, **119**, 191–202.

Golbe, L.I., Iorio, G.D., Bonavita, V., Miller, D.C. and Duvoisin, R.C. (1990). A large kindred with autosomal dominant Parkinson's disease. *Annals of Neurology*, **27**, 276–82.

Goldberg, E. (1989). Gradiential approach to neocortical functional organization. *Journal of Clinical and Experimental Neuropsychology*, **11**(4), 489–517.

Goldberg, E. and Costa, L.D. (1981). Hemisphere differences in the acquisition and use of descriptive systems. *Brain and Language*, **14**, 144–73.

Golden, C.J., Hammeke, T.A. and Purisch, A.D. (1978). Diagnostic validity of a standardised neuropsychological battery derived from Luria's neuropsychological tests. *Journal of Consulting and Clinical Psychology*, **46**, 1258.

Golden, C.J., Hammeke, T.A. and Purisch, A.D. (1980). *Manual for the Luria–Nebraska Neuropsychological Battery*. Los Angeles: Western Psychological Services.

Goldman-Rakic, P.S. (1987). Circuitry of primate prefrontal cortex and regulation of behaviour by representational memory. In F. Plum (ed.), *Handbook of Physiology: The nervous system*, volume 5. Bethesda: American Physiology Society.

Goldman-Rakic, P.S. (1988). Topography of cognition: parallel distributed networks in primate association cortex. *Annual Review of Neuroscience*, **11**, 137–56.

Goldman-Rakic, P.S. (1992). Working memory and the mind. *Scientific American*, **267**(3), 73–9.

Goldman-Rakic, P.S. (1995). Cellular basis of working memory. *Neuron*, **14**, 477–85.

Goldman-Rakic, P.S. (1996). Multiple working memory domains and the concept of the central executive. In A.C. Roberts, T.W., Robbins, T.W. and L. Weiskrantz (eds), *Cognitive and Executive functions of the Prefrontal Cortex*, Philosophical Transactions: Biological Sciences. London: Royal Society, in press.

Goldman-Rakic, P.S. and Brown, R.M. (1981). Regional changes of monoamines in cerebral cortex and subcortical structures of aging rhesus monkeys. *Neuroscience*, **7**, 419–24.

Goldstein, J.H., Harman, J., McGhee, P.E. and Karasik, R. (1975). Test of an information-processing model of humor: physiological response changes during problem- and riddle-solving. *Journal of General Psychology*, **92**, 59–68.

Goldstein, K. (1936). The significance of the frontal lobes for mental performance. *Journal of Neurological Psychopathology*, **17**, 27–40.

Goldstein, K. (1939). *The organism*. New York: Academic Press.

Goldstein, K. and Scheerer, M. (1941). Abstract and concrete behaviour: an experimental study with special test. *Psychology Monographs*, **53**, 2.

Goldstein, L.H., Bernard, S., Fenwick, P.B.C., Burgess, P.W. and McNeil, J. (1993). Unilateral frontal lobectomy can produce strategy application disorder. *Journal of Neurology, Neurosurgery and Psychiatry*, **56**, 274–6.

Goldstein, S.G., Filskov, S.B., Weaver, L.A. and Ives, J.O. (1977). Neuropsychological effects of electroconvulsive therapy. *Journal of Clinical Psychology*, **3**, 798–806.

Gollin, E.S. (1960). Developmental studies of visual recognition of incomplete objects. *Perceptual and Motor Skills*, **11**, 289–98.

Goodale, M.A. and Milner, A.D. (1992). Separate visual pathways for perception and action. *Trends in Neuroscience*, **15**, 20–5.

Goodale, M.A., Milner, A.D., Jakobson, L.S. and Carey, D.P. (1991). Perceiving the world and grasping it: a neurological dissociation. *Nature*, **349**, 154–6.

Goodale, M.A., Meenan, J.P., Bulthoff, H.H., Nicolle, D.A., Murphy, K.J. and Raciot, C.I. (1994). Separate neural pathways for the visual analysis of object shape in perception and prehension. *Current Biology*, **4**, 604–10.

Goodglass, H. (1976) Agrammatism. In H. Whitaker and H.A. Whitaker (eds), *Studies of Neurolinguistics*. New York: Academic Press.

Goodglass, H. (1993). *Understanding Aphasia*. New York: Academic Press.

Goodglass, H. and Quadfasel, F.A. (1954). Language laterality in left-handed aphasics. *Brain*, **77**, 521–48.

Gordon, H.W. (1980). Degree of ear asymmetries for perception of dichotic chords for illusory chord localization in musicians of different levels of competence. *Journal of Experimental Psychology: Human perception and performance*, **6**, 516–27.

Gordon, H.W. and Sperry, R.W. (1969). Lateralization of olfactory perception in the surgically separated hemispheres of man. *Neuropsychologia*, **7**, 111–20.

Gorenstein, E.E. (1982). Frontal lobe functions in psychopaths. *Journal of Abnormal Psychology*, **91**, 368–79.

Gott, P.S. (1973). Language after dominant hemispherectomy. *Journal of Neurology, Neurosurgery and Psychiatry*, **36**, 1082–8.

Gottfries, C.G. (1990). Neurochemical aspects of dementia disorders. *Dementia*, **1**, 56–64.

Grafman, J., Jones, B. and Salazar, A. (1990). Wisconsin Card Sorting Test performance based on location and size of neuroanatomical lesions in Vietnam veterans with penetrating head injuries. *Perceptual and Motor Skills*, **71**, 1120–2.

Grailet, J.M., Seron, X., Bruyer, R., Coyette, F. and Frederix, M. (1990). Case report of visual integrative agnosia. *Cognitive Neuropsychology*, **7**, 275–309.

Grant, D.A. and Berg, E.A. (1948). A behavioural analysis of degree of reinforcement and ease of shifting to new responses in a Weigl-type card sorting problem. *Journal of Experimental Psychology*, **38**, 404–11.

Gray, J.A. (1982). *The Neuropsychology of Anxiety: An enquiry into the septo-hippocampal system*. Oxford: Oxford University Press.

Gray, J.A. (1995). A model of the limbic system and basal ganglia: applications to anxiety and schizophrenia. In M.S. Gazzaniga (ed.), *The Cognitive Neurosciences*. Cambridge, MA: MIT Press.

Green, G.L. and Lessell, S. (1977). Acquired cerebral dyschromatopsia. *Archives of Ophthalmology*, **95**, 121–28.

Greene, J.D.W. and Hodges, J.R. (1996a). Identification of famous faces and famous names in early Alzheimer's disease. *Brain*, **119**, 111–28.

Greene, J.D.W. and Hodges, J.R. (1996b). Identification of remote memory: Evidence from a longitudinal study of dementia of Alzheimer type. *Brain*, **119**, 129–42.

Grossi, G., Semenza, C., Corazza, S. and Volterra, V. (1996). Hemispheric specialization for sign language. *Neuropsychologia*, **34**(7), 737–40.

Gruzelier, J.H. (1981). Hemispheric imbalances masquerading as paranoid and nonparanoid syndromes? *Schizophrenia Bulletin*, **7**, 662–73.

Gruzelier, J.H. (1984). Hemispheric imbalance in schizophrenia. *International Journal of Psychology*, **1**, 227–40.

Gruzelier, J.H. and Hammond, N.V. (1980). Lateralized deficits and drug influences on the dichotic listening of schizophrenic patients. *Biological Psychiatry*, **15**, 759–79.

Guariglia, C., Padovani, A., Pantano, P. and Pizzamiglio, L. (1993). Unilateral neglect restricted to visual imagery. *Nature*, **364**, 235–7.

Guitton, D., Buchtel, H.A. and Douglas, R.M. (1982). Disturbances of voluntary saccadic eye movement mechanisms following discrete unilateral frontal lobe removals. In G. Lennerstrand, D.S. Lee and E.L. Keller (eds), *Functional Basis of Ocular Motility Disorders*. Oxford: Pergamon.

Gur, R.E. (1978). Left hemisphere dysfunction and left-hemisphere overactivation in schizophrenia. *Journal of Abnormal Psychology*, **87**, 226–38.

Gur, R.C., Gur, R.E., Orbist, W.D., Skolnick, B.E. and Reivich, M. (1987). Age and regional cerebral blood flow at rest and during cognitive activity. *Archives of General Psychiatry*, **44**, 617–21.

Gur, R.C., Ragland, J.D., Resnick, S.M., Skolnick, B.E., Jaggi, J., Muenz, L. and Gur, R.E. (1994). Lateralised increases in cerebral blood flow during performance of verbal and spatial tasks: relationship with performance level. *Brain and Cognition*, **24**, 244–58.

Gurland, B.J. (1981). The borderland of dementia: the influence of socio-cultural characteristics on rates of dementia occurring in the senium. *Ageing*, **15**, 61–84.

Habib, M., Gayraud, D., Olivia, A., Regis, J., Salamon, G. and Khalil, R. (1991). Effects of handedness and sex on the morphology of the corpus callosum: a study with brain magnetic resonance imaging. *Brain and Cognition*, **16**, 41–61.

Hadziselimovic, H. and Cus, M. (1966). The appearance of the internal structures of the brain in relation to the configuration of the human skull. *Acta Anatomica*, **63**, 289–99.

Hagen, C. (1973). Communication abilities in hemiplegia: effect of speech therapy. *Archives of Physical and Medical Rehabilitation*, **54**, 454–63.

Hager, J.C. and Ekman, P. (1985). The asymmetry of facial actions is inconsistent with models of hemispheric specialization. *Psychophysiology*, **22**, 307–18.

Hakuta, K. (1986). *Mirror of Language*. New York: Basic Books.

Halgren, E. (1992). Emotional neurophysiology of the amygdala within the context of human cognition. In J.P. Aggleton (ed.), *The Amygdala: Neurobiological aspects of emotion, memory and mental dysfunction*. New York: Wiley/Liss.

Halligan, P.W. and Cockburn, J.M. (1993). Cognitive sequelae of stroke: visuospatial and memory disorders. *Critical Reviews in Physical and Rehabilitation Medicine*, **5**(1), 57–81.

Halligan, P.W. and Marshall, J.C. (1991). Left neglect for near but not far space in man. *Nature*, **350**, 498–500.

Halligan, P.W. and Marshall, J.C. (1994). *Spatial Neglect: Position papers on theory and practice*. Hove, UK: Lawrence Erlbaum Associates.

Halligan, P.W., Marshall, J.C. and Wade, D.T. (1992). Contrapositioning in a case of visual neglect. *Neuropsychological Rehabilitation*, **2**(2), 125–35.

Halpern, D.F. and Coren, S. (1988). Do right handers live longer? *Nature*, **333**, 213.

Halpern, D.F. and Coren, S. (1990). Handedness and life span. *New England Journal of Medicine*, **324**, 998.

Halsey, J.H., Blauenstein, U.W., Wilson, E.M. and Wills, E.L. (1979). Regional cerebral blood flow comparison of right and left hand movement. *Neurology*, **29**, 21–28.

Halstead, W.C. (1940). Preliminary analysis of grouping behaviour in patients with cerebral injury by the method of equivalent and non-equivalent stimuli. *American Journal of Psychology*, **96**, 1263–94.

Halstead, W.C. (1947). *Brain and Intelligence: A quantitative study of the frontal lobes*. Chicago University Press.

Hamilton, C.R. and Vermiere, B.A. (1983). Discrimination of monkey faces by split-brain monkeys. *Behavioural Brain Research*, **9**, 263–75.

Hannay, H.J., Varney, N.R. and Benton, A.L. (1976). Visual localization in patients with unilateral brain disease. *Journal of Neurology, Neurosurgery and Psychiatry*, **39**, 307–13.

Hansen, L., Salmon, D.P. and Galasko, D. (1990). The Lewy body variant of Alzheimer's disease: a clinical and pathological entity. *Neurology*, **40**, 1–8.

Hardyck, C. and Petrinovich, L.F. (1977). Left-handedness. *Psychological Bulletin*, **84**, 385–404.

Hare, R.D. (1978). Electrodermal and cardiovascular correlates of psychopathy. In R.D. Hare and D. Schalling (eds), *Psychopathic Behaviour: Approaches to research*. New York: Wiley.

Hare, R.D. (1984). Performance of psychopaths on cognitive tasks related to frontal lobe function. *Journal of Abnormal Psychology*, **93**, 133–40.

Hari, R. and Salmelin, R. (1997). Human cortical oscillations: a neuromagnetic view through the skull. *Trends in Neurosciences*, **20**(1), 44–9.

Harlow, J.M. (1848). Passage of an iron rod through the head. *Boston Medicine and Surgery Journal*, **39**, 389–93.

Harlow, J.M. (1868). Recovery from the passage of an iron bar through the head. *Massachusetts Medical Society Publications*, **2**, 327–46.

Harman, D.W. and Ray, W.J. (1977). Hemispheric activity during affective verbal stimuli: an EEG study. *Neuropsychologia*, **15**, 157–160.

Harris, A.J. (1957). Lateral dominance, direction confusion and reading disability. *Journal of Psychology*, **44**, 283–94.

Harris, J.E. (1980). We have ways of making you remember. *Concord, The Journal of the British Association for Service to the Elderly*, **17**, 21–27.

Harris, L.J. (1993). Do left-handers die sooner than right-handers? Commentary on Coren and Halpern's (1991) 'Left-handedness: a marker for decreased survival fitness'. *Psychological Bulletin*, **114**(2), 203–34.

Harshman, R.A., Hampson, E. and Berenbaum, S.A. (1983). Individual differences in cognitive abilities and brain organization, Part I: sex and handedness differences in ability. *Canadian Journal of Psychology*, **37**, 144–92.

Hartje, W. (1987). The effect of spatial disorders on arithmetical skills. In G. Deloche and X. Seron (eds), *Mathematical Disabilities: A cognitive neuropsychological perspective*. Hillsdale, NJ: Lawrence Erlbaum Associates.

Haslam, D.R. (1970). Lateral dominance in the perception of size and pain. *Quarterly Journal of Experimental Psychology*, **22**, 503–7.

Hata, T., Meyer, J.S. and Tanahashi, N. (1987). Three-dimensional mapping of local cerebral perfusion in alcoholic encephalopathy with and without Wernicke–Korsakoff syndrome. *Journal of Cerebral Blood Flow and Metabolism*, **7**, 35–44.

Hatta, T. and Koike, M. (1991). Left-hand preference in frightened mother monkeys in taking up their babies. *Neuropsychologia*, **29**, 207–9.

Haug, H. and Eggers, R. (1991). Morphometry of the human cortex cerebri and corpus callosum during aging. *Neurobiology of Aging*, **12**, 336–8.

Haxby, J.V., Grady, C.L., Koss, E., Horwitz, B., Heston, L., Schapiro, M., Friedland, R.P. and Rapoport, S.I. (1990). Longitudinal study of cerebral metabolic asymmetries and associated neuropsychological patterns in early dementia of the Alzheimer's type. *Archives of Neurology*, **47**, 753–60.

Heaton, R.K. (1981). *Wisconsin Card Sorting Test Manual*. Odessa, FL: Psychological Assessment Resources.

Hebb, D.O. (1939). Intelligence in man after large removals of cerebral tissue: report of four frontal lobe cases. *Journal of General Psychology*, **21**, 73–87.

Hebb, D.O. (1941). Human intelligence after removal of cerebral tissue from the right frontal lobe. *Journal of General Psychology*, **25**, 257–65.

Hebb, D.O. (1945). Man's frontal lobes: a critical review. *Archives of Neurology and Psychiatry*, **54**, 10–24.

Hebb, D.O. (1949). *Organization of Behaviour*. New York: Wiley.

Hecaen, H. (1962). Clinical symptomatology in right and left hemispheric lesions. In V.B. Mountcastle (ed.), *Interhemispheric Relations and Cerebral Dominance*. Baltimore: Johns Hopkins University Press.

Hecaen, H. (1976). Acquired aphasia in children and the ontogenesis of hemispheric functional specialisation. *Brain and Language*, **3**, 114–34.

Hecaen, H. (1978). Les Apraxies ideomotrices essai de dissociation. In H. Hecaen and M. Jeannerod (eds), *Du controle moteur a l'organisation du geste*. Paris: Masson.

Hecaen, A. and Ajuriaguerra de J. (1956). Agnosie visuelle pour les objets inanimés par lésion unilaterale gauche. *Revue Neurologique*, **94**, 222–3.

Hecaen, A. and Albert, M.L. (1978). *Human Neuropsychology*. New York: Wiley.

Hecaen, A. and Angelergues, R. (1962). Agnosia for faces. *Archives of Neurology (Chicago)*, **7**, 92–100.

Hecaen, A. and Angelergues, R. (1963). *La cetite psychique*. Paris: Masson.

Hecaen, H. and Rondot, P. (1985). Apraxia as a disorder of signs. In E. Roy (ed.), *Neuropsychological Studies of Apraxia and Related Disorders*. Elsevier: Amsterdam.

Hecaen, A., Goldblum, M.C., Massure, M.C. and Ramier, A.M. (1974). Une nouvelle observation d'agnosie d'objet. Déficit de l'association ou de la categorisation, specifique de la modalité visuelle. *Neuropsychologia*, **12**, 447–64.

Heilman, K.M. (1975). A tapping test in apraxia. *Cortex*, **11**, 259–63.

Heilman, K.M. (1979). Apraxia. In K.M. Heilman and E. Valenstein (eds), *Clinical Neuro-psychology*. New York: Oxford University Press.

Heilman, K.M. and Rothi, L.J.G. (1993). Apraxia. In K.M. Heilman and E. Valenstein (eds), *Clinical Neuropsychology* (3rd edition). New York: Oxford University Press.

Heilman, K.M. and Valenstein, E. (1979). Mechanisms underlying hemispatial neglect. *Annals of Neurology*, **5**, 166–70.

Heilman, K.M., Rothi, L.J.G. and Valenstein, E. (1982). Two forms of ideomotor apraxia. *Neurology*, **32**, 342–46.

Heilman, K.M., Valenstein, E. and Watson, R.T. (1994). The what and how of neglect. In P.W. Halligan and J.C. Marshall (eds), *Spatial Neglect: Position papers on theory and practice*. Hove, UK: Lawrence Erlbaum Associates.

Helkala, E.L., Laulumaa, V., Soinninen, H. and Riekkinen, P.J. (1988). Recall and recognition memory in patients with Alzheimer's and Parkinson's diseases. *Annals of Neurology*, **24**, 214–17.

Hellige, J.B. (1991). Cerebral laterality and metacontrol. In F. Kitterle (ed.), *Recent Advances in Laterality*. Hillsdale, NJ: Lawrence Erlbaum Associates.

Hellige, J.B. and Michimata, C. (1989). Visual laterality for letter comparison: effects of stimulus factors, response factors and metacontrol. *Bulletin of the Psychonomic Society*, **27**, 441–4.

Hellige, J.B., Taylor, A.K. and Eng, T.L. (1989). Interhemispheric interaction when both hemispheres have access to the same stimulus information. *Journal of Experimental Psychology: Human perception and performance*, **15**, 711–722.

Henriques, J.B. and Davidson, R.J. (1991). Left frontal hypoactivation in depression. *Journal of Abnormal Psychology*, **100**, 535–45.

Hermann, B.P. and Wyler, A.R. (1988) Effects of anterior frontal lobectomy on language function: a controlled study. *Annals of Neurology*, **23**, 585–8.

Hermann, D.O. (1988). Development of the Wechsler Memory Scale – Revised. *Clinical Neuropsychology*, **2**, 102.

Hermann, H.T. and Zeevi, Y.Y. (1991) Interhemispheric interactions and dyslexia. In J.F. Stein (ed.), *Vision and Visual Dyslexia*. London: Macmillan.

Heschl, R.L. (1878). *Die vordere quere Schlafenwindung des menschlichen Grosshirns*. Vienna: Wilhelm Braumuller.

Hicks, R.A. and Beveridge, R. (1978). Handedness and intelligence. *Cortex*, **14**, 304–7.

Hier, D.B. and Kaplan, J. (1980) Are sex differences in cerebral organization clinically significant? *Behavioural and Brain Sciences*, **3**, 238–9.

Hier, D.B., LeMay, M., Rosenberger, P.B. and Perlo, V.P. (1978). Developmental dyslexia. *Archives of Neurology*, **35**, 90–2.

Hines, M., Chui, L., McAdams, L.A., Bentler, P.M. and Lipcamon, L. (1992). Cognition and the corpus callosum: verbal fluency, visuospatial ability and language lateralization related to midsaggital surface areas of callosal subregions. *Behavioural Neuroscience*, **106**, 3–14.

Hiscock, M. and Kinsbourne, M. (1995). Phylogeny and ontogeny of cerebral lateralization. In R.J. Davidson and K. Hugdahl (eds), *Brain Asymmetry*. Cambridge, MA: MIT Press.

Hiscock, M., Inch, R., Jacek, C., Hiscock-Kalil, C. and Kalil, K.M. (1994). Is there a sex difference in human laterality? I. An exhaustive survey of auditory laterality studies from six neuropsychology journals. *Journal of Clinical and Experimental Neuropsychology*, **16** (3), 423–35.

Hoeft, H.J. (1957) Klinisch-anatomischer Breitrag zur Kenntnis der Nachsprechaphasie. *Deutsch. Z. Nervenheilk.*, **175**, 560–94.

Hoffman, J.J., Hall, R.W. and Bartsch, T.W. (1987). On the relative importance of 'psycho-pathic' personality and alcoholism on neuropsychological measures of frontal lobe dysfunction. *Journal of Abnormal Psychology*, **96**, 158–60.

Holland, A.L. and Forbes, M.M. (1993). *Aphasia Treatment: World perspectives*. Chichester: Wiley.

Holligan, C. and Johnston, R.S. (1988). The use of phonological information by good and poor readers in memory and reading tasks. *Memory and Cognition*, **16**(6), 522–32.

Holloway, R.L. and Lacoste, M-C. de (1986). Sexual dimorphism in the human corpus callosum: an extension and replication study. *Human Neurobiology*, **5**, 87–91.

Holmes, G. (1918). Disturbances of visual orientation. *British Journal of Opthamology*, **2**, 449–68.

Holmes, G. (1931). Discussion on the mental symptoms associated with cerebral tumors. *Proceedings of the Royal Society of Medicine*, **24**, 997–1000.

Hoptman, M.J. and Davidson, R.J. (1994). How and why do the two cerebral hemispheres interact? *Psychological Bulletin*, **116**(2), 195–219.

Horn, J.L. and Cattell, R.B. (1967). Age differences in fluid and crystalized intelligence. *Acta Psychologia*, **26**, 107–29.

Horvath, T.B. and Davis, K.L. (1990). Central nervous system disorders in aging. In E.L. Schneider and J.W. Rowe (eds), *Handbook of the Biology of Aging* (3rd edition). San Diego, CA: Academic Press.

Hounsfield, G.N. (1973). Computerized transverse axial scanning (tomography). Part I: description of the system. *British Journal of Radiology*, **46**, 1016–22.

Hubel, D.H. and Wiesel, T.N. (1979). Brain mechanisms of vision. *Scientific American*, **241**, 150–62.

Huber, W., Poeck, K. and Springer, L. (1991). *Sprachstorungen*. Stuttgart: TRIAS.

Hugdahl, K. (1995). Dichotic listening: probing temporal lobe functional integrity. In R.J. Davidson and K. Hugdahl (eds), *Brain Asymmetry*. Cambridge, MA: MIT Press.

Hughlings-Jackson, J. (1870) On voluntary and automatic movements. *British Medical Journal*, **2**, 641–2.

Hughlings-Jackson, J. (1874). On the nature of the duality of the brain. *Medical Press and Circular*, **1**, 19.

Hughlings-Jackson, J. (1931). In J. Taylor (ed.), *Selected Writing of John Hughlings-Jackson*. London.

Hulme, C. (1988). Short-term memory development and learning to read. In M. Gruneberg, P. Morris and R. Sykes (eds), *Practical Aspects of Memory: Current research and issues* Volume 2, *Clinical and Educational Implications*. Chichester: Wiley.

Hulme, C. and Roodenrys, S. (1995). Practitioner review: verbal working memory development and its disorders. *Journal of Child Psychology and Psychiatry*, **36**(3), 373–98.

Humphreys, G.W. and Riddoch, M.J. (1987a). *To See or not to See: A case study of visual object processing*. Hove, UK: Lawrence Erlbaum Associates.

Humphreys, G.W. and Riddoch, M.J. (1987b). The fractionation of visual agnosia. In G.W. Humphreys and M.J. Riddoch (eds), *Visual Object: A cognitive neuropsychologial approach*. London: Lawrence Erlbaum Associates.

Humphreys, G.W. and Riddoch, M.J. (1993). Object agnosias. *Balliére's Clinical Neurology*, **2**, 339–59.

Hynd, G.W. and Semrud-Clikeman, M. (1989). Dyslexia and neurodevelopmental pathology: relationships to cognition, intelligence, and reading skill acquisition. *Journal of Learning Disabilities*, **22**(4), 204–16.

Hynd, G.W., Semrud-Clikeman, M., Lorys, A.R., Novey, E.S. and Eliopulos, D. (1990) Brain morphology in developmental dyslexia and attention deficit disorder/ hyperactivity. *Archives of Neurology*, **47**, 919–26.

Inglis, J. and Lawson, J.S. (1981) Sex differences in the effects of unilateral brain damage on intelligence. *Science*, **212**, 693–5.

Ioannides, A.A. (1991). Comparison of MEG with other functional imaging techniques. *Clinical, Physical and Physiological Measurement*, **12**, 23–28.

Irle, E. and Markowitsch, H.J. (1982). Thiamine deficiency in the cat leads to severe learning deficits and to widespread neuroanatomical damage. *Experimental Brain Research*, **48**, 199–208.

Ishai, S., Furukawa, T. and Tsukagoshi, H. (1989). Visuospatial processes of line bisection and the mechanisms underlying unilateral spatial neglect. *Brain*, **112**, 1485–1502.

Iversen, S.D. and Mishkin, M. (1970). Perseverative interference in monkey following selective lesions of the inferior prefrontal convexity. *Experimental Brain Research*, **11**, 376–86.

Ivnik, R.J., Sharbrough, F.W. and Laws, E.R. (1987). Effects of anterior temporal lobectomy on cognitive function. *Journal of Clinical Psychology*, **43**, 128–37.

Jacobson, R. (1986). Disorders of facial recognition, social behaviour and affect after combined bilateral amygdalotomy and subcaudate tractotomy: a clinical and experimental study. *Psychological Medicine*, **16**, 439–50.

Jacobson, R.R. and Lishman, W. (1987). Selective memory loss and global intellectual deficits in alcoholic Korsakoff's syndrome. *Psychological Medicine*, **17**, 649–55.

Jacobson, R.R. and Lishman, W. (1990). Cortical and diencephalic lesions in Korsakoff's syndrome: a clinical and CT scan study. *Psychological Medicine*, **20**, 63–75.

Jacobson, R.R., Acker, C. and Lishman, W.A. (1990). Patterns of neuropsychological deficit in alcoholic Korsakoff's syndrome. *Psychological Medicine*, **20**, 321–34.

Jakobson, L.S., Archibald, Y.M., Carey, D.P. and Goodale, M.A. (1991). A kinematic analysis of reaching and grasping movements in a patient recovering from optic ataxia. *Neuropsychologia*, **29**, 803–9.

James, W. (1884). What is emotion? *Mind*, **19**, 188–205.

James, W. (1890). *The Principles of Psychology*. New York: Henry Holt.

Janowic, J. (1993). Tourette's syndrome: phenomenology, pathophysiology, genetics, epidemiology and treatment. In S.H. Appel (ed.), *Current Neurology*, volume 13. Chicago: Mosby Yearbook.

Janowsky, D.S., El-Yousef, M.K., Davis, J.M., Hubbard, B. and Sekerke, H.J. (1972). Cholinergic reversal of manic symptoms. *Lancet*, **1**, 1236–7.

Janowsky, J.S., Shimamura, A.P., Kritchevsky, M. and Squire, L.R. (1989a). Cognitive impairment following frontal lobe damage and its relevance to human amnesia. *Behavioural Neuroscience*, **103**, 548–60.

Janowsky, J.S., Shimamura, A.P. and Squire, L.R. (1989b). Memory and metamemory: Comparisons between patients with frontal lobe lesions and amnesic patients. *Psychobiology*, **17**, 3–11.

Jeannerod, M. (1986). Mechanisms of visuomotor coordination: a study in normal and brain-damaged subjects. *Neuropsychologia*, **24**, 41–78.

Jeannerod, M. (1997). *The Cognitive Neuroscience of Action*. Oxford: Blackwell.

Jeannerod, M., Decety, J. and Michel, F. (1994). Impairment of grasping movements following a bilateral posterior parietal lesion. *Neuropsychologia*, **32**, 369–80.

Johnson, D.J. and Blalock, J.W. (1987). *Adults with Learning Disabilities*. Orlando, FL: Grune and Stratton.

Johnson, D.J. and Grant, J.O. (1989). Written narratives of normal and learning-disabled children. *Annals of Dyslexia*, **39**, 140–58.

Johnson, J.S. and Newport, E.L. (1989). Critical period effects in second language learning: the influence of maturational state on the acquisition of English as a second language. *Cognitive Psychology*, **21**, 60–99.

Johnstone, J., Galin, D., Fein, G., Yingling, C., Herron, J. and Marcus, M. (1984). Regional brain activity in dyslexic and control children during reading tasks: visual probe event-related potentials. *Brain and Language*, **21**, 233–54.

Jones-Gotman, M. and Milner, B. (1977). Design fluency: the invention of nonsense drawings after focal cortical lesions. *Neuropsychologia*, **15**, 653–74.

Jones-Gotman, M. and Zatorre, R.J. (1993). Odor recognition memory in humans: role of right temporal and orbitofrontal regions. *Brain and Cognition*, **22**, 182–98.

Kandel, E. (1991). Brain and behaviour. In E. Kandel, J.H. Schwartz and T.M. Jessell (eds), *Principles of Neural Science*. New York: Elsevier.

Kaplan, E., Goodglass, H. and Weintraub, S. (1983). *Boston Naming Test*. Philadelphia: Lea and Febiger.

Kapur, N. and Butters, N. (1977). Visuoperceptive deficits in long-term alcoholics with Korsakoff's psychosis. *Journal of Studies on Alcohol*, **40**, 791–6.

Kapur, N., Thompson, S., Cook, P., Lang, D. and Brice, J. (1996). Anterograde but not retrograde memory loss following combined mammillary body and medial thalamic lesions. *Neuropsychologia*, **34**(1), 1–8.

Karnath, H.O. (1994). Disturbed coordinate transformation in the neural representation of space as the crucial mechanism leading to neglect. In P.W. Halligan and J.C. Marshall (eds), *Spatial Neglect: Position papers on theory and practice*. Hove, UK: Lawrence Erlbaum Associates.

Karnath, H.O., Christ, K. and Hartje, W. (1993). Decrease of contralateral neglect by neck muscle vibration and spatial orientation of trunk midline. *Brain*, **116**, 383–96.

Katz, R.B., Shankweiler, D. and Liberman, I.Y. (1981). Memory for item order and phonetic recoding in the beginning reader. *Journal of Experimental Child Psychology*, **32**, 474–84.

Kaufmann, W.E. and Galaburda, A.M. (1989) Cerebrocortical microdysgenesis in neurologically normal subjects – a histopathologic study. *Neurology*, **39**(2), 238–244.

Kaye, W.H., Sitaram, N., Weingartner, H, Elbert, M.H., Smallberg, G. and Gillin, J.C. (1982). Modest facilitation of memory in dementia with combined lecithin and anticholinesterase treatment. *Biological Psychiatry*, **17**, 275–80.

Keane, M.M., Gabrieli, J.D.E., Mapstone, H.C., Johnson, K.A. and Corkin, S. (1995). Double dissociation of memory capacities after bilateral occipital-lobe or medial temporal-lobe lesions. *Brain*, **118**, 1129–48.

Keenan, S.S. and Brassel, E.G. (1974). A study of factors related to prognosis for individual aphasic patients. *Journal of Speech and Hearing Disorders*, **39**, 257–69.

Kendell, R.E. (1981). The present status of electroconvulsive therapy. *British Journal of Psychiatry*, **139**, 265–83.

Kenin, M. and Swisher, L. (1972). A study of pattern of recovery in aphasia. *Cortex*, **8**, 56–68.

Kennard, M.A. (1936). Age and other factors in motor recovery from precentral lesions in monkeys. *American Journal of Physiology*, **115**, 138–46.

Kennard, M.A. (1940). Relation of age to motor impairment in man and subhuman primates. *Archives of Neurology and Psychiatry*, **44**, 377–97.

Kennard, M.A. (1942). Cortical reorganisation of motor function: studies on series of monkeys of various ages from infancy to maturity. *Archives of Neurology and Psychiatry*, **48**, 227–40.

Kennedy, H., Meisserel, C. and Dehay, C. (1991). Callosal pathways and their compliancy to general rules governing the organization of corticocortical connectivity. In B. Drehrer and S.R. Robinson (eds), *Neuroanatomy of the Visual Pathways and their Development*. Boca Raton, FL: Chemical Rubber Company.

Kershner, J.R., Henninger, P. and Cooke, W.L. (1984). Written recall induces a right hemisphere linguistic advantage for digits in dyslexic children. *Brain and Language*, **21**, 105–22.

Kertesz, A. (1979). *Aphasia and Associated Disorders*. New York: Grune and Stratton.

Kertesz, A. (1981). Anatomy of jargon. In J. Brown (ed.), *Jargonaphasia*. New York: Academic Press.

Kertesz, A. (1987). Recovery of language disorders. In S. Finger, T.E. LeVere, C.R. Almli and D.G. Stein (eds), *Brain Injury and Recovery: Theoretical and controversial issues*. New York: Plenum.

Kertesz, A. (1988). What do we learn from aphasia? In S.G. Waxman (ed.), *Advances in Neurology*, volume 47, *Functional Recovery in Neurological Disease*. New York: Raven Press.

Kertesz, A. (1993). Recovery and treatment. In K.M. Heilman and E. Valenstein (eds), *Clinical Neuropsychology* (3rd edition). New York: Oxford University Press.

Kertesz, A. (1995). Recovery in aphasia and language networks. *Neurorehabilitation*, **5**(2), 103–13.

Kertesz, A. and McCabe, P. (1977). Recovery patterns and prognosis in aphasia. *Brain*, **100**, 1–18.

Kertesz, A. and Poole, E. (1974). The aphasia quotient: the taxonomic approach to measurement of aphasic disability. *Canadian Journal of Neurological Science*, **1**, 7–16.

Kertesz, A., Sheppard, A. and Mackenzie, R. (1982). Localisation in transcortical sensory aphasia. *Archives of Neurology*, **39**, 475.

Kertesz, A., Dennis, S., Polk, M. and McCabe, P. (1989). The structural determinants of recovery in Wernicke's aphasia. *Neurology*, **39**, suppl. 1, 177.

Kim, M. and Davis, M. (1993). Lack of temporal gradient of retrograde amnesia in rats with amygdala lesions assessed with the fear-potentiated startle paradigm. *Behavioural Neuroscience*, **107**, 1088–92.

Kimura, D. (1961). Some effects of temporal lobe damage on auditory perception. *Canadian Journal of Psychology*, **15**, 156–65.

Kimura, D. (1963). Right temporal lobe damage: perception of unfamiliar stimuli after damage. *Archives of Neurology*, **8**, 264–71.

Kimura, D. (1964) Left–right differences in the perception of melodies. *Quarterly Journal of Experimental Psychology*, **16**, 355–8.

Kimura, D. (1967). Functional asymmetry of the brain in dichotic listening. *Cortex*, **3**, 167–78.

Kimura, D. (1969). Spatial localization in left and right visual fields. *Canadian Journal of Psychology*, **23**, 445–58.

Kimura, D. (1982). Left hemisphere control of oral and brachial movements and their relationship to communication. *Philosophical Transactions of the Royal Society of London*, Series B, **298**, 135–49.

Kimura, D. (1983) Sex differences in cerebral organization for speech and praxic functions. *Canadian Journal of Psychology*, **37**, 19–35.

Kinsbourne, M. (1987). Mechanisms of unilateral neglect. In M. Jeannerod (ed.), *Neurophysiological and Neuropsychological Aspects of Spatial Neglect*. Amsterdam: North-Holland.

Kinsella, G. and Ford, B. (1985). Hemi-inattention and the recovery patterns of stroke patients. *International Rehabilitation Medicine*, **7**, 102.

Kippur, N., Thompson, S., Cook, P., Land, D. and Brice, J. (1996). Anterograde but not retrograde memory loss following combined mammillary body and medial thalamic lesions. *Neuropsychologia*, **34**(1), 1–8.

Kish, S.J., Shannak, K. and Hornykiewicz, O. (1988). Uneven pattern of dopamine loss in the striatum of patients with idiopathic Parkinson's disease: pathophysiologic and clinical implications. *New England Journal of Medicine*, **318**, 876–81.

Kleist, K. (1934). *Gehirnpathologie*. Leipzig: Barth.

Kluver, H. and Bucy, P.C. (1939). Preliminary analysis of functions of the temporal lobes in monkeys. *Archives of Neurology and Psychiatry*, **42**, 979–1000.

Knopman, D.S., Selnes, O.A., Niccum, N., Rubens, A.B., Yock, D. and Larson, D. (1983). A longitudinal study of speech fluency in aphasia: CT correlates of recovery and persistent nonfluency. *Neorology*, **33**, 170–78.

Kohn, B. and Dennis, M. (1974). Selective impairments of visuo-spatial abilities in infantile hemiplegics after right hemidecortication. *Neuropsychologia*, **12**, 505–12.

Kolb, B. and Milner, B. (1981). Performance of complex arm and facial movements after focal brain lesions. *Neuropsychologia*, **19**, 505–14.

Kolb, B. and Whishaw, I.Q. (1987). Mass action and equipotentiality reconsidered. In S. Finger, T.E. LeVere, C.R. Almli and D.G. Stein (eds), *Brain Injury and Recovery: Theoretical and controversial issues*. New York: Plenum.

Kolb, B. and Whishaw, I.Q. (1989). Plasticity in the neocortex: mechanisms underlying recovery from early brain damage. *Progress in Neurobiology*, **32**, 235–76.

Koller, W., Vetere-Overfeld, B., Gray, C., Alexander, C. Cin, T., Dolezal, J., Harsarein, R. and Tanner, C. (1990). Environmental risk factors in Parkinson's disease. *Neurology*, **40**, 1218–22.

Kolodny, A. (1929). Symptomatology of tumor of the frontal lobe. *Archives of Neurology and Psychiatry*, **21**, 1107–27.

Kopelman, M.D. (1991). Non-verbal, short-term forgetting in the alcoholic Korsakoff syndrome and Alzheimer-type dementia. *Brain*, **114**, 117–37.

Kopelman, M.D. (1995). The Korsakoff syndrome. *British Journal of Psychiatry*, **166**, 154–73.

Korsakoff, S.S. (1889a). Psychic disorder in conjunction with peripheral neuritis. *Neurology*, **5**, 394–406.

Korsakoff, S.S. (1889b). Etude medico-psychologique sur une forme des maladies de la memoire. *Revue Philosophie*, **20**, 501–30.

Kosslyn, S.M. (1987). Seeing and imagining in the cerebral hemispheres: a computational approach. *Psychological Review*, **94**, 148–75.

Kosslyn, S.M. and Intriligator, J.M. (1992). Is cognitive neuropsychology plausible? The perils of sitting on a one-legged stool. *Journal of Cognitive Neuroscience*, **4**(1), 96–106.

Krashen, S.D. (1973). Lateralization, language learning and the critical period: some new evidence. *Language Learning*, **23**, 63–74.

Kratskin, I.L. (1995). Functional anatomy, central connections, and neurochemistry of the mammalian olfactory bulb. In R.L. Doty (ed.), *Handbook of Olfaction and Gustation*. New York: Marcel Dekker.

Kratz, K.E., Spear, P.D. and Smith, D.C. (1976). Postcritical-period reversal of effects of monocular deprivation on striate cells in the cat. *Journal of Neurophysiology*, **39**, 501–11.

Kreindler, A. and Fradis, A. (1968). *Performances in Aphasia: A neurodynamical, diagnostic and psychological study*. Paris: Gauthier-Villars.

Kreuter, C., Kinsbourne, M. and Trevarthen, C. (1972). Are disconnected cerebral hemispheres independent channels? A preliminary study of the effect of unilateral loading on bilateral finger tapping. *Neuropsychologia*, **10**, 453–61.

Kreutzberg, G.W. (1996). Microglia: a sensor for pathological events in the CNS. *Trends in Neuroscience*, **19**(8), 312–18.

Kronfol, Z., Hamsher, K. de S., Digire, K. and Waziri, R. (1978). Depression and hemispheric functions: changes associated with unilateral ECT. *British Journal of Psychiatry*, **132**, 560–67.

Kubanis, P. and Zornetzer, S.F. (1981). Age-related behavioural and neurobiological changes: a review with an emphasis on memory. *Behavioural and Neural Biology*, **31**, 115–72.

Kusch, A., Gross-Glenn, K., Jallad, B., Lubs, H., Rabin, M., Feldman, E. and Duara, R. (1993). Temporal lobe surface area measurements on MRI in normal and dyslexic readers. *Neuropsychologia*, **31**(8), 811–21.

Kutas, M. and Hillyard, S.A. (1980). Reading senseless sentences: brain potentials reflect semantic incongruity. *Science*, **207**, 203–5.

Kutas, M., McCarthy, G. and Donchin, E. (1975). Differences between sinistrals' and dextrals' ability to infer a whole from its parts: a failure to replicate. *Neuropsychologia*, **13**, 455–64.

Kwong, K.K., Belliveau, J.W., Chesler, D.A., Goldberg, I.E., Weisskoff, R.M., Poncelet, B.P., Kennedy, D.N., Hoppel, B.E., Cohen, M.S., Turner, R., Cheng, H-M., Brady, T.J. and Rosen, B.R. (1992). Dynamic magnetic resonance imaging of human brain activity during primary sensory stimulation. *Proceedings of the National Academy of Sciences*, **89**, 5675–9.

Lacoste-Utamsing, C. de and Holloway, R.L. (1982) Sexual dimorphism in the human corpus callosum. *Science*, **216**, 1431–2.

Ladavas, E. (1994). The role of visual attention in neglect: a dissociation between perceptual and directional motor neglect. In P.W. Halligan and J.C. Marshall (eds), *Spatial Neglect: Position papers on theory and practice*. Hove, UK: Lawrence Erlbaum Associates.

Lader, M.H. and File, S.E. (1987). The biological basis of benzodiazepine dependence. *Psychological Medicine*, **17**, 539–47.

Laitinen, L.V., Bergenheim, A.T. and Hariz, M.I. (1992). Leskell's posteroventral pallidotomy in the treatment of Parkinson's disease. *Journal of Neurosurgery*, **77**, 487–8.

Lamantia, A-S. and Rakic, P. (1990). Cytological and quantitative characteristics of four cerebral commissures in the rhesus monkey. *Journal of Comparative Neurology*, **291**, 520–37.

Lambert, A.J. (1991). Interhemispheric interaction in the split-brain. *Neuropsychologia*, **29**, 941–8.

Landis, T., Cummings, J.L., Benson, F. and Palmer, E.P. (1986). Loss of topographic familiarity: an environmental agnosia. *Archives of Neurology (Chicago)*, **43**, 132–6.

Landwehrmeyer, B., Gerling, J., Wallesch, C.S. (1990). Patterns of task-related slow brain potentials in dyslexia. *Archives of Neurology*, **47**, 791–7.

Langston, J.W. (1985). Mechanism of MPTP toxicity: more answers, more questions. *Trends in Pharmacological Sciences*, **6**, 375–8.

Lansky, L.M., Feinstein, H. and Peterson, J.M. (1988). Demography of handedness in two samples of randomly selected adults (*N* = 2083). *Neuropsychologia*, **26**, 465–77.

Lapierre, D., Braun, C.M.J. and Hodgins, S. (1995). Ventral frontal deficits in psychopathy: neuropsychological test findings. *Neuropsychologia*, **33**(2), 139–51.

Laplane, D., Talairach, J., Meininger, V., Bancaud, J. and Orgogozzo, J.M. (1977). Clinical consequences of corticectomies involving the supplementary motor area in man. *Journal of Neurological Sciences*, **34**, 301–14.

Larrabee, G.J. (1990). Cautions in the use of neuropsychological evaluation in legal settings. *Neuropsychology*, **4**, 239–47.

Larsen, J., Hoien, T., Lundberg, I. and Odegaard, H. (1990) MRI evaluation of the size and symmetry of the planum temporale in adolescents with developmental dyslexia. *Brain and Language*, **39**, 289–301.

Lashley, K.S. (1938). Factors limiting recovery after central nervous lesions. *Journal of Nervous and Mental Diseases*, **88**, 733–55.

Lashley, K.S. (1951). The problem of serial order in behaviour. In L.A. Jeffries (ed.), *Cerebral Mechanisms in Behaviour: The Hixon Symposium*. New York: Wiley.

Lasonde, M., Sauerwein, H., Chicoine, A-J. and Geoffroy, G. (1991). Absence of disconnexion syndrome in callosal genesis and early callosotomy: brain reorganization or lack of structural specificity during ontogeny? *Neuropsychologia*, **29**, 481–495.

Lassen, N.A., Ingvar, D.H. and Skinhoj, E. (1978). Brain function and blood flow. *Scientific American*, **239**, 62–71.

Lawson, R. (1878). On the symptomatology of alcoholic brain disorders. *Brain*, **1**, 182–94.

Lazarus, R.S. (1966). *Psychological Stress and the Coping Process*. New York: McGraw-Hill.

Lea, M. (1986). *A British Supplement to the Manual of the Wechsler Adult Intelligence Scale – Revised*. San Antonio: Psychological Corporation.

LeDoux, J.E. (1987). Emotion. In F. Plum and V.B. Mountcastle (eds), *Handbook of Physiology V. The Nervous System: Higher functions of the brain*. Washington, DC: American Physiological Society.

LeDoux, J.E. (1995a). In search of an emotional system in the brain: leaping from fear to emotion and consciousness. In M.S. Gazzaniga (ed.), *The Cognitive Neurosciences*. Cambridge, MA: MIT Press.

LeDoux, J.E. (1995b). Emotion: clues from the brain. *Annual Review of Psychology*, **46**, 209–35.

LeDoux, J.E., Sakaguchi, A. and Reis, D.J. (1984). Subcortical efferent projections of the medial geniculate nucleus mediate emotional responses conditioned by acoustic stimuli. *Journal of Neuroscience*, **4**(3), 683–98.

LeDoux, J.E., Cicchetti, P., Xagoraris, A. and Romanski, L.M. (1990). The lateral amygdaloid nucleus: sensory interface of the amygdala in fear conditioning. *Journal of Neuroscience*, **10**, 1062–9.

Lehmkuhl, G., Poeck, K. and Willmes, K. (1983). Ideomotor apraxia and aphasia: an examination of types and manifestations of apraxic syndromes. *Neuropsychologia*, **21**, 199–212.

Lehto, J. (1996). Are executive function tests dependent on working memory capacity? *Quarterly Journal of Experimental Psychology*, **49A**(1), 29–50.

Leng, N.R.C. and Parkin, A.J. (1988). Double dissociation of frontal dysfunction in organic amnesia. *British Journal of Clinical Psychology*, **27**, 127–9.

Leng, N.R.C. and Parkin, A.J. (1995). The detection of exaggerated or simulated memory disorder by neuropsychological methods. *Journal of Psychosomatic Research*, **39**(6), 767–76.

Lenneberg, E. (1967). *The Biological Foundations of Language*. New York: Wiley.

Leonard, C.M., Rolls, E.T., Wilson, F.A.W. and Baylis, G.C. (1985). Neurons in the amygdala of the monkey with responses selective for faces. *Behavioural Brain Research*, **15**, 159–76.

Leonard, C.M., Lombardino, L.J., Mercado, L.R., Browd, S.R., Breier, J.I., Agee, O.F. (1996). Cerebral asymmetry and cognitive development in children – a magnetic resonance imaging study. *Psychological Science*, **7**(2), 89–95.

Lesser, R.P., Luders, H, Morris H.H., Dinner, D.S., Klem, G., Hahn, J. and Harrison, M. (1986). Electrical-stimulation of Wernicke's area interferes with comprehension. *Neurology*, **36**(5), 658–663

LeVere, T.E. (1980). Recovery of function after brain damage: a theory of the behavioural deficit. *Physiological Psychology*, **8**, 297–308.

Levin, H.S. and Benton, A.L. (1986). Neuropsychological assessment. In A.B. Baker and R.J. Joynt (eds), *Clinical Neurology*, Volume 1. New York: Harper and Row.

Levin, H.S., Grossman, R.G., Rose, J.E. and Teasdale, G. (1979). Long-term neuropsychological outcome of closed head injury. *Journal of Neurosurgery*, **50**, 412–22.

Levin, H.S., Benton, A.L. and Grossman, R.G. (1982). *Neurobehavioural Consequences of Closed Head Injury*. New York: Oxford University Press.

Levin, H.S., Culhane, K.A., Hartmann, J., Evankovich, K., Mattson, A.J., Harward, H., Ringholtz, G., Ewing-Cobbs, L. and Fletcher, J.M. (1991). Developmental changes in performance on tests of purported frontal lobe functioning. *Developmental Neuropsychology*, **7**(3), 377–95.

Levine, D.N. (1978). Prosopagnosia and visual object agnosia: a behavioural study. *Brain and Language*, **10**, 224–42.

Levitt, P. (1995). Experimental approaches that reveal principles of cerebral cortical development. In M.S. Gazzaniga (ed.), *The Cognitive Neurosciences*. Cambridge, MA: MIT Press.

Levy, J. (1969). Possible basis for the evolution of lateral specialization in the human brain. *Nature*, **224**, 614–15.

Levy, J. (1974). Psychobiological implications of bilateral asymmetry. In S. Dimond and G. Beaumont (eds), *Hemispheric Function in the Human Brain*. New York: Halstead Press.

Levy, J. (1990). The regulation and generation of perception in the asymmetric brain. In C. Trevarthen (ed.), *Brain Circuits and Functions of the Mind: Essays in honour of Roger Sperry*. Cambridge: Cambridge University Press.

Levy, J. and Trevarthen, C. (1976). Metacontrol of hemispheric function in human split-brain patients. *Journal of Experimental Psychology: Human perception and performance*, **2**, 299–312.

Levy, J., Trevarthen, C. and Sperry, R.W. (1972). Perception of chimeric bilateral figures following hemispheric disconnection. *Brain*, **95**, 61–78.

Levy, J., Heller, W., Banich, M. and Burton, L. (1983). Asymmetry of perception in free viewing of chimeric faces. *Brain and Cognition*, **2**, 404–19.

Lewis, D.W. and Diamond, M.C. (1995). The influence of gonadal steroids on the asymmetry of the cerebral cortex. In R.J. Davidson and K. Hugdahl (eds), *Brain Asymmetry*. Cambridge, MA: MIT Press.

Lewis, N.D.C., Landis, C. and King, H.E. (1956). *Studies in Topectomy*. New York: Grune and Stratton.

Lezak, M.D. (1988). IQ: RIP. *Journal of Clinical and Experimental Neuropsychology*, **10**, 351.

Lezak, M.D. (1995). *Neuropsychological Assessment* (3rd edition). New York: Oxford University Press.

Lhermitte, F. (1983). Utilization behaviour and its relation to lesions of the frontal lobes. *Brain*, **106**, 237–55.

Lhermitte, F. and Pillon, B. (1975). La prosopagnosie: role de l'hemisphere droit dans la perception visualle. *Revue de Neurologie*, **131**, 791–812.

Lhermitte, F., Pillon, B. and Serdaru, M. (1986). Human autonomy and the frontal lobes. Part I: Imitation and utilization behaviour – a neuropsychological study of 75 patients. *Annals of Neurology*, **19**, 326–34.

Liberman, I.Y., Mann, V.A., Shankweiler, D. and Werfelman, M. (1982). Children's memory for recurring linguistic and non-linguistic material in relation to reading ability. *Cortex*, **18**, 367–75.

Liepmann, H. (1900). Das Krankheitsbild der Apraxie (motorische Asymbolie). *Monatschrift für Psychiatrie und Neurologie*, **8**, 15–44, 102–132, 182–97.

Liepmann, H. (1905). Der weitere Krankheitsverlauf bei dem einseitig Apraktischen und der Gehirnbefund auf Grund von Serienschnitten. *Monatsschrift für Psychiatrir und Neurologie*, **17**, 283–311.

Liepmann, H. (1920). Apraxia. *Ergebnisse der Gesamten Medizin*, **1**, 516–43.

Liepmann, H. and Maas, O. (1907). Fall von linksseitiger Agraphie und Apraxie bei rechsseitiger Lahmung. *Z. Psychologie und Neurologie*, **10**, 214–27.

Light, L.L. (1991). Memory and aging: four hypotheses in search of data. *Annual Review of Psychology*, **42**, 538–59.

Lindvall, O., Rehncrona, S. and Brundin, P (1989). Human fetal dopamine neurons grafted into the striatum in two patients with severe Parkinson's disease. *Archives of Neurology*, **46**, 615–31.

Linn, M.C. and Petersen, A.A. (1985). Emergence and characterization of sex differences in spatial ability: a meta-analysis. *Child Development*, **59**, 1479–98.

Lissauer, H. (1890). Ein Fall von Seelenblindheit nebst einem Beitrag zur Theorie derselben. *Archiv für Psychiatrie*, **21**, 222–70.

Luders, H. Lesser, R.P., Hahn, J., Dinner, D.S., Morris, H. and Harrison, M. (1985). Language disturbances produced by electrical stimulation of the basal temporal region. *Annals of Neurology*, **18**, 151.

Luders, H. Lesser, R.P., Hahn, J., Dinner, D.S., Morris, H., Resor, S. and Harrison, M. (1986) Basal temporal language area demonstrated by electrical stimulation. *Neurology*, **36**(4), 505–10.

Luders, H., Lesser, R.P., Hahn, J., Dinner, D.S., Morris, H.H., Wyllie, E. and Godoy, J. (1991). Basal temporal language area. *Brain*, **114**, 743–54.

Ludlow, C. (1977). Recovery from aphasia: a foundation for treatment. In M.A. Sullivan and M.S. Kommers (eds), *Rationale for Adult Aphasia Therapy*. Lincoln: University of Nebraska Medical Center.

Lundberg, I., Olofsson, A. and Wall, S. (1980). Reading and spelling skills in the first school years predicted from phonemic awareness skill in kindergarten. *Scandinavian Journal of Psychology*, **21**, 159–73.

Luria, A.R. (1959). Disorders of 'simultaneous perception' in a case of bilateral occipitoparietal brain injury. *Brain*, **83**, 437–49.

Luria, A.R. (1963). *Recovery of Function after Brain Injury*. Macmillan: New York.

Luria, A.R. (1966). *Higher Cortical Functions in Man*. London: Tavistock.

Luria, A.R. (1970). The functional organization of the brain. *Scientific American*, **222**, 3.

Luria, A.R. (1973). *The Working Brain*. London: Penguin.

Luria, A.R., Naydin, V.L., Tsvetkova, L.S. and Vinarskaya, E.N. (1969). Restoration of higher cortical function following local brain damage. In P.J. Vinken and G.W. Bruyn (eds), *Handbook of Clinical Neurology,* volume 3. Amsterdam: North-Holland.

Machiyama, Y., Watanabe, Y. and Machiyama, R. (1987). Neuroanatomical studies of the corpus callosum in schizophrenia: evidence of aberrant interhemispheric fibre connections. In R. Takahashi, P. Flor-Henry and S. Niwa (eds), *Cerebral Dynamics: Laterality and psychopathology*. New York: Elsevier.

MacLean, M., Bryant, P.E. and Bradley, L. (1987). Rhymes, nursery rhymes and reading in early childhood. *Merrill–Palmer Quarterly*, **33**, 255–82.

Macmillan, M. (1995). Experimental and clinical studies of localisation before Flourens. *Journal of the History of Neuroscience*, **4**(3/4), 139–54.

Mahmood, T., Reveley, A.M. and Murray, R.M. (1983). Genetic studies of affective and anxiety disorders. In M. Weller (ed.), *The Scientific Basis of Psychiatry*. London: Ballière/Tindal.

Maier, M. (1995). *In vivo* magnetic resonance spectroscopy: application in psychiatry. *British Journal of Psychiatry*, **167**, 299–306.

Malone, K. and Mann, J.J. (1993). Serotonin and major depression. In J.J. Mann and D.J. Kupfer (eds), *Biology of Depressive Disorders, Part A: A systems perspective*. New York: Plenum.

Mammucari, A., Caltagirone, C., Ekman, P., Friesen, W., Gianotti, G., Pizzamiglio, L. and Zoccolotti, P. (1988). Spontaneous facial expression of emotions in brain-damaged patients. *Cortex*, **24**, 521–33.

Mann, D.M.A., Yates, P.O. and Hawkes, J. (1982). The noradrenergic system in Alzheimer and multi-infarct dementias. *Journal of Neurology, Neurosurgery and Psychiatry*, **45**, 113–19.

Mark, V.W., Kooistra, C.A. and Heilman, K.M. (1988). Hemispatial neglect affected by non-neglected stimuli. *Neurology*, **38**, 1207–11.

Markesbery, W.R., Ehmann, W.D., Hossain, T.I.M., Alauddin, M. and Goodin, D.T. (1981). Instrumental neutron activation analysis of brain aluminium in Alzheimer's disease and aging. *Annals of Neurology*, **10**, 511–16.

Marks, I.M. (1986). Genetics of fear and anxiety disorders. *British Journal of Psychiatry*, **149**, 406–18.

Markus, H.S. and Boland, M. (1992). 'Cognitive activity' monitored by non-invasive measurement of cerebral blood flow velocity and its application to the investigation of cerebral dominance. *Cortex*, **28**, 575–81.

Marr, D. (1982). *Vision*. San Francisco: Freeman.

Marshall, J.C. and Halligan, P.W. (1988). Blindsight and insight in visuospatial neglect. *Nature*, **336**, 766–7.

Marshall, J.C. and Halligan, P.W. (1994). Left in the dark. In P.W. Halligan and J.C. Marshall (1994). *Spatial Neglect: Position papers on theory and practice*. Hove, UK: Lawrence Erlbaum Associates.

Marshall, J.C. and Halligan, P.W. (1996). Hemispheric antagonism in visuo-spatial neglect: a case study. *Journal of the International Neuropsychological Society*, **2**, 412–8.

Martin, A., Wiggs, C.L., Ungerleider, G. and Haxby, J.V. (1996). Neural correlates of category-specific knowledge. *Nature*, **379**, 649–52.

Martin, G.N. (1995a). Olfactory influences on the human EEG. *Journal of Psychophysiology*, **9**(2), 183–4.

Martin, G.N. (1995b). Emotion and the EEG: an olfactory experiment. *Journal of Psychophysiology*, **9**(2), 178–9.

Martin, G.N. (1996). Olfactory remediation: current evidence and possible applications. *Social Science and Medicine*, **43**(1), 63–70.

Martin, G.N. and Gray, C.D. (1996). The effects of audience laughter on men's and women's responses to humor. *Journal of Social Psychology*, **136**(2), 221–31.

Martin, P.R., Rio, D., Adinoff, B. (1992). Regional cerebral glucose utilization in chronic organic mental disorders associated with alcoholism. *Journal of Neuropsychiatry and Clinical Neurosciences*, **4**, 159–67.

Martyn, C.N., Osmond, C., Edwardson, J.A., Barker, D.J.P., Harris, E.C. and Lacey, R.F. (1989). Geographical relationship between Alzheimer's disease and aluminium in drinking water. *Lancet*, **i**, 59–62.

Marzi, C.A., Tassinari, G., Aglioti, S. and Lutzemberger, L. (1986). Spatial summation across the vertical meridian in hemianopics: a test of blindsight. *Neuropsychologia*, **24**, 749–58.

Mayes, A.R. (1988). The memory problems caused by frontal lobe lesions. In A.R. Mayes (ed.), *Human Organic Memory Disorders*. Cambridge: Cambridge University Press.

Mazzocchi, F. and Vignolo, L.A. (1979) Localization of lesions in aphasia: clinical CT scan correlations in stroke patients. *Cortex*, **15**, 627–54.

McCarley, R.W., Faux, S.F., Shenton, M.E., Nestor, P.G. and Adams, J. (1991). Event-related potentials in schizophrenia: their biological and clinical correlates and a new model of schizophrenic pathophysiology. *Schizophrenia Research*, **4**, 209–31.

McCarley, R.W., Shenton, M.E., O'Donnell, B.F., Faux, S.F., Kikinis, R., Nestor, P.G. and Jolesz, F.A. (1993). Auditory P300 abnormalities and left posterior superior temporal gyrus volume reduction in schizophrenia. *Archives of General Psychiatry*, **50**, 190–7.

McCarthy, G., Blamire, A.M., Rothman, D.L., Gruetter, R. and Schulman, R.G. (1993). Echo-planar magnetic resonance imaging studies of frontal cortex activation during word generation in humans. *Proceedings of the National Academy of Sciences*, **90**, 4952–6.

McCarthy, R.A. and Warrington, E.K. (1986). Visual associative agnosia: a clinico-anatomical study of a single case. *Journal of Neurology, Neurosurgery and Psychiatry*, **49**, 1233–40.

McCarthy, R.A. and Warrington, E.K. (1988). Evidence for modality specific meaning systems in the brain. *Nature*, **334**, 428–30.

McCarthy, R.A. and Warrington, E.K. (1990). *Cognitive Neuropsychology: A clinical introduction*. New York: Academic Press.

McCloskey, M. (1993). Theory and evidence in cognitive neuropsychology: a 'radical' response to Robertson, Knight, Rafal and Shimamura (1993). *Journal of Experimental Psychology: Learning, Memory and Attention*, **19**(3), 718–34.

McCloskey, M., Aliminosa, D. and Sokol, S.M. (1991). Facts, rules, and procedures in normal calculation: evidence from multiple single-patient studies of impaired arithmetic fact retrieval. *Brain and Cognition*, **17**, 154–203.

McCrae, D. and Trolle, E. (1956). The defect of function in visual agnosia. *Brain*, **79**, 94–110.

McCulloch, W. (1949). Mechanisms for the spread of epileptic activation in the brain. *Electroencephalography and Clinical Neurophysiology*, **1**, 19–24.

McDonald, C. (1969). Clinical heterogeneity in senile dementia. *British Journal of Psychiatry*, **115**, 267–71.

McGhee, M.G. (1979). Human spatial abilities: psychometric studies and environmental, genetic, hormonal and neurological influences. *Psychological Bulletin*, **86**, 889–918.

McGlone, J. (1977) Sex differences in the cerebral organization of verbal function in patients with unilateral brain lesions. *Brain*, **100**, 775–93.

McGlone, J. (1980) Sex differences in human brain asymmetry: a critical survey. *Behavioural and Brain Sciences*, **5**, 215–64.

McGlone, J. and Davidson, W. (1973) The relation between cerebral speech laterality and spatial ability with special reference to sex and hand preference. *Neuropsychologia*, **11**, 105–13.

McGlone, J. and Kertesz, A. (1973) Sex differences in cerebral processing of visuospatial tasks. *Cortex*, **9**, 313–20.

McGuire, P.K., Silbersweig, D.A., Wright, I., Murray, R.M., David, A.S., Frackowiak, R.S.J. and Frith, C.D. (1995). Abnormal monitoring of inner speech: a physiological basis for auditory hallucinations. *Lancet*, **346**, 596–600.

McKeever, W.F. (1986). The influences of handedness, sex, familial sinistrality, and androgyny on language laterality, verbal ability and spatial ability. *Cortex*, **22**, 521–37.

McKeever, W.F. (1991). Handedness, language laterality and spatial ability. In F.L. Kitterle (ed.), *Cerebral Laterality: Theory and research*. Hillsdale, NJ: Lawrence Erlbaum Associates.

McKhann, G., Drachman, D., Folstein, M., Katzman, R., Price, D. and Stadlan, E.M. (1984). Clinical diagnosis of Alzheimer's disease: report of the NINCDS-ADRDA Work Group under the auspices of the Department of Health and Human Services Task Force on Alzheimer's Disease. *Neurology*, 34, 939–44.

McLellan, D.L. (1991). Functional recovery and the principles of disability medicine. In M. Swash and J. Oxbury (eds), *Clinical Neurology*. Edinburgh: Churchill Livingstone.

McPherson, S.E. and Cummings, J.L. (1996). Neuropsychological aspects of vascular dementia. *Brain and Cognition*, **31**, 269–82.

Meador, K.J., Allen, M.E., Adams, R.J. and Loring, D.W. (1991). Allochiria vs allesthesia. Is there a misrepresentation? *Archives of Neurology*, **48**, 546–9.

Meadows, J.C. (1974). The anatomical basis of prosopagnosia. *Journal of Neurology, Neurosurgery and Psychiatry*, **37**, 489–501.

Mehta, Z. and Newcombe, F. (1991). A role for the left hemisphere in spatial processing. *Cortex*, **27**, 153–67.

Melamed, E., Lavy, S., Shlomo, B., Cooper, G. and Rinot, Y. (1980). Reduction in regional cerebral blood flow during normal aging in man. *Stroke*, **11**(1), 31–4.

Mesulam, M.M. (1986). Frontal cortex and behaviour. *Annals of Neurology*, **19**, 320–5.

Mesulam, M.M. (1990). Large scale neurocognitive networks and distributed processing for attention, language and memory. *Annals of Neurology*, **28**, 597–613.

Miller, E. (1971). Handedness and pattern of human ability. *British Journal of Psychology*, **62**, 111–2.

Miller, E. (1984). *Recovery and Management of Neuropsychological Impairments*. Chichester: Wiley.

Miller, E. (1993). Dissociating single cases in neuropsychology. *British Journal of Clinical Psychology*, **32**, 155–67.

Miller, E.N., Fujuoka, T.A.T., Chapman, L.J. and Chapman, J.P. (1995). Psychometrically matches tasks for assessment of hemispheric asymmetries of function. *Brain and Cognition*, **28**, 1–13.

Miller, N.E. (1995). Clinical–experimental interactions in the development of neuroscience. *American Psychologist*, **50**(11), 901–11.

Milner, A.D. and Goodale, M.A. (1993). Visual pathways to perception and action. In T.P. Hicks, S. Molotchnikoff and T. Ono (eds), *Progress in Brain Research*. Amsterdam: Elsevier.

Milner, B. (1958). Psychological deficits produced by temporal-lobe excision. *Research Publications/Association for Research in Nervous and Mental Disease*, **36**, 244–57.

Milner, B. (1963). Effects of different brain lesions on card sorting. *Archives of Neurology*, **9**, 90–100.

Milner, B. (1964). Some effects of frontal lobectomy in man. In J.M. Warren and G. Akert (eds), *The Frontal Granular Cortex and Behaviour*. New York: McGraw-Hill.

Milner, B., Corkin, S. and Teuber, H-L. (1968). Further analysis of the hippocampal amnesic syndrome: 14 year follow-up study of HM. *Neuropsychologia*, **6**, 217–4.

Milner, B., Corsi, P. and Leonard, G. (1991). Frontal lobe contribution to recency judgements. *Neuropsychology*, **29**, 601–18.

Mirsen, T. and Hachinski, V. (1988). Epidemiology and classification of vascular and multi-infarct dementia. In J.S. Meyer, H. Lechner, J. Marshall and J.F. Toole (eds), *Vascular and Multi-infarct Dementia*. Mount Kisko, NY: Future Publishing.

Mishra, S.P and Brown, K.H. (1983). The comparability of WAIS and WAIS-R IQ and subtest scores. *Journal of Clinical Psychology*, **39**, 754–7.

Mittenberg, W., Zielinski, R.E., Fichera, S.M. and Heilbronner, R.L. (1995). Identification of malingered head injury on the Wechsler Adult Intelligence Scale–Revised. *Professional Psychology: Research and Practice*, **26**, 491–8.

Mohr, J.P., Pessin, M.S., Finkelstein, S., Funkenstein, H.H., Duncan, G.W. and Davis, K.R. (1978) Broca's aphasia: pathologic and clinical aspects. *Neurology*, **28**, 311–24.

Mohr, J.P., Weiss, G.H., Caveness, W.F., Dillon, J.D., Kistler, J.P., Meirowsky, A.M. and Rish, B.L. (1980). Language and motor disorders after penetrating head injury in Viet Nam. *Neurology*, **30**, 1273–9.

Morgan, A.H., Macdonald, P.J. and Macdonald, H. (1971). Differences in bilateral alpha activity as a function of experimental task with a note on lateral eye movements and hypnotizability. *Neuropsychologia*, **9**, 459–69.

Morris, J.S., Frith, C.D., Perrett, D.I., Rowland, D., Young, A.W., Calder, A.J. and Dolan, R.J. (1996). A differential neural response in the human amygdala to fearful and happy facial expressions. *Nature*, **383**, 812–5.

Morris, R.D., Hopkins, W.D. and Bolser-Gilmore, L. (1993). Assessment of hand preference in two language-trained chimpanzees (Pan troglodytes): a multimethod analysis. *Journal of Clinical and Experimental Psychology*, **15**, 487–502.

Morris, R.G., Evenden, J.L., Sahakian, B.J. and Robbins, T.W. (1986). Computer-aided assessment of dementia: comparative studies of neuropsychological deficits in

Alzheimer-type dementia and Parkinson's disease. In S.M. Stahl, S.D. Iversen and E.C. Goodman (eds), *Cognitive Neurochemistry*. New York: Oxford University Press.

Morris, R.G., Downes, J.J., Sahakian, B.J., Evenden, J.L., Heald, A. and Robbins, T.W. (1988). Planning and spatial working memory in Parkinson's disease. *Journal of Neurology, Neurosurgery and Psychiatry*, **51**, 757–66.

Moss, A.R. and Dowd, T. (1991). Does the NART hold after head injury? A case report. *British Journal of Clinical Psychology*, **30**, 179–180.

Muller-Hill, B. and Beyreuther, K. (1989). Molecular biology of Alzheimer's disease. *Annual Review of Biochemistry*, **58**, 287–307.

Munk, H. (1878). Weitere Mittheilungen zur Physiologie der Grosshirnrinde. *Archives of Anatomy and Physiology*, **3**, 581–92.

Munk, H. (1881). *Über die Funktionen der Grosshirnrinde, Gesammelte Mitteilungen aus den Jahren 1877–1880*. Berlin: Hirshwald.

Myers, R.E. (1956). Function of corpus callosum in interocular transfer. *Brain*, **79**, 358–63.

Myers, R.E. and Sperry, R.W. (1958). Interhemispheric communication through the corpus callosum: mnemonic carry-over between the hemispheres. *Archives of Neurology and Psychiatry*, **80**, 298–303.

Nachshon, I. (1980). Hemispheric dysfunctioning in schizophrenia. *Journal of Nervous and Mental Disease*, **168**(4), 241–2.

Naeser, M.A., Hayward, R.W., Laughlin, S.A. and Zatz, L.M. (1981) Quantitative CT scan studies in aphasia. I: infarct size and CT numbers. *Brain and Language*, **12**, 140–64.

Nagahama, Y., Fukuyama, H., Yamauchi, H., Matsuzaki, S., Konishi, J., Shibasaki, H. and Kimure, J. (1996). Cerebral activation during performance of a card sorting test. *Brain*, **119**, 1667–75.

Najlerahim, A. and Bowen, D.M. (1988a). Biochemical measurements in Alzheimer's disease reveal a necessity for improved neuroimaging techniques to study metabolism. *Biochemical Journal*, **251**, 305–8.

Najlerahim, A. and Bowen, D.M. (1988b). Regional weight loss of the cerebral cortex and some subcortical nuclei in senile dementia of the Alzheimer type. *Acta Neuropathologica*, **75**, 509–12.

Nauta, W.J.H. (1971). The problem of the frontal lobe: a reinterpretation. *Journal of Psychiatric Research*, **8**, 167–87.

Nauta, W.J.H. (1973). Connections of the frontal lobe with the limbic system. In L.V. Laitinen and R.E. Livingston (eds), *Surgical Approaches in Psychiatry*. Baltimore: University Park Press.

Neary, D. and Snowden, J. (1996). Fronto-temporal dementia: nosology, neuropsychology and neuropathology. *Brain and Cognition*, **31**, 176–87.

Nebes, R. (1972). Direct examination of cognitive function in the right and left hemispheres. In M. Kinsbourne (ed.), *Asymmetrical Function of the Brain*. Cambridge: Cambridge University Press.

Neils, J. and Aram, D.M. (1986). Family history of children with developmental language disorders. *Perceptual and Motor Skills*, **63**, 655–8.

Nelson, H. (1976). A modified card sorting test sensitive to frontal lobe defects. *Cortex*, **12**, 313–24.

Nelson, H.E. (1982). *National Adult Reading Test (NART): Test Manual*. Windsor: NFER/ Nelson.

Nelson, H.E. and O'Connell, A. (1978). Dementia: the estimation of premorbid intelligence. *Journal of Abnormal Psychology*, **93**, 321–30.

Neri, M., Vecchi, G.P. and Caselli, M. (1985). Pain measurements in right–left cerebral lesions. *Neuropsychologia*, **23**, 123–6.

Neville, H.J. (1989). Neurobiology of cognitive and language processing: effects of early experience. In K. Gibson and A.C. Petersen (eds), *Brain Maturation and Behavioural Development*. Hawthorn, NY: Aldine Gruyter Press.

Newcombe, F. and Marshall, J.C. (1980). Transcoding and lexical stabilisation in deep dyslexia. In M. Coltheart, K.E. Patterson and J.C. Marshall (eds), *Deep Dyslexia*. London: Routledge and Kegan Paul.

Newcombe, F., Mehta, Z. and de Haan, E.H.F. (1994). Category specificity in visual recognition. In M.J. Farah and G. Ratcliff (eds), *The Neuropsychology of High-level Vision*. Hove, UK: Lawrence Erlbaum Associates.

Newman, J.P., Patterson, C.M. and Kosson, D.S. (1987). Response perseveration in psychopaths. *Journal of Abnormal Psychology*, **96**, 145–8.

Nielsen, J.M. (1937). Unilateral cerebral dominance as related to mind blindness. *Archives of Neurology and Psychiatry*, **38**, 108–35.

Nielsen, J.M. (1946) *Agnosia, Apraxia, Aphasia: Their value in cerebral localisation*. New York: Paul Hoeber.

Niedermeyer, E. (1987). The normal EEG of the waking adult. In E. Niedermeyer and F. Lopes DaSilva (eds), *Electroencephalography: Basic principles, clinical applications and related fields*. Germany: Urban and Schwarzenberg.

Nobler, M.S., Sackheim, H.A., Prohovnik, I., Moeller, J.R., Mukherjee, S., Schnur, D.B., Prudic, J. and Devanand, D.P. (1994). Regional cerebral blood flow in mood disorders III. *Archives of General Psychiatry*, **51**, 884–97.

Nobre, A.C. and McCarthy, G. (1994). Language-related ERPs: scalp distributions and modulation by word type and semantic priming. *Journal of Cognitive Neuroscience*, **6**(3), 233–55.

Nobre, A.C. and McCarthy, G. (1995). Language-related field potentials in the anterior-medial temporal lobe. *Journal of Neuroscience*, **15**(2), 1090–8.

Nobre, A.C., Allison, T. and McCarthy, G. (1994). Word recognition in the human inferior temporal lobe. *Nature*, **372**, 260–3.

Norman, D. and Shallice, T. (1986). Attention to action: willed and automatic control of behaviour. In R.J. Davidson, G.E. Schwartz and D. Shapiro (eds), *Consciousness and Self-regulation*, volume 4. New York: Plenum.

Oatley, K. and Jenkins, J.M. (1996). *Understanding Emotions*. Oxford: Blackwell.

Obler, L. (1979). Right hemisphere participation in second language acquisition. In K.C. Diller (ed.), *Individual Differences and Universals in Language Learning Aptitude*. Rowley, MA: Newbury House.

O'Boyle, M.W. and Benbow, C.P. (1990). Handedness and its relationship to ability and talent. In S. Coren (ed.), *Left-handedness: Behavioural implications and anomalies*. Amsterdam: North-Holland.

Obrzut, J.E., Conrad, P.F. and Boliek, C.A. (1989). Verbal and nonverbal auditory processing among left- and right-handed good readers and reading-disabled children. *Neuropsychologia*, **27**, 1357–71.

O'Carroll, R.E. (1995). The assessment of premorbid ability: a critical review. *Neurocase*, **1**, 83–9.

O'Carroll, R.E., Baikie, E.M. and Whittick, J.E. (1987). Does the National Adult Reading Test hold in dementia? *British Journal of Clinical Psychology*, **26**, 315–16.

Oddy, M. (1993). Head injury during childhood. *Neuropsychological Rehabilitation*, **3**(4), 301–20.

Oddy, M. and Humphrey, M. (1980). Social recovery during the year following severe head injury. *Journal of Neurology, Neurosurgery and Psychiatry*, **43**, 798–8.

Oertel, W.H. and Quinn, N.P. (1996). Parkinsonism. In T. Brandt, L.R. Caplan, J. Dichgans, H.C. Diener and C. Kennard (eds), *Neurological Disorders: Course and treatment*. New York: Academic Press.

Ogawa, S., Lee, L.M., Kay, A.R., and Tank, D.W. (1990). Brain magnetic resonance imaging with contrast dependent on blood oxygenation. *Proceedings of the National Academy of Sciences*, **87**, 9868–72.

Ojemann, G.A. (1982) Models of the brain organisation for higher integrative functions derived with electrical stimulation techniques. *Human Neurobiology*, **1**, 243–50.

Ojemann, G. A. (1983). Brain organisation for language from the perspective of electrical stimulation mapping. *Behavioural and Brain Sciences*, **6**, 189–230.

Ojemann, G.A. and Whitaker, H.A. (1978) Language localization and variability. *Brain and Language*, **6**, 239–60.

O'Keefe, J. and Nadel, L. (1978). *The Hippocampus as a Cognitive Map*. Oxford: Oxford University Press.

Olanow, C.W., Kordower, J.H. and Freeman, T.B. (1996). Fetal nigral transplantation as a therapy for Parkinson's disease. *Trends in Neuroscience*, **19**(3), 102–9.

Oldfield, R.C. (1971). The assessment and analysis of handedness: the Edinburgh Inventory. *Neuropsychologia*, **9**, 97–113.

Olton, D.S., Becker, J.T., and Handelmann, G.E. (1979). Hippocampus, space and memory. *Behavioural and Brain Sciences*, **2**, 313–66.

Orton, S.T. (1937). *Reading, Writing and Speech Problems in Children*. New York: Norton.

Ortony, A. and Turner, T.J. (1990). What's basic about basic emotions? *Psychological Review*, **97**, 315–31.

Oscar-Berman, M. (1973). Hypothesis testing and focusing behaviour during concept formation by amnesic Korsakoff patients. *Neuropsychologia*, **11**, 191–8.

Otto, M.W., Yeo, R.A. and Dougher, M.J. (1987). Right hemisphere involvement in depression: toward a neurophysiological theory of negative affective experiences. *Biological Psychiatry*, **22**, 1201–15.

Owen, A.M., Morris, R.G., Sahakian, B.J., Polkey, C.E. and Robbins, T.W. (1996). Double dissociations of memory and executive functions in working memory tasks following frontal lobe excisions, temporal lobe excisions or amygdalo-hippocamectomy in man. *Brain*, **119**, 1597–615.

Pallis, C.A. (1955). Impaired identification of faces and places with agnosia for colours. report of a case due to cerebral embolism. *Journal of Neurology, Neurosurgery and Psychiatry*, **18**, 218–24.

Pandya, D.N. and Barnes, C.L. (1987). Architecture and connections of the frontal lobe. In E. Perecman (ed.), *The Frontal Lobes Revisited*. New York: IRBN Press.

Pandya, D.N. and Seltzer, B. (1986). The topography of commissural fibres. In F. Lepore, M. Ptito and H.H. Jasper (eds), *Two Hemispheres – One Brain: Functions of the corpus callosum*. New York: Liss.

Panksepp, J. (1982). Towards a general psychobiological theory of emotions. *Behavioural and Brain Sciences*, **5**, 407–22.

Papanicolaou, A.C., Eisenberg, H.M. and Levy, R.S. (1983). Evoked-potential correlates of left-hemisphere dominance in covert articulation. *International Journal of Neuroscience*, **20**(3/4), 289–93.

Papero, P.H., Prigatano, G.P., Snyder, H.M. and Johnson, D.L. (1993). Children's adaptive behavioural competence after head injury. *Neuropsychological Rehabilitation*, **3**(4), 321–40.

Papez, J.W. (1937). A proposed mechanism of emotion. *Archives of Neurology and Psychiatry*, **38**, 725–44.

Passingham, R.E. (1995). *The Frontal Lobes and Voluntary Action*. Oxford: Oxford University Press.

Patterson, K.E. and Marcel, A.J. (1977) Aphasia, dyslexia and the phonological coding of written words. *Quarterly Journal of Experimental Psychology*, **29**, 307–18.

Paulesu, E., Frith, U., Snowling, M., Gallagher, A., Morton, J., Frackowiak, R.S.J. and Frith, C.D. (1996). Is developmental dyslexia a disconnection syndrome? Evidence from PET scanning. *Brain*, **119**(1), 143–57.

Pauling, L. (1935). Oxygen equilibrium of haemoglobin and its structural interpretation. *Proceedings of the National Academy of Sciences*, **21**, 186–91.

Pawlik, G. and Heiss, W-D. (1989). Positron emission tomography and neuropsychological function. In E.D. Bigler and R.A. Yeo (eds), *Neuropsychological Function and Brain Imaging*. New York: Plenum.

Pell, M.D. and Baum, S.R. (1997). The ability to perceive and comprehend intonation in linguistic and affective contexts by brain-damaged adults. *Brain and Language*, **57**, 80–99.

Penfield, W. and Jasper, H. (1954) *Epilepsy and the Functional Anatomy of the Human Brain*. Boston: Little Brown.

Penfield, W. and Perot, P. (1963) The brain's record of auditory and visual experience: a final summary and discussion. *Brain*, **86**, 595–696.

Penfield, W. and Rasmussen, T. (1950) *The Cerebral Cortex of Man: A clinical study of localisation of function*. New York: Macmillan.

Penfield, W. and Roberts, L. (1959) *Speech and Brain Mechanisms*. New York: Oxford University Press.

Perenin, M.T. and Vighetto, A. (1988). Optic ataxia: A specific disorder in visuomotor coordination. In A. Hein and M. Jeannerod (eds), *Spatially Oriented Behaviour*. New York: Springer.

Periani, D., Bressi, S., Cappa, S.F., Vallar, G., Alberoni, M., Grassi, F., Caltagirone, C., Cipolotti, L., Franceschi, M., Lenzi, G.L. and Fazio, F. (1993). Evidence of multiple memory systems in the human brain. *Brain*, **116**, 903–19.

Perria, L., Rossalini, G. and Rossi, G.F. (1961). Determination of side of cerebral dominance with Amobarbital. *Archives of Neurology*, **4**, 173–81.

Perris, C., Monakhov, K., von Knorring, L., Botskarev, M. and Nikiforov, A. (1978). Systemic structural analysis of the electroencephalogram of depressed patients: general principles and preliminary results of an international collaborative study. *Neuropsychobiology*, **4**, 207–20.

Perry, E.K., Tomlinson, B.E., Blessed, G., Bergmann, K., Gibson, P.H. and Perry, R.H. (1978). Correlation of cholinergic abnormalities with senile plaques and mental test scores in senile dementia. *British Medical Journal*, **2**, 1457–9.

Perry, E.K., Irving, D., Blessed, G., Fairbairn, A. and Perry, E.K. (1990). Senile dementia of Lewy body type: a clinically and neuropathologically distinct form of Lewy body dementia in the elderly. *Journal of the Neurological Sciences*, **95**, 119–39.

Peters, M. (1992). How sensitive are handedness prevalence figures to differences in handedness classification procedures? *Brain and Cognition*, **18**, 208–15.

Peters, M. (1995). Handedness and its relation to other indices of cerebral lateralization. In R.J. Davidson and K. Hugdahl (eds), *Brain Asymmetry*. Cambridge, MA: MIT Press.

Petersen, S.E., Fox, P.T., Posner, M.I., Mintun, M. and Raichle, M.E. (1988). Positron emission tomographic studies of the cortical anatomy of single-word processing. *Nature*, **331**, 585–9.

Petersen, S.E., Fox, P.T., Snyder, A.Z. and Raichle, M.E. (1990) Activation of extrastriate and frontal cortical areas by visual words and word-like stimuli. *Science*, **249**, 1041–4.

Peterson, J.M. and Lansky, L.M. (1977). Left-handedness among architects: partial replication and some new data. *Perceptual and Motor Skills*, **45**, 1216–8.

Pfeifer, R.A. (1936). Pathologie der Horstrahlung und der corticalen Horsphare. In O. Bumke and O. Foerster (eds), *Handbuch der neurologie*, volume 6. Berlin: Springer.

Piccolino, M. and Pignatelli, A. (1996). Calcium-independent synaptic transmission: artifact or fact? *Trends in Neuroscience*, **19**(4), 120–5.

Pick, A. (1905). *Studien uber motorische Apraxie und ihr nahestehende Erscheinungen*. Leipzig: Deuticke.

Pieczuro, A.C. and Vignolo, L.A. (1967). Studio speimentale sulla aprassia ideomotoria. *Sistema Nervoso*, **19**, 131–43.

Pieniadz, J.M., Naeser, M.A., Kloff, E. and Levine, H.L. (1983). CT scan cerebral hemispheric asymmetry measurements in stroke cases with global aphasia: atypical asymmetries associated with improved recovery. *Cortex*, **19**, 371–91.

Platel, H., Price, C., Baron, J-C., Wise, R., Lambert, J., Frackowiak, R.S.J., Lechevalier, B. and Eustache, F. (1997). The structural components of music perception: a functional anatomical study. *Brain*, 120, 229–43.

Plutchik, R. (1994). *The Psychology and Biology of Emotion*. London: Harper Collins.

Poeck, K. and Lehmkuhl, G. (1980). Das Syndrom der ideatorischen Apraxie und seine Localisation. *Nervenarzt*, **51**, 217–25.

Polich, J. and Kok, A. (1995). Cognitive and biological determinants of P300: an integrative overview. *Biological Psychology*, **41**, 103–46.

Poon, L.W. (1985). Differences in human memory with aging: nature, causes, and clinical implications. In J.E. Birren and K.W. Schaie (eds), *Handbook of the Psychology of Aging* (2nd edition). New York: Van Nostrand Reinhold.

Porac, C. and Coren, S. (1981). *Lateral Preferences and Human Behaviour*. New York: Springer.

Porteus, S.D. (1965). *The Porteus Maze Test. Fifty years of application*. Palo Alto, CA: Pacific Books.

Posner, M. (1980). Orienting of attention. The 7th Sir F.C. Bartlett Lecture. *Quarterly Journal of Experimental Psychology*, **32**, 3–25.

Posner, M. (1993). Interaction of arousal and selection in the posterior attention network. In A. Baddeley and L. Weiskrantz (eds), *Attention, Selection, Awareness and Control. A tribute to Donald Broadbent*. Oxford: Oxford University Press.

Posner, M. (1994). Neglect and spatial attention. In P.W. Halligan and J.C. Marshall (eds), *Spatial Neglect: Position papers on theory and practice*. Hove, UK: Lawrence Erlbaum Associates.

Posner, M. and Raichle, M. (1994). *Images of Mind*. New York: Scientific American Library.

Post, R.M., DeLisi, L.E., Holcomb, H.H., Uhde, T.W., Cohen, R. and Buchsbaum, M.S. (1987). Glucose utilisation in the temporal cortex of affectively ill patients: positron emission tomography. *Biological Psychiatry*, **22**, 545–53.

Potter, H. and Nauta, W.J.H. (1979). A note on the problem of olfactory associations of the orbitofrontal cortex in the monkey. *Neuroscience*, **4**, 361–7.

Pozzilli, C., Bastianello, S., Padovani, A., Passaflume, D., Millefiorini, E., Bozzao, L. and Fieschi, C. (1991). Anterior corpus callosum atrophy and verbal fluency in multiple sclerosis. *Cortex*, **27**, 441–5.

Pramstaller, P.P. and Marsden, C.D. (1996). The basal ganglia and apraxia. *Brain*, **119**, 319–40.

Price, C.J., Wise, R.J.S., Watson, J.D.G, Patterson, K., Howard, D. and Frackowiak, R.S.J. (1994). Brain activity during reading: the effects of exposure duration and task. *Brain*, **117**, 1255–69.

Procter, A.W., Palmer, A.M., Francis, P.T., Lowe, S.L., Neary, D., Murphy, E., Doshi, R. and Bowen, D.M. (1988). Evidence of glutamatergic denervation and possible abnormal metabolism in Alzheimer's disease. *Journal of Neurochemistry*, **50**, 790–802.

Prusiner, S.B. (1987). Prions and neurodegenerative diseases. *New England Journal of Medicine*, **317**, 1571–81.

Rabbitt, P. (1993). Does it all go together when it goes? The nineteenth Bartlett memorial lecture. *Quarterly Journal of Experimental Psychology*, **46A**(3), 385–434.

Rademacher, J., Galaburda, A.M., Kennedy, D.N., Filipek, P.A. and Caviness, V.S. (1993). Topographic variation of the human primary cortices: implications for neuroimaging, brain mapping and neurobiology. *Cerebral Cortex*, **3**, 313–29.

Raichle, M.E. (1994). Images of the mind: studies with modern imaging techniques. *Annual Review of Psychology*, **45**, 333–56.

Raine, A. (1993). *The Psychopathology of Crime*. New York: Academic Press.

Raine, A., Buchsbaum, M.S., Stanley, J., Lottenberg, S., Abel, L. and Stoddard, J. (1993). Selective reductions in prefrontal glucose metabolism in murderers assessed with positron emission tomography. Unpublished.

Rajput, A.H., Offort, K., Beard, C.M. and Kurland, L.T. (1984). Epidemiological survey of dementia in Parkinsonism and control population. In R.G. Hassler and J.F. Christ (eds), *Advances in Neurology*, volume 40. New York: Raven Press.

Ramsay, D.S. (1980). Beginnings of bimanual handedness and speech in infants. *Infant Behaviour and Development*, **3**, 67–77.

Rao, S.M. (1986). Neuropsychology of multiple sclerosis: a critical review. *Journal of Clinical and Experimental Neuropsychology*, **8**, 503.

Rasmussen, T. and Milner, B. (1975). Clinical and surgical studies of the cerebral speech areas in man. In K.J. Zulch, O. Creutzfeldt and G.C. Galbraith (eds), *Cerebral Localization*. New York: Springer.

Rasmussen, T. and Milner, B. (1977). The role of early left brain injury in determining lateralization of cerebral speech functions. *Annals of the New York Academy of Sciences*, **299**, 355–69.

Reed, C.L., Caselli, R.J. and Farah, M.J. (1996). Tactile agnosia. *Brain*, **119**, 875–88.

Reiman, E.M., Raichle, M.E., Robins, E., Butler, F.K., Herscoritch, P., Fox, P.T. and Perlmutter, J. (1986). The application of positron emission tomography to the study of panic disorder. *American Journal of Psychiatry*, **143**, 469–77.

Reiman, E.M., Fusselman, M.J., Fox, P.T. and Raichle, M.E. (1989). Neuroanatomical correlates of anticipatory anxiety. *Nature*, **305**, 527–9.

Reiss, A.L., Abrams, M.T., Singer, H.S., Ross, J.L. and Denckla, M.B. (1996). Brain development, gender and IQ in children. *Brain*, **119**, 1763–74.

Reitan, R.M. and Wolfson, D. (1990). A consideration of the comparability of the WAIS and WAIS-R. *The Clinical Neuropsychologist*, **4**, 80–5.

Reitan, R.M. and Wolfson, D. (1996). Relationships between specific and general tests of cerebral functioning. *The Clinical Neuropsychologist*, **10**(1), 37–42.

Resnick, S.M., Lazar, J., Gur, R.E. and Gur, R.C. (1994). The stability of tachistoscopic measures of hemispheric specialization. *Neuropsychologia*, **32**(11), 1419–30.

Rey, A. (1941). L'examen psychologique dans les cas d'encephalopathie traumatique. *Archives of Psychology*, **28**, 286–340.

Rey, A. (1964). *L'examen clinique en psychologie*. Paris: Presses Univ. France.

Rezai, K., Andreasen, N.C., Alliger, R., Cohen, G., Swayze, V. and O'Leary, D.S. (1993). The neuropsychology of the prefrontal cortex. *Archives of Neurology*, **50**(22), 636–42.

Riddoch, G. (1917). Dissociation of visual perceptions due to occipital injuries, with special reference to appreciation of movement. *Brain*, **40**, 15–47.

Riddoch, M.J. and Humphreys, G.W. (1983). The effect of cueing on unilateral neglect. *Neuropsychologia*, **21**, 589–99.

Riddoch, M.J., Humphreys, G.W., Coltheart, M. and Funnel, E. (1988). Semantic systems or system? Neuropsychological evidence examined. *Cognitive Neuropsychology*, **5**, 3–25.

Rinn, W.E. (1984). The neuropsychology of facial expression: a review of the neurological and psychological mechanisms for producing facial expression. *Psychological Bulletin*, **95**(1), 52–77.

Risberg, J. and Prohovnik, I. (1983). Cortical processing of visual and tactile stimuli studied by non-invasive rCBF measurements. *Human Neurobiology*, **2**, 5–10.

Risse, G.L., Gates, J., Lund, G., Maxwell, R. and Rubens, A. (1989). Interhemispheric transfer in patients with incomplete section of the corpus callosum: anatomic verification with magnetic resonance imaging. *Archives of Neurology*, **46**, 437–43.

Riva, D. and Cazzamiga, L. (1986). Late effects of unilateral brain lesions before and after the first year of age. *Neuropsychologia*, **24**, 423–8.

Rizolatti, G., Umilta, C. and Berlucchi, G. (1971). Opposite superiorities of the right and left cerebral hemispheres in discriminative reaction time to physiognomical and alphabetic material. *Brain*, **94**, 431–42.

Robbins, T.W. and Sahakian, B.J. (1994). Computer methods of assessment of cognitive function. In J.R.M. Copeland, M.T. Abou-Saleh and D.G. Blazer (eds), *Principles and Practice of Geriatric Practice*. Chichester: Wiley.

Roberts, A.C., Robbins, T.W. and Weiskrantz, L. (1996). Cognitive and executive functions of the prefrontal cortex. *Philosophical Transactions: Biological Sciences*. London: Royal Society, in press.

Robertson, I.H. (1990). Does computerised cognitive rehabilitation work? A review. *Aphasiology*, **4**, 381–405.

Robertson, I.H., Halligan, P.W. and Marshall, J.C. (1993). Prospects for the rehabilitation of unilateral neglect. In I.H. Robertson and J.C. Marshall (eds), *Unilateral Neglect: Clinical and experimental studies*. Hove, UK: Lawrence Erlbaum Associates.

Robertson, I.H., Ward, T. and Nimmo-Smith, I. (1994). *The Test of Everyday Attention*. Bury St Edmunds: Thames Valley Test Company.

Robertson, I.H., Ward, T. and Nimmo-Smith, I. (1996). The structure of normal human attention: the Test of Everyday Attention. *Journal of the International Neuropsychological Society*, **2**, 525–34.

Robertson, L.C. and Lamb, M.R. (1991). Neuropsychological contributions to theories of part/whole organisation. *Cognitive Psychology*, **23**, 299–330.

Robinson, R.G. and Benson, D.F. (1981). Depression in aphasic patients: frequency, severity, and clinical pathological correlation. *Brain and Language*, **14**, 282–91.

Rocca, W.A., Amaducci, L.A. and Schoenberg, B.S. (1986). Epidemiology of clinically diagnosed Alzheimer's disease. *Annals of Neurology*, **19**, 415–24.

Rockland, K.S. and Pandya, D.N. (1986). Topography of occipital lobe commissural connections in the rhesus monkey. *Brain Research*, **365**, 174–8.

Roland, P.E. and Friberg, L. (1985). Localization of cortical areas activated by thinking. *Journal of Neurophysiology*, **53**, 1219–43.

Roland, P.E., Larsen, B., Lassen, N.A. and Skinhoj, E. (1980) Supplementary motor area and other cortical areas in organization of voluntary movements in man. *Journal of Neurophysiology*, **43**, 118–36.

Rolls, E.T. (1984). Neurons in the cortex of the temporal lobe and in the amygdala of the monkey with responses selective for faces. *Human Neurobiology*, **3**, 209–22.

Rolls, E.T. (1989). Information processing in the taste system of primates. *Journal of Experimental Biology*, **146**, 141–64.

Rolls, E.T. (1990). A theory of emotion, and its application to understanding the neural basis of emotion. *Cognition and Emotion*, **4**(3), 161–90.

Rolls, E.T. (1995). A theory of emotion and consciousness and its application to understanding the neural basis of emotion. In M.S. Gazzaniga (ed.), *The Cognitive Neurosciences*. Cambridge, MA: MIT Press.

Rolls, E.T. and Baylis, L.L. (1994). Gustatory, olfactory, and visual convergence within the primate orbitofrontal cortex. *Journal of Neuroscience*, **15**, 5437–52.

Rolls, E.T., Sienkiewicz, Z.J. and Yaxley, S. (1989). Hunger modulates the responses to gustatory stimuli of single neurons in the orbitofrontal cortex. *European Journal of Neuroscience*, **1**, 53–60.

Rose, S.P.R. (1992). *The Making of Memory*. New York: Bantam.

Rosenberger, P.B. (1990) Morphological cerebral asymmetries and dyslexia. In G.Th. Pavlidis (ed.), *Perspectives on Dyslexia*, volume 1. Chichester: Wiley.

Rosenberger, P.B. and Hier, D. (1980). Cerebral asymmetry and verbal intellectual deficits. *Annals of Neurology*, **8**, 300–4.

Ross, E.D. (1981). The aprosodias. *Archives of Neurology*, **38**, 561–9.

Ross, E.D. (1983). Right hemisphere lesions in disorders of affective language. In A. Kertesz (ed.), *Localization in Neuropsychology*. New York: Academic Press.

Ross, E.D. (1985). Modulation of affect and nonverbal communication by the right hemisphere. In M-M. Mesulam (ed.), *Principles of Behavioural Neurology*. Philadelphia: Davis.

Ross, E.D. and Rush, J. (1981). Diagnosis of neuroanatomical correlates of depression in brain-damaged patients: implications for a neurology of depression. *Archives of General Psychiatry*, **38**, 1344–54.

Roth, M. (1986). The association of clinical and neurological findings and its bearing on the classification and aetiology of Alzheimer's disease. *British Medical Bulletin*, **42**, 42–50.

Rourke, B.P. and Finlayson, M.A. (1978). Neuropsychological significance of variations in patterns of academic performance: verbal and visual–spatial abilities. *Journal of Abnormal Child Psychology*, **6**, 121–33.

Rubens, A. (1985). Caloric stimulation and unilateral visual neglect. *Neurology*, **35**, 1019–24.

Rubens, A.B. and Benson, D.F. (1971). Associative visual agnosia. *Archives of Neurology*, **24**, 305–16.

Rudge, P. and Warrington, E.K. (1990). Selective impairment of memory and visual perception in splenial tumours. *Brain*, **113**.

Rugg, M.D. and Dickens, A.M.J. (1982). Dissociation of alpha and theta activity as a function of verbal and visuospatial tasks. *Electroencephalography and Clinical Neurophysiology*, **53**, 201–7.

Russell, E. W. (1982). Theory and developments of pattern analysis methods related to the Halstead–Reitan Battery. In P.E. Logue and J.M. Shear (eds), *Clinical Neuropsychology: a multidisciplinary approach*. Chicago: Charles C. Thomas.

Russell, J.A. (1994). Is there universal recognition of emotion from facial expression? A review of cross-cultural studies. *Psychological Bulletin*, **115**, 102–41.

Russo, M. and Vignolo, L.A. (1967). Visual figure–ground discrimination in patients with unilateral cerebral disease. *Cortex*, **3**, 113–27.

Ryan, C. and Butters, N. (1980). Further evidence for a continuum-of-impairment encompassing male alcoholic Korsakoff patients and chronic alcoholic men. *Alcoholism: Clinical and Experimental Research*, **4**, 190–8.

Ryding, E., Bradvik, B. and Ingvar, D.H. (1985). Simultaneous bilateral changes in regional cerebral blood flow (rCBF) from verbal and nonverbal vocal activations. *Journal of Cerebral Blood Flow Metabolism*, **5**(1), 207–8.

Rylander, G. (1939). Personality changes after operations on the frontal lobes: clinical study of 32 cases. *Acta Psychiatrica et Neurologica Scandinavica Supplement*, **20**, 1–81.

Rylander, G. (1943). Mental changes after excision of cerebral tissue. *Acta Psychiatrica et Neurologica Scandinavica Supplement*, **25**, 1–81.

Sackheim, H.A., Greenberg, M.S., Weiman, A.L., Gur, R.C., Hungerbuhler, J.P. and Geschwind, N. (1982). Hemispheric asymmetry in the expression of positive and negative emotions: neurologic evidence. *Archives of Neurology*, **39**, 210–8.

Sacks, O. (1985). *The Man who Mistook his Wife for a Hat*. New York: Summit.

Sacks, O. (1991). *Seeing Voices*. London: Picador.

Sahakian, B., Jones, G., Levy, R., Gray, J. and Warburton, D. (1989). The effect of nicotine on attention, information processing and short term memory in patients with dementia of the Alzheimer's type. *British Journal of Psychiatry*, **154**, 797–800.

Sahakian, B.J. and Owen, A.M. (1992). Computerised assessment in neuropsychiatry using CANTAB. *Journal of the Royal Society of Medicine*, **85**, 399–402.

Salmon, D.P., Butters, N. and Heindel, W.C. (1993). Alcoholic dementia and related disorders. In R.W. Parks, R.F. Zec and R.S. Wilson (eds), *Neuropsychology of Alzheimer's Disease and Other Dementias*. Oxford: Oxford University Press.

Salmon, D.P., Galasko, D., Hansen, L.A., Masliah, E., Butters, N., Thal, L.J. and Katzman, R. (1996). Neuropsychological deficits associated with diffuse Lewy body disease. *Brain and Cognition*, **31**, 148–65.

Salmon, E., Van de Linden, M., Collette, F., Delfiore, G., Maquet, P., Degueldre, C., Luxen, A. and Franck, G. (1996). Regional brain activity during working memory tasks. *Brain*, **119**, 1617–25.

Sanchez-Prieto, J., Budd, D.C., Herrero, I., Vazquez, E. and Nicholls, D.G. (1996). Presynaptic receptors and the control of glutamate exocytosis. *Trends in Neuroscience*, **19**(6), 235–9.

Sanders, B., Wilson, J.R. and Vandenberg, S.G. (1982). Handedness and spatial ability. *Cortex*, **18**, 79–90.

Satz, P. and Sparrow, S.S. (1970). Specific developmental dyslexia: a theoretical formulation. In D.J. Bakker and P. Satz (eds), *Specific Reading Disability: Advances in theory and method*. Rotterdam: Rotterdam University Press.

Saxby, L. and Bryden, M.P. (1984). Left ear superiority in children for processing auditory emotional material. *Developmental Psychology*, **20**, 72–80.

Schacter, D.L. (1987). Implicit memory: history and current status. *Journal of Experimental Psychology: Learning, Memory and Cognition*, **13**, 501–18.

Schachter, S. and Wheeler, L. (1962). Epinephrine, chlorpromazine and amusement. *Journal of Abnormal and Social Psychology*, **65**, 121–8.

Schachter, S.C., Ransil, B.J. and Geschwind, N. (1987). Associations of handedness with hair color and learning-disabilities. *Neuropsychologia*, **25**, 269–76.

Schaffer, C.E., Davidson, R.J. and Saron, C. (1983). Frontal and parietal electroencephalographic asymmetry in depressed and non-depressed subjects. *Biological Psychiatry*, **18**, 753–62.

Schalling, D. and Rosen, A.S. (1968). Porteus maze differences between psychopathic and non-psychopathic criminals. *British Journal of Social and Clinical Psychology*, **7**, 224–8.

Scheibel, M.E., Lindsay, R.D., Tomiyasu, U. and Scheibel, A.B. (1975). Progressive dendritic changes in aging human cortex. *Experimental Neurology*, **47**, 392–403.

Schelleberg, D., Besthorn, C., Pfleger, W. and Gasser, T. (1993). Emotional activation and topographic EEG band power. *Journal of Psychophysiology*, 24–33.

Schiff, B.B. and Gagliese, L. (1994). The consequences of experimentally induced and chronic unilateral pain: reflections of hemispheric lateralization of emotion. *Cortex*, **30**, 255–67.

Schiff, B.B. and Lamon, M. (1989). Inducing emotion by unilateral contraction of facial muscles: a new look at hemispheric specialization and the experience of emotion. *Neuropsychologia*, **27**, 923–35.

Schiff, B.B. and Lamon, M. (1994). Inducing emotion by unilateral contraction of hand muscles. *Cortex*, **30**, 247–54.

Schlaug, G., Jancke, L., Huang, Y. and Steinmetz, H. (1995). *In vivo* evidence of structural brain asymmetry in musicians. *Science*, **267**, 699–701.

Schlesinger, H. (1988). Questions and answers in the development of deaf children. In M. Strong (ed.), *Language Learning and Deafness*. Cambridge: Cambridge University Press.

Schmitt, J.J., Hartje, W. and Willmes, K. (1997). Hemispheric asymmetry in the recognition of emotional attitude conveyed by facial expression, prosody and propositional speech. *Cortex*, **33**, 65–81.

Schneider, G.E. (1969). Two visual systems. *Science*, **163**, 895–902.

Schonell, F. (1942). *Backwardness in the Basic Subjects*. London: Oliver and Boyd.

Schou, M. (1989). Lithium prophylaxis: myths and realities. *American Journal of Psychiatry*, **146**, 573–6.

Schwartz, M., Creasey, H., Grady, C.L., DeLeo, L.M., Frederickson, H.A. and Cutler, N.R. (1985). Computed tomographic analysis of brain morphometrics in 30 healthy men, aged 21 to 81 years. *Annals of Neurology*, **17**, 146–57.

Scott, T.R., Yaxley, S., Sienkiewicz, Z.J. and Rolls, E.T. (1986). Taste responses in the nucleus tractus solitarius of the behaving monkey. *Journal of Neurophysiology*, **55**, 182–200.

Scoville, W. B. and Milner, B. (1957). Loss of recent memory after bilateral hippocampal lesions. *Journal of Neurology, Neurosurgery and Psychiatry*, **20**, 150–76.

Searleman, A. (1977). A review of right hemisphere linguistic abilities. *Psychological Bulletin*, **84**, 503–28.

Searleman, A., Herrmann, D.J. and Coventry, A.K. (1984). Cognitive abilities and left handedness: an interaction between familial sinistrality and strength of handedness. *Intelligence*, **8**, 295–304.

Seeck, M., Mainwaring, N., Ives, J., Blume, H., Dubuisson, D. and Cosgrove, R. (1993). Differential neural activity in the human temporal lobe evoked by faces of family members and friends. *Annals of Neurology*, **34**, 369–72.

Seeman, P. and Niznik, H.B. (1990). Dopamine receptors and transporters in Parkinson's disease and schizophrenia. *FASEB Journal*, **4**, 2737–44.

Segalowitz, S.J. and Berge, B.E. (1995). Functional asymmetries in infancy and early childhood: a review of electrophysiologic studies and their implications. In R.J. Davidson and K. Hugdahl (eds), *Brain Asymmetry*. Cambridge, MA: MIT Press.

Segalowitz, S.J. and Bryden, M.P. (1983). Individual differences in hemispheric representation of language. In S.J. Segalowitz (ed.), *Language Functions and Brain Organisation*. New York: Academic Press.

Segalowitz, S.J., Wagner, W.J. and Menna, R. (1992). Lateral versus frontal predictors of reading skill. *Brain and Cognition*, **20**, 85–103.

Semenza, C. (1996). Methodological issues. In J. G. Beaumont, P.M. Kenealy and M.J.C. Rogers (eds), *Blackwell Dictionary of Neuropsychology*. Oxford: Blackwell.

Serby, M.J., Larson, P.M. and Kalkstein, D. (1992). Olfaction and neuropsychiatry. In M.J. Serby and K.L. Chobor (eds), *Science of Olfaction*. New York: Springer.

Sergent, J. (1987). A new look at the human split brain. *Brain*, **110**, 1375–92.

Sergent, J. (1990). Furtive incursions into bicameral minds: integrative and coordinating role of subcortical structures. *Brain*, **113**, 537–68.

Sergent, J. (1991). Processing of spatial relations within and between the disconnected cerebral hemispheres. *Brain*, **114**, 1025–43.

Sergent, J., Ohta, S. and Macdonald, B. (1992). Functional neuroanatomy of face and object processing: a PET study. *Brain*, **115**, 15–36.

Seymour, P.H.K. (1986). *Cognitive Analysis of Dyslexia*. London: Routledge and Kegan Paul.

Seymour, P.H.K. and MacGregor, C.J. (1984). Developmental dyslexia: a cognitive experimental analysis of phonological, morphemic and visual impairments, *Cognitive Neuropsychology*, **1**(1), 43–82.

Seymour, S.E., Reuter-Lorenz, P.A. and Gazzaniga, M.S. (1994). The disconnection syndrome: basic findings reaffirmed. *Brain*, **117**, 105–15.

Shallice, T. (1981). Phonological agraphia and the lexical route in writing. *Brain*, **104**, 413–29.

Shallice, T. (1982). Specific impairments of planning. *Philosophical Transactions of the Royal Society, London*, **298**, 199–209.

Shallice, T. (1988). *From Neuropsychology to Mental Structure*. Cambridge: Cambridge University Press.

Shallice, T. and Burgess, P.W. (1991). Deficits in strategy application following frontal lobe damage in man. *Brain*, **114**, 727–41.

Shallice, T., Burgess, P.W., Baxter, D.M. and Schon, F. (1989). The origins of utilisation behaviour. *Brain*, **112**, 1587–98.

Shaywitz, B.A., Shaywitz, S.E., Pugh, K.R., Constable, R.T., Skurdlarski, P., Fulbright, R.K., Bronen, R.A., Fletcher, J.M., Shankweiler, D.P., Katz, L. and Gore, J.C. (1995). Sex differences in the functional organisation of the brain for language. *Nature*, **373**, 607–9.

Shepard, R.N. and Metzler, D. (1971). Mental rotation of three-dimensional objects. *Science*, **171**, 701–3.

Sheridan, J. and Humphreys, G.W. (1993). A verbal-semantic category-specific recognition impairment. *Cognitive Neuropsychology*, **10**, 143–84.

Shewan, C.M. and Bandur, D.L. (1986). *Treatment of aphasia: a language-oriented approach*. London: Taylor and Francis.

Shimamura, A.P. (1995). Memory and frontal lobe function. In M.S. Gazzaniga (ed.), *The Cognitive Neurosciences*. Cambridge, MA: MIT Press.

Shimamura, A.P., Salmon, D.P., Squire, L.R. and Butters, N. (1987). Memory dysfunction and word priming in dementia and amnesia. *Behavioural Neuroscience*, **101**, 347–51.

Shimamura, A.P., Jernigan, T.L. and Squire, L.R. (1988). Korsakoff's syndrome: radiological (CT) findings and neuropsychological correlates. *Journal of Neuroscience*, **8**, 4400–10.

Sidtis, J.J., Volpe, B.T., Holtzman, J.D., Wilson, D.H. and Gazzaniga, M.S. (1981). Cognitive interaction after staged callosal section: evidence for transfer of semantic activation. *Science*, **212**, 344–6.

Sieratzki, J.S. and Woll, B. (1996). Why do mothers cradle babies on their left? *Lancet*, **347**, 1746–48.

Silberman, E.K. and Weingartner, H. (1986). Hemispheric lateralization of functions related to emotion. *Brain and Cognition*, **5**, 322–53.

Silbersweig, D.A., Stern, E., Frith, C., Cahill, C., Holmes, A., Grootoonk, S., Deaward, J., McKenna, P., Chua, S.E., Schnorr, L., Jones, T. and Frackowiak, R.S.J. (1995). A functional neuroanatomy of hallucinations in schizophrenia. *Nature*, **378**, 176–79.

Simpson, J., Yates, C.M., Gordon, A. and St Clair, D.M. (1984). Olfactory tubercle choline acetyltransferase activity in Alzheimer-type dementia, Down's syndrome and Huntington's disease. *Journal of Neurology, Neurosurgery and Psychiatry*, **47**, 1138–9.

Sinden, J.D., Hodges, H. and Gray, J.A. (1995). Neural transplantation and recovery of cognitive function. *Behavioural and Brain Sciences*, **18**, 10–35.

Singer, T.P., Trevor, A.J. and Castagnoli, N. (1987). Biochemistry of the neurotoxic action of MPTP. *Trends in Biochemical Sciences*, **12**, 266–70.

Sirigu, A., Zalla, T., Pillon, B., Grafman, J., Agid, Y and Dubois, B. (1995). Selective impairments in managerial knowledge following pre-frontal cortex damage. *Cortex*, **31**, 301–6.

Sittig, O. (1921). Storungen im Verhalten gegunuber farben bei Aphasischen. *Monaschrift für Psychiatrie und Neurologie*, **49**, 159–87.

Skeels, H.M. (1966). Adult status of children with contrasting early life experiences. *Monographs of the Society for Research in Child Development*, **31**, 1–65.

Smith, J.S. and Kiloh, L.G. (1981). The investigation of dementia: results in 200 consecutive admissions. *Lancet*, 2, 824–7.

Snowling, M. and Hulme, C. (1989). A longitudinal case study of developmental phonological dyslexia. *Cognitive Neuropsychology*, **6**, 379–401.

Snowling, M., Stackhouse, J. and Rack, J. (1986). Phonological dyslexia and dysgraphia: a developmental analysis. *Cognitive Neuropsychology*, **3**(3), 309–39.

Snowling, M., Van Wagtendonk, B. and Stafford, C. (1988). Object naming deficits in developmental dyslexia. *Journal of Research in Reading*, **11**, 67–85.

Sohlberg, M.M. and Mateer, C. (1989). Training use of compensatory memory books: a three-stage behavioural approach. *Journal of Clinical and Experimental Neuropsychology*, **11**, 871–91.

Sokol, S.M., McCloskey, M., Cohen, N.J. and Aliminosa, D.(1991). Cognitive representations and processes in arithmetic: Inferences from the performance of brain-damaged subjects. *Journal of Experimental Psychology: Learning, Memory and Attention*, **17**(3), 335–76.

Sokoloff, L., Reivich, M., Kennedy, C., DesRosjers, M.H., Patlak, C.S. *et al.* (1977). The [14 C]deoxyglucose method for the measurement of local cerebral glucose utilization: theory, procedure, and normal values in the conscious and anesthetized albino rat. *Journal of Neurochemistry*, **28**, 897–917.

Son, Y-J., Trachtenberg, J.T. and Thompson, W.J. (1996). Schwann cells induce and guide sprouting and reinnervation of neuromuscular junctions. *Trends in Neuroscience*, **19**(7), 280–5.

Speedie, L.J., Rothi, L.J. and Heilman, K.M. (1982) Spelling dyslexia: a form of cross-cueing. *Brain and Language*, **15**, 340–52.

Spencer, D.D., Robbins, R.J., Noftolin, F., Marek, K.L., Vollmer, T., Leranth, C., Roth, R.H., Price, L.H., Gjedde, A., Bunney, B.S., Sass, K.J., Elsworth, J.D., Kier, E.L., Makuch, R., Hoffer, P.B. and Redmonds, D.E. (1992). Unilateral transplantation of human fetal mesencephalic tissue into the caudate nucleus of patients with Parkinson's disease. *New England Journal of Medicine*, **327**, 1541–8.

Sperry, R.W. (1968). Hemispheric deconnection and unity in conscious awareness. *American Psychologist*, **23**, 723–33.

Sperry, R.W. (1974). Lateral specialization in the surgically separated hemispheres. In F.O. Schmitt and F.C. Worden (eds), *The Neurosciences Third Study Program*. Cambridge, MA: MIT Press.

Sperry, R.W., Gazzaniga, M.S. and Bogen, J.E. (1969). Interhemispheric relationships: the neocortical commissures; syndromes of hemisphere disconnection. In P.J. Vinken and G.W. Bruyn (eds), *Handbook of Clinical Neurology*, volume 4. Amsterdam: North-Holland.

Spiers, P.A. (1987). Acalulia revisited: current issues. In G. Deloche and X. Seron (eds), *Mathematical Disabilities: A cognitive neuropsychological perspective*. Hillsdale, NJ: Lawrence Erlbaum Associates.

Spring, C. (1976). Encoding speed and memory span in dyslexic readers. *Journal of Special Education*, **10**, 35–40.

Squire, L.R. (1982). Comparisons between forms of amnesia: some deficits are unique to Korsakoff's syndrome. *Journal of Experimental Psychology: Learning, Memory and Cognition*, **8**, 560–71.

Squire, L.R. (1994). Declarative and nondeclarative memory: multiple brain systems supporting learning and memory. In D.L. Schachter and E. Tulving (eds), *Memory Systems*. Cambridge, MA: MIT Press.

Squire, L.R. and Moore, R.Y. (1979). Dorsal thalamic lesion in a noted case of human memory dysfunction. *Annals of Neurology*, **6**, 503–6.

Squire, L.R. and Zola-Morgan, S. (1988). Memory: brain systems and behaviour. *Trends in Neurosciences*, **11**, 170–5.

Stahl, S.A. and Murray, B.A. (1994). Defining phonological awareness and its relationship to early reading. *Journal of Educational Psychology*, **86**(2), 221–34.

Starkstein, S.E. and Robinson, R.G. (1991). The role of the frontal lobes in affective disorder. In H.S. Levin, H.M. Eisenberg and A.L. Benton (eds), *Frontal Lobe Function and Dysfunction*. New York: Oxford University Press.

Stein, D.G. and Glaser, M.M. (1995). Some practical and theoretical issues concerning fetal brain tissue grafts as therapy for brain dysfunctions. *Behavioural and Brain Sciences*, **18**, 36–45.

Stein, J.F. (1991). Visuospatial sense, hemispheric asymmetry and dyslexia. In J.F. Stein (ed.), *Vision and Visual Dyslexia*. London: Macmillan.

Steinmetz, H., Jancke, L., Kleinschmidt, A., Schlaug, G, Volkmann, J. and Huang, Y. (1992). Sex but no hand differences in the isthmus of the corpus callosum. *Neurology*, **42**, 749–52.

Steinthal, H. (1871). *Abriss der sprachwissenschaft*. Berlin.

Sternbach, R. (1962). Assessing differential autonomic patterns in emotions. *Journal of Psychosomatic Research*, **6**, 87–91.

Stewart, F., Parkin, A.J. and Hankin, N.M. (1992). Naming impairments following recovery from Herpes Simplex Encephalitis: category-specific? *Quarterly Journal of Experimental Psychology*, **44A**, 261–84.

St James-Roberts, I. (1981). A reinterpretation of hemispherectomy data without functional plasticity of the brain. 1: Intellectual function. *Brain and Language*, **13**, 31–53.

Stoerig, P. and Cowey, A. (1997). Blindsight in man and monkey. *Brain*, **120**, 535–59.

Stoicheff, M.L. (1960). Motivating instructions and language performance of dysphasic subjects. *Journal of Speech and Hearing Research*, **3**, 75–85.

Stone, V.E., Nisenson, L., Eliassen, J.C. and Gazzaniga, M.S. (1996). Left hemisphere representations of emotional facial expressions. *Neuropsychologia*, **34**(1), 23–30.

Strange, P.G. (1992). *Brain Biochemistry and Brain Disorders*. New York: Oxford University Press.

Strauss, E. and Moscovitch, M. (1981). Perception of facial expression. *Brain and Language*, **13**, 308–32.

Stuss, D.T. and Benson, D.F. (1983). Emotional concomitants of psychosurgery. In K.M. Heilman and P. Satz (eds), *Neuropsychology of Human Emotion*. New York: Guilford.

Stuss, D.T. and Benson, D.F. (1986). *The Frontal Lobes*. New York: Raven Press.

Stuss, D.T. and Levine, B. (1996). The dementias: nosological and clinical factors related to diagnosis. *Brain and Cognition*, **31**, 99–113.

Stuss, D.T. and Richard, M.T. (1982). Neuropsychological sequelae of coma after head injury. In L.P. Ivan and D. Bruce (eds), *Coma: Physiopathology, diagnosis and management*. Springfield, IL: Charles C. Thomas.

Stuss, D.T., Gow, C.A. and Hetherington, C.R. (1992). 'No longer Gage': frontal lobe dysfunction and emotional changes. *Journal of Consulting and Clinical Psychology*, **60**(3), 349–59.

Stuss, D.T., Eskes, G.A. and Foster, J.K. (1994). Experimental neuropsychological studies on frontal lobe functions. In F. Boller and H. Splinner (eds), *Handbook of Neuropsychology*, volume IX. Amsterdam: Elsevier.

Subirana, A. (1969). Handedness and cerebral dominance. In P.J. Vinken and G.W. Bruyn (eds), *Handbook of Clinical Neurology*, volume 4. Amsterdam: North-Holland.

Suhara, T., Fukuda, H., Inoue, O., Itoh, T., Suzuki, K., Yamasaki, T. and Tateno, Y. (1991). Age-related changes in human D1 dopamine receptors measured by positron emission tomography. *Psychopharmacology*, **103**, 41–5.

Sungaila, P. and Crockett, D.J. (1993). Dementia and the frontal lobes. In R.W. Parks, R.F. Zec and R.S. Wilson (eds), *Neuropsychology of Alzheimer's Disease and Other Dementias*. Oxford: Oxford University Press.

Sutker, P.B. and Allain, A.N. (1983). Behaviour and personality assessment in men labelled adaptive sociopaths. *Journal of Behavioural Assessment*, **5**, 65–79.

Sutton, J.P., Whitton, J.L., Topa, M. and Moldofsky, H. (1986). Evoked potential maps in learning disabled children. *Electroencephalography and Clinical Neurophysiology*, **65**, 399–404.

Sutton, S., Braren, M., Zubin, J. and John, E.R. (1965). Evoked potential correlates of stimulus uncertainty. *Science*, **150**, 1187–8.

Svebak, S. (1975). Respiratory patterns as predators of laughter. *Psychophysiology*, **12**, 62–5.

Svebak, S. (1977). Some characteristics of resting respiration as predictors of laughter. In A.J. Chapman and H.C. Foot (eds), *It's a Funny Thing, Humour*. Oxford: Pergamon.

Svebak, S. (1982). The effect of mirthfulness upon amount of discordant right–left occipital EEG alpha. *Motivation and Emotion*, **6**, 133–43.

Svennilson, E., Torvik, A., Lowe, R. and Leksell, L. (1960). Treatment of parkinsonism by stereotactic thermolesions in the pallidal region. *Acta Psychiatrica Scandinavia*, **35**, 358–79.

Syndulko, K. (1978). Electrocortical investigations of sociopathy. In R.D. Hare and D. Schalling (eds), *Psychopathic Behaviour: Approaches to research*. New York: Wiley.

Takahashi, N., Kawamura, M., Hirayama, K., Shiota, J. and Isono, O. (1995). Prosopagnosia: a clinical study and anatomical study of four patients. *Cortex*, **31**, 317–29.

Tallal, P. and Katz, W. (1989). Neuropsychological and neuroanatomical studies of developmental language/reading disorders: recent advances. In C. von Euler, I. Landberg and G. Lennenstrand (eds), *Brain and Reading*. London: Macmillan.

Tanner, C.M. (1989). The role of environmental toxins in the aetiology of Parkinson's disease. *Trends in Neurosciences*, **12**, 49–54.

Taylor, M.J. (1993). Maturational changes in ERPs to orthographic and phonological tasks. *Electroencephalography and Clinical Neurophysiology*, **88**, 494–507.

Taylor, M.J. and Keenan, N.K. (1990). Event-related potentials to visual and language stimuli in normal and dyslexic children. *Psychophysiology*, **27**(3), 318–27.

Tegner, R. and Levander, M. (1991). The influence of stimulus properties on visual neglect. *Journal of Neurology, Neurosurgery and Psychiatry*, **54**, 1943–51.

Temple, C.M. and Marshall, J.C. (1983). A case study of developmental phonological dyslexia. *British Journal of Psychology*, **74**, 517–33.

Tenhula, W.N. and Sweet, J.J. (1996). Double cross-validation of the booklet category test in detecting malingered traumatic brain injury. *The Clinical Neuropsychologist*, **10**(1), 104–16.

Terry, R.D., Maslia, H., Salmon, D.P., Butters, N., DeTeresa, R., Hill, R., Hansen, L.A. and Katzman, R. (1991). Physical basis of cognitive alterations in Alzheimer's disease: synapse loss is the major correlate of cognitive impairment. *Annals of Neurology*, **30**, 572–80.

Teszner, D., Tzavaras, A., Gruner, J. and Hecaen, H. (1972). L'asymmetrie droite–gauche du planum temporale: a propos de l'étude anatomique de 100 cerveaux. *Révue Neurologique*, **126**, 444–9.

Teuber, H.L. (1965). Some needed revisions of the classical views of agnosia. *Neuropsychologia*, **3**, 371–8.

Teuber, H.L. (1975). Recovery of function after brain injury in man. *Ciba Foundation Symposium*, **34**, 159–90.

Teuber, H.L. and Mishkin, M. (1954). Judgement of visual and postural vertical after brain injury. *Journal of Psychology*, **38**, 161–75.

Thal, L.J. (1992). Cholinomimetic therapy in Alzheimer's disease. In L.R. Squire and N. Butters (eds), *Neuropsychology of Memory*. New York: Guilford.

Thomas-Anterion, C., Laurent, B., Le Henaff, H., Foyatier-Michel, N. and Michel, D. (1994). Spelling acquisition impairments: a neuropsychological study in 2 adolescents with developmental dysgraphia. *Neurologique*, **150**(12), 827–34.

Thompson, P.D., Filley, C.M., Mitchell, W.D., Culig, K.M., LoVerde, M. and Byynyl, R.L. (1990). Lack of efficacy of hydergine in patients with Alzheimer's disease. *New England Journal of Medicine*, **323**, 445–8.

Tiihonen, J., Kuikka, J., Kupila, J., Partanen, K., Vainio, P., Airaksinen, J., Eronen, M., Hallikainen, T., Paanila, J., Kinnunen, I. and Huttunen, J. (1994). Increase in cerebral blood flow of right prefrontal cortex in man during orgasm. *Neuroscience Letters*, **170**, 241–3.

Tognola, G. and Vignolo, L.A. (1980). Brain lesions associated with oral apraxia in stroke patients: a clinico-neuroradiological investigation with CT scan. *Neuropsychologia*, **18**, 257–71.

Tomarken, A.J. and Davidson, R.J. (1994). Frontal brain activation in repressors and non-repressors. *Journal of Abnormal Psychology*, **103**(2), 339–49.

Tomarken, A.J., Davidson, R.J. and Henriques, J.B. (1990). Resting frontal brain asymmetry predicts affective responses to films. *Journal of Personality and Social Psychology*, **59**(4), 791–801.

Tootell, R.B.H., Dale, A.M., Sereno, M.I. and Malach, R. (1996). New images from human visual cortex. *Trends in Neurosciences*, **19**, 481–9.

Tranel, D. and Damasio, A.R. (1985). Knowledge without awareness: an autonomic index of facial recognition by prosopagnosics. *Science*, **228**, 1453–4.

Tranel, D., Damasio, A.R. and Damasio, H. (1988). Intact recognition of facial expression, gender and age in patients with impaired recognition of face identity. *Neurology*, **38**, 690–6.

Trenerry, M.R., Jack, C.R., Ivnik, R.J., Sharbrough, F.W., Cascino, G.D., Hirschorn, K.A., Marsh, W.R., Kelly, P.J. and Meyer, F.B. (1993). MRI hippocampal volumes and memory function before and after temporal lobectomy. *Neurology*, **43**, 1800–5.

Trevarthen, C. (1987). Subcortical influences on cortical processing in 'split' brains. In D. Ottoson (ed.), *Duality and Unity of the Brain*. London: Macmillan.

Trueblood, W. and Schmidt, M. (1993). Malingering and other validity considerations in the neuropsychological evaluation of mild head injury. *Journal of Clinical and Experimental Neuropsychology*, **15**(4), 578–90.

Tucker, D.M., Watson, R.T. and Heilman, K.M. (1977). Discrimination and evocation of affectively intoned speech in patients with right parietal disease. *Neurology*, **27**, 947–50.

Tucker, D.M., Stenslie, C.E., Roth R.S., and Shearer, S.L. (1981). Right frontal lobe activation and right hemisphere performance decrement during a depressed mood. *Archives of General Psychiatry*, **38**, 169–74.

Tulving, E. and Schacter, D.L. (1990). Priming and human memory systems. *Science*, **247**, 301–6.

Turkewitz, G. (1988). A prenatal source for the development of hemispheric specialisation. In D.L. Molfese and S.J. Segalowitz (eds), *Brain Lateralization in Children: Developmental implications*. New York: Guilford.

Turnbull, O.H. and Matheson, E.A. (1996). Left-sided cradling: comment on Sieratzki and Woll. *Lancet*, **348**, 691.

Tzavaras, A., Phocas, C., Kaprinis, G. and Karavatos, A. (1993). Literacy and hemispheric specialisation for language: dichotic listening in young functionally illiterate men. *Perceptual and Motor Skills*, **77**, 195–9.

Ungerleider, L. and Mishkin, M. (1982). Two cortical visual systems. In D.J. Ingle, M.A. Goodale and R.J.W. Mansfield (eds), *Analysis of Visual Behaviour*. Cambridge, MA: MIT Press.

Vallar, G., Sterzi, R., Bottini, G., Cappa, S. and Rusconi, M.L. (1990). Temporary remission of left hemianesthesia after vestibular stimulation: a sensory neglect phenomenon. *Cortex*, **26**, 123.

Van den Broek, M.D., Bradshaw, C.M. and Szabadi, E. (1993). Utility of the Modified Wisconsin Card Sorting Test in neuropsychological assessment. *British Journal of Clinical Psychology*, **32**, 333–43.

Van den Broek, M.D., Schady, W. and Coyne, H.J. (1995). *Living with Head Injury*. Manchester: Manchester University Press.

Van Horn, J.D., Berman, K.F. and Weinberger, D.R. (1996). Functional lateralization of the prefrontal cortex during traditional frontal lobe tasks. *Biological Psychiatry*, **39**, 389–99.

Van Lancker, D. (1997). Rags to riches: our increasing appreciation of cognitive and communicative abilities of the human right cerebral hemisphere. *Brain and Language*, **57**, 1–11.

Van Strien, J.W. and Bouma, A. (1995). Sex and familial sinistrality differences in cognitive ability. *Brain and Cognition*, **27**, 137–46.

Vargha-Khadem, F., O'Gorman, A.M. and Watters, G.V. (1985). Aphasia and handedness in relation to hemispheric side, age at injury, and severity of cerebral lesion during childhood. *Brain*, **108**, 677–96.

Victor, M., Adams, R.D. and Collins, G.H. (1971). *The Wernicke–Korsakoff Syndrome*. New York: Davis.

Vignolo, L.A. (1964). Evolution of aphasia and language rehabilitation: A retrospective exploratory study. *Cortex*, **1**, 344–67.

Vignolo, L.A. (1969). Auditory agnosia: a review and report of recent evidence. In A.L. Benton (ed.), *Contributions to Clinical Neuropsychology*. Chicago: Aldine.

Voeller, K., Armus, J. and Alhambra, M. (1983) Atypical computed tomographic scans and cerebral asymmetries in dyslexic children and adolescents. *Annals of Neurology*, **14**, 362–3.

Volkow, N.D. and Tancredi, L. (1987). Neural substrates of violent behaviour: a preliminary study with positron emission tomography. *British Journal of Psychiatry*, **151**, 668–73.

Von Cramon, D. and Kerkhoff, G. (1993). On the cerebral organization of elementary visuospatial perception. In B. Gulyas, D. Ottoson and P.E. Roland (eds), *Functional Organization of the Human Visual Cortex*. Oxford: Pergamon.

Von Monakow, C. (1914). *Die Lokalisationim Grosshirn und der abbau der Funktion durch Koertikale Herde*. Wiesbaden: Bergmann.

Wada, J.A. and Rasmussen, T. (1960). Intracarotid injection of sodium Amytal for the lateralization of cerebral speech dominance. *Journal of Neurosurgery*, **17**, 266–82.

Wada, J.A., Clarke, R. and Hamm, A. (1975). Cerebral hemispheric asymmetry in humans: cortical speech zones in 100 adult and 100 infant brains. *Archives of Neurology, (Chicago)*, **32**, 239–46.

Walsh, K.W. (1991). *Understanding Brain Damage: A primer of neuropsychological evaluation.* Edinburgh: Churchill Livingstone.

Wand, P.L. (1987). Concept formation and frontal lobe function. In E. Perecman (ed.), *The Frontal Lobes Revisited.* New York: IRBN Press.

Wapner, W., Hamby, S. and Gardner, H. (1981). The role of the right hemisphere in the apprehension of complex linguistic materials. *Brain and Language*, **14**, 15–33.

Warren, J.M., Abplanalp, J.M. and Warren, H.B. (1967). The development of handedness in cats and rhesus monkeys. In H.W. Stevenson, E.H. Hesss and H.L. Rheingold (eds), *Early Behaviour: Comparative developmental approaches.* New York: Wiley.

Warrington, E.K. (1982). Neuropsychological studies of object recognition. *Philosophical Transactions of the Royal Society of London*, Series B, **295**, 411–23.

Warrington, E.K. (1985). Agnosia: the impairment of object recognition. In P.J. Vinken, G.W. Gruyn and Klawans, H.L. (eds), *Handbook of Clinical Neurology.* Amsterdam: Elsevier.

Warrington, E.K. and James, M. (1967). An experimental investigation of facial recognition in patients with unilateral cerebral lesions. *Cortex*, **3**, 317–26.

Warrington, E.K. and James, M. (1986). Visual object recognition in patients with right hemisphere lesions: axes or features? *Perception*, **15**, 355–66.

Warrington, E.K. and Shallice, T. (1980) Word form dyslexia. *Brain*, **103**, 99–112.

Warrington, E.K. and Shallice, T. (1984). Category specific semantic impairments. *Brain*, **107**, 829–53.

Warrington, E.K. and Taylor, A.M. (1973). Contribution of the right parietal lobe to object recognition. *Cortex*, **9**, 152–64.

Warrington, E.K., James, M. and Maciejewski, C. (1986). The WAIS as a lateralizing and a localizing instrument: a study of 656 patients with unilateral cerebral lesions. *Neuropsychologia*, **24**, 223–39.

Watson, J.B. (1924). *Psychology from the Standpoint of a Behaviourist.* Philadelphia: Lippincott.

Watson, R.T. and Heilman, K.M. (1983). Callosal apraxia. *Brain*, **106**, 391–403.

Wechsler, A.F., Verity, M.A., Rosenschien, S., Fried, I. and Sceibel, A.B. (1982). Pick's disease: a clinical, computed tomographic and histological study with Golgi impregnation. *Archives of Neurology*, **39**, 287–90.

Wechsler, D. (1955). *Manual for the Wechsler Adult Intelligence Scale.* New York: Psychological Corporation.

Wechsler, D. (1981). *Manual for the Wechsler Adult Intelligence Scale – Revised.* New York: Psychological Corporation.

Weddell, R.A. (1994). Effects of subcortical lesion site on human emotional behaviour. *Brain and Cognition*, **25**, 161–93.

Weddell, R.A., Miller, J.D. and Trevarthen, C. (1990). Voluntary emotional facial expressions in patients with focal cerebral lesions. *Neuropsychologia*, **28**, 49–60.

Weekes, B. and Coltheart, M. (1996). Surface dyslexia and surface dysgraphia: treatment studies and their theoretical implications. *Cognitive Neuropsychology*, **13**(2), 277–315.

Weigl, E. (1941). On the psychology of so-called processes of abstraction. *Journal of Abnormal Psychology*, **36**, 3–33.

Weinberger, D.R., Luchins, D.J., Morihisa, J. and Wyatt, R.J. (1982). Asymmetrical volumes of the right and left frontal and occipital regions of the human brain. *Annals of Neurology*, **11**, 97–100.

Weiner, B. (1985). An attributional theory of achievement motivation and emotion. *Psychological Review*, **92**, 548–73.

Weingartner, H., Grafman, J., Boutelle, W., Kaye, W. and Martin, P.R. (1983). Forms of memory failure. *Science*, **221**, 380–82.

Weiskrantz, L. (1986). *Blindsight: A case study and implications*. Oxford: Oxford University Press.

Weiskrantz, L. and Warrington, E.K. (1979). Conditioning in amnesia patients. *Neuropsychologia*, **17**, 187–94.

Wernicke, C. (1874) *Der aphasische symptomenkomplex*. Breslau, Poland: Cohn and Weigert.

West, R.L. (1996). An application of prefrontal cortex function theory of cognitive aging. *Psychological Bulletin*, **120**(2), 272–92.

Wheeler, R.W., Davidson, R.J., and Tomarken, A.J. (1993). Frontal brain asymmetry and emotional reactivity: a biological substrate of affective style. *Psychophysiology*, **30**, 82–9.

Whitehouse, P.J., Lerner, A. and Hedera, P. (1993). Dementia. In K.M. Heilman and E. Valenstein (eds), *Clinical Neuropsychology* (3rd edition). New York: Oxford University Press.

Widner, H., Tetrud, J., Rehncrona, S., Snow, B., Brundin, P., Gustavii, B., Bjorklund, A., Lindvall, O. and Langston, J.W. (1992). Bilateral fetal mesencephalic grafting in two patients with parkinsonism induced by 1-methyl-4-phenyl-1,2,3,6-tretrahydropyridine (MPTP). *New England Journal of Medicine*, **327**, 1556–63.

Wigan, A.L. (1844). *The Duality of the Mind*. London: Longman, Brown and Green.

Wiggins, E.C. and Brandt, J. (1988). The detection of simulated amnesia. *Law and Human Behaviour*, **12**, 57–78.

Wiig, E.H. and Semel, E.M. (1976). *Language Disability in Children and Adolescents*. Ohio: Charles Merrill.

Wikswo, J.P., Gevins, A., Williamson, S.J. (1993). The future of the EEG and MEG. *Electroencephalography and Clinical Neurophysiology*, **87**, 1–9.

Wilcock, G.K., Esiri, M.M., Bowen, D.M. and Hughes, A.O. (1988). The differential involvement of subcortical nuclei in senile dementia of the Alzheimer's type. *Journal of Neurology, Neurosurgery and Psychiatry*, **51**, 842–9.

Wilkins, R.H. (1992). *Neurosurgical Classics*. USA: American Association of Neurological Surgeons.

Willows, D.M., Kruk, R.S. and Corcos, E. (1993). *Visual Processes in Reading and Reading Disabilities*. Hillsdale, NJ: Lawrence Erlbaum Associates.

Wilson, B.A. (1991). Long-term prognosis of patients with severe memory disorders. *Neuropsychological Rehabilitation*, **1**, 117–34.

Wilson, B.A. (1992). Rehabilitation and memory disorders. In L.R. Squire and N. Butters (eds), *Neuropsychology of Memory*. New York: Guilford.

Wilson, B.A. (1995). Rehabilitation. In J. G. Beaumont, P.M. Kenealy and M.J.C. Rogers (eds), *Blackwell Dictionary of Neuropsychology*. Oxford: Blackwell.

Wilson, B.A. and Moffat, N. (1992). *Clinical Management of Memory Problems* (2nd edition). London: Chapman and Hall.

Wilson, R.S., Rosenbaum, G., Brown, G., Rourke, D., Whitman, D. and Grisell, J. (1978). An index of premorbid intelligence. *Journal of Consulting and Clinical Psychology*, **46**, 1554–5.

Wilson, S.L. and McMillan, T.M. (1991). Computer-based assessment in neuropsychology. In J.R. Crawford, D.M. Parker, and M.M. McKinlay (eds), *A Handbook of Neuropsychological Assessment*. Hove, UK: Lawrence Erlbaum Associates.

Winner, E. and Gardner, H. (1977). The comprehension of metaphor in brain-damaged patients. *Brain*, **100**, 719–27.

Witelson, S.F. (1977). Neural and cognitive correlates of developmental dyslexia: age and sex differences. In C. Shagass, S. Gershon and A.J. Friedhoff (eds), *Psychopathology and Brain Dysfunction*. New York: Raven Press.

Witelson, S.F. (1985). The brain connection: the corpus callosum is larger in left handers. *Science*, **229**, 665–8.

Witelson, S.F. (1986). Wires of the mind: anatomical variation in the corpus callosum in relation to hemispheric specialisation and integration. In F. Lepore, M. Petito and H.H. Jasper (eds), *Two Hemispheres – One Brain: Functions of the corpus callosum*. New York: Liss.

Witelson, S.F. (1989). Hand and sex differences in the isthmus and genu of the human corpus callosum: a post-mortem morphological study. *Brain*, **112**, 799–835.

Witelson, S.F. and Pallie, W. (1973). Left hemisphere specialization for language in the newborn: neuroanatomical evidence of asymmetry. *Brain*, **96**, 641–6.

Witt, E.D. and Goldman-Rakic, P.S. (1983a). Intermittent thiamine deficiency in the rhesus monkey. I: Progression of neurological signs and neuroanatomical lesions. *Annals of Neurology*, **13**, 376–95.

Witt, E.D. and Goldman-Rakic, P.S. (1983b). Intermittent thiamine deficiency in the rhesus monkey. II: Evidence for memory loss. *Annals of Neurology*, **13**, 396–401.

Wolff, P.H., Hurwitz, I. and Moss, H. (1977). Serial organization of motor skills in left and right-handed adults. *Perceptual and Motor Skills*, **15**, 539–46.

Wolpert, I. (1924). Die simultanagnosie: Storung der gesamtauffassung. *Z. Gesamte Neurol. Psychiatr.*, **93**, 397–413.

Wood, C.C., Goff, W. and Day, R. (1971). Auditory evoked potential during speech perception. *Science*, **173**, 1248–51.

Wood, E.K. (1988). Less sinister statistics from baseball records. *Nature*, **335**, 1042.

Wood, F.B., Flowers, D.L. and Naylor, C.E. (1991) Cerebral laterality in functional neuroimaging. In F.L. Kitterle (ed.), *Cerebral Laterality: Theory and research*. Hillsdale, NJ: Lawrence Erlbaum Associates.

Woods, B.T. (1980). The restricted effects of right-hemisphere lesions after age one: Wechsler test data. *Neuropsychologia*, **18**, 65–70.

Woods, B.T. (1987). Impaired speech shadowing after early lesions of either hemisphere. *Neuropsychologia*, **25**, 519–25.

Woods, B.T. and Carey, S. (1979). Language deficits after apparent clinical recovery from childhood aphasia. *Annals of Neurology*, **6**, 405–9.

Woods, B.T. and Teuber, H-L. (1978). Mirror movements after childhood hemiparesis. *Neurology*, **28**, 1152–8.

Woodward, S.H. (1988). An anatomical model of hemispheric asymmetry. *Journal of Clinical and Experimental Neuropsychology*, **10**, 68.

Wurtman, R.J. and Wurtman, J.J. (1989). Carbohydrates and depression. *Scientific American*, **260**(1), 50–7.

Wyke, M. (1967). The effect of brain lesions on the rapidity of arm movement. *Neurology*, **17**, 1113–30.

Wyler, F., Graves, R. and Landis, T. (1987). Cognitive task influence on relative hemispheric motor control. *Journal of Clinical and Experimental Neuropsychology*, **9**, 105–16.

Yen, W.M. (1975). Sex-linked major-gene influences on selected types of spatial perform-ance. *Behaviour Genetics*, **5**, 281–98.

Yeni-Komishian, G.H. and Benson, D.A. (1976). Anatomical study of cerebral asymmetry in the temporal lobe of humans, chimpanzees and rhesus monkeys. *Science*, **192**, 387–9.

Yeudall, L.T. and Fromm-Auch, D. (1979). Neuropsychological impairments in various psychopathological populations. In J. Gruzelier and P. Flor-Henry (eds), *Hemisphere Asymmetries of Function and Psychopathology*. New York: Elsevier.

Yeudall, L.T., Fromm-Auch, D. and Davies, P. (1982). Neuropsychological impairment of persistent delinquency. *Journal of Nervous and Mental Disease*, **170**, 257–65.

Young, A.W. (1994a). Covert recognition. In M.J. Farah and G. Ratcliff (eds), *The Neuro-psychology of High-level Vision*. Hove, UK: Lawrence Erlbaum Associates.

Young, A.W. (1994b). Progress and neglect. In P.W. Halligan and J.C. Marshall (eds), *Spatial Neglect: Position papers on theory and practice*. Hove, UK: Lawrence Erlbaum Associates.

Young, A.W., Newcombe, F., de Haan, E.H.F., Small, M. and Hay, D.C. (1993). Face perception after brain injury. *Brain*, **116**, 941–59.

Young, A.W., Aggleton, J.P., Hellawell, D.J., Johnson, M., Broks, P. and Hanley, J.R. (1995). Face processing impairments after amygdalotomy. *Brain*, **118**, 15–24.

Zaidel, D.W. (1996). Left-sided cradling. Comment on Sieratzki and Woll. *Lancet*, **348**, 691.

Zaidel, D.W., Chen, A.C. and German, C. (1995). She is not a beauty even when she smiles: Possible evolutionary basis for a relationship between facial attractiveness and hemi-spheric specialization. *Neuropsychologia*, **33**(5), 649–55.

Zaidel, D.W. and FitzGerald, P. (1994). Sex of the face in Western art: left and right in portraits. *Empirical Studies of the Arts*, **12**, 9–18.

Zajonc, R.B. (1980). Feeling and thinking: preferences need no inferences. *American Psychologist*, **35**, 151–75.

Zarit, S. and Kahn, R. (1974). Impairment and adaption in chronic disabilities: spatial inattention. *Journal of Nervous and Mental Diseases*, **159**, 63.

Zatorre, R.J. (1989). Perceptual asymmetry in the dichotic fused words test and cerebral speech lateralization determined by the carotid Amytal test. *Neuropsychologia*, **27**, 1207–19.

Zatorre, R.J., Evans, A.C., Meyer, E. and Gjedde, A. (1992a). Lateralization of phonetic and pitch discrimination in speech processing. *Science*, **256**, 846–9.

Zatorre, R.J., Jones-Gottman, M., Evans, A.C. and Meyer, E. (1992b). Functional localization and lateralization of human olfactory cortex. *Nature*, **360**, 339–40.

Zatorre, R.J., Meyer, E., Gjedde, A. and Evans, A.C. (1996). PET studies of phonetic processing of speech- review, replication and reanalysis. *Cerebral Cortex*, **6**(1), 21–30.

Zeki, S. (1993). *A Vision of the Brain*. Oxford: Blackwell.

Zurif, E.B. and Carson, G. (1970). Dyslexia in relation to cerebral dominance and temporal analysis. *Neuropsychologia*, **8**, 351–61.

Index